MASS MEDIA LAW

MASS MEDIA LAW

Fifth Edition

Don R. Pember
University of Washington—Seattle

 WCB **Wm. C. Brown Publishers**

Book Team

Editor *Stan Stoga*
Developmental Editor *Linda Harper*
Production Coordinator *Peggy Selle*

Wm. C. Brown Publishers

President *G. Franklin Lewis*
Vice President, Publisher *George Wm. Bergquist*
Vice President, Publisher *Thomas E. Doran*
Vice President, Operations and Production *Beverly Kolz*
National Sales Manager *Virginia S. Moffat*
Advertising Manager *Ann M. Knepper*
Marketing Manager *Kathleen Nietzke*
Production Editorial Manager *Colleen A. Yonda*
Production Editorial Manager *Julie A. Kennedy*
Publishing Services Manager *Karen J. Slaght*
Manager of Visuals and Design *Faye M. Schilling*

Cover image © FourByFive/Robert Llewellyn

Cover design by Jeanne Marie Regan

Library of Congress Catalog Card Number: 89–60363

ISBN 0–697–03019–9

Printed in the United States of America by Wm. C. Brown Publishers,
2460 Kerper Boulevard, Dubuque, IA 52001

10 9 8 7 6 5 4 3 2 1

CONTENTS

PREFACE

The first edition of this book had its genesis almost 15 years ago. And let me tell you something, many aspects of mass media law have changed dramatically during that decade and a half. Because you're reading only the fifth edition, and not the first, second, third, and fourth as well (thank goodness!), this change isn't apparent to you. Let me briefly note some of the differences.

The rights of the student press have been more clearly outlined and limited in the past 15 years. Book banning is a bigger or at least more visible problem today. Attempts by the federal government to cut off the flow of information to the press and the people are more obvious and more frequent.

Libel law is even a bit more complicated today than it was in the mid-1970s (if that is possible), but contrary to what you might hear, the mass media have gained rather than lost ground under libel law. Journalists today have a far broader right to cover the courts than they did in 1975. While material that is legally obscene remains protected today to the same extent it was protected 15 years ago, legal and quasi-legal pressures upon non-obscene sexually-oriented material have sharply grown.

There are far fewer regulations governing both broadcasting and advertising today, but not even all proponents of the First Amendment are sure this is a good idea. And this Spring the Supreme Court agreed to hear its first case on the Newspaper Preservation Act, a law that selectively repealed some of the nation's anti-trust laws as they applied to newspapers. This decision could settle a legal question that has been simmering since the first edition of this text came off the press.

So that is what has changed. Let me tell you something about the book that hasn't changed in 15 years. This text still has a strong bias toward the First Amendment and freedom of expression. The rights to freedom of speech and freedom of the press are easy to defend in the abstract. Every American professes a belief in these constitutional guarantees, but only so long as they remain abstract principles. Arrayed against other tangible values, the often elusive principles embodied in freedom of expression are more difficult to defend. When you stand squarely behind the First Amendment you often end up supporting the right of persons who do things with which you may violently disagree. You support their right to publish and broadcast the name of a rape victim, their right to distribute sleazy, sexually-oriented books and films, their right to express beliefs and join groups whose professed aims are directly antithetical to our democratic principles, and even their right to burn our flag as a part of a political protest. But that is what freedom is all about. If people used their rights of freedom of speech and press to do only what we all support and believe in, we wouldn't need a First Amendment.

A lot of you who read this book aren't planning careers in mass communications. But I think after reading it you will have a better idea about your rights as citizens—because in almost every case the rights of the press are co-equal with the rights of the average citizen. And many of you who are planning careers in mass communication don't expect to be journalists or broadcasters. Advertising and public relations is drawing more and more of you away from journalism and broadcast journalism. And your question is (I know it because I hear it from my own students) why isn't there more in the book relating to public relations and advertising? My answer is this: Nearly everything in the book relates to public relations and advertising as well as journalism. Someone in public relations surely must know the law of libel and privacy. Advertising practitioners must know about copyright and the equal time rules. The real question is, why aren't there more examples of problems that grow out of public relations and advertising? This book is built generally around real life examples, actual cases. There are very few cases in mass communications law that stem from public relations. These disputes just don't seem to generate into litigation. As far as advertising is concerned, there is an entire chapter devoted exclusively to advertising problems. Certainly there are some issues that face persons in public relations and advertising that rarely face journalists. Matters regarding contracts, for example, don't usually concern reporters but may be of interest to a public relations professional. I believe the law of contracts is best taught through a course in business law, not in a communications class. Any time we would spend on these kind of issues would mean less time for other matters, and time is surely short enough as it is. I think it is sufficient to assure you that most of what is contained in this book is relevant to any career in mass communications. Enough said.

Before closing I want to thank some people for helping me on this edition. First, thanks to the crew at Wm. C. Brown Publishers. I received strong support from Stan Stoga, Peggy Selle, and Karen Doland. Next, thanks to my colleagues in the field who gave me their advice and counsel in putting this edition together: John DeMott (Memphis State Univeristy), Robert Drechsel (University of Wisconsin-Madison), Ed Kimbrell (Middle Tennessee State University), Barbara Mack (Iowa State University), James Scotton (Marquette University), Jeffrey Smith (University of Iowa), Michael Vadnie (St. Cloud State University), and John Zelezny (California State University-Fresno). I also want to thank the many students at the University of Washington and at other schools who have given my many suggestions and ideas. Thanks finally to the Pember family for hanging in there one more time.

Don R. Pember
Seattle, Washington
July, 1989

MASS MEDIA LAW

1 THE AMERICAN LEGAL SYSTEM

Probably no nation is more closely tied to the law than the American Republic. From the 1770s, when in the midst of a war of revolution we attempted to legally justify our separation from the motherland, to the 1990s, when citizens of the nation attempt to resolve weighty moral, political, social, and environmental problems through the judicial process, and during the more than two hundred years between, the American people have showed a remarkable faith in the law. One could write a surprisingly accurate history of this nation using reports of court decisions as the only source. Not that what happens in the courts reflects everything that happens in the nation; but as has been observed by Alexis de Tocqueville and others, political issues in the United States often end up as legal disputes. Beginning with the sedition cases in the late 1790s, which reflected the political turmoil of that era, one could chart the history of the United States from adolescence to maturity. As the frontier expanded in the nineteenth century, citizens used the courts to argue land claims and boundary problems. Civil rights litigation in both the midnineteenth and midtwentieth centuries reflects a people attempting to cope with racial and ethnic diversity. Industrialization brought labor unions, workmen's compensation laws, and child labor laws, all of which resulted in controversies that found their way into the courts. As mass production developed and large manufacturers began to create most of the consumer goods used, judges and juries had to cope with new laws on product safety, honesty in advertising, and consumer complaints.

Americans have protested nearly every war the nation has fought—including the Revolutionary War. The record of these protests is contained in scores of court decisions. Prohibition and the crime of the twenties and the economic woes of the thirties both left residue in the law. In the United States, as in most other societies, law is a basic part of existence, as necessary for the survival of civilization as are economic systems, political systems, cultural achievement, and the family.

This chapter has two purposes: to acquaint readers with the law and to present a brief outline of the legal system in the United States. While this is not designed to be a comprehensive course in law and the judicial system—such material can better be studied in depth in an undergraduate political science course—it does provide sufficient introduction to understand the remaining eleven chapters of the book.

The chapter opens with a discussion of the law, giving consideration to the five most important sources of the law in the United States, and moves on to the judicial system, including both the federal and state court systems. A summary of judicial review and a brief outline of how both criminal and civil lawsuits are started and proceed through the courts are included in the discussion of the judicial system. ◆

SOURCES OF THE LAW

There are almost as many definitions of law as there are people who study the law. Some people say that law is any social norm or any organized or ritualized method of settling disputes. Most writers on the subject insist that it is a bit more complex, that some system of sanctions is required before law exists. John Austin, a nineteenth-century English jurist, defined law as definite rules of human conduct with appropriate sanctions for their enforcement. He added that both the rules and the sanctions must be prescribed by duly constituted human authority. Roscoe Pound, an American legal scholar, has suggested that law is really social engineering—the attempt to order the way people behave. For the purposes of this book, it is probably more helpful to consider the law to be a set of rules that attempt to guide human conduct and a set of formal, governmental sanctions that are applied when those rules are violated.

Scholars still debate the genesis of "the law." A question that is more meaningful and easier to answer is: What is the source of American law? There are really five major sources of the law in the United States: the Constitution, the common law, the law of equity, the statutory laws, and the rulings of various executive and administrative bodies and agencies. Historically we can trace American law to Great Britain. As colonizers of much of the North American continent, the British supplied Americans with an outline for both a legal system and a judicial system. In fact, because of the many similarities between British and American law, many people consider the Anglo-American legal system to be a single entity. Today in the United States our federal Constitution is the supreme law of the land. Yet when each of these five sources of law is considered separately, it is more useful to begin with the earliest source of Anglo-American law, the common law.

The Common Law

The **common law,** which developed in England during the two hundred years after the Norman Conquest in the eleventh century, is one of the great legacies of the British people to colonial America. During those two centuries the crude mosaic of Anglo-Saxon customs was replaced by a single system of law worked out by jurists and judges. The system of law became common throughout England; it became the common law. It was also called the common law to distinguish it from the ecclesiastical (church) law prevalent at the time. Initially, the customs of the people were used by the king's courts as the foundation of the law, disputes were resolved according to community custom, and governmental sanction was applied to enforce the resolution. As such, the common law was, and still is, considered "discovered law." It is law that has always existed, much like air and water. When a problem arises, the court's task is to find or discover the proper solution, to seek the common custom of the people. The judge doesn't create the law; he or she merely finds it, much like a miner finds gold or silver.

This, at least, is the theory of the common law. Perhaps at one point judges themselves believed that they were merely discovering the law when they handed down decisions. As legal problems became more complex and as the law began to be professionally administered (the first lawyers appeared during this era and eventually professional judges), it became clear that the common law reflected not so much the custom of the land as the custom of the court—or more properly, the custom of the judges. While judges continued to look to the past to discover how other courts had decided, given similar facts (precedent is discussed in a moment), many times judges were forced to create the law themselves.

This common-law system was the perfect system for the American colonies. Like most Anglo-Saxon institutions, it was a very pragmatic system aimed at settling real problems, not at expounding abstract and intellectually satisfying theories. The common law is an inductive system of law in which a legal rule is arrived at after consideration of a great number of specific instances of cases. (In a deductive system the rules are expounded first and then the court decides the legal situation under the existing rule.) Colonial America was a land of new problems for British and other settlers. The old law frequently did not work. But the common law easily accommodated the new environment. The ability of the common law to adapt to change is directly responsible for its longevity.

Fundamental to the common law is the concept that judges should look to the past and follow earlier court precedents. The Latin expression for the concept is this: *Stare decisis et non quieta movere* (to stand by past decisions and not disturb things at rest). **Stare decisis** is the key phrase: let the decision stand. A judge should resolve current problems in the same manner as similar problems were resolved in the past. When Barry Goldwater sued publisher Ralph Ginzburg for publishing charges that the conservative Republican senator was mentally ill, the judge most certainly looked to past decisions to discover whether in previous cases such a charge had been considered defamatory or libelous. There are ample precedents for ruling that a published charge that a person is mentally ill is libelous, and Senator Goldwater won his lawsuit (*Goldwater* v. *Ginzburg,* 1969).

The Role of Precedent

At first glance one would think that under a system that continually looks to the past, the law can never change. What if the first few rulings in a line of cases were bad decisions? Are we saddled with bad law forever? Fortunately, the law does not operate quite in this way. While following **precedent** is the desired state of affairs (many people say that certainty in the law is more important than justice), it is not always the proper way to proceed. To protect the integrity of the common law, judges have developed several means of coping with bad law and with new situations in which the application of old law would result in injustice.

Imagine for a moment that the newspaper in your hometown publishes a picture and story about a twelve-year-old girl who gave birth to a seven-pound son in a local hospital. The mother and father do not like the publicity and sue the newspaper for invasion of privacy. The attorney for the parents finds a precedent (*Barber* v. *Time,* 1942) in which a Missouri court ruled that to photograph a patient in a hospital room against her will and then to publish that picture in a news magazine is an invasion of privacy.

Now does the existence of this precedent mean that the young couple will automatically win their lawsuit? that the court will follow the decision? No, it does not. For one thing, there may be other cases in which courts have ruled that publishing such a picture is not an invasion of privacy. In fact in 1956 in the case of *Meetze* v. *AP,* a South Carolina court made just such a ruling. But for the moment assume that *Barber* v. *Time* is the only precedent. Is the court bound by this precedent? No. The court has several options concerning the 1942 decision.

First, it can *accept* the precedent as law and rule that the newspaper has invaded the privacy of the couple by publishing the picture and story about the birth of their child. Second, the court can *modify* or change the 1942 precedent by arguing that *Barber* v. *Time* was decided almost fifty years ago when people were more sensitive about going to a hospital, since a stay in a hospital was often considered to reflect badly on a patient, but that hospitalization is no longer a sensitive matter to most people. Therefore, a rule of law restricting the publication of a picture of a hospital patient is unrealistic, unless the picture is in bad taste or needlessly embarrasses the patient. Then the publication is an invasion of privacy. If not, the publication of such a picture is permissible. In our imaginary case, then, the decision turns on what kind of picture and story the newspaper published: a pleasant picture that flattered the couple? or one that mocked and embarrassed them? If the court rules in this manner, it *modifies* the 1942 precedent, making it correspond to what the judge perceives to be contemporary life.

As a third option the court can decide that *Barber* v. *Time* provides an important precedent for a plaintiff hospitalized because of disease—as Dorothy Barber was. But that in the case before the court, the plaintiff was hospitalized to give birth to a baby, a different situation: Giving birth is a voluntary status; catching a disease is not. Consequently the *Barber* v. *Time* precedent does not apply. This practice is called *distinguishing the precedent from the current case,* a very common action.

Finally, the court can *overrule* the precedent. In 1941 the United States Supreme Court overruled a decision made by the Supreme Court in 1918 regarding the right of a judge to use what is called the summary contempt power (*Toledo Newspaper Co.* v. *U.S.,* 1918). This is the power of a judge to charge someone with being in contempt of court, to find that person guilty of contempt, and then to punish him or her for the contempt—all without a jury trial. In *Nye* v. *U.S.* (1941) the High Court said that in 1918 it had been improperly informed as to the intent of a measure passed by Congress in 1831 that authorized the use of the summary power by federal judges. The 1918 ruling was therefore bad, was wrong, and was reversed. (Fuller explanation of summary contempt as it applies to the mass media is given in chapter 6.)

The only courts that can overrule the 1942 decision by the Missouri Supreme Court in *Barber* v. *Time* are the Missouri Supreme Court and the United States Supreme Court.

Obviously the preceding discussion oversimplifies the judicial process. Rarely is a court confronted with only a single precedent. And whether or not precedent is binding on a court is often an issue. Lower federal courts are bound to follow precedents from the appellate court in their circuit or region (see pages 25–27) and from the Supreme Court of the United States. But when focusing upon state law, the courts in the fifty separate states are bound to follow only the court rulings or precedents that have been generated within each state. A court in Arkansas, for example, need only look to the precedents from other Arkansas courts when deciding an issue that involves only Arkansas law. It might be useful to look to court decisions in other states that have similar laws or have had similar cases. But the Arkansas courts are not bound by these other state rulings. Because mass media law is so heavily affected by the First Amendment, state judges are frequently forced to look outside their borders to precedents developed by the federal courts. A state court ruling on a question involving freedom of speech and freedom of the press is necessarily governed by federal court precedents on the same subject.

Lawyers and law professors often debate just how important precedent really is when a court makes a decision. Some persons have suggested what is called the "hunch theory" of jurisprudence. Under this theory a judge or justice decides a case based on instinct or a feeling of what is right and wrong and then seeks out precedents to support the decision.

The imaginary invasion-of-privacy case just discussed demonstrates that the common law can have vitality, that despite the rule of precedent a judge is rarely bound tightly by the past. There is a saying: Every age should be the mistress of its own law. This saying applies to the common law as well as to all other aspects of the legal system.

It must be clear at this point that the common law is not specifically written down someplace for all to see and use. It is instead contained in the hundreds of thousands of decisions handed down by courts over the centuries. Many attempts have been made to summarize the law. Sir Edward Coke compiled and analyzed the precedents of common law in the early seventeenth century. Sir William Blackstone later expanded Coke's work in the monumental *Commentaries on the Law of England*. More recently, in such works as the massive *Restatement of Torts* the task was again undertaken, but on a narrower scale.

Courts began to keep records of their decisions centuries ago. In the thirteenth century unofficial reports of cases began to appear in Year Books, but they were records of court proceedings in which procedural points were clarified for the benefit of legal practitioners, rather than collections of court decisions. The modern concept of fully reporting the written decisions of all courts probably began in 1785 with the publication of the first British Term Reports.

Figure 1.1 Reading a case citation

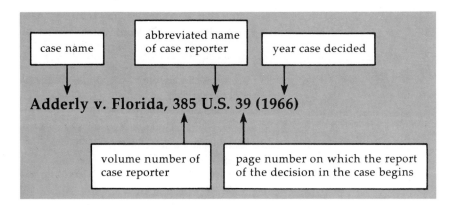

While scholars and lawyers still uncover the common law using the case-by-case method, it is fairly easy today to locate the appropriate cases through a simple system of citation. The cases of a single court (such as the United States Supreme Court or the federal district courts) are collected in a single **case reporter** (such as the *United States Reports* or the *Federal Supplement*). The cases are collected chronologically and fill many volumes. Each case collected has its individual **citation,** which reflects the name of the reporter in which the case can be found, the volume of that reporter, and the page on which the case begins (fig. 1.1). For example, the citation for the decision in *Adderly* v. *Florida* (a freedom-of-speech case) is 385 U.S. 39 (1966). The letters in the middle (U.S.) indicate that the case is in the *United States Reports,* the official government reporter for cases decided by the Supreme Court of the United States. The number 385 refers to the specific volume of the *United States Reports* in which the case is found. The last number (39) gives the page on which the case appears. Finally, 1966 provides the year in which the case was decided. So, *Adderly* v. *Florida* can be found on page 39 of volume 385 of the *United States Reports.*

If you have the correct citation, you can easily find any case you seek. Locating all citations of the cases apropos to a particular problem—such as a libel suit—is a different matter and is a technique taught in law schools. A great many legal encyclopedias, digests, compilations of the common law, books, and articles are used by lawyers to track down the names and citations of the appropriate cases.

There is no better way to sum up the common law than to quote Oliver Wendell Holmes (*The Common Law*, published in 1881):

> The life of the law has not been logic; it has been experience. The felt necessities of the time, the prevalent moral and political theories, intuitions of public policy, avowed or unconscious, even the prejudices which judges share with their fellow-men, have had a good deal more to do than syllogism in determining the rules by which men should be governed. The law embodies the story of a nation's development through many centuries, and it cannot be dealt with as if it contained only the axioms and corollaries of a book of

mathematics. In order to know what it is, we must know what it has been, and what it tends to become. . . . The very considerations which judges most rarely mention, and always with an apology, are the secret root from which the law draws all the juices of life. I mean, of course, considerations of what is expedient for the community concerned.

The Law of Equity

The law of **equity** is another kind of judge-made law. The distinction today between the common law and equity law has blurred. The cases are heard by the same judges in the same courtrooms. Differences in procedures and remedies are all that is left to distinguish these two categories of the law. Separate consideration of the common law and equity leads to a better understanding of both however. The law of equity, as developed in Britain beginning in the fourteenth and fifteenth centuries, is the second basic source of the law in the United States. Equity was originally a supplement to the common law and developed side by side with the common law. During the 1300s and 1400s the king's courts became rigid and narrow. Many persons seeking relief under the common law for very real grievances were often turned away because the law did not provide a suitable remedy for their problems. In such instances the disappointed litigant could take the problem to the king for resolution, petitioning the king to "do right for the love of God and by way of charity." According to legal scholar Henry Abraham (*The Judicial Process*), "The king was empowered to mold the law for the sake of 'justice,' to grant the relief prayed for as an act of grace." Soon the chancellor, the king's secretary or assistant, set up a special office or court to resolve the problems the king's common law courts could not handle. At the outset of the hearing, the aggrieved party had to establish that there was no adequate remedy under the common law and that a special court was needed to hear the case. The office of the chancellor soon became known as the Court of Chancery. Decisions were made on the basis of conscience or fairness or "equity."

British common law and equity law were American law until the Revolution in 1776. After independence was won, the basic principles of common law in existence before the War of Revolution were kept because the cases remained acceptable precedent. After some hesitation, equity was accepted in much the same way.

The rules and procedures under equity are far more flexible than those under the common law. Equity really begins where the common law leaves off. Equity suits are never tried before a jury. Rulings come in the form of **judicial decrees,** not in judgments of yes or no. Decisions in equity are (and were) discretionary on the part of judges. And despite the fact that precedents are also relied upon in the law of equity, judges are free to do what they think is right and fair in a specific case.

Equity provides another advantage for troubled litigants—the restraining order. A judge sitting in equity can order preventive measures as well as remedial ones. Individuals who can demonstrate that they are in peril, or about to suffer a serious irremediable wrong, can usually gain a legal writ such as an injunction or a restraining order to stop someone from doing something. Generally a court issues a temporary restraining order until it can hear arguments from both parties in the dispute and decide whether an injunction should be made permanent.

In 1971 the federal government asked the federal courts to restrain the *New York Times* and the *Washington Post* from publishing what have now become known as the Pentagon Papers (this case is discussed in greater detail in chapter 2). This case is a good example of equity law in action. The government argued that if the purloined documents were published by the two newspapers the nation would suffer irremediable damage; that foreign governments would be reluctant to entrust the United States with their secrets if those secrets might someday be published in the public press; that the enemy would gain valuable defense secrets. The federal government argued further that it would do little good to punish the newspapers after the material had been published since there would be no way to repair the damage. The federal district court temporarily restrained both newspapers from publishing the material while the case was argued—all the way to the Supreme Court of the United States. After two weeks of hearings, the High Court finally ruled that publication could continue, that the government had failed to prove that the nation would be damaged (*New York Times Co. v. U.S.*, 1971).

Statutory Law

Statutory law or legislation is the third great source of United States law. Today there are legislative bodies of all shapes and sizes. The common traits they share are that they are popularly elected and that they have the authority to pass laws. In the beginning of our nation, legislation, or statutory law, really did not play a very significant role in the legal system. Certainly many laws were passed, but the bulk of our legal rules were developed from the common law and from equity law. After 1825 statutory law began to play an important role in our legal system, and it was between 1850 and 1900 that a greater percentage of law began to come from legislative acts than from common-law court decisions.

Several important characteristics of statutory law can best be understood by contrasting them with common law. First, **statutes** tend to deal with problems affecting society or large groups of people, in contrast to common law, which usually deals with smaller, individual problems. (Some common-law rulings affect large groups of persons, but this occurrence is rare.) It should also be noted in this connection the importance of not confusing common law with constitutional law. Certainly when judges interpret the Constitution they make policy that affects us all. However, it should be kept in mind that the Constitution is a legislative document voted upon by the people and is not "discovered law" or "judge-made law."

Second, statutory law can anticipate problems, and common law cannot. For example, a state legislature can pass a statute that prohibits publication of the school records of a student without prior consent of the student. Under the common law the problem cannot be resolved until a student's record has been published in a newspaper or broadcast on television and the student brings action against the medium to recover damages for the injury incurred.

Third, the criminal laws in the United States are all statutory laws—common-law crimes no longer exist in this country and have not since 1812. Common-law rules are not precise enough to provide the kind of notice needed to protect a criminal defendant's right to due process of law.

Fourth, statutory law is collected in codes and law books, instead of in reports as is the common law. When a proposal or bill is adopted by the legislative branch and approved by the executive branch, it becomes law and is integrated into the proper section of a municipal code, a state code, or whatever. However, this does not mean that some very important statutory law cannot be found in the case reporters.

Passage of a law is rarely the final word on the subject. Courts become involved in the process of determining what that law means. While a properly constructed statute sometimes needs little interpretation by the courts, judges are frequently called upon to rule upon the exact meaning of ambiguous phrases and words. The resulting process is called **statutory construction** and is a very important part of the law. Even the simplest kind of statement often needs interpretation. For example, a prohibition stating "it is illegal to distribute an obscene newspaper" is filled with ambiguity. What does *distribution* mean? Can an obscene newspaper be sent through the mail? distributed from house to house? passed out on street corners? Are all of these actions prohibited? What constitutes a newspaper? Is any printed matter a newspaper? Is any printed matter published regularly a newspaper? Are mimeographed sheets and photocopied newsletters considered newspapers? Of course, implicit is the classic question with which courts have wrestled in this country for nearly a century, What is obscenity?

Usually a legislature tries to leave some kind of trail to help a judge find out what the law means. For when judges rule on the meaning of a statute, they are supposed to determine what the legislature meant when it passed the law (the legislative intent), not what they think it should mean. Minutes of committee hearings in which the law was discussed, legislative staff reports, and reports of debate on the floor can all be used to help a judge determine the legislative intent. Therefore when lawyers deal with statutes, they frequently are forced to search the case reporters to find out how the courts interpreted a law in which they are interested.

Constitutional Law   Great Britain does not have a written **constitution.** The United States does have a written constitution, and it is an important source of our law. In fact, there are many constitutions in this country: the federal Constitution, state constitutions, city charters, and so forth. All of these documents accomplish the same ends. First, they provide the plan for the establishment and organization of the government. Next, they outline the duties, responsibilities, and powers of the various elements of government. Finally, they usually guarantee certain basic rights to the people, such as freedom of speech and freedom to peaceably assemble.

Legislative bodies may enact statutes rather easily by a majority vote. It is far more difficult to adopt or change a constitution. State constitutions are approved or changed by a direct vote of the people. It is even more difficult to change the federal Constitution. An amendment may be proposed by a vote of two-thirds of the members of both the United States House of Representatives and the Senate. Alternatively, two-thirds of the state legislatures can call for a constitutional convention for proposing amendments. Once proposed, the amendments must be approved either by three-fourths of the state legislatures or by three-fourths of the constitutional conventions called in all the states. Congress decides upon which method of ratification or approval is to be used. Because the people have an unusually direct voice in the approval and change of a constitution, constitutions are considered the most important source of United States law.

One Supreme Court justice described a constitution as a kind of yardstick against which all the other actions of government must be measured to determine whether the actions are permissible. The United States Constitution is the supreme law of the land. Any law or other constitution that conflicts with the United States Constitution is unenforceable. A state constitution plays the same role for a state: a statute passed by the Michigan legislature and signed by the governor of that state is clearly unenforceable if it conflicts with the Michigan Constitution. And so it goes for all levels of constitutions.

While constitutions tend to be short and infrequently amended, the process of determining what specific areas of these documents mean and whether a specific law or government action violates a certain constitutional provision is a laborious one. Consequently, with the exception of the bare-bones documents themselves, the case reporters are once again the repository for the constitutional law that governs the United States.

Twenty-six amendments are appended to the United States Constitution. The first ten of these are known as the Bill of Rights and provide a guarantee of certain basic human rights to all citizens. Included are freedom of speech and freedom of the press, rights you will come to understand more fully in future chapters.

The federal Constitution and the fifty state constitutions are very important when considering mass-media law problems. All fifty-one of these charters contain provisions, in one form or another, that guarantee freedom of speech and freedom of the press. Consequently, any government action that affects in any way the freedom of individuals or mass media to speak or publish or broadcast must be measured against the constitutional guarantees of freedom of expression. There are several reasons why a law limiting speaking or publishing might be declared unconstitutional. The law might be a direct restriction on speech or press that is protected by the First Amendment. For example, an order by a Nebraska judge that prohibited the press from publishing certain information about a pending murder trial was considered a direct restriction on freedom of the press (see *Nebraska Press Association* v. *Stuart,* chapter 7). A criminal obscenity statute or other kinds of criminal laws might be declared unconstitutional because they are too vague. A law must provide adequate notice to a person of ordinary intelligence that his or her contemplated conduct is prohibited by the law. An Indianapolis pornography ordinance that made it a crime to publish pornographic material was declared void, at least in part, because the law's definition of pornography was not specific enough. The law defined pornography as including depictions of "the subordination of women." It is almost impossible to settle in one's own mind upon a single meaning or understanding of that term, noted Judge Sarah Barker (see *American Booksellers Association* v. *Hudnut,* chapter 8). A statute might also be declared to be unconstitutional because it violates what is known as the overbreadth doctrine. A law is overbroad, the Supreme Court said many years ago, if it does not aim specifically at evils within the allowable area of government control but sweeps within its ambit other activities that constitute an exercise of protected expression. Struthers, Ohio, an industrial community where many people worked at night and slept during the day, passed an ordinance that forbade knocking on the door or ringing the doorbell at a residence in order to deliver a handbill. The Supreme Court ruled that the ordinance was overbroad, that the city's objective could be obtained by passing an ordinance making it an offense for any person to ring a doorbell of a householder who had, through a sign or some other means, indicated that he or she did not wish to be disturbed. As written, however, the law prohibited persons from distributing handbills to all persons—to those who wanted to see and read them as well as those who did not (see *Martin* v. *Struthers,* chapter 2). So there are many reasons why a court might declare a law to be an unconstitutional infringement upon the guarantees of freedom of speech and press.

Administrative Rules

By the latter part of the nineteenth century in the United States the job of governing had become much more complex. Congress was being asked to resolve questions going far beyond such simple matters as budgets, wars, treaties, and the like. Technology created new kinds of problems for the Congress to resolve. Many such issues were complex and required specialized knowledge and expertise that the representatives and senators lacked and could not easily acquire, had they wanted to. Federal administrative agencies were therefore created to deal with these problems.

For example, regulation of the railroads that traversed the nation created numerous problems in the late nineteenth century. Since questions concerning use of these railroads fell within the commerce power of the Congress, that deliberative body was given the task of resolving this complex issue. To deal with these problems, Congress created the first **administrative agency,** the Interstate Commerce Commission (ICC). This agency was established by legislation and funded by Congress. Its members were appointed by the president and approved by the Congress. Each member served a fixed term in office. The agency was independent of the Congress, the president, and the courts. Its task was (and is) to regulate commerce between the states, a matter that concerned pipelines, shipping, and transportation. The members of the board presumably were somewhat expert in the area before appointment and of course became more so during the course of their term.

Hundreds of such agencies now exist at both federal and state levels. In fact, many people speculate that the rules generated by these agencies comprise the bulk of American law today. Each agency undertakes to deal with a specific set of problems that are too technical or too large for the legislative branch to handle. Typical is the Federal Communications Commission (FCC), which was created by Congress in 1934. Its task is to regulate broadcasting in the United States, a job that Congress has really never attempted. Its members must be citizens of the United States and are appointed by the president. The single stipulation is that at any one time no more than three of the five individuals on the commission can be from the same political party. The Senate must confirm the appointments.

Congress sketched the broad framework for the regulation of broadcasting in the Federal Communications Act of 1934, and this act is used by the agency as its basic regulatory guidelines. The agency also creates much law itself in administration of the 1934 act. In interpreting provisions, handing down rulings, developing specific guidelines, and the like, the FCC has developed a sizable body of regulations that bind broadcasters.

Persons dissatisfied with rulings by an agency can go to court and seek a reversal of the action. But courts are strictly limited in their power when reviewing decisions by administrative agencies, and can overturn such a ruling in only these limited circumstances: (1) if the original act that established the commission or agency is unconstitutional, (2) if the commission or agency exceeds its authority, (3) if the commission or agency violates its own rules, or (4) if there is no evidentiary basis whatsoever to support the ruling. The reason for these limitations is simple: These agencies were created to bring expert knowledge to bear on complex problems, and the entire purpose for their creation would be defeated if judges with no special expertise in a given area could reverse an agency ruling merely because they had a different solution to a problem.

The case reporters contain some law created by the administrative agencies, but the reports that each of these agencies themselves publish contain much more such law. These reports are also arranged on a case-by-case basis in chronological order. A citation system similar to that used for the case reporters is used in these reports.

There are other sources of American law. Executives—a governor, a president, a mayor—have the power to make law, in some circumstances, through executive order. The five sources just discussed—common law, law of equity, statutory law, constitutional law, and rules and regulations by administrative agencies—are the most important, however, and are of most concern in this book. First Amendment problems fall under the purview of constitutional law. Libel and invasion of privacy are matters generally dealt with by the common law and the law of equity. Obscenity laws in this country are statutory provisions (although this fact is frequently obscured by the hundreds of court cases in which judges attempt to define the meaning of obscenity). And of course the regulation of broadcasting and advertising falls primarily under the jurisdiction of administrative agencies.

While this section provides a basic outline of the law and is not comprehensive, the information is sufficient to make upcoming material on mass media law understandable.

SUMMARY

There are five important sources of American law. The common law is the oldest source of our law, having developed in England more than six hundred years ago. The law became common throughout Great Britain and reflected the customs of the people. It was easily transported to the New World, and its pragmatic philosophy was highly useful on the rapidly developing North American continent. Fundamental to the common law is the concept that judges should look to the past and follow earlier court rulings called precedents. *Stare decisis* (let the decision stand) is a key concept. But judges have developed the means to change or adapt the common law by modifying, distinguishing, or overruling precedent case law. The common law is not written down in a law book but is collected in volumes that contain the reports of legal decisions. Each case is given its own legal identity through a system of numbered citations.

Equity law, the second source of American law, developed because in some instances the common law was simply too rigid to fairly resolve the real grievances of British subjects. The rules and procedures of equity are far more flexible than those of the common law and permit a judge (equity cases are never heard before a jury) to fashion a solution to unique or unusual problems. A court is permitted under equity law to restrain an individual or a corporation or even a government from taking an action. Under the common law a court can only attempt to compensate the injured party for the damage that results from the action.

Today a great volume of American law is generated by Congress, legislatures, city and county councils, and myriad other legislative bodies. This legislation, called statutory law, is the third important source of American law. All criminal laws are statutes. Statutes usually deal with problems that affect great numbers of people, and statutes can anticipate problems, whereas the common law cannot. All statutes are collected in codes or statute books. Courts become involved in the development of statutes when they are called upon to interpret the meaning of the words and phrases contained in a statute.

Constitutions, the fourth source of our law, take precedence over all other American law. The United States Constitution is the supreme law of the land. Other laws, whether they spring from common law, equity, legislative bodies, or administrative agencies, cannot conflict with the provisions of the Constitution. Courts are often called upon to interpret the meaning of the provisions of our constitutions (one federal and fifty state constitutions) and through this process can often make these seemingly rigid legal prescriptions adaptable to contemporary problems.

There are thousands of administrative agencies, boards, and commissions in the nation that produce rules and regulations. This administrative law, the fifth source of American law, usually deals with technical and complicated matters requiring levels of expertise that members of traditional legislative bodies do not normally possess. Members of these agencies and commissions are usually appointed by presidents or by governors or mayors, and the agencies are supervised and funded by legislative bodies. Their tasks are narrowly defined, and their rulings, while they carry the force of law, can always be appealed.

THE JUDICIAL
SYSTEM

This section gives an introduction to the court system in the United States. Since the judicial branch of our three-part government is the field upon which most of the battles involving communications law are fought, an understanding of the judicial system is essential.

It is technically improper to talk about the American judicial system. There are fifty-one different judicial systems in the United States, one for the federal government and one for each of the fifty states. While each of these systems is somewhat different from all the others, the similarities among the fifty-one systems are much more important than the differences. Each of the systems is divided into two distinct sets of courts—trial courts and appellate courts. Each judicial system is established by a constitution, federal or state. In each system the courts act as the third branch of a common triumvirate of government: a legislative branch, which makes the law; an executive branch, which enforces the law; and a judicial branch, which interprets the law.

Facts Versus the Law

Common to all judicial systems is the distinction between trial courts and appellate courts, and it is important to understand this distinction. Each level of court has its own function: basically, **trial courts** are fact-finding courts and **appellate courts** are law-reviewing courts. Trial courts are the courts of first instance, the place where nearly all cases begin. Juries sit in trial courts, but never in appellate courts. Trial courts are empowered to consider both the facts and the law in a case. Appellate courts consider only the law. The difference between facts and law is significant. The facts are what happened. The law is what should be done about the facts.

The difference between facts and law can be emphasized by looking at an imaginary libel suit that might result when the *River City Sentinel* publishes a story about costs at the Sandridge Hospital.

Ineffective Medications Given to Ill, Injured
SANDRIDGE HOSPITAL OVERCHARGING
PATIENTS ON PHARMACY COSTS

Scores of patients at the Sandridge Hospital have been given ineffective medications, a three-week investigation at the hospital has revealed. In addition, many of those patients were overcharged for the medicine they received.

The *Sentinel* has learned that many of the prescription drugs sold to patients at the hospital had been kept beyond the manufacturer's recommended storage period.

Many drugs stored in the pharmacy (as late as Friday) had expiration dates as old as six months ago. Drug manufacturers have told the *Sentinel* that medication used beyond the expiration date, which is stamped clearly on most packages, may not have the potency or curative effects that fresher pharmaceuticals have.

Hospital spokesmen deny giving patients any of the expired drugs, but sources at the hospital say it is impossible for administrators to guarantee that none of the dated drugs were sold to patients.

In addition, the investigation by the *Sentinel* revealed that patients who were sold medications manufactured by Chaos Pharmaceuticals were charged on the basis of 1988 price lists despite the fact that the company lowered prices significantly in 1989.

The Sandridge Hospital sued the newspaper for libel. When the case got to court, the first thing that had to be done was to establish what the facts were—what happened. Both the hospital and the newspaper presented evidence, witnesses, and arguments to support its version of the facts. Several issues had to be resolved. In addition to the general questions of whether the story had been published and whether the hospital had been identified in the story, the hospital had to supply evidence that its reputation had been injured, that its good name had been damaged, that the story was false, and that the newspaper staff had been extremely careless or negligent in the publication of the report. The newspaper will seek to defend itself by attempting to document the story or raise the defense that the report was privileged in some way. Or the newspaper may argue that even if the story is mistaken, it was the result of an innocent error, not negligence on the part of the staff.

All this testimony and evidence establishes the factual record—what actually took place at the hospital. When there is conflicting evidence, the jury decides whom to believe (in the absence of a jury, the judge makes the decision). Suppose the hospital is able to prove by documents that pharmacists in fact had removed the dated medicine from their shelves and simply stored it to return to the manufacturers. Further, the hospital can show that while it did overcharge some patients for Chaos products, it quickly refunded the excess charge to these patients. Finally, attorneys for the hospital demonstrate that the story was prepared by an untrained stringer for the newspaper who used but a single source—a pharmacist who had been fired by Sandridge for using drugs while on the job—to prepare the story and failed to relate to readers the substance of the evidence (which it had when the story was published) presented by the hospital in court. In such a case, a court would likely rule that the hospital had carried its burden of proof, and that no legitimate defense exists for the newspaper. Therefore, the hospital wins the suit. If the newspaper is unhappy with the verdict, it can appeal.

In an appeal, the appellate court does not establish a new factual record. No more testimony is taken. No more witnesses are called. The factual record established by the jury or judge at the trial stands. The appellate court has the power in some kinds of cases (libel suits that involve constitutional issues, for example) to examine whether the trial court properly considered the facts in the case. But normally it is the task of the appellate court to determine whether the law has been applied properly in light of the facts established at the trial. Perhaps the appellate might rule that even with the documentary evidence it presented, the hospital failed to prove that the newspaper story was false. Perhaps the judge erred in allowing certain testimony into evidence or refused to allow a certain witness to testify. Nevertheless, in reaching an opinion the appellate court considers only the law; the factual record established at the trial stands.

What if new evidence is found or a previously unknown witness comes forth to testify? If the appellate court believes that the new evidence is important, it can order a new trial. However, the court itself does not hear the evidence. These facts are given at a new trial.

The important differences between trial and appellate courts have now been pointed out. Other differences will undoubtedly emerge as the specific structure of each court system is discussed.

In the discussion that follows, the federal court system and its methods of operating are considered first, and then some general observations about state court systems are given, based on the discussion of the federal system.

The Federal Court System

The Congress has the authority to abolish every federal court in the land, save the Supreme Court of the United States. The United States Constitution calls for but a single federal court, the Supreme Court. Article III, Section 1 states: "The judicial power of the United States shall be vested in one Supreme Court." The Constitution also gives Congress the right to establish inferior courts if it deems these courts to be necessary. And Congress has, of course, established a fairly complex system of courts to complement the Supreme Court.

The jurisdiction of the federal courts is also outlined in Article III of the Constitution. The jurisdiction of a court is its legal right to exercise its authority. Briefly, federal courts can hear the following cases:

1. Cases that arise under the United States Constitution, United States law, and United States treaties
2. Cases that involve ambassadors and ministers, duly accredited, of a foreign country
3. Cases that involve admiralty and maritime law
4. Cases that involve controversies when the United States is a party to the suit
5. Cases that involve controversies between two or more states
6. Cases that involve controversies between a state and a citizen of another state (we must remember that the Eleventh Amendment to the Constitution requires that a state give its permission before it can be sued)
7. Cases that involve a controversy between citizens of different states

While special federal courts have jurisdiction that goes beyond this broad outline, these are the circumstances in which a federal court may normally exercise its authority. Of the seven categories of cases just listed, categories one and seven account for most of the cases getting to federal court. For example, disputes that involve violations of the myriad federal laws and disputes that involve constitutional rights such as the First Amendment are heard in federal courts. Also, disputes between citizens of different states—what is known as a diversity of citizenship matter—are heard in federal courts. It is very common, for example, for libel suits and invasion of privacy suits against publishing companies to start in federal courts rather than in state courts. If a citizen of Arizona is libeled by *Time* magazine, the case will very likely be tried in a federal court in the state of Arizona, rather than in a state court. Arizona law will be applied. In 1988, Congress limited federal trial courts to hearing only those diversity cases in which the damages sought to exceed $50,000.

The Supreme Court of the United States is the oldest federal court, having been in operation since 1789. The Constitution does not establish the number of justices who will sit on the High Court. That task is left to the Congress. In 1789 the Congress passed the first judiciary act and established the membership of the High Court at six: a chief justice and five associate justices. This number was increased to seven in 1807, to nine in 1837, and to ten in 1863. The Supreme Court had ten members until 1866, when Congress ruled that only seven justices would sit on the high tribunal. Since 1869 the Supreme Court has had eight associate justices and the chief justice of the United States. (Note the title: not chief justice of the Supreme Court, but the chief justice of the United States.)

No attempt to change the size of the Court has occurred since the 1930s, when President Franklin Roosevelt, unhappy about the manner in which it treated some of his New Deal legislation, proposed enlarging the Court. But the proposal was unpopular with the people and never came to pass.

The Supreme Court exercises both original and appellate jurisdictions. Under its **original jurisdiction,** which is established in the Constitution, the Supreme Court is the first court to hear a case and acts much like a trial court in ascertaining facts and deciding law. But original jurisdiction is rarely exercised. Because the High Court is strictly limited by the Constitution to exercise its original jurisdiction in a few specific instances, and because Congress has given the lower federal courts concurrent jurisdiction with the Supreme Court in those specific instances, few persons begin their lawsuits at the Supreme Court.

The primary task of the Supreme Court is as an appellate tribunal, hearing cases already decided by lower federal courts and state courts of last resort. The appellate jurisdiction of the Supreme Court is established by the Congress, not by the Constitution. A case will come before the Supreme Court of the United States for review in one of two principal ways: on a direct appeal or by way of a writ of certiorari. The certification process is a third way for a case to get to the High Court, but this process is rarely used today.

In some instances a litigant has an apparent right, guaranteed by federal statute, to appeal a case to the Supreme Court. This is called **direct appeal.** For example, if a federal appeals court declares that a state statute violates the United States Constitution or conflicts with a federal law, the state is guaranteed the right to appeal this decision to the Supreme Court. But this is only an apparent right, because since 1928 the Supreme Court has had the right to reject such an appeal "for want of a substantial federal question." This is another way of the Court saying "we think this is a trivial matter." Almost ninety percent of all cases that come to the Supreme Court via the direct appeal process are rejected.

The much more common way for a case to reach the nation's High Court is via a **writ of certiorari.** No one has the right to such a writ. It is a discretionary order issued by the Court when it feels that an important legal question has been raised. Litigants using both the federal court system and the various state court systems can seek a writ of certiorari. The most important requirement that must be met before the Court will even consider issuing a writ is that a petitioner exhaust all other legal remedies. While there are a few exceptions, this generally means that if a case begins in a federal district court (the trial level court) the **petitioner** must first seek a review by a United States court of appeals before bidding for a writ of certiorari. The writ can be sought if the court of appeals refuses to hear the case or sustains the verdict against the petitioner. All other legal remedies have then been exhausted. In state court systems every legal appeal possible must be made within the state before seeking a review by the United States Supreme Court. This usually means going through a trial court, an intermediate appeals court, and finally the state supreme court.

When the Supreme Court grants a writ of certiorari, it is ordering the lower court to send the records to the High Court for review. Each request for a writ is considered by the entire nine-member Court, and an affirmative vote of four justices is required before the writ can be granted. The High Court rejects most of the petitions it receives. Work load is the key factor. Certain important issues must be decided each term, and the justices do not have the time to consider thoroughly most cases for which an appeal is sought. Term after term, suggestions to reduce the Court's work load are made but most are not popular with the Congress or the people in the nation. All citizens believe that they should have the right to appeal to the Supreme Court. Even if the appeal will probably be rejected, and even if the Court may never hear the case, they believe the right to make the appeal should remain.

Hearing a Case

While the operation of state and federal appellate courts varies from state to state and court to court, these courts have a good deal in common in the way in which they hear and decide a case. So by examining how the Supreme Court operates in the following section, we can also learn quite a bit about how other appellate courts operate.

The first thing the Court does is to decide whether it will hear a case, either on appeal or via a writ of certiorari. Once a case is accepted, the attorneys for both sides have the greatest burden of work during the next few months. Oral argument on the case is scheduled, and both sides are expected to submit **legal briefs**—their legal arguments—for the Court to study before the hearing. The greatest burden at this point is on the party seeking appeal, since he or she must provide the Court with a complete record of the lower court proceedings in the case. Included are trial transcripts, lower-court rulings, and all sorts of other materials.

Arguing a matter all the way to the Supreme Court takes a long time, often as long as five years/sometimes longer/from initiation of the suit until the Court gives its ruling. James Hill brought suit in New York in 1953 against Time, Inc., for invasion of privacy. The United States Supreme Court made the final ruling in the case in 1967 (*Time* v. *Hill,* 1967).* Even at that the matter would not have ended had Hill decided to go back to trial, which the Supreme Court said he must if he wanted to collect damages. He chose not to.

After the nine justices study the briefs (or at least the summaries provided by their law clerks), the **oral argument** is held. For a generation schooled on Perry Mason and Owen Marshall, oral argument before the Supreme Court (or indeed before any court) must certainly seem strange. For one thing, the attorneys are strictly limited as to how much they may say. Each side is given a brief amount of time, often no more than an hour or ninety minutes, to present its arguments. In important cases "friends of the court" (**amici curiae**) are allowed to present briefs and to participate for thirty minutes in the oral arguments. For example, the American Civil Liberties Union often seeks the friend status in important civil rights cases.

Deciding a Case

After the oral argument (which of course is given in open court with visitors welcome) is over, the members of the High Court move behind closed doors to undertake their deliberations. No one is allowed in the discussion room except members of the Court itself—no clerks, no bailiffs, no secretaries. The discussion, which often is held several days after the arguments are completed, is opened by the chief justice. Discussion time is limited, and by being the first speaker the chief justice is in a position to set the agenda, so to speak, for each case—to raise what he or she thinks are the key issues. Next to speak is the justice with the most seniority, and after him or her, the next most senior justice. The Court usually has an average of seventy-five items or cases to dispose of during one conference or discussion day; consequently, brevity is valued. Each justice has just a few moments to state his or her thoughts on the matter. After discussion, a tentative vote is taken and recorded by each justice in a small, hinged, lockable docket book. In the voting procedure the junior justice votes first; the chief justice, last.

Under the United States legal system, which is based so heavily upon the concept of court participation in developing and interpreting the law, a simple yes-or-no answer to any legal question is hardly sufficient. More important than the vote, for the law if not for the **litigant,** are the reasons for the decision. Therefore the Supreme Court and all courts that deal with questions of law prepare what are called opinions in which the reasons, or rationale, for

*The Bibliography at the end of each chapter supplies additional information about the sources and legal cases cited in the text. An explanation of how to locate a given case using its citation is provided on page 8.

the decision are given. One of the justices voting in the majority is asked to write what is called the **Court's opinion.** If the chief justice is in the majority, he or she selects the author of the opinion. If not, the senior associate justice in the majority makes the assignment. Either the chief justice or the senior associate justice can write the opinion.

Opinion writing is a difficult task. Getting five or six or seven people to agree to yes or no is one thing; getting them to agree upon why they say yes or no is something else. The **opinion** must therefore be carefully constructed. After it is drafted, it is circulated among all Court members, who make suggestions or even draft their own opinions. The opinion writer incorporates as many of these ideas as possible into the opinion to retain its majority backing. While all this is done in secret, historians have learned that rarely do court opinions reflect solely the work of the writer. They are more often a conglomeration of paragraphs and pages and sentences from the opinions of several justices.

A justice in agreement with the majority who cannot be convinced to join in backing the Court's opinion has the option of writing what is called a **concurring opinion.** This means that the justice agrees with the outcome of the decision but does so for different reasons than those of the majority.

Justices who disagree with the majority can also write an opinion, either individually or as a group, called a **dissenting opinion.** Dissenting opinions are very important. Sometimes, after the Court has made a decision, it becomes clear that the decision was not the proper one. The issue is often litigated again by other parties who use the arguments in the dissenting opinion as the basis for a legal claim. If enough time passes, if the composition of the Court changes sufficiently, or if the Court members change their minds, the High Court can swing to the views of the original dissenters. This is what happened in the case of *Nye* v. *U.S.* (noted earlier) when the High Court repudiated a stand it had taken in 1918 and supported instead the opinion of Justice Oliver Wendell Holmes, who had vigorously dissented in the earlier decision.

Finally, it is possible for a justice to concur with the majority in part and to dissent in part as well. That is, the justice may agree with some of the things the majority says but disagree with other aspects of the ruling. This kind of stand by a justice, as well as an ordinary concurrence, frequently fractures the Court in such a way that in a six-to-three ruling only three persons subscribe to the Court's opinion, two others concur, the sixth concurs in part and dissents in part, and three others dissent. Such splits by the members of the Court have become more common in recent years. In several key mass-media law decisions (*Gannett* v. *DePasquale,* 1979 and *Island Trees* v. *Pico,* 1982, for example) such disarray has left substantial confusion among persons vitally interested in the issues.

The Supreme Court can dispose of a case in two other ways. A **per curiam** (by the court) **opinion** can be prepared. This is an unsigned opinion drafted by one or more members of the majority and published as the Court's opinion. Per curiam opinions are not common, but neither are they rare.

Finally, the High Court can dispose of a case with a **memorandum order**—that is, it just announces the vote without giving an opinion. Or the order cites an earlier Supreme Court decision as the reason for affirming or reversing a lower-court ruling. This device is quite common today as the work load of the High Court increases. In cases with little legal importance and in cases in which the issues were really resolved earlier, the Court saves a good deal of time by just announcing its decision.

One final matter in regard to voting remains for consideration: What happens in case of a tie vote? When all nine members of the Court are present, a tie vote is technically impossible. However, if there is a vacancy on the Court, only eight justices hear a case. Even when the Court is full, a particular justice may disqualify himself or herself from hearing a case. When a vote ends in a tie the decision of the lower court is affirmed. No opinion is written. It is almost as if the Supreme Court had never heard the case.

During the circulation of an opinion, justices have the opportunity to change their vote. The number and membership in the majority may shift. It is not impossible for the majority to become the minority if one of the dissenters writes a particularly powerful dissent that attracts support from members originally opposed to his opinion. This event is probably very rare. Nevertheless, a vote of the Court is not final until it is announced on decision day, or opinion day. The authors of the various opinions—court opinions, concurrences, and dissents—publicly read or summarize their views. Printed copies of these documents are handed out to the parties involved and to the press.

Are lower courts bound to follow United States Supreme Court decisions? The answer to that is yes and no. Since the Supreme Court is the supervisor of the federal courts, lower federal courts are bound closely by the High Court rulings. Still, occasionally lower federal courts are reluctant to follow the lead of the High Court.

The Supreme Court is not empowered to make a final judgment when it reviews a state court decision. All it can do, as Henry Abraham writes in *The Judicial Process,* is "to decide the federal issue and remand it to the state court below for final judgment 'not inconsistent with this opinion.' " However, new issues can be raised at the lower level by the state courts, and the opportunity to evade the ruling of the Supreme Court always exists. One study undertaken by the *Harvard Law Review* showed that of 175 cases remanded to state courts between 1941 and 1951, 22 of the litigants who won at the High Court level ultimately lost in the state courts following the High Court ruling. As pointed out earlier, because courts operate on a case-by-case basis, the opportunity for defiance beyond the instant case is real.

Finally, courts have no real way to enforce decisions and must depend upon other government agencies for enforcement of their rulings. The job normally falls to the executive branch. If perchance the president decides not to enforce a Supreme Court ruling, no legal force exists to compel him to do so.

If former President Nixon, for example, had chosen to refuse to turn over the infamous Watergate tapes after the Court ruled against his arguments of executive privilege, no other agency could have forced him to give up those tapes.

At the same time, there is one force that usually works to see that court decisions are carried out: it is that vague force called public opinion or what political scientists call "legitimacy." People believe in the judicial process; they have faith that what the courts do is probably right. This does not mean that they always agree with court decisions, but they do agree that the proper way to settle disputes is through the judicial process. Jurists help engender this spirit or philosophy by acting in a temperate manner. The Supreme Court, for example, has developed means that permit it to avoid having to answer highly controversial questions in which an unpopular decision could weaken its perceived legitimacy. The justices might call the dispute a political question, a **nonjusticiable matter,** or they may refuse to hear a case on other grounds. When the members of the Court sense that the public is ready to accept a ruling, they may take on a controversial issue. School desegregation is a good example. In 1954 the Supreme Court ruled in *Brown* v. *Board of Education* that segregated public schools violated the United States Constitution. The foundation for this ruling had been laid by a decade of less momentous desegregation decisions and executive actions. By 1954 the nation was prepared for the ruling, and it was generally accepted, even in most parts of the South. The legitimacy of a court's decisions, then, often rests upon prudent use of the judicial power.

Other Federal Courts

The United States Supreme Court is the most visible, perhaps the most glamorous (if that word is appropriate), of the federal courts. But it is not the only federal court nor even the busiest. There are two lower echelons of federal courts, plus various special courts, within the federal system. These special courts, such as the Court of Military Appeals, Court of Claims, Customs Court, and so forth, were created by the Congress to handle special kinds of problems.

Most business in the federal system begins and ends in a district court. This court was created by Congress by the Federal Judiciary Act of 1789, and today in the United States there are nearly one hundred such courts staffed by more than six hundred judges. Every state has at least one United States district court. Some states are divided into two districts: an eastern and western district or a northern and southern district. Individual districts often have more than one judge, sometimes many more than one.

When there is a jury trial, the case is heard in a district court. It has been estimated that about half the cases in United States district courts are heard by a jury.

At the intermediate level in the federal judiciary are the thirteen United States courts of appeal. These courts were also created by the Federal Judiciary Act of 1789. Until 1948 these courts were called circuit courts of appeal, a reflection of the early years of the republic when the justices of the Supreme

Court "rode the circuit" and presided at the courts-of-appeal hearings. While the title Circuit Courts of Appeal is gone, the nation is still divided into circuits, each of which is served by one court of appeal:

First Circuit: Maine, Massachusetts, New Hampshire, Rhode Island, and Puerto Rico

Second Circuit: Connecticut, New York, and Vermont

Third Circuit: Delaware, New Jersey, Pennsylvania, and Virgin Islands

Fourth Circuit: Maryland, North Carolina, South Carolina, Virginia, and West Virginia

Fifth Circuit: Texas, Mississippi, and Louisiana

Sixth Circuit: Kentucky, Michigan, Ohio, and Tennessee

Seventh Circuit: Illinois, Indiana, and Wisconsin

Eighth Circuit: Arkansas, Iowa, Minnesota, Missouri, Nebraska, North Dakota, and South Dakota

Ninth Circuit: Alaska, Arizona, California, Hawaii, Idaho, Montana, Nevada, Oregon, Washington, Guam, and Northern Mariana Islands

Tenth Circuit: Colorado, Kansas, New Mexico, Utah, Oklahoma, and Wyoming

Eleventh Circuit: Alabama, Florida, Georgia, and the Canal Zone

The twelfth and thirteenth circuits are unnumbered. One is the Court of Appeals for the District of Columbia. This is a very busy court since it hears most of the appeals from decisions made by federal administrative agencies. The thirteenth is the Court of Appeals for the Federal Circuit, a court created by the Congress in 1982 to handle special kinds of appeals. This court is especially empowered to hear appeals from patent and trademark decisions of United States district courts and other federal agencies such as the Board of Patent Appeals. It also hears appeals from rulings by the United States Claims Court, the United States Court of International Trade, the United States International Trade Commission, the Merit Systems Protection Board and a handful of other special kinds of rulings. Congress established this court to try to develop a uniform, reliable, and predictable body of law in each of these very special fields. But observers say the new court has not worked as well as hoped since there remains considerable confusion about its jurisdiction. Many of the cases which should be heard by the Court of Appeals for the Federal Circuit are still mistakenly heard by other courts of appeal.

The courts of appeal are appellate courts, which means that they only hear appeals from lower courts and other agencies. These courts are the last stop for nine out of ten cases in the federal system. Each circuit has nine or more judges. Typically a panel of three judges hear a case. In a case of great importance nine or more of the judges hear the case. This is called sitting **en banc.**

Federal Judges

All federal judges are appointed by the president and must be confirmed by the Senate. The appointment is for life. The only way a federal judge can be removed is by impeachment. Nine federal judges have been impeached: Four were found guilty by the Senate, and the other five were acquitted. Impeachment and trial is a long process and one rarely undertaken.

Political affiliation plays a distinct part in the appointment of federal judges. Democratic presidents usually appoint Democratic judges, and Republican presidents appoint Republican judges. Nevertheless, it is expected that nominees to the federal bench be competent jurists. This is especially true for appointees to the courts of appeal and to the Supreme Court. The Senate must confirm all appointments to the federal courts, a normally perfunctory act in the case of lower-court judges. More careful scrutiny is given nominees to the appellate courts. The Senate has rejected twenty-two men nominated for the Supreme Court either by adverse vote or by delaying the vote so long that the appointment was withdrawn by the president or the president left office and the new chief executive nominated a different individual. Most recently Judge Robert Bork's nomination to the Supreme Court was rejected.

While district judges must live in the community in which they work and are therefore clearly sensitive to some public pressure, judges of the courts of appeal and the justices of the Supreme Court are quite isolated from public pressure. Hence, philosophy can change when an individual reaches the Court; judges and justices mature or change in many directions. Liberal President John Kennedy named Justice Byron White to the Supreme Court, but Justice White more often than not has taken the conservative position in recent years. President Richard Nixon thought he had nominated a conservative when he name Judge Harry Blackmun to the Court, and Justice Blackmun lived up to that billing for several years. But recently, Justice Blackmun has often joined with liberals on the court, especially on First Amendment issues.

The State Court System

The constitution of every one of the fifty states either establishes a court system in that state or authorizes the legislature to do so. The court system in each of the fifty states is somewhat different from the court system in all the other states. There are, however, more similarities than differences among the fifty states.

The **trial courts** (or court) are the base of each judicial system. At the lowest level are usually what are called courts of limited jurisdiction. Some of these courts have special functions, like a traffic court, which is set up to hear cases involving violations of the motor-vehicle code. Some of these courts are limited to hearing cases of relative unimportance, such as trials of persons charged with misdemeanors, or minor crimes, or civil suits where the damages sought fall below one thousand dollars. The court may be a municipal court set up to hear cases involving violations of the city code. Whatever the court, the judges in these courts have limited jurisdiction and deal with a limited category of problems.

Above the lower-level courts normally exist trial courts of general jurisdiction similar to the federal district courts. These courts are sometimes county courts and sometimes state courts, but whichever they are, they handle nearly all criminal and civil matters. They are primarily courts of original jurisdiction; that is, they are the first courts to hear a case. However, on occasion they act as a kind of appellate court when the decisions of the courts of limited jurisdiction are challenged. When that happens, the case is retried in the trial court—the court does not simply review the law. This proceeding is called hearing a case **de novo.**

A **jury** is most likely to be found in the trial court of general jurisdiction. It is also the court in which most civil suits for libel and invasion of privacy are commenced (provided the state court has jurisdiction), in which prosecution for violating state obscenity laws starts, and in which many other media-related matters begin.

Above this court may be one or two levels of appellate courts. Every state has a supreme court, although some states do not call it that. In New York, for example, it is called the Court of Appeals, but it is the high court in the state, the court of last resort. Formerly a supreme court was the only appellate court in most states. As legal business increased and the number of appeals mounted, the need for an intermediate appellate court became evident. Therefore, in most states there is an intermediate court, usually called the court of appeals. This is the court where most appeals end. In some states it is a single court with three or more judges. More often, numerous divisions within the appellate court serve various geographic regions, each division having three or more judges. Since every litigant is normally guaranteed at least one appeal, this intermediate court takes much of the pressure off the high court of the state. Rarely do individuals appeal beyond the intermediate level.

State courts of appeal tend to operate in much the same fashion as the United States courts of appeal, with cases being heard by small groups of judges, usually three at a time.

Cases not involving federal questions go no further than the high court in a state, usually called the supreme court. This court—usually a seven- or nine-member body—is the final authority regarding the construction of state laws and interpretation of the state constitution. Not even the Supreme Court of the United States can tell a state supreme court what that state's constitution means. For example, in 1976 the United States Supreme Court ruled that the protection of the First Amendment did not include the right to distribute materials, demonstrate, or solicit petition signatures at privately owned shopping centers (*Hudgens* v. *NLRB*—this case is discussed fully on page 95). In 1980, however, the Supreme Court refused to overturn a decision by the California Supreme Court which declared that students had the right under the California constitution to solicit signatures for a pro-Israeli petition at a private shopping center in Campbell, California. Justice William Rehnquist wrote for the unanimous United States Supreme Court that perhaps the free-speech guarantee in the California constitution is broader than the First Amendment. In any case, the California High Court was the final authority on the state's constitution (*Pruneyard Shopping Center* v. *Robins*).

State supreme court judges—like most state judges—are usually elected. Normally the process is nonpartisan, but because they are elected and must stand for reelection periodically, state court judges are generally a bit more politically motivated than their federal counterparts. In some states the judges or justices are appointed, and several states use an unusual system that both appoints and elects. Under this scheme, called the **Missouri Plan,** the state's high-court judges (and sometimes all judges) are appointed to the bench by the governor from a list supplied by a nonpartisan judicial commission. After a one-year term, the judge must stand before the people during a general election and win popular support. The voter's ballot asks "Shall Judge Smith be retained in office?" If Judge Smith wins support, his next term is usually a long one, up to twelve years. If support is not forthcoming, a new person is selected to fill the seat for one year, and at the end of the term the judge must seek voter approval.

The advantages of the Missouri Plan are appointment of a qualified person initially and eventual citizen participation in the selection process.

Judicial Review

One of the most important powers of courts (and at one time one of the most controversial) is the power of **judicial review**—that is, the right of any court to declare any law or official governmental action invalid because it violates a constitutional provision. We usually think of this in terms of the United States Constitution. However, a state court can declare an act of its legislature to be invalid because the act conflicts with a provision of the state constitution. Theoretically, any court can exercise this power. The Circuit Court of Lapeer County, Michigan, can rule that the Environmental Protection Act of 1972 is unconstitutional because it deprives citizens of their property without due process of law, something guaranteed by the Fifth Amendment to the federal Constitution. But this action isn't likely to happen, because a higher court would quickly overturn such a ruling. In fact, it is rather unusual for any court—even the United States Supreme Court—to invalidate a state or federal law on grounds that it violates the Constitution. Less than 130 federal statutes have been overturned by the courts in the two-hundred-year history of the United States. During the same period, about one thousand state laws and state constitutional provisions have been declared invalid. Judicial review is therefore not a power that the courts use excessively. In fact, a judicial maxim states: When a court has a choice of two or more ways in which to interpret a statute, the court should always interpret the statute in such a way that it is constitutional.

Judicial review is extremely important when matters concerning regulations of the mass media are considered. Because the First Amendment prohibits laws that abridge freedom of the press and freedom of speech, each new measure passed by the Congress, by state legislatures, and even by city councils and township boards must be measured by the yardstick of the First Amendment. Courts have the right, in fact have the duty, to nullify laws and executive actions and administrative rulings that do not meet the standards of the First Amendment. While many lawyers and legal scholars rarely consider constitutional principles in their work and rarely seek judicial review of a statute, attorneys who represent newspapers, magazines, broadcasting stations, and motion-picture theaters constantly deal with constitutional issues, primarily those of the First Amendment. The remainder of this book will illustrate the obvious fact that judicial review, a concept at the very heart of American democracy, plays an important role in maintaining the freedom of the American press, even though the power is not explicitly included in the Constitution.

Lawsuits

The final topic which needs to be understood before mass media law itself is considered is what happens in a lawsuit. The brief discussion of the process which follows is simplified as much as possible. Many good books on the subject are available for persons interested in going further into the intricacies of lawsuits (some are listed in the Bibliography at the end of the chapter).

The party who commences a civil action is called the **plaintiff,** the person who brings the suit. The party against whom the suit is brought is called the **defendant.** In a libel suit the person who has been libeled is the plaintiff and is the one who starts the suit against the defendant—the newspaper, the magazine, the television station, or whatever. To file a civil suit is a fairly simple process. A civil suit is usually a dispute between two private parties. The government offers its good offices—the courts—to settle the matter. A government can bring a civil suit such as an antitrust action against someone, and an individual can bring a civil action against the government. But normally a civil suit is between private parties. (In a criminal action, the government always initiates the action.)

To start a civil suit the plaintiff first picks the proper court, one that has jurisdiction in the case. Then the plaintiff files a **civil complaint** with the court clerk. This complaint, or **pleading,** is a statement of the charges against the defendant and the remedy that is sought, typically money damages. The plaintiff also summons the defendant to appear in court to answer these charges. While the plaintiff may later amend his or her pleadings in the case, usually the initial complaint is the only pleading filed. After the complaint is filed, a hearing is scheduled by the court.

If the defendant fails to answer the charges, he or she normally loses the suit by default. Usually, however, the defendant will answer the summons and prepare his or her own set of pleadings, which constitute an answer to the plaintiff's charges. If there is little disagreement at this point about the facts—what happened—and that a wrong has been committed, the plaintiff and the defendant might settle their differences out of court. The defendant might say, "I guess I did libel you in this article, and I really don't have a very good defense. You asked for $15,000 in damages, would you settle for $7,500 and keep this out of court?" The plaintiff might very well answer yes, because a court trial is costly and takes a long time, and the plaintiff can also end up losing the case. Smart lawyers try to keep their clients out of court if possible and settle matters in somebody's office.

If there is disagreement, the case is likely to continue. A common move for the defendant to make at this point is to file a motion to dismiss, or a **demurrer.** In such a motion the defendant says this to the court: "I admit that I did everything the plaintiff says I did. On June 5, 1989, I did publish an article in which he was called a socialist. But, Your Honor, it is not libelous to call someone a socialist." The plea made then is that even if everything the plaintiff asserts is true, the plaintiff is not legally wronged. The law cannot help the plaintiff. The court might grant the motion, in which case the plaintiff can appeal. Or the court might refuse to grant the motion, in which case the defendant can appeal. If the motion to dismiss is ultimately rejected by all the courts up and down the line, a trial is then held. It is fair play for the defendant at that time to begin argument of the facts, in other words to deny that his newspaper published the article containing the alleged libel.

Before the trial is held, the judge may schedule a conference between both parties in an effort to settle the matter before starting the formal hearing or at least to narrow the issues so that the trial can be shorter and less costly. If this move fails, the trial goes forward. If the facts are agreed upon by both sides and the question is merely one of law, a judge without a jury hears the case. There are no witnesses and no testimony, only legal arguments before the court. If the facts are disputed, the case can be tried before either a jury or, again, only a judge. Note that both sides must waive the right to a jury trial. In this event, the judge becomes both the fact finder and the lawgiver. Now, suppose that the case is heard by a jury. After all the testimony is given, all the evidence is presented, and all the arguments are made, the judge instructs the jury in the law. Instructions are often long and complex, despite attempts by judges to simplify them. **Judicial instructions** guide the jury in determining guilt or innocence if certain facts are found to be true. The judge will say that if the jury finds that X is true and Y is true and Z is true, then it must find for the plaintiff, but if the jury finds that X is not true, but that R is true, then it must find for the defendant.

After deliberation the jury presents its **verdict,** the action by the jury. The judge then announces the **judgment of the court.** This is the decision of the court. The judge is not always bound by the jury verdict. If he or she feels that the jury verdict is unfair or unreasonable, the judge can reverse it and rule for the other party. Needless to say this happens rarely.

If either party is unhappy with the decision, an appeal can be taken. At that time the legal designations change. The person seeking the appeal becomes the **appellant,** or **petitioner.** The other party becomes the **appellee,** or **respondent.** The name of the party initiating the action is usually listed first in the name of the case. For example: Smith sues Jones for libel. The case name is *Smith* v. *Jones.* Jones loses and takes an appeal. At that point Jones becomes the party initiating the action and the case becomes *Jones* v. *Smith.* This change in designations often confuses novices in their attempt to trace a case from trial to final appeal. If Jones wins the appeal and Smith decides to appeal to a higher court, the case again becomes *Smith* v. *Jones.* In a few jurisdictions, the names in the case remain in the order in which the case was first heard throughout the appeal process. *Smith* v. *Jones* would remain *Smith* v. *Jones* until the end in California, for example.

The end result of a successful civil suit is usually awarding of money **damages.** Sometimes the amount of damages is guided by the law, as in a suit for infringement of copyright in which the law provides that a losing defendant pay the plaintiff the amount of money he or she might have made if the infringement had not occurred, or at least a set number of dollars. But most of the time the damages are determined by how much the plaintiff seeks, how much the plaintiff can prove he or she lost, and how much the jury thinks the plaintiff deserves. It is not a very scientific means of determining the dollar amount.

A **criminal suit** is like a civil suit in many ways. The procedures are more formal, are more elaborate, and involve the machinery of the state to a greater extent. The state brings the charges, usually through the county or state prosecutor. The defendant can be apprehended either before or after the charges are brought. In the federal system persons must be indicted by a **grand jury,** a panel of twenty-one citizens, before they can be charged with a serious crime. But most states do not use grand juries in that fashion, and the law provides that it is sufficient that the prosecutor issue an **information,** a formal accusation. After being charged, the defendant is arraigned. An **arraignment** is the formal reading of the charge. It is at the arraignment that the defendant makes a formal plea of guilty or not guilty. If the plea is guilty, the judge then gives the verdict of the court and passes sentence, but usually not immediately, for presentencing reports and other procedures must be undertaken. If the plea is not guilty, a trial is then scheduled.

Some state judicial systems have an intermediate step called a preliminary hearing or preliminary examination. The preliminary hearing is held in a court below the trial court, such as a municipal court, and the state has the responsibility of presenting enough evidence to convince the court—only a judge—that a crime has been committed and that there is sufficient evidence to believe that the defendant might possibly be involved.

In both a civil suit and a criminal case, the result of the trial is not enforced until the final appeal is exhausted. That is, a money judgment is not paid in civil suits until defendants exhaust all of their appeals. The same is true in a criminal case. Imprisonment or payment of a fine is not required until the final appeal. However, if the defendant is dangerous or if there is some question that the defendant might not surrender when the final appeal is completed, bail can be required. Bail is money given to the court to ensure appearance in court.

SUMMARY

There are fifty-one different judicial systems in the nation: one federal system and one for each of the fifty states. Courts within each of these systems are divided into two general classes—trial courts and appellate courts. In any lawsuit both the facts and the law must be considered. The facts or the factual record is an account of what happened to prompt the dispute. The law is what should be done to resolve the dispute. Trial courts determine the facts in the case; then the judge applies the law. Appellate courts, using the factual record established by the trial court, determine whether the law was properly applied by the lower court and whether proper judicial procedures were followed. Trial courts exercise original jurisdiction almost exclusively; that is, they are the first courts to hear a case. Trial courts have very little discretion over which cases they will and will not hear. Appellate courts exercise appellate jurisdiction almost exclusively; that is, they review the work done by the lower courts when decisions are appealed. While the intermediate appellate courts (i.e., courts of appeal; the appellate division) have limited discretion in the selection of cases, the high courts (supreme courts) in the states and the nation generally have the power to select the cases they wish to review.

Federal courts include the Supreme Court of the United States, the courts of appeal, the United States district courts, and several specialized tribunals. These courts have jurisdiction in all cases that involve the United States Constitution, United States law, and United States treaties; in disputes between citizens of different states; and in several less important instances. In each state there are trial-level courts and a court of last resort, usually called the supreme court. In about half of the states there are intermediate appellate courts as well. State courts generally have jurisdiction in all disputes between citizens of their state that involve the state constitution or state law.

Judicial review is the power of a court to declare a statute, regulation, or executive action to be a violation of the Constitution and thus invalid. Because the First Amendment to the United States Constitution guarantees the rights of freedom of speech and freedom of the press, all government actions that relate to the communication of ideas and information face potential scrutiny by the courts to determine their validity.

There are two basic kinds of lawsuits—civil suits and criminal suits. A civil suit is normally a dispute between two private parties in which the government offers its good offices (the courts) to resolve the dispute. The person who initiates the civil suit is called the plaintiff; the person at whom the suit is aimed is called the defendant. A plaintiff who wins a civil suit is normally awarded money damages.

A criminal case is normally an action in which the state brings charges against a private individual, who is called the defendant. A defendant who loses a criminal case can be assessed a fine, jailed, or in extreme cases executed. A jury can be used in both civil and criminal cases. The jury becomes the fact finder and renders a verdict in a case. But the judge issues the judgment in the case. In a civil suit a judge can reject any jury verdict and rule in exactly the opposite fashion, finding for either plaintiff or defendant if the judge feels the jury has made a serious error in judgment. Either side can appeal the judgment of the court. In a criminal case the judge can take the case away from the jury and order a dismissal, but nothing can be done about an acquittal, even an incredible acquittal, as Charles Rembar notes in his book *The Law of the Land*. While a guilty defendant may appeal the judgment, the state is prohibited from appealing an acquittal.

As stated at the outset, this chapter is designed to provide a glimpse, only a glimpse, of both our legal system and our judicial system. The discussion is in no way comprehensive, but it provides enough information to make the remaining eleven chapters meaningful. The chapter is not intended to be a substitute for a good political science course in the legal process. Students of communications law are at a distinct disadvantage if they do not have some grasp of how the systems work and what their origins are.

The United States legal and judicial systems are old and tradition-bound. But they have worked fairly well for these last two hundred years. In the final analysis the job of both the law and the men and women who administer it is to balance the competing interests of society. How this balancing act is undertaken comprises the remainder of this book. The process is not always easy, but it is usually interesting.

| BIBLIOGRAPHY | *Here is a list of some of the sources that have been helpful in the preparation of chapter 1:* |

Books	Abraham, Henry. *The Judicial Process.* 4th ed. New York: Oxford University Press, 1980.
	_____. *The Judiciary: The Supreme Court in the Government Process.* 3d ed. Boston: Allyn & Bacon, 1973.
	Franklin, Marc A., *The Dynamics of American Law.* Mineola, N. Y.: Foundation Press, 1969.

Holmes, Oliver W. *The Common Law*. Boston: Little, Brown & Co., 1881.
Pound, Roscoe. *The Development of the Constitutional Guarantees of Liberty*. New Haven: Yale University Press, 1957.
Rembar, Charles. *The Law of the Land*. New York: Simon & Schuster, 1980.
Roche, John P. *Courts and Rights*. 2d ed. New York: Random House, 1966.

Cases

Barber v. *Time*, 159 S.W.2d 291 (1942).
Branzburg v. *Hayes*, 408 U.S. 665 (1972).
Gannett v. *DePasquale*, 443 U.S. 368 (1979).
Goldwater v. *Ginzburg*, 414 F.2d 324 (1969).
Hudgens v. *NLRB*, 424 U.S. 507 (1976).
Island Trees v. *Pico*, 457 U.S. 853 (1982).
New York Times Co. v. *U.S.*, 403 U.S. 713 (1971).
Nye v. *U.S.*, 313 U.S. 33 (1941).
Pruneyard Shopping Center v. *Robins*, 447 U.S. 74 (1980).
Time, Inc. v. *Hill*, 385 U.S. 374 (1967).
Toledo Newspaper Co. v. *U.S.*, 242 U.S. 402 (1918).
U.S. v. *Barnett*, 376 U.S. 681 (1964).

2 FREEDOM OF THE PRESS

When people reach the final years of their lives, they often ponder how people will remember them. What aspects of their characters and their contributions to society will people cherish? What will be quickly forgotten? So too is it with nations. Historians outline the important contributions made by ancient China, Greece and Rome, by imperial Spain, and by the British Empire. What will historians consider the outstanding contributions of America and Americans? William O. Douglas, former associate justice of the Supreme Court of the United States, suggests that United States technology will not be the most memorable aspect of the nation's life. Instead, it will be our experiment with freedom of expression, an experiment shared with other Western democracies. Freedom of speech and freedom of the press—they are the achievements people will look upon with awe in eons to come.

No one knows whether Justice Douglas will be right. Clearly the attempt by Western democracies during the past three centuries to construct societies based upon the freedom to speak, the freedom to publish, and the freedom to criticize the government is a remarkable effort. Perhaps even more remarkable is that the experiment has worked so well. The guarantee of freedom of expression can be found in the constitution of nearly every nation. Only in a few countries such as the United States, however, are the people and the government dedicated to making the ideal come true. As this chapter is being prepared, for example, the fundamentalist religious leader of Iran has ordered his Moslem followers to kill British author Salmon Rushdie because his book, *Satanic Verses,* is considered blasphemous by some Moslems. And the people in Poland, the Soviet Union, and China are struggling—sometimes against armed military resistance—to gain greater freedom, including freedom of expression.

The purpose of this chapter is to sketch a broad outline of the meaning of freedom of the press in the United States today. Freedom of the press is an element in all aspects of mass media law—libel, invasion of privacy, obscenity, regulation of broadcasting, and so forth. Indeed, in any area in which the law touches mass media, the First Amendment is a material consideration. At the same time, broader general principles defining freedom of expression have been fashioned by the courts in the past half-century. It is these broader principles that we will focus upon in chapter 2. ◆

HISTORICAL DEVELOPMENT	Before freedom of the press can be defined, a brief look at the roots of the idea, roots that wind through many centuries, is necessary. Freedom of the press is not, and was not, exclusively an American idea. We did not invent the concept—in fact, no one invented it. Like Topsy, it just grew from crude beginnings that can be traced back to Plato and Socrates. The concept developed more fully during the past four hundred years. The modern history of freedom of the press really began in England during the sixteenth and seventeenth centuries as printing developed and grew. Today the most indelible embodiment of the concept is the First Amendment to the United States Constitution, forged in the last half of the eighteenth century by the men who built upon their memory of earlier experiences. To understand the meaning of freedom of the press and freedom of speech, it is necessary to understand the meaning of censorship, for viewed from a negative position freedom of expression can be simply defined as the absence of censorship.
Freedom of the Press in England	When William Caxton set up the first British printing press in Westminster in 1476, his printing pursuits were restricted only by his imagination and ability. There were no laws governing what he could or could not print—he was completely free. For five centuries Englishmen and Americans have attempted to regain the freedom that Caxton enjoyed, for shortly after he started publishing, the British Crown began the control and regulation of printing presses in England. Printing developed during a period of great religious struggle in Europe, and it soon became an important tool in that struggle. Printing presses made communication with hundreds of persons fairly easy and in doing so gave considerable power to small groups or individuals who owned and/or could use a printing press.

The British government soon realized that unrestricted publication and printing could seriously dilute its own power. Information is a powerful tool in any society, and the individual or individuals who control the flow and content of the information received by a people exercise considerable control over those people. The printing press broke the Crown's monopoly of the flow of information, and therefore control of printing was essential.

Between 1476 and 1776 the British devised and used several means to limit or restrict the press in England. **Seditious libel** laws were used to punish those who criticized the government or the Crown, and it did not matter whether the criticism was truthful or not. The press suffered under **licensing** laws as well which required printers to get prior approval from the government or the church before printing their handbills or pamphlets or newspapers. Printers were also often required to deposit with the government large sums of money called **bonds.** This money was forfeited if material appeared that the government felt should not have been published. And the printer was forced to post another bond before printing could be resumed. The British also granted special patents and monopolies to certain printers in exchange for their co-operation in printing only acceptable works and in helping the Crown ferret out other printers who broke the publication laws.

British control of the press during these three hundred years was generally successful, but did not go unchallenged. As ideas about democracy spread throughout Europe it became harder and harder for the government to limit freedom of expression. The power of the printing press in spreading ideas quickly to masses of people greatly helped foster the democratic spirit. While British law regulated American printers as well during the colonial era, regulation of the press in North America was never as successful as it was in Great Britain.

Freedom of the Press in Colonial America

There were laws in the United States restricting freedom of the press for almost thirty years before the first newspaper was published. As early as 1662, statutes in Massachusetts made it a crime to publish anything without first getting prior approval from the government, twenty-eight years before Benjamin Harris published the first—and last—edition of *Publick Occurrences*. The second and all subsequent issues of the paper were banned because Harris had failed to get permission to publish the first edition, which contained material construed to be criticism of British policy in the colonies, as well as a report that scandalized the Massachusetts clergy because it said the French king took immoral liberties with a married woman (not his wife).

Despite this inauspicious beginning, American colonists had a much easier time getting their views into print (and staying out of jail) than their counterparts in England. There was censorship, but American juries were reluctant to convict printers prosecuted by the British colonial authorities. The colonial governments were less efficient than the government in England. Also, the British had only limited control over the administration of government in many of the colonies.

The British attempted to use licensing, taxes and sedition laws to control American printers and publishers. Licensing, which ended in England in 1695, lasted until the mid-1720s in the American colonies. Benjamin Franklin's older brother James was jailed in 1722 for failing to get prior government approval for publishing his *New England Courant*. The unpopular government move failed to daunt the older Franklin and licensing eventually ended in the colonies as well. The taxes levied against the press, most of which were genuine attempts to raise revenues, were nevertheless seen as censorship by American printers and resulted in growing hostility toward the Parliament and the Crown. Most publishers refused to buy the stamps and there was little retribution by the British.

Undoubtedly, the most famous case of government censorship in the American colonies was the seditious libel trial of immigrant printer John Peter Zenger, who found himself involved in a vicious political battle between leading colonial politicians in New York. Zenger published the *New York Weekly*

Journal, a newspaper sponsored by Lewis Morris and James Alexander, political opponents of the unpopular colonial governor, William Cosby. Zenger was jailed in November of 1734 after his newspaper published several stinging attacks on Cosby, who surmised that by jailing the printer—one of only two in New York—he could silence his critics. There is little doubt that Zenger was guilty under eighteenth century British sedition law. But his attorneys, including the renowned criminal lawyer Andrew Hamilton, were able to convince the jury that no man should be imprisoned or fined for publishing criticism of the government that was both truthful and fair. Jurors simply ignored the law and acquitted the German printer.

The verdict in the Zenger case was a great political triumph but did absolutely nothing to change the law of seditious libel. In other words, the case did not set an important legal precedent. But the revolt of the American jurors did force colonial authorities to reconsider the use of sedition law as a means of controlling the press. While a few sedition prosecutions were initiated after 1735, there is no record of a successful prosecution in the colonial courts after the Zenger case. The case received widespread publicity both in North America and in England, and the outcome of the trial played an important role in galvanizing public sentiment against this kind of government censorship.

The Zenger trial has today become an accepted part of American journalism mythology. While the case is certainly worth remembering, it doesn't represent the end of British attempts to control the press in the American colonies. Other means were substituted for sedition. Rather than haul printers and editors before jurors who were often hostile to the state, the government instead hauled printers and editors before colonial legislatures and assemblies that were usually hostile to journalists. The charge was not sedition, but breach of parliamentary privilege or contempt of the assembly. There was no distinct separation of powers then, and the legislative body could order the printer to appear, question him, convict him, and punish him. Printers and publishers were thus still being jailed and fined for publications previously considered sedition. Only the means of exacting this punishment had changed.

Yet despite these potent sanctions occasionally levied against publishers and printers, the press of this era was remarkably robust. Researchers who have painstakingly read the newspapers and pamphlets and handbills produced in the last half of the eighteenth century are struck by the seeming lack of concern for government retribution or censorship. Historian Leonard Levy notes in a recent book, *Emergence of a Free Press,* the seeming paradox uncovered by scholars who seek to understand the meaning of freedom of expression during that era. "To one [a scholar] whose prime concern was law and theory, a legacy of suppression [of the press] came into focus; to one who looks at newspaper judgments on public men and measures, the revolutionary controversy spurred an expanding legacy of liberty," he wrote.

But the appearance of such freedom can be deceptive, as political scientist John Roche points out in his book *Shadow and Substance,* for the community often exerted tremendous pressure upon anyone who expressed an unpopular idea. The belief of many persons that freedom was the hallmark of society in America ignores history, Roche argues. In colonial America the people simply did not understand that freedom of thought and expression meant freedom for the other fellow also, particularly for the fellow with hated ideas. Roche points out that colonial America was an open society dotted with closed enclaves—villages and towns and cities—in which citizens generally shared similar beliefs about religion and government and so forth. Citizens could hold any belief they chose and could espouse that belief, but personal safety depended upon the people in a community agreeing with a speaker or writer. If they didn't, the speaker then kept quiet or moved to another enclave where the people shared his ideas. While there was much diversity of thought in the colonies, there was often little diversity of belief within towns and cities, according to Roche.

The propaganda war that preceded the Revolution is a classic example of the situation. In Boston, the patriots argued vigorously for the right to print what they wanted in their newspapers, even criticism of the government. Freedom of expression was their right, a God-given right, a natural right, a right of all British subjects. Many persons, however, did not favor revolution or even separation from England. Yet it was extremely difficult for them to publish such pro-British sentiments in many American cities after 1770. Printers who published such ideas in newspapers and handbills did so at their peril. In cities like Boston the printers were attacked, their shops were wrecked, and their papers were destroyed. Freedom of the press was a concept with limited utility in many communities for colonists who opposed revolution once the patriots had moved the populace to their side.

The plight of the pro-British printer in Boston in the 1770s is not a unique chapter in American history. Today such community censorship still exists—and in some instances is growing. In recent years extreme pressure has been exerted on many retailers, for example, to exclude so-called men's magazines like *Playboy* from their newsstands. Students at universities like Harvard and Yale have attempted to block the appearances of extreme right-wing speakers with whom they disagree. Libraries continue to be the target of those who seek to ban books that they find objectionable. In many of these instances the general public, the masses on the sidelines, find little cause for concern about such attempts at censorship. The public malaise about such conditions is dangerous. No individual's freedom is secure unless the freedom of all is ensured.

SUMMARY

Freedom of the press is a part of the great Anglo-American legal tradition, but it is a right that has been won only through many hard-fought battles. The British discovered the power of the press in the early sixteenth century and devised numerous schemes to restrict publication. Criticism of the government, called seditious libel, was outlawed. Licensing or prior censorship was also common. In addition, the Crown for many years used an elaborate system of patents and monopolies to control printing in England.

While under British law for more than one hundred years, American colonists enjoyed somewhat more freedom of expression than did their counterparts in England. Censorship laws existed before the first printing press arrived in North America, but they were enforced erratically or not at all. Licensing ended in the United States colonies in the 1720s. There were several trials for sedition in the colonies, but the acquittal of John Peter Zenger in 1735 by a recalcitrant jury ended that threat. Colonial legislatures and assemblies then attempted to punish dissident printers by using their contempt power. By the time the American colonists began to build their own governments in the 1770s and 1780s, they had the history of a three-hundred-year struggle for freedom of expression upon which to build.

THE FIRST AMENDMENT

In 1781, even before the end of the Revolutionary War, the new nation adopted its first constitution, the Articles of Confederation. The Articles provided for a loose-knit confederation of the thirteen colonies, or states, in which the central or federal government had little power. The Articles of Confederation did not contain a guarantee of freedom of expression. In fact, it had no bill of rights of any kind. The men who drafted this constitution did not believe such guarantees were necessary. Under these articles states were the most powerful political entities; the national government had few prerogatives. Guarantees of freedom of expression were already a part of the constitutions of most of the thirteen states. The citizens of Virginia, for example, had adopted a new constitution that contained a declaration of rights in June 1776, five years before the Articles of Confederation were written. Freedom of the press was guaranteed as a part of that declaration of rights. Other states soon followed Virginia's lead.

But the system of government created by the Articles of Confederation did not work very well. In the hot summer of 1787, each of the thirteen states sent a handful of its best men to Philadelphia to revise or amend the Articles, to make fundamental changes in the structure of the government.

The New Constitution

It was a remarkable group of men; perhaps no such group has gathered before or since. The members were merchants and planters and professional men, and none were full-time politicians. As a group these men were by fact or inclination members of the economic, social, and intellectual aristocracy of their respective states. These men shared a common education centered around history, political philosophy, and science. Some of them spent months preparing for the meeting—studying the governments of past nations. While some members came to modify the Articles of Confederation, many others knew from the start that a new constitution was needed. In the end that is what they produced, a new governmental charter. The charter was far different from the Articles in that it gave vast powers to a central government. The states remained supreme in some matters, but in other matters they were forced to relinquish their sovereignty to the new federal government.

No official record of the convention was kept. The delegates deliberated behind closed doors as they drafted the new charter. However, some personal records remain. We do know, for example, that inclusion of a bill of rights in the new charter was not discussed until the last days of the convention. The Constitution was drafted in such a way as not to infringe upon state bills of rights. When the meeting was in its final week, George Mason of Virginia indicated his desire that "the plan be prefaced with a Bill of Rights. . . . It would give great quiet to the people," he said, "and with the aid of the state declarations, a bill might be prepared in a few hours." Few joined Mason's call. Only one delegate, Roger Sherman of Connecticut, spoke against the suggestion. He said he favored protecting the rights of the people when it was necessary, but in this case there was no need. "The state declarations of rights are not repealed by this Constitution; and being in force are sufficient." He said that where the rights of the people are involved Congress could be trusted to preserve the rights. The states, voting as units, unanimously opposed Mason's plan. While the Virginian later attempted to add a bill of rights in a piecemeal fashion, the Constitution emerged from the convention and was placed before the people for ratification without a bill of rights.

The new Constitution was not without opposition. The struggle for its adoption was hard fought. The failure to include a bill of rights in the document was a telling complaint raised against the new Constitution. Even Thomas Jefferson, who was in France, lamented, in a letter to his friend James Madison, the lack of a guarantee of political rights in the charter. When the states finally voted on the new Constitution, it was approved, but only after supporters in several states had promised to petition the First Congress to add a bill of rights.

James Madison was elected from Virginia to the House of Representatives, defeating James Monroe for the House seat only after promising his constituents to work in the First Congress toward adoption of a declaration of human rights. When Congress convened, Madison worked to keep his promise.

He first proposed that the new legislature incorporate a bill of rights into the body of the Constitution, but the idea was later dropped. That the Congress would adopt the declaration was not a foregone conclusion. There was much opposition, but after several months, twelve amendments were finally approved by both houses and sent to the states for ratification. Madison's original amendment dealing with freedom of expression states: "The people shall not be deprived or abridged of their right to speak, to write or to publish their sentiments and freedom of the press, as one of the great bulwarks of liberty, shall be inviolable." Congressional committees changed the wording several times, and the section guaranteeing freedom of expression was merged with the amendment guaranteeing freedom of religion and freedom of assembly. The final version is the version we know today:

> Congress shall make no law respecting an establishment of religion, or prohibiting the free exercise thereof; or abridging the freedom of speech, or of the press; or the right of the people peaceably to assemble, and to petition the Government for a redress of grievance.

The concept of the "first freedom" has been discussed often. Historical myth tells us that because the amendment occurs first in the Bill of Rights it was considered the most important right. In fact, in the Bill of Rights presented to the states for ratification, the amendment was listed third. Amendments one and two were defeated and did not become part of the Constitution. The original First Amendment called for a fixed schedule that apportioned seats in the House of Representatives on a ratio many persons thought unfair. The Second Amendment prohibited senators and representatives from altering their salaries until after a subsequent election of representatives. Both amendments were rejected, and amendment three became the First Amendment.

Passage of the last ten amendments did not occur without struggle. Not until two years after being transmitted to the states for approval did a sufficient number of states adopt the amendments for them to become part of the Constitution. Connecticut, Georgia, and Massachusetts did not ratify the Bill of Rights until 1941, a kind of token gesture on the 150th anniversary of its constitutional adoption. In 1791 approval by these states was not needed, since only three-fourths of the former colonies needed to agree to the measures.

Freedom of Expression in the Eighteenth Century

What did the First Amendment mean to the people who supported its ratification in 1790? This is not an idle question. The Bill of Rights was, after all, approved by a vote of the people in the several states. By their votes of approval, they enacted into the supreme law of the land their definitions of such rights as freedom of the press. Technically, the definition of freedom of the press approved by the nation when the First Amendment was ratified in 1791 is what is guaranteed today. To enlarge or narrow that definition requires another vote of the people, a constitutional amendment.

But most people today consider this notion so much legalistic poppycock. The nation has changed dramatically in two hundred years. Television, radio, and film did not exist in 1790, for example. Does this mean that the guarantees of the First Amendment should not apply to these mass media? Of course not. Our Constitution has lasted for two hundred years because it has been somewhat elastic. The Supreme Court of the United States, our final arbiter on the meaning of the Constitution, has helped adapt the document to changing times.

Still, it is important that we respect the document that was adopted almost two hundred years ago. If we stray too far from its original meaning, the document may become meaningless; there will be no rules of government. Anarchy will be but a step away.

What did the First Amendment mean in 1790? Surprisingly, that is not an easy question to answer. The records of the period carry mixed messages. There was really no authoritative definition of freedom of the press and freedom of speech rendered by a body like the Supreme Court. And even the words used by persons of that era may have meant something different in 1790 than they mean in 1990. Most everyone agrees that freedom of expression meant at least the right to be free from **prior restraint** or licensing. Sir William Blackstone, a British legal scholar, published a major four-volume summary of the common law between 1765 and 1769. In this summary, *Commentaries on the Law of England,* Blackstone defined freedom of expression as "laying no previous restraints upon publication." Today we call this no prior censorship. Many scholars argue that freedom of expression surely meant more than simply no prior censorship, that it also protected persons from punishment *after publication* for such offenses as criticizing the government. In other words, the First Amendment precluded prosecutions for seditious libel. After all, they argue, one of the reasons for the American Revolution was to rid the nation of the hated British sedition laws.

The truth is that we probably don't know what freedom of the press meant to American citizens two hundred years ago. The written residue of the period reveals only a partial story. It's very likely that it meant something a little different to different people, just as it does today. Even those individuals who drafted the Bill of Rights probably shared somewhat different views on the meaning of the First Amendment.

Freedom of Expression Today

If we are not certain what the First Amendment meant in 1790, do we know what it means today? More or less. The First Amendment means today what the Supreme Court of the United States says it means. Certainly many people often disagree with the definition of freedom of expression rendered by the High Court. But from the standpoint of the law—and that is what this book is about—the Supreme Court defines the meaning of the First Amendment to the Constitution.

The Supreme Court is a collection of nine justices, not a single individual. Consequently, at any given time there can be nine different definitions of freedom of expression. This has never happened—at least, not on important issues. What has happened is that groups of justices have subscribed to various theoretical positions regarding the meaning of the First Amendment. These theories of the meaning of the First Amendment help justices shape their vote on a question regarding freedom of expression. These theories have changed during the past sixty years, the point at which the First Amendment first came under serious scrutiny by the Supreme Court. It is rare that the justices themselves develop such theories. Most theories are proposed by persons outside the court: legal scholars, lower court judges, even philosophers. At some point a jurist finds a comfortable theory and uses it to assist in interpreting the First Amendment.

Legal theories are sometimes like amorphous wraiths—difficult to handle. Judge Learned Hand, a distinguished American jurist, referred to the propagation of legal theory as "shoveling smoke." With such cautions in mind, we will attempt to identify five important First Amendment theories or strategies that have been used or are used today to help judges develop a practical definition of freedom of expression.

Absolutist theory: The First Amendment declares that "no law" shall abridge the freedom of speech or of the press. "No law" means *no law*. Speech and press are absolutely protected from interference by the government. There are no exceptions. This is what was intended by the men who drafted the First Amendment.

No more than two Supreme Court justices—Hugo Black and William Douglas—have subscribed to this position. Critics of the absolutist theory argue that the key words in the First Amendment are "*freedom* of speech and press," not "no law." The freedom to speak and publish was not an absolute freedom in 1790; limits to this freedom were accepted by the people. What the amendment means, then, is that "no law" may abridge the limited protection given to the rights to speak and publish. If speech and press were to be protected absolutely, the First Amendment would have been written this way: "Congress shall pass no law abridging speech and press." The absolutist theory has received little public support because it lacks the recognition that other important human rights often conflict with freedom of speech and press.

Ad hoc balancing theory: Freedom of speech and press are two of a number of important human rights we value in this nation. These rights often conflict. When conflict occurs, it is the responsibility of the court to balance the freedom of expression with other values. For example, the government must maintain the military to protect the people from aggression. To function, the military must maintain security about many of its weapons, plans, and movements. Imagine that the press seeks to publish information about a secret weapon system. The right to freedom of expression must be balanced with the need for secrecy in the military.

This theory is called *ad hoc* balancing because the scales are erected anew in every case; the meaning of the freedom of expression is determined solely on a case by case basis. Freedom of the press might outweigh the need for the government to keep secret the design of its new rifle, but the need for secrecy about a new fighter plane might take precedence over freedom of expression.

Ad hoc balancing is really not a theory; it is a strategy. Developing a definition of freedom of expression on a case-by-case basis leads to uncertainty. Under *ad hoc* balancing we will never know what the First Amendment means except as it relates to a specific, narrow problem (e.g., the right to publish information about a new army rifle). If citizens cannot reasonably predict whether a particular kind of expression might be protected or prohibited, they will have the tendency to play it safe and keep silent. This will limit the rights of expression of all persons. Also, *ad hoc* balancing relies too heavily in its final determination on the personal biases of the judge or justices who decide a case.

Preferred position balancing theory: Freedom of expression is the foundation of the United States system of government. Without our ability to speak and publish freely, all other rights have little meaning. Of what value is the right to be free from illegal police searches if complaints about the police after such searches have been made cannot be published? Because it is so important, freedom of expression must be given a preferred status when balanced against other rights. Operationally this means that whenever balancing between freedom of expression and some other interest takes place, a court will presume that the limitation upon freedom of speech or freedom of the press is illegal. It is the responsibility of the persons who seek to block the speech or publication to convince a court that their interests should be given preference. For example, imagine that the navy seeks to block the publication of information about a new fighter plane. The navy must prove to the court that the publication of this material will be harmful to the national interests. Those who seek to publish the material are not obliged to convince the court that publication of the matter will be harmless or that the people have a right to see this information. The burden of proof falls on the navy.

Today, courts use this theory more than any other. While it retains some of the negative features of *ad hoc* balancing, by tilting the scales in favor of freedom of expression it adds somewhat more certainty to our definition of freedom of expression. By basing this balancing strategy upon a philosophical foundation (the maintenance of all rights is dependent upon free exercise of speech and press), it becomes easier to build a case in favor of the broad interpretation of freedom of expression under the First Amendment.

Meiklejohnian theory: Philosopher Alexander Meiklejohn presented the legal community with a rather complex set of ideas about freedom of expression in the late 1940s (*Free Speech and Its Relation to Self-Government*).

Meiklejohn looked at the First Amendment in a pragmatic manner and argued that freedom of expression is worth little as an abstract concept; that its primary value is as a means to an end. That end is successful self-government. Freedom of speech and press are protected in the Constitution so that our system of democracy can function, and that is the only reason they are protected. Expression that relates to the self-governing process must be protected absolutely by the First Amendment. There can be no government interference with such expression. Expression that does not relate to the self-governing process is not protected absolutely by the First Amendment. The value or worth of such speech must be balanced by the courts against other rights and values.

Critics of this theory argue in a telling fashion that it is not always clear whether expression pertains to self-government (public speech) or to other interests (private speech). While not providing the specific definition sought by critics, Meiklejohn argued that a broad range of speech is essential to successful self-government. He included speech-related education (history, political science, geography, etc.), science, literature, and many other topics. This theory has been subscribed to by some members of the Supreme Court of the United States, most notably Justice William Brennan. American libel law was radically changed when Brennan led the Supreme Court to give First Amendment protection only to libels published about government officials and others who attempt to lead public policy, a purely Meiklejohnian approach to the problem.

Access theory: In the mid1960s some legal scholars suggested that the First Amendment includes the right of the people to gain access to the mass media to publish or present their own views and ideas. Development of this theory was prompted by economic trends in the nation, which showed a rapidly diminishing number of newspapers. Surely the First Amendment means more than simply the right of rich publishers to print their views. The First Amendment gives the average citizen the right to speak and publish freely. To make this right mean something, newspapers should be forced to open up their news columns to persons with ideas and views different from their own.

The Supreme Court unanimously rejected this notion in 1974 in *Miami Herald* v. *Tornillo*. Chief Justice Warren Burger, writing for the Court, said that the choice of material to go into a newspaper, and the decisions made as to limitations on the size of the paper and to content and treatment of public issues and public officials are decisions that must be made by the editors. The First Amendment does not give the government the right to force a newspaper to publish the views or ideas of a citizen. The *Tornillo* case sounded the legal death knell for this access theory for print media. See *South Wind Motel* v. *Lashutka* (1983) for an example of how courts have rejected the access theory since the *Tornillo* ruling.

However, the access theory was a potent justification for the regulation of broadcasting. The Federal Communication Commission has in the past justified its regulation of the content of broadcasting on the theory that the airwaves belong to the people and that all persons really have a right to see and hear programs that reflect a diverse range of ideas. As Justice Byron White said in the famous case of *Red Lion Broadcasting* v. *FCC* (1969), "It is the right of the public to receive suitable access to social, political, esthetic, moral, and other ideas and experiences, which is crucial here." Using this argument as a foundation, the government has justified the application of the Fairness Doctrine and other rules that can force broadcasters to carry certain kinds of programming. As we will note in chapter 11, this philosophy of broadcast regulation is being undercut today by many factors.

The five theories or strategies just outlined guide jurists across the nation as they attempt to fathom the meaning of these seemingly simple thirteen words: "Congress shall make no law abridging freedom of speech or of the press." In the remainder of this book, we will attempt to tell you what the courts—using these theories—say the First Amendment means. It is appropriate that we begin that discussion now.

SUMMARY

The nation's first constitution, the Articles of Confederation, did not contain a guarantee of freedom of speech and press, but nearly all state constitutions provided for a guarantee of such rights. Citizens insisted that a written declaration of rights be included in the Constitution of 1787, and a guarantee of freedom of expression was a part of the Bill of Rights that was added to the national charter in 1791.

There is a debate within the legal-historical community over the meaning of the First Amendment when it was drafted and approved in the late eighteenth century. Some persons argue that it was intended to block both prior censorship and prosecution for seditious libel. Others argue that it prohibits only prior censorship. We will probably never know what the guarantee of freedom of expression meant to the persons who drafted it, but it is a good bet that citizens had a wide variety of interpretations of the First Amendment when they voted to approve it.

The meaning of the First Amendment today is largely determined through interpretation by the Supreme Court of the United States. Jurists use legal theories to guide them in determining the meaning of the Constitutional guarantee that "Congress shall make no law abridging freedom of speech or of the press." Five such theories are (1) absolutist theory, (2) *ad hoc* balancing theory, (3) preferred position balancing theory, (4) Meiklejohnian theory, and (5) public access theory. Theories two, three, and four have the most supporters on the Supreme Court, and all the theories have assisted members of the High Court to shape the meaning of the First Amendment.

SEDITIOUS LIBEL AND THE RIGHT TO CRITICIZE THE GOVERNMENT

The First Amendment of the United States Constitution states:

> Congress shall make no law respecting an establishment of religion, or prohibiting the free exercise thereof; or abridging the freedom of speech, or of the press; or the right of the people peaceably to assemble, and to petition the Government for a redress of grievances.

The essence of a democracy is the participation by citizens in the process of government. At its most basic level, this participation involves selecting leaders for the nation, the state, and the various local governments through the electoral process. Popular participation also includes examination of government and public officials to determine their fitness for serving the people. Discussion, criticism, and suggestion all play a part in the orderly transition of governments and elected leaders. The right to speak and print, then, is inherent in a nation governed by popularly elected rulers.

Whether the rights of free expression as defined in 1790 included a broad right to criticize the government, this kind of political speech has emerged as a central element of our modern understanding of the First Amendment.

The right to discuss the government, the right to criticize the government, the right to oppose the government, the right to advocate the change of the government—all of these dimensions of free speech and free press are at the center of our political philosophy today. But this has not always been the case. Even today we are sometimes troubled when asked to decide just how far an individual can go in criticizing or opposing the government. Can the use of force or violence be advocated as a means of changing the government? Can a citizen use the essence of democracy, free expression, to advocate the violent abolition of democracy and the establishment of a repressive state in which the rights of free speech and free press would be denied? Americans familiar with the history of the past two hundred years know these are more than academic questions. Some of the fiercest First Amendment battles have been fought over exactly these issues.

Alien and Sedition Acts

The United States wasn't even ten years old when the nation's resolve in protecting freedom of expression was first tested. Intense rivalry between President John Adams' Federalist party and Thomas Jefferson's Republican or Jeffersonian party, coupled with the fear of some that the growing violence in the French Revolution might spread to this country, led to the adoption by the Federalist-dominated Congress of a series of highly repressive measures known as the **Alien and Sedition Acts of 1798.** Three laws dealt with aliens, extending the period of residency prior to naturalization and giving the president extraordinary powers to detain and deport these noncitizen residents of the United States. A sedition law forbade false, scandalous, and malicious publications against the United States government, the Congress, and the president. The new law also punished persons who sought to stir up sedition or urged resistance to federal laws. Punishment was a fine of as much as two thousand dollars and a term in jail of up to two years. This latter statute was aimed squarely at the Jeffersonian political newspapers, many of which were relentless in their attacks upon President Adams and his government.

There were fifteen prosecutions under this law. This doesn't sound like many, but among those prosecuted were editors of eight Jeffersonian newspapers, including some of the leading papers in the nation. Imagine the federal government bringing sedition charges today against the editors of *The New York Times, Washington Post, Miami Herald,* and *Chicago Tribune.* Also prosecuted was a Republican member of Congress, Matthew Lyon. The so-called seditious libel that was the basis for the criminal charges was usually petty at best and hardly threatened our admittedly youthful government. But Federalist judges heard most of the cases and convictions were common.

Far from inhibiting dissent, the laws succeeded only in generating dissension among many of President Adams' supporters. Many argue that Adams lost his bid for re-election in 1800 largely because of public dissatisfaction with his attempt to muzzle his critics. The constitutionality of the laws was never tested before the full Supreme Court, but three members of the Court heard Sedition Act cases while they were on the circuit. The constitutionality of the provisions was sustained by these justices. The Sedition Act expired in 1801 and President Thomas Jefferson pardoned all persons convicted under it, while Congress eventually repaid most of the fines. This was the nation's first peacetime sedition law and it left such a bad taste that another peacetime sedition law was not passed until 1940.

The issue of political dissent did not really enter the national debate again until the end of the 1800s when hundreds of thousands of Americans began to understand that democracy and capitalism were not going to bring them the prosperity promised as an American birthright. The advancing rush of the new industrial society left many Americans behind and unhappy. Tens of thousands sought solace and change in political movements such as socialism and anarchism, movements that were considered by most in the mainstream to be foreign to the United States. Labor unrest in the late nineteenth century often turned violent, radical protests turned bloody. President McKinley was assassinated in 1901. Revolution, clearly unlikely, nevertheless arose as a specter in the minds of millions of Americans. Hundreds of laws were passed by states and cities across the nation to try to limit this kind of political dissent. War broke out in Europe in 1914; the United States joined the conflict three years later. This pushed the nation over the edge and anything that remained of our national tolerance toward political dissent and criticism of the government and economic system vanished. At both the state and the federal level, government struck out at those who sought to criticize or suggest radical change.

World War I is probably the most unpopular war this nation has fought, rivaling the Vietnam conflict in terms of public protest. The war was a replay of the imperial wars of the seventeenth and eighteenth centuries in Europe, except that it was fought with deadly new weapons. Industrialists and farmers saw the opportunity for vast economic gains in supplying war goods and super patriots were thrilled that the United States was actually going to have the opportunity to fight in a real war on the continent. But to millions of people in this nation the war was being fought in their homelands. Their families were dying; their relatives were now our enemies. The economically dispossessed rightly feared as well that the outbreak of war signaled the beginning of a period of internal political repression for those with little power.

Suppression of freedom of expression reached a higher level during World War I than at any other time in our history. Government prosecutions during the Vietnam War, for example, were minor compared with government action between 1918 and 1920. Vigilante groups were active as well, persecuting when the government failed to prosecute.

Two federal laws were passed to deal with persons who opposed the war and United States participation in it. In 1917 the **Espionage Act** was approved by the Congress and signed by President Woodrow Wilson. The measure dealt primarily with espionage problems, but some parts were aimed expressly at dissent and opposition to the war. The law provided that it was a crime to willfully convey a false report with the intent to interfere with the war effort. It was a crime to cause or attempt to cause insubordination, disloyalty, mutiny, or refusal of duty in the armed forces. It also was a crime to willfully obstruct the recruiting or enlistment service of the United States. Punishment was a fine of not more than ten thousand dollars or a jail term of not more than twenty years. The law also provided that material that violated the law could not be mailed.

In 1918 the **Sedition Act,** an amendment to the Espionage Act, was passed, making it a crime to attempt to obstruct the recruiting service. It was criminal to utter or print or write or publish disloyal or profane language that was intended to cause contempt of or scorn for the federal government, the Constitution, the flag, or the uniform of the armed forces. Penalties for violation of the law were imprisonment for as long as twenty years and/or a fine of ten thousand dollars. Approximately two thousand people were prosecuted under these espionage and sedition laws, and nearly nine hundred were convicted. Persons who found themselves in the government's dragnet were usually aliens, radicals, publishers of foreign-language publications, and other persons who opposed the war.

In addition the United States Post Office Department censored thousands of newspapers, books, and pamphlets. Some publications lost their right to the government-subsidized second-class mailing rates and were forced to use the costly first-class rates or find other means of distribution. Entire issues of magazines were held up and never delivered, on the grounds that they violated the law (or what the postmaster general believed to be the law). Finally, the states were not content with allowing the federal government to deal with dissenters, and most adopted sedition statutes, laws against criminal syndicalism, laws that prohibited the display of a red flag or a black flag, and so forth.

Political repression in the United States did not end with the termination of fighting in Europe. The government was still suspicious of the millions of European immigrants in the nation and frightened by the organized political efforts of socialist and communist groups. As the Depression hit the nation, first in the farm belt in the twenties, and then in the rest of the nation by the next decade, labor unrest mushroomed. Hundreds of so-called agitators were arrested and charged under state and federal laws. Demonstrations were broken up; aliens detained and threatened with deportation.

But what about the First Amendment? What happened to the rights of freedom of expression? The constitutional guarantees of freedom of speech and freedom of press were of limited value during this era. The important legal meaning of freedom of expression had developed little in the preceding 125 years. There had been few cases and almost no important rulings before 1920. As you will note as we proceed through this book, the words of the First Amendment—"Congress shall make no law . . ." are not nearly as important as the meaning attached to those words. And that meaning was only then beginning to develop through court rulings that resulted from the thousands of prosecutions for sedition and other such crimes between 1917 and the mid-1930s.

The Smith Act

The Congress adopted the nation's second peacetime sedition law in 1940 when it ratified the **Smith Act,** a measure making it a crime to advocate the violent overthrow of the government, to conspire to advocate the violent overthrow of the government, to organize a group that advocated the violent overthrow of the government, or to be a member of a group that advocated the violent overthrow of the government. The law was aimed directly at the Communist party of the United States. While a small group of Troskyites (members of the Socialist Workers party) were prosecuted and convicted under the Smith Act in 1943, no communist was indicted under the law until 1948 when the nation's top Communist party leaders were charged with advocating the violent overthrow of the government. All were convicted after a nine-month trial and their appeals were denied. In a seven-to-two ruling in 1951 (*Dennis* v. *U.S.*) the Supreme Court of the United States rejected the defendants' arguments that the Smith Act violated the First Amendment.

Government prosecutions persisted during the early fifties. But then, in a surprising reversal of its earlier position, the Supreme Court in 1957 overturned the convictions of West Coast Communist party leaders (*Yates* v. *U.S.*).

Justice John Marshall Harlan wrote for the five-to-two majority that government evidence showed the defendants had advocated the violent overthrow of the government but only as an abstract doctrine, and this was not sufficient to sustain a conviction. Instead there must be evidence that proves the defendants advocated actual *action* aimed at the forcible overthrow of the government. This enhanced burden of proof levied against the government prosecutors made it extremely difficult to use the Smith Act against the communists and prosecutions therefore dwindled. The prosecutions dwindled for other reasons as well however. The times had changed. The cold war was not as intense. Americans looked at the Soviet Union and the communists with a bit less fear. The Communist party of the United States had failed to generate any public support. Its membership had fallen precipitously. In fact, political scientist John Roche has remarked with only a slight wink that it was the dues paid to the party by FBI undercover agents that kept the organization afloat in the mid-to-late fifties.

With the practical demise of the Smith Act, sedition has not been a serious threat against dissent for thirty years. No sedition cases were filed against Vietnam war protestors and the last time the Supreme Court heard an appeal in a sedition case was in 1969 when it overturned the conviction of a Ku Klux Klan leader (*Brandenburg* v. *Ohio*). In 1987 the federal government brought seditious conspiracy charges against nine alleged white supremacists who were members of a group called Aryan Nations. A jury in Ft. Smith, Arkansas, acquitted the defendants, but most of them were already in prison for other convictions. But the government seems undaunted, for it filed seditious conspiracy charges against three men in early 1989. Federal prosecutors brought the charges under the Sedition Act of 1918 and accused the avowed revolutionary white supremacists of conspiring to topple the government. The three men have already been convicted of bombing and bank robbery.

This brief narrative of the past two hundred years does not begin to tell the story of the struggle for political dissent in this nation. Interested students are urged to turn to the Bibliography at the end of this chapter and read on. Missing from the narrative is the struggle undertaken by the courts—especially the Supreme Court—to attempt to reconcile prosecutions for sedition with the nation's constitutional guarantee of freedom of expression. Let's look at those cases more closely.

Tests for First Amendment Infringement

Remarkable as it may seem, the first time the Supreme Court of the United States seriously considered whether a prosecution for sedition violated the First Amendment was in 1919, one hundred and thirty years after the founding of the Republic. The Philadelphia Socialist party authorized Charles Schenck, the general secretary of the organization, to publish fifteen thousand leaflets protesting against the U.S. involvement in the First World War. The pamphlet described the war as a cold-blooded and ruthless adventure propagated in the interest of the chosen few of Wall Street and urged young men to resist the draft. Schenck and other party members were arrested, tried and convicted of violating the Espionage Act (see page 52). The case was appealed all the way to the Supreme Court, with the Socialists asserting that they had been denied their First Amendment rights of freedom of speech and press. Justice Oliver Wendell Holmes penned the opinion for the court and rejected the First Amendment argument. In ordinary times, he said, such pamphlets might have been harmless and protected by the First Amendment. "But the character of every act depends upon the circumstances in which it is done. . . . The question in every case is whether the words used, are used in such circumstances and are of such a nature as to create a clear and present danger that they will bring about the substantive evils that Congress has a right to prevent. It is a question of proximity and degree" (*Schenck* v. *U.S.*, 1919).

How do we reconcile prosecutions for sedition with freedom of expression? According to the Holmes test, Congress has the right to outlaw certain kinds of conduct that might be harmful to the nation. In some instances words, through speeches or pamphlets, can push people toward violating the laws passed by Congress. In such cases publishers or speakers can be punished without infringing upon their First Amendment freedoms. How close must the connection be between the advocacy of the speaker or publisher and the forbidden conduct? Holmes said that the words must create a "clear" (unmistakable? certain?) and "present" (immediate? close?) danger.

Holmes' test means less in the abstract than it does when connected to the facts of the *Schenck* case. In the abstract, an endless debate might be conducted over whether a speech or book presented the requisite clear and present danger. But in rejecting Schenck's appeal, the High Court ruled that these fifteen thousand seemingly innocuous pamphlets posed a real threat to the legitimate right of Congress to successfully conduct the war. To many American liberals this notion seemed farfetched and Holmes was publicly criticized for the ruling. Recently scholars like Fred D. Ragan and Jeremy Cohen have taken Mr. Justice Holmes to task for rendering a naïve and uninformed opinion. But the magic words "clear and present danger" stuck like glue on American sedition law and for more than thirty years American jurists had to work their way around this standard. Holmes changed his mind about his test in less than six months and broke with the majority of the High Court to outline a somewhat more liberal definition of freedom of expression in a ruling on the Sedition Act in the fall of 1919. (See *Abrams* v. *U.S.*, 1919.) But the majority of the Court continued to use the Holmes test to reject First Amendment appeals.

Justice Louis Brandeis attempted to fashion a more useful application of the clear and present danger test in 1927, but his definition of clear and present test was confined to a concurring opinion in the case of *Whitney* v. *California*. The state of California prosecuted Anita Whitney, a sixty-four year-old philanthropist who was the niece of Justice Stephen J. Field, a member of the Supreme Court from 1863 to 1897. She was charged with violating the state's Criminal Syndicalism Act after she attended a meeting of the Communist Labor party. She was not an active member in the party and during the convention had worked against proposals made by others that the party dedicate itself to gaining power through revolution and general strikes in which workers would seize power by violent means. After her conviction she appealed to the Supreme Court.

Justice Edward Sanford wrote the Court's opinion and ruled that California had not violated Miss Whitney's First Amendment rights. The jurist said it was inappropriate to even apply the clear and present danger test. He noted that in *Schenck* and other previous cases, the statutes under which prosecution occurred forbade specific actions, such as interference with the draft. The clear and present danger test was then used to judge whether the words used by the defendant presented a clear and present danger that the forbidden action might occur. In this case, Sanford noted, the state of California law forbade specific words—the advocacy of violence to bring about political change. The Holmes test was therefore not applicable. In addition, the California law was neither unreasonable nor unwarranted.

Justice Brandeis concurred with the majority, but only, he said, because the constitutional issue of freedom of expression had not been raised sufficiently at the trial to make it an issue in the appeal. (If a legal issue is not raised during a trial it is difficult for an appellate court to later consider the matter.) In his concurring opinion, Brandeis disagreed sharply with the majority regarding the limits of free expression. In doing so he added flesh and bones to Holmes's clear and present danger test. Looking to the *Schenck* decision, the justice noted that the Court had agreed that there must be a clear and imminent danger of a substantive evil that the state has the right to prevent before an interference with speech can be allowed. Then he went on to describe what he believed to be the requisite danger (*Whitney* v. *California*):

> To justify suppression of free speech there must be reasonable ground to fear that serious evil will result if free speech is practiced. There must be reasonable ground to believe that the danger apprehended is imminent. There must be reasonable ground to believe that the evil to be prevented is a serious one. Every denunciation of existing law tends in some measure to increase the probability that there will be violation of it. Condonation of a breach enhances the probability. Expressions of approval add to the probability. Propagation of the criminal state of mind by teaching syndicalism increases it. Advocacy of law-breaking heightens it further. But even advocacy of violation, however reprehensible morally, is not a justification for denying free speech where the advocacy falls short of incitement, and there is nothing to indicate that the advocacy would be immediately acted on. The wide difference between advocacy and incitement, between preparation and attempt, between assembling and conspiracy, must be borne in mind. In order to support a finding of clear and present danger it must be shown either that immediate serious violence was to be expected or was advocated, or that the past conduct furnished reason to believe that such advocacy was then contemplated.

Brandeis concluded that if there is time to expose through discussion the falsehoods and fallacies, to avert the evil by the process of education, the remedy to be applied is more speech, not enforced silence.

This truly is a clear and present danger test that even the most zealous civil libertarian can live with. And this is the test that many mistakenly confuse with Holmes's original pronouncement. Unfortunately, this version of the clear and present danger test has never found its way into a majority opinion in a sedition case.

The next major ruling in which the High Court attempted to reconcile sedition law and the First Amendment came in 1951 in the case of *Dennis* v. *U.S.* (See page 53). The eleven Communist Party members had been convicted of advocating the violent overthrow of the government, a violation of the Smith Act. The defendants raised the clear and present danger test as a barrier to their convictions; the actions of a small band of Communists surely did not constitute a clear and present danger to the nation, they argued. Chief Justice Vinson, who wrote the opinion for the court, used neither the clear and present danger test enunciated by Holmes, nor the more expansive version written by Brandeis. He instead created a third test, a clear and probable danger test. Surely the Congress has a right to prevent the overthrow of the government, Vinson said. How likely is it that the words spoken or written by the defendants would lead even to an attempted overthrow? "In each case [courts] must ask whether the gravity of the 'evil' discounted by its improbability, justifies such invasion of free speech as is necessary to avoid the danger," Vinson wrote, quoting a lower court opinion written by Judge Learned Hand.

The test went only slightly beyond the original Holmes test and the Court ruled that the defendants' First Amendment rights had not been violated. If the Brandeis test from *Whitney* had been applied however it is likely the convictions would have gone out the window.

Six years later in *Yates* v. *U.S.* (see page 53) in its next major ruling on the Smith Act, the High Court ignored both clear and present danger and clear and probable danger. Justice John Marshall Harlan wrote for the Court that it was necessary to distinguish between the advocacy of the forcible overthrow of the government as an abstract doctrine and the advocacy of action toward the forcible overthrow of the government. "The essential distinction," Harlan noted, "is that those to whom the advocacy is addressed must be urged to do something now or in the future, rather than merely believe in something." Surely this was a better test, but questions still remained. How specific does this advocacy of action have to be? Contrast two exhortations by a revolutionary speaker. "We must take action, we have waited long enough, we must move to replace the government now." Or "we must demonstrate our resolve by blowing up the selective service office." Obviously the last statement is the advocacy of action. But what about the first statement?

It has been more than twenty years since the Supreme Court heard the case of *Brandenburg* v. *Ohio* (see page 54) and made its last and probably best attempt to resolve the apparent contradiction between sedition law and freedom of expression. In reversing the conviction of a Ku Klux Klan leader the High Court said the law must distinguish between the advocacy of ideas and the incitement to unlawful conduct. "The constitutional guarantees of free speech and free press do not permit a state to forbid or proscribe advocacy of the use of force or of law violation except where such advocacy is directed to inciting or producing imminent lawless action and is likely to incite or produce such actions." This test, which stands as the rule today, comes very close to the Brandeis test from the *Whitney* case. And it provides a fairly safe haven for those who seek to urge others to take action to change the government or to redistribute power in society.

The attempts by the judiciary to accommodate both freedom of expression and the right of the nation to protect itself from violent revolution appear to many to be nothing more than semantic games, moving a noun here, an adjective there. A waste of time at best, some have argued. But these attempts demonstrate three important points. First, the adoption of the First Amendment raised more questions than it answered. The job of answering these questions has fallen to the judiciary; it must define the meaning of this abstract concept. Second, the range of permissible defiance of the government varies with the times, the political climate, the national mood. Finally, in guaranteeing freedom of expression to all, the American people have put themselves at risk, since our system of government contains a Constitution that fosters those who seek to change the status quo.

The *Gitlow* Ruling

Before leaving the discussion of sedition one additional case must be noted; not for its impact upon the law of sedition, but its impact upon the civil liberties enjoyed by all Americans. In 1925 Benjamin Gitlow, a small-time, left-wing agitator asked the U.S. Supreme Court to reverse his conviction for violating the New York criminal anarchy statute. In his appeal to the High Court, he argued that the statute violated his freedom of expression guaranteed by the United States Constitution. In making this plea, Gitlow was asking the Court to overturn a ninety-two-year-old precedent.

In 1833 the Supreme Court of the United States ruled that the Bill of Rights, the first ten amendments to the United States Constitution, were applicable only in protecting citizens from actions of the federal government (*Barron* v. *Baltimore,* 1833). Chief Justice John Marshall ruled that the people of the United States established the United States Constitution for their government, not for the government of the individual states. The limitations of power placed upon government by the Constitution applied only to the government of the United States. In fact, while considering the adoption of the Bill of Rights in 1789, the U.S. Senate rejected a resolution that would have applied to the states as well as the federal government the limits on government action contained in the ten amendments. Applying this rule to the First Amendment meant that neither Congress nor the federal government could abridge freedom of the press, but that the government of New York or the government of Detroit could interfere with freedom of expression without violating the guarantees of the United States Constitution. The citizens of the individual states or cities could erect their own constitutional guarantees in state constitutions or city charters. Indeed, such provisions existed in many places.

As applied to the case of Benjamin Gitlow, then, it seemed unlikely that the First Amendment (which prohibited interference by the federal government with freedom of speech and press) could be erected as a barrier to protect the radical from prosecution by the state of New York. Yet this is exactly what the young socialist argued.

Gitlow's attorneys, especially Walter Heilprin Pollak, did not attack Chief Justice Marshall's ruling in *Barron* v. *Baltimore* directly; instead they went around it. Pollak constructed his argument upon the Fourteenth Amendment to the Constitution, which was adopted in 1868, thirty-five years after the decision in *Barron* v. *Baltimore*. The attorney argued that there was general agreement that the First Amendment protected a citizen's right to liberty of expression. The Fourteenth Amendment says in part, "no state shall deprive any person of life, liberty or property, without due process of law. . . ." Pollak asserted that included among the liberties guaranteed by the Fourteenth Amendment is liberty of the press as guaranteed by the First Amendment. Therefore, a state cannot deprive a citizen of the freedom of the press that is guaranteed by the First Amendment without violating the Fourteenth Amendment. By jailing Benjamin Gitlow for exercising his right of freedom of speech granted by the First Amendment, New York state denied him the liberty assured him by the Fourteenth Amendment. Simply, then, the First Amendment, as applied through the Fourteenth Amendment, prohibits states and cities and counties from denying an individual freedom of speech and press.

The High Court had heard this argument before, but apparently not as persuasively as Mr. Pollak presented it. In rather casual terms Justice Edward Sanford made a startlingly new constitutional pronouncement: "For present purposes we may and do assume that freedom of speech and of the press—which are protected by the First Amendment from abridgement by Congress—are among the fundamental personal rights and 'liberties' protected by the due process clause of the Fourteenth Amendment from impairment by the states."

The importance of the *Gitlow* case is that the High Court acknowledged that the Bill of Rights places limitations upon the actions of states and local government, as well as upon the federal government. The *Gitlow* case states that freedom of speech is protected by the Fourteenth Amendment. In later cases the Court placed freedom of the press, freedom of religion, freedom from self-incrimination, and freedom from illegal search and seizure under the same protection. Today, virtually all of the rights outlined in the Bill of Rights are protected via the Fourteenth Amendment from interference by states and cities, as well as by the federal government. The importance of the *Gitlow* case cannot be underestimated. It truly marked the beginning of attainment of a full measure of civil liberties for the citizens of the nation. It was the key that unlocked an important door.

In the end Gitlow lost his case anyway. He had won a major constitutional victory, but was unable to persuade the High Court that his political agitation was harmless. Justice Sanford ruled that New York state had not violated Gitlow's First Amendment rights when it prosecuted him for publishing his *Left Wing Manifesto,* which the state contended advocated the violent overthrow of the government.

SUMMARY

Within eight years of the passage of the First Amendment, the nation adopted its first (and most wide-ranging) sedition laws, the Alien and Sedition Acts of 1798. Many leading political editors and politicians were prosecuted under the laws, which made it a crime to criticize both the president and the national government. While the Supreme Court never did hear arguments regarding the constitutionality of the laws, several justices of the Supreme Court presided at sedition act trials and refused to sustain a constitutional objection to the laws. The public hated the measures. John Adams was voted out of office in 1800 and was replaced by his political opponent and target of the sedition laws, Thomas Jefferson. The laws left such a bad taste that the federal government did not pass another sedition law until World War I, 117 years later.

Sedition prosecutions in the period of 1915–1925 were the most vicious in the nation's history as war protestors, socialists, anarchists, and other political dissidents became the target of government repression. It was during this era that the Supreme Court began to interpret the meaning of the First Amendment. In a series of rulings stemming from the World War I cases, the High Court fashioned what is known as the clear and present danger test to measure state and federal laws and protests and other expressions against the First Amendment. The test was rigid and was never used to overturn a lower-court conviction, although in 1927 Justice Louis D. Brandeis did fashion a broad and liberal interpretation of the clear and present danger test in his dissent in the case of *Whitney* v. *California.* In 1925 the Court ruled that the guarantees of freedom of speech apply to actions taken by all governments, that freedom of speech under the First Amendment protects individuals from censorship by all levels of government, not just from actions by the federal government. This pronouncement in *Gitlow* v. *New York* opened the door to a much broader protection of freedom of expression in the nation.

The nation's most recent sedition law was adopted in 1940. The Smith Act, as it is known, prohibits the advocacy of the violent overthrow of the government. Following a series of trials and two Supreme Court rulings in the 1950s, the law has become a relatively benign prohibition. The High Court ruled in 1957 in *Yates* v. *U.S.* that to sustain a conviction under the Smith Act, the government must prove that the defendants advocate specific violent or forcible action toward the overthrow of the government. The government found it impossible to do this in the 1950s, and the Smith Act has not been invoked to punish an act of expression for more than twenty-five years. The Supreme Court made its last important attempt to reconcile the First Amendment and the law of sedition in 1969 when it ruled in *Brandenburg* v. *Ohio* that advocacy of unlawful conduct is protected by the Constitution unless it is directed toward inciting or producing imminent lawless action and is likely to incite or produce such action.

PRIOR RESTRAINT

The great compiler of the British law, William Blackstone, defined freedom of the press in the 1760s as freedom from "previous restraint," or **prior restraint.** Regardless of the difference of opinion on whether the First Amendment is intended to protect political criticism, most students of the constitutional period agree that the guarantees of freedom of speech and press were intended to bar the government from exercising prior restraint. Despite the weight of such authority, the media in the United States in the 1980s still faces instances of prepublication censorship.

Prior censorship is difficult to define, as scores of laws and government actions hold the potential for a kind of prior restraint. In privacy law, for example, it is possible under some statutes to stop the publication of material that illegally appropriates a person's name or likeness. In extreme cases the press can be stopped from publishing information it has learned in a criminal case. The two instances just mentioned, as well as others, will be discussed fully in later, more appropriate sections of this book. The purpose of this section is to outline those kinds of prior restraint that seem to fall outside the boundaries of other chapters in the book.

The Supreme Court did not consider the issue of prior restraint until more than a decade after it had decided its first major sedition case. In 1931, in *Near* v. *Minnesota,* the Court struck an important blow for freedom of expression.

Near v. *Minnesota*

City and county officials in Minneapolis, Minnesota, brought a legal action against Jay M. Near and Howard Guilford, publishers of the *Saturday Press,* a small weekly newspaper. Near and Guilford were reformers whose purpose was to clean up city and county government in Minneapolis. In their attacks upon corruption in city government, they used language that was far from temperate and defamed some of the town's leading government officials. Near and Guilford charged that Jewish gangsters were in control of gambling, bootlegging, and racketeering in the city and that city government and its law enforcement agencies did not perform their duties energetically. They repeated these charges over and over in a highly inflammatory manner.

Minnesota had a statute that empowered a court to declare any obscene, lewd, lascivious, malicious, scandalous, or defamatory publication a public nuisance. When such a publication was deemed a public nuisance, the court issued an injunction against future publication or distribution. Violation of the injunction resulted in punishment for contempt of court.

In 1927 County Attorney Floyd Olson initiated an action against the *Saturday Press*. A district court declared the newspaper a public nuisance and "perpetually enjoined" publication of the *Saturday Press*. The only way either Near or Guilford would be able to publish the newspaper again was to convince the court that their newspaper would remain free of objectionable material. In 1928 the Minnesota Supreme Court upheld the constitutionality of the law, declaring that under its broad police power the state can regulate public nuisances, including defamatory and scandalous newspapers.

The case then went to the United States Supreme Court, which reversed the ruling by the state supreme court. The nuisance statute was declared unconstitutional. Chief Justice Charles Evans Hughes wrote the opinion for the Court in the five-to-four ruling, saying that the statute in question was not designed to redress wrongs to individuals attacked by the newspaper. Instead, the statute was directed at suppressing the *Saturday Press* once and for all. The object of the law, Hughes wrote, was not punishment but censorship—not only of a single issue, but also of all future issues—which is not consistent with the traditional concept of freedom of the press. That is, the statute constituted prior restraint, and prior restraint is clearly a violation of the First Amendment.

One maxim in the law holds that when a judge writes an opinion for a court, he should stick to the problem at hand, that he should not wander off and talk about matters that do not really concern the issue before the court. Such remarks are considered **dicta,** or words that do not really apply to the case. These words, these dicta, are never really considered an important part of the ruling in the case. Chief Justice Hughes's opinion in *Near* v. *Minnesota* contains a good deal of dicta.

In this case Hughes wrote that the prior restraint of the *Saturday Press* was unconstitutional, but in some circumstances, he added, prior restraint might be permissible. In what kinds of circumstances? The government can constitutionally stop publication of obscenity, the government can stop publication of material that incites people to acts of violence, and it may prohibit publication of certain kinds of materials during wartime. Hughes admitted, on the other hand, that defining freedom of the press as only the freedom from prior restraint is equally wrong, for in many cases punishment after publication imposes effective censorship upon the freedom of expression.

Near v. *Minnesota* stands for the proposition that under American law prior censorship is permitted only in very unusual circumstances; it is the exception, not the rule. Courts have reinforced this interpretation many times since 1931. Despite this considerable litigation, we still lack a complete understanding of the kinds of circumstances in which prior restraint might be acceptable under the First Amendment, as a series of recent cases (some of which are concerned with national security) illustrate.

Austin v. *Keefe*

A case that to some extent reinforced the *Near* ruling involved the attempt of a real-estate broker to stop a neighborhood community action group from distributing pamphlets about him (*Organization for a Better Austin* v. *Keefe,* 1971). The Organization for a Better Austin was a community organization in the Austin suburb of Chicago. Its goal was to stabilize the population in the integrated community. Members were opposed to the tactics of certain real estate brokers who came into white neighborhoods, spread the word that blacks were moving in, bought up the white-owned homes cheaply in the ensuing panic, and then resold them at a good profit to blacks or other whites. The organization received pledges from most real estate firms in the area to stop these blockbusting tactics. But Jerome Keefe refused to make such an agreement. The community group then printed leaflets and flyers describing his activities and handed them out in Westchester, the community in which Keefe lived. Group members told the Westchester residents that Keefe was a "panic peddler" and said they would stop distributing the leaflets in Westchester as soon as Keefe agreed to stop his blockbusting real estate tactics. Keefe went to court and obtained an injunction that prohibited further distribution by the community club of pamphlets, leaflets, and literature of any kind in Westchester on the grounds that the material constituted an invasion of Keefe's privacy and caused him irreparable harm. The Organization for a Better Austin appealed the ruling to the United States Supreme Court. In May 1971 the High Court dissolved the injunction. Chief Justice Warren Burger wrote, "The injunction, so far as it imposes prior restraint on speech and publication, constitutes an impermissible restraint on First Amendment rights." He said that the injunction, as in the *Near* case, did not seek to redress individual wrongs, but instead sought to suppress on the basis of one or two handbills the distribution of any kind of literature in a city of eighteen thousand inhabitants.

Keefe argued that the purpose of the handbills was not to inform the community, but to force him to sign an agreement. The chief justice said this argument was immaterial and was not sufficient cause to remove the leaflets and flyers from the protection of the First Amendment. Justice Burger added (*Austin v. Keefe*):

> Petitioners [the community group] were engaged openly and vigorously in making the public aware of respondent's [Keefe's] real estate practices. Those practices were offensive to them, as the views and practices of the petitioners are no doubt offensive to others. But so long as the means are peaceful, the communication need not meet standards of acceptability.

The *Keefe* case did a good job of reinforcing the High Court's decision in *Near v. Minnesota*.

Pentagon Papers Case

While it is more famous, another 1971 decision is not as strong a statement in behalf of freedom of expression as either *Near* or *Keefe*. This is the famous Pentagon Papers decision (*New York Times Co. v. U.S.; U.S. v. Washington Post,* 1971). While the political implications of the ruling are very important, the ruling itself is legally quite unsatisfying.

The case began in the summer of 1971 when the *New York Times,* followed by the *Washington Post* and a handful of other newspapers, began publishing a series of articles based on a top-secret forty-seven-volume government study officially entitled "History of the United States Decision-Making Process on Vietnam Policy." The day after the initial article on the so-called "Pentagon Papers" appeared, Attorney General John Mitchell asked the *New York Times* to stop publication of the material. When the *Times's* publisher refused, the government went to court to get an injunction to force the newspaper to stop the series. A temporary restraining order was granted as the case wound its way to the Supreme Court. Such an order was also imposed upon the *Washington Post* after it began to publish reports based on the same material.

At first the government argued that the publication of this material violated federal espionage statutes. When that assertion did not satisfy the lower federal courts, the government argued that the president had inherent power under his constitutional mandate to conduct foreign affairs to protect the national security, which includes the right to classify documents secret and top secret. Publication of this material by the newspapers was unauthorized disclosure of such material and should be stopped. This argument did not satisfy the courts either, and by the time the case came before the Supreme Court, the government argument was that publication of these papers might result in irreparable harm to the nation and its ability to conduct foreign affairs. The *Times* and the *Post* consistently made two arguments. First, they said that the classification system is a sham, that people in the government declassify documents almost at will when they want to sway public opinion or influence a reporter's story. Second, the press also argued that an injunction against the continued publication of this material violated the First Amendment. Interestingly, the newspapers did not argue that under all circumstances prior restraint is in conflict with the First Amendment. Defense attorney Professor Alexander Bickel argued that under some circumstances prior restraint is acceptable, for example, when the publication of a document has a direct link with a grave event that is immediate and visible. Former Justice William O. Douglas noted that this was a strange argument for newspapers to make—and it is. Apparently both newspapers decided that a victory in that immediate case was far more important than to establish a definitive and long-lasting constitutional principle. They therefore concentrated on winning the case, acknowledging that in future cases prior restraint might be permissible.

On June 30 the High Court ruled six to three in favor of the *New York Times* and the *Washington Post*. The Court did not grant a permanent injunction against the publication of the Pentagon Papers, but the ruling was hardly the kind that strengthened the First Amendment. In a very short per curiam opinion, the majority said that in a case involving the prior restraint of a publication, the government bears a heavy burden to justify such a restraint. In this case the government failed to show the Court why such a restraint should be imposed upon the two newspapers. In other words, the government failed to justify its request for the permanent restraining order.

The decision in the case rested upon the preferred position First Amendment theory or doctrine (see page 47). The ban on publication was *presumed* to be an unconstitutional infringement upon the First Amendment. The government had to prove that the ban was needed to protect the nation in some manner. If such evidence could be adduced, the Court would strike the balance in favor of the government and uphold the ban on the publication of the articles. But in this case the government simply failed to show why its request for an injunction was vital to the national interest. Consequently, the High Court denied the government's request for a ban on the publication of the Pentagon Papers on the grounds that such a prohibition was a violation of the First Amendment. Note: The Court did not say that in all similar cases an injunction would violate the First Amendment. It did not even say that in this case an injunction was a violation of the First Amendment. It merely said that the government had not shown why the injunction was needed, why it was not a violation of the freedom of the press. Such a decision is not what one would call a ringing defense of the right of free expression.

In addition to the brief unsigned opinion from the majority, all nine members of the Court wrote short individual opinions. Justices Black and Douglas clung to the absolutist theory and argued that they could conceive of no circumstance under which the government might properly interfere with freedom of expression. Justice Brennan's opinion echoed the unsigned opinion; the government had failed to carry the necessary burden of proof. Justice Potter Stewart said he agreed with Brennan and noted that there was simply too much secrecy in government. Justice Byron White said he supported the Court's decision to refrain from issuing the injunction, but suggested the newspapers might be in violation of an espionage statute and subject to criminal prosecution. And Justice Thurgood Marshall questioned the power of the executive branch to classify documents. All three dissenters, Chief Justice Warren Burger and Justices John Harlan and Harry Blackmun, complained that there had not been sufficient time to properly consider the legal questions. Both Blackmun and Harlan said they were also concerned about the damage to foreign relations and national security that might be caused by the publication of the documents.

What many people at first called the case of the century ended in a fizzle, at least with regard to developing First Amendment law. The press won the day; the Pentagon Papers were published. But thoughtful observers expressed concern over the ruling. A majority of the Court had not ruled that such prior restraint was unconstitutional—only that the government had failed to meet the heavy burden of showing such restraint was necessary in this case.

Progressive
Magazine Case

The fragile nature of the Court's holding became clear in early 1979 when the government again went to court to block the publication of material it claimed could endanger the national security (*U.S.* v. *Progressive*, 1979). Freelance writer Howard Morland had prepared an article, entitled "The H-Bomb Secret: How We Got It, Why We're Telling It." The piece was scheduled to be published in the April edition of the *Progressive* magazine, a seventy-year-old political digest founded by Robert M. LaFollette as a voice of the progressive movement.

Morland had gathered the material for the article from unclassified sources. After completing an early draft of the piece, he sought technical criticism from various scholars. Somehow a copy found its way to officials in the federal government. With the cat out of the bag, *Progressive* editor Erwin Knoll sent a final draft to the government for prepublication comments on technical accuracy. The government said the piece was too accurate and moved into federal court to stop the magazine from publishing the story.

The defendants in the case argued that all the information in the article was from public sources, that any citizen could have gotten the same material by going to the Department of Energy, federal libraries, and the like. Other nations already had this information or could easily get it. Experts testifying in behalf of the magazine argued that the article was a harmless exposition of some exotic nuclear technology.

The government disagreed. It said that while some of the material was from public sources much of the data were not publicly available. Prosecutors and a battery of technical experts argued that the article contained a core of information that had never before been published. The United States also argued that it was immaterial where Morland had gotten his information and whether it had come from classified or public documents. Prosecutors argued that the nation's national security interest permitted the classification and censorship of even information originating in public if, when such information is drawn together, synthesized, and collated, it acquires the character "of presenting immediate, direct and irreparable harm to the interests of the United States." The United States was arguing, then, that some material is automatically classified as soon as it is created if it has the potential to cause harm to the nation. The information in Morland's article met this description, prosecutors argued.

It fell to United States District Judge Robert Warren to evaluate the conflicting claims and reach a decision on the government's request to enjoin the publication of the piece. In a thoughtful opinion in which Warren attempted to sort out the issues in the case, he agreed with the government that there were concepts in the article not found in the public realm—concepts vital to the operation of a thermonuclear bomb. Was the piece a do-it-yourself-guide for a hydrogen bomb? No, Warren said, it was not. "A number of affidavits make quite clear that a sine qua non to thermonuclear capability is a large, sophisticated industrial capability coupled with a coterie of imaginative, resourceful scientists and technicians." But the article could provide some nations with a ticket to bypass blind alleys and help a medium-sized nation to move faster in developing a hydrogen bomb.

To the *Progressive*'s argument that the publication of the article would provide people with the information needed to make an informed decision on nuclear issues, Warren wrote, "This Court can find no plausible reason why the public needs to know the technical details about hydrogen bomb construction to carry on an informed debate on this issue."

Looking to the legal issues in the case, Warren said he saw three differences between this case and the *Pentagon Papers* ruling of 1971. The Pentagon Papers themselves were a historical study; the Morland article focused on contemporary matter. In the *Pentagon Papers* case there had been no cogent national security reasons advanced by the government when it sought to enjoin the publication of the study. The national security interest is considerably more apparent in the *Progressive* case, Warren noted. Finally, the government lacked substantial legal authority to stop the publication of the Pentagon Papers. The laws raised by the government were vague, not at all appropriate. But Section 2274 of the Atomic Energy Act of 1954 is quite specific in prohibiting anyone from communicating or disclosing any restricted data to any persons "with reasons to believe such data will be utilized to injure the United States or to secure an advantage to any foreign nation." Section 2014 of the same act defined restricted data to include information on the design, manufacture, or utilization of atomic weapons.

Warren concluded that the government had met the heavy burden of showing justification for prior restraint. The judge added that he was not convinced that suppression of the objected-to technical portions of the article would impede the *Progressive* in its crusade to stimulate public debate on the issue of nuclear armament. "What is involved here," Warren concluded, "is information dealing with the most destructive weapon in the history of mankind, information of sufficient destructive potential to nullify the right to free speech and to endanger the right to life itself."

When the injunction was issued, the editors of the *Progressive* and their supporters inside and outside the press vowed to appeal the ruling—to the Supreme Court if necessary. Yet there was a distinct uneasiness among even many persons who sided with the publication. Judge Warren had done a professional job of distinguishing this case from the *Pentagon Papers* ruling. There were important differences. The membership on the High Court had changed as well. Black and Douglas, both of whom had voted against the government in 1971, had left the Court, as had Harlan who had voted with the government. Some newspapers, the *Washington Post* and the *New York Times*, for example, expressed the fear that a damaging precedent could emerge from the Supreme Court if the *Progressive* case ultimately reached the high tribunal.

Then in September of 1979, as the *Progressive* case began its slow ascent up the appellate ladder, a small newspaper in Madison, Wisconsin, published a story containing much of the same information as was in the Morland article. When this occurred, the Department of Justice unhappily withdrew its suit against the *Progressive* (*U.S.* v. *Progressive*, 1979). The confrontation between the press and the government in the Supreme Court was averted. Many journalists expressed relief.

But the victory in the *Progressive* case was bittersweet at best. The publication of the article had been enjoined. A considerable body of legal opinion had supported the notion that the injunction would have been sustained by the Supreme Court, rightly or wrongly. It must be remembered that as a legal precedent the decision in the Progressive case has limited value. It was, after all, only a United States district court ruling and doesn't carry the weight of the *Near* decision, for example. From a political standpoint, however, the case had important implications. Prior restraint, which had seemed quite distant in the years succeeding *Near* v. *Minnesota* and in the afterglow of the press victory in the Pentagon Papers case, took on realistic and frightening new proportions.

<table>
<tr><td>Varieties of Prior Restraint</td><td>Not all instances of prior restraint are as blatant or as boldfaced as the censorship in the Progressive case. During the 1980s the Reagan administration became adept at developing schemes that amounted to prior restraint, even though in many instances they didn't look like what we traditionally think of as prior restraint. Nevertheless the government went to incredible lengths to</td></tr>
</table>

block the flow of information on a wide range of subjects to the American press and the American people. Many of these actions will be outlined in chapter 5 when access to information is discussed. For now here are three other instances of government policies resulting in what amounts to a prior restraint.

For decades employees of the Central Intelligence Agency have had to sign agreements at the time they are hired in which they promise not to publish "any information or material relating to the agency, its activities or intelligence activities generally, either during or after the term of employment . . . without specific prior approval of the agency." This gives the agency a right of prior censorship over any books or articles current or former CIA employees might seek to publish. Previous presidential administrations have vigorously enforced this provision (see *U.S.* v. *Marchetti,* 1972) and in 1980 the U.S. Supreme Court, ignoring the obvious First Amendment questions involved, approved of such enforcement by dealing with the matter as a contractual problem rather than a constitutional one. In *Snepp* v. *U.S.* the High Court ruled that sanctions could be imposed against a former agent who sought to publish a book without getting the CIA's prior approval because the agent had breached his "valid CIA employment agreement."

During Reagan's eight-year tenure in the White House the executive branch of the federal government attempted to censor the writing and speeches of a great many more persons. In January of 1983 the White House adopted a budget office proposal limiting the rights of all persons and organizations that receive federal grants from speaking out on many public affairs issues. The proposal, only slightly modified, was adopted a year later and constituted the prior censorship of millions of people. In the spring of 1983 the president issued a National Security Directive that required all government employees with access to "sensitive compartmentalized information" to sign contracts promising they would not publish a book, an article or even submit a letter to the editor containing any information related to intelligence—without first seeking government review and alteration if needed. This provision was to apply for so long as these employees lived. President Reagan changed his mind eleven months later and decided to hold the censorship provisions of the directive in abeyance—perhaps because the Senate had voted 56-to-34 in opposition to the provision.

The federal government exercised another blatant form of censorship in 1983 when it barred American reporters from accompanying the U.S. forces that invaded the island of Grenada in the Caribbean. In the past reporters were allowed to accompany American troops during wartime. Their stories were then censored before they were published or broadcast. There was little censorship in Vietnam, however, and this angered many military officers.

The invasion of Grenada marked the first time reporters were left at home. The government refused to permit American reporters on the island for forty eight hours; and a handful of U.S. reporters on Grenada prior to the invasion were detained. Journalists were told to stay away and a small boat carrying some American journalists was buzzed by a U.S. warplane until it turned back from its attempted journey to the island. During the first two days of the fighting, all the news in American newspapers and on radio and television about the invasion came from the military.

Why should reporters be permitted to accompany the invading force? Aren't they likely to, as Secretary of State George Schultz said, "screw things up?" Won't they reveal our plans to the enemy, making surprise impossible? That hasn't happened in the past. Reporters were even on warships in the English Channel as the Allies prepared to invade the European continent on June 6, 1944. Reporters are needed on the scene if the public expects to get an independent account of the invasion. Was it handled efficiently? Were civilians needlessly harmed? Were the opposing forces as described by the government?

The invasion of Grenada did not go well as a military operation, according to many who have since studied the landings. Veteran Pentagon reporter Arthur T. Hadley, in his book, *Straw Giant*, reports that American forces in the northern part of the island who were commanded by a Marine colonel could not communicate with American forces in the south who were commanded by an Army general because the radio frequencies were not compatible. This incompatibility of communications equipment forced an Army officer to use a credit card to make a telephone call all the way to the Pentagon to try to tell the Navy, standing offshore, that he needed some air support. Also Army helicopters ferrying wounded to a ship offshore for treatment were forbidden to land on the ship because the pilots had not been trained in Navy landing techniques and men died unnecessarily, according to Hadley.

The military and the press worked together after the invasion to try to avoid a similar problem in the future. The result was the formation of a small pool of reporters who could be called at a moment's notice in the event of future military operations. The pool has been activated several times, most notably during the American attack on Libya and the Persian Gulf tanker war. Associated Press reporter Tim Ahern was a member of the pool that was assigned to the American warships that escorted the reflagged Kuwaiti tankers through the Persian Gulf. Ahern said he had twenty-four-hour, unrestricted access to every part of the ship—including the bridge and the combat information center—but not including the radio room. Officers and enlisted soldiers were candid and helpful, he added. He did, however, complain about what he believed was unnecessary censorship of a couple of his stories. For example, U.S. naval officers met with civilian tanker officials in the conference room of one of the tankers. After the meeting they drank some beer. This reference was cut from Ahern's story, the censor contending it would not look good to readers back in the United States. Some photographers and broadcasters had technical difficulties getting their stories out, but most members of the press and the military said they believed the press pool idea has worked very well.

The issue of prior restraint arose again in May of 1986 when CIA Director William Casey threatened to initiate prosecution of *The Washington Post, The Washington Times, The New York Times, Time,* and *Newsweek* if stories about U.S. intelligence gathering capabilities were published. The stories were generated while the government was prosecuting Ronald Pelton, a former intelligence specialist with the National Security Agency, for selling secrets to the Soviets. The stories focused upon a top secret U.S. eavesdropping operation against the Soviet Union, something Pelton had apparently revealed to the Soviets. Casey met with two senior editors at *The Washington Post* and threatened to invoke a thirty-five-year-old federal law that makes it a crime to reveal information about American ciphers, code-breaking, and other communication intelligence functions. *The Post* ultimately published a version of the story, but without three paragraphs containing a description of the interception device. President Reagan called *Post* publisher Katherine Graham and personally asked that the material be deleted. The Justice Department, which had never used the 1950 law cited by Casey to prosecute a journalist, said it was very reluctant to prosecute any reporter under the statute, and the issue died away as the Pelton trial ended.

All the newspapers and magazines had gotten the information about the eavesdropping capability legally. Reporters argued that the government used a double standard by invoking the classification of material to try to block the publication or broadcast of stories. When the government wanted to prove a point or make a case for its own action (as when President Reagan revealed that American intelligence agencies had eavesdropped on communications between Libyan officials and their agents in Germany prior to the bombing of the discotheque in Germany which prompted the air attacks against that African nation) it never hesitated to declassify material. But the government uses classification to block the flow of information that is sometimes embarrassing to the government, journalists argue.

"Fighting-Words" Doctrine

While national security issues are frequently the source of prior restraint problems, other issues can provoke authorities to apply restraint. In 1942, in the case of *Chaplinsky* v. *New Hampshire,* the Supreme Court identified one category of speech in which the application of prior censorship is not necessarily a violation of the First Amendment. Justice Frank Murphy wrote:

> There are certain well-defined and narrowly limited classes of speech, the *prevention* [emphasis added] and punishment of which have never been thought to raise any constitutional problems. These include . . . fighting words—those which by their very utterance inflict injury or tend to incite an immediate breach of the peace. It has been well observed that such utterances are no essential part of any exposition of ideas, and are of such slight social value as a step to the truth that any benefit that may be derived from them is clearly outweighed by the social interest in order and morality.

In the *Chaplinksy* case a Jehovah's Witness in Rochester, New Hampshire, angered citizens when he sought to distribute pamphlets denouncing religion as a fraud. When warned by a law officer of the danger to his safety, the Witness called the marshal a "God-damned racketeer" and a "damned Facist." He was convicted of violating a state statute that forbade any person to "address any offensive, derisive, or annoying words, to any other person who is lawfully in any street or other public place, nor call him by any offensive or derisive name."

The prohibition of this kind of verbal assault is permissible so long as the statutes are carefully drawn and do not permit the application of the law to protected speech. Also, the "fighting words" must be used in a personal, face-to-face encounter—a true verbal assault. In 1972 the Supreme Court ruled that laws on the subject must be limited to words "that have a direct tendency to cause acts of violence by the person to whom, individually, the remark is addressed" (*Gooding* v. *Wilson,* 1972).

The 1977 confrontation in Skokie, Illinois, between Nazi protesters and city officials presents a more contemporary example of a multitude of free-speech problems, including the so-called fighting-words doctrine. In 1976 members of the National Socialist party said they planned to peacefully demonstrate in Skokie, a community with a large Jewish population, to protest the racial integration of nearby Chicago schools. The protest was prohibited by village officials, who said the Nazis had failed to obtain $350,000 worth of liability and property damage insurance as required by a Skokie Park District ordinance.

After the Nazis announced that they planned to protest against the insurance ordinance, the village obtained a temporary restraining order blocking the demonstration and then adopted three new ordinances regarding public marches and protests. In addition to the insurance requirements, the village ruled that a member of a political party cannot march in a military-style uniform and ruled that it is not permissible to disseminate material intended to incite racial hatred. State and federal courts in Illinois invalidated all the ordinances, ruling that they were discriminatory or abridged constitutionally protected rights of free speech (*Collin* v. *Smith*, 1978; *Village of Skokie* v. *National Socialist Party,* 1978).

The Illinois Supreme Court, in refusing to enjoin the display of the swastika and other Nazi symbols, rejected the contention that such display constituted "fighting words" sufficient "to overcome the heavy presumption against the constitutional validity of a prior restraint" (*Village of Skokie* v. *National Socialist Party,* 1978). "Peaceful demonstrations cannot be totally precluded solely because that display [of the swastika] may provoke a violent reaction by those who view it. . . . A speaker who gives prior notice of his message has not compelled a confrontation with those who voluntarily listen."

In *Handbook of Free Speech and Free Press,* authors Jerome Barron and C. Thomas Dienes suggest two key questions in determining whether so-called fighting words might be suppressed. First, is there imminent danger of disorder? Second, does the speaker use provocative language that constitutes fighting words or that incites his audience to a clear and present danger of disorder? Both questions must be answered in the affirmative before the speech can reasonably be restrained.

Freedom of Expression in Schools

Do students working on school publications enjoy the same First Amendment rights against prior restraint as enjoyed by other persons working on newspapers and magazines in the "real world?" The answer to this question is still slowly unfolding. What is clear today is that when answering this question the courts will usually distinguish among the ages of students—high school versus college, for example; and among varieties of student newspapers—those published off campus, those published on campus but independent of the curriculum, and those published as a part of the students' regular classwork.

For centuries, students were presumed to have few constitutional rights of any kind. They were regarded as junior or second-class people and were told it was better to be seen and not heard. Parents were given wide latitude in controlling the behavior of their offspring and when these young people moved into schools or other public institutions, the government had the right to exercise a kind of parental control over them; in loco parentis, in the place of a parent. During the social upheaval of the 1960s and 1970s students began to assert their constitutional rights and in several important decisions the federal courts acknowledged these claims. In 1969, for example, the Supreme Court ruled that students in the public schools do not shed their constitutional rights to freedom of speech or expression at the school house gate (*Tinker* v. *Des Moines Independent School District,* 1969). A small group of students in an Iowa high school decided to wear black arm bands to school to protest the Vietnam War. School officials prohibited the wearing of the armbands because they feared such a symbolic act might disrupt the operation of the school. Five students were suspended for this protest. Justice Abe Fortas, writing for the High Court, said that the school officials must show that students caused a greater interference with normal school operations before they could censor such expression. Students may express their opinions on even controversial subjects like the Vietnam War if they do so "without materially and substantially interfering with the requirements of appropriate discipline in the operation of the school and without colliding with the rights of others."

In the twenty-plus years since the *Tinker* ruling, federal courts have had to struggle with a wide variety of student free expression cases. It is apparent now that the rather benign protest by a handful of students that resulted in the *Tinker* decision presented the courts with a rather simple problem to solve.

Hence the seemingly broad constitutional protection erected in the 1969 ruling has not been fully carried forth when judges are faced with more complex issues dealing with the publication and distribution of student newspapers. Courts have been increasingly reluctant to second-guess the actions of school administrators who are often viewed as being "on the firing line," forced to make quick decisions that may appear to be too stringent in hindsight. The promise of *Tinker,* then, has surely not been fulfilled. No case demonstrates that more clearly than the 1988 ruling in *Hazelwood School District* v. *Kuhlmeier.*

The Kuhlmeier *Case*

In 1983 the principal at East Hazelwood High School near St. Louis censored the school newspaper by completely removing two pages from the publication. The pages contained articles about teenage pregnancy and the impact of parents' divorce on children. The articles on pregnancy included personal interviews with three Hazelwood students (whose names were not used) about how they were affected by their unwanted pregnancies. There was also information about birth control in the story. The story on divorce quoted students—again not identified—about the problems they had suffered when their mothers and fathers had split up. The censorship of the articles was defended on the grounds of privacy and editorial balance. School officials said they were concerned that the identity of the three girls who anonymously discussed their pregnancy might nevertheless become public. School officials said they acted to protect the privacy of the students and the parents in the story on divorce as well. In addition, the principal said the latter story was unbalanced, giving the views of only the students. The federal district court upheld the censorship of the school newspaper, but this decision was overturned by a United States court of appeals. In January of 1988 the Supreme Court reversed the appellate court ruling and ruled that the censorship was permissible under the First Amendment.

At the outset it is important to note that this ruling involved the censorship of a high school newspaper that was published as a part of the school curriculum. The Court strongly suggested that the full force of the ruling would not necessarily apply to a high school paper published as an extracurricular activity, what the Court calls an open forum where any student might contribute stories. Justice Byron White, author of the Court's opinion, noted specifically in a footnote that the Court did not at that time have to decide whether its ruling might also be applied to school-sponsored college and university newspapers. The tone of the ruling, however, and the fact that White consistently used the term "high school" as opposed to "school" suggested to many observers the unlikelihood of the High Court pushing the ruling beyond the doors of a secondary school.

The court of appeals had ruled the censorship of the newspaper unconstitutional because the articles could not have reasonably been forecast to "materially disrupt classwork, give rise to substantial disorder or, invade the rights of others." This is the standard from *Tinker*. But the Supreme Court rejected this standard by distinguishing the *Kuhlmeier* case from the earlier ruling. The *Tinker* ruling, Justice White said in the 5–3 decision, deals with right of educators to silence a student's personal expression that happens to occur on school property. *Kuhlmeier* concerns the authority of educators over school-sponsored publications. "Educators are entitled to exercise greater control over this second form of student expression to assure that participants learn whatever lessons the activity is designed to teach, that readers or listeners are not exposed to material that may be inappropriate for their level of maturity, and that the views of individual speakers are not erroneously attributed to the school," he wrote. Educators do not offend the First Amendment by exercising editorial control over the style and content of student speech in school-sponsored publications so long as their actions are reasonably related to "legitimate pedagogical concerns." This means school officials could censor out material they found "ungrammatical, poorly written, inadequately researched, biased or prejudiced, vulgar or profane, or unsuitable for immature audiences." Justice White stressed at one point in the ruling that the education of the nation's youth is primarily the responsibility of parents, teachers and state and local school officials, not federal judges. Only when the decision to censor has "no valid educational purpose" is the First Amendment directly and sharply involved.

Justice William Brennan wrote a strong dissent for three members of the Court. He complained of the crabbed view of the First Amendment rights of students outlined by Justice White in the court's opinion.

> Instead of teaching children to respect the diversity of ideas that is fundamental to the American system . . . and that our Constitution is a living reality, not parchment under glass, the Court today teaches youth to discount important principles of our government as mere platitudes. The young men and women of Hazelwood East expected a civics lesson, but not the one the Court teaches them today.

Surprisingly, perhaps, the nation's daily press overwhelmingly supported the High Court's ruling, according to the trade publication, *Editor and Publisher*. Freedom of the press, a consensus of the newspaper editorials said, is for those who own one. In the case of a school newspaper, it is the principal who owns the press. Some observers pointed out, however, that a school newspaper is funded by public monies, not the private funds of a publishing company. As such, the comparison between school newspapers and daily newspapers misses the mark.

Though the First Amendment does not fully protect the rights of students who work on school-sponsored newspapers, other means of protection might be found. California, for example, has chosen to expand the protection of these student journalists by statute. As this chapter was being prepared other states were considering similar legislation.

While the *Kuhlmeier* case helps to define the First Amendment rights of high school students publishing a school-sponsored publication, it fails to offer substantial guidance for college students, or for any kind of nonschool-sponsored publication written by a student. Most authorities agree that college or university students enjoy a significantly higher degree of First Amendment freedom than do secondary school students. School officials must demonstrate a "compelling governmental interest" to interfere with the First Amendment rights of students on a public university campus, according to Kay Beth Avery and Robert J. Simpson in a recent article in the *Journal of Law and Education.* But administrators need only show a "reasonable basis" for restraining the rights of high school students, the authors contend. Indeed, in 1973, a United States court of appeals ruled that censorship of constitutionally-protected expression cannot be imposed by university officials by suspending the editors, suppressing circulation, requiring imprimatur of controversial articles, excising repugnant material, withdrawing financial support, or asserting any other form of censorial oversight based on the power of the purse (*Joyner* v. *Whiting*). A 1983 decision by another U.S. Court of Appeals, *Stanley* v. *McGrath,* demonstrates how far the courts are willing to go to protect the college-level press.

At the end of the 1978–79 school year the University of Minnesota *Daily* published its "Finals Edition," which offended thousands of persons both on and off the Twin Cities campus. "The newspaper," wrote University of Minnesota journalism professor Don Gillmor, "through gabble and toilet talk, was designed to irritate Third World students, Blacks, Jews, feminists, gays, lesbians and Christians." Through what it called an exclusive interview with Jesus Christ, the newspaper "revealed" to readers that Christ was a druggie, a bootlegger, a lecher, and a homosexual, for example.

The newspaper, the university administration and the board of regents were inundated with complaints from all segments of the state's population. Hundreds of students were upset enough to begin a drive to change the student-fee support system for the newspaper. The *Daily* is typical of many university newspapers in that a small portion of student activity fees—in this case two dollars per semester—was automatically given to the newspaper. It was suggested that students should be given the right to choose not to support the newspaper. The regents liked this idea as well, and despite the advice of two review committees, which recommended just the opposite, voted in 1980 for a refundable fee system that would permit students to refuse to financially support the newspaper. A court case resulted and in 1983 the U.S. Court of Appeals for the Eighth Circuit ruled that the regents' action violated the First Amendment. If the fee system had been changed, the court said, simply to respond to student complaints of being coerced into supporting views in the newspaper that they opposed, there would be no problem. But the *Daily* carried a wide variety of views, something for virtually everyone on campus. More importantly, it was clear under the circumstances that the fee system was changed because the regents were unhappy with the 1979 Finals Edition.

"Several Regents testified that one of the reasons that they voted in favor of the resolution was that students should not be forced to support a paper which was sacrilegious and vulgar," the court noted. The heavy political pressure on the regents and their two resolutions deploring the content in the Finals Edition added weight to the conclusion that they were attempting to punish the newspaper. Finally, the University of Minnesota has several state campuses, but the fee-support system was changed only on the Twin Cities campus, home of the offending newspaper. "Our study of the record . . . leaves us with the definite and firm conviction that this change in funding would not have occurred absent the public hue and cry that the *Daily's* offensive contents provoked. Reducing the revenues available to the newspaper is therefore forbidden by the First Amendment," the court concluded (*Stanley* v. *McGrath*, 1983).

Reducing the financial support for a student newspaper is clearly something a school administrator or school board can do—but only if it is done for the proper reasons. Any hint that censorship is behind the reduction could result in such an action running afoul of the First Amendment.

The high school press is not nearly as well-insulated from censorial problems. School officials can exercise control over the press—even the nonschool-sponsored newspaper that is distributed on campus—on many grounds.

One ground might be academic propriety. Under *Kuhlmeier*, school officials may censor the paper for any legitimate pedagogical or academic reason. An off-campus paper that is distributed on campus may be pre-screened by school authorities and blocked if it presents a "clear and present likelihood that it will cause a material and substantial disruption of the proper and orderly operation and discipline of the school or school activities" (see *Bystrom* v. *Findley High School*, 1987).

School papers may be censored if they attempt to publish content that could result in the invasion of the rights of others. This means authorities may screen the paper in order to protect the school district or college from liability for a libel or invasion of privacy suit, or to protect the rights of students who might be harmed through such publication. Administrators may scrutinize newspapers under health and welfare concerns and block the publication of advertising, for example, for drug paraphernalia. (See *Williams* v. *Spencer*, 1980.) In both of the previous situations, secondary school administrators have a great deal more leeway in making a decision to censor a publication than do college or university administrators, according to most authorities.

Finally, school officials may censor a school publication for reasons of obscenity, vulgarity, or indecency. Avery and Simpson argue that college or university newspapers will likely to be held to a standard of legal obscenity, as defined in *Miller* v. *California* (see chapter 8). But this has not been clearly established by the federal courts. The *Miller* test is the same standard applied to popular magazines or newspapers. But secondary school administrators are empowered to use a far less rigorous standard that is quite broad and somewhat vague—pervasive indecency or vulgarity. This is a standard that has been shaped by case law in broadcasting (see *FCC* v. *Pacifica,* chapter 11) and by a 1986 Supreme Court ruling involving an assembly speech by a high school student. In a 7–2 ruling, the High Court said it was permissible for a Spanaway, Washington, high school to suspend a student who had used sexual metaphor and innuendo in a speech to a school assembly to tout the virility of a candidate for student government office. Some of the six hundred students who attended the assembly responded to the speech with hooting and yelling. While Chief Justice Burger, who wrote the Court's opinion, at one point called the speech obscene, nothing in Matthew Fraser's short speech met the legal definition of obscenity (see chapter 8). In fact, the speech was reprinted in stories about the case in many newspapers and magazines.

Burger stressed, in his opinion, the marked distinction between the *Tinker* case, which focused upon a political message, and the purely sexual content of Fraser's speech. "The undoubted freedom to advocate unpopular and controversial views in schools and classrooms must be balanced against the society's countervailing interest in teaching students the boundaries of socially appropriate behavior," the Chief Justice wrote. The schools could reasonably conclude, he said, that the essential lessons of civil, mature conduct cannot be conveyed in a school that tolerates "lewd, or offensive speech." Burger added that the "pervasive sexual innuendo in Fraser's speech was plainly offensive to both teachers and students. Dissenter Justice John Paul Stevens questioned whether "a group of judges who are at least two generations and three thousand miles away from the scene of the crime" were as well qualified as Fraser to determine whether the speech would offend his contemporaries, who went on to elect the candidate for whom he spoke. (*Bethel School District* v. *Fraser,* 1986.)

There is little doubt that student journalists tend to enjoy fewer First Amendment rights than their real world counterparts. This is especially true for high school students. While they may not shed their constitutional rights of free expression at the school house gate, as Justice Fortas wrote in 1969, they can certainly carry what rights they do have as student journalists in a far smaller basket than a professional American reporter or editor.

One additional note. Most of the First Amendment guarantees for students apply only to students in public schools. Officials at private institutions appear—at this time—to enjoy wider powers of censorship.

Book Banning

Another problem related to school censorship arose in the early 1980s and has remained a thorny legal problem ever since. The banning of books in libraries—especially school libraries—reached epidemic proportions by mid-decade. Conservative Christian organizations have been at the forefront of these efforts across the nation, but other individuals not usually associated with censorship activities have been active as well. Blacks in many communities have complained about Mark Twain's *The Adventures of Huckleberry Finn* and urged it be banned because of what they felt was racist language.

Vulgarity or descriptions of sexual behavior are more common reasons pressure groups have sought to have books removed from library shelves. But book censors have also complained about books that depict unorthodox family arrangements; speculations about Christ; sexual explicitness (even in a biological context); unflattering portraits of American authority; criticism of American authority and business and corporate practices; and radical political philosophy. The list of books that have been attacked is long, but here are a few titles that have consistently come under fire:

Jaws by Peter Benchley
Several books by Judy Blume, a best-selling children's author
The Pill Versus the Springhill Mine Disaster and other novels by Richard Brautigan
Manchild in the Promised Land by Claude Brown
Kramer vs. Kramer by Avery Corman
Catch-22 by Joseph Heller
Sons by Evan Hunter
Valley Forge by MacKinlay Kantor
One Flew Over the Cuckoo's Nest by Ken Kesey
The Thorn Birds by Colleen McCullough
The Godfather by Mario Puzo
One Day in the Life of Ivan Denisovitch by Aleksander Solzhenitsyn
The American Heritage Dictionary
The Dictionary of American Slang
Trial of the Catonsville Nine by Daniel Berrigan
Our Bodies, Ourselves by the Boston Women's Health Book Collective
The Art of Loving by Erich Fromm
Boss: Richard J. Daley of Chicago by Mike Royko
The Electric Kool-Aid Acid Test by Tom Wolfe
Show Me a sex education book
Tarzan by Edgar Rice Burroughs
Oliver Twist by Charles Dickens
Mother Goose
The Bible

Also included in the list of frequently censored books are *A Farewell to Arms, 1984, Brave New World, The Catcher in the Rye, The Merchant of Venice, The Grapes of Wrath, Huckleberry Finn,* and *Stuart Little.*

In recent years much of the censorship attack has shifted to public school curriculum materials. Textbooks—especially those that discuss evolution—have been the target of protests in many school districts. Groups with names like Citizens for Excellence in Education have also attacked drug programs mounted by junior and senior high schools. In Oak Harbor, Washington, members of a local chapter of Citizens for Excellence in Education attempted to force the school board to remove a fourth grade reader in the *Impressions* series. Complaints about the reader, which contains a myriad of well-known stories and essays, included assertions that the stories taught the occult and witchcraft, encouraged children to steal and disobey their parents, and taught New Age religion. For example, members of the pressure group argued that a condensed version of *The Wizard of Oz* contained in the book "teaches children that human traits like courage and compassion are gained through one's own efforts and not bestowed as gifts from God."

In this case the school board voted unanimously to retain the book, but in many other instances local pressure succeeded in forcing the opposite decision. Unfortunately most school board members are woefully unprepared to deal with an organized campaign against parts of the school curriculum or books contained in the library. And the courts have given little guidance in this matter. The Supreme Court has looked at this issue but once, and its somewhat ambiguous ruling left many questions unanswered.

Members of the Board of Education of the Island Trees School District in Eastern New York removed nine books from the high school library. Included among the banished books were *The Fixer* by Bernard Malamud, *Slaughterhouse Five* by Kurt Vonnegut, *The Naked Ape* by Desmond Morris, *Soul on Ice* by Eldridge Cleaver, and the *Best Short Stories by Negro Writers*. Student Council President Steven Pico and four other students challenged this action in the United States district court. They argued that their First Amendment rights to read these books had been violated. But United States District Judge George Pratt rejected these arguments and ruled that a school board has the right to remove books that are irrelevant, vulgar, immoral and in bad taste. The First Amendment was not violated by such action, Pratt ruled, citing a seven-year-old United States Court of Appeals decision (*President's Council District 25* v. *Community School Board,* 1972). The judge's ruling came on the board of education's motion for summary judgment. No trial was ever held to establish the facts, including the school board's motives for removing these volumes (*Pico* v. *Island Trees,* 1979).

The United States Court of Appeals for the Second Circuit reversed Judge Pratt's order and ordered the district court to hold a trial. The court stood by its earlier decision that permitted school authorities to remove vulgar or immoral books from the school library. But Steven Pico and the other students should have been given a chance at trial to persuade the court that the school board's ostensible justification for removing the books (that they were in bad taste, vulgar, etc.) was merely a pretext for the suppression of freedom of speech. The board could not ban the books if their decision to remove them was based on their political or moral disagreement with the content of the works.

In March 1982 the Supreme Court heard arguments in the case and three months later affirmed the court of appeals and returned the case to district court for trial. However the High Court was fractured into several groups, and seven different opinions were written.

The Court's opinion was written by Justice William Brennan. A school board cannot, under the First Amendment, remove books from a school library simply because it disapproves of the political ideas or philosophies expressed in the books, wrote Justice Brennan. Books may be removed if they are persuasively vulgar or if they are educationally unsuitable. But the First Amendment guarantees to students a right to receive ideas, and the board of education cannot interfere with that right simply because it disagrees with those ideas. Brennan mustered the support of Justices Thurgood Marshall and John Stevens behind his opinion.

Justice Harry Blackmun concurred with all of Brennan's opinion except his reference to a "right to receive ideas," a controversial notion Brennan has promulgated in recent years. Blackmun said he based his opinion on a principle narrower and far more basic than the right to receive ideas. The state may not suppress exposure to ideas for the sole purpose of suppressing exposure to those ideas, he wrote. The fifth vote in the five-to-four decision came from Justice Byron White, who seemed dismayed at Brennan's exploration of constitutional issues. A trial was needed, he said, to find out what motivated the removal of the books. When the facts are established, he wrote, the Court can develop constitutional law on the matter.

Chief Justice Warren Burger and Justices Lewis Powell, William Rehnquist, and Sandra O'Connor all dissented. All the dissenting opinions reflected the position that it was the responsibility of the school board, not of a federal court, to run the school. "The plurality [Brennan, Marshall, Blackmun, and Stevens] concludes that the Constitution requires school boards to justify to its teenage pupils the decision to remove a particular book from a school library," Burger wrote. Other dissenters echoed Burger's complaint.

The ruling was particularly unsatisfactory because the Court failed to provide any clear guidance on an issue that is plaguing scores of school libraries across the nation. The splits within the Court left even a careful reader of the decision with little certainty about how the Court would act in a subsequent case. Four justices said school boards cannot remove books from a library for political or moral reasons; four justices said school boards can remove books for any reason; and Justice White refused to say where he stands on the issue. "We should not decide constitutional questions until it is necessary to do so," he wrote. Even the language in the Court's opinion lacks clarity. Brennan said that a book can be removed from the shelves if it is "persuasively vulgar" or "educationally unsuitable." What do these terms mean?

No court decision since 1982 has helped to clarify the meaning of the ruling in *Pico*. The High Court's decision clearly established a First Amendment right of access to the information in books already held in secondary school libraries. School boards no longer have the broad discretion once exercised to remove works they personally find offensive. And school boards must exercise great caution to assure that when they are operating in what they consider the best interests of their students, they do not tread on educationally relevant information, noted Donald J. Dunn in an article in the *Law Library Journal.* But work still needs to be done, for the Supreme Court has not dispelled all the confusion surrounding the book removal issue. Other courts, if not the Supreme Court, will have to refine the broad and even vague standards enunciated in *Pico* before the issue will be clearly resolved.

The brief survey just presented by no means exhausts the catalog of attempts by the government to exercise prior restraint. Innovative efforts abound each year. Here are two recent examples.

In the mideighties the Securities and Exchange Commission (SEC) sought to restrain the publication of an investment newsletter. The publisher, Christopher Lowe, had been previously convicted of serious misconduct as an investment advisor, and the SEC said his continued attempts to advise the public on investments was a violation of the federal Investment Advisors Act of 1940. The Supreme Court, however, ruled that Lowe's newsletter was a bonafide newspaper and exempt from the restrictions of the 1940s law (*Lowe v. SEC,* 1985).

In 1984 the federal government launched a criminal investigation against Antoni Gronowicz, the author of a book entitled *God's Broker,* in hopes of blocking the distribution of this biography of Pope John Paul II. Gronowicz claimed to have conducted a series of personal interviews with the Pope, something the Vatican denied. The United States Attorney's office in Philadelphia instituted a grand jury investigation into possible mail and wire fraud violations. If the book was indeed a hoax, the government argued, then attempts to sell it or promote it amounted to fraud. In the face of this controversy, the publisher withdrew the book from distribution. Gronowicz refused to comply with a subpeona and was ultimately held in contempt of court. (See chapter 7.) He claimed that the purpose of the investigation was to establish the truth or falsity of the contents of his book, and this amounted to a violation of his First Amendment rights. The United States Court of Appeals for the Third Circuit rejected this argument, however, and sustained the contempt citation. (See in re *Gronowicz.*) Gronowicz petitioned the Supreme Court to hear his appeal, but he died in October of 1985 and the High Court refused to hear arguments in the case or take any action. Sandra Disbrow, writing in the *Albany Law Review,* described the decision in the case as a dangerous one. "Authors, especially of nonfiction works, must live with the fear that their work product might displease influential people," she wrote. And that displeasure could easily be translated into a criminal investigation, using a device like the mail fraud statutes to argue that an effort to promote or sell an untruthful book is the commission of a fraudulent act.

SUMMARY   While virtually all American legal scholars agree that the adoption of the First Amendment in 1791 was designed to abolish prior restraint in this nation, prior censorship still exists by virtue of an opinion of the Supreme Court in 1931. In *Near* v. *Minnesota* Chief Justice Charles Evans Hughes ruled that while prior restraint is unacceptable in most instances, there are times when it must be tolerated if the republic is to survive. The most vivid example cited by Hughes is the prior restraint of the publication of information that may assist the enemy during wartime. Hughes's "wartime" exception has been translated today to mean a "national security" exception, and in recent years in two important cases the press has been stopped from publishing material that courts believed to be too sensitive. While the Supreme Court finally permitted the *New York Times* and the *Washington Post* to publish the so-called Pentagon Papers, the newspapers were blocked for two weeks from printing the material. And in the end the High Court merely ruled that the government had failed to make its case, not that the newspapers had an absolute right to publish the material. The *Progressive* magazine was enjoined from publishing an article about the hydrogen bomb. Only the publication of the material by a small newspaper in Wisconsin thwarted government efforts to permanently stop publication of the material.

Chief Justice Hughes said in 1931 that prior restraint is also permissible in instances in which a speaker or publisher is attempting to incite violence. The Supreme Court has developed a "fighting-words" doctrine, which has been applied in several instances to block expression that might incite others to violence. In a recent case involving a protest by members of the Nazi party in Illinois however, both federal and state courts ruled that members of an audience have an obligation to restrain themselves, and expression cannot be prohibited merely because the speaker has chosen to appear before a volatile group.

Student journalists enjoy a more limited protection against prior restraint than other journalists. College and university officials have considerably less power to interfere with the student press than do their counterparts in high schools. High school administrators are considered the publishers of newspapers associated with the school curriculum and may censor out any material in the school paper so long as their efforts are related to "legitimate pedagogical concerns." This includes material that might cause disruptions in the school, that might invade the rights of others, that might create liability for the school, or that is considered vulgar or indecent. Papers published off-campus but distributed on the school grounds can also be scrutinized for acceptability. Book banning in school libraries, something that emerged anew in the early 1980s, continues as a problem. A plurality of the Supreme Court ruled in 1982 that the removal of books from the shelves of school libraries cannot be motivated because school members disagree with the political ideas or philosophies in the books. Books can be removed, however, if they are considered persuasively vulgar or educationally unsuitable. The Court was badly split in the decision and the ruling was murky. The issue remains to be clarified.

TIME, PLA
AND MAN
RESTRICTI

Justification of the previously noted instances of prior restraint—both inside and outside the schools—was based on the content of the article or the speech; that is, what was written or said provoked the prior censorship. Prior censorship can also be justified, however, on the basis of where or when a particular expression is scheduled to occur. In these instances the content of the publication or speech is not considered material in determining whether the prior restraint is justified or whether it is prohibited by the First Amendment. Such rules are called **time, place, and manner restrictions** and focus on when, where, or how the expression is to be made public.

During the past fifty years courts have developed a series of guidelines or tests that are used when a judge is asked to determine whether or not a particular instance of censorship is a reasonable time, place and manner rule. The court will first ask whether the law or order is content neutral; that is, whether the application of the rule depends upon the content of the speech or publication. Laws that are not content neutral are frequently invalid on that basis alone. Some laws that are not content neutral are invalid on their face. For example, when the city of Brentwood, Tennessee, adopted an ordinance that said commercial handbills could not be delivered in any public place, but that newspapers, political, and religious material could be delivered in this manner, the Tennessee Supreme Court ruled that the law was not content neutral (*H & L Messengers* v. *Brentwood,* 1979). In other instances, a law appears to be content neutral but is not because it vests in some authority the power to use the content of the message to determine whether or not to enforce or apply the law. An Alamogordo, New Mexico, city ordinance banned door-to-door solicitations except by religious or charitable organizations. The city manager had the authority to determine what was and was not a legitimate religious cause. A federal district court declared the law invalid because of this content consideration (*Weissman* v. *Alamogordo,* 1979).

A legitimate time, place and manner rule must be reasonable as well as content neutral. In determining whether or not a law is reasonable a court will ask the following questions:

> Does the law constitute a complete ban on a type of communication; are other alternative means of distributing the message available?
>
> Has the state articulated a compelling state or public interest to justify this restraint on speech?

Is the law precisely or narrowly tailored so that it furthers this state interest, but does not restrain more expression than is actually required?

A law or ordinance may be declared invalid for failing to successfully pass any of the above tests. For example, pollsters for news organizations often like to talk with voters after they leave the polling place. This allows the researcher to find out what kinds of people (ethnic background, income level, education, etc.) are voting for what candidate. State laws that have attempted to ban such exit polling have been struck down, in part at least, because there is simply no other way for the press to ask such questions. Telephone interviews after the election would not allow the pollster to generate the same kind of data (see page 91). A law might also be struck down because the state interest in controlling a certain form of expression is insignificant. Laws limiting the placement of newsstands on city streets are frequently declared invalid because city officials are unable to articulate a good reason why such newsstands should be limited (see page 88). Finally, the law must be drafted so as to limit no more speech than is needed to advance the state interest. A city certainly has a legitimate interest in keeping sound trucks from blaring a message when people are trying to sleep. But a law which altogether bans such amplification devices is surely not narrowly cast.

The manner in which a court applies these rules or tests is often dependent upon the setting or forum in which the communication takes place. The First Amendment requires that courts protect to a far greater extent expression that occurs in a public forum—such as a public park—than expression that occurs in a private forum—a solicitor knocking on the door of a private home for example. The public forum category has been refined recently to a greater extent by many courts. (See *San Diego Committee* v. *Grossmont Union High School*, 1986.) There are public places which by long tradition have been devoted to assembly or debate. The rights of the state to limit expression in a public park or on a street corner are sharply limited. There are some public forums that the state itself has opened for use by the public for expression such as a city-owned auditorium or the grounds of a state fair. The state has more power to regulate speech in such a setting than it does in the previous kind of public forum. Finally, there are public places which have not by tradition nor designation been the setting for public communication. A prison or a military base are examples of these. The state has its greatest authority to control speech in such settings.

Before looking at the application of time, place and manner rules in a variety of public and private settings, let's first recall the important Supreme Court ruling in *Lovell* v. *Griffin* (1938) which established that the First Amendment protects the distribution as well as the publication of messages and ideas.

The city of Griffin, Georgia, had an ordinance that prohibited distribution of circulars, handbooks, advertising, and literature of any kind without first obtaining written permission from the city manager. Under the law, the city manager had considerable discretion as to whether to give permission. Alma Lovell was a member of the Jehovah's Witnesses religious sect, an intense and ruggedly evangelical order that suffered severe persecution in the first half of this century. But the Witnesses doggedly continued to spread the Word, passing out millions of leaflets and pamphlets and attempting to proselytize anyone who would listen.

Alma Lovell didn't even attempt to get a license before she circulated pamphlets, and she was arrested, convicted, and fined fifty dollars for violating the city ordinance. When she refused to pay the fine, she was sentenced to fifty days in jail. At the trial the Jehovah's Witnesses freely admitted the illegal distribution, but argued that the statute was invalid on its face because it violated the First Amendment guarantees of freedom of the press and freedom of religion.

On appeal the Supreme Court agreed that the law did indeed violate freedom of the press. Chief Justice Charles Evans Hughes wrote, "We think that the ordinance is invalid on its face" because it strikes at the very foundation of freedom of the press by subjecting it to license and censorship. The city argued that the First Amendment applies only to newspapers and regularly published materials like magazines. The High Court disagreed, ruling that the amendment applies to pamphlets and leaflets as well: "These indeed have been historic weapons in the defense of liberty, as the pamphlets of Thomas Paine and others in our own history abundantly attest. The press in its historic connotation comprehends every sort of publication which affords a vehicle of information and opinion."

Lawyers for Griffin also argued that the First Amendment was not applicable because the licensing law said nothing about publishing, but only concerned distribution. Again the Court disagreed, noting that liberty of circulation is as essential to freedom of expression as liberty of publication. Chief Justice Hughes wrote, "Without the circulation, the publication would be of little value."

Public Streets

Nineteen months after the *Lovell* decision the Supreme Court decided a second distribution case, a case involving laws in four different cities. The four cases were decided as one (*Schneider* v. *New Jersey,* 1939). A Los Angeles ordinance prohibited the distribution of handbills on public streets on the grounds that distribution contributed to the litter problem. Ordinances in Milwaukee, Wisconsin, and Worcester, Massachusetts, were justified on the same basis—keeping the city streets clean.

An Irvington, New Jersey, law was far broader, prohibiting street distribution or house-to-house calls unless permission was first obtained from the local police chief. The police department asked distributors for considerable personal information and could reject applicants the law officers deemed not of good character. This action was ostensibly to protect the public against criminals.

The Supreme Court struck down all four city ordinances. Justice Owen Roberts wrote for the Court that cities can certainly enact regulations in the interest of public safety, health and welfare. Pedestrians, for example, could be prohibited from blocking a street or sidewalk in order to distribute pamphlets. And a city can certainly punish persons who litter the streets with paper. But a community cannot justify an ordinance that prohibits the distribution of handbills—conduct that is protected under the First Amendment—by asserting an interest in keeping the streets clean. The fourth ordinance, the one in Irvington, was declared unconstitutional because it was not content neutral. It gave police the discretion to determine who could express their ideas and who could not, Roberts said.

The following year the Supreme Court voided another anti-solicitation law, one enacted in New Haven, Connecticut. Solicitation of money for religious causes was prohibited unless the solicitors first gained the approval of local officials, whose job it was to determine what was and was not a "bona fide object of charity." Justice Roberts, writing for a unanimous court, ruled that a community could, in order to protect its citizens from fraudulent solicitations, require strangers in the community to establish identity and authority to act for the cause they purport to represent. A community could also adopt reasonable rules limiting the time such door-to-door solicitation might be made.

> But to condition the solicitation of aid for the perpetuation of religious views or systems upon a license, the grant of which rests in the exercise of a determination by state authority as to what is a religious cause, is to lay a forbidden burden upon the exercise of a liberty protected by the Constitution (*Cantwell* v. *Connecticut,* 1940).

Airports

The regulation of expression in airports and other public transportation terminals has been an issue as well. Milwaukee was one of many communities that tried to regulate solicitations and distribution at its airport on the grounds that the passageways and corridors at General Billy Mitchell Field were too narrow and crowded to allow such activity. The United States District Court for Eastern Wisconsin ruled that the county airport is a public forum and that county rules that require prior permission before any solicitation can take place violate the First Amendment: "Crowded conditions may require restrictions to ensure the efficient operation of the airport," the court ruled. But such conditions did not justify sweeping rules that totally excluded solicitation by many persons and groups (*International Society for Krishna Consciousness* v. *Wolke,* 1978). Other courts have made similar rulings with regard to airport regulations.

In a similar manner the United States Supreme Court ruled that officials of the Minnesota State Fair can regulate solicitations on the fair grounds during the annual summer event. Anyone who seeks to sell or distribute merchandise or even hand out written material is required to work from booths rented for a small fee from fair officials. Booths are provided on a first-come, first-serve basis, and the rule applies to everyone—commercial, nonprofit, and charitable organizations—equally. The International Society for Krishna Consciousness challenged the rule, arguing it violated their religious freedom as well as their freedom of expression. Justice White and four other members of the High Court disagreed.

White reiterated that in order for a time, place, and manner rule to be acceptable it must (1) be content neutral, (2) serve a significant governmental interest, and (3) leave ample alternative channels for the communication of the information. The Minnesota State Fair rules are content neutral; they apply to all equally. The state has a strong interest in maintaining the orderly movement of crowds at the fairgrounds. The grounds are small, only 125 acres; crowds are heavy, up to 160,000 persons on a weekend day. The fairgrounds are not like a public street, White said, which is always open and normally uncongested. Finally, the members of the Society for Krishna Consciousness can perform their ritualistic solicitation outside the fairgrounds. Members can mingle with the crowds on the grounds, talk with people, and propagate their views. They can even have a booth on the fairgrounds. There are alternative means to communicate their information. "The Minnesota State Fair is a limited public forum in that it exists to provide a means for a great number of exhibitors temporarily to present their products or views . . . to a large number of people in an efficient fashion," Justice White wrote. Considering these limits, the rules are reasonable (*Heffron* v. *International Society,* 1981).

The Supreme Court in 1988 struck down an attempt by city officials in the small Ohio community of Lakewood to control the placement and appearance of newsstands on the public sidewalks (*Lakewood* v. *Plain Dealer Publishing Co., 1988*). This was the first High Court ruling on this topic in decades and marked both the growing amount of litigation on this topic as well as the growing importance of these vending machines to the newspaper industry. The development of satellite communication transmission and regional printing plants has made possible the same day sale of national newspapers in cities all over America. Street sales through vending machines of the *New York Times,* the *Wall Street Journal, USA Today* and other publications have increased the number of stands on most public sidewalks. Many municipal officials have argued that the machines cause congestion and are unsightly, and hundreds of new local ordinances have been adopted.

In Lakewood the city tried to subject placement of the stands to permit fees, insurance requirements, design standards, and any other "such terms and conditions" the mayor deems necessary and reasonable. The United States

Court of Appeals for the Sixth Circuit (*Plain Dealer* v. *Lakewood*, 1986) ruled that ordinance was unconstitutional because it allowed the granting of permits to be contingent upon the mayor's unbridled discretion. The law was not narrowly tailored because it didn't contain any standards for the mayor to use when granting and denying permits, the court ruled.

The Supreme Court affirmed this ruling in a 4–3 vote in 1988. Justice William Brennan noted at the outset that licensing schemes fostered two kinds of problems. The first is self-censorship. Speakers will choose not to speak if they must first get a license to permit them to speak. The second problem is the difficulty of effectively detecting, reviewing and correcting content-based censorship that might be disguised by a licensing plan. In focusing on the Lakewood licensing system Brennan stated "It is apparent that the face of the ordinance itself contains no explicit limits on the mayor's discretion. Indeed, nothing in the law as written requires the mayor to do more than make the statement, 'It is not in the public interest' when denying a permit application." The city argued that it must be presumed that the mayor would act in good faith, but Brennan remained unpersuaded. "To allow these illusory 'constraints' to constitute the standards necessary to bound a licensor's descretion renders the guaranty against censorship little more than a high-sounding ideal" (*Lakewood* v. *Plain Dealer Publishing Co.*, 1988).

Is any regulation of newsstands permissible? Yes, as long as the ordinances meet the normal tests for time, place and manner rules. They must be content neutral, there must be written rules, and the rules must be reasonable. The New York Court of Appeals recently struck down attempts by New York City to block the placement of stands containing course catalogs for a company called "The Learning Annex" on city street corners. Stands for newspapers were permitted. Persons seeking to place a stand needed to gain permission from the office of the city attorney. But there were no guidelines—city officials approved or disapproved of applications almost at whim. The state's high court ruled that the city certainly had the right to regulate the newsstands so long as it accommodated First Amendment interests. But it had to have properly drawn regulations (*New York City* v. *American School Publications*, 1987). The city of Newport, Rhode Island, tried to ban the placement of stands altogether on aesthetic and safety grounds. A United States district court threw out the ordinance. There was no evidence that the stands were broken, rusted and poorly maintained, as the city asserted. And even if stands were ugly, the court ruled, lots of things on city streets (fire hydrants, utility poles, traffic signs) are also ugly. The city also failed to show that nothing short of a total ban on the newsstands would alleviate the alleged safety risks (*Providence Journal* v. *Newport*, 1987).

What kind of regulations are permissible? Generally, fees or license costs are permissible. Some states require that the fees can be no higher than need be to cover the actual administrative cost of providing the permit. (See *Jacobsen* v. *Crivaro*, 1988.) Regulations regarding the location of the stands are also permissible, so long as they are reasonable. Rules that prohibit the placing of stands too close to fire hydrants or crosswalks are clearly acceptable. And it is possible to ban newsstands completely from some parts of a community. In the aforementioned *Plain Dealer* case the United States Court of Appeals for the Sixth Circuit said it was permissible for Lakewood, Ohio, to ban the boxes completely from residential parts of the community. The city justified the ban on traffic safety, maintaining a clear right-of-way for pedestrians on the narrower sidewalks, and aesthetics. The court said this was permissible since there were many alternative means of getting those papers to readers in that area—home delivery, newsstands in the city center, and sales at small convenience stores (*Plain Dealer* v. *Lakewood*, 1986). But the government must justify such a total ban. (See, for example, *Chicago Newspaper Publishers Association* v. *Wheaton*, 1988, where a total ban on residential placement was declared improper.) New York State tried to block the placement of *USA Today* newsstands at rest areas along a freeway. A United States district court said the effort was invalid because the state could not identify any government interest let alone a significant government interest in such a total ban (*Gannett* v. *White*, 1987).

Finally, rules on clustering or limits on the number of stands on a single corner are possible. California courts approved a Glendale ordinance that permits only eight newsstands in any one location and sixteen on each side of a block. The ordinance also employed a preference system for newspapers wishing to place stands on the streets, giving priority to newspapers that are published most frequently and circulated most widely in Los Angeles County. The court said that space was limited and the city had an obligation to allocate it. The preference for one kind of newspaper over another was "simply a means of balancing the problem of public demand and supply" (*Socialist Labor Party* v. *Glendale*, 1978).

Several states and cities have attempted to regulate the placement of billboards, with mixed results. The problem in such regulation is coping with the rights of store owners to advertise their businesses. The dilemma is best illustrated by a 1981 United States Supreme Court ruling on a San Diego billboard ordinance. The ordinance prohibited all outdoor advertising except on-site commercial signs that promoted goods or services offered by businesses on the premises. That is, owners of hardware stores could erect on their property signs that advertised materials sold in the hardware store. Acknowledging that the ban was prompted by substantial state interests in the aesthetic quality of the city and in traffic safety, the Supreme Court nevertheless struck down the city law. The flaw in the ordinance was the broad exemption granted for on-site commercial speech. "Insofar as the city tolerates billboards at all," Justice White wrote in the plurality Court opinion, "it cannot choose to limit their content to commercial messages." The law is not content neutral; it reaches into the realm of protected speech, he wrote. To be constitutional, then, the ordinance must allow noncommercial (Save the Whales, Abortion

Is a Crime, etc.) on-site billboards as well. A total ban on billboards, if properly justified, might also be acceptable (*Metromedia* v. *San Diego,* 1981; see also *Donnelly* v. *Campbell,* 1980; *Metromedia* v. *Baltimore,* 1982; and *Norton* v. *Arlington Heights,* 1982).

Polling Places

A serious controversy arose in the early 1980s over a practice employed by the major television networks of projecting the winner of the presidential election before the polls had closed in the western United States. The networks attempted to make these projections on the basis of data gathered from voters who were questioned as they left the polling place. Officials in many states argued that the practice was harmful. If some voters thought the election had already been decided, they would not vote, and this failure to vote might change the outcome of local elections for Congress or state offices. While there was considerable anecdotal evidence that some people who said they had planned to vote changed their minds after hearing the network projections, scientific evidence was far less ascertainable. Regardless, there was no constitutional way to bar the networks from making the projections; a ban on such pronouncements would surely be a prior restraint. So states like Washington attempted instead to block exit polling by the networks, hoping that if the researchers could not gather their data, they would not be able to make their projections. Washington State amended its law prohibiting the disruption of polling places to forbid within three hundred feet of the voting place exit polling or public opinion polling of voters. The law was quickly challenged and after several trips up and down the appellate ladder, the United States Court of Appeals for the Ninth Circuit ruled in 1988 that the state statute was unconstitutional. Clearly the law was not content neutral—it proscribed a certain category of speakers, exit pollers, from asking questions on a specific subject, voting behavior. But the court said it was still willing to accept the restriction if it was narrowly tailored to accomplish a compelling government interest, and was the least restrictive means to accomplish this interest. The state argued it had a strong interest in preventing disruption at the polling places, but the court pointed out that this law prevents all polling, that which is disruptive, and that which is not. As such it was too broad. Also, the statute was not the least restrictive means to accomplish the state's goal, the court said. There is already another state law prohibiting disruption at the polls. A less restrictive law might have reduced the size of the polling ban from three hundred to perhaps one hundred feet. Or the state could have required pollsters to inform voters that they did not have to answer questions. Or the state could require polling places to have separate entrances and exits. Judges on the court of appeals said they recognized the real intent of the law—to prevent the broadcast of election projections. This is an impermissible purpose, the court said. A general interest in insulating voters from outside influences is insufficient to justify speech regulation, (*Daily Herald* v. *Munro,* 1988). A United States district court in Florida struck down a similar statute in that state that barred exit polling within 150 feet of the polling place on similar grounds (*CBS* v. *Smith*, 1988). Laws in Minnesota (*CBS, Inc.* v. *Growe*, 1988) and Georgia (*NBC* v. *Cleveland*, 1988) were also overturned.

Other Public Forums

Public streets, airports, and state fairs are some of the public forums that have been discussed thus far in relation to permissible time, place, and manner rules. In the early 1980s federal courts were asked to examine two other communication forums and to determine (1) whether they were public forums and (2) whether decisions made regarding their use violated the First Amendment. The forums were mailboxes and public television stations.

For nearly fifty years the Congress has prohibited deposit of unstamped mailable matter in a letter box in front of someone's home. The rule was adopted in 1934 when the postal service was losing revenues because many organizations and businesses were hand delivering circulars, letters, bills, and other mailable material and depositing them in homeowners' mailboxes. The law is justified today by the government on three grounds:

1. The law protects postal revenues.
2. The law facilitates the efficient and secure delivery of the mail.
3. The law promotes a mail patron's privacy.

Number one has just been discussed. A mailbox filled with nonstamped junk can crowd out real mail, slowing the delivery of the mail. Thieves can use the delivery of circulars as a ruse to examine the contents of a mailbox and then steal checks and other valuable material. Finally, the mail received by an individual should be private, not exposed to other persons who are hand delivering circulars or other matter.

The postal regulation was challenged by the Council of Greenburgh Civic Association, which delivered pamphlets and notices to local residents by placing them in mailboxes. The local postmaster ordered the practice stopped. The council said the postal regulation violated their rights under the First Amendment. The Supreme Court disagreed in a seven-to-two ruling. In his majority opinion Justice William Rehnquist rejected the notion that a mailbox is a public forum. He wrote that a mailbox was much like a military base, a jail or a prison, or the advertising space in a city transit system. "In all these cases, this Court recognizes that the First Amendment does not guarantee access to property simply because it is owned or controlled by the government," Rehnquist wrote. "It is a giant leap from the traditional 'soap box' to the letter box designated as an authorized depository of the United States mails, and we do not believe the First Amendment requires us to make that leap," he added. Because the mailbox is not a public forum, there is no need to evaluate whether the statute is a reasonable time, place, and manner rule. However, Rehnquist added, there are ample reasons to support the law, even if the mailbox were considered a public forum. He cited the government's justifications for the law (see one through three above). He also noted that there are numerous alternative means that the civic council could use to communicate information to residents. Justices Brennan and White said that they believed the mailbox to be (or at least be like) a public forum, but that the rules were reasonable. Marshall and Stevens dissented (*Postal Service* v. *Council,* 1981).

In the early 1980s federal courts were asked to determine whether a public television station is a public forum; that is, whether the public has a right to participate in determining the programming shown on a government-funded station. The issue arose when several public television stations refused to air a controversial program about a Saudi Arabian princess who supposedly had a nonsanctioned love affair and was subsequently executed for her indiscretion. The Saudi government put pressure on the United States government to block the showing of the program, but the State Department refused to interfere. Viewers who wanted to see the program brought lawsuits against stations that chose not to broadcast it. In 1982 the United States Court of Appeals for the Fifth Circuit ruled that managers of public television stations enjoy the same rights as managers of commercial stations—to select programming on the basis of their own judgment. Acknowledging that the First Amendment traditionally has been used to protect the people from the government, this did not preclude the government from exercising editorial control over its own medium of expression. "To find that the government is without First Amendment protection is not to find that the government is prohibited from speaking or that private individuals have the right to limit or control the expression of the government," the court said (*Muir* v. *Alabama Educational Television Commission,* 1982).

Private Forums

The cases just noted concern public forums. Courts have generally tolerated more restrictions upon expression exercised in private forums—shopping centers and private residences, for example. Residential distribution and solicitation have consistently been a vexing problem as the rights of freedom of expression are measured against the rights of privacy and private property.

Private Homes

In 1943 the Supreme Court faced an unusual ordinance adopted by the city of Struthers, Ohio, which totally prohibited door-to-door distribution of handbills, circulars, and other advertising materials. The law also barred anyone from ringing doorbells to summon householders for the purpose of distributing literature or pamphlets.

Justice Hugo Black wrote the opinion for the majority in the divided Court. He said the arrest of Thelma Martin, another Jehovah's Witness, for ringing doorbells in behalf of her religious cause was a violation of her First Amendment rights. Door-to-door distributors can be a nuisance and can even be a front for criminal activities, Justice Black acknowledged. Further, door-to-door distribution can surely be regulated, but it cannot be altogether banned. It is a valuable and useful means of the dissemination of ideas and is especially important to those groups that are too poorly financed to use other expensive means of communicating with the people. Black said a law that makes it an offense for a person to ring the doorbell of householders who have appropriately indicated that they are unwilling to be disturbed would be lawful and constitutional. However, the city of Struthers cannot by ordinance make this decision on behalf of all its citizens—especially when such a rule clearly interferes with the freedom of speech and of the press. "The right of freedom of speech and press has broad scope. The authors of the First Amendment knew that novel and unconventional ideas might disturb the complacent, but they chose to encourage a freedom which they believed essential if vigorous enlightenment was ever to triumph over slothful ignorance" (*Martin v. City of Struthers,* 1943).

Nearly ten years later, in 1951, the High Court was confronted with still another case of door-to-door solicitation. This case, however, concerned solicitation of subscriptions for nationally circulated magazines (*Breard v. Alexandria,* 1951). The Alexandria, Louisiana, ordinance in question prohibited door-to-door solicitation for sale of goods, wares, or merchandise without the prior consent or invitation of the homeowner. Jack H. Breard, who was employed by a Pennsylvania magazine subscription company, appealed his conviction all the way to the Supreme Court on the grounds that the law violated his First Amendment rights. This time the divided Court ruled against the solicitor, stating that the restriction was not a violation of the First Amendment.

Justice Stanley Reed distinguished the early cases from the *Breard* case by arguing that *Breard* was a case of door-to-door sale of wares, not of propagation of ideas or religious faith. "This kind of distribution is said to be protected because the mere fact that money is made out of the distribution does not bar the publications from First Amendment protection. We agree that the fact that periodicals are sold does not put them beyond the protection of the First Amendment. The selling, however, brings into the transaction a commercial feature," Reed wrote. He added that there are many other ways to sell magazines besides intruding upon the privacy of a householder through door-to-door techniques. Justices Black, Douglas, and Vinson disagreed with Justice Reed, arguing that the High Court had turned its back on earlier free expression decisions. "The constitutional sanctuary for the press must necessarily include liberty to publish and circulate. In view of our economic system, it must also include freedom to solicit paying subscribers," Black wrote. The jurist added that homeowners could themselves place the solicitor on notice by using a sign that they did not wish to be disturbed.

The majority opinion in the *Breard* case, which distinguishes commercial solicitation and distribution from noncommercial solicitation and distribution, has been seriously undercut recently by the Supreme Court's rulings that commercial speech is also entitled to the protection of the First Amendment (these rulings are discussed in chapter 10). For example, the United States Court of Appeals for the Third Circuit recently invalidated a township ordinance that prohibited the distribution of advertising matter without first getting consent of the homeowner. *Ad World,* which publishes *Piggy Back,* a sixteen-page tabloid that is filled mostly with advertising but that also carries a few community announcements and bits of consumer information, challenged the ordinance. The court ruled, "The line between commercial and noncommercial speech cannot be drawn by some magic ratio of editorial to advertising content. The important question is whether the publication as a whole relates solely to the economic interests of the speaker and its audience." The court said that an ordinance aimed at "purely commercial advertising" might be constitutional, but only if the community can justify the need for such a law. Doylestown Township argued that the accumulation of free newspapers on a doorstep might tip off burglars that the homeowner is out of town. But the township offered no evidence to support this argument. Also the township failed to show why the homeowner should not be called upon to request that delivery be stopped if the delivery of *Piggy Back* was not desired (*Ad World* v. *Doylestown,* 1982).

Shopping Centers

The problem of dealing with distribution of materials at privately owned shopping centers has also been a troubling one. In 1968, in *Amalgamated Food Employees Local 590* v. *Logan Valley Plaza,* the Supreme Court ruled that the shopping center was the functional equivalent of a town's business district and permitted informational picketing by persons who had a grievance against one of the stores in the shopping center. Four years later in *Lloyd Corp.* v. *Tanner* (1972), the Court ruled that a shopping center can prohibit the distribution of handbills on its property when the handbilling is unrelated to the shopping center operation. Protesters against nuclear power, for example, cannot use the shopping center as a forum. Persons protesting against the policies of one of the stores in the center, however, can use the center to distribute materials.

In 1976 the Supreme Court recognized the distinctions it had drawn between the rules in the *Logan Valley* case and the rules in the *Lloyd Center* case for what they were—restrictions based on content. The distribution of messages of one kind was permitted, while the distribution of messages about something else was banned. In *Hudgens* v. *NLRB* (1976), the High Court ruled that if, in fact, the shopping center is the functional equivalent of a municipal street, then restrictions based on content cannot stand. But rather than to open the shopping center to the distribution of all kinds of material, *Logan Valley* was overruled, and the Court announced that "only when . . . property has taken all the attributes of a town" can property be treated as public. Distribution of materials at private shopping centers can be prohibited.

Just because the First Amendment does not include within its protection of freedom of expression the right to circulate material at a privately owned shopping center does not mean that such distribution might not be protected by legislation or by a state constitution. That is exactly what happened in California. In 1974 in the city of Campbell, California, a group of high school students took a card table, some leaflets, and unsigned petition forms to the popular Pruneyard Shopping Center. The students were angered by a recent anti-Israel United Nations' resolution and sought to hand out literature and collect signatures for a petition to send to the president and Congress. The shopping center did not allow anyone to hand out literature, speak, or gather petition signatures, and the students were quickly chased off the property by a security guard. They filed suit in court, and in 1979 the California Supreme Court ruled that the rights of freedom of speech and petitioning are protected under the California Constitution, even in private shopping centers, as long as they are "reasonably exercised." (*Robins* v. *Pruneyard Shopping Center,* 1979). The shopping center owners appealed the ruling to the U.S. Supreme Court, arguing that the High Court's ruling in *Lloyd* v. *Tanner* prohibited the states from going further in the protection of personal liberties than the federal government. But six of the nine justices disagreed, ruling that a state is free to adopt in its own constitution individual liberties more expansive than those conferred by the federal constitution (*Pruneyard Shopping Center* v. *Robins,* 1980).

Since 1980, courts in Washington, Massachusetts, and New York have ruled that under their state constitutions, citizens could exercise rights of free expression at private shopping centers, according to an unpublished master's thesis by Kenneth Schiffler at the University of Washington. Courts in Pennsylvania and New Jersey have ruled that persons have a right to exercise rights of free expression on the grounds of private colleges.

Finally, in an interesting decision that focused upon the mail rather than upon the mailbox, the Supreme Court ruled that the New York Public Service Commission could not restrict the content of inserts Consolidated Edison, a private utility company, put in billing envelopes. The utility company used the inserts to promote the value of nuclear power to its customers. The commission passed a regulation prohibiting utilities from using bill inserts to discuss political matters, including the desirability of future development of nuclear power. Justice Powell, who wrote the seven-to-one ruling, said the regulation was not content neutral. "The First Amendment means that government has no power to restrict expression because of its message, its ideas, its subject matter or content," he wrote. In addition, the state was hard pressed to outline a compelling or substantial state interest it was attempting to protect through such a regulation (*Consolidated Edison* v. *Public Service Commission,* 1980).

As noted previously, other examples of prior restraint can be found within the law. Films may be censored before they are shown, for example (see chapter 9). Under certain circumstances the press may be prohibited from publishing material that might prejudice a defendant's chance for a fair trial (see chapter 7). Such examples will be noted as other aspects of mass media law are discussed.

SUMMARY

The prior restraint of expression is permissible under what are known as time, place, and manner regulations. That is, the government can impose reasonable regulations about when, where, and how individuals or groups may communicate with other persons. Time, place, and manner rules apply to both public forums (settings owned or controlled by a government, such as a public street or an airport) and private forums (privately owned settings, such as residences and shopping centers). In order to be constitutional, time, place, and manner restraints must meet certain criteria:

1. The regulation should be content neutral; that is, application of the rule should not depend upon the content of the communication.

2. The regulation must serve a substantial governmental interest, and the government must justify the rule by explicitly demonstrating this interest.

3. There cannot be total prohibition of the communication. The speakers or publishers must have reasonable alternative means of presenting their ideas or information to the public.

4. The rules cannot be broader than they need to be to serve the governmental interest. For example, the government cannot stop the distribution of literature on all public streets if it only seeks to stop the problem of congestion on public streets that carry heavy traffic.

BIBLIOGRAPHY

Here is a list of some of the sources that have been helpful in the preparation of chapter 2:

Books

Alexander, James. *A Brief Narrative on the Case and Trial of John Peter Zenger.* Edited by Stanley N. Katz. Cambridge: Harvard University Press, 1963.

Barron, Jerome, and Dienes, C. Thomas. *Handbook of Free Speech and Free Press.* Boston: Little, Brown & Co., 1979.

Chafee, Zechariah. *Free Speech in the United States.* Cambridge: Harvard University Press, 1941.

Cohen, Jeremy. *Congress Shall Make No Law.* Ames, Iowa: Iowa State University Press, 1989.

Gerald, J. Edward. *The Press and the Constitution.* Minneapolis: University of Minnesota Press, 1948.

Hadley, Arthur T. *Straw Giant.* New York: Avon Books, 1987.

Levy, Leonard. *Emergence of a Free Press.* New York: Oxford University Press, 1985.

Meiklejohn, Alexander. *Free Speech and Its Relation to Self-Government.* New York: Harper & Brothers, 1948.

Peterson, H. C., and Fite, Gilbert. *Opponents of War, 1917–1918*. Seattle: University of Washington Press, 1957.

Roche, John P. *Shadow and Substance*. New York: Macmillan Co., 1964.

Rutland, Robert. *The Birth of the Bill of Rights*. Chapel Hill: University of North Carolina Press, 1955.

Siebert, Frederick. *Freedom of the Press in England, 1476–1776*. Urbana: University of Illinois Press, 1952.

Smith, James M. *Freedom's Fetters*. Ithaca, N.Y.: Cornell University Press, 1956.

Articles

Ahern, Tim. "White Smoke in the Persian Gulf." *Washington Journalism Review,* October, 1987, p. 16.

Avery, Kay Beth, and Simpson, Robert J. "The Constitution and Student Publications: A Comprehensive Approach." 16 *Journal of Law and Education* 1, 1987.

Bender, John R. "Regulating Newsracks." *presstime,* October, 1987, p. 32.

Buckley, T. D. Jr. "Student Publications, the First Amendment, and State Speech." 34 *Cleveland State Law Review* 267, 1986.

Denniston, Lyle. "School Principal as Censor." *Washington Journalism Review,* March, 1988, p. 12.

Disbrow, Sandra J. "In Re Grand Jury Matter (Gronowicz): Authors, Mail Fraud, and the First Amendment." 51 *Albany Law Review* 117, 1986.

Dunn, Donald J. "Pico and Beyond: School Library Censorship Controversies." 77 *Law Library Journal* 435, 1984–85.

"Editorials support censorship decision." *Editor and Publisher,* Jan. 23, 1988.

Gillmor, Donald M. "The Fragile First." 8 *Hamline Law Review* 277, 1985.

Hamilton, Patricia Anne. "Freedom of Expression in Public Schools: Regulation of Student Newspapers and Other Publications." 18 *Cumberland Law Review* 181, 1987.

Karp, Walter. "Liberty Under Seige." *Harpers,* November, 1985.

Pember, Don R. "The Pentagon Papers: More Questions Than Answers." 48 *Journalism Quarterly* 403, 1971.

———. "The Smith Act as a Restraint on the Press." 10 *Journalism Monographs* 1, 1969.

Ragan, Fred D. "Justice Oliver Wendell Holmes, Jr., Zechariah Chafee, Jr., and the Clear and Present Danger Test for Free Speech: The First Year, 1919." 53 *Journal of American History* 24, 1971.

Smith, Jeffrey A., "Prior Restraint: Original Intentions and Modern Interpretations." 28 *William and Mary Law Review* 439, 1987.

Cases

Abrams v. *U.S.,* 250 U.S. 616 (1919).

Ad World v. *Doylestown,* 672 F.2d 1136 (1982).

Amalgamated Food Employees Local 590 v. *Logan Valley Plaza,* 391 U.S. 308 (1968).

Barron v. *Baltimore,* 7 Pet. 243 (1833).

Bethel School District v. *Fraser,* 478 U.S. 675 (1986).

Brandenburg v. *Ohio,* 395 U.S. 444 (1969).

Breard v. *Alexandria,* 341 U.S. 622 (1951).

Bystrom v. *Fridley High School,* 822 F.2d 747 (1987).

Cantwell v. *Connecticut,* 310 U.S. 296 (1940).

CBS v. *Smith,* 681 F.Supp. 794 (1988).

CBS, Inc. v. *Growe,* 15 M.L.R. 2275 (1988).

Chaplinsky v. *New Hampshire,* 315 U.S. 568 (1942).

Chicago Newspaper Publishers Association v. *Wheaton,* 697 F.Supp. 1464 (1988).

Collin v. *Smith,* 578 F.2d 1197, cert. den. 439 U.S. 916 (1978).

Consolidated Edison v. *Public Service Commission*, 447 U.S. 529 (1980).
Daily Herald v. *Munro*, 838 F.2d 380 (1988).
Dennis v. *U.S.*, 341 U.S. 494 (1951).
Gannett v. *White*, 14 M.L.R. 2037 (1987).
Gitlow v. *U.S.*, 268 U.S. 652 (1925).
Gooding v. *Wilson*, 405 U.S. 518 (1972).
in re *Gronowicz*, 764 F.2d 983 (1985); cert den. 106 S.Ct. 193 (1986).
H & L Messengers v. *Brentwood*, 577 SW 2d 444 (1979).
Hazelwood School District v. *Kuhlmeier*, 108 S.Ct. 562 (1988).
Heffron v. *International Society*, 452 U.S. 640 (1981).
Hudgens v. *NLRB*, 424 U.S. 507 (1976).
International Society for Krishna Consciousness v. *Wolke*, 453 F.Supp 869 (1978).
Island Trees v. *Pico*, 457 U.S. 853 (1982).
Joyner v. *Whiting*, 477 F.2d 456 (1973).
Kuhlmeier v. *Hazelwood School District*, 795 F.2d 1368 (1986).
Lakewood v. *Plain Dealer Publishing Co.*, 108 S.Ct. 2138 (1988).
Lloyd Corp. v. *Tanner*, 407 U.S. 551 (1972).
Lovell v. *Griffin*, 303 U.S. 444 (1938).
Lowe v. *SEC*, 472 U.S. 181 (1985).
Martin v. *City of Struthers*, 319 U.S. 141 (1943).
Metromedia v. *Baltimore*, 583 F.Supp. 1183 (1982).
Metromedia v. *San Diego*, 453 U.S. 490 (1981).
Miami Herald v. *Tornillo*, 418 U.S. 241 (1974).
NBC v. *Cleveland*, 697 F.Supp. 1204 (1988).
Near v. *Minnesota*, 283 U.S. 697 (1931).
New York City v. *American School Publications*, 509 N.E.2d 311 (1987).
New York Times Company v. *U.S.*; *U.S.* v. *Washington Post*, 713 U.S. 403 (1971).
Organization for a Better Austin v. *Keefe*, 402 U.S. 415 (1971).
Plain Dealer v. *Lakewood*, 794 F.2d 1139 (1986).
President's Council District 25 v. *Community School Board*, 457 F.2d 566 (1972).
Providence Journal v. *Newport*, 665 F.Supp 107 (1987).
Pruneyard Shopping Center v. *Robins*, 447 U.S. 74 (1980).
Red Lion Broadcasting v. *FCC*, 395 U.S. 367 (1969).
Robins v. *Pruneyard Shopping Center*, 592 P.2d 341 (1979).
San Diego Committee v. *Grossmont High School*, 12 M.L.R. 2329 (1986).
Schenck v. *U.S.*, 249 U.S. 47 (1919).
Schneider v. *New Jersey*, 308 U.S. 147 (1939).
Snepp v. *U.S.*, 444 U.S. 507 (1980).
Socialist Labor Party v. *Glendale*, 82 Cal.App.3d 722 (1978).
Stanley v. *McGrath*, 719 F.2d 279 (1983).
Tinker v. *Des Moines School District*, 393 U.S. 503 (1969).
U.S. v. *Marchetti*, 466 F.2d 1309 (1972).
U.S. v. *Progressive*, 467 F.Supp 990 (1979).
Village of Skokie v. *National Socialist Party*, 373 NE.2d 21 (1978).
Weissman v. *Alamogordo*, 472 F.Supp. 425 (1979).
Whitney v. *California*, 274 U.S. 357 (1927).
Williams v. *Spencer*, 622 F.2d 1200 (1980).
Yates v. *U.S.*, 354 U.S. 298 (1957).

3 LIBEL

Defamation, or **libel,** is undoubtedly the most common legal problem faced by journalists and others who work in the mass media. In simple terms libel is the publication or broadcast of a statement that injures someone else's reputation, that lowers that person's esteem in the community. While reporters, writers and editors at newspapers, magazines and broadcasting stations obviously face the greatest danger from a libel suit, advertising copywriters, public relations practitioners, in-house magazine editors, and scores of others in the communications business can easily fall into the many snares that are a part of modern defamation law.

Journalists face the biggest problem because the very nature of contemporary journalism creates a fertile soil for the growth of libel problems. News media today carry massive amounts of information about vast numbers of persons, and each news item is a potential libel problem. The common stuff of news includes accusations, innuendo, assertions or references that are often critical of someone. Despite the special care exercised by most in journalism in the preparation of these news reports, many practices of modern journalism exacerbate the libel problem.

All editors—even those for the company magazines or trade association newsletters—face deadlines. The rush to get a story completed before press time or air time fosters an atmosphere in which errors are more likely to occur. The need for headlines creates problems for those in print media; the ten second audio tease causes the same difficulties for those in broadcasting. There is a need to compress often complicated information into a few words in both instances, and this can often result in exaggeration or misstatement of the charges carried in the story. Journalists are frequently aggressive seekers of information, and during the last fifteen years the emphasis by many in the news media on investigative reporting has resulted in the publication and broadcast of stories that are embarrassing and even harmful to influential people. A libel suit, justified or not, is often the injured person's response. Finally, the publication or broadcast of news and information is a complex process. A story often goes through many hands before it is ultimately printed or broadcast. And each person who handles the story has an opportunity to change it in a way that may result in defamation. A word is accidently dropped out, changing *not* guilty to guilty; names are transposed, resulting in the victim becoming the perpetrator of the crime; or letters are switched and the phrase "he vied to gain support from the commission" becomes "he lied to gain support from the commission."

Libel has existed as a legal problem for persons involved in mass communications for almost eight hundred years. But today it seems to be a special problem, especially for the American news media. There seem to be more libel suits than ever before, the press seems to be losing more of these cases than it has in the past, the judgments won by plaintiffs seem to be significantly higher, and the cost of defending a lawsuit seems to be skyrocketing for newspapers, magazines and broadcasting stations. Appearances may be deceiving, however. There is no real evidence that there are more libel suits today than in the past; it may just seem like there are more because of the massive publicity given a few cases involving plaintiffs like Carol Burnett, William Westmoreland, Ariel Sharon, and Wayne Newton. And in the end, the press wins about ninety percent of the lawsuits, according to an exhaustive study of libel actions undertaken by a team of researchers at the University of Iowa. It is true though that libel judgments are getting bigger, and defense costs are increasing. Let's examine each of these elements briefly before discussing the impact contemporary libel law has had on the press. ◆

THE LIBEL CLIMATE

The Iowa Libel Research Project, conducted by Professors Randall P. Benzanson, Gilbert Cranberg, and John Soloski, examined almost one thousand libel and privacy suits filed between 1974 and 1984. As a part of this examination the researchers learned a great deal about who sues for libel and why, information that is completely detailed in their book, *Libel Law and the Press*. One of the most interesting findings in the report is that about three-fourths of all plaintiffs said they would have been satisfied if the news medium would have published or broadcast a correction, retraction or apology. This finding supports an earlier conclusion drawn by Stanford law professor Marc Franklin, based on his study of a smaller number of libel suits. Plaintiffs bring lawsuits not to win money damages, but because they are frustrated by their treatment by the mass media. And this frustration is usually engendered after they have attempted to resolve the issue in some other fashion and are rebuffed by the news organization. This suggests, then, that if in fact there is an epidemic of libel suits in this nation, the press has the means to quell it without changing anything that is published or broadcast. A simple willingness to correct errors, if they have occurred, or to permit the aggrieved person to tell his or her side of the story in the newspaper or on the air would solve many of the problems. The lawsuit is perceived by the plaintiff as the last resort to gain some kind of satisfaction.

In some cases however, the plaintiff will accept nothing less than a lawsuit. And the goal of the litigation sometimes has little to do with restoring a reputation or winning satisfaction. Its aim is to harass or even punish the news medium. Liberty Lobby, for example, has made something of a habit of suing the press, according to *Baltimore Sun* reporter Lyle Denniston. During the past fifteen years Liberty Lobby has brought six different libel suits, always against someone who has suggested that the organization was either racist, anti-Semitic, or both. Liberty Lobby has lost every case; in fact, not one suit has even reached a jury. But it has cost the defendants hundreds of thousands of dollars to defend these actions. In a recent lawsuit brought by Liberty Lobby against the *Wall Street Journal*, United States court of appeals judge Robert Bork saw the defamation claim for what it was and dismissed the suit:

> This suit epitomizes one of the most troubling aspects of modern libel litigation; the use of the libel complaint as a weapon to harrass. Despite the patent insufficiency of a number of appellant's claims, it has managed to embroil a media defendant in over three years of costly and contentious litigation. The message to this defendant and the press is clear: discussion of Liberty Lobby is expensive. However well-documented a story, however unimpeachable a reporter's source, he or she will have to think twice about publishing where litigation, even to a successful motion for summary judgment, can be very expensive. (*Liberty Lobby* v. *Dow Jones,* 1988)

A researcher who studies only trial records would clearly conclude that the press loses most libel suits. Between 1984 and 1986, for example, mass media defendants lost seventy-two percent of all libel suits at trial, according to a study by the Libel Defense Resource Center. The percentage is even higher if only cases tried before a jury are considered; the press lost almost eighty percent of these suits. But these losses are usually reversed on appeal. As we have noted, in the end, the press wins almost nine out of ten defamation cases. Why such a disparity?

Several answers are suggested. Many people argue that jury verdicts today represent more a general anti-press mood by the public rather than a careful consideration of the allegations in the lawsuit. It is asserted that average citizens view the press as somewhat intrusive and too powerful, and view reporters as arrogant and elitist. Jurors have the opportunity to humble the press in a jury verdict; or at least attempt to enforce some kind of standard of behavior. There is undoubtedly truth in these assertions. And the law makes it somewhat easier for the jury to do so. Libel law is exceedingly complex, as you will soon discover. Frequently, trial judges—who rarely see more than a single libel case in a lifetime—make errors of law that are corrected upon appeal. Jury instructions frequently reflect these errors or are exceedingly complicated. Juries can misunderstand what they are expected to do, or even ignore the instructions. A lawsuit filed by William Tavoulareas, president of Mobil Oil, against the *Washington Post* demonstrates what can happen. In this case the foreman of the jury, a highly persuasive young man, convinced the jury that contrary to the judge's instructions, the newspaper rather than the plaintiff should carry the burden of proof on key issues. The jury was not convinced that the *Post* had proved its case and ruled for Tavoulareas. The judge threw out the jury verdict upon learning this.

Damage awards by juries are skyrocketing. Between 1980 and 1988 there were forty libel damage awards in excess of one million dollars. In fact, by 1986 the average damage award topped one million dollars. The vast majority of these big awards are reduced or thrown out on appeal. But a kind of a milestone was reached in April of 1988 when the Supreme Court let stand an award of three million dollars that CBS must pay to the Brown and Williamson Tobacco Corporation. This was the first time an appellate court had ever affirmed a judgment of more than one million dollars in a libel suit. "For years we've been like the Dutch boy with his finger in the dike, trying to keep back an affirmed award over a million dollars," said Henry J. Kaufman, general counsel of the Libel Defense Resource Center in New York. The three million dollar award could have very important psychological meaning, he added.

The award of these huge sums frequently has little to do with injury to the plaintiff, Bezanson and Cranberg pointed out in an article in *The New York Times.* Entertainer Wayne Newton won a five million dollar award from NBC, for supposed loss of reputation. After the defamatory broadcast, however, his reputation was sufficiently solid to get a loan of nineteen million dollars. He was also awarded the Presidential Medal of Freedom, dined at the White House, was visited at home by President Reagan, had a Las Vegas street named after him, and was named Nevada's "Republican Man of the Year." Most of the five million dollars was in punitive damages (see p. 187), not necessarily based on the actual harm to Newton.

While damage judgments increase, defense costs rise accordingly. Lawyers fees typically amount to eighty percent of the cost to a news medium defending a libel suit. Lawyers fees also usually chew up fifty percent of the plaintiff's damage award. The Iowa Libel Research Project revealed that it took four years for the typical libel suit to be resolved, and the average cost to the defendant in attorney's fees was ninety thousand dollars. As there is occasionally a huge damage award, so too there are cases in which defense costs are astronomical. ABC allegedly spent seven million dollars defending itself against a series of lawsuits by an organization called Synanon. It cost CBS several million to defend itself against William Westmoreland's libel action. The *Washington Post* spent over one million to fight the suit brought by William Tavaloureas.

Impact of the Libel Climate

The dramatic changes in the atmosphere in which libel law is litigated and the outcome of these lawsuits has had an impact on nearly everyone. Many libel plaintiffs, persons who are often only seeking to regain a part of their reputation or to soothe their considerable emotional turmoil, have discovered that it is no fun to undertake a lawsuit against the press. Almost two-thirds of plaintiffs questioned by researchers in the Iowa Libel Project said they were dissatisfied with their litigation experience. Few won large damage settlements; most got nothing at all. Oftentimes the libelous accusations were originally published in a local newspaper or broadcast to a single community. When the suit is filed however, the accusations are rehashed before a wider audience through publicity about the case. The wear and tear on the general well-being of a libel plaintiff became painfully evident in 1985 when a once robust General William Westmoreland appeared before a press conference and told the public he was dropping his almost thirty-month lawsuit against CBS. The suit may have cost CBS several million dollars to defend (estimates are between six and ten million dollars), but it also took its toll on the former military leader who appeared to have aged considerably during the two-and-one-half years.

For the press the impact of contemporary libel litigation has struck first in the pocketbook, then in the news columns and news programming. The costs to the press in fighting (and occasionally losing) such lawsuits have been documented. At least one newspaper has been forced to the brink of bankruptcy. The *Alton* (Illinois) *Telegraph* would have gone under had it been forced to pay the 9.2 million dollar judgment against it. The publishers ultimately managed to settle the case for 1.4 million dollars and stave off extinction. Until recently, libel insurance premiums had risen dramatically in lieu of what happened in the courtroom. Some news media have been forced to drop their coverage because the premiums were too high. CBS dropped its coverage in 1986, according to a report in *Channels* magazine. In other instances the insurer has dropped the news medium. In 1987, Fireman's Fund, one of a few libel insurance carriers, informed the publisher of the *Wangell* (Alaska) *Sentinel* that it was cancelling the weekly's libel coverage. The reason: the *Sentinel* runs names of residents who appear on the local police blotter and otherwise doesn't fit the image of a noncontroversial, small-town newspaper that insurance carriers prefer.

The dangers of libel suits have forced many news media into cutting back on aggressive investigative reporting and avoiding coverage of some topics. The *New York Times* quoted one media attorney who said, "more and more I see unflattering adjectives removed, incisive analyses of people and events watered down, and risky projects dropped." The chill has also affected the book industry. Macmillan, a New York publisher, recently withdrew a book on the Bingham newspaper family of Louisville, Kentucky, that was to have been published within a month. The book was in print, but had not yet been bound. The family had obtained an advance copy of the book and lawyers prepared a five-inch-thick legal memorandum challenging the book's content, according to the *New York Times*. In February of 1989 Simon & Schuster announced it had changed its mind and would not publish a book by Peter Golenbock which purported to outline charges of improprieties in the North Carolina State University basketball program. Lawsuits were threatened when excerpts from the book were published in January. It is of course possible that both these books are flawed; but such actions by publishers have in the past been quite rare. One commentator has noted that broadcasters and editors are basing their decision to air or publish a story on whether a suit is likely to be filed, not whether the material is defamatory. As such, the law has become oppressive in the eyes of many persons and is affecting what each of us can view or read. In this way, the current libel climate has had a deleterious impact far beyond the courtrooms and the newsrooms; it now affects all Americans in their living rooms as well.

Proposals for Change   Many proposals have been put forth in an attempt to ameliorate this situation. At the simplest level, the number of suits could be reduced if news media gave an injured party an opportunity to talk back, to let the potential libel plaintiff use the airwaves or news columns to try to win back his or her self-respect or dignity or to heal perceived wounds. The copious correction of erroneous stories that are published or broadcast would also help. The press has improved measurably in this regard in the past two decades, but too often the error in the headline on the front page of the second section is corrected in agate type on the inside of page four. Few publications are willing to be as generous as was the *New York Times* on July 13, 1987, when it proclaimed in large type at the top of its front page that the newspaper had made a significant error two days earlier in a story on Colonel Oliver North.

Many persons have argued that most libel actions could be more quickly and cheaply handled in an arbitration setting, rather than in court. An Iowa Dispute Resolution Program in Iowa, a part of the Iowa Libel Project, is attempting to resolve issues of falsity or reputational damage through a kind of mediation process. A media participant in the process agrees to publicize the findings of the process; the plaintiff carries the burden of proof. The mediator is chosen from a list of five names submitted to each side for review. By May of 1988 the program was going into its second year. Mediation had taken place in forty cases, but no case had yet gone all the way through the process. In Florida, experimentation was under way with a seven-member panel of arbitrators. The process was similar to that taking place in Iowa with the publication of findings by the offending medium offered in lieu of damages. In late 1988 a committee of lawyers, journalists and others working under the auspices of the Annenberg Washington Program in Communication Policy Studies of Northwestern University, proposed what they called a Libel Reform Act. Under the proposal libel plaintiffs would first have to seek a retraction or the right to reply to a defamatory article or broadcast. If a retraction or reply was granted the matter would end. If not, the plaintiff could go on to seek either a declaratory judgment from a court or file a lawsuit. If the plaintiff sought a declaratory judgment as a means of solving the dispute, the defendant would lose some of his or her First Amendment libel protection. The only question decided by the declaratory judgment is whether the statement at issue is true or false. The plaintiff could win only expenses, not money damages. The proposal received a relatively cool reception from both the press and the legal community.

The press is currently attempting to discourage lawsuits that have little merit by filing counteractions against plaintiffs. It is possible for the defendant to file civil actions against a plaintiff for abuse of process or malicious prosecution, or engage in other actions to try to win back at least attorney's fees and court costs. To win an abuse of process action it must be shown that the libel action was filed for purposes having little to do with remedying the alleged injury to the plaintiff's reputation. A finding of malicious prosecution might result if it can be shown that a lawsuit was begun in malice, without much hope that it could succeed, and that in fact the suit failed. None of these counteractions have been notably successful, as the legal system is reluctant to take any action that would inhibit a legitimately injured person from attempting to use the law to win damages. Finally, the fact that some courts have recently forced plaintiffs to pay the defendant's attorney's fees when it was ruled that the libel suit was a frivolous lawsuit may act as a deterrent to nonmeritorious claims. (See *Mitchell* v. *The Herald Co.,* 1988, for example.)

One of the best weapons against a libel suit is knowledge of the law, an understanding of what is or what is not legally publishable. Clearly many plaintiffs may still threaten suit, but few are likely to follow through if the reporter or editor has followed the law and the ethical practices of journalism and can demonstrate this clearly to a plaintiff's attorney.

LAW OF DEFAMATION

The law of defamation is ancient; its roots can be traced back several centuries. Initially the law was an attempt by government to establish a forum for persons involved in a dispute brought about by an insult or by what we today call a defamatory remark. One man called another a robber and a villain. The injured party sought to avenge his damaged reputation. A fight or duel of some kind was the only means of gaining vengeance before the development of libel law. It was obvious that fights and duels were not satisfactory ways to settle such disputes, so government offered its "good offices" to solve these problems. Slowly the law of defamation evolved.

Today the process of going to court to avenge one's honor is highly institutionalized. In addition, some scholars in the field suggest that the purpose of the law has subtly changed as well. While protection of reputation still remains a primary objective of the law of defamation, the law is also seen as a means of gaining press accountability. Standards of responsible journalism and professional conduct are frequently applied to the press in determining liability, and in this way society and the government, via the court system, are taking a role in defining acceptable journalistic practices.

In other parts of the world, different schemes are used to accomplish similar ends. In continental Europe libel suits are uncommon. When a newspaper defames a person, that person has the right—under law—to strike back, using the columns of the same newspaper to tell his side of the story; so to speak, to blast the writer or the editor. This right is called the right of reply, and it exists in the United States in a far less advanced form, as is noted near the end of this chapter. Many people favor the notion; that is, letting the parties fight it out in print or by broadcast. They say it is far better to set out after the truth in this fashion than to rattle the chains on the courthouse door every time an insult is flung in the public press.

Parts of the law of libel do not really concern those who work in mass communications. For example, elements of libel deal with allegations contained in private communications, a letter from one person to another, a job recommendation from a former employer to a prospective employer. The material in this chapter focuses on public communications—material that is published or broadcast via the mass media, using that term in its broadest sense to include advertising, company magazines, trade association newsletters, press releases and the like. Similarly, because newspapers, broadcasting stations, magazines and the like tend to focus on material considered to be of public concern, courts often treat them differently from nonmedia defendants. (See *Philadelphia Newspapers, Inc.* v. *Hepps,* 1986, for example.) Unless otherwise stated it can be presumed the discussion in the remainder of this chapter focuses upon the rights and responsibilities of media defendants.

Additionally, it must be remembered that libel law is essentially state law. It is possible to describe the dimensions of the law in broad terms that transcend state boundaries, and that is what this chapter attempts to do. But important variations in the law from state to state exist, as will be demonstrated later in this chapter in the discussion of fault requirements. It is important for students to focus on the specific elements of the law in their states after gaining an understanding of the general boundaries of the law.

Another complex problem in the law has to do with whether a communication is a libel (written defamation) or a **slander** (an oral defamation). The law in many states distinguishes between the two. The problem was simple one hundred years ago. Because of the state of technology, a public communication, one meant for a wide audience, was a printed communication—a newspaper, magazine, or handbill. Therefore a law that dealt with libel more harshly than with slander made sense; libel caused more severe damage. A libel lasted longer than a slander since a libel was printed, more people saw it, and it was generally considered to be planned defamation, not words accidentally spoken in the heat of argument. Film, radio, and television have made these distinctions meaningless. If a performer defames someone on "The Tonight Show," the defamation still has immense impact and is heard by millions despite the fact that the defamation is not printed. Today it is a general rule that a published defamation, whether it is in a newspaper, on radio or television, in the movies, or what have you, is a libel. And libel rules apply.

The purpose of this chapter is to give persons in mass communications guidance and rules to apply in the process of gathering, writing, publishing and broadcasting news, information or advertising. People who want to learn to litigate a lawsuit should go to law school. This author's goal is to keep media practitioners out of libel suits or at least to keep them from losing libel suits.

The chapter is divided into two basic parts. The first section deals with the nature of a defamation suit: definitions of libel, what a plaintiff must prove in a libel suit, words that tend to be defamatory, and so forth. The second section outlines the various defenses—legal excuses for publishing defamatory matter—for a libel suit.

ELEMENTS OF LIBEL

There are many definitions of defamation, and they are all about the same. A few typical definitions follow.

In their book *Libel,* Phelps and Hamilton include this definition:

> Defamation is a communication which exposes a person to hatred, ridicule, or contempt, lowers him in the esteem of his fellows, causes him to be shunned, or injures him in his business or calling.

The legal encyclopedia *Corpus Juris* defines libelous words as follows:

> . . . words which have a tendency to disgrace or degrade the person or hold him up to public hatred, contempt, ridicule or cause him to be shunned and avoided; the words must reflect on his integrity, his character, and his good name and standing in the community. . . . The imputation must be one which tends to affect the plaintiff in a class of society whose standard of opinion the court can recognize. It is not sufficient, standing alone, that the language is unpleasant and annoys and irks plaintiff and subjects him to jests or banter, so as to affect his feelings.

The *Restatement of Torts* (2nd ed.), a compilation by the American Law Institute of what it thinks the common law says, defines libel this way:

> . . . a communication which has the tendency to so harm the reputation of another as to lower him in the estimation of the community or to deter third persons from associating with him.

Here is a shorter definition: Defamation is any communication that holds a person up to contempt, hatred, ridicule, or scorn.

Each of the four preceding definitions reveals common and important elements of defamation:

1. Defamation is a communication that damages the reputation of a person, but not necessarily the individual's character. Your character is what you are; your reputation is what people think you are. Reputation is what the law protects. A person without a reputation cannot be libeled. The Alabama Supreme Court ruled that a libel plaintiff, a prison inmate who had five convictions on theft charges and was declared a habitual criminal, could not possibly show damage to

his reputation; he had no reputation. He was libel proof. The suit was based on a published statement that the inmate's lawsuit against the state was "frivolous." (*Cofield* v. *Advertiser Co.,* 1986).

2. To be actionable defamation, the words must actually damage a reputation. There must be some harm done to the individual's reputation. Without proof of this harm, the party who claims injury should not be able to recover damages for the injury. But the awarding of damages by juries is hardly a science and often a plaintiff is compensated for suffering emotional harm or loss of self-esteem. Such awards should only be possible if the suffering or loss of esteem is a direct result from the actual harm to reputation.

3. At least a significant minority of the community must believe that the plaintiff's reputation has been damaged, but the minority must not be an unrepresentative minority. A Delaware superior court ruled that it was not defamatory for a television newscaster to refer to a convict as "an alleged FBI informant." The plaintiff complained that the statement hurt his reputation among his fellow prisoners at the state penitentiary. Conceding that the "informant" label might harm his prison reputation, the court ruled that "it is not one's reputation in a limited community in which attitudes and social values may depart substantially from those prevailing generally which an action for defamation is designed to protect." The public in general would not think any less of the plaintiff for being an informant for the FBI (*Saunders* v. *WHYY-TV,* 1978). To summarize this point: The defamation must lower a person's reputation in the eyes of a significant number of people, and unless unusual circumstances exist, these people must fairly reflect representative views.

Persons can be injured through a libel in numerous ways. The statement may simply hurt their reputation, or it may be that lowering their reputation deprives them of their right to enjoy social contacts, which is a fancy way of saying that their friends don't like them any more or their friends want to avoid them. A man's or woman's ability to work or hold a job or make a living may be injured. A person need only be injured in *one* of these three ways to have a cause of action for libel. If plaintiffs can show actual harm in any one of these areas, chances are good they will recover some damages. That is one of the reasons libel law exists—to compensate the plaintiff for injury. There are other reasons. A libel suit can help vindicate the plaintiff, help restore the damaged reputation. A victorious plaintiff can point a finger at the newspaper or television station and say, "See, they were wrong, they lied, they made an error." A damage judgment is also considered punishment for the defendant. Editors and broadcasters who have to pay a large damage award may be more cautious in the future. It can stand also as an example to other journalists to avoid such behavior.

Any living person can bring a civil suit for libel. A dead person can't sue; that's obvious. Nor can the relatives of someone who has died sue in behalf of the deceased. A high school student named Stephen Smith was murdered in 1985. In a story about the death a local newspaper quoted one of Smith's teachers who suggested the young man had been on drugs, drank a lot, was aggressive, and talked without making much sense. Smith's parents sued the teacher and the newspaper, but the suit failed. Relatives cannot sue for defamatory statements against the deceased made after his or her death (*Smith v. Dameron,* 1987). Note, however, that if a living person is defamed, brings suit, and then dies before the matter is settled by the court, it is possible in some states that have what are called **survival statutes** for relatives to continue to pursue the lawsuit (see *MacDonald* v. *Time,* 1983, and *Canino* v. *New York News,* 1984, for example). A business corporation can sue for libel, as can a nonprofit corporation, if it can show that it has lost public support and contributions because of the defamation. There is a division in judicial opinion about whether unincorporated associations like labor unions and political action groups can sue for libel. Some court rulings say no; others say yes. Find out what the law is in your state. Cities, counties, agencies of government, and governments in general cannot bring a civil libel suit. This question was decided years ago and is settled law (see *City of Chicago* v. *Tribune Co.,* 1923).

PROVING THE INITIAL ELEMENTS

One important key to understanding any lawsuit is to understand the concept of the burden of proof. Which party must prove what? While this sounds like a trivial matter to many lay persons, it is a very significant element in a lawsuit. Remember, under our adversarial legal system, the court does nothing but evaluate and analyze the material that is brought before it by the adversaries. Judges and juries don't go out and look for evidence themselves. So the matter of who must bring the evidence before the court is a critical one. If a plaintiff, for example, is required to prove a specific element in a case and fails to bring sufficient evidence before the court to convince the judge or jury, the plaintiff loses the case. Theoretically, the defendant can just sit on his or her hands and do nothing until the plaintiff has brought forth the needed material to prove the point. But this is not likely to happen; the defendant is more likely to fight the plaintiff every step of the way, arguing that the evidence is not acceptable or insufficient to prove the point.

In a libel case the plaintiff bears the initial burden of proof. He or she must establish these five separate elements of the case in order to have any chance of winning.

1. That the libelous communication was published.
2. That he or she (the plaintiff) was identified as the target of the libelous material.
3. That the words or picture complained of are defamatory.

4. That the libelous allegations or statements are false. (This condition must be met only if the libelous statements focus upon a matter of public concern. See page 126 for a further explanation of this.)
5. That the libelous material was published due to neglect or disregard or carelessness; that its publication was not the result of an honest error.

Each of these five elements will be outlined in detail shortly. Items four and five are probably only required if the plaintiff is suing a mass media defendant. These are fairly recent additions to the law of libel and the courts have not yet fully resolved the question of how far they should be extended. (See *Columbia Sussex* v. *Hay*, 1981; *Mutafis* v. *Erie Insurance Exchange*, 1985; and *Philadelphia Newspapers, Inc.* v. *Hepps*, 1986.) Since this book is about mass media law, it is written with the assumption that plaintiffs will generally have to prove the falsity of the matter. Usually, by definition, courts presume that what is published or broadcast is of public concern. The fifth element, proof of fault, is also presumed to be a requirement to be met by the plaintiff for purposes of this discussion.

Publication

Before the law recognizes a statement or comment as a civil libel (**criminal libel** is different; see page 189), the statement must be published. In the eyes of the law, **publication** occurs when one person, in addition to the writer and the person who is defamed, sees or hears the material.* Think of the situation as a kind of triangle. The writer or broadcaster (ultimately the defendant) is at the first point; the subject of the defamatory statement (ultimately the plaintiff) is at the second point; and a third person is at the third point. All three are necessary for a libel suit. In defamation by the mass media, publication is virtually presumed. In fact, some cases are on record in which courts ruled that if a statement was published in a newspaper or broadcast over television, it is presumed that a third party saw it or heard it (*Hornby* v. *Hunter*, 1964).

Technically, every republication of a libel is a new libel. Judge Leon Yankwich (*It's Libel or Contempt If You Print It*) wrote more than two decades ago:

> In brief, the person who repeats a libel assumes responsibility for the statement and vouches for its truth as though it had been of his own making

---

*This statement may confuse some people who see it as a contradiction of an earlier statement that to be defamatory something must lower an individual's reputation in the eyes of a significant minority of the community. It is not a contradiction. Publication is what is being discussed here: how many people must see something before the law considers it to have been published. The earlier remark refers to damage to an individual: how many people must think less of a person upon hearing or reading the statement. It is necessary for the plaintiff to convince the court that a significant number of people in the community think less of him or her because of the libelous remark, but it is not necessary that the plaintiff show that these people have actually seen the libelous remark, only that they would think less of the plaintiff if they had seen it.

or on his own information, no matter how emphatically the qualifying words show that the statement is made on the basis of a source other than the writer himself.

Imagine this hypothetical situation for a moment. A newspaper called the *River City Sentinel* is being sued for libel for asserting that Steve Jones has contracted AIDS. Another newspaper, the *Ames Daily Advertiser,* informs its readers about the suit and notes that the *Sentinel* reported that Jones had AIDS. In this circumstance the *Advertiser* has republished the libel. (In this case the republication is probably permissible because of the libel defense called qualified privilege. [See pp. 164–174.])

Another republication problem has to do with attribution, one of the great myths of American journalism. For example, most good reporters know that it is libelous to label someone a murderer. But a remarkably high percentage of professionals erroneously believe you can label someone a murderer, so long as you attribute the statement to a third party. "Jones killed his wife" is obviously defamatory. So is "Jones killed his wife, according to neighbor Ned Block." The newspaper or broadcasting station has simply republished Block's original libel of Jones. (The relationship between quoting an official as the source of a libelous assertion and fault, another element of the case that must be proved by the plaintiff, is discussed on pages 150–151.) Because of the republication rule, nearly everyone in the chain of production of a news story is technically liable in a lawsuit.

Identification

The second element in a libel suit is **identification:** the injured party must show the court that the allegedly defamatory statement is "of and concerning him, her, or it." Failing to do this, the plaintiff will lose the suit. Author William Peter Blatty sued the *New York Times* for libel when the newspaper refused to list one of the writer's novels on its best-selling book list. Blatty, who wrote *The Exorcist* among other thrillers, argued that his book had sold more than enough copies to be included on the list, and that the newspaper, by keeping him off the list, was publishing a false and defamatory statement about him. But the California Supreme Court dismissed the case, noting that because Blatty was not on the list, he could not establish that anything the *New York Times* implied was "of and concerning him" (*Blatty* v. *The New York Times,* 1986). This was surely an unusual suit, but it makes the point; the plaintiff must be identified. And it is important to note that not all readers or viewers need to know to whom the libel refers. Some authorities say it is sufficient if only a single person can identify the subject of the report.* A person can be

---

*This situation should not be confused with damage to the plaintiff. Only one person has to see a story for it to have been published. Some authorities (e.g., Phelps and Hamilton) also say that only one person has to identify the plaintiff. However, when a judge and jury consider whether the material is defamatory and damaging to the plaintiff, they must decide whether the statement can lower the plaintiff's reputation in the eyes of a significant minority of the community.

identified in a number of ways. He or she may be explicitly named. The individual can be described, for example as the host of "The Tonight Show" or the city's superintendent of public works. A picture or a drawing, even without a caption, can be sufficient if the likeness is recognizable. Even descriptive circumstances can sometimes point the finger at someone. Several years ago a New York gossip columnist wrote, "Palm Beach is buzzing with the story that one of the resort's richest men caught his blonde wife in a compromising spot the other day with a former FBI agent." A man named Frederick Hope sued the Hearst Corporation (for whom the columnist worked) for libel. Hope, who was a former member of the Federal Bureau of Investigation (FBI), convinced the jury that the article identified him. He had recently joined the county attorney's staff and had been given considerable local publicity. His background as a former FBI man was given special prominence. He was also able to show that he was the only former G-man who ran with Palm Beach high society. Hope claimed that many of his friends would put these two facts together and know that the columnist referred to him. Hope won a $58,000 judgment (*Hope* v. *Hearst Corp.,* 1961).

It is also possible to put two stories together to make an identification. Imagine that this story was broadcast on Monday: "A fugitive wanted by the FBI for bank robbery was injured today when the automobile in which he was riding was struck by a train." No name appears here, so there is no problem. Tuesday's story appears to be safe as well: "John Smith who was severely injured yesterday when the automobile in which he was riding was struck by a train. . . ." Smith can put two stories together and claim that he has been identified as the fugitive and bank robber.

If a libelous statement does not make an explicit identification, then the plaintiff must somehow prove that the defamatory words refer to him or her. There have been a handful of cases recently in which plaintiffs have sued for libel, arguing that they have been fictionally portrayed in a novel. This is not as difficult to prove as it sounds, as some publishers have recently discovered. The U.S. Court of Appeals for the Second Circuit ruled in 1980 that an identification might be established if "a reasonable reader rationally suspects that the protagonist is in fact the plaintiff, notwithstanding the author's and publisher's assurances that the work is fiction." To do this, the court said, the plaintiff must show that the fictional work "designates the plaintiff in such a way as to let those who knew her understand that she was the person meant. It is not necessary that all the world should understand the libel; it is sufficient if those who knew the plaintiff can make out that she is the person meant" (*Geisler* v. *Petrocelli,* 1980). What courts tend to do in such cases is first look at the similarities between the character and the plaintiff, and then look at the dissimilarities. In the early 1980s Lisa Springer sued Viking Press, alleging that she had been depicted as a character in Robert Tine's novel, *State of Grace.* The heroine of the fictional work was Lisa Blake, the mistress of a ruthless Italian industrialist, a woman who had an unusual sexual appetite.

Springer had had a personal relationship with the author just before the book was published, and both she and the fictional Lisa Blake had similar physical characteristics, attended college, and even lived on the same street in New York. But the court found that the dissimilarities between the two were more striking, noting that Springer lived a fairly modest, quiet life, while the fictional Blake inhabited a far more luxurious world. "The dissimilarities both in manner of living and in outlook are so profound that it is virtually impossible to see how one who had read the book and who knew Lisa Springer could attribute to Springer the lifestyle of Blake" (*Springer* v. *Viking Press,* 1982).

One of the most common problems in libel is careless identification that results in a case of mistaken identity. Years ago the *Washington Post* ran a story about a District of Columbia attorney named Harry Kennedy who was brought back from Detroit to face charges of forging a client's name. The attorney charged was Harry P. L. Kennedy, a man who used his middle initials when he gave his name. The *Post* left out the middle initials. Harry F. Kennedy, another District of Columbia attorney who did not use his middle initial in business, sued the newspaper and won a substantial judgment (*Washington Post* v. *Kennedy,* 1924). That was sloppy journalism.

Most journalists learn early that complete identification is required when an individual in a news story is discussed. The identification should include the name, John Smith; the address, 2185 Pine Street; the age, 34; and if possible the occupation, carpenter. This complete identification clearly separates this John Smith from any other John Smith in the area. Complete identification protected the now defunct *Washington Star* newspaper in a lawsuit brought by a man who was erroneously named a suspect in a shooting. When prominent physician Michael Halberstam was shot in the nation's capital, the *Star* reported that police had arrested a suspect named "Jerry Summerlin, 22, of the 5500 block of Dana Place N.W." This address is just a block from Dr. Halberstam's home in the District of Columbia. The *Star* also reported that the suspect had been hit by the victim's car and was in the District General Hospital. The assailant was really Bernard Welch, who refused to provide any identification to police. The court ruled that Summerlin had not been libeled because he had not been identified. Summerlin was not twenty-two years old, lived in Silver Springs, Maryland, and was not in the District General Hospital after the shooting. In fact the *Star* had got everything correct in its identification of the shooting suspect except the name. By adding the details of identification, the newspaper saved itself from a libel judgment (*Summerlin* v. *Washington Star,* 1981).

A troublesome question regarding identification is group identification. Can a member of a group sue when the group as a whole is libeled? Remember, the plaintiff must show the court that the injurious remarks are "of and concerning him or her." If the group is very small the plaintiff usually has little difficulty convincing a court that identification has occurred. If the editor of a company's employee newsletter asserts that the three-person employee benefit board is incompetent, each member could claim identification. On the other hand, if the group is very big it is improbable that a suit will stand. The Oklahoma Supreme Court ruled that a single doctor of osteopathy could not sue for libel based on the assertion that doctors of osteopathy generally are less competent than medical doctors (*McCullough* v. *Cities Service,* 1984). The owner of a dog breeding farm was similarly blocked in an attempt to sue the *Midnight Globe* for an article claiming that certain United States Department of Agriculture dog breeding farms raised the animals under inhumane conditions. There are 955 such farms, the U.S. Court of Appeals for the Tenth Circuit noted, far too many for a single farm owner to be identified (*Weatherhead* v. *Globe International,* 1987).

But what about the groups in between very small and very big? The *Restatement of Torts (2d)* says this:

> One who publishes defamatory matter concerning a group of class of persons is subject to liability to an individual member of it, but only if (A) the group or class is so small that the matter can reasonably be understood to refer to the individual, or (B) the circumstances of publication reasonably give rise to the conclusion that there is particular reference to him.

There is really no magic number; it is not possible to say for example that a group with more than forty is safe, or that groups with less than twenty-five pose problems. Courts will look at the circumstances as well as the number in the group. A police undercover agent reported to the owner of a paper mill in Maine that employee Harry Hudson had been drinking on the job. The agent was assigned to the mill to look for illegal drug use. A dozen workers at the mill were ultimately fired, eleven for illegal drug use, and Hudson for drinking on the job. A local television station subsequently reported that twelve workers had been terminated at the mill for involvement with illegal drugs. No names were given, but the mill was identified. Hudson sued and argued that it was common knowledge in the small community who the twelve workers were—and as such he had been erroneously identified as an illegal drug user. The station sought to have the suit dismissed, but the Maine Supreme Court refused, ruling that it was a jury question whether or not the broadcast had identified Hudson (*Hudson* v. *Guy Gannett Broadcasting,* 1987).

A U.S. district court in Minnesota ruled that statements in Peter Matthiessen's book, *In the Spirit of Crazy Horse,* about "FBI agents" did not identify agent David Price, who sued Viking Press, the publisher of the book, for defamation. The group "FBI agents" is too large, the court said (*Price* v. *Viking Press,* 1985).

The question in a Massachusetts newspaper, "Is it true that a Bellingham cop locked himself and a female companion in the back of a cruiser in a town sandpit and had to radio for help?" did not specifically identify any single member of the community's twenty-one-member police department (*Arcand* v. *Evening Call,* 1977). There was no liability.

Finally, a federal court ruled that a small group of editors and reporters for the Manchester *Union-Leader* newspaper could not maintain a lawsuit against the *Boston Globe* because of critical comments published in the *Globe* about the New Hampshire publication. The *Union-Leader*, which was published for many years by William Loeb, a very controversial figure in journalism, was described in a *Globe* editorial as "probably the worst newspaper in America." The *Globe* said that Loeb "runs a newspaper by paranoids for paranoids." Three editors and twenty-four other employees including some reporters brought suit against the *Globe*, but a United States district court in Massachusetts dismissed the action. "Defamation of a large group gives rise to no civil action on the part of an individual member of the group unless he can show special application of the defamatory matter to himself," the court ruled. Three hundred twenty-five persons were employed at the newspaper. The group was too large. Admitting that the general references to the paper probably hurt the editors more than other employees because they were ostensibly responsible for what appeared in the *Union-Leader*, the court ruled that no special application or particular reference to these three persons could be inferred from the general criticism of the newspaper (*Loeb* v. *Globe Newspaper*, 1980).

Despite these victories by the press, caution is urged upon reporters who describe even a very large group in a defamatory manner. Caution is especially appropriate if only a small number of the defamed group live in the community. If the charge is made that all astrologers are frauds and there is only one astrologer in the community, the remark can be dangerous. The plaintiff could convince a sympathetic jury that he or she has been severely harmed by the remark. Saying "all" members of a group are corrupt is worse than saying "most" members are corrupt. Saying "most" is worse than saying "some," and saying "some" is worse than saying "one or two."

Defamation

The third element in the plaintiff's case are the words themselves. There are two kinds of defamatory words. The first kind consists of words that are libelous on their face, words that obviously can damage the reputation of any person. Words like *thief, cheat,* and *traitor* are libelous per se—there is no question that they are defamatory.

The second kind of words are innocent on their face and become defamatory only if the reader or viewer knows other facts. To say that Jane Adams had a baby appears safe enough. But if the reader knows that Ms. Adams is not married, then the words are libelous.

The distinction between these two kinds of words was once more important than it is now. At one time plaintiffs had to prove they were specifically harmed by the words in the second category, usually called "libelous per quod." Damage was presumed from the words in the first category, usually called "libelous per se." All plaintiffs today must prove they were damaged by the publication of the libel. Still, in many jurisdictions, courts have erected significant barriers that make it more difficult for persons who sue for libel per quod to win their case than persons who sue for words that are clearly defamatory on their face.

The law in most states tries to define words that are libelous. But these laws rarely go beyond the general description of libel, words that hold someone up to ridicule, hatred, scorn, etc. That probably is not sufficient to define what is defamatory and what is not. On the other hand, the presentation of a catalog of defamatory words is not within the scope of this text. We will attempt to outline general categories of words that frequently cause problems. But the simplest test is to ask yourself a question. If I say this about Mr. X, will it harm his reputation? Before outlining common categories of words, a few other points—some of which are probably pretty obvious—should be noted.

Because the meanings of words change over time, what is defamatory today may not be considered defamatory tomorrow. Calling someone a socialist today would probably not harm their reputation. But socialists were once feared and hated, and the use of the word was considered highly derogatory. The word slacker once had a specific meaning; during the First World War it described a person who sought to avoid military service. That meaning does not attach to the word today.

At a libel trial a judge and jury are supposed to consider the words in light of their ordinary meaning unless the evidence is persuasive that the defendant meant something else when the statement was published. As a general rule, the judge will decide as a matter of law whether particular words are capable of conveying a defamatory meaning. Sometimes even negative descriptions of a person won't qualify as libel. Comedienne Martha Raye recently sued late night television host David Letterman for a parody of her ads for denture cleaner. The ads always began, "Here is Martha Raye, actress, denture wearer." Letterman told his audience that he had seen "the most terrifying commercial on television last night, featuring Martha Raye, condom user." The court said that the words were not defamatory. "No one could reasonably understand this passage as expressing that plaintiff actually uses condoms, that she is promiscuous, that she actually had made a condom commercial, or any other statement of fact," the California Superior Court judge ruled, dismissing the case (*Raye* v. *Letterman,* 1987).

If the judge rules the words are capable of a defamatory meaning, the fact finder—the jury, if there is one—is to determine whether the words in fact convey a defamatory meaning. For example, a United States court of appeals ruled that it was a jury question whether or not a statement alleging that a researcher charged five thousand dollars per day to testify as a witness in civil law suits suggested that because of the high fee, his testimony was for sale to the highest bidder. If made, such an inference would clearly be libelous, the court ruled. It then sent the case back to trial to determine if such an inference was possible. (*McBride* v. *Merell Dow,* 1984).

Innuendo as opposed to a flat assertion can be defamatory. Read the following actual news item from the *Boston Record:*

> The Veterans Hospital here suspected that 39-year-old George M. Perry of North Truro, whose death is being probed by federal and state authorities, was suffering from chronic arsenic poisoning.
>
> State police said the body of Perry, and of his brother, Arthur, who is buried near him, would probably be exhumed from St. Peter's Cemetery in Provincetown.
>
> George Perry died in the VA hospital last June 9, forty-eight hours after his tenth admission there. . . . His brother, who lived in Connecticut and spent two days here during George's funeral, died approximately a month later. About two months later, in September, George's mother-in-law, seventy-four-year-old Mrs. Mary F. Mott, who had come to live with her daughter, died too. Her remains were cremated.

While the story lacked a good deal in journalistic clarity, an Ellery Queen or a Perry Mason is not needed to get the gist of what the reporter was saying. Mrs. Perry murdered her husband, her brother-in-law, and her mother. Lizzie Borden strikes again! The insinuations are that Arthur died after visiting the plaintiff's home and that the mother had "died too." Isn't it too bad that her remains were cremated? This story cost the Hearst Corporation, publishers of the *Boston Record,* $25,000 (*Perry* v. *Hearst Corp.,* 1964).

A libel suit cannot be based on an isolated phrase wrenched out of context. The article as a whole must be considered. A story about baseball's legendary base stealer, Maury Wills, might contain the sentence "Wills might be the best thief of all time," referring to his base-stealing ability. Wills cannot sue on the basis of that single sentence. The story itself makes it clear the kind of thievery the writer is discussing. Nevertheless, a libelous remark in a head-line—even though it is cleared up in the story that follows—can be the basis for a libel suit.

Also, a headline cannot go beyond the story and say more than the story says. In Mississippi, *The Commercial Dispatch* newspaper published a story about three men who had pleaded guilty to charges of illegally transferring cattle from one county to another without having the animals tested for a bacterial disease. But the headline on the story said, "Three Plead Guilty to Cattle Theft." That the true facts were contained in the story did not immunize the newspaper from a successful libel suit based upon the headline, according to the Mississippi Supreme Court. (*Whitten* v. *Commercial Dispatch,* 1986).

A federal court in Seattle ruled that reader habits can also be material in a libel case. Suit was brought against the *Seattle Post-Intelligencer* for a story it published about the redemption of a home mortgage by a local attorney. The headline and the first four or five paragraphs suggested that the attorney had done something illegal or unethical. The remainder of the story—which was about fifty paragraphs long and jumped from page to page after leaving the front page—explained that what the attorney had done was not illegal or unethical, that his actions were fair and aboveboard. The court admitted expert testimony on reader habits, which indicated that people tend not to finish such long stories, that many people stop reading as soon as the story is continued on the inside pages of a newspaper. The plaintiff argued that in the minds of most readers, the libelous opinion created by the first part of the story was not corrected, since they did not finish the story. The jury awarded the attorney one hundred thousand dollars in damages (*McNair* v. *Hearst Corp.,* 1974).

Factual statements can obviously be defamatory. What about an opinion? "I think Mayor Frank Jones is doing a rotten job of running this city." An opinion cannot be defamatory. In 1974, in a very important case, the Supreme Court of the United States ruled (*Gertz* v. *Welch,* 1974):

> Under the First Amendment there is no such thing as a false idea.
> However pernicious an opinion may seem, we depend for its correction not on the conscience of judges and juries but on the competition of other ideas.

The *Restatement of Torts (2d)* states that an opinion statement can be defamatory only if "it also expresses, or implies the assertion of a false and defamatory fact which is not known or assumed by both parties to the communication." We will talk much more about statements of opinion when we examine the defense of fair comment.

Accusation of a Crime   Probably the category of words responsible more than any other for the greatest number of libel suits pertains to crime and criminal acts. Any imputation that a man or woman has done something illegal—from murder to jaywalking—is libelous. The statement can be a straightforward charge: John Smith is an arsonist or John Smith was convicted of arson. The imputation can be indirect: John Smith makes his living using matches and gasoline. The statement might note only that John Smith has spent much of his life in jail because fire fascinates him. A description might be used: John Smith went to the Fuddle Paint Company, poured gasoline on an outside wall, and then lit a match. Maybe John has a nickname—John the Torch. Each of these statements and many more you can think of accomplish the same end: they defame poor John Smith.

It is also libelous to call John an "alleged arsonist." According to the dictionary, to allege means "to assert without proof." The police assert that John is an arsonist when they arrest him and charge him with that crime. What the journalist should do is avoid the shorthand version—alleged arsonist—and tell us what she knows. Instead of saying alleged arsonist, say "Smith, who has been charged by police with arson." If the police have only arrested Smith for questioning about an arson fire, describe him that way; "Smith, who is being questioned by police in connection with an arson fire." Otherwise, if he is called an alleged arsonist, and is never charged with that crime, a jury might decide it was the newspaper or broadcasting station who made the allegation that he was an arsonist.

It has been said that the United States is a nation overly concerned with sex. Sexual references, comments about sexual morality, sexual abnormality, and so forth, all constitute bases for libel suits. Supposedly, we are in the midst of a sexual revolution, but many people are not aware of the fact. For a woman to be sleeping with a man to whom she is not married may be perfectly normal in some parts of our society, but is still not acceptable behavior in other parts of our society. If such a charge were made against a woman, a libel suit would probably stand. Woman's virtue is strongly protected by our courts via the libel suit. Any charge made in any fashion that a woman may be unchaste or may not be virtuous is dealt with harshly by a court. Charges of rape come within this category as well.

Similarly, comments about sexual abnormality are dangerous. John is gay or John is queer, Jane is a lesbian, Frank is an exhibitionist—all are defamatory remarks. Caution must be exercised as well in stories about less exotic sexual concerns: calling a man impotent can be libelous. Charges of wife swapping and failure to fulfill "marital obligations" are also defamatory.

Personal Habits and Characteristics

Much of a person's reputation is concerned with personal habits. Is he honest, ethical, and kind? Does he pay his bills on time or is he a deadbeat? Is she clean, does she drink too much liquor, does she use cocaine, does she smoke pot? Statements regarding all such behaviors have been and will continue to be the subjects of libel suits. To call a man dishonest is defamatory. Likewise are charges that he is unkind to his children and unethical in the way he conducts his financial affairs. She drinks too much, she is a drunkard, she is always potted or smashed, she is an alcoholic, she is a member of Alcoholics Anonymous, she is on the juice, she was arrested for drunken driving—all of these charges are libelous. The same is true of statements regarding the use of drugs and marijuana. A good credit rating is very important today; therefore any charge that reflects on financial standing—the Smiths live beyond their means, they are broke, they don't pay their bills, they owe money all over town—is defamatory.

An imputation of a certain kind of disease can be dangerous. Syphilis, gonorrhea, and genital herpes all suggest loose sexual behavior and uncleanliness frowned upon by many. Diseases that can cause a person to be shunned—contagious diseases such as smallpox, infectious hepatitis or AIDS—are other examples. A former Philadelphia Eagles football player tried to sue the team when the management incorrectly asserted that he had contracted polycythemia vera, a blood disorder. He lost the suit because the court ruled that the alleged affliction was neither contagious nor loathesome, and contracting it did not in any way suggest socially repugnant behavior. The assertion was wrong, but it was not defamatory (*Chuy* v. *Philadelphia Eagles,* 1979). Mental illness is another very sensitive area; it is surely defamatory to charge that someone is psychotic or insane.

If a person professes to belong to a specific faith, a charge that reflects on his or her commitment to or acceptance by that faith can be defamatory. To say that a Catholic was denied the right of Holy Communion is a serious charge, for to most people it suggests some ghastly kind of behavior by the excommunicant. The same rule applies to political and patriotic affiliations. To charge that a person had been stripped of citizenship is defamatory. Charging someone with being a traitor or a spy or with urging sedition or anarchy or revolution are all defamatory statements.

It can be libelous to ridicule someone, to make that person appear foolish. Ridicule is a difficult area to describe because not all ridicule is defamatory. Many humorous stories about people have been ruled to be safe. Newspapers are frequently the victims of false obituaries, and generally courts rule that such stories are not libelous to the person alleged to have died (*Cohen* v. *New York Times,* 1912; *Decker* v. *Princeton Packet,* 1988).

A plaintiff sued the *New York Post* for the intentional infliction of emotional distress when the newspaper mistakenly published a death notice. But the New York Court of Appeals has defined this emerging tort very narrowly, ruling that recovery could only be based on defamation and malicious prosecution, willful and outrageous humiliation intentionally inflicted by conduct exceeding all bounds usually tolerated by decent society, or deliberate harrassment. Publication of the death notice was not libelous, the New York Supreme Court ruled, nor did it meet the other two criteria (*Rubenstein* v. *New York Post,* 1985).

Ridicule which can be libelous is that which makes the plaintiff appear to be uncommonly foolish, which carries a kind of sting that hurts. Everyone must die, and therefore a false obituary really says nothing derogatory about the plaintiff. It is just a joke at his expense. But a story in a New England newspaper about a man so thrifty that he built his own casket and dug his own grave was ruled to be libelous ridicule. The story made the man appear to be foolish, weird, and unnatural. A fifty dollar judgment was awarded (*Powers* v. *Durgin-Snow Publishing Co.,* 1958). How can reporters tell the difference between the two kinds of stories? The distinction is often very difficult. Extreme care is needed to avoid problems.

Libel law probably goes farthest in protecting persons in their business and occupations. Any comment that injures an individual's ability to conduct a business, harms them in their job, or makes it more difficult for them to pursue their occupation is generally defamatory. Comments about business ethics, about competence to do a job, about honesty, about financial solvency—these and many more can form the basis of a successful lawsuit. And business people are generally more likely to sue. They tend to be more acquainted with law generally and more comfortable with a legal suit. And while fear of dragging one's personal life through a courtroom to sue for something published about a home life or sexual practice often deters a would-be plaintiff, the same cannot be said for suits based upon comments about a business practice. This should not deter reporters and others from writing about persons in business and industry however. Corporations and business people frequently have vast power and play a major role in the life of a community or the people who live there. In some towns what the major business decides to do or not do is more important than any action taken by the city government. Business officials should be given the same scrutiny as public officals.

There are some interesting quirks in libel law as it relates to comments about the way an individual does business. To report that a businessperson or professional person has made an error is not always defamatory. Business and professional people are not expected to be perfect. Everyone makes a mistake now and then. A story, for example, that suggests a physician has misdiagnosed a case or that a real estate developer has botched a deal may not be considered defamatory under what is called the *single mistake rule*. The community would not think less of a doctor or businesswoman who made a single error, the reasoning goes. Hence, the statement is not defamatory. Stories that suggest a pattern of incompetence, that go beyond asserting a single error, are defamatory however. (See *Hentell* v. *Knopf,* 1982.) The single mistake rule should not be used as an excuse for sloppy reporting, but it can come in handy if an error is inadvertently made.

Corporations that believe their credit has been damaged or their reputation has been harmed can do exactly what an individual plaintiff can do and sue for this injury. The list of kinds of defamatory accusations is long. Assertions that a company is involved in illegal business or that it fails to pay its bills on time or that it deliberately manufactures unsafe products or that it is trying to break a union are all libelous. The law, however, does not hold a public business responsible for the bad behavior of its customers. Several years ago Louis Stillman sued Paramount Pictures for a remark in the movie "Country Girl" that punch-drunk fighters could be found at Stillman's Gym in New York City. The court rebuffed the gym owner's argument that the remark reflected on him and his business. Proprietors of public business have no control over who comes in to use the facilities. Moviegoers know this and would not think anything less of Stillman because of the comment (*Stillman* v. *Paramount,* 1957). The owner of a Biloxi lounge sued for a story that said a man had been killed in a fight in the bar. Actually the fight took place outside, about one-half block down the street. The Mississippi Supreme Court refused to hold the newspaper responsible, ruling that there was nothing in the story that harmed the lounge or its owner (*Chatham* v. *Gulf Publishing,* 1987). A suggestion that the proprietor of a public business encourages rowdy behavior, or tolerates fighting, or permits drug deals to be made is a different matter. In these cases the story does reflect on the behavior of the owner and would be libelous.

Criticism of a product falls into a different legal category called "disparagement of property." While such criticism is often called **trade libel,** it is not really libel at all, but product disparagement. What is the difference? A plaintiff finds it significantly harder to win a trade libel case than to win a garden-variety libel suit. First, consider some examples of trade libel. Bango rifles fail to eject empty cartridges. Crumo bread gets stale in one day. DooDad motorcycles fail to stop within a safe distance. The remarks are aimed at the products, not at the companies. There is no implication that the manufacturer intentionally makes a bad product, tries to cheat customers, or conducts its business fraudulently. DooDad may make the best motorcycles it can make; they just turn out to be unsafe.

Since the company itself is not presumed to be hurt, the law raises some stiff barriers to a successful trade libel suit. First, the plaintiff, the manufacturer of the product, must prove that the statement is untrue. Proof is difficult, but not too difficult for the kinds of statements just given. If DooDad is able to demonstrate to the court that some of its motorcycles brake to a stop within a safe distance, the company then shows the falsity of the charge. It is much safer to refer to individual products. For example, rather than say that DooDad motorcycles do not stop safely, report that of the ten motorcycles tested none stopped safely or that of the Bango rifles tested, none ejected cartridges properly. The manufacturer will then have to refute this evidence, not merely find examples of the product that are in good working order.

Next, the plaintiff will have to show special damage—actual monetary loss because of the comments. Loss of orders attributable to the unfavorable report is such evidence, and testimony from potential customers who failed to purchase the maligned product because of the comment can be used to support the damage claim. Finally, the plaintiff has to prove that the false remarks were motivated by ill will, bad feeling, or gross carelessness. The plaintiff can prove this if he or she can show that the negative remarks were published "to get him (or her)" and that the writer doesn't like him or her. The plaintiff might also be able to prove that the writer was grossly negligent in checking the truth of the statement. Before the plaintiff can collect for trade libel, all three charges must be proved: falsity, damage, and malicious motives or extreme carelessness.

Evaluate the following three statements on the basis of the foregoing discussion of trade libel:

1. DooDad autos are superior to Acme cars.
2. Acme cars stop running after about one year.
3. Acme cars stop running after about one year because the company has a plan to force customers to buy a new car every year.

Is statement one libelous? It contains no libel, no disparagement, no anything. Nothing negative was said about Acme; only a positive statement about DooDad cars was made. Statement two? This statement is trade libel, an attack upon the product. Statement three? Here we have garden-variety libel. The comment states that Acme purposefully sells automobiles that break down after one year and reflects upon the integrity of the business itself.

Banks and Insurance Companies

One other point should be made before we leave this topic. In addition to the protections businesses and corporations have against libel, many states have laws that prohibit critical and untrue comments about banks, insurance companies, and other such organizations. What these laws are designed to do is to protect such organizations from attack upon their fiscal integrity to avoid turning customers against them and destroying them. After all, a bank has only its fiscal integrity and other people's money to sell.

Suits under such statutes are rare, but occasionally they do occur. Newspaper or broadcasting station soon discover that the many protections the press enjoys in a libel suit often do not apply when a suit is brought under such a law. Check the insurance laws and the banking laws in your state. If such laws exist, find out how the courts interpreted the laws. This check might save a lot of grief some time in the future.

SUMMARY

A plaintiff bears the initial burden of proof in a libel suit and must prove:

1. That the libel was published
2. That the plaintiff was identified
3. That the words were defamatory

Publication can be established if the plaintiff can show that one additional person besides the plaintiff and the defendant has seen the material. An individual can be identified for purposes of a libel suit by a name, nickname, or photograph or even through a report of circumstances. Statements made about a very large group of people cannot be used as the basis for a libel suit by a single member of that group. However, if the group is smaller, all the members might be able to sue for comments made about the entire group. A statement is defamatory if it lowers the reputation of the injured party. The most common kinds of defamatory statements reflect such matters as suggestions of criminal behavior or sexual impropriety, comments about personal habits or characteristics, statements reflecting upon patriotism or political beliefs, and reports about competence and qualifications in an individual's occupation or business. Corporations and other businesses can be defamed; the manufacturer of a product that has been criticized can sue for product disparagement.

PROOF OF FALSITY   Libel plaintiffs who sue the mass media must generally prove that the defamatory statements are false. This statement must be qualified, because it is not completely accurate, and to make this qualification you must be introduced to one of the anomalies of libel law, something that will be discussed at far greater length on pages 132–149.

The world of libel plaintiffs is divided into two groups, public persons and private persons. A public person is a government official, an elected officer, someone who is leading a public crusade, a prominent entertainer, a visible religious or business leader. A private person is someone who is not a public person. As you will soon see, the law makes it far more difficult for a public person, as opposed to a private person, to win a libel suit.

In every instance a public-person plaintiff must prove that the libelous remarks are not truthful. But the Supreme Court has ruled that a private-person plaintiff must prove the falsity of the libelous statements only when the subject of the statement is a matter of public concern (*Philadelphia Newspapers v. Hepps,* 1986). What is a matter of public concern? The Supreme Court has not given a definition, but in another case noted that whether a statement dealt with a matter of public concern must be determined on the basis of the statement's "content, form and context" (*Dun & Bradstreet v. Greenmoss,* 1985). Not a very clear definition.

The legal definition of a "matter of public concern" will undoubtedly be litigated heavily in the years to come and someday a good set of criteria will be developed. It is this author's belief that this definition will be a broad definition, perhaps as broad as this: if something is published in a newspaper or magazine of general circulation or aired on radio or television, this must be a matter of public concern. Please note, this is only an educated guess at this point.

Most plaintiffs, then, must prove that the defamatory material is false. In those few instances when a private person sues for a story that is not a matter of public concern, the defendant must prove that the material is truthful. How does one prove falsity or truth?

The first rule of proving truth or falsity is that the evidence presented in court must go to the heart of the libelous charge.

The proof must be direct and explicit. If there is conflicting evidence, the fact finder—the judge or the jury—will decide who is telling the truth. Every word of a defamatory charge need not be truthful, only the part that carries the gist or the sting.

What the court is looking for is substantial truth. For example, a Michigan newspaper published that a land developer had been "Charged in Shopping Mall Fraud." The story said Harlan Orr had been charged with fifteen counts of fraud, outlined what it called his "phony shopping mall investment scheme," and referred to his behavior as an "alleged swindle." Orr sued for libel. He admitted that the basic facts of the story were true: he had been charged with five counts of the sale of unregistered stock, with eight counts of failure to disclose information, and two acts of deceit. Orr had told potential investors in his scheme that J.C. Penney Company had already leased space in his proposed shopping center. That was not true. What Orr objected to was the use of the words "fraud," "swindle," and "phony" scheme. The United States Court of Appeals for the Sixth Circuit overturned a jury verdict in behalf of Orr and ruled that the article was substantially true. The word *fraud* is an accurate and appropriate description of a violation of the Michigan security laws, the court said. The word *swindle* is a common colloquialism for the term *defraud*. The J.C. Penney scheme was "phony." The court admitted that the words in the story could mean more; they could mean a "flimflam." But they could be used also to mean what Orr had done (*Orr* v. *Argus Press,* 1978).

Extraneous errors don't always equal falsity. An article in *Hustler* magazine noted that *Penthouse* magazine publisher Robert Guccione "is married and also has a live-in girlfriend." Guccione was married and had a live-in girlfriend from 1966 to 1979. But at the time the story in *Hustler* was published he was divorced. The court said calling Guccione an adulterer in 1983 was substantially true, considering the long duration of his earlier adulterous conduct (*Guccione* v. *Hustler,* 1986). The Vermont Supreme Court made a similar ruling when it rejected a suit by a plaintiff who had been arrested and charged with receiving stolen property valued at $505. UPI initially reported that the property was valued at fifty thousand dollars, and both a television station and newspaper carried that report. The court said the difference between fifty thousand dollars and five hundred dollars doesn't change the gist of the libel—the man was arrested and charged with receiving stolen property (*Weisburgh* v. *Mahody,* 1986).

But the story must have some truth to it. Two men were apprehended at the Galleria Shopping Center in Little Rock, Arkansas, after police had received a call that a design store was being robbed. The two men were handcuffed, searched, placed in a patrol car, and taken to the police station. The action was videotaped by reporters from KARK-TV. The police made no comment to the reporters at the scene, and a clerk in the store gave the reporter what was later described as a "vague response." Nevertheless, KARK told the viewers of the "10 O'Clock News" that quick action by police had stopped a robbery at the Custom Design store. "Details are sketchy, however it appears that two suspects backed their car up to the store in order to rob it. For a time, the two men allegedly held a store clerk hostage," the broadcaster reported, as videotape of the incident was telecast. In fact, police had released the two men at 9 P.M., an hour earlier, after deciding no robbery attempt had even taken place. Reporters had not followed up on the apprehension and went on the air with little more than rumors. The station attempted to argue that the story was truthful; two men were apprehended. But the Supreme Court of Arkansas refused to permit the tactic. Literal truth is not necessary, the court noted. Only the gist of the libel need be true. But in this story nothing was true. There was no robbery attempt, no hostage-taking; the plaintiffs were involved in no crime whatsoever (*KARK-TV* v. *Simon,* 1983).

How does the court evaluate the truth of the charge? The jury does this with guidance from the judge. The judge will probably give the jury a test to use in evaluating the evidence against a defamatory charge. One of the commonly used tests comes from a 1934 New York case, *Fleckstein* v. *Friedman.* Defendant Benny Friedman, a former all-star professional football player, charged that some of the players in the National Football League were sadists and bullies. Friedman named names in his *Collier's* magazine story, and one of the players identified, William Fleckstein, sued.

In attempting to prove the truth of the charge, Friedman demonstrated some of the tactics used by these rough players. In instructing the jury in this case, the judge said:

> . . . a workable test of truth is whether the libel as published would have a different effect on the mind of the reader from that which the pleaded truth would have produced. When truth is so near to the facts as published that fine and shaded distinctions must be drawn and words pressed out of their ordinary usage to sustain a charge of libel, no legal harm has been done.

In simpler terms this is what the court said: After reading the article, readers were left with a certain opinion of William Fleckstein, a negative opinion since he was called a bully and a sadist in the story. Now, if persons who had not seen the story had a similar opinion of Fleckstein after seeing the evidence Friedman presented in court, Friedman had then succeeded in proving the truth of his statements. Today this test would be applied to the plaintiff's proof of falsity. If the proof offered by the plaintiff in court leaves a different impression in the minds of the jurors than the published defamation has left, this would likely constitute proof of falsity.

One more point should be stressed about truth and falsity. Correctly quoting someone or accurately reporting what someone else has told you does not necessarily constitute publishing a truthful statement. Imagine that John Smith tells a reporter that the police chief changes arrest records of certain prisoners to simplify their getting bail and winning acquittal. This charge, attributed to John Smith, is contained in the reporter's story which is subsequently published. The police chief sues for libel. It is not sufficient for the reporter to prove merely that the statement in the story was an accurate copy of what Smith said. Even if the reporter's story contained an exact duplicate of Smith's charge, truth can be sustained only by proving the substance of the charge, that the police chief has altered arrest records. It is the truth of the libelous charge that is at issue, not merely of the accuracy of the quote in the story. Accuracy, then, is not always the same thing as truth.

SUMMARY   The plaintiff in lawsuits against the mass media generally must prove the falsity of damaging statements on matters of public concern. The evidence presented in court must go to the heart of the libelous charge; it must relate to the gist or the basic substance of the libel. Minor errors in a story will not necessarily result in a finding of falsity.

PROOF OF FAULT

In 1964, for the first time, the Supreme Court of the United States ruled that a libel plaintiff war required to show that a libel defendant had been at fault when the defamatory material was published. Until that time civil libel law had been governed by what is known as the doctrine of **strict liability.** Under this doctrine a libel defendant was responsible for harming a plaintiff regardless of how cautious and careful he or she had been in publishing the material. Even though the story had been checked in every way possible, even though the reporters and editors completely believed that the material was truthful and accurate, if the story was false and defamatory the plaintiff would likely win the defamation suit.

The case that first sounded the death knell for the doctrine of strict liability was *New York Times* v. *Sullivan,* decided in 1964 by the Supreme Court. This is one of the most important First Amendment cases ever decided and is worth reflecting upon for a few moments.

A difficult and often violent struggle for civil rights was taking place in much of the deep South in the early 1960s. Blacks, often accompanied by whites, set out to challenge a wide range of voting, accommodation, and education laws that had left them as second-class citizens through various nonviolent acts of civil disobedience. Network television news was still in its early adolescence in this era; NBC and CBS carried only fifteen minutes of news each night. The story of the civil rights movement was carried throughout the nation via a handful of prestigious and frequently liberal newspapers, especially the *New York Times.* Segregationist leaders in the South hated these newspapers, which each day carried stories and pictures of another peaceful civil rights protest that had been met with violence or some other illegal act by city, county or state officials, or angry southern citizens.

On March 29, 1960, the *Times* carried a full-page editorial-advertisement entitled "Heed Their Rising Voices." The ad was placed by an ad hoc coalition of civil rights leaders called "The Committee To Defend Martin Luther King and the Struggle for Freedom in the South." The text of the ad leveled charges against public officials in the South who, the committee contended, had used violence and illegal tactics to try to quell the peaceful civil rights struggle. The basic thrust of the charges contained in the advertisement was true; but the ad was filled with small, factual errors. Several public officials in Alabama brought suit against the newspaper. The first case to go to trial was one brought by Montgomery, Alabama, police commissioner L. B. Sullivan, who sought five hundred thousand dollars in damages for false and defamatory statements about the conduct of the Montgomery police department. A trial court ruled on behalf of Sullivan and his five hundred thousand dollar judgment was upheld by the Alabama Supreme Court. This despite the fact that only thirty five copies of the issue of the *New York Times* containing the ad were circulated in Montgomery County.

The Supreme Court unanimously reversed the decision, ruling that Sullivan could not recover damages in this case unless he proved that the *New York Times* published the false and defamatory advertisement knowing it was false, or that the paper exhibited reckless disregard for the truth when it printed the material (*New York Times* v. *Sullivan,* 1964). Justice William Brennan called these latter elements—knowledge that the ad was false, or reckless disregard for the truth or falsity of the ad—actual malice. Henceforth, the High Court ruled, all public officials who sought to win a libel suit based on defamatory allegations about the manner in which they conducted their public office would have to prove actual malice, proof that the newspaper or broadcasting station was seriously at fault.

The Court's rationale rests on at least three important pillars. First, this was after all, a kind of seditious libel case. A government official had been criticized for the manner in which he conducted his public office. The newspaper was being punished for publishing this criticism. True the editor was not being thrown in jail, the more typical punishment in a sedition case. But a half-million dollar fine is strong medicine. The nation had fairly well washed its hands of seditious libel a decade earlier in the Smith Act cases. (See p. 53.) This ruling by the High Court made it much harder for a public official to accomplish the ends of seditious libel through the means of a civil law suit.

Brennan said the court recognized as well that this case was being considered against the background of a profound and long-standing national commitment to the principle that debate on public issues should be uninhibited, robust, and wide open. Erroneous statement is inevitable in such a debate, the associate justice wrote. Persons who are fearful of being sued if they make an error during the debate will likely not speak or write. Freedom of expression needs breathing space to survive. Whatever is added to the field of libel, Brennan noted, is taken from the field of free debate.

Finally, as a public official, Sullivan voluntarily assumed a position in government, a position in which he must surely have expected criticism and complaint. As police commissioner he stood on the public podium and had ready access to the print and broadcast media to refute any charges that were leveled at him. He had at his disposal effective means of rebutting criticism and rebuilding his reputation if harmed.

A handful of states had followed a similar rule prior to the 1964 Supreme Court ruling. (See *Coleman* v. *MacLennan,* 1908, for example.) In *New York Times* v. *Sullivan* the Supreme Court ruled that the First Amendment required that all state courts and lower federal courts follow this rule. And as the United States Constitution is the supreme law of the land, legislation cannot be drafted to modify or abolish the actual malice rule. Many government officials don't like this rule, stating that they believe they have lost the ability to protect their reputations, that they are being sacrificed on the altar of public debate. And there is probably some truth to this assertion. For in the end, what the Supreme Court has done is to make it much harder for some kinds of persons to use the law to repair damage to their reputation in order that persons generally can have the benefit of a free and open debate.

By the end of the 1960s the federal courts had extended the actual malice fault requirement to persons called public figures. A U.S. Court of Appeals in 1966 ruled that libel plaintiff Linus Pauling, a Nobel-prize winning physicist who was a visible and active participant in the movement to ban atmospheric testing of nuclear weapons, would have to demonstrate that the *St. Louis Globe-Democrat* exhibited actual malice when it incorrectly published that the Nobel laureate had been convicted of contempt of Congress. That is, that the editors of the paper knew that charge was false but published it anyway, or demonstrated reckless disregard of whether that statement was true or false (*Pauling* v. *Globe-Democrat,* 1966). One year later the Supreme Court took similar action in a pair of cases, *AP* v. *Walker* and *Curtis Publishing Co.* v. *Butts.* The rationale for extending the rule to public figures mirrors at least two pillars that support the original Sullivan ruling. Persons outside of government frequently try to lead public debate on important issues. They should not be any more immune to criticism and complaints than public officials. Also, such persons normally have the ability to attract the media to refute the libel, to correct the mistake, to rebuild their reputations. Again, the Supreme Court ruled, the First Amendment requires that such public figures be required to show actual malice on the part of the defendant.

In 1974 the Supreme Court filled out the picture by ruling that henceforth, even private persons must prove fault in order to win a libel suit filed against a mass medium (*Gertz* v. *Welch*). In this case, however, the High Court gave the states some flexibility in applying a fault standard. Remember, previously the Court had ruled that the First Amendment requires that public officials and public figures must show actual malice to win their libel suits. With private persons, however, the Court ruled that the First Amendment only mandates that the libel plaintiff show at least negligence or the failure of the defendant to exercise reasonable care. This is a lower level of fault; it is easier for a plaintiff to show negligence than actual malice. The Court did say however, that a state may require a private-person libel plaintiff to show a higher degree of fault; actual malice or gross negligence for example.

Most states have explicitly or implicitly chosen to require private-person libel plaintiffs to show only negligence. Courts in Colorado (*Walker* v. *Colorado Springs Sun, Inc.,* 1975); Indiana (*AAFCO Heating and Air Conditioning Co.,* v. *Northwest Publications, Inc.,* 1974); New York (*Chapadeu* v. *Utica Observer-Dispatch, Inc.,* 1975); and Alaska (*Gay* v. *Williams,* 1979) have opted for a higher fault standard for private-person plaintiffs when the subject matter of the libelous material concerns a matter of public interest. To find out the rule in your state locate the most recent state supreme court ruling on libel. Undoubtedly within the text of this decision the court will discuss the level of fault applicable to private-person plaintiffs.

Several words have been used in the past few pages that beg for fuller explanation. Who is a public official? Who is a public figure? How do you define negligence? How do you define actual malice? In the next section of the book an attempt will be made to add flesh to these bones, to make these legal concepts come a bit more alive. Before moving to that, let's briefly summarize the fault rules to this point.

1. Private persons who sue the media for defamation must at least prove that the material was published through negligence. Negligence is defined in the law as the failure to exercise reasonable care.

2. Public persons—both public officials and public figures—who sue the media for defamation have to prove that the defendant exhibited actual malice when the material was published. Actual malice is defined in the law as publishing with the knowledge that the libelous assertion is false, or with reckless disregard for whether it is true or false.

PUBLIC PERSONS VERSUS PRIVATE PERSONS

All libel plaintiffs who sue the mass media must prove that the defendant in the case was at fault, that the publication or broadcast of the libelous material was not simply the result of an innocent error. Public officials and public figures have to prove a higher level of fault than do private individuals. But who are public officials and public figures in the eyes of the law? Before exploring this issue a brief caution is warranted. One of the problems in the law of libel is that courts have taken perfectly good words which most of us use daily and have attached a slightly different meaning to these words. Students need to exercise caution because of this. Most of us could probably agree on a general definition of a public figure, for example. But in libel law the courts have given these words a slightly different meaning. What we need to remember is the legal definition of these words, not the common, ordinary, everyday definition.

Two questions must be asked to determine whether a libel plaintiff should be considered a public official.

1. Who is this plaintiff; that is, what kind of job does this person have?
2. What was the allegedly libelous story about?

Let us consider these questions separately.

A public official is someone who works for a government and draws a salary from the public payroll. Included are persons from the president of the United States to a patrolman on a beat. Yet not all persons who are government employees qualify as public officials under the law of libel. In 1966 when the Supreme Court was confronted with a lawsuit from a former director of a county ski area, Justice Brennan attempted to define those persons in government who would fall under the rubric public official. "It is clear," he wrote, "that the 'public official' designation applies at the very least to those among the hierarchy of government employees who have or appear to the public to have substantial responsibility for or control over the conduct of governmental affairs" (*Rosenblatt* v. *Baer,* 1966). Brennan added that the person must hold a position that invites public scrutiny of the person holding it, entirely apart from the scrutiny and discussion occasioned by the particular charges in the controversy.

This latter dimension is terribly important. The Supreme Court demonstrated this in 1979 when it refused to consider the research director of a public mental hospital to be a public official. There could be little doubt that Ronald Hutchinson was a well-paid public employee. In addition to his state salary, he was the recipient of about a half-million dollars in public funds for his research on aggression in animals. Senator William Proxmire, who apparently thought the expenditure of public money on such research was wasteful and foolish, named the public agencies that funded the scientist's research recipients of one of his Golden Fleece awards for making a "monkey out of the American taxpayer." In the libel suit that followed, the Supreme Court ruled that there was little public interest in Hutchinson's job before he was made the butt of Proxmire's joke. Chief Justice Burger said that those charged with defamation cannot by their own conduct create their own defense by making the plaintiff a public person (*Hutchinson* v. *Proxmire,* 1979). In other words, Hutchinson's position was not one that invited public scrutiny, apart from the scrutiny and discussion caused by the defamatory charges.

State courts have not always followed this rule to the letter. In *Press* v. *Verran* (1978) the Tennessee Supreme Court ruled that a junior state social worker was a public official because her job carried with it "duties and responsibilities affecting the lives, liberty, money or property of a citizen or that may enhance or disrupt his enjoyment of life. . . ." The Washington Supreme Court in 1979 said that the administrator of a small county motor pool, who worked without direct supervision, had two assistants, and could independently spend up to five hundred dollars of county money on open charge accounts at several local parts dealers, was a public official. "The public quite naturally has a legitimate and continuing interest in how local tax revenues are spent by those county employees vested with the power to utilize the public purse," wrote Chief Justice Robert Utter for the court (*Clawson* v. *Longview Publishing Co.,* 1979). The defamation in this case was an allegation that the plaintiff had used small amounts of county funds to repair private vehicles. Similarly, police officers, who are relatively low-level government employees, have frequently been held to be public officials because they hold the power of life and death over the citizens in a community (see *Malerba* v. *Newsday,* 1978).

It is safe to conclude that any government employee who periodically stands for election is a public official. Appointed officials can also meet the established criteria. The Washington Supreme Court recently ruled that a research analyst for the state Senate Energy and Utilities Committee was a public official. She was a top expert in nuclear waste management and was the major source of information to senators on all matters concerning radioactive waste (*Price* v. *Washington State Senate,* 1986).

What about a consulting firm that advises a government on a controversial but important government policy question? The Iroquois Research Institute was hired by Fairfax County, Virginia, to evaluate the historical and archeological value of an island in the Potomac River on which the county hoped to construct water-intake facilities. Lowes Island was the subject of a great zoning controversy in the community, and when Iroquois reported that the work could be done without harming the island, the research institute became the focus of sharp criticism. The *Loudoun* (Va.) *Times Mirror* published a story that challenged the competence of Iroquois researchers, and a libel suit followed. The United States Court of Appeals for the Fourth Circuit ruled that the consulting firm could not be considered a public official in terms of the libel suit. The court said that the institute made no recommendations to the county, participated in no policy determinations, and exercised no discretion. In short, it had no control over the conduct of governmental affairs. "Its position was not of such apparent importance that the public has an independent interest in its qualifications," the court ruled. The court conceded that in some instances a consultant employed by the government entity can be classified a public official, but not this time (*Artic* v. *Loudoun Times Mirror,* 1980).

The context in which the defamation occurs is often important. A planner with a state geological survey office might not normally hold a position that invites public scrutiny. But if this person is appointed by the governor to conduct a study of the feasibility of constructing a hazardous waste dump site near the state capital, this special assignment brings with it closer public scrutiny. In such a case a person who was not a public official might suddenly become one in terms of libel law.

This leads to the second question in determining who is a public official in a libel suit: What is the nature of the supposedly libelous story?

A person who works for the government in a position of authority may not be termed a public official for the purposes of a lawsuit if the allegedly libelous story does not pertain either (1) to the plaintiff's official conduct—the manner in which the official conducts the official public role or (2) to the plaintiff's general fitness to hold public office.

Stories that fall under the first category are obvious. These stories focus upon how well or how badly public officials handle their job. Stories in the second category are far more troublesome for journalists.

If the mayor is drunk when he attempts to preside at a meeting of the city council, his personal habits directly affect his fitness for office. But what if the mayor has a serious drinking problem that does not visibly affect his work? And what if a newspaper erroneously reports, following the mayor's arrest for drunken driving, that it was the third arrest for such an offense? Will the mayor be forced to prove actual malice in the libel suit that follows? This is a tough question. As a rule of thumb, the lower persons are on the scale of public officialdom, the more their private lives will be protected by the law. Because of the immense responsibilities, almost everything the president of the United States does reflects upon his fitness to hold the job. The private life of a United States senator is probably less open to public scrutiny than the private life of a president, but more investigation of the senator's private life will be permitted than of the life of an elected prosecutor of Clinton County, Michigan.

Public Figures

The concept of the public figure was introduced into libel law in the mid-1960s. However it was not until 1974 that the category was divided into two subcategories by the Supreme Court—all-purpose public figures and limited public figures. Initially, in his opinion in *Gertz* v. *Welch* (1974), Justice Lewis Powell attempted to outline the essence of the public-figure category:

> Hypothetically, it may be possible for someone to become a public figure through no purposeful action of his own, but the instances of truly involuntary public figures must be exceedingly rare. For the most part those who attain this status have assumed roles of especial prominence in the affairs of society.

Powell then noted that there were two separate categories of persons who might be classified public figures:

> Some [persons] occupy positions of such pervasive power and influence that they are deemed public figures for all purposes. More commonly, those classed as public figures have thrust themselves to the forefront of particular public controversies in order to influence the resolution of the issues involved. In either event, they invite attention and comment.

After reading Justice Powell's words in the *Gertz* case one certainly gets the impression that he knows who is and is not a public figure, and can easily tell the difference between an all-purpose public figure and a limited public figure. But others—including many, many judges—have had a difficult time figuring out who falls into what category. There have only been a handful of people deemed to be all-purpose public figures. Entertainers Johnny Carson (*Carson* v. *Allied News*, 1976) and Wayne Newton (*Newton* v. *NBC*, 1985) have both been declared all-purpose public figures. So has conservative political writer William F. Buckley (*Buckley* v. *Littel*, 1976). What about businessman Lee Iacocca; is he an all-purpose public figure? Or test pilot Chuck Yeager? Or Jacqueline Kennedy Onassis? These are all tough questions without answers at the moment. Professors Jerome Barron and Thomas Dienes suggest in their *Handbook of Free Speech and Free Press* "It is almost as if the courts are saying that a plaintiff will have to be totally exposed to constant media attention in order to be classified as a total [all-purpose] public figure." Barron and Dienes suggest the keys might be instant national recognition and constant media exposure.

On a national level this definition of a general or all-purpose public figure may be accurate, but there is another way of looking at the problem: the general notoriety of a person within the area in which the libel is circulated. It is quite probable that there are persons in small communities who might have the status of all-purpose public figures. Consider the woman who lives in a community of 6,500 persons. She was formerly the mayor, has served on the school board in the past, and has been a perennial choice for president of the Parent-Teacher Association. She is the president of the largest real estate company in town, is a director on the board of the local bank, and owns the local pharmacy and dry cleaner's. She is active in numerous service clubs, is a leader in various civic projects, and is instantly recognizable on the street by virtually all of the town's residents. Her family founded the town 150 years earlier. If she is libeled in a community newspaper whose circulation remains almost exclusively in the community, it could be argued persuasively that this woman is a all-purpose public figure in the community. (See *Steere* v. *Cupp*, 1979, where the Kansas Supreme Court ruled such an individual was a total or all-purpose public figure.) In 1982, the Montana Supreme Court ruled that investment and commodity adviser Larry Williams was an all-purpose public figure for his libel suit based on a Democratic party press release that erroneously charged that he had been under federal indictment for political dirty tricks. The court listed the following activities by Williams, which convinced the court that he was an all-purpose public figure: he published an investment advisory service; he wrote three books on stocks; he was the subject of an article in *Forbes* magazine and another article in the *Wall Street Journal;* he frequently gave speeches and ran unsuccessfully for the United States Senate; he was chairman of the Republican party in Montana; and he was an active member of the National Taxpayers Union (*Williams* v. *Pasma*, 1982).

But what if the defamatory material circulates outside the local community, as well, to persons who may not be familiar with the plaintiff? This question arose in 1985 in a libel suit by businessman George Martin against the *Chariho Times* in Rhode Island. Martin was clearly well known in the village of Shannock, where he owned and had developed a considerable amount of property over a period of fifteen years. The *Times* was widely read by the three hundred residents of the village, and a trial court ruled that Martin was a local all-purpose public figure. On appeal Martin argued that the newspaper had three thousand subscribers, a far larger readership than just among the village residents by whom he was so well known. The Rhode Island Supreme Court, noting that Martin's fame had spread beyond the Shannock Village limits, added that "very few individuals will be known to all subscribers or purchasers of any publication." Wally Butts and Major General Edwin Walker were not known to all subscribers of the *Saturday Evening Post,* yet were declared to be public figures by the Supreme Court, the Rhode Island justice noted, recalling that famous 1967 decision (see pages 154–155). "It is sufficient to attain a public figure status that the plaintiff should have been known to a substantial portion of the publication's readership," the court ruled. And Martin met this test (*Martin* v. *Wilson Publishing,* 1985).

Limited Public Figures

Regardless of these examples, few persons fall into the category of all-purpose public figure. Far more important for journalists is Justice Powell's second category, the limited public figure. The Supreme Court has spent more time since 1974 on defining who is and who is not a limited public figure than on any other aspect of libel law. The High Court wrote opinions in four libel suits in the five years following the *Gertz* ruling, and in three of the four cases a central question was whether the plaintiff was a limited public figure (*Time, Inc.* v. *Firestone,* 1976; *Wolston* v. *Reader's Digest,* 1979; and *Hutchinson* v. *Proxmire,* 1979). The fourth case was *Herbert* v. *Lando* (1979), which focused upon the discovery procedures in a libel action. When the essential elements are extracted from *Gertz* and the three subsequent public figure cases, certain basic criteria in the definition of a limited public figure emerge.

In *Gertz* v. *Welch* plaintiff Elmer Gertz was a well-known and widely respected Chicago attorney who had gained prominence in civil rights disputes in that city. He had written several books and articles, and on many occasions had served on commissions and committees in Chicago and Cook County. When a young man was slain by a Chicago police officer, Gertz agreed to represent the family in a civil action against the officer. The policeman had been tried and convicted of murder in the shooting, but Gertz played no role in that criminal action. His only role in the entire matter was as an attorney representing the family in the action for civil damages. He became the subject of a vicious attack by *American Opinion,* a magazine published by the John Birch Society, which accused him of being a communist fronter, a Leninist, and the architect of a frame-up against the police officer. It also charged that Gertz had a long police record.

In the libel suit that followed, the Supreme Court ruled that despite his prominence in the civil rights area, Elmer Gertz was not a public figure for the purposes of this lawsuit. The words of Justice Powell stand as an important guideline (*Gertz* v. *Welch,* 1974):

> It is preferable to reduce the public figure question to a more meaningful context by looking to the nature and extent of an individual's participation in the particular controversy giving rise to the defamation.

The key phrase is "extent of an individual's participation in the particular controversy giving rise to the defamation." To be a limited public figure, the plaintiff must be shown to have played a prominent role in the particular controversy giving rise to the defamation, the controversy prompting publication of the defamatory statement or comment. Gertz would have been a limited public figure if the dispute in the case had involved civil rights in Chicago. He would have had to prove actual malice in such circumstances. But the particular controversy that gave rise to the article in *American Opinion* was the murder of the young man and the subsequent trial of the police officer. Gertz was not an important participant in that issue. He was simply acting as an attorney—which is his profession—in representing the family of the youth in a civil action. He was acting as a private individual and as such had only to prove simple negligence.*

Two years later the Court ruled that a socially prominent Palm Beach woman was not a public figure with regard to the divorce action in which she was involved. The case, *Time, Inc.* v. *Firestone* (1976), resulted from a short notice published in *Time* magazine that Russell Firestone was granted a divorce from his wife on grounds of extreme cruelty and adultery. Firestone was in fact granted a divorce from his wife, but on grounds that neither member of the couple was "domesticated." Mary Alice Firestone sued *Time* for libel, claiming she had been called an adulteress. *Time* argued that her prominence in the Palm Beach community made her a public figure. On the record she clearly appeared to be a public figure, a leading member of the "Four Hundred of Palm Beach Society," an "active member of the sporting set," a person whose activities attracted considerable public attention. She even maintained a clipping service to keep track of her publicity. The divorce case became a *cause celebre* in the community, prompting forty-three articles in a Miami newspaper and forty-five stories in the Palm Beach newspapers. She held several press conferences during the course of the seventeen-month legal dispute.

---

*The case of *Gertz* v. *Welch,* which began in 1969, finally ended in the summer of 1982 when a four hundred thousand dollar judgement against *American Opinion* was upheld by the United States Court of Appeals for the Seventh Circuit (*Gertz* v. *Welch,* 1982).

Nevertheless, the Supreme Court refused to acknowledge that Mary Alice Firestone was a public figure in the context of the divorce case, the subject of the *Time* article that was defamatory. Justice William Rehnquist wrote:

> Respondent did not assume any role of especial prominence in the affairs of society, other than perhaps Palm Beach society, and she did not thrust herself to the forefront of any particular public controversy in order to influence the resolution of the issues involved in it.

Time argued that because the trial was well publicized, it must be considered a public controversy and Mary Alice Firestone a public person. "But in doing so," Justice Rehnquist wrote, "petitioner seeks to equate 'public controversy' with all controversies of interest to the public." The justice said that a divorce proceeding is not the kind of public controversy referred to in *Gertz*. While there was public interest in the proceedings, the case was not an important public question.

Rehnquist also pointed out that Mrs. Firestone was not a voluntary participant in the divorce proceeding. She was forced to go into public court to dissolve her marriage. The subtle difference, then, that Rehnquist points to is the difference between voluntarily becoming involved in a public controversy, and voluntarily becoming involved in something that results in a controversy. Firestone did the latter—she voluntarily went to court to get a divorce, and the divorce trial resulted in the controversy. Justice Powell did note in *Gertz* that "it may be possible for someone to become a public figure through no purposeful action of his own, but the instances of truly involuntary public figures are exceedingly rare."

The meaning of *Gertz* and *Firestone* was reemphasized in 1979 in two rulings by the Supreme Court that clearly indicated that the High Court intended the limited-public-figure category to be narrow. In both cases, *Hutchinson* v. *Proxmire* and *Wolston* v. *Reader's Digest,* the Supreme Court reversed rulings by lower federal courts, rulings that had declared that the plaintiffs were in fact limited public figures.

The facts in the *Hutchinson* case were mentioned earlier. The plaintiff was the research director at a public mental hospital in Michigan. He was also the recipient of about five hundred thousand dollars in federal grants to support his research on animal aggression. Believing that such research was unimportant, Senator William Proxmire bestowed his monthly Golden Fleece Award on several federal agencies that had funded Hutchinson's research for nearly seven years. In the process the Wisconsin lawmaker accused Hutchinson of putting the "bite" on the American taxpayer and making "a monkey" out of the American people. Hutchinson sued.

Chief Justice Burger refused to consider the plaintiff a public figure. He said there was no controversy about the research until Proxmire's defamatory comments about Dr. Hutchinson. The scientist did not thrust himself or his views into a public dispute or issue. In fact, Burger said, the defendants "have not identified such a particular controversy; at most they point to concern about general public expenditures." Hutchinson, the chief justice noted, at no time assumed any role of public prominence in the broad question of concern about expenditures. The researcher, then, had no part in the controversy that gave rise to the defamation, according to Burger. Simply taking public money to do research is not enough to make a person like Hutchinson into a public figure, the Court ruled. "If it were, everyone who received or benefited from the myriad public grants for research could be classified as a public figure. . . ."

Finally, the chief justice drew upon a basic rationale for the distinction between private and public persons and said that "we cannot agree that Hutchinson had such access to the media that he should be classified as a public figure." His access, Burger noted, was limited to responding to Proxmire's announcement of the Golden Fleece Award. The decision of the Court was eight to one in favor of Hutchinson's status as a private figure. The single dissenting vote by Justice Brennan was based solely on how the Court had responded to another question, not to the public-figure issue.

The facts in the *Wolston* case are somewhat more complicated. Ilya Wolston was identified in a 1974 book, *KGB: The Secret Works of Soviet Secret Agents,* as a Soviet agent. His description as such stemmed from events that had taken place nearly twenty years earlier when a federal grand jury in New York State was investigating the activities of Soviet agents in the United States. Wolston's aunt and uncle, Myra and Joe Soble, were well-publicized American Communists who were arrested in January 1957 and charged with spying. Wolston himself was interviewed by the Federal Bureau of Investigation (FBI) and testified several times before the New York grand jury. In July 1958 he failed to respond to a grand jury subpoena. His failure to appear was publicized in the press. He said he had not testified because he was in a state of mental depression. Later he changed his mind and offered to give testimony. He subsequently pleaded guilty to a charge of contempt and was sentenced to three years' probation. During the six weeks between the time he refused to testify and his sentencing, fifteen news stories were published about Ilya Wolston in New York and Washington newspapers. He was never indicted for espionage.

Wolston's libel suit was based on his misidentification in the *KGB* book published by *Reader's Digest.* The publication argued that because of his contempt conviction in 1958, Wolston was a limited public figure for purposes of a discussion of Soviet agents and espionage. Eight members of the Supreme Court disagreed. Justice William Rehnquist, writing for the majority, stated that Wolston did not "inject" himself into any controversy, that he was dragged into the controversy when the government pursued him during the investigation of Soviet agents. "The mere fact that petitioner voluntarily chose not to appear before the grand jury, knowing that his action might be attended by publicity, is not decisive on the status of public figure," Rehnquist said. The justice noted that Wolston played a minor role in whatever controversy there might have been over Soviet espionage, that he had never talked about this matter with the press. "We decline to hold that his mere citation for contempt rendered him a public figure for purposes of comment on the investigation of Soviet espionage."

Rehnquist stressed that Wolston had made no effort to influence the public on the resolution of any issue. The plaintiff did not in any way seek to arouse public sentiment in his favor or against the investigation. Quoting his own opinion in the *Firestone* (1976) case, Rehnquist wrote:

> While participants in some litigation may be legitimate "public figures," either generally or for the limited purpose of that litigation, the majority will more likely resemble respondent [Mary Firestone or Ilya Wolston], drawn into a public forum largely against their will in order to attempt to obtain the only redress available to them or to defend themselves against actions brought by the state or by others.

The question now is, what can we learn from the language in these Supreme Court rulings? Three basic points seem to emerge:

1. Limited public figures normally must voluntarily step into the public spotlight. The Court said it would be exceedingly rare for someone to be an involuntary public figure. Such instances as rising to deny charges made against you and going to court to end a marriage or to defend yourself from government charges do not represent voluntary behavior. They represent a response to the behavior of someone or something else.

2. A limited public figure is someone who plays a role in the resolution of an important public or social issue. A messy divorce, an investigation of aggression in animals, a charge of contempt for failure to testify before a grand jury are not the kinds of "affairs of society" that the Court considers to be important. One gets the impression that the justices are looking to the discussion of social issues (abortion, discrimination), economic issues (taxpayers' revolt, city budget), educational problems (busing, minimum competency requirements), governmental rulings (censorship, arms control), and the like, to find the kinds of persons they would consider limited public figures. A public controversy might be defined as a controversy in which the resolution of the issues will affect the general public or at least a wider group of persons than those individuals involved in the controversy.

3. There must have been some attempt by the plaintiff to influence public opinion in the resolution of these issues. This speaks to the basic point made by Justice Powell in the *Gertz* case—the nature and extent of the individual's participation in the particular controversy giving rise to the defamation. In *Hutchinson* the issue was wasteful expenditures, but Dr. Hutchinson had said little, if anything, about

that before being libeled by Senator Proxmire. Similarly, Ilya Wolston had said nothing about the issue of Soviet agents in this country—which is what the defendant contended was the issue in *Wolston* v. *Reader's Digest* (1979).

Inherent in an attempt to influence the outcome of a public issue is the ability of the plaintiff to get access to the mass media. The plaintiff generally must have some means of speaking out on the issue or of responding to criticism. Also, the media cannot create the controversy by defaming the plaintiff and then argue that the role of the plaintiff is important to the resolution of the issue. These are the key points, then, in determining whether an individual is a limited public figure:

1. There must be an important public controversy.
2. The plaintiff must inject himself or herself voluntarily into the controversy.
3. The plaintiff must attempt to influence public opinion about the resolution of the issue and have some access to the press to accomplish this feat.

Lower Court Rulings

After reading the four cases just outlined, the definition of a limited public figure may seem straightforward and fairly easy to apply. Nothing could be further from the truth. Many lower courts have been in utter confusion in attempting to apply the three criteria outlined above. Some cases simply don't fit neatly into the package and as such the law remains clouded with decisions by lower courts that seem to be off the mark established by the Supreme Court. What follows is a short review of some lower court rulings. These decisions are really only illustrative of how some courts have tried to apply the criteria established by the Supreme Court. Their value as precedent is dubious, except in those jurisdictions where these rulings are binding. Even then, another judge, looking at a similar set of facts, might find sufficient differences between the two cases to reach an opposing conclusion.

Illustrative of this confusion are two recent decisions, both dealing with lawsuits filed against newspaper defendants by wealthy farmers. In the first case, *Blake* v. *Gannett Co.,* the plaintiff was a well-to-do Mississippi corporate farmer who had been investigated, along with several other farmers, by the federal government in connection with loans they received from the Farmers Home Administration. Plaintiff Blake had not reported all his assets while he was receiving the federal loans, according to the newspaper. The Mississippi Supreme Court ruled that Blake was not a limited public figure, that the controversy in the case was about the federal loans to the farmers, and that Blake was just one of the subjects of this overall investigation. The loans were of legitimate public concern; Blake was not, the court ruled in 1988.

At about the same time a Wisconsin Court of Appeals ruled that another wealthy farmer, Joseph Weigel, who was one of a group of farmers who owned land adjacent to a state park, was a public figure when he sued for a story alleging that his refusal to adopt soil conservation practices led to pollution problems in a lake in the park. The federal government claimed that these landowners allowed animal manure and pesticides to run off into the lake and a nearby river, causing serious pollution. The court ruled that even if Weigel did not seek publicity, as the largest landowner in the area, his activities put him into the vortex of a public controversy (*Weigel* v. *Capital Times Co.*, 1988).

Putting these cases side by side is not done to confuse you; only to show you that the courts themselves are often confused, or at least inconsistent.

In reporting a move by dissident stockholders of the Koehring Company of Wisconsin to oust the firm's management, *Business Week* erroneously reported that William Denny, one of the leaders of the group of dissidents, had been fired from Koerhing. Because of his public visibility in the expulsion campaign, the publication argued that Denny was a limited public figure. The Wisconsin Supreme Court disagreed, noting that a stockholders fight was not a public controversy. Its resolution would have an impact only upon those persons with a financial interest in the company. (*Denny* v. *Mertz*, 1980). (See also *Levine* v. *CMP Publications*, 1984.) The Georgia Supreme Court recently reached the same conclusion in a libel suit brought by a group of plastic surgeons who were suing for defamation because of an article published in the *Journal of the American Medical Association* about a dispute among physicians over whether specialists in otolaryngology should perform plastic surgery. The court ruled that the doctors were not public figures because the controversy was a private dispute within the medical community (*Georgia Society of Plastic Surgeons* v. *Anderson*, 1987).

The Delaware Supreme Court declared that an inventor who invited the press to a demonstration of an automobile that ran on compressed air was not a public figure. The Delaware *News Journal* made an error in a story about the demonstration, which had taken place in 1977. The newspaper argued that Ronald Re, the inventor, was a public figure because he had thrust himself into the public spotlight to try to resolve the energy crisis by demonstrating an automobile he had designed that did not need gasoline. But the state's high court disagreed, stating that the energy crisis was merely a matter of public concern and interest, not a controversy, which the court said must involve a dispute. Many people are trying to find a way to save energy, the court said. There is surely public interest in this issue. But it is not a public controversy as defined by the leading U.S. Supreme Court rulings (*Gannett* v. *Re*, 1985).

When KSL-TV broadcast a news segment on animal cruelty in 1974, the station identified W. Garth Seegmiller as a rancher who failed to take care of his horses. The station charged that a number of the animals were malnourished and two had died. The story contained several errors and Seegmiller sued. KSL argued that cruelty to animals was an important public issue. The Utah Supreme Court agreed with that argument, but declared that the plaintiff was not a voluntary participant in attempting to resolve the controversy. "On the contrary, he was plucked by the defendant from the anonymity of private life and thrust against his will into the limelight," the state's high court noted. Even if he had been guilty of a misdemeanor, the court ruled, that fact by itself would not be sufficient to compel the conclusion that he is a public figure" (*Seegmiller* v. *KSL-TV,* 1981).

The Minnesota Supreme Court recently rendered a similar ruling when it decided that Donald Jacobson was not a public figure in connection with a story about his legal travails. Jacobson had been tried and convicted of arson and insurance fraud, but his conviction was reversed, (*Jacobson* v. *Rochester Communications,* 1987). The court agreed there had been considerable publicity about the case, but like Mary Alice Firestone, Jacobson had been forced to go to court to defend himself. The justices noted that they were not saying a criminal defendant might never be a public figure; only that such a person doesn't automatically become a public figure.

On the other hand, the Washington Court of Appeals ruled in 1986 that two women who frequently brought suit against the state, the city and the school district were limited public figures. The pair argued the cases themselves as pro se litigants, and were described by the executive secretary of the Washington Association of Prosecuting Attorneys as "constitutional crazies." They had received lots of publicity—and had never won a case. As plaintiffs in lawsuits they had voluntarily sought to influence the resolution of numerous public issues, the court ruled (*Camer* v. *Seattle Post-Intelligencer,* 1986). And the United States Court of Appeals for the Tenth Circuit ruled in 1988 that a libel plaintiff who had taken his minor son from his wife during a custody fight, and then appeared in disguise on two nationally televised talk shows to discuss his views on a father's custody rights, was a limited purpose public figure. The plaintiff initiated the libel action when a newspaper published a story saying he had been jailed in a previous custody battle (*Anderson* v. *Rocky Mountain News,* 1988).

A book-banning controversy arose at San Rafael High School in California when the members of an Elks lodge complained about a textbook being used in an American government class. The book was used in a unit on political philosophies and contained writings from the underground of the sixties, articles on revolution, drugs, and sex. The board of education held several public meetings to discuss the issue. Virginia Franklin, who taught the class, testified at the meetings, but took no other part in the dispute. The *Elks Magazine* published a story on the controversy, but erroneously reported that teacher Franklin had been fired from a previous job for "teaching the same sort of rot." In the libel suit that followed, the California Court of Appeals rejected the magazine's contention that Franklin was a public figure. Her only voluntary overt act had been to order several copies of the book for the class. Her testimony was mandated by the school district. "There is no showing that appellant [Franklin] ordered the book for the purpose of inciting controversy. She declares without contradiction that she did not anticipate controversy. It is not clear that, but for the vigorous reaction of Lodge 1108 [the Elks] there would ever have been a controversy," the court noted (*Franklin* v. *Lodge 1108,* 1979). (Please note that in other cases teachers have been declared to be public officials. See *Johnson* v. *Corinthian Television,* 1978, Oklahoma Supreme Court, for example.)

In 1980 the United States Court of Appeals in the District of Columbia ruled that Eric Waldbaum, former head of the nation's second largest consumer cooperative, was a public figure with regard to a story about his dismissal as president of that organization. The court ruled that Waldbaum had played an active role in attempting to bring consumer-related issues before the public through the media and was a limited public figure in his role with the cooperative (*Waldbaum* v. *Fairchild Publications,* 1980). The United States Court of Appeals for the Second Circuit ruled in 1980 that John Yiamouyiannis, long an outspoken foe of the fluoridation of public water supplies, was a limited public figure in a lawsuit he brought against Consumers Union for criticizing him and his research on the subject (*Yiamouyiannis* v. *Consumers Union,* 1980).

Finally, the United States Court of Appeals for the Fifth Circuit recently ruled that the president of a Guatemalan soft drink bottling company that had been in the news for its violent anti-union activities was a public figure for the purposes of a libel suit filed against columnist Jack Anderson. Anderson quoted federal government officials who reportedly had said that John C. Trotter was firmly committed to destroying the union at the Central American bottling plant, and that union officials had been assassinated and their successors had been harassed with death threats. The court, applying a test used by the Court of Appeals in the District of Columbia, asked three questions to determine Trotter's status. First, was there a public controversy? Next, did the plaintiff play a prominent role in that controversy? Finally, were the defamatory allegations germane to the plaintiff's participation in the controversy? All three questions were answered affirmatively in this case. The violence at the bottling plant was a legitimate issue of public concern. The plaintiff was the chief executive of the company and had extensive control over its policy toward unions. And Anderson's comments were certainly germane to Trotter's role in the controversy (*Trotter* v. *Anderson,* 1987).

If someone is a public figure today, will they remain a public figure several years from now? The United States Court of Appeals for the Sixth Circuit faced this question in 1981 when a lawsuit was filed by a woman who had been involved in a celebrated trial years earlier, in 1931. Victoria Price Street was the chief witness against the so-called Scottsboro Boys in a sensational rape trial in Alabama. In a National Broadcasting Company (NBC) dramatization of the long legal struggle, the viewer is left with the strong impression that Victoria Street falsely accused the young men of rape. NBC thought that Mrs. Street was dead. When she sued for libel, the television network argued that she was a limited public figure in connection with the Scottsboro Boys trial. The plaintiff conceded that she may have been a public figure during the trial, but pointed out that that was forty years ago. The court of appeals sided with the network, ruling that "once a person becomes a public figure in connection with a particular controversy, that person remains a public figure thereafter for purposes of later commentary or treatment of that controversy" (*Street* v. *NBC,* 1981). Mrs. Street appealed the decision to the Supreme Court of the United States, which accepted the case. But before arguments were heard, NBC and Mrs. Street agreed upon an out-of-court settlement. Apparently NBC was fearful that it would lose the case in the Supreme Court. There have been at least two other rulings that support this position. In 1984 the Mississippi Supreme Court decided in *Newsom* v. *Henry* that a man who ran for public office in 1967 and lost was still a public figure in 1984 for the purposes of a libel action based on a recent story about the 1967 election campaign. And the United States Court of Appeals for the Second Circuit ruled in 1988 that the "passage of time will not necessarily change an individual's status as a public figure" (*Contemporary Mission* v. *New York Times,* 1988). In this suit a group of Catholic priests sued for libel for a story written in 1980 about their activities in the late 1960s and early 1970s when they left the Monfort Fathers in St. Louis and founded their own order. This sectarian feud generated considerable publicity and the publicity continued as the priests defied the church and had three of their members ordained by a Ghanian Catholic bishop. Some members of the order became popular folk singers. The mission then founded a large mail order business that resulted in many consumer complaints. Ultimately its nonprofit status was revoked by the Internal Revenue Service. The *Times* story recounted this history and for these purposes the priests were still public figures, the court ruled.

Businesses as Public Figures

Businesses and corporations have, on occasion, been deemed to be limited public figures. It is difficult, however, to discern a real pattern in the court opinions in this area. In 1980 the United States Court of Appeals for the Third Circuit ruled that a company accused of misrepresentation was a limited public figure because it used unusual techniques to advertise its low-priced, inspected, ungraded, frozen, tenderized, boxed beef, which attracted great public attention to itself (*Steaks Unlimited* v. *Deaner,* 1980). A United States district court rendered a similar decision in 1988 when it ruled that a Texas bulk meat retailer who had done business in such a way as to generate many consumer complaints, government legal actions, and considerable media attention, was a public figure for purposes of the controversy concerning the sale of bulk meat (*Brueggemeyer* v. *ABC,* 1988). In another case the Bose Corporation was deemed to be a limited public figure in a lawsuit against *Consumer Reports* magazine over a review of Bose stereo speakers because the audio equipment manufacturer advertised the speakers in a highly unconventional manner that precipitated a public discussion of the merits of the product. The *Consumer Reports* article that criticized the speaker system did not create a controversy, the court ruled. Bose had done this by using a market strategy that emphasized the unconventional design of the 901 speakers (*Bose* v. *Consumers Union,* 1981). So when a company attempts to draw attention to itself in an unusual way, it may become a limited public figure.

On the other hand, simply doing business in a normal manner—even if it involves advertising and promotion—does not turn a business into a public figure. Thomas Jadwin promoted a double tax-exempt no-load bond mutual fund he had developed by placing ads in newspapers, distributing thirteen thousand copies of the fund prospectus and sales literature, and issuing more than two dozen press releases. But the Minnesota Supreme Court ruled in 1985 that he was not a public figure for purposes of a lawsuit based on a newspaper article about the fund because his accomplishments and activities "are not unlike countless other finance professionals. . . ." Soliciting media attention for such an offering is normal, the court said. "To hold, in effect, that soliciting public investment automatically transforms any small businessman into a public figure would, in our view, expand the category beyond the limits contemplated by *Gertz*" (*Jadwin* v. *Minneapolis Star,* 1985). The United States Court of Appeals for the First Circuit made a similar ruling in 1980. *The Boston Globe* published four articles critical of commercial fishing boats manufactured by the Bruno and Stillman Company. A libel suit followed and the court ruled that the company was not a public figure. There had been no controversy or public discussion about the boats before the libelous stories were published. "The mere selling of products itself cannot easily be deemed a public controversy," the court said (*Bruno and Stillman* v. *Globe Newspapers,* 1980).

Another criterion has been used to establish whether or not a business is a limited public figure. In 1984 a United States district court in Kansas ruled that the Beech Aircraft Company was a limited public figure for the purposes of a libel suit against the *Aviation Consumer Magazine,* which had published a story about Beech aircraft that had been involved in accidents. The court said that "The defamatory statements relate to part of Beech's business that is federally regulated and arose in the context of a federal investigation." By entering into a regulated activity like the manufacture of aircraft, the company, in essence, invited public scrutiny, the court said (*Beech Aircraft* v. *National Aviation Underwriters,* 1984). And in 1988 the United States Court of Appeals for the Eleventh Circuit ruled that two owners of jai alai frontons in Florida were public figures in their libel suit brought against ABC. The court ruled the pair had put themselves in the public eye by becoming involved in a heavily-regulated industry (*Silvester* v. *ABC,* 1988). But the Supreme Court of Oregon did not even consider the rationale that a regulated business is a public figure when it ruled that the Bank of Oregon was not a limited public figure for purposes of a lawsuit against the *Williamette Week* newspaper. "There simply is no public controversy into which plaintiffs arguably thrust themselves. Merely opening one's doors to the public, offering stock for public sale, advertising, etc., even if considered a thrusting of one's self into matters of public interest, is not sufficient to establish a public figure," the court ruled. *Williamette Week* had suggested that the bank was wrongfully diverting depositors' money and credit to another bank customer, something federal regulators of the banking industry would certainly find interesting. But the court did not discuss this aspect of the case (*Bank of Oregon* v. *Independent News,* 1985).

There is reason for caution, then, when communicating about businesses, even those that have a high visibility in the marketplace. Conducting business in a normal, albeit public manner, is not sufficient to make a corporation or company into a limited public figure. And there is no guarantee that even heavily regulated business, like banks, attain this status simply by virtue of being regulated.

An outline of these cases was presented to give you some insight into how the courts have applied the criteria established by the Supreme Court to determine whether a libel plaintiff is a limited public figure. The simplest way to determine whether a particular individual would be considered a public figure is to apply the test given us by Justice Powell. Determine the extent and the nature of the individual's participation in the controversy giving rise to the defamation. What is the controversy? How did the plaintiff get involved in the controversy? What was the plaintiff's role in the controversy? The answers to these questions will normally lead to the correct answer.

Other Public Figures

Given the contrariness of this aspect of libel law, it should come as no surprise that a line of case law is apparently developing that flies in the face of many of the prescriptions uttered by the Supreme Court; most notably the admonition by Justice Powell and others that the "instances of truly involuntary public figures are exceedingly rare." Courts have ruled that persons who engage in certain lines of work, or undertake certain kinds of behavior, automatically bring attention to themselves. Persons who choose to do things that draw them regularly into regional or national view, and lead to fame and notoriety in the community, are public figures for purposes of a libel suit, even though they make no attempt to resolve any kind of public controversy. Thus far this rationale has been applied to professional athletes (*Chuy* v. *Philadelphia Eagles,* 1979) and professional criminals or members of the underworld (*Rosanova* v. *Playboy,* 1976, affirmed 1978). True, such persons have not voluntarily stepped into the public spotlight to resolve a public issue. But the courts have said that if society chooses to direct massive public attention to a particular sphere of activity like sports or crime, those who enter that sphere and invite attention will be deemed limited public figures in libel actions based on statements that relate to those activities.

A good example of this emerging definition of a public figure is found in the case of *Marcone* v. *Penthouse,* a 1985 ruling by the United States Court of Appeals for the Third Circuit. Frank Marcone is a Philadelphia lawyer who gained great notoriety by representing members of national motorcycle gangs when they ran afoul of the law. He enjoyed socializing with members of the gangs as well and was indicted for participating in illegal drug trafficking. In a libel action against *Penthouse* magazine, which made a slight error in a story written about Marcone, the court of appeals ruled that Marcone was a public figure because of his status. Surely, Marcone did not thrust himself into the public spotlight by attempting to resolve an important public controversy. But the court said that multiple factors—including his legal representation of the gang members, his indictment on drug charges, and the fact that he went on trips and socialized with gang members—when added together, pushed Marcone into the public-figure category. Intense media attention was engendered through this behavior and it did not matter that Marcone did not desire the status of a public person. "The purpose of the First Amendment would be frustrated if those persons and activities that most require public scrutiny could wrap themselves in a veil of secrecy and thus remain beyond the reach of public knowledge," the court said (*Marcone* v. *Penthouse,* 1985).

It is important to note the difference between this case and others. Unlike Elmer Gertz, Frank Marcone not only represented clients, he also spent a great deal of time with them. And the clients were notorious. And unlike Ilya Wolston, Frank Marcone voluntarily engaged in a course of conduct that involved him with organized crime and was not a passive respondent to a legal process, the court noted. This emerging status test for public figures is surely a tentative standard at this time and is probably limited to only a few kinds of persons.

SUMMARY

Under the fault requirement all persons who sue a mass medium for libel must prove that the defendant was somehow at fault in publishing the defamatory material, that the publication (or broadcast) did not result from an innocent error. What the courts call a "public person" must normally prove that the defendant acted with actual malice in publishing the libel; that is, the defendant knew the material was false but still published it or exhibited reckless disregard for the truth. What the courts define as "private persons" must prove at least that the defendant acted negligently, that is, in such a way as to create an unreasonable risk of harm. The courts have ruled that there are three kinds of "public persons":

1. *Public officials:* Persons who work for a government in a position of authority, who have substantial control over the conduct of governmental affairs, and whose position in government invites independent public scrutiny beyond the general public interest in the qualifications and performance of all government employees.

Libelous comments must focus upon the plaintiff's official conduct (the manner in which the plaintiff conducts his or her job) or upon the plaintiff's general fitness to hold public office.

2. *All-purpose public figures:* Persons who occupy persuasive power and influence in the nation or in a community, persons who are usually exposed to constant media attention.

3. *Limited public figures:* Persons who voluntarily inject themselves into an important public controversy in order to influence public opinion regarding the resolution of that controversy. The key elements are

   a. Public controversy, the resolution of which must affect more persons than simply the participants. The outcome must have an impact upon people in a community.

   b. Plaintiffs who voluntarily thrust themselves into this controversy. An individual who has been drawn involuntarily into a controversy created by someone else (such as the press) is not a limited public figure.

   c. Plaintiffs who attempt to influence the outcome of the controversy, to shape public opinion on the subject. This implies that a plaintiff has some access to the mass media to participate in the public discussion surrounding the controversy.

Additionally, highly visible persons engaged in professional sports or underworld activities have been deemed to be limited public figures by virtue of their occupational status by some courts.

THE MEANING OF FAULT

We have attempted to establish which persons must prove what level of fault in a libel suit. In most states private persons must prove only negligence, public persons must prove actual malice. But remember in a few states the courts have created an additional level fault called gross negligence or something like that. And in some circumstances private persons have to meet this added burden, which is higher than simple negligence, but less than actual malice. Let's now try to define the two most common levels of fault, negligence and actual malice.

Negligence

Negligence is a term that has been commonly used in tort law for centuries, but has only recently been applied to libel law. In simple terms, negligence implies the failure to exercise ordinary care. In deciding whether to adopt the negligence or the stricter actual malice fault requirements, state courts are providing their own definitions of the standard. Washington State adopted a "reasonable care" standard. Defendants are considered negligent if they do not exercise reasonable care in determining whether a statement is false or will create a false impression (*Taskett* v. *King Broadcasting,* 1976). The Tennessee Supreme Court has adopted a "reasonably prudent person test:" What would a reasonably prudent person have done or not have done in the same circumstance? Would a reasonably prudent reporter have checked the truth of a story more fully? Would such a reporter have waited a day or so to get more information? Would a reasonably prudent reporter have worked harder in trying to reach the plaintiff before publishing the charges? (See *Memphis Publishing Co.* v. *Nichols,* 1978.) In Arizona, negligence has been defined as conduct that creates unreasonable risk of harm. "It is the failure to use that amount of care which a reasonably prudent person would use under like circumstances," the Arizona Supreme Court ruled (*Peagler* v. *Phoenix Newspapers,* 1976).

Negligence may result from many kinds of behavior. A reporter who trusts an inherently untrustworthy source may be deemed to be negligent. Failure by a reporter to check statements in a story that he or she does not understand may be ruled to be negligent behavior. Misreading a file or not including all the pertinent information from a file when preparing a story could be deemed to be a failure to exercise reasonable care. Carelessness in handling a news story might also result in a finding of negligence.

There are a growing number of cases defining negligence, some of which are quite helpful. Here is a sample of how the courts are defining a failure to exercise reasonable care. The Massachusetts Supreme Judicial Court ruled in 1985 that a newspaper or broadcasting station is not negligent when it publishes or broadcasts a story carried by the Associated Press or United Press International without first independently verifying allegations contained in the story. The two wire services are recognized throughout the industry as trustworthy, accurate news sources, and requiring independent verification of wire service stories would place too heavy a burden on the press. Of course, if it appears likely that the story probably contains an error, the publication or broadcasting station should undoubtedly try to verify the report (*Appleby* v. *Daily Hampshire Gazette,* 1985).

Courts have been reluctant to find negligence when a reporter bases a story on the report of a normally reliable "official" source. A Florida court of appeals ruled that a story based upon an inaccurate report from an immigration officer was not published negligently. The same officer had provided consistently accurate information in the past (*Karp* v. *Miami Herald,* 1978). On the other hand, the Massachusetts Supreme Judicial Court ruled that a jury might find negligence in a case where a television reporter relied on a source for a story whom local police described as not having been reliable in the past. In this case the reporter testified that even he found some of the informant's claims to be way off the mark on crucial points (*Jones* v. *Taibbi,* 1987).

The South Carolina Supreme Court ruled that the failure of a reporter to examine a public judicial record when writing about a criminal case could be negligence. The plaintiff in the case had been arrested with four other men and charged with pirating stereo audio tapes. Two months later four of the men arrested pleaded guilty to the charges, but the charges were dismissed against the plaintiff. The newspaper published a story saying that the plaintiff had also pleaded guilty to the charges. The reporter had gotten his information about the case in a telephone conversation with the prosecuting attorney. The attorney testified that he had given the reporter the correct information. Six days elapsed between the dismissal of charges and the erroneous story. The South Carolina high court concluded that the correct information was available to the reporter in the court records and that he could have looked at this material before publishing the story. He instead chose to rely upon a telephone conversation and in doing so got the story fouled up. The jury could readily conclude that the reporter was negligent, the court ruled (*Jones* v. *Sun Publishing,* 1982). In a similar case in Washington state, the supreme court ruled that there was no evidence of negligence when a reporter relied on erroneous information from a city attorney in attempting to explain a court order. The plaintiff was convicted in municipal court of assault. A superior court later dismissed the charges. Legally this meant that the municipal court conviction was voided as well. The news story related that the superior court had dismissed the charges, but also reported that the plaintiff had been convicted in municipal court. Nowhere in the superior court dismissal order—which was read to the reporter over the telephone—did it state that the municipal court charges were dismissed as well. The reporter checked with a city attorney on this point, and he confirmed her impression that the dismissal did not negate the previous conviction. There is no evidence of negligence in this case, the state's high court ruled. The reporter exercised reasonable care by checking with the city attorney, who she might reasonably presume to understand the meaning of the dismissal order (*Lamon* v. *Butler,* 1988).

The North Carolina Court of Appeals ruled that failure to retract a libelous statement is not evidence of fault of any kind (*Walters* v. *Sanford Herald,* 1976). But the Arizona Supreme Court ruled that it was reasonable to expect a reporter to attempt to verify charges made by two former employees of the Phoenix Better Business Bureau about a local automobile dealer. The former employees charged the businessman with misrepresentation in advertising. The reporter did not attempt to verify the statements by calling the Better Business Bureau to determine the truth of the charges. This was negligent conduct, the court ruled (*Peagler* v. *Phoenix Newspapers,* 1976).

Finally, the Virginia Supreme Court ruled that when a newspaper published a very negative story about a local teacher, based largely on complaints from parents who called the newspaper, it exhibited negligence. Parents were quoted in the article as saying the teacher was erratic, disorganized, forgetful, unfair, and demeaning to students. The reporter who wrote the story talked to a couple of students, the principal, and two of the teacher's colleagues, but got very little information. As such, the story was very one-sided. The court said that the reporter could have contacted many more students to try to verify the accusations since there was no deadline pressure. It was obvious, the court ruled, that the parents who contacted the reporter bore the teacher ill-will. This should have pushed the reporter to do a more thorough job (*Richmond Newspapers v. Lipscomb,* 1987).

The definition of the term *negligence* will undoubtedly vary from state to state and possibly from judge to judge within a state. It is going to be some time before any kind of broad, consistently applied guidelines emerge. The United States Supreme Court will be of little help in this case, as it appears to be the intention of the Court to leave the matter to the states.

While the uncertainty in this area of the law exists, reporters and editors need to put a premium on *reasonable caution.* Newspapers and broadcasting stations should attempt to develop their own standards of care, and these should be applied in publishing and broadcasting the news. The Tennessee Supreme Court noted in 1978 that the negligence standard was *not* a "journalistic malpractice test" (*Memphis Publishing Co. v. Nichols,* 1978). Liability will be based upon a departure from supposed standards of care set by publishers themselves. Reporters need to become better bookkeepers and undertake to keep records on how and when they investigate the veracity of libelous charges. The key term is "good faith effort." So long as the press makes a good faith effort to establish the truth or falsity of libelous charges, it does not appear that negligence will be a serious problem.

Actual Malice

Defining actual malice is somewhat easier than defining who is and who is not a public figure or public official. In *New York Times Co. v. Sullivan* (1964) Justice Brennan defined actual malice as "knowledge of falsity or reckless disregard of whether the material was false or not." The two parts of this definition should be considered separately.

Knowledge of Falsity

"Knowledge of falsity" is a fancy way of saying "lie." If the defendant lied and the plaintiff can prove it, actual malice has then been shown. But plaintiffs are rarely in a position to show that the defendant lied. Furthermore, not many defendants, at least not many mass media defendants, lie. However, this did occur on at least one occasion. In 1969 Barry Goldwater was able to convince a federal court that Ralph Ginzburg published knowing falsehoods about him during the 1964 presidential campaign in a "psychobiography" carried in Ginzburg's *Fact* magazine. Ginzburg sent questionnaires to hundreds of psychiatrists asking them to analyze Goldwater's mental condition. Ginzburg published only those responses that agreed with the magazine's predisposition that Goldwater was mentally ill and changed the responses on other questionnaires to reflect this point of view. Proof of this conduct, plus evidence of other kinds of similar practices, led the court of appeals to conclude that Ginzburg had published the defamatory material with knowledge of its falsity (*Goldwater* v. *Ginzburg,* 1969; see also *Morgan* v. *Dun & Bradstreet, Inc.,* 1970).

A few months after the initial decision in the *Sullivan* case, the Supreme Court defined reckless disregard for the truth in a **criminal libel** action (*Garrison* v. *Louisiana,* 1964) as "a high degree of awareness of probable falsity" of the material or statements. In 1968, in *St. Amant* v. *Thompson,* the High Court said that before a court can conclude that reckless disregard for the truth exists, "there must be sufficient evidence to permit the conclusion that the defendant in fact entertained serious doubts as to the truth of his publication." Failure to investigate in and of itself is not sufficient evidence to prove actual malice, wrote Justice White.

Both are good definitions of reckless disregard for the truth, but they are not much help to the working journalist who needs a more practical measure of reckless disregard. The Supreme Court has to an extent provided that as well. Look at *New York Times Co.* v. *Sullivan,* for example. All that was required to check the truth of the charges made in the advertisement that ultimately became the basis for the libel suit was for someone to compare the assertions in the advertisement with clippings in the newspaper's files, a simple matter. Yet the Court in that case did not indicate that such a check was really called for. There was no reason for the advertising staff to doubt the veracity of the claims in the document. The newspaper had every reason to believe that the charges contained in the advertisement were true.

A better practical definition of reckless disregard evolved from the cases of *Curtis Publishing Co.* v. *Butts* and *AP* v. *Walker* (1967). In developing the criteria that follow, Justice Harlan said he was attempting to determine whether the plaintiffs in these cases had seriously departed from the standards of responsible reporting. He did not call his opinion a definition of reckless disregard. Some of the other members of the Court did, however, refer to these standards as a measure of reckless disregard, and so have many lower federal and state courts.

These two appeals came before the Supreme Court at about the same time and were joined and decided as one case. In the first case Wally Butts, the athletic director at the University of Georgia, brought suit against the *Saturday Evening Post* for an article it published alleging that Butts and University of Alabama football coach Paul "Bear" Bryant had conspired prior to the annual Georgia-Alabama football game to "fix" the contest. The *Post* obtained its information from a man who said that while making a telephone call, he had been accidentally plugged into a phone conversation between Butts and Bryant. George Burnett, who had a criminal record, told the *Post* editors that he had taken careful notes. The story was based on these notes.

In the other case Major General (retired) Edwin Walker, a political conservative and segregationist from Texas, brought suit against the Associated Press (AP) and a score of publications and broadcasting stations for publishing the charge that he led a mob of white citizens against federal marshals who were attempting to preserve order at the University of Mississippi during the crisis over the enrollment of James Meredith. The AP report, which was wrong, was filed by a young AP correspondent on the scene.

The Court ruled that in the *Butts* case the *Post* had exhibited highly unreasonable conduct in publishing the story but that in the *Walker* case no such evidence was present. Again, it is important to note that while Justice John Marshall Harlan did not call the conduct reckless disregard at the time, most authorities accept these cases as good indicators of what the court means by reckless disregard. Look at the details of each case.

In the *Butts* case the story was not what would be called a hot news item. It was published months after the game occurred. The magazine had ample time to check the report. The source of the story was not a trained reporter, but a layperson who happened to be on probation on a bad-check charge. The *Post* made no attempt to investigate the story further, to screen game films to see if either team had made changes in accord with what Bryant and Butts supposedly discussed. Many persons were supposedly with Burnett when he magically overheard this conversation and none were questioned by the *Post*. The magazine did little, then, to check the story, despite evidence presented at the trial that one or two of the editors acknowledged that Burnett's story needed careful examination.

In the *Walker* case different circumstances were present. It was a hot story, one that had to get out on the wires right away. It was prepared in the "heat of battle" by a young, but trained, reporter who in the past had given every indication of being trustworthy. All but one of the dispatches from the correspondent said the same thing: Walker led the mob. So there was internal consistency. Finally, when General Walker's previous actions and statements are considered, the story that he led a mob at Ole Miss was not terribly out of line with his prior behavior. There was nothing to cause AP to suspect that the story was wrong as, for example, would be a report that the Archbishop of New York led a mob down Fifth Avenue. A red light should signal those kinds of instances that should suggest further checking because the story doesn't sound very likely.

When all this is sorted out, three key factors emerge:

1. Was the publication of the story urgent? Was it a hot news item? Or was there sufficient time to check the facts in the story fully?

2. How reliable was the source of the story? Should the reporter have trusted the news source? Was the source a trained journalist? Should the editor have trusted the reporter?

3. Was the story probable? Or was the story so unlikely that it cried out for further examination?

These factors make up a fairly good operational definition of reckless disregard and are the kinds of considerations a court might take a close look at in determining the reasonableness of the conduct of an editor or a broadcaster.

By combining the two conceptual definitions from *Garrison* and *St. Amant* and the practical guidelines from *Butts* and *Walker,* you should have a pretty good idea of the meaning of actual malice. The standard from *St. Amant,* the requirement of evidence that the defendant in fact entertained serious doubts as to the truth of the material, is a significant burden for the plaintiff to overcome. In addition, in bringing forward evidence to prove to the jury that the defendant did "entertain serious doubts," the plaintiff must meet a rigorous burden of proof. The normal evidentiary test in civil suits—the plaintiff must prove with a preponderance of evidence—has been abandoned in cases involving the *Times* rule. Instead the plaintiff must prove with "convincing clarity," must bring forth "clear and convincing evidence," that there was reckless disregard. If there is doubt in a juror's mind, the vote must be for the defendant. This standard makes the *Times* rule even more difficult for the plaintiff to meet.

In 1984 the United States Supreme Court ruled that it was not actual malice when an engineer at *Consumer Reports* magazine knowingly changed the wording of the results of a test panel that had evaluated an audio speaker system, even though his testimony that he didn't think he had changed the meaning of the statement was unbelievable. *Bose Corporation* v. *Consumer's Union,* (1984) is better known for its ruling that federal appeals courts, when reviewing findings of actual malice in a libel action, must exercise their own judgment in determining whether actual malice was actually shown with convincing clarity and are not restricted by an erroneous standard of review used by a lower court. But the High Court did speak to the question of actual malice as well. In its review of the Bose 901 speakers, *Consumer Reports* magazine said the sound from the speakers "tended to wander about the room." This statement was written by engineer Arnold Seligson, who supervised the test. But the listener panel had actually said that the sound tended to move along the wall, in front of and between the two speakers. At the trial Seligson testified that he believed the two statements meant the same thing. The district court found this testimony incredible and said that Seligson obviously knew he had changed the meaning of the statement. This was evidence of actual malice. The Supreme Court disagreed, saying Seligson's testimony, in and of itself, was not evidence, of actual malice. "He had made a mistake," Justice John Paul Stevens wrote, "and when confronted with it he refused to admit it and steadfastly attempted to maintain that no mistake had been made—that the inaccurate was accurate. That attempt failed, but the fact that he made the attempt does not establish that he realized the inaccuracy at the time of publication."

The lower courts have been somewhat more consistent in determining what is actual malice than they have been in deciding who is a public figure. Courts have found actual malice to exist for instance when defendants fail to investigate a story weakened by an inherent improbability or internal inconsistency. A lower court has also found actual malice when a reporter's own notes revealed she was aware of facts contradicting the libelous assertions and when the plaintiff was able to show that the reporter knew of facts disproving the libelous assertion. When the only "source" of a story denied giving the reporter the information used as the basis for the defamatory charge, the court presumed the story was fabricated and found actual malice. A look at some lower court rulings is also helpful to more closely define reckless disregard.

A reporter for the *St. Louis Globe-Democrat,* preparing a story on deadline, told a rewrite man on the desk that a city alderwoman admitted at a meeting to having had two abortions. The rewrite man, working close to deadline, botched the story and attributed the admission to another alderwoman, who happened to be an outspoken foe of abortion. The Missouri Supreme Court said this was negligence, but not reckless disregard for the truth. Deadline pressure was considered a critical issue by the court (*Glover* v. *Herald Co.,* 1977).

The United States Court of Appeals for the Eleventh Circuit ruled that evidence of actual malice existed when the Liberty Lobby published a story in its *Spotlight* magazine claiming that the CIA was planning to frame Howard Hunt, a man involved in the Watergate scandal, for the assassination of John F. Kennedy. The author of the story was a former CIA agent who had serious legal difficulties with the agency. The court said he should not have been trusted as a source without considerable questioning. The editors made no independent attempt to verify the story, even though there was ample time to check it out. The story was inherently improbable. The editors testified that they believed it, but the court ruled that a jury does not have to believe the editors' professions of belief (*Hunt* v. *Liberty Lobby,* 1983). (See also *Liberty Lobby* v. *Jack Anderson,* 1984.)

Evident ill will on the part of the reporter or source of the story in and of itself is not evidence of actual malice. The Kentucky Court of Appeals recently ruled that just because there was evidence in a case that a reporter was out to get the subject of a critical report, this was not evidence that the reporter in fact entertained serious doubts about the truth or falsity of the assertions in the story—some of which turned out to be mistaken (*E. W. Scripps* v. *Ball,* 1987).

The United States Court of Appeals for the District of Columbia hammered this point even more forcefully in 1987 in overturning a ruling that the *Washington Post* had libeled William Tavoulareas, the former chief of Mobil Oil. The *Post* had published an article stating that Tavoulareas had used his power in the oil business to "set up" his son in the business of managing Mobil tankers and other ships. Tavoulareas sued, a jury ruled in his behalf, but the trial judge set aside the verdict, saying there was no evidence of actual malice in this case. The court of appeals reversed the ruling, noting that there was indeed ample evidence of actual malice. Evidence that the newspaper followed a sensationalistic and adversarial policy provides a motive for knowing falsehood and is evidence of actual malice, the three-judge panel ruled. In addition, there was evidence that a reporter on the story had expressed a desire to "get" the plaintiff while the story was being prepared. This can also lead to the conclusion that there was actual malice, the court ruled.

The *Post* asked and received a rehearing by the full circuit court and by a 7–1 vote this court wiped out the three-judge panel ruling. The court ruled that although the charge of nepotism did defame Tavoulareas, it was a substantially true charge. But the court went much farther in its discussion of actual malice. The court ruled that a newspaper's adversarial policy to produce hard-hitting investigative stories is not evidence of actual malice unless it can be shown that there is "distorting pressure . . . for high-impact stories *without regard for accuracy.*" (The court's emphasis.) There was no evidence, the court noted, that anyone on The *Post* staff understood that the newspaper's policy meant that journalists could advance their careers by being reckless in preparing their stories.

Next, the court ruled that the reporter's comments that he was out to "get" the plaintiff, hoping to do harm in the process, was not, in and of itself, evidence of a willingness to publish falsehoods. Such comments "seem to us well within the everyday parlance of an investigative reporter" the court said. Merely taking an adversarial stand does not prove hostility to the truth, the judges added (*Tavoulareas* v. *The Washington Post Co., 1987*).

Although certain behavior, such as a reporter's vengeful posture, or the reliance on an untrustworthy source, may not individually support a claim of actual malice, several such items taken together may be sufficient. To wit the case of a county prosecutor and a Seattle television station. A reporter at the station got a tip that prosecutor Donald Herron was under investigation by the FBI for improper bail procedures. Reporter Don McGaffin tried to contact Herron, but could only reach one of his assistants. The assistant confirmed the tip, but would say no more. McGaffin reportedly got angry at the stonewall and shouted, "You will regret doing this. I will get you."

McGaffin investigated the connection between Herron and local bail bondsmen and campaign contributions. In a story broadcast on KING-TV McGaffin reported the federal investigation and said that Herron was not asking for forfeiture of bonds for persons who skipped out on court appearances. This saved the bail bondsmen considerable money. McGaffin noted that bail bondsmen had contributed half of all campaign funds used by Herron in the previous election. This was incorrect; public records, which McGaffin said he looked at, clearly showed that bail bondsmen contributed only about two percent of Herron's campaign money. McGaffin testified that he had gotten some of his information for the story from Herron's opponent in the recently bitterly-fought election campaign, and some of this material was apparently not completely verified. KING-TV claimed that the case should be dismissed because as a public official Herron had to prove actual malice, and there was no such evidence.

In a 4–3 vote, the Washington Supreme Court disagreed, noting that four elements, when taken together, could be evidence of actual malice in this case. These were:

> The hostile exchange with the assistant prosecuting attorney and McGaffin's alleged subsequent threat.

> The reporter's assertion that he did look at campaign finance records and the fact that he still came up with the figure that half of Herron's campaign contributions came from bail bondsmen raises the possibility of fabrication of that portion of the story.

> The fact that McGaffin relied in some instances on information given to him by Herron's former election opponent, a questionable source.

> The fact that sometime after the suit was filed, but before it went to trial, KING-TV destroyed the audio tapes of both broadcasts that contained the libelous charges, keeping only a videotape copy.

Individually, none of these would be sufficient to show actual malice, the court ruled. But taken together, they could be sufficient for a jury to make such a finding (*Herron* v. *King Broadcasting,* 1987).

If a broadcaster rehearses with a person she is about to interview, asks the subject to rephrase certain statements made against a third party to make them stronger, and then tells the interviewee not to worry, that she would pay any legal fees if problems arose because of the interview evidence of actual malice? The Ohio Supreme Court said no in 1988. The truth or falsity of the statement was not altered by the rehearsal or by making the charges stronger, the court said. "The distinction between sensationalism and investigate journalism lies in the attitude of the publisher toward the truth." Here the truth was not sacrificed, the court ruled (*Perez* v. *Scripps-Howard Broadcasting,* 1988).

What happens if the plaintiff denies the allegations before they are printed or broadcast, but they are printed or broadcast anyway? Is this evidence of actual malice? Courts have generally said no, that such a prepublication denial, by itself, is not sufficient to show actual malice (*Roberts* v. *Dover,* 1981). Similarly refusal to retract a story is not by itself considered actual malice either. And in 1988 the Illinois Supreme Court ruled that a newspaper's failure to solicit a public official's reaction to a critical charge made against the official does not constitute actual malice. (*Costello* v. *Capital Cities Communications, Inc.,* 1988.)

SUMMARY

In a lawsuit against a mass medium, a private person must prove that the defendant was at least negligent in publishing the defamatory matter. Negligence has been defined as the failure to exercise reasonable care or as acting in such a way as to create a substantial risk of harm. In some states, in certain cases private persons will be required to prove more than simple negligence. They may be required to prove gross negligence, which is a standard that implies a greater degree of carelessness on the part of the defendant. An individual who has been declared to be a public person for the purposes of a libel suit must prove actual malice. Actual malice is defined as knowledge of falsity or reckless disregard of the truth. Transmitting a story with the knowledge of its falsity means that the publishers of the story knew it was not true but still communicated it to the public. To prove reckless disregard for the truth, the plaintiff must show that the publisher of the defamation had a "high degree of awareness of the probable falsity of the material" when it was published or that the publisher in fact "entertained serious doubts about the truth of the material" before it was published. The courts have established a set of three criteria that are used to help determine whether material was published with reckless disregard of the truth. The jurists tend to look at these factors:

1. Whether there was time to investigate the story or whether the material had to be published quickly
2. Whether the source of the information appeared to be reliable and trustworthy
3. Whether the story itself sounded probable or farfetched

If the item was hot news, if the source was a trained journalist, and if the information in the story sounded probable, there can be no finding of reckless disregard. However, if there was plenty of time to investigate, if the source of the material was questionable, or if the information in the story sounded completely improbable, courts are more likely to permit a finding of reckless disregard for the truth.

SUMMARY JUDGMENT

No attempt is made in this book to teach anyone how to try a libel suit; students need to go to law school to find that out. But even journalists should know about one procedural matter in a libel suit. This is called "a motion for **summary judgment.**" After plaintiffs have made all their allegations in a lawsuit, but before the actual trial has begun, defendants can ask the court for a summary judgment. The United States Court of Appeals for the District of Columbia described a summary judgment in this way (*Nader* v. *deToledano*, 1979):

> . . . a summary judgment should be granted if (1) taking all reasonable inferences in the light most favorable to the nonmoving party [the plaintiff in

this case], (2) a reasonable juror, acting reasonably, could not find for the nonmoving party, (3) under the appropriate burden of proof.

Here's a hypothetical example of how this works. Imagine that Rudy Rinaldo, who publishes the newsletter for the Wyoming Cattlemen's Association, inadvertently libels rancher Tom Brand. Brand will present his complaint, containing all of his allegations and arguments to the court. A judge will look at the complaint. If there is any disagreement on the facts in the case, the judge will presume that Brand, the plaintiff, has stated the facts correctly. Brand will also be given the benefit of the doubt in any other instance that might be questionable. After reviewing the case in this manner, if the judge believes that a jury could not possibly rule in Brand's favor, he or she can dismiss the case summarily, or grant a summary judgment.

The summary judgment has proved to be especially useful in libel suits, especially when public persons sue and must prove actual malice. Whether or not the defendant exhibited actual malice is considered a "constitutional fact," something that can be determined by a judge. If the plaintiff lacks substantial evidence of the existence of actual malice, a motion for summary judgment will generally be granted. In fact, since 1980, courts have dismissed about three-quarters of all libel suits filed against mass media defendants. This percentage is even higher if only suits brought by public persons are counted. The existence of these judgments has dramatically helped the press stave off libel litigation in the past ten years, and as such is a very important part of the law. Judge Sarokin of the United States District Court in New Jersey explained this importance in a 1985 libel ruling;

> Possibly the giants of the industry have both the finances and the stamina to run the risk in such situations [the threat of a libel suit]. But the independent will of smaller magazines, newspapers, television and radio stations undoubtedly bends with the spectre of a libel action looming. Even if convinced of their ultimate success on the merits, the costs of vindication may soon be too great for such media defendants to print or publish that which may entail any risk of a court action. If that is the result, it is a sorry state of affairs for the media, and, more important, for the country. Therefore, probably more than any other type of case, summary judgments in libel actions should be readily available and granted where appropriate. (See *Schiavone Construction* v. *Time,* 1985.)

Some judges don't like summary judgment in libel suits because they believe the proof of actual malice calls a defendant's state of mind into question—and this is a matter better considered at a trial. But in 1986 the Supreme Court of the United States emphasized the importance of this process when it ruled in *Anderson* v. *Liberty Lobby* that libel suits filed by public officials and public figures in federal courts must be summarily dismissed before the trial unless the plaintiff can prove libel and fault with convincing clarity. This ruling was hailed by many in the mass media as a ruling that will encourage district court judges to dispose of weak libel claims at early stages of litigation.

STATUTE OF LIMITATIONS

For nearly all crimes and most civil actions there is a **statute of limitations.** Courts do not like stale legal claims. They have plenty of fresh ones to keep them busy. Prosecution for most crimes except homicide and kidnapping must be started within a specified period of time. For example, in many states if prosecution is not started within seven years after an armed robbery is committed, the robber cannot be brought to trial. He or she is home free. (However, the robber can still be prosecuted for failing to pay income tax on money taken from a bank, but that is another story.)

The duration of the statute of limitations for libel actions differs from state to state, varying from one to six years. In most states the duration is one or two years. What this means is that a libel suit must be started within one or two years following publication of the offending material. The date of publication on a newspaper determines when the duration of the statute begins. In television and radio the statute of limitations begins on the day the program is telecast or broadcast. Magazines pose a somewhat different problem. The publication date on the magazine rarely coincides with the date the publication is actually distributed. Magazines dated November are usually distributed in October, sometimes even in late September. Courts have ruled that the statute of limitations begins on the date that a magazine is distributed to a substantial portion of the public. *Time* magazine was sued in New Jersey, which has a one-year statute of limitations, for an article published in an issue dated February 18, 1980. The suit was filed on February 17, 1981. But the magazine proved that a substantial portion of the magazine had been distributed to subscribers and newsstands before February 17, 1980. The United States district court ruled that the statute of limitations had expired by February 17, 1981 (*MacDonald* v. *Time,* 1981). In a similar suit Don Wildmon failed in his attempt to sue *Hustler* magazine for an article published in the November 1978 issue. Wildmon filed his suit on October 9, 1979, but the magazine proved that the November 1978 issue of *Hustler* had gone on sale on October 3, 1978, and subscriber copies had been mailed one to two weeks earlier. The United States district court dismissed the suit because the one-year statute of limitations in Mississippi had expired (*Wildmon* v. *Hustler,* 1980).

The libel republication rule can be a factor in considering the statute of limitations. In many states buying a back issue of a publication is considered new publication, and the statute of limitations starts over. More and more jurisdictions have rejected this rule and substituted the single publication rule. This rule states that the entire edition of a newspaper or magazine is a single publication and that isolated sales in the months or years to come do not constitute republication. Therefore the statute of limitations starts on the day the edition hit the newsstands and ends one or two or three years later. The statute cannot be reactivated by a later sale (see *Morgan* v. *Hustler Magazine,* 1987, for example). About one-half of the states have this progressive rule. Find out if your state does.

Is it possible for a plaintiff who has not filed a libel suit within the statute of limitations in his home state to file an action in another state that has a longer statute of limitations? The answer is yes, so long as the libel has been circulated in this other state. The Supreme Court clarified this question in two 1984 rulings, *Keeton* v. *Hustler* and *Clader* v. *Jones*. Kathy Keeton, a resident of New York, sued *Hustler* magazine, an Ohio corporation, for libel in the state of New Hampshire. *Hustler* challenged the action, arguing that the suit should be brought in New York or Ohio but not New Hampshire, which has a six-year statute of limitations. Only about fifteen thousand copies of the one-million-plus circulation of the magazine are sold in New Hampshire, the defendant argued. A court of appeals ruled that the plaintiff had too tenuous a contact with New Hampshire to permit the assertion of personal jurisdiction in that state, but the Supreme Court unanimously reversed the ruling. *Hustler's* regular circulation of magazines in New Hampshire is sufficient to support an assertion of jurisdiction in a libel action, Justice William Rehnquist wrote. "False statements of fact harm both the subject of the falsehood and the readers of the statement: New Hampshire may rightly employ its libel laws to discourage the deception of its citizens," the justice continued. The state may extend its concern to the injury that in-state libel causes to a nonresident as well, he added (*Keeton* v. *Hustler,* 1984).

The same day, the High Court ruled that California courts could assume jurisdiction in a case brought by a California resident against the authors of a story that was written and published in a newspaper in Florida but circulated in California. Shirley Jones sued Ian Calder and John South for an article they wrote and edited in Florida and that was then published in *National Enquirer*. The *Enquirer* has a national circulation of about five million and distributes about six hundred thousand copies each week in California. A trial court ruled that Jones could certainly sue the publishers of the *Enquirer* in California, but not the reporters. Requiring journalists to appear in remote jurisdictions to answer for the contents of articles upon which they worked could have a chilling impact upon the First Amendment rights of reporters and editors, the court said. But again a unanimous Supreme Court disagreed, with Justice Rehnquist noting that the article was about a California resident who works in California. Material for the article was drawn from California sources and the brunt of the harm to both the career and the personal reputation of the plaintiff will be suffered in California, he added. "An individual injured in California need not go to Florida to seek redress from persons who, though remaining in Florida, knowingly cause the injury in California," Rehnquist wrote. The justice said that the potential chill on protected First Amendment activity stemming from libel actions is already taken into account in the constitutional limitations on the substantive law governing such suits. "To reinforce those concerns at the jurisdictional level would be a form of double counting," he said (*Calder* v. *Jones,* 1984).

SUMMARY A libel suit must be started before the statute of limitations expires. Each state determines how long this period will be. In most states it is one, two, or three years. A libel suit started after the expiration of the statute of limitations will be dismissed.

TRADITIONAL LIBEL DEFENSES

The First Amendment provides defendants in libel suits considerable protection. The defendant in a lawsuit filed against a newspaper or other mass medium is in fact well defended by the constitutional requirements placed upon the plaintiff. But there were defenses for libel even before the ruling in *New York Times* v. *Sullivan.* These emerged through the common law and via statutes in many states. Truth, privileged communication, fair comment, consent, and right of reply all work to protect the libel defendant—no matter who he or she might be. The applicability of each of these defenses in a particular case is determined by the facts in the case—what the story is about, how the information was gained, and the manner in which it was published.

Truth

Traditionally, truth has been regarded as an important libel defense that completely protected defendants in lawsuits for defamation. To use this defense, the defendant was required to prove the truth of the libelous allegations he or she published. Truth is still a defense in a libel action, but it has lost much of its importance in light of recent rulings that require most libel plaintiff's to carry the burden of proving a defamatory allegation to be false when the story focuses on a matter of public concern. In those few instances when a private-person plaintiff sues for a libelous statement that does not focus on something of public concern and therefore does not have to show the falsity of the matter as a part of proving negligence, the libel defendant can escape liability in the case by showing that the defamatory matter is true. But the defendant carries the burden of proof; truth becomes a defense. The same rules apply to proving truth that apply to proving falsity, only they are reversed. The defendant must show that the allegations are substantially true. Extraneous errors will not destroy the defense. See pages 126–128 to refresh your memory on these matters.

Privileged Communications

Traditionally in the United States we value robust debate as a means of discovering those elusive truths that we continually pursue. The law takes pains to protect this debate, making sure that speakers are not unduly punished for speaking their minds. Article 1, Section 6, of the federal Constitution provides that members of the Congress are immune from suits based on their remarks on the floor of either house. This is called a privilege. The statement in question is referred to as a privileged communication.

Today, privilege attaches to a wide variety of communications and speakers. Anyone speaking in a legislative forum—congressmen and -women, senators, state representatives, city councilmembers, and so forth—enjoys this privilege. Even the statements of witnesses at legislative hearings are privileged. But the comments must be made in the legislative forum. The Supreme Court ruled in 1979 that while a speech by a senator on the floor of the Senate would be wholly immune from a libel action, newsletters and press releases about the speech issued by the senator's office would not be protected by the privilege. Only that speech which is "essential to the deliberations of the Senate" is protected, and neither newsletters to constituents nor press releases are parts of the deliberative process (*Hutchinson* v. *Proxmire,* 1979).

Similarly, the privilege attaches to communications made in judicial forums—courtrooms, grand jury rooms, and so forth. Judges, lawyers, witnesses, defendants, plaintiffs, and all other persons are protected so long as the remark is uttered during the official portions of the hearing or the trial. Finally, persons who work in the administrative and executive branches of government enjoy privilege as well. Presidents, mayors, governors, department heads—official communications or official statements by these kinds of persons are privileged. In 1959 in *Barr* v. *Mateo* the Supreme Court suggested that the privilege applies to any publication by government officials that is in line with the discharge of their official duty. This case involved a press release from a department head explaining why two federal employees had been fired. "A publicly expressed statement of the position of the agency head," the Court ruled, "announcing personnel action which he planned to take in reference to the charges so widely disseminated to the public was an appropriate exercise of the discretion which an officer of that rank must possess if the public service is to function effectively."

More recently the court of appeals in New York State ruled that a press release issued by an assistant attorney general concerning the investigation of possible fraudulent activities by fund raisers was protected from a lawsuit by privilege. The court said that since the attorney general as an executive official enjoys absolute privilege while exercising the functions of his office, the same privilege applies to his subordinates, who exercise delegated powers (*Gautsche* v. *New York,* 1979). The difference in the treatment of the assistant attorney general by the New York court and Senator Proxmire by the United States Supreme Court over essentially the same item—a press release—stems from the different roots of the privilege. Congressional privilege stems directly from the United States Constitution and is limited by the constitutional language. The privilege applied to the state attorney general stems from the common law. Also, the functions of the two offices are different. Senators are supposed to deliberate and make legislative policy. Reporting to the public on the results of an official investigation is one of the governmental functions of an attorney general.

The privilege just discussed is an **absolute privilege.** The speaker cannot be sued for defamation on the basis of such a remark. A similar kind of a privilege applies also to certain kinds of private communications. Discussions between an employer and an employee are privileged; the report of a credit rating is privileged; a personnel recommendation by an employer about an employee is privileged. These kinds of private communications remain privileged so long as they are not disseminated beyond the sphere of those who need to know.

Qualified Privilege

What is called **qualified privilege** goes far beyond the absolute immunity granted to speakers at public and official meetings and the conditional immunity granted to certain types of private communications. Under the qualified privilege an individual may report what happens at an official governmental proceeding or transmit the substance of an official government report or statement and remain immune from libel even if the publication of the material defames someone. This is how the privilege is outlined in the *Restatement of Torts (2d):*

> The publication of defamatory matter concerning another in a report of any official proceeding or any meeting open to the public which deals with matters of public concern is conditionally privileged if the report is accurate and complete, or a fair abridgement of what has occurred.

Actually, this definition of the privilege in the Restatement is a bit conservative, as courts continually extend the protection of qualified privilege to reports of more diverse kinds of government activity. This qualified privilege is sometimes called the privilege of the reporter, as opposed to the absolute immunity noted previously, which is often referred to as the privilege of the participant. The use of the term reporter signifies someone who reports on what has happened, as opposed to the journalistic meaning of the term, a newspaper or television reporter.

At the start it is important to note that this is a conditional privilege; that is, the privilege only works as a libel defense if certain conditions are met. First, the privilege only applies to reports of certain kinds of meetings, hearings, proceedings, reports, and statements. Second, the law requires that these reports be a fair and accurate or truthful summary of what took place at the meeting, or what was said in the report. In the past there was a third condition—that the report containing the defamatory charges was published or broadcast in order to inform the people, not simply to hurt the plaintiff. It is generally considered today that this third condition no longer applies; the defendant's motivation for publishing or broadcasting the material is irrelevant. (See *Shiavone* v. *Time,* 1983.)

The defendant bears the burden of proving that the privilege applies to the libelous material. The court will determine whether the particular occasion (meeting, proceeding, report) is privileged. The jury will determine whether the defendant's report of the occasion is a fair and accurate report. Let's first examine the kinds of occasions which courts have found to be covered by the privilege.

Quite obviously, the privilege applies to meetings of organizations such as Congress, state legislatures, city councils, county councils, and so forth. The privilege also applies to the reports of meetings of committees of such organizations, as well as to stories about petitions, complaints, and other communications received by these bodies. The only requirement that must be met with regard to this aspect of the privilege is that the official body, such as a city council, must officially receive the complaint or petition before the privilege applies. If the Citizens for Cleaner Streets bring to a city council meeting a petition charging the street superintendent with incompetence and various and sundry blunders in his job, publication of these charges is privileged as soon as the city council officially accepts the petition. Nothing has to be done with the document. It must merely be accepted.

The privilege likely applies to stories about the news conferences of members of a legislative body following a session, to stories about what was said during a closed meeting by the body, and to what was said during an informal gathering of legislators before or after the regular session. If what is said or what occurs during these kinds of events is of great public interest and there is a compelling public need to know, the privilege then likely applies. The privilege of the reporter also applies to actions that take place in judicial forums: testimony and depositions of witnesses, arguments of attorneys, pronouncements of judges, and so forth. Stories about trials, decisions, jury verdicts, court opinions, judicial orders and decrees, and grand jury indictments are all protected by the privilege.

Probably the most serious problem a reporter on the court beat has to face is what to do when a lawsuit is initially filed. Under our legal system a lawsuit is started when a person files a complaint with a court clerk and serves a summons on the defendant. The complaint is filled with charges, most of which are usually libelous. Can a reporter use that complaint as the basis for a story?

The states are divided on this question. In some states a complaint is not considered privileged until a judge takes some kind of action on the lawsuit. This action may only be the scheduling of an appearance by the litigants, or it may be more. But a judge must get involved in the matter before the complaint becomes a privileged document. In other states the complaint becomes privileged as soon as it has been filed with the court clerk and a summons has been issued (see *Cox* v. *Lee Enterprises,* 1986). It is important for you to determine which rule governs civil complaints in your state. The simplest way to do this is to look for opinions on this question in cases decided by your state high court.

Stories about those parts of the judicial process that are closed to public view are not protected by the privilege. Frequently, court sessions for juveniles and divorce proceedings are closed in order to further a public policy. The legislature or the courts feel obligated to discourage publicity about what occurs during such hearings. A few years ago the *New York Daily News* published a series of articles about a sensational divorce case, one in which the wife accused the husband of keeping a harem of women in a private plane that he used for business trips. When the husband sued the newspaper for libel, the *Daily News* argued that it had taken its report directly from court records and trial testimony.

In New York, however, divorce proceedings are closed to the public. The state's high court ruled that the legislature deemed it to be in the public interest to close divorce proceedings to public scrutiny (*Shiles* v. *News Syndicate Co.,* 1970):

> Since, then, such matrimonial actions were and are not proceedings which the public had the right to hear and see, it follows—and it has been consistently held—that the privilege generally accorded to reports of judicial proceedings is unavailable to reports of matrimonial actions.

Reports of the statements and proceedings conducted by mayors, department heads, and other persons in the administrative and executive branches of government are generally privileged. The best guideline is that the privilege is confined to stories about actions or statements that are official in nature, the kinds of things that are substantially "acts of state." By law, administrators are required to prepare certain reports and to hold certain hearings, and the privilege certainly covers stories on these activities. Although not required by law, other actions are unmistakably part of the job. Reports on these affairs are undoubtedly protected as well. The California Supreme Court, for example, ruled that a report on organized crime prepared for the state attorney general by a special commission was a privileged document once it was released to the press and public (*Kilgore* v. *Younger,* 1982). An Ohio court ruled that reports of health inspections of restaurants are privileged (*McCain* v. *KTVY, Inc.,* 1987). And a New York Supreme Court recently ruled that reports of investigations by an environmental agency are privileged also (*Quarcini* v. *Niagara Falls Gazette,* 1987). Even stories based on confidential government documents that focused on possible government misconduct were declared to be privileged under Massachusetts law (*Ingerere* v. *ABC,* 1984).

Reports of police activities also fall under the heading of executive actions. It is fairly well settled that a report that a person has been arrested and charged with a crime is privileged. Official statements made by police about an investigation are probably privileged in many instances. The United States Court of Appeals for the Second Circuit recently ruled that public statements made by the head of the New York City office of the Federal Bureau of Investigation about an FBI search of law offices in Brooklyn are privileged. The Cable News Network had quoted the FBI agent as describing the offices as the headquarters for a dangerous, left-wing group that sought to topple the United States government (*Foster* v. *Turner Broadcasting,* 1988). The United States Court of Appeals for the Third Circuit ruled that information obtained legally by *Time* magazine from FBI investigatory documents is also protected by a qualified privilege (*Medico* v. *Time,* 1981). Caution needs to be exercised here, however. The privilege surely does not apply to every statement made by every police officer on every topic. In reading between the lines of the few court rulings on these questions, the evident key in these cases is that the individual quoted is an official spokesperson for the department or agency, or the documents represent the work of the agency, not a single member of the agency or an individual's notes or personal investigatory files.

The privilege is not confined to those instances of reporting official government proceedings. The Washington Supreme Court recently ruled that the reporting of the charges on recall petitions is privileged (*Herron* v. *Tribune Pub. Co.,* 1987). An Idaho court has ruled that the privilege applied to a story about a meeting called by citizens to protest the actions of a judge. It clearly was not an official meeting, but concerned important public business, the conduct of a public official. The court said, "There is a general doctrine that what is said at a public meeting, at which any person of the community or communities involved might have attended and heard and seen for himself, is conditionally privileged for publication" (*Borg* v. *Boas,* 1956).

The *Restatement of Torts (2d)* says that reports of what occurs at meetings open to the public at which matters of public concern are discussed are privileged. Paul Ashley, libel authority and author of *Say It Safely* (1976), wrote that the privilege probably applies to a public meeting even though admission is charged, so long as everyone is free to pay the price. "By supplying them with information about public events," Ashley writes, "the publisher is acting as the 'eyes and ears' of people who did not attend."

In such a circumstance, the report of a public meeting, the key element undoubtedly is the subject of debate. Was it of public concern? Was it of limited public concern? Was it a purely private matter? Using the standard of public concern, we can look at some kinds of nonofficial public meetings and try to determine whether the privilege applies.

1. Meeting of local Rotary Club: probably of private concern; not privileged.
2. Meeting of board of directors of United Fund: of public concern; privileged.
3. Meetings of local bar association or medical society: of limited public concern; privileged.
4. Meeting of stockholders of General Motors Company: about private business and of private concern; not privileged.
5. Meeting of county Democratic party: of public concern; privileged.

At this point how far the privilege will extend in protecting nonofficial public meetings cannot be said. Traditionally each state handles this problem differently, and therefore you should seek guidance from local statutes and court decisions.

Neutral Reportage

The privilege has grown in another direction in some parts of the country with the development of what many libel authorities call the defense of **"neutral reportage."** One thing that must be remembered about neutral reportage is that it is by no means accepted as a legitimate defense in all states, or even in most states.

The neutral reportage privilege developed most directly from an interesting suit in New York State concerning the annual Audubon Society Christmas bird count. The *New York Times* printed charges made by an official of the Audubon Society that any scientist who argues that the continued use of the pesticide DDT has not taken a serious toll of bird life is "someone who is being paid to lie about it or is parroting something he knows little about." The implication was, of course, that certain scientists were being paid by the pesticide industry to lie about the impact of the chemicals on wildlife. The *Times* story included the names of several scientists given to the reporter by Robert Arbib, the official at the Audubon Society. Some of these scientists sued for libel, but the Court of Appeals for the Second Circuit ruled the story published by the *Times* containing the libelous charges was privileged. The court ruled this way even though reporter John Devlin might have believed the charges made by Arbib were false when he published them. The court called the privilege "neutral reportage" and described it in the following manner (*Edwards* v. *National Audubon Society*, 1977):

> When a responsible prominent organization like the National Audubon Society makes serious charges against a public figure, the First Amendment protects the accurate and disinterested reporting of those charges, regardless of the reporter's private views regarding their validity. What is newsworthy about such accusations is that they were made. . . . The public interest in being fully informed about controversies that often rage around sensitive issues demands that the press be afforded the freedom to report such charges without assuming responsibility for them. We must provide immunity from defamation where the journalist believes, reasonably and in good faith, that his report accurately conveys the charges made.

In simple terms the neutral reportage rule may be stated this way: publication of an accurate account of information about a public figure from a reliable source by a reporter who doubts the truth of the assertions is still privileged. When charges are made by responsible agencies or persons, the public should hear these charges, even when the journalist doubts their veracity. It is newsworthy that the charges have been made; that fact alone might add materially to the public debate on the issue.

As applied in a handful of courts since the *Edwards* case the neutral reportage privilege seems to have four distinct requirements:

1. The story must be newsworthy; it must be of public interest.
2. The individual who has been libeled must be a public figure.
3. The reporter must accurately report the libelous charges *and* present all sides of the controversy.
4. The publication must play the role of an impartial transmitter of information and not espouse the libelous charges.

A United States district court recently denied the application of the neutral reportage privilege in a libel suit because the target of the charges was not a public figure (*Dresbach* v. *Doubleday*, 1982). The United States Court of Appeals for the Second Circuit ruled the neutral reportage inapplicable in a case in which the defendant publication not only inaccurately reported the charges against the public figure, but also vigorously supported these charges in a personal attack upon the plaintiff. Obviously, the reportage ceased to be neutral (*Cianci* v. *New Times*, 1980).

Neutral reportage remains a limited privilege. In 1985, for example, the South Dakota Supreme Court rejected neutral reportage as a defense (*Janklow* v. *Viking Press*, 1985). Other courts have taken similar action (see *Dickey* v. *CBS*, 1978; *Postill* v. *Booth Newspapers*, 1982; and *Hellman* v. *McCarthy*, 1984). Other courts have accepted it (see, for example, *Orr* v. *Lynch*, 1978; *Krauss* v. *Champaign News Gazette*, 1978; *Wade* v. *Stocks*, 1981; *El Amin* v. *Miami Herald*, 1983; and *Palmer* v. *Seminole*, 1983). The Supreme Court of the United States will probably be asked to decide upon the viability of the defense. Until such a definitive ruling, neutral reportage remains a creative effort in a few jurisdictions to expand the range of permissible reporting.

Abuse of Privilege

Whether qualified privilege applies to a particular story is only part of the problem. The privilege can also be destroyed if the story in question is not a fair and accurate or true report of what took place. *Fair* means balanced. If at a public meeting speakers both attack and defend John Smith, the story should reflect both the attack and the defense. A story that focuses just on the charges is not fair, and the privilege will have been abused. Similarly, if the story concerns a continuing kind of an affair—a legislative hearing, a trial, and so forth—in which testimony is given for several days, the press is obligated to publish stories about each day's events if the privilege is to be used. There has to be balance. If a story about a civil suit based upon the charges listed in the complaint is prepared, it is important to get the defendant's response as well. Balance is the key.

An accurate or true report means just that; it should honestly reflect what took place or what was said. An attorney named Frank Marcone was indicted in Pennsylvania for allegedly giving money to other persons to invest in drug trafficking, such as buying marijuana. The indictment was later dismissed. *Penthouse* magazine published a story in which it said that Marcone had "contributed down payments of up to twenty five thousand dollars on grass transactions. Charges against him were dropped because he cooperated with further investigations." *Penthouse* argued this was a privileged story, since it relied upon the grand jury indictment, a privileged document. But an indictment is an allegation or charge that someone has done something. *Penthouse* reported that Marcone had in fact provided money for drug purchases. The story was not a fair and accurate report of the indictment. The magazine could have said Marcone had been indicted for providing money to purchase drugs or that there were allegations that he had provided money to purchase drugs. The story as published went beyond the official document (*Marcone* v. *Penthouse,* 1982). The Appellate Division of the New York Supreme Court recently handed down a similar ruling in a case involving television station WROC. The station reported that the plaintiff, Gerald Dibble, had been indicted on charges of fraud, embezzlement, and securities violations, when in fact he had been indicated on a single count of second degree grand larceny. This was not an accurate report of the charges, the court said (*Dibble* v. *WROC-TV,* 1988).

Small errors in the story will not destroy the privilege. When a California newspaper reported on a tax fraud trial it stated that the defendant in the case had failed to report $436,000 in taxable income. Actually, the plaintiff's gross income, not his taxable income, was $436,000. The California Court of Appeals ruled that this small error did not destroy the privilege (*Jennings* v. *Telegram-Tribune,* 1985). Attorney F. Lee Bailey wrote in a book that Lawrence D. Murray, a former San Francisco assistant district attorney, was arrested for driving under the influence of alcohol and for assault and battery of police officers. In fact Murray was arrested for being intoxicated in a public place and resisting arrest. "The slight inaccuracy in the details will not prevent a judgment for the defendant," a federal judge ruled, "if the inaccuracy does not change the complexion of the affair so as to affect the reader of the article differently than the actual truth would." The error in Bailey's book was a small one (*Murray* v. *Bailey,* 1985).

The fact finder will determine whether or not the defendant has fairly summarized the report or the testimony. In 1983 Brown and Williamson, a cigarette manufacturer, sued Chicago broadcast journalist Walter Jacobson for libel when he attacked the company in a program on WBBM-TV. Jacobson used as the foundation of his story a Federal Trade Commission report on the tobacco industry. The FTC document focuses upon a report from a market-research firm about the development of an advertising strategy that portrays smoking cigarettes as a kind of illicit pleasure in an effort to make smoking more attractive to young smokers. Brown and Williamson rejected this illicit pleasures strategy, but the FTC concluded that the company adopted "many of the ideas contained in this report in the development of a Viceroy advertising campaign." A Brown and Williamson internal report called the "Viceroy

Strategy" is cited by the FTC as evidence. The commission, quoting from the Brown and Williamson Viceroy report, describes the company's advertising strategies. The "Viceroy Strategy" report did not refer to young smokers or "starters," but did discuss an advertising campaign featuring "young adults in situations that the vast majority of young people would probably experience and in situations demonstrating adherence to a 'free and easy, hedonistic lifestyle.' " Jacobson reported that Brown and Williamson used an advertising strategy that tried to hook children on cigarettes, "to addict children to poison," basing his statements on the FTC report. The United States Court of Appeals for the Seventh Circuit ruled that a jury should decide whether the television journalist's comments were a fair and accurate summary of the FTC report (*Brown and Williamson v. Jacobson and CBS*, 1983). In the autumn of 1985, a jury in Chicago ruled that Jacobson's comments were not an accurate summary of the report and awarded the cigarette maker more than five million dollars in damages. An appellate court ultimately reduced the damage award to three million dollars (*Brown and Williamson v. Jacobson*, 1987).

The story should also be in the form of a report. If defendants fail to make it clear that they are reporting something that was said at a public meeting or repeating something that is contained in the public record, the privilege may be lost. The law says the reader should be aware that the story is a report of what happened at a public meeting or at an official hearing or is taken from the official record. These facts should be noted in the lead and in the headline if possible, as noted in the following example.

At City Council Session
MAYOR BLASTS CONTRACTOR WITH CHARGES OF FRAUD

Mayor John Smith during a city council meeting today charged the Acme Construction Company with fraudulent dealings.

The United States Court of Appeals for the District of Columbia ruled that qualified privilege did not apply to a magazine summary of statements contained in an official report from the National Transportation Safety Board. The report is an official record; it is clearly covered by the reporter's privilege. But the statements in the magazine gave readers no clue that they were in fact a summary of an official document. "The challenged [defamatory] assertion is simply offered as historical fact without any particular indication of its source," the court said. The reader was left with the impression that the author of the article reached the conclusion contained in the defamatory allegations based upon his own research (*Dameron v. Washingtonian*, 1985).

Finally, the privilege protects only that part of a story based on an official proceeding or a public record or report. Anything added to the story from outside these sources will not be protected by the qualified privilege.

The privilege of the reporter is a very important defense and protects the press in a large percentage of the stories that are printed or telecast. Privilege is much easier to use than truth, since all the defendant must prove is that the event, meeting, or report was in fact a privileged occasion and the story was a fair and true report.

SUMMARY

The publication of defamatory material in a report of a public meeting, legislative proceeding, or legal proceeding or in a story that reflects the content of an official government report is conditionally privileged. The privilege extends to the meetings of all public bodies, to all aspects of the legal process, to reports and statements issued by members of the executive branch of government, and even to nonofficial meetings of the public in which matters of public concern are discussed. Such reports cannot be the basis for a successful libel suit as long as the report presents a fair (balanced) and accurate (truthful) account of what took place at the meeting or what is contained in the record.

OPINION AND FAIR COMMENT

The privilege of fair comment, which permits the publication or broadcast of defamatory opinions on matters of public interest, has been a part of the law of libel for several hundred years. Like the privilege of the reporter noted above, it is a conditional privilege. Opinion statements, supported by facts, about matters of public concern, are protected by this privilege. If someone says that the mayor is a fink because he reduced the budget for parks and recreation, that's fine; that's a fair comment.

But the United States Supreme Court ruling in *Gertz* v. *Welch* in 1974 contained a short paragraph that has seriously confused the law of libel (and the fair comment defense) as it relates to opinion. Justice Powell noted in *Gertz:*

> We begin with the common ground. Under the First Amendment there is no such thing as a false idea. However pernicious an opinion may seem, we depend for its correction not on the conscience of judges and juries, but on the competition of other ideas.

It appears by this statement that the High Court was granting absolute First Amendment protection to statements of opinion. As such, this protection goes considerably beyond the traditional conditional protection offered to opinion through the defense of fair comment. But is that what the Supreme Court did? We probably don't yet know. "It remains to be determined whether the common-law predecessor of the constitutional privilege for opinions, the fair comment, has become obsolete," wrote Jeffrey E. Thomas in the *California*

Law Review in 1986. The courts seem split on the question, with some saying yes, fair comment is obsolete (*Kotlikoff* v. *Community News,* 1982) and others saying no, the defense is still workable (*Cianci* v. *New Times Publishing Co.,* 1980).

Does it really matter whether the courts apply the First Amendment privilege as defined by Justice Powell in *Gertz* or the common law defense of fair comment? Ostensibly yes, because fair comment is a conditional, common law privilege, and the First Amendment privilege appears to be without condition. Looking at the law from this point of view there appears to be two critical differences between the constitutional privilege and fair comment. To apply fair comment, the opinion must be focused upon a subject of public interest. Also, if the fair comment defense is to work, the opinion must be accompanied by factual support. On its face, the constitutional privilege seems to be without such conditions. But in practice it is doubtful that that is the case. The Supreme Court, for example, has shaped a good share of the law of libel around the notion of expanded protection for material about public persons and stories about public concerns. It seems doubtful such thinking would be abandoned and the First Amendment privilege for statements of opinion be applied to any and all opinion, regardless of the focus of the comments. Additionally, courts applying the First Amendment opinion privilege have already been forced to cope with the problem of opinion statements that suggest untruthful factual allegations. And in those instances where a statement of opinion implies the existence of undisclosed defamatory facts, the opinion statement may be treated as a statement of fact. So the question of whether or not facts exist to support an opinion cannot be ignored, even if the First Amendment privilege is applied as opposed to the common law fair comment defense. At this point then, whether or not the defense of fair comment is obsolete or not is probably unimportant. Persons working in the mass media should be comforted to know that some courts have found absolute protection for statements of opinion based on Justice Powell's language in *Gertz*. But there is always the possibility that a state court might regard Powell's language as compelling dicta, but nothing more, and insist that the traditional conditions of the fair comment defense be met before the opinion statement is protected. We will first examine the condition that must be met in applying either the First Amendment privilege or the common law defense—that the defamation must be in the form of an opinion. Then we will look briefly at the two additional conditions that clearly attach to the fair comment defense, and will likely be considered in applying the constitutional privilege: the public interest requirement and the existence of facts needed to support the opinion.

Statement of Opinion

Both the First Amendment privilege and the defense of fair comment protect statements of opinion, regardless of how outrageous or preposterous the statement may be. As a federal court once noted, an opinion can be good, bad, or indifferent, immature, premature, or ill-founded. A newspaper in Alaska once called the late Drew Pearson "the garbage man of the Fourth Estate." The court permitted this comment (*Pearson* v. *Fairbanks Publishing Co.,* 1966). Decades ago the *Des Moines Leader* published this review of a vocal trio, the Cherry Sisters (*Cherry* v. *Des Moines Leader,* 1901):

> Effie is an old jade of fifty summers, Jessie is a frisky filly of forty, and Addie, the flower of the family, a capering monstrosity of thirty-five. Their long skinny arms, equipped with talons at the extremities, swung mechanically, and anon waved frantically at the suffering audience. The mouths of their rancid features opened like caverns, and sounds like the wailing of damned souls issued therefrom. They pranced around the stage with a motion that suggested a cross between the danse du'ventre and fox trot—strange creatures with painted faces and hideous mien. Effie is spavined, Addie is stringhalt, and Jessie, the only one who showed her stockings, has legs with calves as classic in their outlines as the curves of a broom handle.

This review was considered fair comment.

Wealthy real estate developer Donald Trump sued the *Chicago Tribune* when its architecture critic called Trump's plan to build a 150-story building in New York City a "Guinness Book of World's Records architecture proposal." Paul Gapp said the 150-story building "would be one of the silliest things anyone could inflict on New York or any other city" and called Trump's suggestion that his building would balance the World Trade Center located on the other side of Manhattan "eyewash." A United States district court said the prose was a highly subjective personal judgment and consequently protected opinion (*Trump* v. *Chicago Tribune,* 1985).

The *Barre* (Vt.) *Times Argus* was sued for libel when it quoted one political candidate who called his opponent "a horse's ass, a jerk, an idiot and paranoid." The Vermont Supreme Court ruled that the words may be insulting, abusive, unpleasant, and objectionable, but they are opinions protected by the First Amendment (*Blovin* v. *Anton,* 1981).

The editor in chief of *El Diario-La Prensa* in New York City recently compared actions of the mayor of Elizabeth, New Jersey, to those of Adolph Hitler and Fidel Castro and the United States Court of Appeals for the Third Circuit called this protected expression (*Dunn* v. *Gannett New York,* 1987). An editorial on a Chicago television station, reporting on something called a "metabolic theory of cancer treatment," referred to the plaintiff chiropractor as part of an "international network of medical quackery" whose patients were victims of "cancer con artists" and "unscrupulous charlatans." The United States district court called this protected opinion (*Kirk* v. *CBS,* 1987). And a New York Supreme Court referred to a statement made by reporter Les Payne that civil rights leader Roy Innis had "put out a contract on me" as rhetorical hyperbole, clearly an exaggerated opinion that no one would mistake for fact (*Innis* v. *Payne,* 1985). But the defamation—no matter how intemperate— must be in the form of an opinion. What is the difference between fact and opinion? This is a question that is more difficult to answer than it first appears.

In fact, American courts have spent considerable time in the past ten years trying to develop a test or tests to try to distinguish between statements of opinion and statements of fact.

Some courts have attempted to use a simple test to try to distinguish between fact and opinion: Can the statement be proved? This test works well for some kinds of statements. John robbed a bank—obviously a statement of fact because it can be proved. Or John is ugly—a statement of opinion because it cannot be proved. But what about the statement John is a fascist? What does this mean? Such words do not easily lend themselves to proof (see *Buckley v. Littell,* 1976). So courts have developed other, more complex tests to try to distinguish between fact and opinion.

By early 1986 a test developed by Judge Starr of the United States Court of Appeals for the District of Columbia seemed to be gaining use in other federal courts. The test was developed by Starr in a 1984 case called *Ollman v. Evans* in which a professor of political science sued columnists Rowland Evans and Robert Novak for calling him a Marxist and speculating that his appointment as chairman of the department of politics and government at the University of Maryland might lead to the use of the classroom for indoctrination, rather than education.

Starr outlined four criteria to be used to determine whether the defamatory statements were protected opinion or statements of fact:

1. What is the common usage or meaning of the language? What do the words mean in their ordinary usage? Do the words have sufficiently specific meaning to convey facts?

2. To what degree are the statements verifiable? Can they be proved? Some statements are simply incapable of being judged true or false and reflect opinions about personal taste, aesthetic judgments, or religious belief.

3. What is the specific context in which the statement occurs? "The degree to which a statement is laden with factual content or can be read to imply facts depends upon the article or column, taken as a whole, of which the statement is a part," Starr wrote. The language of an entire column may signal, for example, that a single statement that may appear factual when standing alone, is actually a statement of opinion.

4. The broader social and journalistic contexts into which the language falls should also be considered. "Some types of writing or speech by custom or convention signal to readers or listeners that what is being read or heard is likely to be opinion, not fact," Starr wrote. Rhetoric is exaggerated in labor disputes. Political debate is usually exaggerated as well. And the world of sports provokes opinions from

many persons about the relative merits of individual performers. The journalistic context should also be considered. Readers and viewers expect to find factual statements in the news columns and in broadcast news reports. On the other hand, they expect to find opinions in editorials, editorial columns, reviews, and commentary.

Applying his test to the facts in *Ollman,* Judge Starr ruled that the objectionable material was opinion, not fact. The statements were contained in an editorial column on the "Op-Ed" page of the newspaper. Readers don't consider such material factual hard news. In the column itself the authors made it clear they were not setting forth specific conclusions, but simply raising questions. The cautionary language suggests that the statements should be treated as opinion. Words like *Marxist* and *political activist* are simply not words that have specific factual meaning today, Starr said (*Ollman* v. *Evans,* 1984).

This test has been criticized by some as being as subjective as the simple true/false test outlined on the previous page. But other courts have started to use the Ollman test. In March of 1985 the United States Court of Appeals for the Second Circuit used parts of the test to determine whether comments made about a restaurant called Mr. Chow were fact or opinion. The reviewer complained that the sweet-and-sour pork contained more dough than meat, that the rice was soaking in oil, that the pancakes were the thickness of a finger, and that other things weren't right as well. Looking at the context of the statements, the court noted that restaurant reviews are well-recognized as vehicles for opinion, not facts. The words used suggest opinion as well—the fried rice was too oily or the meat was too doughy. Finally, only one of the objectionable statements properly lent itself to a test of truth or falsity. The matter of the amount of oil in which rice should be fried or the thickness of pancakes or the amount of dough in sweet-and-sour pork are questions of personal taste, the court said. But the statement that the Peking Duck was made up of only one dish instead of the traditional three does lend itself to proof (*Mr. Chow* v. *Ste. Jour. Azur S.A.,* 1985).

The United States Court of Appeals for the Eighth Circuit applied the *Ollman* test in *Janklow* v. *Newsweek,* a suit brought by William Janklow against the magazine for suggesting that the former South Dakota attorney general had prosecuted Sioux activist Dennis Banks to gain revenge because of a personal feud. The trial court ruled that the comments were opinion, but the court of appeals overturned this decision. But upon a motion by *Newsweek,* the court of appeals agreed to rehear the case en banc and by a 7–3 vote ruled that the language in the magazine article was opinion, not statements of fact. The defamatory allegations lacked the precision of facts and were not really verifiable. The words could be read in several plausible ways. While the report was in the news columns of the weekly news magazine, the court noted that magazines like *Newsweek* and *Time* have a tradition of more colorful or feisty language than a daily newspaper. This freer style should signal to readers that opinion should be expected. Finally, the general context of the remarks was the discussion of how well or how badly government officials carry out their duties, a subject that lies at the heart of the First Amendment. Robust and vigorous debate must be expected in this arena, the court said (*Janklow* v. *Newsweek,* 1986). Other courts have tried to use different tests to determine what is fact and what is opinion. In 1987, for example, the United States Court of Appeals for the First Circuit used a variation of the *Ollman* test to reach the conclusion that a headline in the Block Island (Rhode Island) Times was opinion, not a statement of fact. The newspaper carried a first-person account by one of its staff recounting what had happened when he and his wife had tried to take advantage of an offer of a lobster dinner if they would look at a time-sharing condominium. When the writer refused to respond to the sales pitch, the dinner offer was cancelled. The article was negative but clearly not inaccurate. The headline on the page-one story was "Selling Time-sharing on the Street," but when the story was jumped inside, the one word headline "Scam" was used to identify the story. The condo owner sued for that word, claiming it accused him of something illegal. The court said there was no precise meaning for the word scam. The fact that X is a scam can't be proved or disproved. The story was written in the first person, something that should alert readers that it was an opinion piece. Finally, the issue of selling the condos had been controversial in the region for some time; the social context of the story carried a strong public interest (*McCabe* v. *Rattiner,* 1987).

The *Ollman* test is surely not the only way to determine whether something is opinion or fact. Other judges have generated, and will continue to generate, their own criteria. A state supreme court could, for example, generate its own guidelines that would bind courts in that state. Has the supreme court in your state done that already?

Nevertheless, most tests will look something like the *Ollman* test and consider the words themselves, the ability to verify the statements, and probably the context of the remarks.

Legitimate Public Interest

Under the defense of fair comment, the focus of the defamatory opinion statement must be something of legitimate public interest. The courts will probably seek a similar—if perhaps broader—standard in applying the constitutional privilege. The courts have granted a wide range of topics as fair game for comment. Educational, charitable, and religious institutions are eligible for comment, as are quasi-public organizations such as bar associations, medical societies, and other professional groups. Manufacturers who place products on the market must expect criticism; businesses that cater to the public, such as restaurants, theaters, and galleries, are subject to the same treatment. Any solicitation for public support, such as an advertisement, is fair game, as are artistic and creative efforts such as movies, plays, operas, books, paintings, recitals, comic strips, and television and radio programs. The work of journalists and broadcasters may be commented upon. The performances of those who seek to entertain the public—actors, musicians, athletes, and the like—are also considered legitimate targets for fair comment. In the 1930s a football coach sued a newspaper for its criticism of his team and his coaching abilities. The court found little sympathy for the plaintiff (*Hoeppner* v. *Dunkirk Printing Co., 1930*):

> When the plaintiff assumed the position of . . . coach to the football team of the Dunkirk High School, he was no exception to the habits and customs which have become a part of the game. His work and the play of his team were matters of keen public interest; victories would be heralded, defeats condemned. The same enthusiasm which welcomed the home-coming of the Roman conqueror now finds expression in the plaudits of the bleachers and the grandstand. The conquered now appear not in chains, but what may be far worse, amidst ridicule and derision—the boos of the crowd.

More recently, the Illinois Court of Appeals ruled that when the chairman of a university department described the scholarship of one of the faculty members in the department as "neither the quantity nor the quality of . . . work [that] justifies a grant of tenure" it was a fair comment. It was an opinion on the man's public work. "Once published material is placed into the stream of ideas and it cannot be defamation when that material is critiqued, be it by a reviewer or a superior" (*Byars* v. *Kolodziej,* 1977). A broad range of subjects, then, come under the purview of the privilege.

If a statement of opinion is focused on an individual, the courts will generally require that the comment deal with the public rather than private aspects of the individual's life. That is, while Elvis Presley's performances may have been legitimate targets of criticism, his private life was not. Similarly, while a book might be the fair subject even of scathing critical analysis, fair comment is no license to undertake scathing criticism of the author or the author's life.

Factual Basis

The basis for the defense of fair comment, and for the constitutional privilege as well for that matter, is the notion that both our democratic system of government and our culture are enhanced by the free exchange of ideas and opinions. Almost two hundred years ago Great Britain's Lord Ellenborough wrote that "Liberty of criticism must be allowed, or we should have neither purity of taste nor of morals. Fair discussion is essentially necessary to the truth of history and the advancement of science" (*Tabart* v. *Tipper,* 1808). It is on this rationale that the law gives fairly free sway to those who choose to express their opinions about a wide range of topics.

Those who read or hear the opinions of others certainly have the right to express their own opinions on the topic. But unless they know the factual basis for these opinions of others, readers and listeners cannot really develop their own thoughts on the topic. To wit: the president of the Better Government Association says that the mayor has done a lousy job during his first term in office. I have a right to make up my own mind on that matter, to form my own opinion. So I need the factual basis for the opinion expressed by the mayor's critic. Or: a film critic calls Ron Howard's latest movie the worst film of the year. Why? Give me an explanation that will allow me to make up my own mind. For this reason the defense of fair comment has been premised for several centuries upon the condition of factual support for opinion statements.

Under fair comment the facts may be outlined in the article or broadcast that contains the opinion. For example

> In 1986 Mayor Robert Allen bought six road graders for the city, none of which were needed or used. Two years later he spent five hundred thousand dollars of the people's money upon an auditorium which stands vacant 350 nights a year. Last year he sent four of his staff to Europe to study how mass transit is operated there, and three of the cities his staff visited have no mass transit system. Mayor Allen has been squandering taxpayers' money for too long; he is wasteful and pays little heed to need for fiscal caution.

The opinion—that Allen has been squandering taxpayers' money—was supported by the factual statements in the first part of the story.

But the facts do not have to be explicitly outlined so long as both parties to the communication—the writer and the readers, for example—know the facts or can assume their existence. The *Wilmington* (Del.) *News-Journal,* in an editorial about a local public official who had just pled guilty to a charge of official misconduct, added this sentence: "Other men in quite recent local memory abused their offices and forfeited their right to them: former County Director Melvin A. Slawik. . . ." Slawik had pled guilty three years earlier to a charge of obstruction of justice. He sued the newspaper for libel, but the Delaware Supreme Court ruled the phrase "abused their offices" was an opinion protected by fair comment. What about facts to support the opinion? The court ruled that since Slawik's departure from office had received intensive publicity when it occurred, the facts upon which the newspaper's opinion were based were well known in the community (*Slawik* v. *News-Journal,* 1981).

To use the defense of fair comment successfully then, the factual basis for the opinion must be disclosed with the opinion, or must be generally known to the audience of the defamatory communication.

No such condition is apparent in applying the constitutional privilege as enunciated in *Gertz.* Justice Powell simply said that there was no such thing as a false idea; that pernicious opinions should be corrected by other opinions, not judges and juries. But in fact, the way in which the privilege has been applied by the courts and interpreted by the American Law Institute, (the national keeper of tort law via the highly influential *Restatement of Torts 2d.*), seems to belie this assumption. It appears that in order for the privilege to be successfully applied a factual basis supporting the opinion must be disclosed unless it is generally known by the audience.

In applying the constitutional privilege, courts have described two kinds of opinion statements—pure opinion statements and what are called mixed opinion/fact statements. In the commentary of the most recent *Restatement of Torts* (see section 566, comment b), a pure opinion statement is defined as one in which the opinion is based on a set of generally known facts, or facts fully disclosed by the speaker or publisher. Such statements are absolutely protected. In a mixed opinion/fact situation, the opinion appears to be based on undisclosed facts. The existence of the undisclosed facts may lead the reader or viewer to a negative and possibly defamatory view of the subject of the commentary. Let's look at two examples of this latter situation, the first hypothetical, the second from real life.

Imagine you read this paragraph in an editorial in your newspaper:

> The chief of police is a disgrace and should be fired. The way he treats his wife is shameful. If he was an average citizen he would have been put in jail long ago.

The words in the paragraph are opinion statements; the chief is a disgrace, he should be fired, he treats his wife shamefully. As such they are protected. But what do you think the chief has done to deserve this attack? Does he beat his wife? Does he refuse to take care of her? Did he try to hit her with his police car? We don't know why the editorial writer thinks the chief is a disgrace and should be fired. The factual scenarios each of us may conjure up in our own minds might be far worse than what has really taken place. The negative opinion statements in the paragraph are protected by the First Amendment. But the factual conclusions we reach in our own mind about the chief, because the true facts have not been stated, harm the reputation as well, and may be the basis for a successful libel suit. These are not protected by the First Amendment.

Here is a real-life example. In 1980 Paul Healy, a physician and president of the Pawtucket (Rhode Island) YMCA, was chairing a meeting of the board of directors of the organization. There was a protest taking place about four hundred yards away from the building in which the meeting was being held; some individuals were angry that two YMCA employees had been forced to resign or were fired. During the closed meeting one of the protesters collapsed. Dr. Healy was told what had happened. Healy asked if he could be of assistance, but was told that two persons were already giving the victim CPR and a medical aid unit was on its way. So the meeting went on. The protester subsequently died.

The story was heavily publicized. The newspaper reported that one of the protesters had collapsed, that Dr. Healy was told of the problem, and that he continued to chair the board meeting. The newspaper stories quoted both a relative of the victim and another protester as being critical of Dr. Healy for not helping the victim. The critical comments were defamatory but were clearly opinion statements, and as such protected. But the Rhode Island Supreme Court refused to grant the defendant's motion for dismissal because the newspaper had failed to disclose a critical fact in he story—that Dr. Healy had asked if he could help, but was told he was not needed (*Healy* v. *New England Newspapers, Inc.,* 1987).

Imagine that you read in the newspaper a criticism by a protester of a physician who, despite being only four hundred yards away, does not help another protester who has collapsed. What is your opinion of the doctor? Now read the same criticism, but add this fact: the doctor asked if he could help, but was told he was not needed. Your opinion of the doctor would undoubtedly be different, more positive. The difference in the two instances—the undisclosed fact—is what turns pure privileged opinion into mixed unprivileged opinion and fact.

Many of you probably think this is a lot of legal mumbo jumbo, and maybe it is. What is important is the bottom line. In attempting to apply either the defense of fair comment, or in arguing that opinion statements are protected by the First Amendment, courts are going to look for facts to support those opinions. Without a factual basis either disclosed along with the opinion, or generally known, the court will disallow the fair comment defense. If the facts are not disclosed or generally known, a court will likely rule that the existence of these undisclosed facts creates a negative and defamatory impression about the plaintiff, and while the opinion statements might be privileged, this defamatory impression is not.

SUMMARY

Both the defense of fair comment and the First Amendment privilege protect statements of opinion in a libel action. The defense of fair comment is a conditional privilege that is hundreds of years old. The First Amendment privilege stems from a comment made by Justice Lewis Powell in a 1974 case called *Gertz* v. *Welch* that there is no such thing as a false idea; that pernicious opinions need to be corrected by other opinions, not by the law. There is a serious question whether the fair comment defense has been completely supplanted by the constitutional privilege. Regardless, similar conditions appear to attach to both. The libelous statement must be an opinion, not a statement of fact. Courts have developed tests to try to distinguish between the two categories of words. Usually these tests involve considering the meaning of the specific words, whether or not the assertions are subject to proof, the journalistic context of the statement, and the social, political, or cultural setting that give rise to the defamatory comment. The fair comment defense only works when the opinion statements focus upon something of legitimate public interest. It is likely, but not yet clear, that courts will insist that opinion statements privileged by the First Amendment focus as well on a matter of public concern. In addition, under both fair comment and the First Amendment, the factual basis of opinion statements should be disclosed with the opinion, or generally known by the audience.

CONSENT

There are two additional libel defenses. Both defenses have been used on occasion to successfully ward off a libel suit, but their foundations are tenuous. They have been accepted in some courts and rejected in other courts. Reliance upon either of them as the only defense is therefore not advised. However, both make excellent backup defenses, to be used with privilege or fair comment. The two defenses are **consent** and **right of reply.**

As one authority notes, an otherwise actionable defamation may be privileged if the plaintiff consented to its publication. Imagine that Frank Jones, a reporter for the *River City Sentinel,* hears rumors that John Smith is a leader of organized crime. Jones visits Smith and tells him that he has heard these rumors. Then Jones asks Smith if he cares if the rumors are published in the newspaper. Smith says it is OK with him, and Jones writes and publishes the story. In this instance Smith consented to publication of the defamation.

Now this event is not too likely to happen, is it? Cases of consent are extremely rare. Courts insist that the plaintiff either know or have a good reason to know the full extent of the defamatory statement in advance of its publication before consent can be said to exist.

At least one authority (Phelps and Hamilton) has suggested that while the kind of direct consent just noted is difficult to obtain, indirect consent is a viable defense. Indirect consent means that individuals were informed of the defamatory charges against them and were asked to comment upon the charges. The logic behind this defense is that if the newspaper publishes the response to the charges, it must publish the charges as well. For example, let us look at Smith and Jones again. Frank Jones tells John Smith that the police have called Smith "a big-time gangster." Jones says he is going to print the charge and then asks Smith, "Would you care to comment on the charge?" Smith denies the charge and claims that he is a legitimate businessman. He calls the man who made the charge a liar. Again, the logic of the defense suggests that if Smith's denial is printed, the charge that he denies must also be printed.

This reasoning may be logical, but few courts have accepted it. On record are one or two cases in which this kind of indirect consent by itself worked to defeat a libel suit (*Pulverman* v. *A. S. Abell Co.,* 1956). A very imaginative judge is needed to accept these arguments.

This does not mean, however, that it is not good policy to get a comment from the defamed party before the story is published. The facts may be wrong, and the subject of the story can then point out errors and save the newspaper from a suit. Even if the story is correct, the reporter's attempt to get both sides of the story, to discover the truth, will impress a jury if a suit does result. The reporter's efforts will demonstrate that there was no malice in printing the story, that the reporter honestly sought the truth, and that the plaintiff was given a chance to explain the charges. This policy is far more effective than giving the plaintiff the chance to reply after having been defamed. At that point, the offer looks like an afterthought. Similarly, even if the subject of the story cannot be reached, it is good policy for the journalist to tell readers that an effort was made to contact the person or that the person refused to comment. A reporter can have no worse experience than to testify in a libel suit that he or she made no attempt to contact the plaintiff before printing the story. "You mean you didn't even try to find out from the plaintiff whether the charges were true or not? You didn't have the decency to make a simple phone call?" the plaintiff's attorney will ask as the jury sits up attentively.

Indirect consent can help in a defense, but it is rare indeed for it to defeat a libel suit when standing by itself. As with other defenses, publication of materials for malicious reasons, and not for public enlightenment, can invalidate the protection.

RIGHT OF REPLY

Right of reply is a better defense than consent, is used more often, and is somewhat more substantial. The basis of right of reply is simple: The one who has been libeled may answer in kind. John Smith calls Steve Wilson a cheat, a fraud, and a common thief. Wilson has the right to answer Smith in kind. He can defame Smith in response.

The right of reply is based on the broader concept of self-defense; in fact, it is often referred to as *the* self-defense. As in self-defense, right of reply does have limitations. If a woman walks down the street and someone begins to pepper her with a peashooter, she has the right to stop her assailant, to protect herself. She does not have the right to pull out a .44-magnum pistol and pump three or four slugs into her attacker. Her defense then far exceeds the threat of the original attack. The same is true in a libel case. If a woman has been defamed, she may respond in kind. She may defame her attacker, but her reply cannot exceed the provocation; she cannot hit back harder than she was hit.

In a famous lawsuit two American journalists assailed one another in print. Newsman Quentin Reynolds suggested that columnist Westbrook Pegler had once called a third journalist, Heywood Broun, a liar. This bothered Broun, Reynolds wrote, to the extent that he could not sleep. Broun became ill and finally died. Pegler was incensed by this comment, claiming it charged him with moral homicide. So he attacked Reynolds, calling him sloppy, a sycophant, a coward, a slob, and a four-flusher. Pegler accused Reynolds of public nudism, of being a war profiteer, and of being an absentee war correspondent. Pegler also attacked the deceased Broun, calling him a liar and someone who made his living by controversy.

In the libel suit that followed, Pegler raised the defense of right of reply. The court agreed that Pegler's comments about Broun bore a resemblance to a reply but determined that the columnist had gone too far in his attack on Quentin Reynolds. This portion of the article had no conceivable relationship to a reply. Reynolds was awarded $175,000 from Pegler, the *New York Journal-American,* and the Hearst Corporation (*Reynolds* v. *Pegler,* 1955).

The right of reply can in the right circumstances work as a defense. Where does the press fit in? Many authorities argue that the press has the right to carry the reply and remain immune from suit. In several cases it was held that where the plaintiff's charge was made in a newspaper, the newspaper was privileged to carry the defendant's reply (*Fowler* v. *New York Herald,* 1918). Otherwise the right of reply is of no avail to the defendant; no one would be able to see or read the reply if the defendant were denied use of the press. Similarly, it was held that the reply can even be carried in a newspaper or a medium different from the medium used for the attack.

In *Cases and Materials on Torts,* law professor Harry Kalven wrote:

> The boundaries of this privilege are not clearly established and it gives rise to questions amusingly reminiscent of those raised in connection with self-defense: How vigorous must the plaintiff's original aggression have been? Must the original attack itself have been defamatory? What if it [the original attack] is true or privileged? How much verbal force can the defendant use in reply? Can he defend third parties?

Questions like these continue to reduce the true effectiveness of the defense of right of reply. It is useful as a second defense, to back up either the privilege of the reporter or of fair comment, perhaps. Beyond this use its value is limited, at least at this point.

DAMAGES

If the court gets to the point in a libel suit of assessing **damages,** it is obvious that the plaintiff has met all requirements, including proving fault, and that none of the defenses just outlined have worked. How damages are assessed is not an essential piece of information for a journalist to carry; yet some feeling for the subject is useful. Libel law operates with four kinds of damages today. In each instance, before any damages can be awarded, the plaintiff must prove one thing or another to the court.

Actual Damages

The most common libel damages are called **actual damages,** or damages for actual injury. Plaintiffs have to convince the jury that they have suffered actual harm. What kind of harm? Not physical harm, obviously. The best definition of actual damages (as they are now defined) comes from the *Gertz* case. Justice Powell wrote that actual injury is not limited to out-of-pocket loss or money loss, which is how many authorities defined actual damages prior to this decision. Powell said, "Indeed, the more customary types of actual harm inflicted by defamatory falsehood include impairment of reputation and standing in the community, personal humiliation, and mental anguish and suffering." This statement is a very broad definition of actual damage. How can someone prove that he or she has suffered mental anguish? What is evidence of personal humiliation? These are very hard questions to answer. Libel damages have never been precise, and this formulation does not promise additional precision. The plaintiff has to bring evidence of some kind of injury. The jury will be the key factor in making the determination of how much harm and how much damage.

In 1985 the Supreme Court made a ruling in *Dun & Bradstreet* v. *Greenmoss Builders* that somewhat modified the High Court's 1974 *Gertz* v. *Welch* ruling on damages. In the *Dun and Bradstreet* ruling, the court relieved a heavy burden of proof from private persons who were suing for libel on the basis of statements that do *not* focus upon an issue of public concern.* These changes are reflected in the summaries below.

Special Damages

Special damages are specific items of pecuniary loss caused by published defamatory statements. Special damages must be established in precise terms, much more precise terms than those for the actual damages just outlined. If a plaintiff can prove that he or she lost $23,567.19 because of the libel, that amount is then what the plaintiff can ask for and what will likely be awarded if he or she can convince the jury of the validity of the case. Special damages represent a specific monetary, and only monetary loss as the result of the libel. Most plaintiffs do not seek special damages. However, in some cases special damages are all that can be sought. In trade libel, for example, the only award a plaintiff can get is special damages.

Presumed Damages

Presumed damages are damages that a plaintiff can get without proof of injury or harm. A public person plaintiff or a private person plaintiff suing for a libelous statement that focuses on a matter of public concern can only be awarded presumed (sometimes called general or compensatory damages) on a showing of actual malice, knowledge of falsity, or reckless disregard of the truth. However, a private person suing on the basis of a libelous statement that focuses on a private matter and not a public concern, need only show negligence to collect presumed damages.

Punitive Damages

Lawyers used to call **punitive damages,** or exemplary damages, the "smart money." Punitive damage awards are usually very large. The other kinds of damages just discussed are designed to compensate the plaintiff for injury. Punitive damages are designed to punish defendants for their misconduct and to warn other persons not to act in a similar manner.

A public person plaintiff or a private person plaintiff suing for a libelous statement that focuses on a matter of public concern can only win punitive damages upon a showing of actual malice, knowledge of falsity, or reckless

---

*Some people have viewed the ruling in *Dun & Bradstreet* in a far broader fashion. But it is this author's belief, based on the consensus of authorities, that the ruling applies only to the matter of damages, not to the question of fault generally.

disregard for the truth. A private person suing for libel based on remarks made about a private matter, and not a public concern, can win punitive damages on a showing of negligence.

Punitive damages are the most onerous aspect of any libel suit, and many persons think they are grossly unfair. Consequently, some state courts have abolished punitive damages—regardless of a showing of actual malice. Massachusetts (see *Stone* v. *Essex County Newspapers,* 1975) and Washington (see *Taskett* v. *King Broadcasting,* 1976) are two such states.

Some have argued that the high punitive damage awards violate the excessive fines clause of the Eighth Amendment to the U.S. Constitution. The Supreme Court heard such arguments in 1989 in a case that did not involve the mass media and did not involve libel. In *Browning-Ferris Industries* v. *Kelco Disposal Inc.* the high court rejected these arguments and refused to put a lid on what many believe to be the excessive punitive damage judgements. Whether persons in the mass media will continue to pursue this argument remains to be seen.

One additional point should be made clear about damages. All plaintiffs can attempt to prove actual malice in the hope of getting punitive and presumed damages, and it is only if they meet this burden that they can collect the smart money.

Retraction Statutes

The phrase "I demand a retraction" is common in the folklore of libel. What is a **retraction?** A retraction is both an apology and an effort to set the record straight. Let us say you blow one as an editor. You report that Jane Adams was arrested for shoplifting, and you are wrong. In your retraction you first tell readers or viewers that Jane Adams was not arrested for shoplifting, that you made a mistake. Then you might also apologize for the embarrassment caused Ms. Adams. You might even say some nice things about her. At common law a prompt and honest retraction is usually relevant to the question of whether the plaintiff's reputation was actually harmed. After all, you are attempting to reconstruct that part of her reputation which you tore down just the day before. She might have difficulty proving actual harm.

A good example of correction, or retraction, occurred about eight years ago and involved, of all things, *Playboy's Book of Wines.* The slick-paper wine book erroneously charged on page sixty three that a leading Italian winery, Bolla Vineyards, doctored its wine. As one writer noted, "All hell broke loose" when the American distributor of Bolla wines saw the reference. Playboy Press reached an agreement with the vintners in which it called back all five thousand copies of the book already distributed, sliced the two offending pages out of those copies, replaced them with two new pages containing flattering references to Bolla, stopped publication of the book until corrections could be made, and issued multiple apologies. In late 1983 Random House recalled almost sixty thousand copies of a biography of Barbara Hutton, entitled *Poor Little Rich Girl,* because of errors in the book about one of the physicians who treated the heiress to the Woolworth fortune. This largest book recall in history was an extreme measure, but it was necessary to prevent a possible lawsuit.

In the several states that have retraction statutes, a plaintiff must give the publisher an opportunity to retract the libel before a suit may be started. If the publisher promptly honors the request for a retraction and retracts the libelous material in a place in the newspaper as prominent as the place in which the libel originally appeared, the impact will reduce and in some instances cancel any damage judgment the plaintiff might later seek in a lawsuit. Failure to seek a retraction limits the plaintiff's right to bring a lawsuit against the publisher. About thirty-one states have retraction laws of one kind or another.

In at least two states retraction statutes adopted by the legislature have been ruled to be unconstitutional. In both Arizona (*Boswell* v. *Phoenix Newspapers,* 1986) and Montana (*Madison* v. *Yunker,* 1978) the state high courts have ruled that the state constitution gives citizens the right to sue for injury to person, property, or character. The retraction statute diminishes that right and is hence unconstitutional, the courts ruled.

Retraction laws make good sense. It is the truth we seek, after all; a successful libel suit results in compensating the plaintiff monetarily but it is not very effective in correcting the errors in people's minds resulting from publication of the defamation.

SUMMARY

To collect damages in a libel suit, plaintiffs must demonstrate to the court that there was actual harm to their reputations. These are called *actual damages.* If plaintiffs can demonstrate specific items of monetary loss, *special damages* may be awarded. Plaintiffs may also seek to win *punitive damages.* In nearly thirty-one states, a timely retraction of the libel can reduce damages significantly and even lessen the likelihood of a libel suit. These rules are governed by state laws called *retraction statutes.*

CRIMINAL LIBEL

Since this book is for persons in the media or persons who plan to work in the media, there is really little reason to spend time discussing criminal libel. But it is there and is difficult to ignore. So here are a few well-chosen words on the subject.

The bulk of this chapter deals with civil libel—one person suing another for defamation. In most states, however, libel can be a crime as well. That is, there are criminal libel statutes, laws that make certain kinds of defamation a crime. For the most part these laws go unused today, relics of the past. But they are not forgotten and in some states, especially southern states, prosecutions do occur. For example, in the summer of 1988, the editor of a small weekly newspaper in Kingstree, South Carolina, was indicted for criminal libel after he wrote that two local politicians were involved in "corrupt dealings". Jim Fitts, editor of the weekly, *The Voice,* faced a possible fine of five thousand dollars and a year in jail. The state criminal libel law had only been used three times in the past forty years. As will be noted shortly, the difficulty in prosecuting such a case made it unlikely that Fitts would ever be convicted. And as a matter of fact charges were eventually dropped against Fitts.

The authorities in most states are unwilling to take on someone else's trouble and sue for criminal libel so long as a civil remedy is readily available. A prosecutor has very little to gain from such an action. In fact, he or she would probably be roundly criticized for instituting criminal libel charges. In an age when people are mugged, robbed, raped, and murdered with alarming frequency, damage to an individual's reputation—or even to the reputation of a large number of persons—somehow does not seem too serious. Several years ago in New York, a judge stated this proposition very well (*People* v. *Quill,* 1958):

> The theory, in simplest terms, is that when an individual is libeled, he has an adequate remedy in a civil suit for damages. The public suffers no injury. Vindication for the individual and adequate compensation for the injury done him may be obtained as well in the civil courts. Thus the rule has always been that the remedy of criminal prosecution should only be sought where the wrong is of so flagrant a character as to make a criminal prosecution necessary on public grounds.

Despite the fact that they are rarely used, criminal libel statutes remain on the books in most states. In Louisiana the law is defined in this manner:

> Defamation is the malicious publication or expression in any manner, to any one other than the party defamed, of anything which tends:
>   (1) To expose any person to hatred, contempt, ridicule or to deprive him or her of the benefit of public confidence or social intercourse; or
>   (2) To expose the memory of one deceased to hatred, contempt or ridicule; or
>   (3) To impair any person, corporation or association of persons in his or her or their business occupations.
>   Whoever commits the crime of defamation shall be fined not more than three thousand dollars or imprisoned for not more than one year or both.

As you can see, the crime of defamation is very similar to the tort of defamation: a person can get into trouble in both instances by doing about the same thing. It can be seen from the statute quoted that it is possible to criminally libel a dead person. Since the deceased cannot sue to protect their own good names, it only makes sense to allow the state to intercede. Criminal libel differs from civil libel in several other ways as well.

First, in a few states criminal libel is tied to causing or potentially causing a breach of the peace. This charge used to be quite common. If a publication, speech, or handbill so provoked the readers or listeners that violence became possible or did in fact occur, criminal libel charges might result. In 1966 the

United States Supreme Court undermined most of the "breach of the peace" statutes, as well as the actions of those states that brought criminal libel actions under the common law. The case was *Ashton v. Kentucky* and involved a mining dispute in Hazard, Kentucky. An agitator was arrested for circulating a pamphlet that contained articles attacking the chief of police, the sheriff, and a newspaper editor, among others. At the criminal libel trial, the judge defined the offense as "any writing calculated to create a disturbance of the peace, corrupt public morals or lead to any act, which when done, is indictable."

The Supreme Court reversed the conviction. Writing for a unanimous court, Justice William O. Douglas said the crime, as defined by the trial court, was too general and indefinite. It left the standard of responsibility—whether something is illegal or not—wide open to the discretion of the judge. Also, Douglas noted, the crime is determined not by the character of the person's words, not by what that person says or writes, but rather by the boiling point of those who listen to or read those words. The law makes someone a criminal simply because his or her neighbors have no self-control and cannot refrain from violence. This decision was an important factor, but only one factor, in the passing of "breach of the peace" as an aspect of criminal libel. It is extremely rare for such a case to occur today.

In the past it was possible to criminally libel a large group or race of people. The Supreme Court upheld such a law in 1952, a law that made it a crime to libel any race, color, creed, or religion. The case originated in Illinois where a white racist named Joseph Beauharnais distributed insulting literature at a time when blacks were attempting to integrate the white Chicago suburb of Cicero. Beauharnais's words were strong at a time when police and other officials had their hands full keeping the peace. He was arrested, tried, and fined two hundred dollars for his pamphleteering.

Beauharnais argued that his conviction violated the First Amendment. In a five-to-four vote, the Court upheld the conviction on the grounds that libelous utterances are not within the protection of the First Amendment. Justice Felix Frankfurter wrote that if an utterance directed at an individual may be the object of criminal penalties, the High Court could not then deny the right of a state to make criminal as well such utterances aimed at a well-defined group (*Beauharnais v. Illinois,* 1952).

The rationale for this decision was eroded, if not completely undercut, by the *New York Times* decision: Libelous utterances are protected by the First Amendment in an increasing number of instances. There is serious doubt in the minds of most press-law scholars whether the *Beauharnais* ruling remains viable today. It is very likely, given the opportunity, that the Supreme Court would overturn that decision.

The High Court has heard one criminal libel case since the *New York Times* ruling. The Court ruled in *Garrison v. Louisiana* (1964) that when the defamation of a public official is the basis for a criminal libel suit, the state has to prove actual malice on the part of the defendant; that is, knowledge of falsity, reckless disregard for the truth, or falsity of the matter. Justice Brennan wrote that the reasons that persuaded the Court to rule that the First Amendment protected criticism of public officials in a civil libel suit apply with equal force in a criminal libel suit. "The constitutional guarantees of freedom of expression compel application of the same standard to the criminal remedy," he added. However, the question of what the Court would do with a group libel suit of the kind it faced in 1952 is still not answered.

Criminal libel is not a real problem for journalists and broadcasters. Of the few criminal libel cases on record since World War II, cases in which the media were the defendants can be counted on one hand. Normally the action is brought against the writer of the article or the speaker of the words, not against the medium publishing the comments.

As was noted at the beginning of this chapter, libel is probably the most common legal problem journalists and broadcasters face today. The fear of publishing a libel is something the press lives with day in and day out. Virtually every story contains the potential for a libel suit.

The press is much better protected today than it was twenty-three years ago before the *New York Times* decision. The *New York Times* ruling has helped the press in many ways. In the past, plaintiffs with only the remote possibility of victory were lured to court by the possibility of large windfall judgments. Recent cases have made the smart money tougher to get. Also, infusion of good, solid First Amendment idealism and logic into the law has made judges at all levels far more sensitive to the needs of the press. These events have been very helpful. While "freedom of the press" may be legally vague, a judge or jury who thinks about the First Amendment is likely to be more receptive to the arguments of the defense.

INTENTIONAL INFLICTION OF EMOTIONAL DISTRESS

While persons working in mass communications continue to struggle with the libel imbroglio, a new threat to the right to publish has emerged in the past two decades—a tort called the intentional infliction of emotional distress. Lawsuits alleging this tort injury first appeared in the late nineteenth century, according to Susan Kirkpatrick in an article in the *Northwestern University Law Review.* But it wasn't recognized by the *Restatement of Torts,* the synthesis of tort law published by the American Law Institute, until 1948. In 1965 the *Restatement* provided for the first time a definition of the tort, which has four parts.

1. The defendant's conduct was intentional or reckless.
2. The defendant's conduct was extreme and outrageous.
3. The defendant's conduct caused the plaintiff emotional distress.
4. The emotional distress was severe.

In practice, Kirkpatrick said, courts really focus upon a single criteria—whether the defendant acted outrageously. Or as one court put it, the defendant's conduct went beyond all possible bounds of decency and was regarded as atrocious and utterly intolerable in a civilized community.

It is obvious that this tort covers a wide range of behavior in addition to publishing or broadcasting something about a plaintiff. There have always been fears of an epidemic of such suits, but this has failed to materialize. In fact it has really only been in the past fifteen years that allegations of emotional distress have been made against the mass media. Lawyer Terrance C. Mead wrote in 1983, after examining tort action brought against the mass media over a five-year period, that the fear of such an epidemic was probably unwarranted. It was simply too hard for a plaintiff to win such a suit against the press. But in the mid 1980s there was cause for grave concern when a United States court of appeals ruling seemingly opened the door for a great many more emotional distress suits, especially those aimed at those editorial writers and cartoonists who used the press to satirize and lampoon persons in the public eye.

The case began in November of 1983 when *Hustler* magazine published a parody of a Campari liquor ad. The real Campari ads were interviews with celebrities who talked about their first taste of the liquor, but with a clear suggestion of sexual connotation. The *Hustler* parody was a fictitious interview with the Reverend Jerry Falwell, who described his first time as an incestuous encounter with his mother. Falwell was also characterized by the parody as a drunkard. There was a small disclaimer at the bottom of the parody and it was listed in the table of contents as fiction.

Falwell sued the magazine for libel, invasion of privacy and intentional infliction of emotional distress. The trial judge dismissed the invasion of privacy claim, but sent the other two to the jury. Jurors rejected the libel claim on the grounds that the parody was so far-fetched, no person could possibly believe that it described actual facts about Falwell. The jury did award the Baptist preacher two hundred thousand dollars in damages for emotional distress.

Hustler appealed the ruling, but a unanimous three-judge panel of the United States Court of Appeals for the Fourth Circuit upheld the damage award, noting that all the proof that was needed in such a case was that the item was sufficiently outrageous as to cause emotional harm, and that it was published intentionally (*Falwell* v. *Flynt,* 1986). While most of the nation's journalists did not condone the *Hustler* style of parody, they nevertheless viewed the decision as a serious threat to freedom of expression. The sturdy First Amendment barrier built up to protect the mass media from libel suits brought by persons in the public eye was neatly circumvented by Falwell in this case. Because of his presence as a spokesman for the conservative religious right in this nation, Falwell would likely be considered an all-purpose public figure in a libel action and be forced to prove actual malice before he could collect damages. In this suit he did not even have to show negligence. Nor did the broad First Amendment protection granted statements of opinion apply outside the law of libel. In the future persons suing for satire or parody could avoid having to surmount the constitutional barriers in libel law by instead filing an action for intentional infliction of emotional distress.

Hustler appealed to the Supreme Court and in 1988, in a unanimous ruling, the High Court reversed the appellate court ruling. Chief Justice Rehnquist, noting that most persons would see the *Hustler* parody as gross and repugnant, nevertheless rejected Falwell's argument that because he was seeking damages for severe emotional distress rather than reputational harm a standard different than that applied in libel should apply. "Were we to hold otherwise," the Chief Justice wrote, "there can be little doubt that political cartoonists and satirists would be subjected to damages awarded without any showing that their work falsely defamed its subject". Rehnquist added

> The appeal of the political cartoon or caricature is often based on exploration of unfortunate physical traits or politically embarrassing events—an exploration often calculated to injure the feelings of the subject of the portrayal. The art of the cartoonist is often not reasoned or evenhanded, but slashing and one-sided.

Falwell contended it was making a mockery of serious political cartoons to compare them to the *Hustler* parody, which was truly outrageous. The law should protect even public figures from such outrageous caricatures. Rehnquist disagreed, noting the outrageousness standard of liability would not work.

> "Outrageousness" in the area of political and social discourse has an inherent subjectiveness about it which would allow a jury to impose liability on the basis of jurors' tastes and views or perhaps on the basis of their dislike of a particular expression.

The Court ruled that in order for a public figure or public official to win an emotional distress claim, it would be necessary to prove three things.

1. That the parody or satire amounted to statement of fact, not an opinion.
2. That it was a false statement of fact.
3. That the person who drew the cartoon or wrote the article knew it was false, or exhibited reckless disregard for the truth or falsity of the material. In other words, proof of actual malice is necessary.

Most authorities, like Lyle Denniston, who has covered the Supreme Court for many years for the *Baltimore Sun,* believe that this ruling means there is little chance left for public figures to win emotional distress claims for even the most outrageous parody. As such, it has certainly sounded the death knell for at least one important line of emotional distress claims against the mass media.

BIBLIOGRAPHY

Here is a list of some of the sources that have been helpful in the preparation of chapter 3:

Books

American Law Institute, *Restatement of the Law of Torts.* 2d ed. Philadelphia: American Law Institute, 1975.

Ashley, Paul. *Say It Safely.* 5th ed. Seattle: University of Washington Press, 1976.

Bezanson, Randall P., Cranberg, Gilbert, and Soloski, John. *Libel Law and the Press.* New York: The Free Press, 1987.

Libel Law: A Report of the Libel Reform Project. Washington D.C.: The Annenberg Washington Program, 1988.

Prosser, William L. *Handbook of the Law of Torts.* St. Paul, Minn.: West Publishing Co., 1963.

Smolla, Rodney. *Suing the Press.* New York: Oxford University Press, 1986.

Yankwich, Leon R. *It's Libel or Contempt If You Print It.* Los Angeles: Parker & Sons Publications, 1950.

Articles

Anderson, David. "Presumed Harm: An Item for the Unfinished Agenda of Times v. Sullivan." 62 *Journalism Quarterly* 24, 1985.

"Court Denounces Use of Libel Suit as a Weapon." *Editor and Publisher,* February 13, 1988.

Franklin, Marc A., and Bussel, Daniel. "The Plaintiff's Burden in Defamation: Awareness and Falsity." 25 *William and Mary Law Review* 825, 1984.

Gleason, Timothy W. "The Fact/Opinion Distinction in Libel." 10 *Hastings Journal of Communications and Entertainment Law* 763, 1988.

Goodchild, Seth. "Media Counteractions: Restoring the Balance to Modern Libel Law." 75 *Georgetown Law Journal* 315, 1986.

Jones, Alex S. "Iowa Experiment Offers Arbitration for Settling Libel Disputes Out of Court." *The New York Times,* May 4, 1987.

———. "Libel Awards: Million-Dollar Barrier is Breached." *The New York Times,* April 13, 1988.

Kirkpatrick, Susan. "Falwell v. Flynt: Intentional Infliction of Emotional Distress as a Threat to Free Speech." 81 *Northwestern University Law Review* 993, 1987.

Languardt, Arlen W. "Media Defendants, Public Concerns, and Public Plaintiffs: Toward Fashioning Order from Confusion in Defamation Law." 49 *University of Pittsburgh Law Review* 91, 1987.

Lee, Douglas E. "Public Interest, Public Figures, and the Corporate Defamation Plaintiff: *Jadwin* v. *Minneapolis Star and Tribune.*" 81 *Northwestern University Law Review* 318, 1987.

Mather, Michael. "Experience with *Gertz* 'Actual Injury' in Defamation Cases." 38 *Baylor Law Review* 917, 1986.

Mead, Terrance C. "Suing Media for Emotional Distress: A Multi-Method Analysis of Tort Law Evolution." 23 *Washburn Law Journal* 24, 1983.

O'Connor, Clint. "Setting the Paper of Record Straight." *Washington Journalism Review,* September, 1987.

Smolla, Rodney A. "*Dun & Bradstreet, Hepps, and Liberty Lobby:* A New Analytic Primer on the Future Course of Defamation." 75 *Georgetown Law Journal* 1519, 1987.

Smothers, Ronald. "Editor Faces Criminal Libel Charges." *The New York Times,* June 28, 1988.

Thomas, Jeffrey. "Statements of Fact, Statements of Opinion, and the First Amendment." 74 *California Law Review* 1001, 1986.

AAFCO Heating and Air Conditioning Co. v. Northwest Publications, Inc., 321 N.E.2d 580 (1974).

Anderson v. Liberty Lobby, 477 U.S. 242 (1986).

Anderson v. Rocky Mountain News, 15 M.L.R. 2058 (1988).

Appleby v. Daily Hampshire Gazette, 395 Mass. 2 (1985).

Arcand v. Evening Call, 567 F.2d 1163 (1977).

Artic v. Loudoun Times Mirror, 624 F.2d 518 (1980).

Asnton v. Kentucky, 384 U.S. 195 (1966).

Bank of Oregon v. Independent News, 963 P.2d 35 (1985).

Barr v. Mateo, 353 U.S. 171 (1959).

Beauharnais v. Illinois, 343 U.S. 250 (1952).

Beech Aircraft v. National Aviation Underwriters, 11 M.L.R. 1401 (1984).

Blake v. Gannett, 529 So. 2d 595 (1988).

Blatty v. New York Times, 728 P.2d 1177 (1986).

Blouin v. Anton, 431 A.2d 439 (1981).

Borg v. Boas, 231 F.2d 788 (1956).

Bose v. Consumers Union, 508 F.Supp. 1249 (1981); rev'd. 629 F.2d 189 (1982); aff'd 446 U.S. 485 (1984).

Boswell v. Phoenix Newspapers, 730 P.2d 186 (1986).

Brown and Williamson v. Jacobson, 713 F.2d 262 (1983); 644 F.Supp. 1240 (1986); 827 F.2d 1119 (1987).

Brueggemeyer v. ABC, 684 F.Supp. 452 (1988).

Bruno and Stillman v. Globe Newspapers, 633 F.2d 583 (1980).

Buckley v. Littell, 539 F.2d 882 (1976).

Byars v. Kolodziej, 363 N.E.2d 628 (1977).

Calder v. Jones, 465 U.S. 783 (1984).

Camer v. Seattle Post-Intelligencer, 723 P.2d 1195 (1986).

Canino v. New York News, 475 A.2d 478 (1984).

Carson v. Allied News, 529 F.2d 206 (1976).

Chapadeau v. Utica Observer-Dispatch, Inc., 341 N.E. 2d 569 (1975).

Cherry v. Des Moines Leader, 86 N.W. 323 (1901).

Chuy v. Philadelphia Eagles, 595 F.2d 1265 (1979).

Cianci v. New Times Publishing, 639 F.2d 54 (1980).

City of Chicago v. Tribune Publishing Co., 139 N.E.2d 86 (1923).

Clawson v. Longview Publishing Co., 589 P.2d 1223 (1979).

Cofield v. Advertiser Co., 486 So.2d 434 (1986).

Cohen v. New York Times, 138 N.Y.S. 206 (1912).

Coleman v. MacLennan, 98 P.2d 281 (1908).

Columbia Sussex v. Hay, 627 S.W.2d 270 (1981).

Contemporary Mission v. New York Times, 665 F.Supp 248 (1987); 842 F.2d 612 (1988).

Costello v. Capital Cities Communications, Inc., 15 M.L.R. 2407, 1988.

Cox v. Lee Enterprises, 723 P.2d 238 (1986).

Curtis Publishing Co. v. Butts, AP v. Walker, 388 U.S. 130 (1967).

Dameron v. Washingtonian, 779 F.2d 736 (1985).

Decker v. Princeton Packet, 541 A.2d 292 (1988).

Denny v. Mertz, 318 N.W.2d 141 (1980).

Dibble v. WROC-TV, 530 N.Y.S. 2d 388, 1988.

Dickey v. CBS, 583 F.2d 1221 (1978).

Dresbach v. Doubleday, 8 M.L.R. 1793 (1982).

Dun & Bradstreet v. Greenmoss, 472 U.S. 749 (1985).

Dunn v. Gannett New York, 833 F.2d 446 (1987).

Edwards v. National Audubon Society, 556 F.2d 113 (1977).
El Amin v. Miami Herald, 9 M.L.R. 1079 (1983).
Falwell v. Flynt, 797 F.2d 1270 (1986); rev'd *Hustler Magazine v. Falwell*, 108 S.Ct. 876 (1988).
Fleckstein v. Friedman, 195 N.E. 537 (1934).
Foster v. Turner Broadcasting, 844 F.2d 955 (1988).
Fowler v. New York Herald, 172 N.Y.S. 423 (1918).
Franklin v. Lodge 1108, 97 Cal. App.3d 915 (1979).
Gannett v. Re, 496 A.2d 553 (1985).
Garrison v. Louisiana, 379 U.S. 64 (1964).
Gautsche v. New York, 415 N.Y.S.2d 280 (1979).
Gay v. Williams, 486 F.Supp. 12 (1979).
Geisler v. Petrocelli, 616 F.2d 636 (1980).
Georgia Society of Plastic Surgeons v. Anderson, 363 S.E.2d 710 (1987).
Gertz v. Welch, 418 U.S. 323 (1974).
Glover v. Herald Co., 549 S.W.2d 858 (1977).
Goldwater v. Ginzburg, 414 F.2d 324 (1969).
Guccione v. Hustler, 800 F.2d 298 (1986).
Healy v. New England Newspaper, Inc., 520 A.2d 147 (1987).
Hellman v. McCarthy, 10 M.L.R. 1789 (1984).
Hentell v. Knopf, 8 M.L.R. 1908 (1982).
Herbert v. Lando, 441 U.S. 153 (1979).
Herron v. King Broadcasting, 746 P.2d 295 (1987).
Herron v. Tribune Publishing Co., 736 P.2d 249 (1987).
Hoeppner v. Dunkirk Printing Co., 172 N.E. 139 (1930).
Hope v. Hearst Corp., 294 F.2d 681 (1961).
Hornby v. Hunter, 385 S.W.2d 473 (1964).
Hudson v. Guy Gannett Broadcasting, 521 A.2d 714 (1987).
Hunt v. Liberty Lobby, 720 F.2d 631 (1983).
Hutchinson v. Proxmire, 443 U.S. 111 (1979).
Ingerere v. ABC, 11 M.L.R. 1227 (1984).
Innis v. Payne, 12 M.L.R. 1403 (1985).
Jacobson v. Rochester Communications, 410 N.W.2d 830 (1987).
Jadwin v. Minneapolis Star, 367 N.W.2d 476 (1985).
Janklow v. Newsweek, 788 F.2d 1300 (1986).
Janklow v. Viking Press, 378 N.W.2d 875 (1985).
Jennings v. Telegram-Tribune, 210 Cal. Rptr. 485 (1985).
Johnson v. Corinthian Television, 583 P.2d 1101 (1978).
Jones v. Sun Publishing, 292 S.E.2d 23 (1982).
Jones v. Taibbi, 512 N.E. 2d 260 (1987).
KARK-TV v. Simon, 656 S.W. 702 (1983).
Karp v. Miami Herald, 359 So.2d 580 (1978).
Keeton v. Hustler, 465 U.S. 770 (1984).
Kilgore v. Younger, 180 Cal. Rptr. 657 (1982).
Kirk v. CBS, 14 M.L.R. 1263 (1987).
Kotlikoff v. Community News, 444 A.2d 1086 (1982).
Krauss v. Champaign News Gazette, 375 N.E.2d 1362 (1978).
Lamon v. Butler, 722 P.2d 1373 (1986); 751 P.2d 842 (1988).
Levine v. CMP Publications, 738 F.2d 660 (1984).
Liberty Lobby v. Dow Jones, 838 F.2d 1287 (1988).
Liberty Lobby v. Jack Anderson, 746 F.2d 1563 (1984).
Loeb v. Globe Newspapers, 489 F.Supp. 481 (1980).

MacDonald v. *Time*, 7 M.L.R. 1981 (1981).
MacDonald v. *Time*, 554 F.Supp. 1053 (1983).
McBride v. *Merrell Dow*, 717 F.2d 1460 (1984).
McCabe v. *Rattiner*, 814 F.2d 839 (1987).
McCain v. *KTVY Inc.*, 738 P.2d 960 (1987).
McCullough v. *Cities Service*, 676 P.2d 833 (1984).
McNair v. *Hearst Corp.*, 494 F.2d 1309 (1974).
Madison v. *Yunker*, 589 P.2d 126 (1978).
Malerba v. *Newsday*, 406 N.Y.S.2d 552 (1978).
Marcone v. *Penthouse*, 533 F.Supp. 353 (1982); 754 F.2d 1072 (1985).
Martin v. *Wilson Publishing*, 497 A.2d 322 (1985).
Medico v. *Times*, 634 F.2d 134 (1981).
Memphis Publishing Co. v. *Nichols*, 569 S.W.2d 412 (1978).
Morgan v. *Dun & Bradstreet, Inc.*, 421 F.2d 1241 (1970).
Morgan v. *Hustler Magazine*, 653 F.2d 711 (1987).
Mr. Chow v. *Ste. Jour. Azur S.A.*, 759 F.2d 219 (1985).
Murray v. *Bailey*, 11 M.L.R. 1369 (1985).
Mutafis v. *Erie Insurance Exchange*, 775 F.2d 593 (1985).
Nader v. *DeToledano*, 408 A.2d 31 (1979).
Newsom v. *Henry*, 443 So. 2d 817 (1984).
Newton v. *NBC*, 12 M.L.R. 1252 (1985); 677 F.Supp. 1066 (1987).
New York Times Co. v. *Sullivan*, 376 U.S. 254 (1964).
Ollman v. *Evans*, 750 F.2d 970 (1984).
Orr v. *Argus Press*, 586 F.2d 1108 (1978).
Orr v. *Lynch*, 401 N.Y.S.2d 897 (1978).
Palmer v. *Seminole*, 9 M.L.R. 2151 (1983).
Pauling v. *Globe-Democrat*, 362 F.2d 188 (1966).
Peagler v. *Phoenix Newspapers*, 547 P.2d 1074 (1976).
Pearson v. *Fairbanks Publishing Co.*, 413 P.2d 711 (1966).
People v. *Quill*, 177 N.Y.S.2d 380 (1958).
Perez v. *Scripps-Howard Broadcasting*, 55 Ohio St.3d 215 (1988).
Perry v. *Hearst Corp.*, 334 F.2d 800 (1964).
Philadelphia Newspapers v. *Hepps*, 475 U.S. 767 (1986).
Postill v. *Booth Newspapers*, 325 N.W.2d 511 (1982).
Powers v. *Durgin-Snow Publishing Co.*, 144 A.2d 294 (1958).
Press v. *Verran*, 589 S.W.2d 435 (1978).
Price v. *Viking Press*, 625 F.Supp. 641 (1985).
Price v. *Washington State Senate*, 12 M.L.R. 2035 (1986).
Pulverman v. *A. S. Abell Co.*, 228 F.2d 797 (1956).
Quarcini v. *Niagra Falls Gazette*, 13 M.L.R. 2340 (1987).
Raye v. *Letterman*, 14 M.L.R. 2047 (1987).
Reynolds v. *Pegler*, 223 F.2d 429 (1955).
Richmond Newspapers v. *Lipscomb*, 362 S.E.2d 32 (1987).
Roberts v. *Dover*, 525 F.Supp. 987 (1981).
Rosanova v. *Playboy*, 411 F.Supp 440 (1976); aff'd 580 F.2d 859 (1978).
Rosenblatt v. *Baer*, 383 U.S. 75 (1966).
Rubenstein v. *New York Post*, 488 N.Y.S.2d 331 (1985).
St. Amant v. *Thompson*, 390 U.S. 727 (1968).
Saunders v. *WHYY-TV*, 382 A.2d 257 (1978).
Schiavone v. *Time*, 569 F.Supp. 684 (1985).
Seegmiller v. *KSL-TV*, 626 P.2d 968 (1981).
Shiles v. *News Syndicate Co.*, 261 N.E.2d 251 (1970).
Silvester v. *ABC*, 839 F.2d 1491 (1988).

Slawik v. *News-Journal*, 428 A.2d 15 (1981).
Smith v. *Dameron*, 14 M.L.R. 1879 (1987).
Springer v. *Viking Press*, 457 N.Y.S.2d 246 (1982).
Steaks Unlimited v. *Deaner*, 623 F.2d 624 (1980).
Steere v. *Cupp*, 602 P.2d 1267 (1979).
Stillman v. *Paramount Pictures*, 147 N.E.2d 741 (1957).
Stone v. *Essex County Newspapers*, 330 N.E.2d 161 (1975).
Street v. *NBC*, 645 F.2d 1227 (1981).
Summerlin v. *Washington Star*, 7 M.L.R. 2460 (1981).
Tabart v. *Tipper*, 1 Camp. 350 (1808).
Taskett v. *King Broadcasting*, 546 P.2d 81 (1976).
Time, Inc. v. *Firestone*, 424 U.S. 448 (1976).
Trotter v. *Anderson*, 818 F.2d 431 (1987).
Trump v. *Chicago Tribune*, 616 F.Supp. 1434 (1985).
Wade v. *Stocks*, 7 M.L.R. 2200 (1981).
Waldbaum v. *Fairchild Publications*, 627 F.2d 1287 (1980).
Walker v. *Colorado Springs Sun, Inc.* 538 P.2d 450 (1975).
Walters v. *Sanford Herald*, 228 S.E.2d 766 (1976).
Washington Post v. *Kennedy*, 3 F.2d 766 (1976).
Weatherhead v. *Globe International*, 832 F.2d 1226 (1987).
Weisburgh v. *Mahady*, 511 A.2d 304 (1986).
Whitten v. *Commercial Dispatch*, 487 So.2d 843 (1986).
Wildmon v. *Hustler*, 508 F. Supp. 87 (1980).
Williams v. *Pasma*, 565 P.2d 212 (1982).
Wolston v. *Reader's Digest*, 443 U.S. 157 (1979).
Yiamouyiannis v. *Consumers Union*, 619 F.2d 932 (1980).

The right to privacy is one of the newest legal concepts we will discuss in this text. That might surprise you, but it is true. The notion that each human being needs privacy to sustain his or her life was quite foreign to most Americans two hundred years ago. At least they didn't write or talk about it very much. Some argue that is because Americans did not then lack privacy; this was, after all, a sparsely populated rural nation. True, but it was also a nation in which most families shared small two and three room homes, where strangers ate at common dining tables in inns and roadhouses and shared the cramped quarters of public transportation, and where the insidious but well-organized gossippers in most small American communities stripped most residents of all but their deepest-held secrets.

It wasn't until the end of the nineteenth century that the need for a right to privacy became a public issue. Of course the nation had changed dramatically. America was rapidly becoming an urban nation. The streets of many cities were clogged with poor immigrants or first generation Americans. Big city daily newspapers used a variety of sensational schemes to attract these potential readers. Editors often played out the lives of the "rich and famous" on the pages of their newspapers, permitting their readers to vicariously enjoy wealth, status, and celebrity.

It was this kind of journalism that apparently pushed two Boston lawyers, Samuel D. Warren and Louis D. Brandeis, to use the pages of the *Harvard Law Review* to propose a legally recognized right to privacy. Warren, the scion of a prominent Boston family, urged his friend (and future Supreme Court justice) Brandeis to help him write the piece, "The Right to Privacy." The article appeared in 1890 and can be legitimately regarded as the fountain from which the modern law of privacy has flowed.

The pair argued, "Instantaneous photographs and newspaper enterprise have invaded the sacred precincts of private and domestic life; and numerous mechanical devices threaten to make good the prediction that 'what is whispered in the closet shall be proclaimed from the house-tops.' " Warren and Brandeis said they were offended by the gossip in the press, which they said had overstepped in every direction the obvious bounds of propriety and decency:

> To satisfy a prurient taste the details of sexual relations are spread broadcast in the columns of the daily papers. To occupy the indolent, column upon column is filled with idle gossip, which can only be procured by intrusion upon the domestic circle. . . .
> The common law has always recognized a man's house as his castle, impregnable, often, even to its own officers engaged in the execution of its commands. Shall the courts thus close the front entrance to constituted authority, and open wide the back door to idle or prurient curiosity?

To stop this illicit behavior, the two young lawyers proposed that the courts recognize the legal right of privacy; that is, citizens should be able to go to court to stop such unwarranted intrusions and also secure money damages for the hardship they suffered from such prying and from publication of private material about them.

Today most Americans seem almost schizophrenic about the right to privacy. Ask the question: Do you value the right to privacy? and the answer will almost always be yes. But many of us behave in ways that tend to belie that assertion. Most of us readily give up vast amounts of personal and private information to participate in our buy-now, pay-later economy. How much privacy will you sacrifice to hop on the Visa or Mastercard bandwagon? On election day most Americans will unhesitatingly tell researchers outside polling places for whom they voted. We tolerate, if not support, invasions of privacy by business via two-way mirrors in dressing rooms or video cameras in discount stores. While most Americans profess a dislike for the gossip-mongering press, the sale of the supermarket tabloids has notably increased in the past decade, and these are publications that show little respect for anyone's private life. Invasion of privacy by the government is also condoned. There was considerable public support for the decision of the Supreme Court upholding a Georgia law prohibiting sodomy, despite the professed belief of many that what happens in the bedroom is nobody else's business. Most Americans support mandatory drug testing (usually of others) as a legitimate weapon in the war on drugs. And there has been a surprising amount of public support for efforts by a wide range of moral activists to block the sale of erotic publications and videos, even though most Americans would argue that what a person reads or watches should be a private matter. (See chapter 8.)

In the coming years threats to our privacy will grow even stronger. Computer data banks get larger and more sophisticated each day. For example, in 1989 the Federal Bureau of Investigation proposed that its National Crime Information Center computers, which already contain 20 million records, be expanded to include records on persons suspected of criminal activity as well as those charged with a crime. The arrival of two-way cable television which permits enhanced personal, business, and educational interaction via the fiber-optic wire can literally turn a private life into an open book if legislation to regulate it is not adopted. The worst scenarios of several generations of science fiction writers are almost at hand. And yet there seems to be little public spirit or action to design a future in which privacy interests take precedence. ◆

THE LAW OF PRIVACY

While the *right* to privacy encompasses a vast array of problems and ideas, the *law* of privacy, the subject of this chapter, is far narrower. It was thirteen years from the time the Warren and Brandeis article was first published until the first state recognized the law of privacy. The state of New York adopted a law which prohibited the commercial exploitation of an individual and called it a right to privacy. The concept contained in the law was not even mentioned in the famous *Harvard Law Review* article. Slowly over the next eighty years more and more states proclaimed a legal protection for some kind of a right to privacy. Today the courts or legislatures in virtually all the states have recognized some kind of a legally enforceable right to privacy. Some states have adopted the law via a statute; in most states the courts have found a legitimate claim to privacy in the common law.

But the recognition of a right merely states a legal conclusion. It does not, by itself, provide a full set of legal principles that can be used to grant relief to a plaintiff. The law has grown over the past one hundred years by fits and starts. It has a somewhat ragged profile. Some parts of the right to privacy bear little resemblance to the plan proposed by Warren and Brandeis in 1890. In fact the right to privacy today contains dimensions that have little to do with what we traditionally think of as privacy. Invasion of privacy today encompasses not just one, but four, legal wrongs. They are different and should be thought of as separate wrongs. Let us briefly summarize these four wrongs and then study each of them in depth.

The first kind of invasion of privacy is called appropriation and is defined as taking a person's name, picture, photograph, or likeness and using it for commercial gain without permission. This is technically the only right of privacy guaranteed in some of the states that have privacy statutes. The laws are limited to outlawing this one kind of behavior. But as a matter of fact, judicial construction of these laws has allowed them to encompass many of the other aspects of invasion of privacy as well.

Intrusion is the second type of invasion of privacy, an area of the law growing rapidly today, and is what most people think of when invasion of privacy is mentioned. Intrusion upon the solitude and into the private life of a person is prohibited.

The third arm of the law prohibits publication of private information—truthful private information—about a person. What is truthful private information? Gossip, substance of private conversations, and details of a private tragedy or illness have all been used as the basis of a suit.

Finally, the publication of material that places a person in a false light is the fourth category of the law of privacy. This is an outgrowth of the first area of the law, appropriation, and doesn't at first glance seem like an invasion of privacy at all. But it is, and it seems to be a growing area of the law since in some jurisdictions it appears to be easier to win a false light suit than a libel suit when either cause of action might be filed based on the facts in the case.

A caveat of sorts is appropriate before the law of privacy is discussed. The laws as outlined in this chapter are the legal limits of behavior. These are not necessarily the same as the ethical or moral limits of behavior. For example, the law says in most instances it is permissible to publish the name of the victim of a rape, once that name appears in a public police or court document. But is that the right thing to do? The victim often faces embarrassment and further humiliation. Some victims may choose not to prosecute simply because of a fear of this publicity. And what is gained through the publication of the name? These are questions reporters and editors have to ask themselves and each other. There are a lot of other, similar questions that might be raised as well. Today, more than ever, many readers and viewers are asking the mass media to exercise restraint in certain areas, restraint that often falls well within the boundaries of what is legal. Journalists would do well to ponder these requests. Publish and be damned is still an appropriate response in some situations. But more often a thoughtful journalist will take a different tack.

APPROPRIATION

Appropriation is the oldest, and in many ways the least ambiguous, of the four types of invasion of privacy. Two of the earliest cases remain good examples of this area of the law:

1. In 1902 young Abigail Roberson of Albany, New York, awoke one morning to find her picture all over town on posters advertising Franklin Mills Flour. Twenty-five thousand copies of the advertisement had been placed in stores, warehouses, saloons, and other public buildings. Abigail said she felt embarrassed and humiliated, that she suffered greatly from this commercial exploitation, and she therefore sued for invasion of privacy. But she lost her case, and the state's high court ruled (*Roberson* v. *Rochester Folding Box Co.,* 1902):

> . . . an examination of the authorities leads us to the conclusion that the so-called "right of privacy" has not yet found an abiding place in our jurisprudence, and, as we view it, the doctrine cannot now be incorporated without doing violence to settled principles of law by which the profession and the public have long been guided.

Following this decision a great controversy arose in New York, led by the press, much of which expressed outrage at the way the court had treated Abigail. The controversy settled on the state legislature, which during the following year, 1903, adopted the nation's first privacy law. The statute was very narrow; that is, it prohibited a very specific kind of conduct. Use of an individual's name or likeness without the individual's consent for advertising or trade purposes was made a minor crime. In addition to the criminal penalty, the statute allowed the injured party to seek both an injunction to stop the use of the name or picture and money damages. This was the first privacy statute.

2. Two years later Georgia became the first state to recognize the right of privacy through the common law. Paolo Pavesich, an Atlanta artist, discovered that a life insurance company had used his photograph in newspaper advertisements. Pavesich's photograph was used in a before-and-after advertisement to illustrate a contented, successful man who had bought sufficient life insurance. A testimonial statement was also ascribed to the artist. He sued

for twenty five thousand dollars and won his case before the Georgia Supreme Court, which ruled (*Pavesich* v. *New England Mutual Life Insurance Co.,* 1905)

> . . . the form and features of the plaintiff are his own. The defendant insurance company and its agents had no more authority to display them in public for the purpose of advertising the business . . . than they would have had to compel the plaintiff to place himself upon exhibition for this purpose.

Before the ramifications of this aspect of the law are discussed, let us ask the question, For what are plaintiffs compensated in an invasion of privacy suit? What is their damage? In a libel case the reputation is damaged, a fairly invisible injury. But in a privacy suit the damage is even more invisible: the damage is the humiliation, embarrassment, and general bother that an ordinary person might experience from invasion of privacy. In other words, the damage is personal. The right of privacy is a personal right.

Use of Name or Likeness

Everybody knows what a name is, and it is therefore unnecessary to dwell on that term. It should be noted, however, that stage names, pen names, pseudonyms, and so forth, count the same as real names in the eyes of the law. If the name of rock star Elton John is used in an advertisement for dental floss without his permission, the suit cannot be defended on the basis that since Elton John's real name is Reginald Kenneth Dwight, his "name" was not appropriated illegally. It should also be noted that the law of privacy protects only people's names. Company names, trade names, and corporate names are not protected. Only people enjoy the right of privacy. Businesses, corporations, schools, and other "things" are not protected under the law. However, the use of a trade name like Kodak or Crest can create other serious legal problems. (See chapter 9.)

What is a likeness? Obviously a photograph, a painting, and a sketch—anything that suggests to readers and viewers that the plaintiff is pictured—is a likeness. Federal courts in New York State ruled recently that a sketch of a black man sitting in the corner of a boxing ring was, for purposes of an invasion-of-privacy suit, the "likeness" of former heavyweight champion Muhammed Ali. The boxer looked a little like Ali, and the photograph was accompanied by a verse that referred to the boxer as "the Greatest" (*Ali* v. *Playgirl,* 1978). ABC Records lost the right-to-privacy suit brought by classical guitarist Jean Pierre Jumez over an album cover. As part of a promotional scheme to attract the attention of young people, ABC packaged Jumez's record in an album that depicted a bearded man playing a guitar. The hairy-legged individual, whose face was obscured, was dressed in a tuxedo jacket but wore no pants. Jumez contended record buyers would think the picture was of him. "Any sufficiently clear representation of a living person is violative of the [New York] statute if it is used for commercial purposes without the subject's consent," the court ruled. Since the face of the man was obscured, record buyers could not tell whether the picture was of Jumez or not. But since the artist's name was on the album cover, people might surely believe Jumez was the individual in the picture (*Jumez* v. *ABC Records,* 1978).

Whether or not a likeness or representation of a plaintiff has been appropriated is often a jury question. Susan Cohen sued a cosmetics maker in 1984 after the firm published an ad containing what Cohen said was a photo of herself and her daughter bathing in a stream while nude. But only the backs and the sides of the bathers can be seen, and the company argued no appropriation had taken place because the plaintiffs were not identifiable. Cohen's husband said he recognized his wife and daughter, as did friends of the family. A lower court dismissed the suit, ruling that the plaintiff's identities cannot be determined from the picture. But the appellate division of the New York Supreme Court overturned the dismissal. The requirement that a portrait or picture of a plaintiff be appropriated "does not require that there be an identifiable facial representation as a prerequisite to relief," the court said. A jury should decide whether the advertisement contains a recognizable likeness (*Cohen* v. *Herbal Concepts,* 1984).

Does using a look-alike in an advertisement constitute appropriating someone's likeness? Performers who look like or sound like someone more famous were in demand for public appearances and to work in advertising during the 1980s. Barbara Reynolds, a woman who bears a striking resemblance to Jackie Kennedy Onassis, was featured in a Christian Dior ad, along with three real celebrities. Reynolds was made up and dressed to look like Onassis, who sued, arguing that her likeness had been appropriated for the advertisement. The New York Supreme Court agreed, noting that the law prohibits the use of a representation "which conveys the essence and likeness of an individual." Reynolds, as Reynolds, could pose for ads or make public appearances, but she could not attempt to convey the appearance of someone else, someone much better known (*Onassis* v. *Christian Dior,* 1984). Phil Boroff, who might easily be mistaken for Woody Allen, appeared in several ads for firms like National Video and Men's World. In April 1986 he appeared in a Men's World ad in *Newsday* holding a clarinet, very reminiscent of the character played by Allen in the film "Annie Hall." Beneath the photo, in small, lightfaced type, were these words: "This is a Ron Smith celebrity look-alike." Allen sued. A United States District Court ruled that despite the disclaimer, and despite the fact that it was Phil Boroff, not Woody Allen in the photo, "the use of Boroff's photograph in their [Men's World] advertisement creates a likelihood of consumer confusion over plaintiff's endorsement or involvement" (*Allen* v. *Men's World Outlet,* 1988). A bigger, bolder disclaimer might have solved the legal problem, the judge ruled.

Voice impersonations, a fairly common phenomenon in radio and television commercials, have resulted in far fewer suits. Singer Bette Midler recently sued the Ford Motor Company which had featured a Midler sound-alike singing a song popularized by the performer in the 1960s. Ford first asked Midler to do the commercial, but she refused. They hired another singer who had worked for Midler as a back-up singer for ten years. Midler sued for unfair competition and invasion of privacy. The United States Court of Appeals for the Ninth Circuit ruled that she could maintain a cause of action for invasion of privacy under California common law. "The singer manifests herself in the song. To impersonate her voice is to pirate her identity," the court ruled. Not every voice imitation to advertise goods is necessarily actionable, the court noted; however "we hold that when a distinctive voice of a professional singer is widely known and is deliberately imitated in order to sell a product, the sellers have appropriated what is not theirs and have committed a tort in California" (*Midler* v. *Ford Motor Co.,* 1988). Advertisers undoubtedly can reduce the risk of a lawsuit by preceding the ad with a clear explanation: "Here's singer Judy Jones for Ford" or with a subsequent explanation: "The preceding was a voice impersonation of Bette Midler." But this takes some of the sizzle out of the ad and still may not completely blunt a privacy action. Perhaps it is best to simply avoid copying someone else's identity for commercial purposes.

What are advertising and trade purposes? While minor differences exist among the states—especially among the states with statutes—a general guideline can be set down: advertising or trade purposes are commercial uses; that is, someone makes money from the use. Here are examples of the kinds of actions that are clearly commercial use:

1. Use of a person's name or photograph in an *advertisement* on television, on radio, in newspapers, in magazines, on posters, on billboards, and so forth.
2. Display of a person's photograph in the window of a photographer's shop to show potential customers the quality of work done by the studio.
3. A testimonial falsely suggesting that an individual eats the cereal or drives the automobile in question.

In Utah a broadcaster announced the name of a person on the "Dialing for Dollars" television feature. The individual sued, arguing that the program was simply an advertising device used by the station to attract viewers and that since no consent had been given for the use of the name over the air, the use was an invasion of privacy. The Utah Supreme Court agreed with the plaintiff, declaring that the name had been used to promote a commodity—the television station (*Jeppson* v. *United Television,* 1978).

What about this argument? A newspaper runs a photograph of John Smith on the front page after his car rolled over several times during a high-speed police pursuit. Smith sues for invasion of privacy, arguing that his picture on the front page of the newspaper attracted readers to the paper, resulted in the sale of newspapers, and therefore was used for commercial or trade purposes. Despite the arguments of many persons—even today—courts have consistently rejected this claim.

This plea was first made in 1907 by a New Yorker who objected to having his picture appear on the front page of the *New York World*. The state supreme court rejected the argument, noting that surely the intent of the state legislature was not to prohibit a newspaper or magazine from publishing a person's name or picture in a single issue without his consent (*Moser* v. *Press Publishing Co.*, 1908). Two years later another New York court reiterated this stand, ruling that advertising and trade purposes referred to commercial use, not to the dissemination of information (*Jeffries* v. *New York Evening Journal*, 1910). The United States Supreme Court has ruled that the fact that newspapers and books and magazines are sold for profit does not deny them the protection of liberty of expression (*Time, Inc.* v. *Hill*, 1967).

Anyone who has worked in journalism for very long knows that material created for promotional or trade purposes is often published or broadcast under the guise of news or information. For example, *Seventeen* magazine features what it calls its make-over section each month. Teenage girls are given clothing, cosmetics, and considerable advice to use to try to improve their appearance. The article accompanying the before-and-after pictures discusses the make over, and the brand names of products are prominently mentioned. The teenagers are paid and are supposed to sign permission forms, but one young woman inadvertently did not sign a model release. She sued and argued that her name and likeness had been appropriated for trade purposes. She lost. A court ruled that the article about grooming, makeup, and clothing was newsworthy to the teenage audience at which it was aimed. Mention of the brand names of products was incidental to the article and pictures (*Lopez* v. *Triangle Communications*, 1979).

A professional model argued that the use of a picture of her modeling a jacket in the "Best Bets" column of the *New York* magazine was an illegal appropriation of her likeness for advertising purposes. The column features short articles and photos about new and unusual products and services, and the photo of the model carried this caption:

> Yes Giorgio—from Giorgio Armani. Based on his now classic turn on the bomber jacket, this cotton-twill version with "fun fur" collar features the same cut at a far lower price—about $225. It'll be available in the stores next week. Henry Post Bomber Jacket/Barney's, Bergdorf Goodman, Bloomingdale's.

The plaintiff said this was an advertisement and that in order to get a product featured in the "Best Bets" column, a merchant had to advertise in the magazine. The New York Court of Appeals disagreed that use of the photo was an appropriation, ruling that the "newsworthiness exception applies not only to reports of political happenings and social trends, but also to news stories and articles of consumer interest, including developments in the fashion world." The plaintiff argued that she certainly was not newsworthy. The court said that was immaterial—the jacket she modeled was newsworthy (*Stephano* v. *News Group W Publications*, 1984).

Most recently the New York Supreme Court rejected an appropriation claim by Charles T. Welch, an actor who had appeared in a well-known cigarette commercial in the late 1960s. The commercial was included in a collection of classic television commercials in 1986, and this collection was shown on television and licensed for showing and sale by Group W Productions. Welch sued Group W, claiming the defendant was making money by showing the commercial containing his likeness. The court disagreed, noting that the law does not preclude the use of a person's likeness in material that is newsworthy or of public interest. The classic commercials were a part of our social history, the court suggested. It is not material that Group W made money by showing the film. "It is the content of the material that determines whether it is newsworthy (*Welch* v. *Group W Productions,* 1987).

Where there is a broad general rule there is generally an exception. Courts have been far more hospitable toward appropriation suits brought by a person whose name or likeness has appeared in nonadvertising matter in erotic or pornographic magazines or books. (See *Creel* v. *Crown Publishers,* 1985, for example.) Some judges have been reluctant to rule that such material is newsworthy or is a matter of public interest. The commercial nature of the publication, then, dictates a ruling for the aggrieved plaintiff. We are, after all, known by the company we keep.

Incidental Uses

Certain uses of a person's name or likeness in an advertisement have been ruled to be "incidental uses" and not an invasion of privacy. The use of a person's name or likeness in an advertisement *for* a magazine or a newspaper or a television program is usually not regarded as an appropriation if the photo or name has been or will be a part of the news or information content.

The controversy that sparked this rule involved actress Shirley Booth. She was photographed in Jamaica, and the picture was published in a feature story in *Holiday* magazine. *Holiday* then used the same picture to advertise the magazine itself. The full-page advertisement told readers that the picture was typical of the material appearing in *Holiday* magazine and urged people to advertise in the periodical or subscribe to *Holiday*. Ms. Booth did not object to her photograph in the feature story, only to its use in the subsequent advertisement. The courts, however, refused to call the use an invasion of privacy. The New York Supreme Court ruled that the strength of a free press depends upon economic support from advertisers and subscribers, and hence a publication or broadcasting station must promote itself. Since the picture in this case was first used in an information story, its subsequent use in a promotion for the magazine was really only "incidental" to its original use and was merely to show the quality and content of the magazine. The picture was not used to sell spaghetti or used cars. Hence the use did not constitute an invasion of privacy (*Booth* v. *Curtis Publishing Co.,* 1962).

This incidental use rule, which some call the "Booth rule," is slowly developing as more and more case law emerges from the courts. Originally it was felt that only republication or rebroadcast of previously used material was protected. That is, if a youngster's photo appeared on the front page of the newspaper, the newspaper could later *republish* that photo in an advertisement proclaiming the value of the newspaper to both readers and advertisers. Some courts still follow that somewhat narrow rule. (See *Lawrence* v. *A.S. Abell Co.,* 1984.) Courts have also ruled that it is permissible for a newspaper or magazine to use previously published material in a television advertisement for the newspaper or magazine (*Friedan* v. *Friedan,* 1976). An Oregon court ruled that it was permissible for a television station to use film it had shot, but never used, to promote a program soon to be broadcast. In this case news film of the plaintiff, a victim of a traffic accident, had not been used on the news. Nor was the plaintiff's picture used in the documentary program on emergency medical assistance systems the film clip promoted (*Anderson* v. *Fisher Broadcasting,* 1986). How far can a news or information medium push this rule? It is hard to say. Former New York Jet quarterback Joe Namath found he had no legal means to stop *Sports Illustrated* from using his photograph (which had previously illustrated a story in the magazine) on posters, television advertisements and insert cards to try to lure subscribers to the publication (*Namath* v. *Sports Illustrated,* 1976). Ten years later, another Time, Inc. company, Time-Life Books, was taken to court over the use of a plaintiff's photo to advertise a series of books on the Vietnam War. Edward Tellado's picture had been taken in Vietnam while he and other GIs waited in a battle zone for a helicopter. The AP photo was published in newspapers and ultimately sold to Time-Life Books. The photo was never used in any of the books in the series, but Time-Life used Tellado's picture in millions of direct mail advertisements promoting the book series. A United States district court in New Jersey refused to grant the book company a summary judgment and sent the case back for trial to determine whether the use of the photo was predominantly commercial or of news or historic value (*Tellado* v. *Time-Life Books,* 1986).

Clearly the use of a name or photo to promote a medium cannot be an explicit or even implied endorsement of the medium. Cher won a lawsuit against *Forum* magazine after it used her photo to promote an edition of the publication. The advertisements clearly implied that the actress-singer endorsed *Forum,* which was not true. That issue of the magazine did contain an interview with Cher, but the court ruled that the advertisments went far beyond establishing the news content and quality of the publication for potential readers (*Cher* v. *Forum International,* 1982). On the other hand, *The Village Voice* regularly uses a cover from a recent edition as an advertisement for new subscribers. The reproduced cover is always embellished by the addition of a cartoon balloon emanating from the mouth of the personality featured on the cover. The balloon usually contains the words "We'll be right over," or "What's your address?" Ramon Velez, an activist in New York, sued *The Village Voice,* arguing that the use of his photo in this way implied an endorsement. The appellate division of the Supreme Court disagreed, noting that no reasonable reader would believe that the plaintiff had endorsed *The Village Voice* (*Velez v. VV Publishing Corp.,* 1988). The fact that the entire cover and not just Velez's photo had been used probably helped the defendant in this case.

There are at least a couple of other instances when the unauthorized use of a name or likeness in an advertisement would not create liability. Surely it is permissible to use someone's name or likeness in a political advertisement: "Vote for Jones, not Smith." Similarly, the unauthorized use of an individual's name in an issue-oriented advertisement would not stand as an appropriation. If an environmental group wants to castigate the Secretary of Interior, and publishes his or her picture and name in an advertisement urging citizens to fight against some federal policy, the Secretary of Interior is without recourse to sue for appropriation.

Consent as a Defense

The law prohibits only the unauthorized use of a name or picture. In those states that have privacy statutes, the law specifically requires that the consent be a written authorization from the subject. In the remainder of the states, the law is more ambiguous on the question. Nevertheless, defendants are forced to prove they do have written consent if and when a lawsuit arises. Therefore, it only makes sense to obtain written consent. An example of a standard consent or release form appears on page 213.

The problems that can arise from the defense of consent are numerous, and in each case they are more severe when written consent has not been obtained. For example, it is always possible for the person to withdraw consent after it has been given. Columbia Broadcasting System (CBS) prepared a fictional television drama about the kidnapping of Jackie Gleason. Gleason played himself in the story, and an actor played the part of Gleason's manager. The manager's real name was used in the script. Suddenly the manager decided after the program was filmed that he did not want his name included in the program. Despite the fact that he had worked on the play for many weeks, planning and writing, a New York court said that inclusion of the plaintiff's name in the film against his will constituted an invasion of privacy (*Durgom v. CBS,* 1961). While this suit falls under category four of invasion of privacy, the rules are the same for both appropriation and falsehood. Columbia Broadcasting was therefore forced to write the plaintiff out of the script and reshoot part of the production.

Had the network gained written consent from the subject, and had it paid the plaintiff for using his name in the play, he would have found it much harder—if not impossible—to revoke consent at the last minute. Written consent has a distinct advantage. The safest rule is to always get written consent.

Photographers especially are advised to carry copies of a standard release form in their gadget bags so that when that once-in-a-lifetime picture comes along, the one they are certain to sell for ten thousand dollars, they can obtain written consent from the subject on the spot.

There are times when even written consent does not work as a defense, and the media must be aware of such situations:

1. Consent given today may not be valid ten years hence, especially if it is gratuitous oral consent. In Louisiana a man named Cole McAndrews gave permission to the owner of a health spa to use his before-and-after pictures in advertisements for the gym. But the owner, Alvin Roy, waited ten years to use the photographs, and in the interim McAndrews's life had changed considerably. He sued Roy, who argued that it was McAndrews's responsibility to revoke the consent if he no longer wanted the pictures used. But a Louisiana court of appeals agreed instead with the plaintiff. Judge Robert D. Jones wrote (*McAndrews* v. *Roy,* 1961):

> We are of the opinion that it would be placing an unreasonable burden on the plaintiff to hold he was under duty to revoke a gratuitous authorization given many years before. As the defendant was the only person to profit from the use of the pictures then, under all the circumstances, it seems reasonable that he should have sought renewal of the permission to use the old pictures.

Reauthorization is needed when a name or photograph is used many years after consent was first given. A professional actor in New York gave the manufacturer of artificial Christmas trees permission to use his picture in a commercial for one year. When the commercial was used after one year, he sued for appropriation, and the New York High Court sustained his privacy suit against the challenge by the defendant that only an action for breach of contract should be permitted (*Welch* v. *Mr. Christmas Tree,* 1982).

2. Some persons cannot give consent. A teenage girl is perfect to appear in an Acme Shampoo advertising campaign. She agrees to pose and signs a release authorizing use of her picture in the advertisements. The pictures are great, the advertisements are great, everything is great—until notice arrives that the model is suing for invasion of privacy! But she signed the permission form. Right. But she was only sixteen years old, and under the law minors cannot give consent. Parental consent is required in such instances. If parents or guardians do give consent for the use of a minor's name or picture, under the common law in many states it is possible for the minors to revoke that consent when they reach the legal age. When Brooke Shields was ten years old, a photographer was given permission by Brooke's mother to use a picture he had taken of the child model. The appellate division of the New York Supreme Court ruled that Brooke could revoke that consent when she became an adult (*Shields* v. *Gross,* 1982). But the state's high court reversed this ruling. The court of appeals said it recognized that such a revocation was possible under the common law, but the New York state privacy statute specifically permits parents to give written consent on behalf of a minor child. The statute,

the court said, derogates, or replaces, the common law rule. Brooke Shields had no recourse, since her mother had previously given written permission for the use of the photograph (*Shields* v. *Gross*, 1983).

Other people are unable to give consent as well. CBS was sued on behalf of David Delan by his guardian for including the young man in its film "Any Place But Here," a documentary about mental illness. Delan had been hospitalized for more than five years as a psychotic at the Creedmor State Hospital in New York. He was legally incompetent to sign a consent form, and the network failed to gain a signed release from a physician. A psychologist gave CBS permission to film David, but the New York state law specifically requires the signature of a medical doctor on the release agreement before patients in the state's mental hospitals can be photographed or interviewed (*Delan* v. *CBS*, 1981). CBS ultimately prevailed in the case when the appellate division of the New York Supreme Court ruled that the broadcast was not made for advertising or trade purposes, and therefore consent from David Delan was not required (*Delan* v. *CBS*, 1983). But the point made by the trial court is well taken. Persons who are unable to give consent because, for one reason or another, they are wards of the state are risky subjects for publications or broadcasts that are made for advertising or trade purposes.

It is important to know that the person from whom consent is obtained is legally able to give consent.

3. Finally, consent to use a photograph of a person in an advertisement or on a poster cannot be used as a defense if the photograph is materially altered or changed. Several years ago a well-known and well-paid New York fashion model posed for pictures to be used in an advertising campaign for a bookstore. After the photography session, model Mary Jane Russell signed this standard release form:

> The undersigned hereby irrevocably consents to the unrestricted use by Richard Avedon [the photographer], advertisers, customers, successors, and assigns, of my name, portrait, or picture for advertising purposes or purposes of trade, and I waive the right to inspect or approve such completed portraits, pictures, or advertising matter used in connection therewith.

It sounds as though she signed her life away, and with regard to the pictures Avedon took she did. However, the bookstore sold one of the photographs to a maker of bed sheets. The bedding manufacturer had a reputation for running sleazy advertising and consequently had trouble getting first-class models to pose for advertising pictures. The manufacturer substantially retouched the Avedon photographs, changing the context. Mary Jane Russell sued for invasion of privacy, but the manufacturer answered by telling the court that the model had given irrevocable consent for anyone to use those pictures, that she had waived her right to inspect the completed pictures and the advertising, and so forth.

The court agreed that Mary Jane had given up her right of privacy with regard to the pictures Avedon took. But the picture used by the sheet maker in its advertising was not the same picture taken by Avedon. It had been altered. And Mary Jane won her case. Justice Matthew Levy of the New York Supreme Court wrote (*Russell* v. *Marboro Books*, 1959):

> If the picture were altered sufficiently in situation, emphasis, background, or context, I should think that it would no longer be the same portrait, but a different one. And as to the changed picture, I would hold that the original written consent would not apply and that liability would arrive when the content of the picture has been so changed that it is substantially unlike the original.

What is substantial alteration? It probably means something other than minor retouching, but how much retouching is permissible before a privacy suit can accrue is difficult to say. This is one of the few cases on this legal point. Persons who want to retouch a photograph should be careful, even when they have written consent. They might change the picture sufficiently so that the consent would not apply.

The reference to altering the context of a picture arose recently in New York when a model sued and won after her seminude photograph was used to advertise an allegedly obscene movie. She had signed a release permitting the use of her photograph for "any purpose whatsoever," but the New York Supreme Court ruled that "any purpose whatsoever" does not include a "degrading use" (*Dittner* v. *Troma*, 1980).

Right of Publicity

In 1953, a distinguished American jurist, Jerome Frank, noted in an appropriation case that some plaintiffs might indeed be embarrassed and humiliated to see their name or face used to promote cornflakes or shampoo. Yet other plaintiffs, Frank argued, were not upset because they were humiliated; they were angry because they had not been paid for the commercial exploitation of their name or likeness (*Haelan Laboratories, Inc.* v. *Topps Chewing Gum*, 1953). Judge Frank identified what he called the "right of publicity," the right of persons to control the commercial exploitation of their name or likeness. The logic behind this assertion is that persons have a property right in their name just as they can have a property right in a book or a piece of land.

The relative youth and somewhat ambiguous state of the law of privacy resulted in most courts ignoring Judge Frank's ideas for many years. However, recently several jurisdictions have accepted the idea of this property right ancillary to the right of privacy.

Right of publicity cases generally involve persons who have developed a significant property right in their name through their exploits. Athletes, entertainers, writers, and other celebrities have all argued that the use of their name without consent and without compensation deprived them of rightful income. In cases in 1967 and 1970, courts ruled that several professional athletes, like Arnold Palmer and Jack Nicklaus, have the right to enjoy the fruits of their own industry free from unjustified interference and that celebrities have a legitimate proprietary interest in their public personality. These cases involved the use of the athletes' names and pictures in board games without compensation or permission (*Palmer v. Schonhorn Enterprises,* 1967, and *Uhlaender v. Henricksen,* 1970). A judge noted that the celebrity's "identity, embodied in his name, likeness, statistics and other personal characteristics, is the fruit of his labors and a type of property." However, in New Jersey a court said that even noncelebrities enjoy a property right in their identity when it ruled that a real estate company could not use a family's name and picture in its advertisements without permission (*Canessa v. J. I. Kislak,* 1967). "However little or much plaintiff's likeness and name may be worth," the judge wrote, "defendant, who has appropriated them for his commercial benefit, should be made to pay for what he has taken. . . ."

Some courts have simply refused to recognize the claims of the right of publicity. When comedian Pat Paulsen announced his candidacy for president in 1968, unauthorized campaign posters of the comedian were published. Paulsen sued, claiming appropriation of his likeness (*Paulsen v. Personality Posters,* 1968). But the court refused to compensate the entertainer, arguing that by declaring for president, even in jest, he had lost his right to privacy regarding his picture. And in 1988 a United States district court in New York turned back the plea of Ginger Rogers that her identity had been illegally exploited by the Fredrico Fellini film "Ginger and Fred." The film is a fictional work that depicts a reunion between two dancers who, decades earlier, had made a living in Italian cabarets by imitating Fred Astaire and Ginger Rogers. Rogers name was used as a reference in the film and in the title of the film. The court ruled that the law has been unwilling to recognize a right of publicity cause of action where the plaintiff's name was used in connection with a matter of public interest, be it news or entertainment (1988, aff'd., *Rogers v. Grimaldi,* 1989).

In its only ruling on the subject, the Supreme Court of the United States left many observers bewildered when it ruled that it is a violation of the right to publicity for a television station to broadcast news film of an entertainer's entire performance (*Zacchini v. Scripps-Howard Broadcasting Co.,* 1977). In a case that clearly proves the old judicial maxim that hard cases make bad law, the High Court overturned a decision by the Ohio Supreme Court and ruled that Hugo Zacchini, "The Human Cannonball," had indeed been harmed by the broadcast. The case was a hard one for at least two reasons. Zacchini's performance—being shot out of a cannon into a net—took only about fifteen seconds and consequently fit neatly into a small segment on a thirty-minute newscast. Obviously, such is not the case with most performers. Also, Zacchini had specifically asked the television station employees not to film the act, which was playing at a local county fair. A cameraman filmed it anyway. Zacchini argued that the television broadcast hurt his ability to make a living. Why should people pay to get into the fair to see his act if they had seen it on the television news? Justice Byron White and four other members of the Court agreed. The broadcast of the film of Zacchini's *entire* performance posed a substantial threat to the economic value of that performance, Justice White wrote. It went to the heart of his ability to earn a living as an entertainer, he added. Yet the ruling raised more questions than it answered. In previous right-of-publicity cases, the defendant had gained monetarily by exploiting the plaintiff's name or likeness. Yet in this case the television station had made no monetary gain from showing the short film of Zacchini being shot from a cannon. The cannon shot was a news item, like an automobile accident or a street parade.

White made the point that the station televised the *entire act*. But what does this mean? Zacchini took several minutes to do his act—adjusting the net, preparing to get into the cannon, building the suspense. The film lasted but fifteen seconds and included only the actual cannon shot. Would a newspaper be prohibited from publishing a detailed word description of the feats of Zacchini? If Zacchini were seriously injured in performing this stunt, could the accident be safely filmed? The dissenters in the case argued strongly—but to little avail—that the important question to be decided was not whether Zacchini's *entire act* was broadcast, but the purpose for which the film was used. Had the station filmed the shot, promoted it, built a show around it, and got advertisers to pay money to sponsor it? Such action would clearly be an exploitation of Zacchini. But this was a routine newscast, Justice Powell noted. There was no violation of any right.

The Zacchini case will probably have little impact upon the emerging—and often confusing—right of publicity. White's ruling was based largely on the fact that the television station telecast the *entire act*. Since few performers have such abbreviated acts, there seem to be few persons who could use the ruling as a precedent in a similar suit.

The right of privacy is a personal right and generally ends upon the death of the individual. But the right of publicity—based upon a theory of property rights—does not necessarily terminate upon death. In some instances it may be passed on to benefit the heirs, like any other part of the estate. The law on this question, which has only been raised recently, is currently being decided on a state-by-state basis. In about eight states legislation has been adopted. In Kentucky, for example, a 1984 law states that the name or likeness of a person who is a public figure shall not be used for commercial profit for a period of fifty years from the date of death without the written consent of the heirs. Tennessee and California have similar laws, and statutes in Florida, Nebraska, Oklahoma, Utah, and Virginia all speak in some way to the question of the rights of heirs.

Litigation of this question in other states has produced a ragged profile for the law, one that seems to be heading in three different directions. In some states, courts have ruled that the right to publicity is not descendible; it may not be passed on to heirs. (See *Reeves* v. *United Artists,* 1983, for example.) But this is clearly the minority rule today. In other states, courts have ruled that the right of publicity may be passed on to heirs, but only if the deceased had attempted to exploit this right while he or she was alive. In other words, the public figure had to have capitalized on his or her fame to create the property right to pass on to the heirs. This is the direction in which the California law was proceeding prior to the adoption of a state statute. (See *Lugosi* v. *Universal,* 1979 and *Acme* v. *Kuperstock,* 1983.) Finally, some state courts have ruled that the right may be passed on to heirs, regardless of whether the deceased attempted to exploit it while he or she was alive. (See *The Martin Luther King Center* v. *American Heritage Products,* 1982.)

Large advertising agencies have routinely sought permission from estates to insure that clients are not embarrassed by lawsuits. When IBM chose Charlie Chaplin's "Little Tramp" character to promote its line of personal computers, the company sought a license from the owner of the rights, Bubbles, Inc., before beginning the campaign. Licensing fees can be very expensive, sometimes as much as ten thousand dollars for the use of a character or likeness in one sixty-second commercial, according to an article in *The New York Times*. It is advisable for anyone seeking to use the name or likeness of a dead celebrity in an advertisement to gain permission from the heirs. While the courts and legislatures in most states have not yet decided whether or not the right to publicity is descendible, the clear trend is toward protecting that right for use by the heirs.

SUMMARY

Appropriation of a person's name or likeness for commercial or trade purposes without permission is an invasion of privacy. Use of an individual's photograph, a sketch of the person, a nickname, or a stage name are all considered use of a name or likeness. However, the publication of news and information in magazines, books, newspapers, and news broadcasts is not considered a trade purpose, even though the mass medium may make a profit from such publication. Consequently, persons who are named or pictured in news stories or other such material cannot sue for appropriation. Also, a news medium may republish or rebroadcast news items or photographs already carried as news stories in advertising for the mass medium to establish the quality or kind of material carried by the medium.

Anyone who seeks to use the name or likeness of an individual for commercial or trade purposes should gain written consent from that person. Even written consent may be invalid as a defense in an invasion of privacy suit if the consent was given many years before publication, if the person from whom the consent was gained cannot legally give consent, or if the photograph or other material that is used is substantially altered.

Courts have also recognized what is known as the right to publicity. Right to publicity actions are most often instituted by well-known persons who believe the unauthorized use of their name or likeness has deprived them of an opportunity to reap financial gain by selling this right to the user. The United

States Supreme Court has ruled that it is a violation of the right to publicity for a television news station to broadcast an entertainer's complete act without permission, even if this is done in the context of a news broadcast. In some states the right to publicity can be passed on to heirs like any other piece of property, which means that a performer's estate can control the use of his or her name and likeness after the performer's death.

INTRUSION   The intrusion category is what a lot of people think of when they hear the phrase "right to privacy." Wiretapping, using cameras with telephoto lenses, peeping-Tom actions, bugging rooms, and using supersensitive microphones and hidden transmitters are the kinds of behavior that many people—especially people outside the press—associate with violations of the right to privacy. This kind of behavior does occur, people are caught, and lawsuits do result. Until recently such suits were simply not brought against mass-media defendants. Even now such litigation is relatively rare.

The press does not often go in for this kind of snooping, or at least does not get caught frequently. Probably the earliest known intrusion case involving the press occurred in 1926 when a reporter for the *Washington* (D.C.) *Herald* stole a picture from the home of Mrs. Louise Peed, who had nearly died from asphyxiation when a gas jet was carelessly left open in the home of a friend she was visiting. The court held the newspaper responsible because it had published the plaintiff's picture, not because it had stolen the picture (*Peed* v. *Washington Times Co.,* 1927). A similar suit in Los Angeles a few years later failed altogether (*Metter* v. *Los Angeles Examiner,* 1939).

The *Peed* case points out a very important aspect of intrusion in invasion of privacy. In appropriation cases and in cases based upon publication of private information or publication of falsehoods, the legal wrong occurs when the picture or story is published. It must be published. A photographer who takes a picture of a skier, enlarges it to eight-by-ten inches, and hangs it on his or her kitchen wall has not invaded the skier's privacy. However if the photographer were to publish the picture in an advertisement, for example, appropriation, an illegal invasion of privacy occurs. If a newspaper reporter uncovers private information about a teacher's life but keeps the information confidential, no invasion of privacy occurs. Only when the reporter publishes this information might a lawsuit succeed.

In intrusion, on the other hand, the legal wrong is committed as soon as the intrusion takes place, whether or not the fruits of the intrusion are published. If your home is bugged, someone intrudes upon your privacy. Invasion of privacy occurred regardless of whether the content of the overheard conversations are published. If a reporter breaks into a private office and copies information from a private file, his act would probably be considered an invasion of privacy, an intrusion.

Intrusion cases are not too common. Those that have occurred seem to fall into a handful of categories. Here are some examples of the kinds of intrusion problems faced by the mass media.

Publication of Material Obtained Through Intrusion

In two cases in the late sixties, federal courts in Washington, D.C., established the principle that a news medium that publishes material obtained via intrusion by someone not connected with the medium cannot be held liable for the intrusion. In the two instances, the late newspaper columnist Drew Pearson obtained documents from private files of the Liberty Lobby, a right-wing, political group in Washington, and from the files of former Connecticut Senator Thomas Dodd. Employees of both Dodd and Liberty Lobby took the files from the private offices, made copies of them (which were given to Pearson), and then returned the purloined files. In both cases the court ruled that the publishers could not be held responsible for the actions of the intruders (*Liberty Lobby* v. *Pearson,* 1968; *Pearson* v. *Dodd,* 1969).

Judge J. Skelly Wright wrote in the *Dodd* case:

> If we were to hold appellants liable for invasion of privacy on these facts, we would establish the proposition that one who receives information from an intruder, knowing it has been obtained by improper intrusion, is guilty of a tort. In an untried and developing area of tort law, we are not prepared to go so far, . . .

This principle was supported in 1978 by a Maryland circuit court when several former and current members of the University of Maryland basketball team sued the *Baltimore Evening Star* for publishing an article that revealed portions of their academic records. Somebody gave the newspaper the information. There was no evidence presented that the reporters had either personally inspected the records or asked someone else to do it. Consequently, no suit could be maintained by the athletes on the intrusion theory (*Bilney* v. *Evening Star,* 1979).

Possessing Stolen Property

There is, however, another aspect of intrusion that can result in a problem for a journalist. If a reporter has original files that belong to someone else, a suit based on the doctrine of conversion could possibly be maintained. Conversion means to unlawfully convert someone else's property for your own use. This is property law and would be applicable only if journalists have the actual files—someone else's property—in their possession. In both the *Dodd* and *Liberty Lobby* cases just noted, the plaintiffs attempted to sue for conversion, but columnist Pearson did not have the original files, only copies of those files. Hence, no conversion had occurred.

In California the publisher and a reporter of the *Los Angeles Free Press* were found guilty of possession of stolen goods after they bought a list of names of undercover narcotic agents stolen from the attorney general's office. Art Kunkin and Robert Applebaum were freed upon appeal to the state's high court, but only because there was insufficient evidence to prove that they had known the list was stolen when they purchased it (*People* v. *Kunkin,* 1973). If the state could have adduced any evidence at all that the pair had knowledge that the list was stolen, the conviction would have stood. As it was, the thief was a former employee of the attorney general's office, and Kunkin and Applebaum said they thought he still worked for the attorney general. The thief also asked that they return the list to him after it was copied, presumably to return it to the proper file, the two journalists said.

This whole area of the law is gray. Of course, if employees of the publication are the intruders, liability might result, depending upon whether they acted on their own or at the employer's suggestion. In any case, intruders are always liable if they are caught, regardless of what use is made of the purloined material.

Journalists should ask tough questions of their sources of documents and files. Did you steal it? Did you copy it illegally? If a jury can be convinced that the journalist knew it was obtained illegally, or should have known it was obtained illegally (secret files, for example, can normally only be obtained illegally), a suit based on property law, not on privacy, might then in fact hold up.

News Gathering

While reporters may not engage in stealing or breaking and entering, they sometimes undertake other kinds of intrusions. These intrusions are harder to define, and generally involve the use of snooper aids; that is, hidden cameras, telephoto lens, and hidden microphones.

No broad, general proposition can be stated here, and we must rely instead upon examples. Hopefully, as more and more cases are litigated, the gaps will be filled and a rule formulated. Reporters have the right to photograph persons in public places, even when they do not know they are being photographed. These people are present in a public, not a private, place and are visible to anyone passing by. A ruling by the United States Court of Appeals for the Eighth Circuit supports this proposition. An attorney who was jailed for drunken driving became angry when jailed and began hitting and banging on the cell door, hollering and cursing and calling police officers names. The sounds were recorded by a television reporter, who played them during a newscast. The attorney sued for invasion of privacy, but the appellate court ruled that there was no zone of privacy in a jail cell. The court ruled that the reporter "could not be prevented from reporting the statements he could so easily overhear aurally; use of a device to record them cannot create a claim for privacy when one would not otherwise exist." The court noted that undoubtedly the plaintiff had not made his boisterous outbursts with any expectation of privacy at all (*Holman* v. *Central Arkansas Broadcasting,* 1979).

On record is a case in which harassment, not invasion of privacy, was charged. The photographer was Ron Galella, whose whole life seemed to revolve around taking pictures of Jacqueline Kennedy Onassis. He went everywhere she went, blocked her path, made a general nuisance of himself. When he was not around Mrs. Onassis, he followed the Kennedy children. In one instance his penchant for getting close almost resulted in a serious accident for young John Kennedy when the horse he was riding bolted after being frightened by Galella. The Secret Service, which guards the Kennedy children and Mrs. Onassis, went to court to stop Galella. A federal court enjoined the photographer from coming within twenty-four feet of Mrs. Onassis and within thirty feet of the children, from blocking their movement in any way, from doing anything that might put them in danger or might harass, alarm, or frighten them and from entering the children's play area at school (*Galella* v. *Onassis,* 1973). In 1982 a United States district court in New York found Galella in contempt of court for violating this order on twelve separate occasions. The photographer faced a severe fine and possible imprisonment (*Galella* v. *Onassis,* 1982).

The lawsuit against Galella was based on harassment. Could an invasion of privacy suit for intrusion have worked as well for Mrs. Onassis? No. Taking pictures on a public street or in a public schoolyard is not considered an intrusion. In an intrusion suit the courts will ask, Was there any legitimate expectation of privacy or solitude for the plaintiff when the photograph was taken? There can be none in a public setting. What can be seen on a public street or in a public park is open to public scrutiny.

A pharmacist in Seattle, Washington, sued KING-TV for invasion of privacy after the television station photographed the interior of his pharmacy through the front window. The druggist had been charged with cheating the state out of Medicaid funds. He refused to talk with reporters after the charges were made, so the KING-TV camera operator placed the camera against the outside of the store's front window and photographed the druggist as he talked on the telephone. The filming was done from the exterior of the building, from a place open to the public. The court ruled that an intrusion must be something that the general public would not be free to view. In this case any passerby could have seen what was recorded on film by the KING-TV camera operator. There was no unwarranted intrusion (*Marks* v. *King Broadcasting,* 1980). A key question in such an intrusion case, then, is did the plaintiff have a reasonable expectation of privacy? Or was the plaintiff in a public place? Theresa Stressman was in a restaurant in Iowa when a television news crew began videotaping in the room. She asked the camera operator not to tape her, but she was photographed anyway and the pictures were shown on the television news. She sued, arguing the videotaping had been an intrusion. Lower courts dismissed the suit, but the Iowa Supreme Court sent the case back to trial, noting that the plaintiff could conceivably recover damages if she could prove that she had a legitimate expectation of privacy. Clearly, if she was in a public dining room no such expectation could exist. But if she was in a private room in the restaurant, not in public view, an illegal intrusion may have occurred, the court ruled (*Stressman* v. *American Blackhawk Broadcasting,* 1987).

There are other instances when an invasion of privacy suit based upon photography may very well stand. For example, imagine that a homeowner has a fenced-in yard with a pool. The pool area is hidden from public view by a fence and foliage. Surely someone at pool side would legitimately enjoy the expectation of privacy. But a photographer climbs a nearby hill and using a supertelephoto lens takes photographs of persons swimming in the pool. This action could very likely be considered an intrusion. Or imagine that a photographer films the interior of a home through a crack in the draperies while standing on private property surrounding the home. This is a scene that a passerby would not see. This, too, is fertile ground for an intrusion suit. Many problems also surround the use of hidden cameras and recording devices, as the next series of cases readily demonstrates.

A disabled veteran and journeyman plumber named A. A. Dietemann practiced healing using clay, minerals, and herbs. Dietemann practiced his version of medicine in his home. It was there that two *Life* magazine reporters who had agreed to work with Los Angeles law enforcement people visited the healer. Jackie Metcalf and William Ray pretended they were married, and Ms. Metcalf complained of a lump in her breast. Dietemann diagnosed the ailment as due to rancid butter she had eaten eleven years, nine months, seven days previously. While the "doctor" examined Ms. Metcalf, Ray photographed him with a secret camera. The conversation between the reporters (who did not reveal that they were reporters) and the healer was also broadcast via a hidden microphone to investigators waiting in a car outside.

Dietemann was arrested weeks later and charged with practicing medicine without a license. *Life* photographers took more pictures at the time of the arrest, and in an article on medical quackery included those pictures with pictures taken by the hidden camera. Dietemann sued for invasion of privacy. *Life* magazine said the pictures were informational and newsworthy and were protected. The court agreed that the pictures were indeed newsworthy but ruled that the photos taken with the hidden camera had been obtained by intruding upon Dietemann's privacy. The magazine had the right to publish the pictures; the publication did not constitute an invasion of privacy. It was the use of the secret camera and microphone that turned the relatively routine news-gathering venture into an illegal intrusion into Dietemann's privacy. Judge Shirley Hufstedler wrote (*Dietemann* v. *Time, Inc.,* 1971):

> One who invites another into his home or office takes a risk that the visitor may not be what he seems, and that the visitor may repeat all he hears and observes when he leaves. But he does not and should not be required to take the risk that what is heard and seen will be transmitted by photography or recording, or in our modern world, in full living color and hi-fi to the public at large or any segment of it that the visitor might select.

Recognizing that news gathering is an integral part of news dissemination, Judge Hufstedler said she still did not believe there was a need to use mechanical devices in gathering information:

> The First Amendment is not a license to trespass, to steal, or to intrude by electronic means into the precincts of another's home or office. It does not become such a license simply because the person subjected to the intrusion is reasonably suspected of committing a crime.

The magazine protested, saying the story was simply an example of good investigative reporting. Judge Hufstedler was unimpressed:

> Investigative reporting is an ancient art; its successful practice long antecedes the invention of miniature cameras and electronic devices. The First Amendment has never been construed to accord newsmen immunity from torts or crimes committed during the course of news gathering.

The facts in the *Dietemann* case are significant. And as more and more intrusion cases are decided, this ruling stands out as an atypical decision; one tied very closely to the unusual facts in this case. The reporters were in the plaintiff's home, almost as uninvited visitors, taking secret pictures and making a clandestine recording of the conversation. Cases since 1971 demonstrate the narrow bases of the *Dietemann* ruling.

In 1975 Arlyn Cassidy and several other Chicago police officers were acting as undercover agents, investigating massage parlors in the city. The owner of one massage parlor where police previously had made arrests believed he was being harassed by the lawmen and invited a television news camera crew to come in and secretly film an encounter between an undercover agent and a model at the parlor. The camera was set up behind a two-way mirror and was filming when officer Cassidy came in, paid thirty dollars for deluxe lingerie modeling, and subsequently arrested the girl for solicitation. Three other agents came into the room at about the same time the television news crew burst through another door, filming as they left the building. The officers sued the station for intrusion, using the *Dietemann* case as precedent.

But an Illinois appellate court ruled in favor of the journalists, distinguishing the *Dietemann* case in some important ways. First, Cassidy and the other plaintiffs were public officers acting in the line of duty as the filming took place. Second, the film crew was not in a private home, but in a public business. And third, the crew was on hand at the invitation of the operator of the premises. "In our opinion," the court ruled, "no right of privacy against intrusion can be said to exist with reference to the gathering and dissemination of news concerning discharge of public duties" (*Cassidy* v. *ABC,* 1978).

In 1979 a Kentucky circuit court ruled that it was not an intrusion when a young woman, at the instigation of a newspaper, secretly recorded a conversation she had with an attorney. Kristie Frazier met with attorney John T. McCall after she was indicted on a drug charge. According to Ms. Frazier, the attorney said he would guarantee that he could get her "off the hook" if she could come up with ten thousand dollars. He said he would return nine thousand dollars if he failed to have her set free. Setting a fee in a criminal case in such a manner is considered unethical conduct for an attorney.

Ms. Frazier recognized the unusual fee arrangement and went to the offices of the *Louisville Courier-Journal*. Reporters were interested in Ms. Frazier's allegations against McCall but were unwilling to take her word for what had been said in the private conversation. They gave her a small tape recorder and told her to propose a second meeting with McCall—to try to trap him into repeating what he had said earlier. McCall repeated his proposal, Ms. Frazier recorded it secretly, and the *Courier-Journal* published the transcript. McCall sued for intrusion, but lost.

The court distinguished *Dietemann* by noting that Frazier—who may or may not have been an agent of the newspaper—was in McCall's office at his invitation. There was no intrusion into McCall's private affairs because they were also the affairs of Ms. Frazier. "A lawyer, an officer of the court, discussing in a public court with a potential client, is not in seclusion within the meaning of the law," the court ruled. "Human dignity demands the rights of privacy be enforced, but when the rights of privacy encroach upon the most sacred trust the public possesses, namely, the judicial system, then those rights must give way," the judge added (*McCall v. Courier-Journal*, 1979). The trial court ruling for the newspaper was upheld in March 1980 by a Kentucky court of appeals.

Cassidy and *McCall* have chipped away at some of the fears the press had after the *Dietemann* case. The California case must be viewed as a fairly narrow ruling. Remember, the intrusion in *Dietemann* took place in the plaintiff's home, and Anglo-American courts have protected a citizen's home from government intrusions for centuries. ("A man's home is his castle," ruled Lord Chief Justice Sir Edward Coke in the early seventeenth century.) Remember also that the reporters carried hidden electronic devices into the plaintiff's home. The courts have suggested that different rules apply in public places and in business offices, especially when public officers (such as police officers and attorneys, who are considered officers of the court) are being scrutinized in the performance of their duty.

A federal court in Missouri dismissed an intrusion suit against a television station after an employee posed as someone who sought the help of an alcoholic treatment program, and then secretly videotaped and recorded a meeting between hospital employees and a bogus prospective patient. The judge, however, refused to dismiss charges of fraud, eavesdropping, and negligence against the station. The station then filed a counter suit against the hospital for malicious prosecution, defamation and assorted other claims. No resolution of the dispute has been reported (*W.C.H. of Waverly, Mo., Inc.* v. *Meredith Corp.*, 1986).

But this case makes an important point. Reporters need to be cautious when they secretly record a conversation. In many states only the consent of a single party is needed to record a conversation. The reporter does not need the permission of the other party. But many states have two-party consent laws; that is, both participants in the conversation must agree to the recording. Secret recording in such states is not permitted. Minor criminal penalties accrue when the law is violated. The secret recording might also be the basis for a privacy action. Check the laws where you reside and work.

Some persons have expressed concern that an intrusion may occur if a reporter poses as someone other than a reporter to gain a story. That is not likely; the fact that reporters posed as patients in the *Dietemann* case does not appear to be a material consideration. This conclusion is strengthened by the decision in *Rifkin* v. *Esquire,* 1982, when a United States district court in California ruled that no invasion of privacy took place when reporters posed as a friend of the plaintiff, Stan Rifkin, in order to get information about Rifkin from his friends and neighbors. The court said this did not constitute an intrusion upon plaintiff Rifkin's solitude. However, this is not to suggest that a reporter may pose as a government official or someone else of authority in order to get a story. Impersonating a government official is generally forbidden by state statute. In New Jersey, a newspaper reporter interviewed the mother of a homicide victim, supposedly identifying herself to the woman as a county official, "a lady from the morgue." She was found to have violated a state law that makes it a crime "to falsely pretend to hold a position in the public service with the purpose to induce another to submit to such pretended official authority." The journalist was fined five hundred dollars and was required to serve thirty days community service (*New Jersey* v. *Cantor,* 1987).

Because intrusion is such a new area of the law, no good defenses have been developed. A heavy burden rests upon the plaintiff to prove that the behavior by the reporter or cameraman was in fact an intrusion, an invasion of privacy. If invasion of privacy can be established, there are no good "legal excuses" with which to defend this behavior. In addition to the legal problems involved, members of the press themselves have begun to raise ethical questions about such behavior. Defending illegal behavior on the grounds that it is in the public interest is an excuse that the American people seemed to reject when the members of the Nixon White House used it in 1973 and 1974. There are few causes that are "good enough" to justify illegal intrusion upon the privacy of others. Intrusion as an aspect of invasion of privacy should really not be a problem to journalists who conduct their business in an ethical fashion. Still, the paucity of good guidelines at this time can be somewhat frightening. Until there is more law to guide the press, journalists are advised to be guided by the common sense, conscience, and integrity one normally expects from responsible adults. (See pp. 262–265 in chapter 5 for more material relating to legal problems involved in news gathering.)

SUMMARY

Intruding upon an individual's solitude is an invasion of privacy. While the press is not often the subject of intrusion privacy suits, cases have occurred more often in recent years. An invasion of privacy takes place as soon as the intrusion has been made. Publication of the fruits of the intrusion is irrelevant in such cases. Journalists will not normally be held responsible for intrusion if they publish material that other persons have obtained through an intrusion. However, the journalist may be charged with the possession of stolen goods if in fact the material was stolen and the news person is aware of that fact.

Courts will not permit a successful intrusion suit based upon the recording of events that take place in public places. The court will permit a suit only if the plaintiff in the case can prove that at the time the intrusion was made, there was a "legitimate expectation of solitude"; that is, the plaintiff was in a place where he or she could expect to be alone. Courts are sensitive about protecting the privacy of a home and are likely to rule it is an intrusion to secretly film or record what occurs there. Courts are less sensitive about protecting what takes place in a business office.

PUBLICITY ABOUT PRIVATE FACTS

The most controversial aspect of the right of privacy in the current decade is that aspect of the law which penalizes the publication of private information about a person. The *Restatement of the Law of Torts* (2d) defines this section of the law this way:

> One who gives publicity to a matter concerning the private life of another is subject to liability to the other for invasion of his privacy, if the matter publicized is of a kind that
> a. would be highly offensive to a reasonable person, and
> b. is not of legitimate concern to the public.

This, of course, is the kind of privacy protection that Warren and Brandeis sought in 1890. Strangely, as we will see shortly, American courts have been most reluctant to curb this kind of journalism, for it touches at the very foundation of our long-held notions about freedom of the press. The North Carolina Supreme Court recently ruled that, that State did not even recognize this variety of the law of privacy, calling it "constitutionally suspect," and claiming that plaintiffs who had a legitimate cause of action could find legal relief in some other tort area outside of privacy (*Hall* v. *Post,* 1988). Most American judges find it difficult, if not impossible, to impose liability upon a newspaper or broadcasting station for the publication or broadcast of truthful information. This attitude has angered many persons, who suggest that members of the press use this freedom irresponsibly to probe and publicize intimate information about the famous and the not-so-famous or to prey upon the private lives of victims of crime and other tragedy. While most journalists don't do this, those who do have generated a strong antipress feeling among large and often vocal segments of the public. The reluctance of judges to rule for plaintiffs in these private facts cases has suggested to some scholars that this area of privacy has no real validity. But that is not the case, for occasionally judges are willing to draw the line. Reporters need to be aware of the guidelines that do exist, as generous as they are. Reporters also need to reflect upon their ethical and moral responsibilities as well as their legal liabilities.

Most courts use a two-step evaluation in considering whether this kind of invasion of privacy has occurred. This method also lends itself to presentation of a simple explanation of the law. First, the determination must be made that private facts about a person's life have indeed been publicized, which requires examination of two concepts: publicity and private facts. The information or facts publicized must be private, not known to other persons. And these facts must have been publicized. The plaintiff must prove both elements. If there *has been* publicity about private facts, a second evaluation must be made. The questions asked are, (1) Would this publicity be highly offensive to a reasonable person? and (2) Was the matter published of legitimate public concern? In this second stage, a kind of balancing process normally results, with the importance to the public of the revelation of the private material being weighed against how offensive the publication is to the plaintiff. While guidelines do exist, the balancing process often tends to be quite subjective, and matters of personal taste and sensitivity frequently play a role in the outcome. Reporters should spend time in considering how to present important but sensitive material in the least offensive manner.

This category of right to privacy can be best understood by considering each of the two elements of the law individually.

Publicity

The words *publicity* and *publication* mean different things in privacy law than they do in libel law. In defamation, *publication* means to communicate the material to a single third party. The word *publicity* in privacy law implies far more. It means that the material is communicated to the public at large or to a great number of people, making it certain that the facts will shortly become public knowledge. Needless to say this kind of publicity can usually be presumed when a story is published in a newspaper or broadcast over radio and television.

Private Facts

Before there can be an invasion of privacy, it must be demonstrated that the material publicized was indeed private. What happens in public is considered public information. A fan at a Pittsburgh Steeler football game urged a news photographer to take his picture. The photographer did, but when the photograph was published in *Sports Illustrated,* the fan sued for invasion of privacy, arguing that the photograph revealed that his trousers were unzipped and that this was quite embarrassing. The District Court for Eastern Pennsylvania ruled against the plaintiff, primarily because the picture was taken in a public place with the defendant's knowledge and encouragement. It was not private information (*Neff* v. *Time, Inc.,* 1976). Similarly, the United States Court of Appeals for the D.C. Circuit refused to find liability for the broadcast of news film that showed two men on a public street being escorted by police officers. Plaintiff Darryl Harrison argued that the pictures were embarrassing because they portrayed him as being a criminal. But the court ruled that an action for invasion of privacy cannot be maintained for pictures of events that take place in public view. The photographer in this case was standing on a public sidewalk while he took the pictures (*Harrison* v. *Washington Post,* 1978). A Massachusetts court of appeals ruled that no privacy exists when a person is standing in a line at a government building. The plaintiff in the case was photographed while standing in a line of persons waiting to collect unemployment benefits at the state employment security office. "The appearance of a person in a public place necessarily involves doffing the cloak of privacy which the law protects," the court ruled (*Cefalu* v. *Globe Newspaper,* 1979; see also *Arrington* v. *New York Times,* 1982).

Three revelers at a San Francisco Exotic Erotic Halloween Ball brought suit against *Penthouse* when it published their pictures in the magazine. They complained they had not given permission to the photographer to take their pictures; in fact, they had not even known the pictures were taken. A California court of appeals said that was immaterial. It doesn't make the facts any less public. Thousands of other persons attending the ball saw the plaintiffs. These were not private facts (*Martin* v. *Penthouse,* 1986).

If a large segment of the public is already aware of supposedly intimate or personal information, it is not private. Oliver Sipple, a man who deflected a gun held by a woman who tried to assassinate President Gerald Ford, sued the *San Francisco Chronicle* after a columnist noted that Sipple was a homosexual and that that may be the reason Ford had never thanked his benefactor for his heroic act. But Sipple's suit failed, in part at least, because his sexual orientation was hardly a secret in San Francisco. A California court of appeals noted that Sipple routinely frequented gay bars, marched in parades with other homosexuals, openly worked for the election of homosexual political candidates and that many gay publications had reported stories about his activities in the homosexual community. That he was a homosexual was not a private fact, the court ruled (*Sipple* v. *Chronicle Publishing,* 1984).

In 1975 the United States Supreme Court ruled that the broadcast or publication of the name of a rape victim that was included in the public record during a criminal trial could not be considered an invasion of privacy. At that time, at least four states had statutes making the publication of such information an invasion of privacy. The rationale for such laws was generally accepted: nonpublication would save victims from embarrassment and might, in turn, encourage more women to report such incidents. Decreased reporting of names might therefore result in more prosecutions of rapists. There had been at least two decisions prior to the 1975 ruling upholding these laws. (See, for example, *Nappier* v. *Jefferson Standard Life Insurance Co.,* 1963.) When an Atlanta, Georgia, television station broadcast the name of a young woman who had been raped and murdered, her parents sued. In *Cox Broadcasting Co.* v. *Cohn* (1975), the United States Supreme Court overturned the Georgia state court ruling and held that the press cannot be held liable for invasion of privacy for reporting information already part of the public record. Justice Byron White noted that most persons depend upon the mass media for information about the operations of the government via public meetings and the public record. Judicial proceedings are an important part of our governmental system and are something in which the public has always expressed a great interest. By making judicial records and proceedings public, the state of Georgia must have concluded that the public interest was being served (*Cox Broadcasting Co.* v. *Cohn,* 1975):

> We are reluctant to embark on a course that would make public records generally available to the media but forbid their publication if offensive to the sensibilities of the supposed reasonable man. Such a rule would make it very difficult for the press to inform their readers about the public business and yet stay within the law. The rule would invite timidity and self-censorship and very likely lead to the suppression of many items that would otherwise be put into print and that should be made available to the public.

Quoting the *Restatement of Torts* (*2d*), which attempts to summarize the law of torts, the Court said, "There is no liability when the defendant merely gives further publicity to information about the plaintiff which is already public. Thus there is no liability for giving publicity to facts about the plaintiff's life which are matters of public record."

Since 1975 the impact of the decision in *Cox* v. *Cohn* has been felt nationwide. A 1982 New Jersey ruling is a good example. When the victim of a sexual assault in Willingboro, New Jersey, reported the crime, she asked police to keep her name and address confidential. The hospital at which she was treated routinely gave out her name, and a reporter for the *Burlington County Times* followed up the story by talking with a police officer who was investigating the case. Three stories were published about the incident, and in each the plaintiff was identified. Details of the attack were not included, however. In her invasion of privacy suit, the plaintiff argued that this case was different from *Cox* v. *Cohn* where the reporter got the information from an official court record. This story was obtained orally from a police officer. But the New Jersey Superior Court rejected the plaintiff's argument. "The fact that the story was derived directly from a person in charge of the investigation and not from a written record of such investigation . . . does not distinguish [this case from] *Cox* in the opinion of the court." The police officer was an official source, the court ruled. This was a matter of great public interest (*Griffith* v. *Rancocas Valley Hospital et al.,* 1982).

The legal question of how far the decision in *Cox* v. *Cohn* goes is not yet resolved. In that ruling the court said a news medium could not be punished for reprinting the name of the victim of a rape when that name had appeared in public court documents or public court testimony. In 1989 the Supreme Court pushed the boundaries of that decision out a bit farther when it ruled that a Florida newspaper was not liable for an invasion of privacy when it inadvertently published the name of the victim of a rape, a name that had been obtained from police records that had been open to public inspection. "Where the government has made certain information publicly available, it is highly anomalous to sanction persons other than the source of its release," said Justice Thurgood Marshall, writing for the court in the 6–3 ruling. Marshall said the ruling by the court did not preclude imposing civil sanctions in the future for publication of the name of a victim of a rape. But in such a case such sanctions would have to be "overwhelmingly necessary" to advance the privacy interests of the victim (*Florida Star* v. *B.J.F.*, 1989).

Legal resolution of the issue—if that should come—won't end the matter, however. Many persons, both inside and outside the field of journalism, raise the question of whether the limited public good that derives from publishing or broadcasting a victim's name really outweighs the probable harm done to the victim through further publicity about his (or her) plight.

If these two Supreme Court rulings do stand for the broad proposition that any information taken from any public record cannot be considered a private fact for purposes of a lawsuit, reporters still need to exercise caution. Government agencies keep many kinds of records; some are public, some are not. If a reporter inadvertently gains access to a nonpublic document and uses names from that document, he or she may not have any protection from a charge of invasion of privacy. For example, a Florida newspaper that published material taken from confidential records in a child abuse case was found guilty of an invasion of privacy. The parents in the case had been charged but acquitted of aggravated child abuse in a closed proceeding. State law declares that the numerous records that accumulate in such a case are confidential. Persons in the state's attorney office gave a reporter the material in the file. When sued by the parents the newspaper argued that when the state official gave the confidential material to the reporter, the documents became public. The court disagreed, "While the state attorney was the custodian of the file and burdened with the responsibility not to disclose, it was the newspaper who [sic] published the private facts thus fulfilling the element of public disclosure." The trial court had presumed injury in the case, but a Florida court of appeals overruled this finding, ruling that damages must be proved (*Cape Publications* v. *Hitchner*, 1987). Reporters need to be knowledgeable about what is and what is not public information. Ignorance will not work as a defense.

Offensive Material

If the determination has been made that private facts about a person's life have been published, a court must then ask two subsequent questions:

1. Would the publication of the material offend a reasonable person?

2. Was the published material of legitimate public concern?

Frequently courts are faced with the real dilemma that while revelation of the material was extremely offensive and embarrassing, its publication, was of great importance for the public. Except in extremely unusual circumstances, the press will win such decisions. The judiciary places great weight upon the role of the press as an agent to inform and enlighten the public upon matters of interest and importance. Judges have ruled time and again that it is the responsibility of the press to bring such "newsworthy" information to the people. And courts have been hesitant to define narrow limits upon what the public needs to know or upon the kinds of information in which the people have a genuine interest. And remember, the publication of the material must be offensive to a reasonable person. The feelings of a hypersensitive person or someone who is especially sensitive do not count. Peggy Jo Fry sued the *Ionia* (Michigan) *Sentinel-Standard* for invasion of privacy when it reported that her husband and another woman had died in a fire that destroyed a cottage near Lake Michigan. The story mentioned that Ted Fry had been seen with Rita Hill at a tavern prior to the fire and related details about Fry's wife and children. The court ruled that these details were simply not highly offensive to a reasonable person (*Fry* v. *Ionia Sentinel-Standard*, 1980). Another Michigan woman sued Knight-Ridder Newspapers after the *Miami Herald* published a story about the murder of her daughter. The plaintiff in the case was mentioned incidently in the story. It was noted that four of her six children were deaf and that she was a hard-working woman who had great faith in her daughter's ability to succeed in life. The court said such information is not offensive (*Andren* v. *Knight-Ridder Newspapers*, 1984).

Generally, if journalists stick to their job—reporting what is newsworthy—there is little to worry about. But privacy is an emotional subject. There are times when the revelation of details is highly offensive, and even seemingly newsworthy reports lose their immunity from a successful invasion of privacy suit.

Several years ago a woman with a rather unusual disorder—she ate constantly, but still lost weight—was admitted to a hospital. The press was tipped off and descended upon her room, pushed past the closed door, and took pictures against the patient's will. *Time* magazine ran a story about the patient, Dorothy Barber, whom in inimitable "*Time* style" it called "the starving glutton." Mrs. Barber sued and won her case. The judge said the hospital is one place people should be able to go for privacy (*Barber* v. *Time, Inc.,* 1942). More than the privacy of the hospital visit influenced the ruling, because there are several decisions in which persons in hospitals have been considered to be the subject of legitimate concern and did not therefore enjoy the right to privacy. The story about the unusual disorder was surely offensive, almost mocking. The disorder was not contagious, and the implications for the general public were minimal. The *Time* story seemed to focus upon Mrs. Barber almost as if she were a freak, and in doing so the revelation of this information was highly offensive to any reasonable person.

A Georgia housewife took her two sons to the county fair and finally succumbed to their pressure to be taken through the fun house. As she left the building, an air jet blew Mrs. Flora Bell Graham's dress up over her head, and she was exposed from the waist down except for her underclothing. As fate would have it, a local photographer was nearby and captured the moment on film. The picture was featured in the Sunday edition of the local newspaper as a publicity piece for the fair. Mrs. Graham sued. By logical analysis one could suggest that she should not have won. The event took place in public. Many people saw her. She could not be readily identified in the picture because her dress was over her head. However, persons who knew the children, who were also in the picture, could make the connection between mother and children. Mrs. Graham did win (*Daily Times-Democrat* v. *Graham*, 1962). She had suffered an immense amount of embarrassment from the most intimate kind of revelation, and the public value of the photograph was extremely low.

More recently a woman successfully sued her plastic surgeon for publicly displaying "before and after" pictures of her at a department store presentation about plastic surgery and on a television appearance promoting the presentation. The plaintiff argued that only the members of her immediate family and a few close friends were aware she had undergone the cosmetic surgery. A jury ruled that the revelation of such personal medical facts was offensive to a reasonable person, and the United States Court of Appeals for the District of Columbia sustained the ruling (*Vassiliades* v. *Garfinckel's*, 1985). The court let the department store and other defendants off the hook because of evidence that the doctor had given assurances that he had consent to use the pictures.

Finally, the South Carolina Supreme Court recently affirmed a jury verdict against a newspaper that in publishing a story about teenage pregnancies had identified a young man—a minor—as the father of an illegitimate child. The teenage mother of the baby had given the reporter the father's name. The reporter talked to the young man who understood that the newspaper was doing a survey on teenage pregnancy. He said he was never told that his name might be used in the story. The newspaper argued that the information—including the boy's name—was of great public interest. The state supreme court said that was a jury question, and a jury ruled it was not of great public interest (*Hawkins* v. *Multimedia*, 1986).

While the four cases cited do not stand alone, they are unusual. Far more often courts rule that public concern over the issues involved outweighs any embarrassment to plaintiffs. Several factors have been cited in weighing the public concern or interest in a particular matter.

In determining whether something is of public concern, courts have focused upon such factors as what the story is about, who the story is about, when the incidents described in the story took place, and sometimes where they took place. Factual stories, reports, or broadcasts that have great public interest have generally been protected in invasion of privacy suits. The courts have been quite liberal in defining public interest, not as something people should read about but as something they do read about, something in which people are interested.

A twelve-year-old girl who gave birth to a baby (*Meetze* v. *AP,* 1956), the suffocation of two children in an old refrigerator (*Costlow* v. *Cuismano,* 1970), the sterilization of an eighteen-year-old girl (*Howard* v. *Des Moines Register,* 1979), the death of a young man from a drug overdose (*Beresky* v. *Teschner,* 1978), the activities of a bodysurfer (*Virgil* v. *Time,* 1975), and other subjects have all been ruled to be of legitimate concern and interest to the public. Even the seemingly frivolous subject of romance was declared to be newsworthy by a New York court that found no liability in the broadcast of a television film of a man and a woman walking hand in hand along Madison Avenue. The couple objected to being photographed; he was married to another woman, she was engaged to be married to another man. The court said that the film, used to show people behaving in a romantic fashion in order to explore the prevailing attitudes on this topic, is newsworthy (*DeGregorio* v. *CBS,* 1984).

The courts have been most generous to the press in their understanding of American reading and viewing habits. In a 1975 ruling in California, the United States Court of Appeals for the Ninth Circuit noted that "in determining what is a matter of legitimate public interest, account must be taken of the customs and conventions of the community; and in the last analysis what is proper becomes a matter of community mores" (*Virgil* v. *Time,* 1975). Thirty-five years earlier another federal judge noted that the public enjoyed reading about the problems, misfortunes, and troubles of their neighbors and other members of the community. "When such are the mores of the community, it would be unwise for a court to bar their expression in the newspapers, books, and magazines of the day," Judge Charles Clark wrote (*Sidis* v. *F-R Publishing Co.,* 1940).

Even the way a story is presented is normally not a factor: sensationalism and sensational treatment generally do not remove the protection of newsworthiness. Concerning the story of the suffocation of the two young children, the parents found the sensational treatment of the story as objectionable as the story itself. However, the court ruled that the manner in which the article was written was not relevant to whether the article was protected by the constitutional guarantees of free speech and free press—which, by the way, it was. In another case a Boston newspaper published a horrible picture of an automobile accident in which the bloodied and battered body of one of the victims was clearly visible and identifiable, and the court rejected the plaintiff's claim. The Massachusetts Supreme Court noted, "Many things which are distressing or may be lacking in propriety or good taste are not actionable" (*Kelley* v. *Post Publishing Co.,* 1951).

What the story is about, then, is an important aspect of determining whether it is newsworthy. American readers, viewers, and listeners are believed to have a wide range of interests that often focus on grotesque events and the tragedy, unhappiness, and misfortune of other persons.

Who the story is about is also taken into account in determining whether the material is of legitimate public concern. As in the law of libel, stories about public officials and persons who thrust themselves into the public eye are looked at much differently than are stories about private persons. A story that Mayor John Smith has a serious drinking problem would not be considered an invasion of privacy; the same story about barber Bill Brown might in fact be an invasion of privacy. How far can the press go in publishing details of the private life of so-called public persons? That is a difficult question to answer. Certainly the public status of the individual is important. Probably few details of the life of a president are considered private in terms of the law, but a circuit judge in a rural county, also an elected official, would probably enjoy considerably more privacy. In an interesting case in California, federal courts were asked to determine how far the press can go in looking into the private life of a public person.

The story focused upon Mike Virgil, widely regarded in southern California as one of the best bodysurfers along the Pacific Coast. *Sports Illustrated* decided to publish a feature on bodysurfing, and writer Curry Kirkpatrick chose to emphasize the prowess of Virgil. Virgil was known for his almost total disregard for personal safety and talked freely with the writer about his private life, as well as about his surfing. He told Kirkpatrick that he was reckless in private as well and described several incidents to demonstrate this attitude. These incidents included putting out a burning cigarette with his mouth, burning a hole in his wrist with a cigarette, diving headfirst down a flight of stairs, and eating live insects. But after the interview Virgil had second thoughts about the story and asked *Sports Illustrated* not to include the material about his private life. The magazine published the story as Kirkpatrick had written it, and Virgil sued. The Court of Appeals for the Ninth Circuit ruled that the line between private and public information "is to be drawn when the publicity ceases to be the giving of information to which the public is entitled, and becomes a morbid and sensational prying into private lives *for its own sake* [emphasis added]." In applying this standard to the Virgil case, the United States district court ruled that "any reasonable person reading the article would conclude that the personal facts concerning the individual were revealed in a legitimate journalistic attempt to explain his extremely daring and dangerous style of bodysurfing" (*Virgil* v. *Sports Illustrated,* 1976). Judge Thompson ruled that no one could reasonably conclude that these personal facts were included for any inherent morbid, sensational, or curiosity appeal they might have. If *Sports Illustrated* had published these personal details about Virgil without any other information, it might have been an invasion of privacy. But in the context of the story about his public life as a surfer, the publication was not an invasion of privacy.

An Iowa court used the same sort of standard when ruling that a story about a girl who had been sterilized when she was eighteen years old was not an invasion of privacy. The story focused upon the activities at a county juvenile home that had come under investigation by the state. As an example of what occurred there, the *Des Moines Register* recounted the story of a girl who was sterilized against her will because a psychiatrist reported to officials that she was "impulsive" and "hair-triggered" and would probably have sexual problems in the future. The girl's name was used, but was not prominent in the story. The court ruled that the paper had not pried into the girl's life simply to shock or outrage the community. The facts were presented to demonstrate to the community the kind of unethical, even illegal, activities taking place at the home. As such, the material was of legitimate public concern (*Howard* v. *Des Moines Register,* 1979). But was it necessary to use the victim's name in this story? Was it not possible for the newspaper to present this story to readers without identifying an unfortunate victim of this county home? The Iowa high court ruled it was legitimate to conclude that the name was an essential ingredient in the story (*Howard* v. *Des Moines Register,* 1979):

> In the sense of serving an appropriate news function, the disclosure [of the name] contributed constructively to the impact of the article. It offered a personalized frame of reference to which the reader could relate, fostering perception and understanding. Moreover, it lent specificity and credibility to the report. In this way the disclosure served as an effective means of accomplishing the intended news function. . . . Moreover, at a time when it was important to separate fact from rumor, the specificity of the report would strengthen the accuracy of the public perception of the merits of the controversy.

The United States Court of Appeals for the Tenth Circuit used this same argument to refute charges of invasion of privacy brought by a physician against the periodical *Medical Economics*. The story in the magazine was entitled "Who Let This Doctor in the O.R.? The Story of a Fatal Breakdown in Medical Policing," and described several patients of an anesthesiologist who suffered fatal or severely disabling injuries in the operating room. The article focused upon the lack of self-policing by physicians and the lack of disciplinary action by hospitals. To document these allegations the author of the story discussed the plaintiff anesthesiologist's psychiatric and related personal problems. Her picture and name were included in the story. While the plaintiff conceded the story was newsworthy, she argued that the publication of her photograph, name, and private facts revealing her psychiatric and marital histories added nothing to the story and were an invasion of privacy. The court disagreed, stating that the inclusion of the name and photograph strengthened the impact and credibility of the article. "They obviate any impression that the problems raised in the article are remote or hypothetical, thus providing an aura of immediacy and even urgency that might not exist had plaintiff's name and photograph been suppressed," the court said. The plaintiff's psychiatric and marital problems were connected to the newsworthy topic by the rational inference that her personal problems were the underlying causes of the acts of alleged malpractice (*Gilbert* v. *Medical Economics,* 1981).

What courts often look for in these kind of cases, then, is a nexus between the admittedly private and embarrassing information and the newsworthy subject of the story. How far the press can go in reporting the private life of public persons often depends not only upon what was said—how private the information is—but also upon why the material was used. When an individual's public life is explained, many parts of that person's private life are of legitimate public concern.

It is important at this point in our discussion of public persons and public figures to note that we are not using these terms as they are used in the law of libel. Recall, when discussing defamation, the label "public figure" had a distinct and quite narrow meaning. That is not the definition of public person used in privacy law. Also, libel law tends to reject the concept of the "involuntary public figure," a private individual who just happens to get caught in a big story. Since 1929 American courts have recognized that involuntary public figures do exist in privacy law. The Kentucky Supreme Court first noted such a person and gave this definition of the status (*Jones* v. *Herald Post Co.,* 1929):

> The right of privacy is the right to live one's life in seclusion, without being subjected to unwarranted and undesired publicity. In short, it is the right to be let alone. . . . There are times, however, when one, whether willing or not, becomes an actor in an occurrence of public or general interest. When this takes place he emerges from his seclusion, and it is not an invasion of his right of privacy to publish his photograph with an account of such occurrence.

The court later noted that private citizens can become "innocent actors in great tragedies in which the public has a deep concern." The scope, therefore, of the rubric involuntary public figure is wide. In Kansas City not too long ago, a young man was arrested by police outside the local courthouse on suspicion of burglary. Local television news cameramen filmed the arrest, and it was broadcast on televison that night. The young man, however, had been released by police, who admitted they had arrested the wrong man. An invasion of privacy suit followed, but the courts rejected it, stating that the plaintiff must show a serious, unreasonable, unwarranted, and offensive invasion of private affairs before recovery can be allowed (*Williams* v. *KCMO Broadcasting Co.,* 1971):

> In the case at bar, plaintiff was involved in a noteworthy event about which the public had a right to be informed and which the defendant [television station KCMO] had a right to publicize. This is true even though his involvement therein was purely involuntary and against his will.

An Illinois appeals court ruled in 1978 that a story that reported the death of a boy from an apparent drug overdose and then went on to outline details of the youth's life was not an invasion of privacy. The subject was of legitimate concern; in addition, the youth became an involuntary public figure by his actions within the drug culture in the community. "It is not necessary for an individual to actively seek publicity in order to be found in the public eye," the court ruled (*Beresky* v. *Teschner,* 1978).

Some have speculated that because the Supreme Court has ruled in libel cases that a public figure must be a voluntary participant in a controversy or public event, a similar rule might be applied in the law of privacy. But there seems to be nothing on record to suggest that will happen. Indeed, two factors strongly mitigate against such a development. First, to abandon the involuntary public figure rule in privacy law would be to radically reshape a part of the law that is over sixty years old. That seems unlikely. Second, remember we are dealing not with defamatory falsehoods in privacy law, but with truthful accounts of private affairs. American judges have been extremely reluctant to find liability where the charge is based on truthful or factual material. A narrowing of the definition of public figure to meet the criteria established in libel law would significantly enlarge the scope of liability. The records suggest most American jurists oppose such a move.

Sometimes the people who are close to public figures also lose some of their privacy. In 1971 in Pennsylvania the state high court ruled that the *Saturday Evening Post* was not liable for the publication of the names of the children of an entertainer in a story relating that the entertainer, Lillian Corabi, was accused of masterminding a complex burglary (*Corabi* v. *Curtis Publishing Co.,* 1971). The court said that "Tiger Lil" Corabi was a public figure and that anyone could legitimately publish her biography without consent and could include the names of the members of her family.

When a white southern civil rights leader published his autobiography, it was not an invasion of privacy to include information about his brother's wife, according to a United States district court. In *Brother to a Dragonfly,* author Will D. Campbell portrayed his life and his relationship to his deceased brother Joe, whom he regarded as a major inspiration in his life. Joe was a pharmacist who became addicted to drugs. This resulted in a dramatic change in his personality, and at times he seriously abused his wife, Carlyne, who was also mentioned several times in the book. She sued for invasion of privacy.

"The fact that she [the plaintiff] was the wife of a close and influential family member of the author justifies her inclusion in the book," the United States district court ruled. "Joe's problems with drugs and the profound effect that had on the author justifies the extent of her inclusion" (*Campbell* v. *Seabury Press*, 1979).

| Recounting the Past | A great number of privacy suits have resulted from both published and broadcast stories about people who were formerly in the public eye. In these cases the plaintiffs have consistently argued that the passing of time dims the public spotlight and that a person stripped of privacy because of great notoriety regains the protection of privacy after several years. Courts have not accepted this argument very often. The general rule is that once persons become public figures they pretty much remain public figures, despite attempts to avoid publicity. Two kinds of stories fall into this category: (1) stories that merely recount a past event (fourteen years ago today Walter Denton jumped off the Golden Gate Bridge and survived) and do not tell readers what the subject of the story does today and (2) stories that recount a past occurrence and attempt to focus as well on what the participant does today (fourteen years ago Walter Denton jumped off the Golden Gate Bridge and survived, and today he is principal of Madison High School). |

Stories that fall in the first category are protected in almost every instance. In 1975 the Kansas Supreme Court, for example, ruled it was not an invasion of privacy when a newspaper republished in a "Looking Backward Column" a story that a police officer had been suspended and then fired in 1964 after a complaint from a citizen. The court said that "official misconduct is newsworthy when it occurs, and remains so for so long as anyone thinks it worth retelling." The court added, "Once these facts entered the public domain, they remained there . . . plaintiff could not draw himself like a snail into his shell" (*Rawlins* v. *The Hutchinson Publishing Co.*, 1975). And the New Jersey Supreme Court recently ruled that the publication of a book about crimes that took place eight years earlier was not an invasion of privacy, despite the lapse of time. Joseph Kallinger and his son were apprehended by police in 1975 after their criminal rampage that included killing, robbing and raping. In 1983 a professor of criminal justice at City University of New York published a book about Kallinger's life and crimes. One of Kallinger's victims sued, arguing that replaying this tragedy in public print was traumatic, disturbing and would be highly offensive. The court agreed with that assessment, but ruled that the case failed because the facts revealed were not private but public, and "even if they were private, they are of legitimate concern to the public." The lapse of time did nothing to insulate the plaintiff from such publicity. The facts were taken from the public trial record in the case, and the court noted that the Supreme Court ruling in *Cox* v. *Cohn* was not limited to contemporaneous events (*Romaine* v. *Kallinger*, 1988).

The second kind of story is more problematic. There have been too few cases to establish a clear guideline. Some courts have clearly gone on record permitting the "where-are-they-now" kind of story. But even these judges have suggested that stories designed to purposely embarrass or humiliate a person because of his or her past conduct might not be tolerated under all circumstances (see *Kent* v. *Pittsburgh Press,* 1972; *Sidis* v. *F-R Publishing Co.,* 1940; and *Bernstein* v. *NBC,* 1955). The North Carolina Court of Appeals recently refused to grant a summary judgment to a newspaper that had been sued for invasion of privacy for recounting a woman's search for a child she had given up for adoption seventeen years earlier. The woman returned to Salisbury, North Carolina, looking for the girl she had left there in 1966. All of the adoption records were sealed under state law, but she found out the name and address of her daughter through a newspaper advertisement. A newspaper story later identified the girl and her adoptive parents, all of whom were extremely upset by the publicity. The court said that the question of whether the story was newsworthy and immune from a lawsuit depended upon a standard of reasonableness in light of community mores. This is a jury question, the court ruled, not something that should be decided on a motion for summary judgment. The judges noted that whether the story of the adoption, which was likely a public issue in 1967, had become a private matter by 1984, was another question the jury should decide. In making this judgment, the court said, the jurors should consider whether state laws on the confidentiality of jury records reflects on the newsworthy nature of the story. The North Carolina Supreme Court later dismissed the case, noting the state did not recognize the private facts element of privacy law (*Hall* v. *Post,* 1987, 1988).

There is a real risk in running a story about a local banker that includes the fact that he was arrested for car theft twenty years earlier. A judge may ask: Of what relevance is this information about past deeds? Surely if the man is running for public office, the public deserves to have this information. No privacy suit would stand in such a case. Oftentimes such stories are published or broadcast for inspirational reasons—see how this person pulled him- or herself up by the bootstraps and succeeded despite the odds. In such cases the subjects of the stories will usually consent to the use of this information because they are proud of their accomplishments. But if, for example, the editor publishes this information to hurt a banker because an application for a loan was rejected, a court may very well rule that an invasion of privacy has taken place. This is another area where the journalist has to exercise judgment and ask: Why am I publishing this potentially embarrassing information? If there is good cause, the journalist will find the courts will bar an action for invasion of privacy.

The publication of private facts generates many lawsuits, but few are successful. The key to avoiding successful litigation in this area is for the news person to stick to reporting the news. It is when the journalist makes a foray into nonnewsworthy private lives of average persons in order to titillate or amuse readers or viewers that this area of invasion of privacy can prove extremely troublesome.

SUMMARY

It is an invasion of privacy to publicize private information about another person's life if the publication of this information would be embarrassing to a reasonable person and the information is not of legitimate public interest or concern. To publicize means to communicate the information to a large number of people. There is no liability for giving further publicity to information that is already considered public. The press is free, for example, to report even embarrassing and sensitive matters contained in public records. The information that is publicized must be considered offensive to a reasonable person; the law does not protect hypersensitive individuals.

Courts use many strategies to determine whether information has legitimate public concern. Stories that have great interest have legitimate public concern. Stories about both voluntary and involuntary public figures are normally considered of legitimate public concern. When private information is published or broadcast, it is important that there is a connection between the revelation of the embarrassing private information and the newsworthy aspects of the story. Embarrassing details about a person's private life cannot be publicized simply to amuse or titillate audiences. News stories that recount past events—including embarrassing details of an individual's life—are normally protected from successful privacy suits. However, courts will normally insist upon a good reason for attempting to relate these embarrassing past events to an individual's current life or work.

FALSE-LIGHT PRIVACY

The fourth category of invasion of privacy looks, at first glance, as if it has little to do with what we traditionally think of as privacy. It has nothing to do with digging into a person's past, taking pictures with a telephoto lens, or using someone's picture to advertise toothpaste. What this category of invasion of privacy bans is the publication of false information about a person. The law states that it is an invasion of privacy to publish material that puts an individual in a false light. There are two qualifications to this rule. First, the published false information must be highly offensive to a reasonable person. Second, it must be shown—as in libel—that the publisher of the information was somehow at fault, exhibiting either actual malice or negligence (more about this later in this section).

False-light cases come in a wide variety of shapes and colors. Some involve blatant fictionalization of otherwise true stories; others result from simple errors in news stories. A false-light privacy suit resembles a defamation action.

But it has one important difference. In order to maintain a libel action, the plaintiff must show that the material has damaged his or her reputation, that the material is in fact defamatory. In false-light cases the plaintiff must only show that the published material is considered highly offensive by a reasonable person. It is not unusual for a plaintiff to file both an action for invasion of privacy and libel at the same time. Some states, however, have rules that limit a plaintiff to one cause of action based on a single set of facts. The plaintiff must choose either libel or invasion of privacy. Let us first look at some typical examples of false-light invasion of privacy to try to develop some guidelines on the subject.

Fictionalization

Radio and television writers who dramatize true stories are commonly the victims of false-light suits. Years ago the National Broadcasting Company (NBC) dramatized the heroism of a naval officer who, as a passenger on a flight from Honolulu to California, was responsible for saving many lives when the plane crash-landed at sea. The drama stuck to the hard facts of the story, but of course dialogue between passengers and crew was added. In addition, the naval officer was somewhat humanized; he smoked a cigarette and prayed before the crash. The court that heard the officer's privacy suit ruled that these embellishments constituted fictionalization and resulted in an invasion of privacy (*Strickler* v. *NBC,* 1958).

Newspapers and magazine writers have been caught when they dramatized true stories in the same manner by adding dialogue, changing the scene slightly, and so forth. A writer for a Philadelphia newspaper uncovered an interesting divorce suit involving a teenage couple. The boy married the girl only to spite her parents, who did not like him. The newspaper story described the couple as they secretly planned the marriage, as they walked to the justice of the peace, and so forth. Dialogue between the couple was invented. A suit resulted, and the newspaper lost the case because the story was written "in a style used almost exclusively by writers of fiction" (*Acquino* v. *Bulletin Co.,* 1959). Note, the court did not say that the story was fiction, because it was not. The basic facts were true, but they were presented in a fictional style.

Such opinions are not always the rule. Other courts in other cases have said that minor fictionalization, the creation of dialogue, does not constitute invasion of privacy in an otherwise true story (*Carlisle* v. *Fawcett Publishing Co.,* 1962). The foregoing examples point up the confused state of the law in this area.

The simplest way to avoid a suit for false light, if the truth is embellished in any way, is to change the names of the characters in the story. This strategy will work in every case except in those stories that are about a specific person. It does not make much sense to do a character sketch about Mick Jagger if you must refer to him throughout the piece as John Smith because parts of the story are embellished or fictionalized.

On the opposite side of the fictionalization coin is the problem of using the name of a real person in what is clearly a work of fiction. Sometimes this occurs coincidentally. An author writes a novel that includes the character Marie Platt. A real Marie Platt exists and sues, arguing that by using her name in the book the author has put her into a false light. Such suits don't go very far. (See *People* v. *Scribner's and Sons,* 1954.) Ms. Platt's only hope of succeeding is to convince the jury that not only was her name used but that the author of the novel has appropriated her identity as well.

For example, the author and publisher of a book entitled *Match Set* was sued by a woman who had the same name as the central character in the novel. Both women were named Melanie Geisler. The character in the novel is a female transsexual tennis player who is induced to participate in tennis fraud. The plaintiff in the case worked for a small publishing company for six months and was acquainted with the defendant author who also worked at the same company for a short time. The plaintiff and the fictional Melanie Geisler share many physical characteristics. The real Melanie Geisler argued that the similarity of names and physical descriptions, coupled with the fact that she and the author were acquainted for a short time, led many persons to believe the book was about her. The United States Court of Appeals for the Second Circuit ruled that a reasonable person could come to such a conclusion, rejected the defendant's motion for dismissal, and sent the case back for trial (*Geisler* v. *Petrocelli,* 1980). Some authors can face a problem even if the plaintiff does not have the same name as a character in the novel. In a Florida case a novelist knowingly used a real person with whom she was acquainted as the basis for a character in a book. She was sued for invasion of privacy and lost the case. The court ruled that because the character described in the novel was so unusual, many persons in the community recognized her even though the name had been changed (*Cason* v. *Baskin,* 1947).

What about novels like E. L. Doctorow's *Ragtime* in which famous people play an incidental part in a fictional story? The courts in at least one jurisdiction, New York, have ruled that such incidental use of the name and character of real notable people is not an invasion of privacy so long as it is evident to readers that the book is a work of fiction and that individuals named are included simply to add color to the book (*Hicks* v. *Casablanca,* 1978).

Does the disclaimer published in the front of a book asserting that the novel is a work of fiction protect the publisher? In many instances no. Roman Catholic Archbishop Paul Marcinkus recently sued NAL Publishing to try to block the distribution of a novel written by A. J. Quinnell in which an archbishop figures as a character. Marcinkus formerly headed the Vatican bank and in 1982 was accused by Italian authorities of being associated with the collapse of Banco Ambrosiano of Milan. In the novel, the fictional plot centers upon a plan developed by three Vatican officials—including the plaintiff—to assassinate Soviet leader Yuri Andropov in order to prevent further attempts on the Pope's life.

In a prefatory note, the publisher printed the standard disclaimer, noting that names, characters, places and incidents are used fictitiously. But the publisher added, "Some real people such as . . . Paul Marcinkus . . . appear as characters in the book to give a sense of historical accuracy. However, their action and motivations are entirely fictitious and should not be considered real or factual."

While the New York Supreme Court refused to grant the injunction blocking the distribution of the book, it did not dismiss the case. It cannot be said as a matter of law, Justice Ethel Danzig ruled, that readers will assume the work is fiction. That is a question for a factfinder. Also, the justice noted that the use of Marcinkus' name in advertising for the book might constitute an illegal appropriation (*Marcinkus* v. *NAL Publishing, 1987*).

The standard (admittedly based on a handful of cases) that seems to be emerging is this: if the use of the name, as in the *Hicks* case noted above, is simply incidental to what readers will clearly recognize is a fictional work, there will be no liability. But if the fictional nature of the work is not clear, if readers might be confused, a false light action might stand—regardless of what is published in the disclaimer.

False Statements

Today most false-light cases do not involve blatant fictionalization. They instead result from news and feature stories that are either intentionally or unintentionally embellished. Typical of the first sort of case is one in which a writer for a national newspaper told his readers that a mystery surrounded the suicide death of a mother. The woman killed herself after murdering her children, and the writer said that police, family, and friends were baffled because she had been a happy, normal woman. Her husband sued, charging false light. He was able to show that the woman had a history of psychiatric care and mental illness. She was quite despondent before the incident, and her death was really not a mystery at all. The court ruled that the publication had put the woman in a false light (*Varnish* v. *Best Medium, 1968*).

Photographs are a more common source of false-light cases than are stories. The late, great *Saturday Evening Post* seemed to have a penchant for false-light cases, most of which involved photographs. Years ago the magazine published a picture of a little girl who was brushed by a speeding car in an intersection and lay crying in the street. The girl was the victim of a motorist who ignored a red traffic light, but in the magazine the editors implied that she had caused the accident herself by darting into the street between parked cars. The editors simply needed a picture to illustrate a story on pedestrian carelessness and plucked this one out of the files. The picture was totally unrelated to the story, except that both were about people being hit by cars.

Eleanor Sue Leverton sued the *Post* and won. Judge Herbert F. Goodrich ruled that the picture was clearly newsworthy in connection with Eleanor's original accident (*Leverton* v. *Curtis Publishing Co.,* 1951):

> . . . but the sum total of all this is that this particular plaintiff, the legitimate subject for publicity for one particular accident, now becomes a pictorial, frightful example of pedestrian carelessness. This, we think, exceeds the bounds of privilege.

WJLA-TV in the nation's capital was sued in a case that graphically demonstrates how a broadcasting station or publication can and cannot use unrelated pictures to illustrate a story. The station broadcast a story on a new medical treatment for genital herpes. The report appeared on both the 6 P.M. and 11 P.M. newscasts. Both reports carried the same opening videotape of scores of pedestrians walking on a busy city street. Then the camera zoomed in on one woman, Linda Duncan, as she stood on a corner. Duncan turned and looked at the camera. She was clearly recognizable. On the 6 P.M. news there was no narration during this opening footage. The camera focused on the plaintiff Duncan and then the tape cut to a picture of the reporter, who was standing on the street, and said, "For the twenty million Americans who have herpes, it's not a cure." The remainder of the story followed. But for the 11 P.M. news, the reporter's opening statement was read by the news anchor as viewers watched the opening videotape, including the close-up of Linda Duncan. A defense motion to dismiss the privacy and defamation actions was granted as it related to the 6 P.M. newscast. The court said there was not a sufficient connection between pictures of the plaintiff and the reporter's statement. But the court denied a summary judgment relating to the 11 P.M. broadcast. "The coalescing of the camera action, plaintiff's action (turning toward the camera), and the position of the passerby caused plaintiff to be the focal point on the screen. The juxtaposition of this film and commentary concerning twenty million Americans with herpes is sufficient to support an inference that indeed the plaintiff was a victim," the court ruled. A jury should decide whether the connection was strong enough (*Duncan* v. *WJLA-TV,* 1984).

Sometimes an error simply occurs, and there is little anyone can do about it. A newspaper in Oklahoma recently published an article concerning the death of a former local schoolteacher who had been convicted of murder and who was reportedly mentally ill. But the photo used to accompany the story was that of Frenche Colbert, who lived in Phoenix, Arizona. Colbert's picture had been sent to the newspaper years earlier when he graduated from law school. Somehow, his photo got mixed up with that of the schoolteacher. There is no question that this publication put Colbert in a false light (*Colbert* v. *World Publishing,* 1987).

A simple precaution will protect publishers and broadcasters against many false-light suits. Refrain from using unrelated photos to illustrate stories and articles. When you want to publish a story in the employee magazine about worker carelessness as a prime cause of industrial accidents, control the impulse to pull a random picture from the files of one of the employees working on the assembly line. That employee could contend that you are suggesting she is careless. Similarly, don't use film file of kids hanging around the parking lot at a local park to illustrate your news story on neighborhood complaints about drug dealing in the park. Juxtaposing the wrong pictures with the wrong words could give viewers the impression that you are suggesting one of these kids is selling or using drugs.

Highly Offensive Material

Before a plaintiff can win a false-light case, the court must be convinced that the material that is false is highly offensive to a reasonable person. While there are on record a handful of cases where nonoffensive material was the basis for a successful false-light suit (see *Molony* v. *Boy Comics Publishers,* 1946), these cases are old and should not be regarded as authoritative today. Typical of modern decisions is the case of *Cibenko* v. *Worth Publishers.* The plaintiff is a New York–New Jersey Port Authority police officer whose photograph appeared in a college sociology text. In a section of the book entitled "Selecting the Criminals," the picture depicts a white police officer (Cibenko) in a public place apparently prodding a sleeping black with his nightstick. The caption for the picture states:

> The social status of the offender seems to be the most significant determinant of whether a person will be arrested and convicted for an offense and of the kind of penalty that will be applied. In this picture a police officer is preventing a black male from falling asleep in a public place. Would the officer be likely to do the same if the "offender" were a well-dressed, middle-aged white person?

Officer Cibenko claimed the photograph and caption made him appear to be a racist, and this was false. A United States district court in New Jersey disagreed and ruled that there was no offensive meaning attached to the photograph and caption, especially not a highly offensive meaning (*Cibenko* v. *Worth Publishers,* 1981). A U.S. District Court in Maine recently dismissed a suit by a man who had fallen out of the hatch of a small airplane, but managed to cling to the door rails until the pilot made an emergency landing. An article in *National Enquirer* embellished the story somewhat, adding material on what the plaintiff had thought about as he clung to the airplane. The reporter had never communicated with the accident victim, so couldn't have known what went through his mind. The court ruled that the description of physical sensations and predicable fears, though possibly exaggerated or maybe even fanciful, was not offensive to a reasonable person (*Dempsey* v. *National Enquirer Inc.,* 1988).

The Fault Requirement

Since 1967 plaintiffs in false-light suits have been required to carry a fault requirement much like the one applied in libel cases. The case in which this fault requirement was applied to invasion of privacy was the first mass media invasion of privacy suit ever heard by the United States Supreme Court. In the early 1950s the James Hill family was held captive in their home for nearly twenty-four hours by three escaped convicts. The fugitives were captured by police shortly after leaving the Hill home. The incident became a widely publicized story. A novel, *The Desperate Hours,* was written about a similar incident, as were a play and a motion-picture script. *Life* magazine published a feature story about the drama, stating that the play was a reenactment of the ordeal suffered by the James Hill family. The actors were even taken to the home in which the Hills had lived (now vacant) and were photographed at the scene of the original captivity.

James Hill sued for invasion of privacy. He complained that the magazine had used his family's name for trade purposes and that the story put the family in a false light. *The Desperate Hours* did follow the basic outline of the Hill family ordeal, but it contained many differences. The fictional Hilliard family, for example, suffered far more physical and verbal indignities at the hands of the convicts than did the Hill family.

The family won money damages in the New York state courts, but the Supreme Court of the United States vacated the lower court rulings and sent the case back for yet another trial. The Hill family gave up at this point, and no subsequent trial was held.

Justice William Brennan, in a five-to-four ruling, declared that the family's name and photographs had not been used for trade purposes. Brennan reminded all concerned that informative material published in newspapers and magazines is not published for purposes of trade (see pages 207–208), even though these publications generally are considered profit-making businesses.

Turning to the false-light action, Brennan applied the same First Amendment standards he had developed in the *New York Times* v. *Sullivan* libel suit to this category of invasion of privacy litigation. "We hold that the constitutional protections for speech and press preclude the application of the New York [privacy] statute to redress false reports of matters of public interest in the absence of proof that the defendant published the report with knowledge of its falsity or in reckless disregard of the truth," (*Time, Inc.* v. *Hill,* 1967).

In the last twenty years, however, the Supreme Court has substantially modified the fault requirement in libel. Since 1974 and the case of *Gertz* v. *Welch,* the Supreme Court has insisted that public persons must prove actual malice to win a libel suit, but that states may permit private persons to win a libel judgment with proof of simple negligence, not actual malice. Six months after its ruling in *Gertz,* the Supreme Court issued a ruling in a false-light invasion of privacy case, *Cantrell* v. *Forest City Publishing Co.* In this case the High Court ruled that there was evidence to show that the defendant had acted with reckless disregard for the truth. But because the plaintiff had managed to bear the higher burden of proof in the case and was able to prove actual malice, the Supreme Court didn't decide whether the *Gertz* ruling had changed the law of privacy as well as the law of libel. "This case presents no occasion to consider whether a state may constitutionally apply a more relaxed standard of liability for a publisher or broadcaster of false statements injurious to a private individual under a false-light theory of invasion of privacy or whether the constitutional standard announced in *Time, Inc.* v. *Hill* applies to all false-light cases," wrote Justice Stewart for the Court.

Whether the *Gertz* variable fault standard is applicable to false-light privacy cases as well as libel cases is an actively contested question in the courts today. And there doesn't seem to be a clear trend. In some jurisdictions courts have concluded that the actual malice rule is not constitutionally mandated in all false-light cases—just those in which the plaintiff is a public person. For example, the United States Court of Appeals for the Fifth Circuit (see *Wood* v. *Hustler,* 1984), the West Virginia Supreme Court of Appeals (see *Crump* v. *Beckley Newspapers,* 1984), and the appellate division of the New York Supreme Court (see *Fils Aime* v. *Enlightment Press,* 1986) have all ruled that a lower level of fault such as negligence should apply in false-light suits brought by private persons. The New York Court ruled that "Given the similarity of issues raised in defamation and privacy claims, particularly as they implicate First Amendment concerns, there would seem to be no reason why the same standards of fault should not be applied on both types of cases."

On the other hand, courts in Arkansas (*Dodrill* v. *Arkansas Democrat Co.,* 1979), Kentucky (*McCall* v. *Courier-Journal and Louisville Times Co.,* 1981), Connecticut (*Goodrich* v. *Waterbury Republican-American, Inc.,* 1982), Oregon (*Dean* v. *Guard Publishing Co.,* 1985), and Oklahoma (*Colbert* v. *World Publishing,* 1987) have ruled that private person plaintiffs in false-light cases must still prove actual malice. The Oklahoma Supreme Court ruled "There is simply no room in the framework of our society for permitting one party to sue on the event of every intrusion into the psychic tranquility of an individual. If recovery for damage done is to be afforded at all, there must be some test by which to weed out those suits premised on mere discord between individuals while preserving those where the conduct of individuals involved has clearly exceeded tolerable bounds of social deportment."

It is not now possible to predict the outcome of this disagreement among the courts. It is possible that the Supreme Court will step in and require that all plaintiffs in false-light cases follow the *Time, Inc.* v. *Hill* rule and prove actual malice. That is unlikely. What is more likely is that the Court will rule that the states may make their own decision in the case—as is occurring now— or avoid the question completely, which would have the same result. In any case, the plaintiff who seeks to prove either negligence or actual malice in a false-light privacy case must meet exactly the same requirements as the libel plaintiff. (See pp. 150–160.)

SUMMARY

It is an invasion of privacy to publish false information that places an individual into what is called a false light. However, this false information must be considered offensive to a reasonable person. Also, the plaintiff must prove that the information was published negligently, with knowledge of its falsity or with reckless disregard for the truth.

One common source of false-light privacy suits is any drama that adds fictional material to an otherwise true story. The use of fictional rather than real names in such a drama will normally preclude a successful invasion of privacy suit. The coincidental use of a real name in a novel or stage play will not stand as a cause of action for invasion of privacy. Most false-light cases, however, result from the publication of false information about a person in a news or feature story. Pictures of persons who are not involved in the stories the pictures are used to illustrate frequently provoke false-light privacy suits.

Before the discussion of the right of privacy comes to an end, we need to recall a few points. First, remember that only people have the right of privacy. Corporations, businesses, and governments do not enjoy the legal right of privacy as such. Second, unlike libel, the law of privacy does provide that the plaintiff may seek an injunction to stop an invasion of privacy. Courts are very hesitant to enjoin tortious conduct however, unless the plaintiff can show that the action will cause irreparable injury and that the tortious conduct will likely be continued. Such was the case in the *Galella-Onassis* suit. A plaintiff is far more likely to get an injunction in either an intrusion or an appropriation case than in a private-facts or false-light suit. Normally courts refuse to grant injunctions, because they believe an adequate legal remedy is available or because they believe that the injunction could constitute prior censorship in violation of the First Amendment. The plaintiff bears an immense burden in convincing a court that prior restraint is called for. While it is possible to get an injunction, it is difficult. Third, it is impossible to civilly libel a dead person, but a few state privacy statutes make it possible for an heir to maintain an action for invasion of privacy.

Although privacy law is not as well charted as libel law and although there are fewer privacy cases, suits for invasion of privacy are a growing menace to journalists. If journalists stick to the job of responsibly reporting the news, they may rest assured that the chance for a successful privacy suit is slim.

BIBLIOGRAPHY

Here is a list of some of the sources that have been helpful in the preparation of chapter 4:

Books

Pember, Don R. *Privacy and the Press.* Seattle: University of Washington Press, 1972.

Articles   Levine, Marla E. "The Right of Publicity as a Means of Protecting Performers' Style." 14 *Loyola of Los Angeles Law Review* 129, 1980.

Pember, Don R. "The Burgeoning Scope of Access Privacy and the Portent for a Free Press." 64 *Iowa Law Review* 1155, 1979.

Pember, Don R., and Teeter, Dwight L. "Privacy and the Press Since *Time, Inc.* v. *Hill.*" 50 *Washington Law Review* 57, 1974.

Pilgrim, Tim A. "Docudramas and False-Light Invasion of Privacy." *Communications and the Law,* June, 1988.

Prosser, William L. "Privacy." 48 *California Law Review* 383, 1960.

Sims, Andrew B. "Right of Publicity: Survivability Reconsidered." 49 *Fordham Law Review* 453, 1981.

Cases   *Acme* v. *Kuperstock,* 711 F.2d 1538 (1983).

Acquino v. *Bulletin Co.,* 190 Pa. Super. 528 (1959).

Ali v. *Playgirl,* 447 F.Supp. 723 (1978).

Allen v. *Men's World Outlet,* 679 F.Supp. 360 (1988).

Anderson v. *Fisher Broadcasting,* 712 P.2d 803 (1986).

Andren v. *Knight-Ridder Newspapers,* 10 M.L.R. 2109 (1984).

Arrington v. *New York Times,* 55 N.Y.2d 433 (1982).

Barber v. *Time, Inc.,* 159 S.W.2d 291 (1942).

Beresky v. *Teschner,* 381 N.E.2d 979 (1978).

Bilney v. *Evening Star,* 406 A.2d 652 (1979).

Boddie v. *ABC,* 731 F.2d 333 (1984).

Booth v. *Curtis Publishing Co.,* 11 N.Y.2d 907 (1962).

Campbell v. *Seabury Press,* 614 F.2d 395 (1979).

Canessa v. *J. I. Kislak,* 235 A.2d 62 (1967).

Cantrell v. *Forest City Publishing Co.,* 95 S.Ct. 465 (1974).

Cape Publications v. *Hitchner,* 514 So.2d 1156 (1987).

Carlisle v. *Fawcett Publishing Co.,* 210 Cal. App.2d 733 (1962).

Cason v. *Baskin,* 159 Fla. 131 (1947).

Cassidy v. *ABC,* 377 N.E.2d 126 (1978).

Cefalu v. *Globe Newspaper,* 391 N.E.2d 935 (1979).

Cher v. *Forum International,* 692 F.2d 634 (1982).

Cibenko v. *Worth Publishers,* 510 F.Supp. 761 (1981).

Cohen v. *Herbal Concepts,* 473 N.Y.S.2d 426 (1984).

Corabi v. *Curtis Publishing Co.,* 273 A.2d 899 (1971).

Costlow v. *Cuismano,* 311 N.Y.S.2d 92 (1970).

Cox Broadcasting Co. v. *Cohn,* 95 S.Ct. 1029 (1975).

Crump v. *Beckley Newspapers,* 320 S.E.2d 70 (1984).

Daily Times-Democrat v. *Graham,* 162 So.2d 474 (1962).

DeGregorio v. *CBS,* 43 N.Y.S.2d 922 (1984).

Delan v. *CBS,* 445 N.Y.S.2d 898 (1981); 458 N.Y.S.2d 608 (1983).

Dietemann v. *Time, Inc.,* 499 F.2d 245 (1971).

Dittner v. *Troma,* 6 M.L. Rept. 1991 (1980).

Duncan v. *WJLA-TV,* 10 M.L.R. 1395 (1984).

Durgom v. *CBS,* 214 N.Y.S.2d 752 (1961).

Florida Star v. *B.J.F.,* No. 87–329, (1989).

Friedan v. *Friedan,* 414 F.Supp. 77 (1976).

Fry v. *Ionia Sentinel-Standard,* 300 N.W.2d 687 (1980).

Galella v. *Onassis,* 487 F.2d 986 (1973); 533 F.Supp. 1076 (1982).

Geisler v. *Petrocelli,* 616 F.2d 636 (1980).

Gilbert v. *Medical Economics,* 665 F.2d 305 (1981).

Griffith v. *Rancocas Valley Hospital,* 8 M.L.R. 1760 (1982).

Haelan Laboratories, Inc. v. *Topps Chewing Gum,* 202 F.2d 866 (1953).
Hall v. *Post,* 355 S.E.2d 819 (1987); 15 M.L.R. 2329 (1988).
Harrison v. *Washington Post,* 391 A.2d 781 (1978).
Hawkins v. *Multimedia,* 344 S.E.2d 145 (1986).
Hendry v. *Conner,* 303 Minn. 317 (1975).
Holman v. *Central Arkansas Broadcasting,* 610 F.2d 542 (1979).
Holmes v. *Curtis Publishing Co.,* 303 F.Supp. 522 (1969).
Howard v. *Des Moines Register,* 283 N.W.2d 789 (1979).
Jeffries v. *New York Evening Journal,* 124 N.Y.S. 780 (1910).
Jeppson v. *United Television,* 580 P.2d 1087 (1978).
Jones v. *Herald Post Co.,* 18 S.W.2d 972 (1929).
Jumez v. *ABC Records,* 3 M.L.R. 2324 (1978).
Kelley v. *Post Publishing Co.,* 327 Mass. 275 (1951).
Kent v. *Pittsburgh Press,* 349 F.Supp. 622 (1972).
Leverton v. *Curtis Publishing Co.,* 192 F.2d 974 (1951).
Liberty Lobby v. *Pearson,* 390 F.2d 489 (1968).
Lopez v. *Triangle Communications,* 421 N.Y.S.2d 57 (1979).
Lugosi v. *Universal,* 160 Cal. App.3d 323 (1979).
McAndrews v. *Roy,* 131 So.2d 256 (1961).
McCall v. *Courier-Journal,* 4 M.L.R. 2337 (1979); affd. 6 M.L.R. 1112 (1980).
Marks v. *King Broadcasting,* 618 P.2d 572 (1980).
Martin Luther King Center v. *American Heritage Products,* 296 S.E.2d 697 (1982).
Martin v. *Penthouse,* 12 M.L.R. 2058 (1986).
Meetze v. *AP,* 95 S.E.2d 606 (1956).
Metter v. *Los Angeles Examiner,* 95 P.2d 491 (1939).
Molony v. *Boy Comics Publishers,* 65 N.Y.S.2d 173 (1946).
Moser v. *Press Publishing Co.,* 109 N.Y.S. 963 (1908).
Namath v. *Sports Illustrated,* 39 N.Y.2d 897 (1976).
Nappier v. *Jefferson Standard Life Insurance Co.,* 322 F.2d 502 (1963).
Neff v. *Time, Inc.,* 406 F.Supp. 858 (1976).
Onassis v. *Christian Dior,* 472 N.Y.S.2d 254 (1984).
Palmer v. *Schonhorn Enterprises, Inc.,* 232 A.2d 458 (1967).
Patterson v. *Tribune Co.,* 146 So.2d 623 (1962).
Paulsen v. *Personality Posters,* 299 N.Y.S.2d 501 (1968).
Pavesich v. *New England Mutual Life Insurance Co.,* 122 Ga. 190 (1905).
Pearson v. *Dodd,* 410 F.2d 701 (1969).
Peed v. *Washington Times Co.,* 55 Wash. 182 (1927).
People v. *Kunkin,* 100 Cal. Rptr. 845 (1972); revd. 107 Cal. Rptr. 184 (1973).
Reeves v. *United Artists,* 572 F.Supp. 1231 (1983).
Rifkin v. *Esquire,* 8 M.L.R. 1384 (1982).
Roberson v. *Rochester Folding Box Co.,* 171 N.Y. 538 (1902).
Rogers v. *Grimaldi,* 695 F.Supp. 112 (1988), aff'd 16 M.L.R. 1648 (1989).
Russell v. *Marboro Books,* 183 N.Y.S.2d 8 (1959).
Shields v. *Gross,* 451 N.Y.S.2d 419 (1982); 58 N.Y.2d 338 (1983).
Sidis v. *F-R Publishing Co.,* 113 F.2d 806 (1940).
Sipple v. *Chronicle Publishing,* 154 Cal. App.3d 1040 (1984).
Stephano v. *News Group W Publications,* 485 N.Y.S.2d 220 (1984).
Stressman v. *American Blackhawk Broadcasting Co.,* 416 N.W.2d 685 (1987).
Strickler v. *NBC,* 167 F.Supp. 68 (1958).
Tellado v. *Time-Life Books,* 634 F.Supp. 904 (1986).
Time, Inc. v. *Hill,* 385 U.S. 374 (1967).

Uhlaender v. *Henricksen*, 159 F. Supp. 1277 (1970).
Varnish v. *Best Medium*, 405 F.2d 608 (1968).
Vassiliades v. *Garfinckel's*, 492 A.2d 580 (1985).
Virgil v. *Time, Inc.*, 527 F.2d 1122 (1975); 424 F.Supp. 1286 (1976).
W.C.H. of Waverly, Mo., Inc. v. *Meredith*, 13 M.L.R. 1648 (1986).
Welch v. *Group W Productions*, 15 M.L.R. 1062 (1987).
Welch v. *Mr. Christmas Tree*, 57 N.Y.2d 143 (1982).
Williams v. *KCMO Broadcasting Co.*, 472 S.W.2d 1 (1971).
Wood v. *Hustler*, 736 F.2d 1084 (1984).
Zacchini v. *Scripps-Howard Broadcasting Co.*, 433 U.S. 562 (1977).

5 GATHERING INFORMATION: RECORDS AND MEETINGS

One of the truly revolutionary changes in American journalism in the past two hundred years has been the fundamental shift in emphasis in the American press from journals of opinion, commentary, and some small bits of "intelligence" to the predominance of publications that offer readers a steady diet of news and information. The "news" paper as we know it simply did not exist in the era of the founding of the American Republic. And the significant legal battles that faced the eighteenth-century editor developed over the right to criticize, ridicule, and even libel the government and government officials. Sedition law was the primary legal problem faced by leading journalists who used their newspapers and pamphlets to form and lead political opinion.

To the editor of the 1990s the law of sedition is about as relevant as a hand-operated printing press. News and information are today the lifeblood of most newspapers, many magazines, and significant sections of the radio and television industry. Gathering and publishing news about government and government officials has become the central task of many journalists.

Most journalists consider the press in the United States to be the eyes and ears of the people with regard to their government, a function often referred to as "a watchdog role." It is the responsibility of the press to inform the people about their government—whether it is operating efficiently, whether it is living up to its constitutional requirements, whether it is treating its citizens fairly, whether its officials are acting responsibly and honestly. This interest in reporting on the activities of government has grown markedly since the 1930s, most particularly since the social and political upheavals of the late sixties and early seventies. Paradoxically, as the journalist's appetite for reporting news of government has grown, so too has grown the societal interest in government secrecy and the right to privacy. The modern reporter who seeks to scrutinize the operation of government at any level is frequently faced with legal impediments that stem from the countervailing interests in secrecy and privacy.

Government secrecy is not a new idea, but it has blossomed with new vigor since World War II. Secrecy results from many conditions. The cold war of the fifties provoked government to actions inconsistent with an open, democratic society. In the name of national security, thousands and thousands of documents are classified as confidential or secret. Ten years ago *Science* magazine reported that nearly fourteen thousand persons in the federal government had the power to classify material. More than four million documents were classified each year, and the Departments of Defense, State, and Energy and the Central Intelligence Agency were the most prolific classifiers. Scientific data that relate in obscure ways to sophisticated weapon systems, military plans and procedures, maps, photographs, and documents and papers relating to foreign policy and strategic materials—all are sifted, stamped, and filed away beyond the view of the press or the public. The problem grew considerably worse in 1980 with the election of Ronald Reagan as president. Reagan and his advisers were extremely sensitive about America's adversaries gaining access to important military, diplomatic, and scientific secrets. Hence, the administration enacted and proposed everything from lie detector tests and prepublication review contracts for government employees to significantly tightening government information release policies. And the federal government successfully prosecuted an analyst who worked at the Naval Intelligence Support Center and sold a classified photograph of the construction of a Soviet aircraft to the British publication, *Jane's Defence Weekly,* which published it. (See *U.S. v. Morison,* 1988.)

The tremendous growth of bureaucracy at all levels of government has also resulted in cutting off public access to many governmental processes and operations. In his classic analysis of bureaucracy as a form of social organization, Max Weber argued that preoccupation with secrecy is an inherent characteristic of administrative organizations. Weber asserted that this preoccupation is based partially on the functional need to keep certain phases of administrative operation a secret to maintain a competitive edge over rival administrative units. Weber also noted that it is not uncommon that this secrecy is transformed into an obsession; that is, an action begun simply as a means to achieve organizational objectives often becomes an end in itself.

The ineptness, dishonesty, and stupidity of some government officials are also conditions that provoke secrecy in government. An inefficient, unethical, or dishonest government official can find the cloak of secrecy a convenient means of covering up misfeasance or malfeasance in office.

The emergence of the right to privacy as an obstacle to gathering news and information about government is an even more recent phenomenon. Citizens of the United States have used the law of privacy as a means of redressing excesses by the press and others for nearly a century. (This dimension of privacy is fully explored in chapter 4.) As our government at all levels has become more entwined in our personal lives through massive programs of public assistance, education, financial aid, and health care, the amount of information the government possesses about individual citizens has dramatically increased. Similarly, as the scope of government regulation of business, industry, financial institutions, transportation, and other activities has enlarged, government knowledge about confidential business practices, manufacturing processes, and related matters has grown as well. And as this storehouse of information about both people and institutions has grown, government has more often raised the right of privacy of these citizens or institutions as a barrier to the scrutiny of its own operations.

The purpose of this chapter is to explore the problems of gathering news and information in a society that manifests a growing interest in secrecy and privacy but that at the same time gives at least lip service to a growing interest in watching government more closely than ever. The chapter has five main sections:

1. The right to gather information from government, which is implied or may be inferred from the common law and the First Amendment to the United States Constitution
2. Federal open records and open meetings laws
3. State open records and open meetings laws
4. Federal and state statutes that specifically preclude public access to information held by the government
5. Public and press access to evidence that is presented in a court of law

While this chapter is generally comprehensive in coverage of the federal statutes and guidelines, only an overview of state law is offered. But this does not mean that state law is not important. For most reporters state laws governing access to records and meetings are more important than federal laws because local journalists spend more time reporting on local and state governments. To be a successful reporter, a journalist must have a good working knowledge of state laws governing access to information. This knowledge is as much a part of the reporter's trade as a pencil or a notebook. A reporter without full knowledge of state laws governing access to information will simply not get all the information and news to which the public is entitled. We will all be losers. Information about state laws can be obtained from teachers and professors, from press organizations within the state (such as the Society of Professional Journalists and Women in Communication, Inc.), from attorneys who represent newspapers and broadcasting stations, and from the statutes and court decisions themselves. ◆

NEWS GATHERING, THE COMMON LAW, AND THE CONSTITUTION

Persons unacquainted with the legal problems involved in news gathering are usually startled to discover that there is no clear common law right to gather news or information. Despite the tradition of open government both in this country and in Great Britain, the common law provides only bare access to government documents and to meetings of public agencies. In Great Britain, where the common law developed, complete and total access to Parliament, for example, was not guaranteed until 1874, and even then the House of Commons could exclude the public by a majority vote. Initially the public was excluded because members of Parliament feared reprisal from the Crown for statements made during floor debate. Later this fear subsided, but secret meetings continued in order to prevent voters from finding out that many members of the legislative body were not faithful in keeping promises to constituents.

Secrecy in England had a direct impact upon how colonial legislatures conducted their business. The Constitutional Convention of 1787 in Philadelphia was conducted in secret. The public and the press had almost immediate access to sessions in the United States House of Representatives, but it was not until 1794 that spectators and reporters were allowed into the Senate chamber. While today access is guaranteed to nearly all sessions of Congress, much (maybe even most) congressional business is conducted by committees that frequently meet in secret.

Common law precedents exist that open certain public records to inspection by members of the public, but distinct limitations have been placed upon this common law right. For example, under the common law a person seeking access to a record must have an "interest" in that record. And most often this interest must relate to some kind of litigation in which the person who seeks the record is a participant. Also, only those records "required to be kept" by state law are subject to even such limited disclosure under the common law. Many important records kept by the government are not "required to be kept" by law. Hence, the common law must be found wanting as an aid in the process of news gathering.

| The Constitution and News Gathering | The United States Constitution is another source of the law in this nation. Does this document provide any assistance to the citizen who seeks to scrutinize government records or attend meetings of government bodies? Surprisingly, perhaps, the First Amendment plays a rather insignificant role in defining the rights of citizens and journalists in the news-gathering process. The amendment was drafted in an age when news gathering was not a primary function of the press. The congressional records of the drafting and adoption of the First Amendment fail to support the notion that the protection of the news-gathering process was to be included within the scope of freedom of the press. The adoption of antecedents to the First Amendment, such as the free speech provisions of the Virginia Declaration of Rights, and the letters and publications of men like Adams, Madison, and Jefferson are also found wanting in support of this idea. On August 15, 1789, during the House debate on the adoption of the First Amendment, James Madison, its principal author in the Congress, stated that if freedom of expression means nothing more than that "the people have a right to express and communicate their sentiments and wishes, we have provided for it already" (in what was to become the First Amendment). "The right of freedom of speech is secured; the liberty of free press is expressly declared to be beyond the reach of this government; the people may therefore publicly address their representatives, may privately address them, or declare sentiments by petition to the whole body," Madison added. |

One is hard pressed to find within this description of the First Amendment guarantee of freedom of expression expansive notions about the right to gather news and information. The First Amendment was seen as a means by which the public could confront its government, not necessarily report on its activities.

The United States Constitution is a living document, and as Justice Oliver Wendell Holmes reminded us, each age should be the mistress of its own law. Courts are not precluded today from finding a right to gather news under the First Amendment, even if such a right was not thought to exist in 1791. Has this happened? Have the courts ruled that the First Amendment supports the right to gather news and information? The answer to this is not completely clear. There seem to be a small but growing number of court rulings that the First Amendment protects the rights of any citizen—not just reporters—to at least attend certain kinds of hearings or meetings, and of course attending such hearings or meetings is fundamental to news gathering.

The Supreme Court of the United States has considered the First Amendment and the right to gather news in several different contexts. In 1964 the Court ruled that the constitutional right to speak and publish does not carry with it the unrestrained right to gather information. This ruling came in an unusual case concerning the right of a United States citizen to travel to Cuba in violation of a State Department ban on such travel (*Zemel* v. *Rusk,* 1964). This ruling was regarded as the law until the 1970s.

Beginning in 1972 in a series of cases involving specific news-gathering problems, the Court attempted to shape the narrow boundaries of the constitutional right to gather news and information.

In *Branzburg* v. *Hayes* in 1972 the High Court suggested for the first time that the United States Constitution provides at least a limited right to gather news and information. The case involved the assertions by a trio of journalists that reporters enjoyed the right under the First Amendment to refuse to reveal to a grand jury the names of confidential news sources, since such a revelation would interfere with their ability to gather news from other confidential sources (this case is discussed more on pages 313–315). Justice Byron White, who wrote the Court's opinion for the four-man plurality, disagreed with the reporters' arguments. But, he added, "Nor is it suggested that news gathering does not qualify for First Amendment protection; without some protection for seeking out the news, freedom of the press could be eviscerated." White could find no connection, however, between news gathering and the reporters' reluctance to reveal the names of confidential news sources. Two years later the High Court considered the right to gather news in federal and state prisons.

Access to Prisons

In *Pell* v. *Procunier* (1974) reporters in California attempted to interview specific inmates at California prisons. In *Saxbe* v. *Washington Post* (1974) reporters from that newspaper sought to interview specific inmates at federal prisons at Lewisburg, Pennsylvania, and Danbury, Connecticut. In both instances the press was barred from conducting the interviews. The United States Bureau of Prisons rule, which is similar to the California regulation, states:

> Press representatives will not be permitted to interview individual inmates. This rule shall apply even where the inmate requests or seeks an interview.

At issue was not access to the prison system. The press could tour and photograph prison facilities, conduct brief conversations with randomly encountered inmates, and correspond with inmates through the mails. Outgoing correspondence from inmates was neither censored nor inspected, and incoming mail was inspected only for contraband and statements that might incite illegal action. In addition, the federal rules had been interpreted to permit journalists to conduct lengthy interviews with randomly selected groups of inmates. In fact, a reporter in the *Washington Post* case did go to Lewisburg and interview a group of prisoners.

The argument of the press in both cases was that to ban interviews with specific inmates abridged the First Amendment protection afforded the newsgathering activity of a free press. The Supreme Court disagreed in a five-to-four decision in both cases. Justice Stewart's opinion was subscribed to by Chief Justice Burger, and Justices Blackmun, White, and Rehnquist. Justice Stewart wrote that the press already had substantial access to the prisons and that there was no evidence that prison officials were hiding things from reporters. Stewart rejected the notion that the First Amendment gave newsmen a special right of access to the prisons. "Newsmen have no constitutional right of access to prisons or their inmates beyond that afforded the general public," the justice wrote. Since members of the general public have no right to interview specific prisoners, the denial of this right to the press does not infringe upon the First Amendment.

The High Court did not disagree with the findings of the district court in the *Saxbe* case that face-to-face interviews with specific inmates are essential to accurate and effective reporting about prisoners and prisons. What the Court seemed to say was that while the First Amendment guarantees freedom of expression, it does not guarantee effective and accurate reporting. In fact, about five months after the *Saxbe* and *Pell* decisions, in a speech at the Yale Law School Sesquicentennial Convocation, Justice Stewart made this exact point:

> The press is free to do battle against secrecy and deception in government. But the press cannot expect from the Constitution any guarantee that it will succeed. There is no constitutional right to have access to particular governmental information, or to require openness from the bureaucracy. The public's interest in knowing about its government is protected by the guarantee of a free press, but the protection is indirect. The Constitution itself is neither a Freedom of Information Act nor an Official Secrets Act. The Constitution, in other words, establishes the contest, not its resolution.

In 1978 the High Court split along similar lines on a case involving press access rights to a county jail. An inmate at the Santa Rita County, California, jail committed suicide in 1975. Following the death and a report by a psychiatrist that jail conditions were bad, KQED television in San Francisco sought permission to inspect and take pictures in the jail. Sheriff Houchins announced that the media could certainly participate in one of the six tours of the jail facility that were given to the public each year. However, the tours did not visit the disciplinary cells nor the portion of the jail in which the suicide had taken place. No cameras or tape recorders were allowed, but photographs of some parts of the jail were supplied by the sheriff's office.

Reporters at KQED took a jail tour, but were not happy at the limits placed upon them. Sheriff Houchins contended that unregulated visits through the jail by the press would infringe on the inmates' right of privacy, could create jail celebrities out of inmates that would in turn cause problems for jailers, and would disrupt jail operations. Houchins noted that reporters did have access to inmates—they could visit individual prisoners, could visit with inmates awaiting trial, could talk by telephone with inmates, could write letters to prisoners, and so forth. But KQED argued that it had a constitutionally protected right to gather news and challenged the limits (*Houchins* v. *KQED*, 1978).

Chief Justice Warren Burger wrote the opinion for the court in the four-to-three decision in which neither Justice Blackmun nor Justice Marshall took part. "Neither the First Amendment nor the Fourteenth Amendment mandates a right of access to government information or sources of information within the government's control," Burger asserted. The chief justice seemed troubled by the argument of KQED that only through access to the jail could the press perform its public responsibility (*Houchins* v. *KQED*, 1978):

> Unarticulated but implicit in the assertion that the media access to jail is essential for an informed public debate on jail conditions is the assumption that the media personnel are the best qualified persons for the task of discovering malfeasance in public institutions. . . . The media are not a substitute for or an adjunct of government. . . . We must not confuse the role of the media with that of government. . . .

Looking back at the dictum in *Branzburg* that "news gathering is not without its First Amendment protections," Burger said this must be looked at in its context—forcing a reporter to disclose to a grand jury information received in confidence. "There is an undoubted right to gather news 'from any source within the law . . .' but that affords no basis for the claim that the First Amendment compels others—private persons or government—to supply information." Problems at the jail can be investigated by citizens' task forces or grand juries, Burger said, public bodies that can be coerced to disclose what they have discovered. There is no way to force a journalist who has been given special access to the jail to publish the information gained in such an inspection.

In 1980 in a case that many commentators hailed as the beginning of a general constitutionally guaranteed "right to know," the Supreme Court ruled that the First Amendment does establish for all citizens the right to attend criminal trials (*Richmond Newspapers* v. *Virginia*). (See chapter 7 for a full discussion of this case.) But while Chief Justice Burger's opinion was quite explicit regarding the First Amendment and attendance at criminal trials, it was obscure regarding the larger constitutional right to gather news in other contexts. And the High Court has done nothing in the past decade to clarify its position on this question. Although it has decided a number of right of access cases since *Richmond Newspapers* (see *Press-Enterprise Co., v. Superior Court,* 1984, for example), the Supreme Court has never explicitly recognized this right outside of criminal proceedings.

Lower courts have added considerably more legal precedent to the notion that news gathering is protected by the First Amendment. In one of the earliest recorded decisions on the question, a federal district judge in Rhode Island ruled that when public records are restricted from examination and publication, "the attempt to prohibit their publication is an abridgement of the freedom of the speech and press" (*Providence Journal Co. et al.* v. *McCoy et al.,* 1950). The case involved two newspapers seeking to examine tax cancellation and abatement records. The Pawtucket city council gave permission to one newspaper (the paper that supported the city government in power) but refused to give similar access to an opposition newspaper. A United States court of appeals upheld the lower court ruling, but on the grounds that denying one newspaper access to information given to another is a violation of the guarantee of equal protection of the laws, not necessarily a violation of the First Amendment. The lower court precedent, then, has limited value. In 1977 the United States Court of Appeals for the Fifth Circuit ruled that "Newsgathering is protected by the First Amendment," but nevertheless upheld a ban by the state of Texas against a reporter who sought to film the execution of a convicted felon (*Garrett* v. *Estelle,* 1977). In 1981 a United States district court in the nation's capital ruled that the White House staff could not totally exclude camera crews from the Cable News Network from the pool of television photographers covering the president because the First Amendment includes "a right of access to news and information concerning the operations and activities of government" (*CNN* v. *ABC et al.,* 1981). In 1984 the United States Court of Appeals for the Third Circuit extended the qualified First Amendment right of access to attend criminal trials outlined in the *Richmond Newspapers* case to civil trials (*Publicker Industries* v. *Cohen,* 1984). (See chapter 7 for more on this case.)

In 1985 a federal court in Utah ruled that the public and the press had a First Amendment right to attend a formal administrative fact finding hearing by the Mine Safety and Health Administration (MSHA). The hearing was held to investigate the causes of a mine fire that killed twenty-seven people. Under federal law the Secretary of Labor is permitted to hold an open hearing, but is not compelled to. MSHA officials decided to close this fact finding hearing. The First Amendment is not without limits, the court said, but "It is doubtful that there are any governmental interests compelling enough to warrant complete closure of the MSHA hearing" (*Society of Professional Journalists* v. *Secretary of Labor,* 1985). The United States Court of Appeals for the Tenth Circuit overturned this ruling in October of 1987, ruling that because the investigative hearings had ended by the time the United States District Court ruled, the issue was moot (*Society of Professional Journalists* v. *Secretary of Labor,* 1987). In Louisiana a United States district court ruled that a Parish Sheriff's policy of routinely excluding certain reporters from press conferences, and withholding routine notification of newsworthy material from these same reporters amounted to a violation of the First Amendment. The reporters worked for a newspaper that had opposed the sheriff in his bid for re-election. The court said their was no rationale for the sheriff's conduct; he was unable to demonstrate a compelling state interest that was being served by the policy (*Times-Picayune Publishing Corp.* v. *Lee,* 1988).

Finally, a United States district court in Ohio ruled in 1988 that the press and public have a qualified First Amendment right of access to the legislative process—in this case a city council meeting. The Cleveland City Council closed its doors in November of 1986, shutting out reporters and citizens alike. Council members made no attempt to defend the action by claiming that confidential or privileged material was on the agenda. They simply asserted that they had a right to close the meeting. The press challenged the closure, arguing that it violated the city charter, the Ohio open meeting law, and the First Amendment. Federal District Judge Aldrich focused exclusively on the First Amendment in his decision, ruling that "A presumption always operates in favor of open government meetings, which presumption can be overcome only by a formal showing of a need for privacy or confidentiality" (*WJW* v. *Cleveland,* 1988).

While these cases are not all the lower court rulings that speak to the First Amendment right to gather news, they do represent what seems to be a growing trend toward a more expansive reading of the constitutional rights of news gatherers. Why haven't courts more quickly and clearly moved to the position that the First Amendment protects news gathering? There are some obvious reasons. The consequences of establishing such an unambiguous right could, it is thought, arm the press with a key that it could use to unlock all doors and thereby give reporters access to all material held by the government, all meetings of government agencies and departments. Few believe this is a good idea, but not many seriously believe it would happen if a qualified but clear First Amendment protection of news gathering were enunciated.

There is perhaps a stickier problem, one outlined by Lynn C. Malmgren in a 1974 *Villanova Law Review* article. "The reluctance of the courts to recognize distinctly a news-gathering right in the press stems from a valid concern with the administrative problems and from the logical necessity of making the determination of what constitutes the press for the purposes of constitutional protection." If the right of the press to gather news is merely the same as the right of the public to gather news, then the press may go only where the public may go, Malmgren notes. But if the press has a special right, reporters would have access to many more areas than the public. In that case, who is a reporter? what is the press? Most court decisions so far specifically rule that it is the right of the press *and the public* to attend meetings, hearings, or trials that is guaranteed, not just the right of reporters. The specter of all citizens clamoring to see records or attend hearings has irrationally frightened some judges out of granting any First Amendment rights to gather news and information.

Trespass

As the previous section illustrates, the press has been successful in some small ways in using the First Amendment as a kind of sword to gain access to meetings and records. Journalists have failed almost completely however, in using the First Amendment as a kind of shield to ward off civil and criminal prosecutions for committing illegal acts such as trespass while gathering news. The trespass prosecutions are the most common problem, and have been occurring with alarming regularity since a 1976 Florida ruling. A photographer and a reporter were invited by police and fire officials into a house that had been gutted by fire. The owner of the house, who was not on the premises at the time of the fire, later brought suit for trespass against the journalists. The journalists were exonerated in this instance, but only because the homeowner had not objected at the time the newspaper people entered the home. The Florida Supreme Court said it was common custom for the press to inspect private premises after a serious fire or a crime and that this common custom constituted a kind of indirect consent to the trespass. But it was clear from the court's opinion that had the homeowner been at the scene of the fire and objected to the reporter and photographer coming on the property, common custom or not, the journalists would have been guilty of trespass (*Florida Publishing Co.* v. *Fletcher,* 1976).

As if to emphasize what could have happened to the reporters in Florida, a state court in New York sustained a trespass action against a broadcasting film crew stemming from an incident at an exclusive New York City restaurant. The news crew had been sent to visit various restaurants cited by local authorities for health code violations. The crew entered the restaurant with its cameras rolling and floodlights on. Although the proprietor of the restaurant commanded the reporters to leave, the journalists stayed with the cameras and continued to film until they were physically escorted from the premises. In the meantime, customers ducked under tables, and some fled without paying their bills.

The broadcasting company, CBS, attempted to defend its action by using the First Amendment as a shield to protect itself from the trespass suit. The court disagreed. "Clearly, the First Amendment is not a shibboleth before which all other rights must succumb," the judge ruled (*Le Mistral, Inc.* v. *CBS*, 1978):

> This court recognizes that the exercise of the right of free speech and free press demands and even mandates the observance of the co-equal duty not to abuse such right, but to utilize it with right reason and dignity. Vain lip service to "duties" in a vacuous reality wherein "rights" exist, sovereign and independent of any balancing moral or social factor, creates a semantical mockery of the very foundation of our laws and legal system.

In a subsequent trespass action that mirrored the facts in *Fletcher,* the New York Supreme Court in Monroe County followed the *Le Mistral* precedent closely. A Humane Society investigator obtained a search warrant to enter a home whose occupants had been the object of numerous complaints of cruelty to animals. The investigator invited reporters and film crews from three television stations to accompany him in this foray. The journalists went inside the home, despite the protests of one of the occupants, filmed the interior of the home, and then broadcast the news story. In a lawsuit that followed, the television stations attempted to raise the defense of "implied consent through custom and usage" accepted by the Florida courts in the *Fletcher* case, but the New York court disagreed vigorously.

The so-called implied consent to enter a private home is a custom created by the press itself, the judge noted. "This is a boot-strapping argument," he said, that does not eliminate the trespass in this case. News people do not stand in any favored position with regard to trespass, the judge said. "If the news media were to succeed in compelling an uninvited and nonpermitted entry into one's private home whenever it chose to do so, this would be nothing less than a general warrant equivalent to the writs of assistance which were so odious to the American colonists," he added (*Anderson* v. *WROC-TV,* 1981).

Reporters in Oklahoma were found guilty of criminal trespass when they followed protestors into restricted areas during demonstrations at a nuclear facility. The Oklahoma Court of Criminal Appeals ruled that journalists enjoyed reasonable access to the events taking place in areas set aside by authorities for the press and for legal protests and did not need to trespass to get the story (*Stahl* v. *Oklahoma,* 1983). The fact that reporters could have legally viewed this news event without trespassing is an important element in this ruling.

More recently courts in Wisconsin and California have upheld trespass claims against the press. A federal judge in Milwaukee ruled that a reporter for the *Ripon Commonwealth-Press,* who was working on a story on the execution of search warrants, had committed a trespass when she entered a private home upon the invitation of the police chief. The homeowner asked police who the reporter was and the chief replied, "She's with us." The journalist was never asked to leave, and took many photos while in the home. While the plaintiff filed the action under a Wisconsin privacy act, the judge nevertheless instructed the jury that the reporter had committed a trespass, and the jury awarded the plaintiff one dollar in nominal damages (*Heiser* v. *Ripon Commonwealth-Press,* 1986).

An NBC field producer accompanied a team of Los Angeles City Fire Department paramedics when they rushed to the home of a heart attack victim. The victim's wife said she was distracted by the police and emergency personnel and did not notice the camera crew. She said she was shocked when she later saw the pictures on television. She sued for trespass, invasion of privacy and intentional infliction of emotional distress. A superior court in Los Angeles County dismissed all claims, but they were reinstated a year later by the California Court of Appeals. The court rejected a First Amendment defense, noting that "One seeking emergency medical attention does not thereby open the door for persons without any clearly identifiable and justifiable official reason who may wish to enter the premises where the medical aid is being administered" (*Miller* v. *National Broadcasting Co.,* 1986).

But a charge of trespass is not the only problem that faces a reporter in news gathering. The New Jersey Supreme Court upheld the disorderly person conviction of a press photographer who was charged with impeding a police officer in the performance of his duty at the scene of a serious traffic accident. The photographer was standing near the wreckage when the state trooper, who feared a fire might begin and who also wanted to preserve the accident scene for investigation, ordered the area cleared of spectators. The news photographer moved back five feet, but when he refused to move any farther, he was arrested.

The journalist, Harvey J. Lashinsky, argued that the state's disorderly person statute was inapplicable to him because he was a member of the press. The state's high court disagreed, noting that "the constitutional prerogatives of the press must yield under appropriate circumstances to other important and legitimate interests." Acknowledging that the press does play a special role in society, the court nevertheless said that the photographer clearly impeded the officer by refusing his request to leave the area. While the officer was arguing with the journalist, he could have been giving assistance to the accident victims and beginning the investigation of the crash (*State* v. *Lashinsky,* 1979).

Reporters also need to be aware that the First Amendment will not immunize them from prosecutions that might result from violating statutes that require two-party or all-party consent to record, film, or broadcast a conversation. In most states and the District of Columbia you can record a conversation to which you are a party without informing other persons in the conversations. But the states of California, Delaware, Florida, Illinois, Louisiana, Maryland, Massachusetts, Michigan, Montana, New Hampshire, Oregon and Washington all have laws that require the consent of more than one person or all persons before a conversation can be recorded. Nineteen states and the federal government have passed eavesdropping laws as well. And nine states, Alabama, Delaware, Georgia, Hawaii, Maine, Michigan, New Hampshire, South Dakota and Utah have laws that expressly prohibit the unauthorized use (such as secret use) of cameras in private places. It is important for reporters to know what the state law is regarding such matters and to follow it. Courts have not in the past permitted a First Amendment defense in such cases.

The brief discussion of these cases makes it clear that the courts will insist that reporters, like all other citizens, obey the law; their status as members of the press, which is granted protection under the First Amendment, is generally immaterial when they are called upon to account for their behavior while gathering news for publication and broadcast.

SUMMARY

Access to information held by the government has been a problem faced by citizen and journalist alike for centuries. Changes in both the size and nature of government in recent years have exacerbated this age-old difficulty. The common law offers little assistance to persons attempting to inspect government records. The United States Constitution was drafted at a time when news gathering was not the central role of the press. There is little evidence to suggest that the right to gather news was intended to be guaranteed by the First Amendment. Federal courts have in recent years suggested that gathering news and information is entitled to some protection under the United States Constitution, but they have been stingy in granting such protection. The United States Supreme Court has limited the right of reporters to gather information at prisons and jails to the same rights enjoyed by other citizens. And the High Court has also rejected the notion that the limited protection granted news gathering entitles journalists special rights to protect the identities of their confidential news sources. The Supreme Court did rule that all citizens have the right to attend criminal trials, but the High Court has not extended this First Amendment right beyond the criminal justice system. Lower courts have found broader, albeit qualified constitutional rights of access. Courts have not permitted, however, the use of the First Amendment to immunize reporters from legal consequences that result when the law is broken while news is being gathered.

FEDERAL STATUTES AND NEWS GATHERING

Neither the common law nor the Constitution has provided the clear and well-defined right of access to government information that most citizens believe is needed. Beginning in the early 1950s, there have been concerted efforts by press and citizen lobbying groups to pass statutes that guarantee to public and press alike the right to inspect records and other information held by the government and to attend meetings held by public agencies. These laws exist in almost every state. In addition, there are federal open records and open meetings laws. Let us look at the federal legislation first.

The Freedom of Information Act

Between 1789 and 1966 access to the records of the federal government was largely an unsettled question. Various housekeeping laws, administrative procedure statutes, had been passed by Congress, but none were aimed at providing the kind of access to government records that both the press and a large segment of the population believed necessary for the efficient operation of our democracy. Before 1966 the laws Congress passed were really laws authorizing information to be withheld, rather than laws forcing government agencies to open their files. Also, reporters could do little when requests for information were denied. In 1966 after many years of hearings and testimony and work, Congress adopted the **Freedom of Information Act** (FOIA), which was ostensibly designed to open up records and files long closed to public inspection. Today, hundreds of thousands of FOIA requests are made to the federal government each year.

Adopting a freedom of information law is one thing; the way the government administers and interprets that law is another. "From Lyndon Johnson's reluctant signing of the FOIA in 1966, every administration since has viewed it with some degree of distaste," said Professor Lotte Feinberg, an FOIA expert at John Jay College of Criminal Justice. But no administration worked more diligently to undermine the basic purpose of the law than that of Ronald Reagan. During that eight-year term Jack Landau, executive director of the Reporter's Committee on Freedom of the Press, noted that "The Reagan administration's policies are causing the most significant media access restrictions on government information since the end of voluntary censorship in World War II."

When Reagan took office his attorney general, William French Smith, told all executive branch department heads that they were to comply with the letter of the law, but not its spirit. If there is a legal basis to withhold a document, withhold it, Smith said. This was a distinct departure from previous administrations. Under President Jimmy Carter, for example, department heads were instructed not to withhold a document, even if it were legally possible to do so, unless it was important to the public interest to do so. Under Reagan there was a considerable growth in the classification of government documents (see pp. 270–273). In addition, his administration supported several amendments to the FOIA that have limited the effectiveness of the law, and Reagan staff gave at least tacit approval to various actions by agencies to avoid complying with the federal statute.

There was considerable budget cutting during the Reagan administration, and this exacerbated the problems. Many agencies cut their staffs, and did not fill vacancies among employees who were charged with filling FOIA requests. The government also stopped publishing vast numbers of information-oriented publications. Between 1983 and 1988, one out of four of the government's sixteen thousand publications was eliminated, according to Eileen Cooke, director of the American Library Association's Washington office. The forty-five-thousand-member association was so concerned that it published a report, "Less Access to Less Information By and About the U.S. Government," in 1988. "A policy has emerged which is less than sympathetic to the principles of freedom of access," the report noted.

How can an administration interfere with the application of a statute? After all, isn't it all spelled out in the law? There are many ways for an agency to foil attempts to gain access to records held by the government. Steve Weinberg, the executive director of Investigative Reporters and Editors, lists many of them in an article published in the *Washington Journalism Review* entitled, "Hits and Misses, FOIA at Twenty." Here are some of Weinberg's examples:

Charging high fees for searching and copying

Claiming the documents are lost, or have been transferred to another agency

Failing to meet the ten-day time limit for a response, claiming that short staffing has caused the delay

Blacking out information on the document indiscriminately

What this all means is that while the FOIA is a reasonably good law, and has been interpreted in a generally fair manner by the courts, the basic purpose of the law can be frustrated by an uncooperative administration. Nevertheless, FOIA requests continue to pour in to the government. Over 300,000 requests were filed in a recent fiscal year. Most requests were completely or partially filled. During that same year, United States district courts— the first judicial point of appeal if a request is turned down—heard almost six hundred FOIA cases.

In the next few pages we will sketch the broad outlines of the federal Freedom of Information Act, focus upon the nine areas of exempted information, suggest some ways in which a journalist or citizen can use the law.

Agency Records

One can write an open records law in two basic ways. The first way is to declare that the following kinds of records are to be accessible for public inspection and then list the kinds of records that are open. The second way is to proclaim that all government records are open for public inspection except the following kinds of records and then list the exceptions. Congress approved the second kind of law in 1966, and it went into effect in 1967. The law has been amended several times, with substantial changes being enacted in 1974 and 1976.

The United States Freedom of Information Act gives any person access to all the records kept by all federal agencies, unless the information falls into one of nine categories of exempted material. An agency has been defined under the law as:

> . . . any executive department, military department, government corporation, government-controlled corporation or other establishment in the executive branch of government (including the executive office of the president), or any independent regulatory agency.

The laws govern records held by agencies in the executive branch of government and all the independent regulatory agencies like the Federal Trade Commission, the Federal Aviation Agency, and the Securities and Exchange Commission. The law does not cover records held by Congress or the federal courts. Some agencies associated with the executive branch of government also fall outside the purview of the law. In 1985 the United States Court of Appeals for the District of Columbia ruled that the Council of Economic Advisors, which works closely with the president on economic matters, is not covered by the law because it exists solely to advise and assist the president and makes no policy on its own. The agency has no regulatory power, it cannot issue rules or regulations. While the FOIA does govern some operations in the executive office of the president, the law does not reach "the president's immediate personal staff or units in the executive office whose *sole function* is to advise and assist the president," the court ruled (*Rushforth* v. *Council of Economic Advisors,* 1985).

What is a record? While Congress did not specify the physical characteristics of a record, records include not only documents written on paper, but also films, tapes, and probably even three-dimensional materials such as weapons that have been used as evidence in criminal cases. The United States Court of Appeals for the Ninth Circuit ruled in 1979 that computer tapes are records for the purposes of the law (*Long* v. *IRS*).

Few disagreements have arisen about the definition of either an agency or a record. But there has been considerable litigation about the nature of an "agency record." Courts have ruled that there must be a connection between the agency and the record before the FOIA is applicable. If the agency creates the record and possesses and controls the record, it is an agency record under the law. Mere possession of a record created by others does not necessarily bring the material under the FOIA. A transcript of a congressional hearing that was in the possession of the Central Intelligence Agency for thirty years is not an agency record, according to the United States Court of Appeals for the District of Columbia. The "record" had been created by Congress, which is not governed by the FOIA (*Goland* v. *CIA,* 1978). A report prepared by members of Ronald Reagan's staff prior to his inauguaration as president but possessed by a high official in the Department of Health and Human Services (HHS) is not an agency record, a United States district court recently ruled. "In this case, although copies of the report are physically located in HHS, the report was not generated by HHS, is not within the control of HHS, and indeed never entered the department's files or was ever used by the department for any purpose," Judge Gesell ruled (*Wolfe* v. *Department of Health and Human Services,* 1982).

Similarly, the United States Court of Appeals for the District of Columbia ruled in 1984 that telephone message slips and desk calendars were not agency records because neither were necessarily related to agency business. The message slips simply alerted an official that a call had been received; the desk calendars were created for personal convenience, to help officials organize personal and agency business appointments (*BNA* v. *Baxter* and *Environmental Defense Fund* v. *Office of Management and Budget,* 1984). What about records that were created by an agency but are no longer possessed by the agency? The Reporter's Committee on Freedom of the Press raised this question before the Supreme Court of the United States in 1980. At issue were transcripts and summaries of telephone conversations made by Henry Kissinger while he was secretary of state. When Kissinger left his post in government, reporters asked the State Department to see copies of these materials. The agency said it could not comply with the request because Kissinger had donated the material to the Library of Congress; the State Department did not possess the records. The Reporter's Committee sued, arguing that these were agency records which should be disclosed by the Department of State under the FOIA. Justice William Rehnquist, who wrote the Supreme Court's opinion, ruled that it was unnecessary to decide whether these telephone notes were agency records, since the covered agency—the Department of State— had not withheld the documents from the reporters. "The FOIA is directed only at requiring agencies to disclose those 'agency records' for which they have chosen to retain possession or control," Rehnquist added (*Kissinger* v. *Reporter's Committee,* 1980). While the facts in this case cloud the issue somewhat (were the telephone transcripts the personal property of Kissinger or something created by the agency?), the case strongly suggests that the Freedom of Information Act cannot be used to gain access to records no longer possessed by an agency.

One of the most vexing problems regarding the definition of agency records has to do with material created for an agency by a private consulting firm. Many persons argue that when the Congress amended the FOIA in 1974, it intended that the law cover all entities that "performed governmental functions and controlled information of public interest." This phrase was contained in a House of Representatives report (93rd Cong., 2d sess., H. Rept. 876) that focused on the amendment. This language surely would place many government consultants under the aegis of the FOIA, according to Anne Wright in an article in the *Georgetown Law Journal*. But the courts have not rigorously applied the law to consulting agencies, even though in some cases these firms do a tremendous amount of government work. Wright reports that in fiscal year 1979, the federal government spent $2.3 billion on consulting services. Seven federal agencies relied on consultants to meet more than forty percent of their congressionally mandated reporting requirements, according to the legal scholar.

In 1980 the Supreme Court ruled that the FOIA does not normally apply to materials generated and retained by consulting firms. The National Institute of Arthritis, Metabolism, and Digestive Diseases (NIAMDD) hired private consultants to study the effectiveness of certain diabetes treatments. The consultants kept the raw data generated by the study, but NIAMDD had access to the data. The consultants concluded in their reports that the use of certain drugs in diabetes treatment increased the risk of heart disease. Access to the raw data was sought by persons outside government. The agency's refusal to grant access to the material was supported by the Supreme Court, which ruled that data generated by a privately controlled organization that has received federal grants are not agency records. Even though NIAMDD used federal money to have the consultants create the data in question, the High Court refused to agree that this amounted to "creating" the records themselves. "We agree with the opinions of the courts below . . . that an agency [the federal agency] must first either create or obtain a record as a prerequisite to it becoming an agency record within the meaning of the FOIA," wrote Justice Rehnquist for the majority of the Court (*Forsham* v. *Harris*, 1980).

FOIA Exemptions

Before the FOIA becomes applicable, then, the information that is sought must be considered an agency record under the law. Agency records may be inspected and copied by the public, unless they fall into one of the nine categories of exempt material. As noted previously, federal agencies are not required to withhold documents from disclosure, even if they fall within an exemption to the FOIA (*Chrysler Corp.* v. *Brown*, 1979). They may choose to disclose this information. But if records or documents properly fall under one of the nine exemptions, access to this material may be properly denied under the law.

Let us look at each exemption separately, try to illuminate its meaning, and note any important court interpretations of the language in the law. The Freedom of Information Act exempts the following nine categories of materials from disclosure.

Exemption One: Matters specifically authorized under criteria established by an executive order to be kept secret in the interest of national defense or foreign policy and in fact properly classified pursuant to such an executive order. This exemption deals with a wide range of materials, from the highest secrets of state to more or less mundane matters. The United States

Court of Appeals for the District of Columbia recently ruled, for example, that the army's compilation of combat units' operation readiness reports was properly classified as confidential and exempt from disclosure under the Freedom of Information Act (*Taylor* v. *Army,* 1982).

As originally adopted in 1966, this exemption excluded from disclosure any document or record that the president, through executive order, chose to classify in the name of national security. Courts, including the Supreme Court, ruled that there could be no challenge to the classification of the document or record, no judicial examination of whether the material was sensitive or even related to national security (see *Epstein* v. *Resor,* 1970 and *EPA* v. *Mink,* 1973). The exemption was abused by administrations, especially during the Nixon presidency, and was amended by the Congress in 1974. The change in the law has given the courts the power to inspect classified documents to determine whether they have been properly classified.

What is supposed to happen is this: The president (undoubtedly his staff) establishes criteria in an executive order for the classification of sensitive documents and records. Material is then classified according to the executive order by members of various government agencies such as the Department of Defense, the National Security Agency, and others. This material is exempt from disclosure. But a citizen seeking a document or record can challenge the classification of any document and ask a court to determine whether the material has been properly classified, using the criteria established by the president. A judge cannot question the criteria established by the executive branch but can only determine whether the records or documents were properly classified according to those criteria.

For example, a federal court was asked to determine whether the navy had properly classified videotape it had taken of the crash of a jet fighter aboard the USS *Nimitz.* The accident, which occurred in 1981, killed fourteen people and caused one hundred million dollars in damage to the carrier and other planes. A congressional investigation of the crash turned up evidence that flight-deck crew members may have been under the influence of drugs at the time of the incident. Since the navy routinely videotapes all carrier takeoffs and landings, there was tape of the accident. Reporter David Browde sought access to the videotape but was turned away. The navy said the material was exempt from release for national security reasons. Analysis of the videotape would reveal operational capabilities of the navy's supercarriers, Secretary of the Navy John Lehman said. Browde went to court, but Judge John Pratt ruled that the navy had shown that it had properly classified the videotape. A United States court of appeals refused to review the ruling (*Browde* v. *Navy,* 1983).

In fact, courts have been very reluctant to second-guess the administration on the classification of documents. The law states that a court *may* determine whether the material was properly classified; it does not state that the court *must* do so. And most courts refuse even to examine the documents. The

Court of Appeals for the Fourth Circuit turned down a request that it privately examine specific secret materials to see whether the documents were classified properly. The court claimed it lacked the expertise to make such a judgment and told the complainant to file a complaint with the agency denying access originally (*Knopf* v. *Colby,* 1975).

In taking this tack the courts seemed to reflect the reluctance of Congress itself to view the FOIA as a means to reform the classification process or to bring about systematic review of individual decisions. The Senate-House Conference Committee report on the 1974 amendment, for example, noted:

> The executive departments responsible for national defense and foreign policy matters have unique insights into what adverse effects may occur as a result of public disclosure of a particular classified record. Accordingly, the conferees expect that federal courts . . . will accord substantial weight to an agency's affidavits concerning the details of the classified status of a disputed record.

Judicial reluctance to second-guess the executive branch on the classification of national security materials became a much more serious problem when President Ronald Reagan sharply tightened the national security classification regulations. President Jimmy Carter had required government agencies to consider the public interest as well as the government interest before classifying any document. Under the Carter administration most documents automatically were declassified after six years unless the federal agency reviewed the material and requested reclassification for six more years. Also under President Carter, government agencies had to prove that "identifiable damage" to national security would result if the information was not classified.

President Reagan changed these policies in an executive order issued in April 1982 (Executive Order 12356). The order ended the explicit consideration of public interest before classification and directed officials to opt for the highest level of secrecy possible when classifying material. The order also permitted classification of materials if the agency could show "any damage," rather than "identifiable damage," to the national security. Material was no longer automatically declassified after six years. Reagan's executive order also permitted the reclassification of material that has already been made public. The National Security Agency recently took documents off public shelves at a Virginia Military Institute library that had been available to the public for years and classified them (see *Peterzell* v. *Faurer,* 1986). These rules went into effect on August 1, 1982. Reagan added strong support for this executive order in March 1983 when he signed a directive ordering all federal employees with access to sensitive information to sign a nondisclosure agreement as a condition of gaining access to this information. The FBI was given enhanced authority to investigate so-called leaks, and federal employees could be forced to take lie detector tests during investigations of these leaks, under provisions of the presidential directive.

A new President, George Bush, took office in January of 1989, as this chapter was being prepared. At that time there was no clear indication whether Bush would continue to follow Reagan's narrow policy regarding access to information, or would offer a more moderate proposal, following the Carter model. While the President promised a kinder and more gentle administration, he at one time was the Director of the Central Intelligence Agency, a body obsessed with secrecy.

Exemption Two: Matters related solely to the internal personnel rules and practices of an agency. This exemption covers what are known as "house-keeping" materials: vacation schedules, coffee-break rules, parking-lot assignments, and so forth. Little harm would result if these materials were made public; the exemption is offered simply to relieve the agencies of the burden of having to maintain such material in public files.

The most controversial aspect of exemption two is whether it applies to agency staff manuals. For example, a citizen recently sought access to a Bureau of Alcohol, Tobacco, and Firearms staff manual entitled *Surveillance of Premises, Vehicles, and Persons.* The bureau released all but twenty pages of the manual, which it said described internal personnel rules and practices of the agency. The United States Court of Appeals for the District of Columbia ruled in favor of the agency in the lawsuit that followed. The court noted that during the debate on the FOIA in Congress, members spoke without contradiction that exemption two was designed to protect law enforcement investigatory manuals from disclosure (*Crooker* v. *Bureau,* 1981). Other federal courts agree (see *Hardy* v. *Bureau of Alcohol, Tobacco, and Firearms,* 1980).

Exemption Three: Matters specifically exempted from disclosure by statute (other than section 552b of this title) provided that such statute (a) requires that the matters be withheld from the public in such a manner as to leave no discretion on the issue, or (b) establishes particular criteria for withholding or refers to particular types of matters to be withheld. This exemption is designed to protect from disclosure information required or permitted to be kept secret by dozens of other federal laws. A wide range of records fall under this exemption, including census bureau records, public utility information, trade secrets, patent applications, tax returns, bank records, veterans benefits, and documents held by both the Central Intelligence Agency and the National Security Agency.

Courts generally ask three questions when determining whether exemption three applies to a specific record or document:

1. Is there a specific statute that authorizes or requires the withholding of information?
2. Does the statute designate specific kinds of information or outline specific criteria for information that may be withheld?
3. Does the record or information that is sought fall within the categories of information that may be withheld?

If all three questions are answered yes, disclosure can be legally denied.

In the mid-1980s the Central Intelligence Agency (CIA) used both Congressional amendments and court action relating to this exemption to close off public scrutiny of much of its work. For the last several years, CIA officials have lobbied Congress for an amendment to the FOIA totally exempting the agency from the provisions of the law. They got something close to that in 1984 when Congress voted to exempt all operational files from release under the Freedom of Information Act. To be exempt a CIA file must deal with the conduct of foreign intelligence operations, background investigations of informants, liaison arrangements with foreign governments, or scientific or technical means of gathering foreign intelligence. The director of the CIA designates certain files as being exempt, using the criteria established by Congress. The law provides for judicial review of whether the files are properly designated, but as previously noted, judicial review has not worked well as it relates to national security documents and there is no reason to suspect it will work any better in this case.

In the spring of 1985, the Supreme Court ruled that another category of CIA material is not available for public inspection. From 1952 to 1966 the CIA funded 185 researchers at eighty universities to study the effects of mind-altering substances on humans. In 1963 the CIA's inspector general investigated the clandestine project and reported to the agency director that people were unwittingly being used as guinea pigs for some of the experiments. CIA files on the project were declassified in 1970, and Congressional reports on the project received publicity in mid-decade. John Sims, an attorney, filed an FOIA request with the CIA in 1977, asking for the names of institutions and individuals who had participated in the experiments. The CIA would disclose only the institutions and individuals who agreed to the release of their names. The agency said that such names were exempt from disclosure under the National Security Act of 1947, which states, "The Director of Central Intelligence shall be responsible for protecting intelligence sources and methods from unauthorized disclosure." The institutions and individuals were intelligence sources, the agency argued.

A United States court of appeals ruled that an intelligence source was an individual or institution that provides the CIA with information on a confidential basis (*Sims* v. *CIA,* 1983). The Supreme Court disagreed, saying that this definition of an intelligence source was too narrow and that such a narrow definition of a source interferes with the broad authority granted to the director of the agency under the National Security Act, to protect all sources of information, not only those guaranteed confidentiality. The agency was free to withhold the information (*Sims* v. *CIA,* 1985).

In recent years, federal agencies have cited nearly one hundred different statutes to try to justify withholding documents. In some instances courts have rejected these attempts, but frequently the denial goes unchallenged, according to researchers at the Reporters Committee on Freedom of the Press.

Courts have upheld denial of access to records based on laws governing the Census Bureau, Consumer Products Safety Commission, Internal Revenue Service, the Patent and Trademark Office, the Postal Service, National Security Agency, Central Intelligence Agency and a few others. It is expected that more and more government agencies will in the future seek specific Congressional exemption from provisions of the FOIA.

Exemption Four: Trade secrets and financial information obtained from any person and privileged or confidential. Two kinds of information are exempt from disclosure under this exemption—trade secrets and financial information. The trade secret exemption has not been heavily litigated, although recently the United States Court of Appeals for the District of Columbia fashioned a definition of a trade secret that considerably narrows the exemption. In litigation initiated by Ralph Nader's Public Citizen Health Research Project, the court said a trade secret is "an unpatented, commercially valuable plan, appliance, formula, or process which is used for the making, preparing, compounding, treating, or processing of articles or materials which are trade commodities, and that can be said to be the end product of either innovation or substantial effort." The court rejected a broader definition of a trade secret proposed by the Food and Drug Administration: "any . . . compilation of information which is used in one's business and which gives him an opportunity to obtain an advantage over competitors who do not know or use it" (*Public Citizen Health Research Group* v. *Food and Drug Administration,* 1983).

The "financial information" exemption applies only to information supplied to the government by individuals or private business firms. It is this second section of the exemption that has undergone the most thorough judicial interpretation. The *Miami Herald* sought records from the Small Business Administration (SBA) regarding loans made to small contractors that had become delinquent. The SBA attempted to block the disclosure by citing exemption four. Courts have interpreted exemption four to apply only if the disclosure of the information will impair the government's ability to obtain information in the future or cause substantial harm to the competitive position of the person from whom the information was obtained. The SBA failed to present any evidence that the delinquent borrowers would suffer competitive harm if this information were disclosed. In fact, there was no evidence presented that the borrowers were even in competition with anyone. A United States court of appeals ordered the material disclosed (*Miami Herald* v. *Small Business Administration,* 1982). The federal courts have rigorously applied the criteria outlined above in the *Miami Herald* case. To block disclosure the government must clearly demonstrate that the provider of the information will suffer considerably more than mere embarrassment or a small loss of business.

American business generally has been unhappy about this application of the FOIA, fearful that the release of some information might give competitors an edge of some sort, or worried that unhappy consumers might use the law to discover information that might be helpful in litigation against the business. Exemption four, as well as exemption eight (which focuses upon banking reports) and exemption nine (oil and gas well data) are aimed at giving American corporations some protection. But corporate America has lobbied for more protection. Rebuffed by Congress in 1986, business sought and received help from Ronald Reagan. Executive Order 12600 requires all federal agencies to provide early notification to a business when "arguably" confidential business data is about to be released under the FOIA. As of January 1, 1988, all submitters of confidential information will be advised of an upcoming FOIA disclosure when the records are less than ten months old and have been designated by the submitter as confidential. The submitter can then object to the release. If the agency decides to release the information despite the objections, it must provide a written explanation to the submitter.

This doesn't sound like a major impediment to the release of data, but it can cause difficult problems for someone seeking information. Imagine a journalist is seeking information from a federal agency about an auto manufacturer. Once the agency tells the company that it is about to release the information, the company attorneys can spring into action, attempting to block the release. Failing that, the manufacturer can attempt to put pressure on the journalist, or more likely his or her publication or broadcasting station, and try to block the publication or broadcast of the data. This is even before the story is completed. Also, if an agency employee realizes that her release of information will require a written explanation to the submitter, it might be easier to refuse access to the material and force the individual seeking it to go to court. Small problems undoubtedly; but they all add up and clearly frustrate the notion that what the people's government is doing is the people's business.

Exemption Five: Interagency and intraagency memorandums and letters which would not be available by law to a private party in litigation with the agency. This exemption is described in an FOI Service Center bulletin as designed to protect working papers, studies, and reports prepared within an agency or circulated among government personnel as the basis of a final agency decision. In addition, this exemption shields from disclosure communications between an agency and its attorney, material normally not disclosed due to the attorney-client privilege.

Two recent cases demonstrate the kinds of materials covered by exemption five. A request was made for material on the United States Air Force report on the use of herbicides in Vietnam. The government provided the final report prepared by the Air Force, but refused to give out portions of the first draft of the report, which were never included in the final report. The court of appeals upheld the government's refusal. The court said (*Russell* v. *Air Force,* 1982):

> There are essentially three policy bases for this privilege. First, it protects creative debate and candid consideration of alternatives, within an agency, and thereby improves the quality of the agency policy decisions. Second, it

protects the public from the confusion that would result from premature exposure to discussions occurring before the policies affecting it had actually been settled upon. And third, it protects the integrity of the decision-making process itself by confirming that "officials should be judged by what they decided, not for matters they considered before making up their minds."

The portions of the first draft of the report sought by the plaintiff in the case were considerations, not decisions and part of the decision-making process designed to be protected by this exemption. Factual portions of predecisional documents are not normally exempt. For example, imagine there is a long policy memorandum containing advisory recommendations on a proposed jet fighter and the cost of the construction of the warplane. While the advisory recommendations are exempt, the factual cost data is not and must be segregated out of the memo and released upon request.

In another instance, the same court ruled against the government when it attempted to use exemption five. In the late 1970s the United States attorney general set up a task force to investigate charges that a Federal Bureau of Investigation (FBI) informant inside the Ku Klux Klan had committed illegal acts while in the Klan, including shooting a civil rights worker. A 302-page report was produced, and *Playboy* magazine sought a copy of the document. The FBI resisted, citing several exemptions including exemption five. The court ruled that while some parts of the report (i.e., names and identifying data) were exempt from the law under other exemptions (exemption seven), the entire report was not protected under exemption five. This exemption is designed to protect the deliberative process, to protect opinions and recommendations from which government decisions are made, the court said. It does not protect purely factual material appearing in documents in a form that is totally severable without compromising the private remainder of the documents (*Playboy* v. *Justice Department,* 1982).

The United States Court of Appeals for the District of Columbia recently ruled that exemption five goes so far as to shield draft book manuscripts from disclosure. An historian working for the Office of Air Force History (OAFH) prepared a draft history of the role of the United States Air Force in South Vietnam in the early 1960s. Senior OAFH officers rejected the manuscript—the second time such a manuscript was turned down. A reporter sought a copy of the manuscript, believing it might contain information about unreported war crimes. The Air Force turned down the request, arguing that disclosure of the manuscript might reveal the deliberative editorial process used by the Air Force. The court agreed. "The simple comparison of the draft with the final manuscript would expose an editorial judgment made by Air Force personnel," the court ruled. This exposure of the editorial judgment would inhibit creative debate and candid considerations in the future, the court added (*Dudman Communications Corp.* v. *Air Force,* 1987).

In 1984 the United States Supreme Court ruled that confidential statements obtained during an Air Force investigation of an air crash are protected from disclosure under exemption five. The public is entitled to all such memorandums or letters that a private party could discover in litigation with the agency, wrote Justice John Paul Stevens for a unanimous court. But the material in question would not normally or routinely be open to discovery in a civil proceeding (the discovery process in litigation enables one party to gain access to evidence, testimony, and other material held by the other party, prior to the trial). The High Court ruled that exemption five incorporates the civil discovery privilege; Congress did not intend to create a situation in which litigants could use the FOIA to circumvent discovery privileges (*U.S.* v. *Weber Aircraft Corp.,* 1984). In 1988, however, the Supreme Court took another look at exemption five as it relates to discovery privileges and reached a different conclusion. Two federal inmates both sought copies of their presentence investigation reports. These reports are prepared by probation officers for use by district courts before sentencing. They are then forwarded to the Bureau of Prisons and finally to the Parole Commission. Some parts of these reports were clearly not to be disclosed because both a federal statute and federal court rules preclude the release of information that relates to confidential sources, diagnostic opinions, and other information that may harm prisoners or third parties. (These rules apply through exemption three.) But the government sought to block the release of the remainder of the reports on the grounds that they are normally considered privileged communications in civil or criminal discovery proceedings. Chief Justice Rehnquist agreed, that courts have been very reluctant to give third parties access to presentence reports. But he noted, "There is no indication, however, that similar restrictions on discovery of presentence investigation reports have been recognized by the courts when the individual requesting discovery is the subject of the report." Rehnquist and four other members of the Court said they believed it was entirely reasonable to treat a claim of privilege under exemption five differently as to one class of those who make requests than as to another class. Here, there was good reason to differentiate between third party requests and requests by the subject of the report. The inmates won their case (*Justice Department* v. *Julian,* 1988).

The long-term ramifications of the *Julian* decision might be far more important than the immediate impact, which is clearly narrow. This is the first time the Supreme Court ever differentiated between types of requesters in resolving an FOIA dispute. In other words, it is the first time the Court said this exemption clearly precludes giving the information to some kinds of persons, but not to other kinds of persons. Whether or not this becomes an important element in litigating FOIA cases remains to be seen.

Exemption five is also called the executive privilege exemption. **Executive privilege** is an old concept in the history of the Republic. Since 1794, beginning with President George Washington, American chief executives have asserted that the president enjoys a common law privilege to keep secret all presidential papers, records, and other documents. Washington asserted the privilege when Congress called for all papers and records in the possession of the president that would facilitate its investigation of the negotiation of the Jay Treaty, a controversial agreement with Great Britain. Washington refused to comply with the congressional demand, citing executive privilege. Andrew Jackson refused to give Congress information relating to a boundary dispute in Maine. Millard Fillmore refused a request from the Senate that he provide that body with information regarding negotiations with the Sandwich (Hawaiian) Islands.

In modern times, however, the heads of agencies within the executive branch have asserted that they also enjoy a kind of limited executive privilege. Exemption five covers the kinds of documents—working papers, memorandums, and so forth—traditionally claimed exempt from public scrutiny by executive privilege. The purpose of the exemption is to protect the confidentiality of the decision-making process. However, exemption five is often used as a shield to avoid disclosing all manner of material totally unrelated to decision making. Legal memorandums, correspondence, minutes and transcripts, staff analyses, interpretations and opinions, and recommendations of experts and consultants have all been at one time or another declared to fall within the boundaries of exemption five.

In 1974 in *U.S. v. Nixon,* the Supreme Court sharply limited the boundaries of the traditional executive privilege. In this case several of the famous White House tapes were subpoenaed by the special prosecutor for use in the criminal trial of some of the Nixon aides. The former president argued that the tapes were protected by executive privilege. He said that revelation of the material on the tapes would damage the integrity of the decision-making process and that under our system of separation of powers, the courts were precluded from reviewing his claim of privilege. He also argued that even if his claim of absolute executive privilege should fail, the court should at least hold as a matter of constitutional law that his privilege superseded the subpoena.

However, in a unanimous opinion (eight-to-nothing, since Justice Rehnquist did not participate in the decision) the Burger Court rejected the notion of absolute privilege in this case. The Court said that an absolute privilege can be asserted only when the material in question consists of military or diplomatic secrets. When other kinds of information are involved, privilege of the president must be balanced against other values—in this case, against the operation of the criminal justice system. The need for the privilege must be weighed against the need for the information. Courts will have to make these decisions from private examination of the materials in question.

How does this decision affect exemption five? Since exemption five is based on the notion of the executive privilege and since the courts have said such an absolute privilege does not exist in the absence of military or diplomatic secrets, agencies that claim exemption five as reason to deny access will have to allow the courts to scrutinize the material in question and evaluate whether the need for secrecy outweighs the benefits of disclosure. The mechanical process of the past under which agencies could gain the exemption merely by asserting that the material in question fell under the purview of the fifth exemption is probably gone. Now when they are challenged, agencies will have to prove to a judge that the material does in fact come within the fifth exemption. Disclosure of much such material withheld in the past should be ensured.

Exemption Six: Personnel and medical files and similar files the disclosure of which would constitute a clearly unwarranted invasion of privacy. This exemption is designed to shield from public view personal and private information held in government files about millions of Americans. There has been considerable litigation involving exemption six, and it is possible to outline a fairly authoritative interpretation of its meaning.

The exemption protects "personnel and medical and similar files." What are similar files? They are files that contain highly personal information, similar to the kinds of personal information that can be found in medical and personnel files. In February 1981 the United States Court of Appeals for the District of Columbia suggested that "similar files" were files *like* medical and personnel files (*Washington Post* v. *State Department,* 1981). But fifteen months later the Supreme Court of the United States rejected that interpretation and said that that phrase "similar files" had a broad meaning and covered a wide range of different kinds of files. What is being protected from disclosure, Justice William Rehnquist wrote for the unanimous Court, is a kind of *information,* not a kind of *file.* An individual's medical and personnel files contain highly personal information about that individual. A file is a "similar file" if it contains the same kind of highly personal information (*State Department* v. *Washington Post,* 1982). A United States district court recently reversed a ruling by the National Aeronautics and Space Administration (NASA) that the voice communications tape, recorded aboard the Challenger space shuttle before it exploded in January of 1987, was a file similar to a medical or personnel file and should not be made public. To fall under the reach of exemption six a file must contain some kind of personal information, the court said. The tape contains nothing about the astronauts or their family members (*New York Times* v. *NASA,* 1987). In 1988 a United States court of appeals affirmed this ruling (*New York Times* v. *NASA,* 1988). Be careful here. Not every file that contains personal information will be considered a "similar file." "The test is not merely whether the information is in some sense personal, but whether it is of the same magnitude—as highly personal or as intimate in nature—as contained in personnel or medical records," according to the United States Court of Appeals for the First Circuit (*Kurzon* v. *Health and Human Services,* 1981; see also *Miami Herald* v. *Small Business Administration,* 1982).

Establishing that a file contains personal information is only the first step or the "threshold question" in the application of exemption six. The court must ask two additional questions:

1. Would the release of this information constitute an invasion of personal privacy?
2. If it will, is this invasion of privacy clearly unwarranted?

Whether an invasion of privacy is warranted or unwarranted will be determined largely by the public benefit that may be derived from the release of the information. The government normally carries the burden of proving that the release of certain information amounts to a "clearly unwarranted" invasion of privacy. But the person seeking the information generally will have to demonstrate that there is public interest in the release of the material. He or she cannot rely solely on the fact that the government has failed to meet its burden of proof. In a 1976 decision the Supreme Court said that exemption six does not protect from disclosure every incidental invasion of privacy, but rather "only such disclosures as constitute clearly unwarranted invasions of personal privacy" (*Department of the Air Force* v. *Rose,* 1976).

The United States Court of Appeals in the District of Columbia recently ruled that the release of records that list the description, quantity, and price of prescription drugs ordered for members of Congress by the United States Navy would not necessarily be an unwarranted invasion of privacy. The navy operates the Office of the Attending Physician for the Congress. Researchers for *Congressional Quarterly* sought access to the records. There was no attempt to gain access to the names of members of Congress who were given the prescription drugs. The navy contended, however, that researchers could put the list of the drugs together with other information and discover quite a bit about the personal health of the members of Congress. A federal district court granted a summary judgment to the navy based on this argument, but the court of appeals ruled that the navy would have to prove this contention before it could block release of the data.

The Supreme Court has previously said that the invocation of exemption six requires threats to privacy interests more palpable than mere possibilities. In this ruling the appellate court noted, "Even if each drug is only prescribed for a single disease, it is fanciful to assume that without more . . . [than the] knowledge that someone among six hundred possible recipients was probably using the drug [only probably, because it might, of course, have been ordered merely to replenish an inventory], would lead to the conclusion that beneficiary X has disease Y." Even if release of the data did reveal information about the health of members of Congress, it is not necessarily an unwarranted invasion of privacy, the Court said. The drugs are made available free to the beneficiaries, and the public has an interest in knowing such things as the extent to which the Office of the Attending Physician prescribes name-brand drugs, as opposed to generic drugs, or whether drugs that the Food and Drug Administration says are ineffective are prescribed (*Arieff* v. *Navy,* 1983).

In another recent ruling a United States district court ordered the FBI to release the names of three FBI officials who had been censured for the bureau's domestic surveillance operations in the 1970s. Reporter Carl Stern got copies of the letters of censure, but the names were deleted. The court rejected the claim of invasion of privacy, noting that such considerations do not exist "when relatively high-placed officials entrusted with the performance of important public business actually jeopardize an agency's integrity by covering up government wrong doing" (*Stern* v. *FBI,* 1983).

Exemption Seven: Records or information compiled for law enforcement purposes, but only to the extent that the production of such law enforcement records or information (a) could reasonably be expected to interfere with enforcement proceedings, (b) would deprive a person of a right to a fair trial or an impartial adjudication, (c) could reasonably be expected to constitute an unwarranted invasion of personal privacy, (d) could reasonably be expected to disclose the identity of a confidential source, including a state, local or foreign agency or authority or any private institution which furnished information on a confidential basis, and, in the case of a record or information compiled by criminal law enforcement authority in the course of a criminal investigation or by an agency conducting a lawful national security intelligence investigation, information furnished by confidential source, (e) would disclose techniques and procedures for law enforcement investigations or prosecutions, or would disclose guidelines for law enforcement investigations or prosecutions if such disclosure could reasonably be expected to risk circumvention of the law, or (f) could reasonably be expected to endanger the life or physical safety of any individual.

In addition, another section of the FOIA permits law enforcement agencies to refuse to confirm or deny the existence of (1) records concerning a criminal investigation, if disclosure could reasonably be expected to interfere with enforcement proceedings, (2) informant records requested by third parties, if the informant's status as an informant has not been officially confirmed, and (3) classified records of the FBI pertaining to foreign intelligence, counterintelligence, and international terrorism investigations.

Exemption seven was heavily amended in 1986. The section permitting law enforcement agencies to refuse to confirm or deny the existence of some kinds of records was added at that time as well. Application of the new exemption is two-tiered. The first or threshold question is:

1. Was the information or record sought compiled for law enforcement purposes?
   If it was not compiled for law enforcement purposes, the exemption does not apply. But if it was compiled for law enforcement purposes, the second question must be asked:

2. Would the release of the record or information result in any one of the consequences outlined in (a) through (f)?

A good example of this approach came in *Cohen* v. *EPA*. Neil Cohen sought 142 names of persons and companies that had received notices from the Environmental Protection Agency regarding their potential liability for the release of hazardous substances into the environment. The agency released six names but declined to reveal the other 136. It argued that these were law enforcement records and their release would interfere with enforcement proceedings. A federal district court agreed that these were law enforcement records but could not see how their release would interfere with the agency's attempts to enforce the environmental laws (*Cohen* v. *EPA*, 1983).

Summaries of investigatory records compiled for law enforcement purposes are also protected by exemption seven, according to a 1982 ruling by the Supreme Court of the United States. In 1969 the White House requested that the FBI summarize and transmit to the president information in its files concerning particular individuals who had criticized the administration. Howard Abramson sought to see these summaries in 1976. The FBI said the documents were shielded by exemption seven; these were investigatory records gathered for law-enforcement purposes. Abramson agreed that as long as the information was in the FBI files, it was exempt from disclosure but that when it was taken out of the files, summarized, and sent to the White House, it was no longer an investigatory record compiled for law enforcement purposes. The High Court disagreed in a five-to-four ruling. "We hold that information initially contained in a record made for law-enforcement purposes continues to meet the threshold requirements of exemption seven where that recorded information is reproduced or summarized in a new document prepared for a nonlaw enforcement purpose," Justice Byron White wrote for the majority. He said there was no question that exemption seven would shield the data if the FBI had given verbatim records to the White House. Summarization of this data does not withdraw the material from the protection of exemption seven. In a sharp dissent Justice William Brennan accused the majority of rewriting the law and said the Court was rejecting a logical and straightforward interpretation of the statute and replacing it with one less plausible (*FBI* v. *Abramson*, 1982).

In one of the first court tests of the new language of exemption seven, the government asserted that the release of computerized arrested records or rap sheets held by the FBI could reasonably be expected to constitute an unwarranted invasion of personal privacy. The rap sheets contain information indicating arrests, indictments, acquittals, convictions and sentences on about 24 million people in this nation. These computerized files are compilations of what are generally public records held by state and local law enforcement agencies across the nation. The Justice Department has simply put together all the bits and pieces of information about an individual held by the various police agencies into a single, computerized file.

CBS reporter Robert Schnake sought such information from the FBI on Charles Medico. The agency denied the request, citing the personal privacy factor in exemption seven. A U.S. District Court supported the agency, saying the material sought by Schnake would be personal to Medico. But the United States Court of Appeals in the District of Columbia reversed, noting that the government cannot assert a privacy interest in records it holds when the records are already available from state and local authorities (*Reporters Committee for Freedom of the Press* v. *Department of Justice,* 1987). In the Spring of 1989, the Supreme Court reversed this ruling in an important 9–0 decision which seemingly went beyond the case at hand to focus on the threat to personal privacy that exists from the widespread use of computers to store personal information. The privacy interest in a rap sheet is substantial, wrote Justice John Paul Stevens for the court. "The substantial character of that interest is affected by the fact that in today's society the computer can accumulate and store information that would have otherwise surely been forgotten long before a person attains the age of 80, when the F.B.I.'s rap sheets are discarded," Stevens added. Stevens rejected the argument that because arrests and convictions are almost always public knowledge when they happen, an individual has only a minimal privacy interest in a Federal compilation of such information. Federal computers, he said, make easily available information that would be difficult to obtain by other means. "Plainly there is a vast difference between the public records that might be found after a diligent search of courthouse files, county archives, and local police stations throughout the county and a computerized summary located in a single clearinghouse of information," Stevens noted. Justices William Brennan and Harry Blackmun concurred in the court's decision, but suggested that barring the disclosure of these records under any circumstance, which is the thrust of the court's ruling, is not sound policy (*Justice Department* v. *Reporters Committee,* 1989).

Exemption Eight: Matters contained in or related to examination, operating, or condition reports prepared by, on behalf of, or for the use of any agency responsible for the regulation and supervision of financial institutions. This is a little-used exemption that is designed to prevent the disclosure of sensitive financial reports or audits that, if made public, might undermine the public confidence in banks, trust companies, investment banking firms, and other financial institutions.

Exemption Nine: Geological and geophysical information and data, including maps concerning wells. People who drill oil and gas wells provide considerable information about these wells to the government. This exemption prevents speculators and other drillers from gaining access to this valuable information.

Government departments must answer requests for records and documents within ten days. If an appeal is filed after a denial, the agency has only twenty days to rule upon the appeal. Each agency must publish quarterly, or more frequently, an index of the documents and records it keeps.

Agencies are required to report to Congress each year and must include in the report a list of the materials to which access was granted and to which access was denied and the costs incurred. If a citizen or a reporter has to go to court to get the agency to release materials and the agency loses the case, the agency may be assessed the cost of the complainant's legal fees and court costs. Finally, agency personnel are now personally responsible for granting or denying access, a requirement federal agencies object to strenuously. An employee of an agency who denies a request for information must be identified to the person who seeks the material, and if the access is denied in an arbitrary or capricious manner, the employee can be disciplined by the Civil Service Commission.

Agencies may charge fees to cover the actual cost of searching for and copying the records that are sought. These fees can be very high if a large amount of material is requested. The Reporters Committee on Freedom of the Press estimates that search charges range from eleven dollars to twenty-eight dollars per hour, depending upon the agency. Computer searches might cost considerably more. Photocopying costs are usually fifteen cents per page. In 1986 Congress passed legislation that set out specific fee provisions for four kinds of requesters:

1. Commercial use requesters must pay fees for document search, duplication, and review.
2. Noncommercial requesters from educational or scientific institutions pay no search fees and receive one hundred pages of free duplication.
3. Representatives of the news media pay no search fees and receive copies of one hundred pages free.
4. All other requesters receive two hours of search time and one hundred pages at no charge.

Persons who are actively working for an organization that publishes or broadcasts the news to the public are considered representatives of the news media. The definition of news provided by this law is vague: information about current events or of current interest to the public.

Anyone who seeks information under the FOIA is entitled to a fee waiver where the disclosure of the information is "in the public interest because it is likely to contribute significantly to public understanding of the operations or activities of the government and is not primarily in the commercial interest of the requester." However, agencies in the Reagan administration applied this

SAMPLE FOI ACT REQUEST LETTER

Your address
Day time phone number
Date

Freedom of Information Office
Agency
Address

FOIA Request

Dear FOI Officer:

Pursuant to the federal Freedom of Information Act, 5 U.S.C. § 552, I request access to and copies of (here, clearly describe what you want. Include identifying material, such as names, places, and the period of time about which you are inquiring. If you think they will help to explain what you are looking for, attach news clips, reports, and other documents describing the subject of your research).

I agree to pay reasonable duplication fees for the processing of this request in an amount not to exceed $ _____ . However, please notify me prior to your incurring any expenses in excess of that amount.[1]

(*Suggested request for fee benefit as a representative of the news media:*) As a representative of the news media I am only required to pay for the direct cost of duplication after the first 100 pages. Through this request, I am gathering information on (subject) that is of current interest to the public because (give reason). This information is being sought on behalf of (give the name of your news organization) for dissemination to the general public. (If a freelancer, provide information such as experience, publication contract, etc., that demonstrates that you expect publication.)

(*Optional fee waiver request:*) Please waive any applicable fees. Release of the information is in the public interest because it will contribute significantly to public understanding of government operations and activities.[2]

If my request is denied in whole or part, I ask that you justify all deletions by reference to specific exemptions of the act. I will also expect you to release all segregable portions of otherwise exempt material. I, of course, reserve the right to appeal your decision to withhold any information or to deny a waiver of fees.

As I am making this request as a journalist (author, or scholar) and this information is of timely value, I would appreciate your communicating with me by telephone, rather than by mail, if you have questions regarding this request.[3] I look forward to your reply within 10 business days, as the statute requires.

Thank you for your assistance.

Very truly yours,

Your Signature

Footnotes

1. Most agencies will not consider your request properly filed unless you state something about the fees—either your willingness to pay or your request for a fee waiver. By setting an amount up front, the agency will begin to process your request, and you can retain some control over the ultimate amount you will have to pay.
2. You may wish to address each criterion for waiver, except that, as a representative of the news media you need not show how you will use the information to contribute to public understanding or that its use is noncommercial. An author or scholar may show how ultimately the information will be available to the public. A library may identify researchers who will use it.
3. It is always a good idea to call the agency's FOI office several days after your request is mailed, to be sure of its arrival and to talk directly with the officer processing your request. Quite often you can resolve any minor problems concerning your request at that time and avoid delays.

Sample FOIA request letter, from *How to Use the FOI Act,* 6th ed., FOI Service Center Publication, 800 18th St. N.W., Washington, D.C., 20006.

standard rather narrowly and many requesters in the news media found they were unable to qualify for the waiver under agency interpretation of the rules. Because fees can be high, it makes sense to try to find out how much it will cost to retrieve documents before you authorize a search and copying.

The Freedom of Information Act is not difficult to use. (See sample FOIA request letter p. 286.) For only three dollars it is possible to get a highly informative booklet, *How to Use the Federal FOI Act,* published by the FOI Service Center, 800 18th Street N.W., Washington, D.C., 20006. Longtime right-of-access proponent Sam Archibald offers these suggestions to journalists on making the law work:

1. Find out which agencies have the material in which you are interested. The *United States Government Manual* lists all federal agencies, explains what they are supposed to do, and usually lists local addresses and telephone numbers.

2. Call or write the agency to get background information about the material and information in which you are interested.

3. When you have determined what records you seek, write an official request for the material. Address it to the head of the agency, describe as specifically as possible the material you seek, and state that the request is made under the Freedom of Information Act: 5 United States Code, Section 552.

4. If your request is rejected, file an appeal with the head of the agency. Send along the copy of the rejection letter and make a strong argument as to why you think the material is not exempt.

5. If the appeal is rejected—and you really want to get the material—go to court. This final point, more than any other, needs to be emphasized. As long as government agencies are confident that the press and public will not bother with lawsuits, the tendency to withhold information will be reinforced. But strong sanctions can be applied against government officials who are found to have deliberately withheld material illegally. Sanctions can only be applied, however, after judicial determination of the matter. The application of this kind of pressure on a regular basis by the press and the public can have generally positive impact in the battle for open government.

Reporter Steve Weinberg, in an article in the *Columbia Journalism Review,* adds these additional tips for using the FOIA. Be specific in your request. Know exactly what you want. To do this you must study the agency indexes closely. Try to direct FOIA requests to regional or local offices when possible. It is easier to communicate with a local office, and very often the people who operate these offices are not as "hardened" as their counterparts in Washington. Offer to pay reasonable fees in your request letter; if not, the agency will write you back in ten days and ask if you are willing to pay the fees. This will simply delay any action on your request.

Finally, many old journalistic hands argue that formal FOI requests should be a last resort. Jack Briggs of the *Tri-City* (Washington) *Herald* advises reporters to:

Ask informally for documents—a formal FOI request often takes much longer.

Look to public court records for information that it takes longer to get through an FOIA request.

Cultivate trusted sources within federal agencies.

Follow up FOIA requests with telephone calls.

Don't kick and scream, unless kicking and screaming is justified. And don't forget to occasionally praise the FOIA officer who helps you.

Federal Open Meetings Law

In 1976 Congress passed and the president signed into law the Government in Sunshine Act, the **federal open meetings law.** The statute affects approximately fifty federal boards, commissions, and agencies "headed by a collegial body composed of two or more individual members, a majority of whom are appointed to such position by the president with the advice and consent of the Senate." These public bodies are required to conduct their business meetings in public. Notice of public meetings must be given one week in advance, and the agencies are required to keep careful records of what occurs at closed meetings. The law also prohibits informal communication between officials of an agency and representatives of companies and other interested persons with whom the agency does business unless this communication is recorded and made part of the public record.

Courts have strictly interpreted the requirement that the law only applies to bodies whose members are appointed by the president. In 1981 the United States Court of Appeals for the District of Columbia ruled that the Government in Sunshine Act did not govern meetings of the Chrysler Loan Guarantee Board, a body created by the Congress to oversee federal loan guarantees for the financially troubled automaker. Persons who serve on the board are not actually named by the president, but serve because they hold other federal offices (i.e., secretary of the treasury, comptroller general, chairman of the Federal Reserve). "If Congress had wanted to subject the board to the provisions of the Sunshine Act, it could have so provided when the board was established," the court noted (*Symons* v. *Chrysler Corporation Loan Guarantee Board,* 1981). A board or agency must also have some independent authority to act or take action before the law applies. A United States court of appeals ruled that the law does not apply to the president's Council of Economic Advisors (CEA). The sole function of the CEA is to advise and assist the president, the court said. It has no regulatory power. It cannot fund projects, even though it may appraise them. It has no function, saving advising and assisting the president. Hence, it is not subject to either the FOIA or the Government in Sunshine Act (*Rushforth* v. *Council of Economic Advisors,* 1985). The same rationale—that the Government in Sunshine Act does not cover advisory bodies—was used to block access to meetings of a panel of experts convened in 1986 by the federal Energy Department to determine whether a nuclear reactor in Washington state could melt down, as did the Chernobyl reactor in the Soviet Union (*National Resources Defense Council Inc.,* v. *Secretary of Energy,* 1986). Even agencies or commissions that fall under the aegis of the law may meet behind closed doors. The 1976 law lists ten conditions or exemptions under which closed meetings might be held. The first nine of these exemptions mirror the exemptions in the Freedom of Information Act. The tenth exemption focuses upon situations in which the agency is participating in arbitration or is in the process of adjudicating or otherwise disposing of a case.

A court of appeals in Washington, D.C., recently ruled that agencies may not automatically hold budget deliberations behind closed doors. "The Sunshine Act contains no express exemption for budget deliberations as a whole. Specific items discussed at budget meetings might, however, be exempt and might justify closing portions of a commission meeting on an individual and particularized basis," Judge Skelly Wright ruled. In each case the agency must defend its closure of the meeting by demonstrating that the discussion would focus on material excluded from public disclosure by one of the ten exemptions (*Common Cause* v. *Nuclear Regulatory Commission,* 1982). The tenth exemption was used to block access to a meeting of the Nuclear Regulatory Commission. The NRC was discussing the reopening of the nuclear power plant at Three Mile Island in Pennsylvania. The federal district court ruled that this meeting would likely focus upon the final adjudication of the federal action involving the nuclear reactor and hence could be closed to press and public (*Philadelphia Newspapers* v. *Nuclear Regulatory Commission,* 1983).

There has been relatively little litigation under the Government in Sunshine Act, and reporters who work in Washington, D.C., report that compliance with the law is not good. The same problems existed in the early years of operation of the Freedom of Information Act. Constant pressure and frequent litigation against agencies that refused to comply with the FOIA finally made the law effective. The same pressure is needed to make the Government in Sunshine Act live up to its promise.

SUMMARY

Statutes provide public access to both federal records and meetings held by federal agencies. The federal records law, the Freedom of Information Act, makes public all records held by agencies within the executive branch of government and the independent regulatory commissions. Courts have given a broad meaning to the term *record* but have ruled that an agency must normally create and possess such a record before it becomes subject to the Freedom of Information Act. Nine categories of information are excluded from the provisions of the law. These include exemptions for national security, agency working papers, highly personal information, and law enforcement files. Agencies must publish indexes of the records they hold and must permit copying of these materials. It is important to follow specific procedures when making a Freedom of Information Act request to see certain records or documents.

The Government in Sunshine Act is the federal open meetings law. This law reaches about fifty agencies in the executive branch and the regulatory commissions. Members of these organizations are not permitted to hold secret meetings unless they will discuss material that falls into one of ten categories. These categories mirror the Freedom of Information Act exemptions but also include a provision that permits closed-door meetings to discuss attempts to arbitrate or adjudicate certain cases or problems. This is a newer law and does not seem to work as well as does the Freedom of Information Act.

STATE LAWS ON MEETINGS AND RECORDS

It is not as easy to talk about access at the state level as it is at the federal level, for we are dealing with hundreds of different statutes. (Most states have multiple laws dealing with access to meetings, access to records, and other access situations.) We can at best make a few generalizations. Harold Cross made some of the most astute generalizations in 1953 in his pioneering book *The People's Right to Know.* Cross was really the first scholar to present a comprehensive report on access problems. In his book he listed four issues or questions common to every case of access:

1. Is the particular record or proceeding public? Many records and meetings kept or conducted by public officers in public offices are not really public at all. Much of the work of the police, though they are public officers and work in public buildings, is not open to public scrutiny.

2. Is public material public in the sense that records are open to public inspection and sessions are open to public attendance? Hearings in juvenile courts are considered public hearings for purposes of the law, but they are rarely open to the public.

3. Who can view the records and who can attend the meetings open to the public? Many records, for example, might be open to specific segments of the public, but not to all segments. Automobile accident reports by police departments are open to insurance company adjusters and lawyers, but such records are not usually open to the general public.

4. When records and meetings are open to the general public and the press, will the courts provide legal remedy for citizens and reporters if access is denied?

The last question is probably not as important today as it was when Cross wrote his book in 1953, for at that time access to many public records and meetings in the states was based on the common law. Today this fact is no longer true. Access to meetings and records is nearly always governed by statute, and these statutes usually, but not always, provide a remedy for citizens who are denied access. This provision is more widespread in open meeting laws, which tend to be more efficient in providing access, than in open records laws, which are still weak and vague in many jurisdictions.

State Open
Meetings Laws

Virtually all states have some kind of constitutional or legislative provision regarding the need for open meetings. All fifty states have specific statutes that mandate open meetings, and these laws range from good to awful. The need for **open-meeting laws** is obvious. There never was a solid common law right to attend the meetings of public bodies, and as noted earlier, the constitutional provisions regarding freedom of expression have proved inadequate with regard to access.

Many states have good laws with strong sanctions to be used against public officials who fail to live up to the legislative mandate. The Exxon Education Foundation released a study comparing all fifty laws on twenty-three different criteria and found the laws in Florida and Tennessee to be the best and the Pennsylvania law the weakest.

William R. Wright II, writing in a recent edition of the *Mississippi Law Review* ("Open Meeting Laws: An Analysis and a Proposal"), outlined the basic provisions of state open-meeting laws. According to Wright, the most vital provision of such a law is a strong, clear statement by the legislature to open up the deliberations and actions of the government to the people. If a provision of the law is questioned in court, a strong legislative declaration in favor of open access can be used to persuade a judge that if a section of the law is vague, it should be interpreted to grant access rather than to restrict access, since that is what the legislature wants.

In Washington the state's open meeting law begins as follows:

> The legislature finds and declares that all . . . public agencies of this state and subdivisions thereof exist to aid in the conduct of the people's business. It is the intent of this chapter that their actions be taken openly and that their deliberations be conducted openly.

State legislatures have usually written their open-meeting laws in one of two ways. Some state legislatures have declared that all meetings will be open, except specific meetings, and then list the meetings to be open. Other states list the agencies that must hold open meetings. Generally excluded from the provisions of an open-meeting law in either case are meetings of the legislature itself, of legislative committees, of parole and pardon boards, of law enforcement agencies, of military agencies such as the national guard, of public hospital boards, and so forth.

Wright says that a good law should specifically define a meeting by giving the number of members of the board or commission who must be present to constitute a public meeting (a quorum? at least two? etc.), by stating that all deliberative stages of the decision-making process are considered meetings and must be open to the public, and by stating that social gatherings and chance encounters are not considered meetings and are therefore excluded from the provisions of the law. Some laws are not this specific and merely refer to all meetings, all regular or special meetings, all formal meetings, or whatever.

The exclusion of chance meetings and social gatherings is often troublesome to the press, especially in small towns. It is not uncommon that all members of the school board or the city council happen to have dinner at the same restaurant just before a meeting. If the dinner is obviously a ploy to avoid the law, a suit can be brought against the members. Often it is difficult to prove that the dinner is anything other than a chance encounter or a social gathering. But a good law specifies that all gatherings at which public business is discussed must be open, not just official decision-making sessions.

Most open-meeting laws provide for closed or **executive sessions** in certain kinds of cases. Meetings at which personnel problems are discussed are an obvious example. A public airing of a teacher's personal problems could be an unwarranted invasion of privacy. The discussion of real estate transactions is another obvious example. When a school board considers buying a parcel of land for a new high school, premature public disclosure of this fact could cost the taxpayers money should the owner raise the price of the property or speculators buy it and force the school district to pay far more than it is worth. Meetings involving public safety are sometimes best conducted in private rather than in public. Usually laws will permit an official body to meet with its attorney behind closed doors if potential or actual litigation is on the agenda. This is merely an extension of the traditional lawyer-client privilege. Labor negotiations may also be held in private in about half the states. All but thirteen state open-meeting laws contain a provision that no final action can be taken at an executive session, that the board or commission must reconvene in public before a final determination can be made on any issue.

Most open-meeting statutes require not only that meetings be open to the public, but also that the public be notified of both regular and special meetings far enough in advance that they can attend if they wish. Time requirements vary, but normally a special meeting cannot be held without an announcement a day or two in advance.

Virtually all laws provide some kind of injunctive or other civil remedy if the law is violated; almost half the statutes provide for criminal penalties if the statute is knowingly violated. In many states any action taken at a meeting that was not public, but should have been public, is null and void. The action must be taken again at a proper meeting. Most laws provide fines and short jail terms for public officers who knowingly violate the law, but prosecution is rare.

While a few laws date from the nineteenth century, the open-meeting laws in most states are a relatively new phenomenon. Such laws, which owe their passage to strong, forceful pressure from the press, have developed largely since 1950. In 1959 only twenty states had such laws. Formation in the early 1970s of the public lobby Common Cause gave great impetus to the passage of open-meeting laws. In 1972 and 1973, alone, nine states passed such statutes.

What should a reporter do when asked to leave a meeting that he or she believes should be open to the press and public? First, find out who has denied you access to the meeting and ask for the legal basis of this denial. Never leave a meeting voluntarily; but if ordered to leave do so and contact your editor immediately. Resistance is not advised, for criminal charges may be filed against you. While open meeting laws provide a good means of access to proceedings, the reporter possesses what is probably a more powerful weapon—the power of publicity. Public officials don't like stories about secret meetings. A photo essay showing a meeting room door open, closing, and closed, accompanied by a caption citing appropriate parts of the open meetings law, will often get a reporter back into a proceeding faster than a court action.

State Open Records Laws

Every state in the union also has some kind of **open-records law.** The access laws either follow the federal formula—all records are open except the following—or list the kinds of records that the public does have a right to inspect. In a useful article in the *George Washington Law Review,* attorneys Burt Braverman and Wesley Heppler ("A Practical Review of State Open Records Laws") outlined the basic dimensions of the state freedom of information laws.

Most state laws permit inspection of records by any person, but a few limit access to public records to citizens of the state. The reason persons want to see a record is normally considered immaterial when determining whether they can gain access to the record. The freedom of information laws provide access to records held by public agencies in the state, and normally these statutes provide a broad definition of these agencies. Normally included are state offices, departments, divisions, bureaus, boards and commissions. Records kept by local government agencies (cities, counties, villages) are also included, as are those kept by school districts, public utilities and municipal corporations. These state laws do not normally govern records kept by courts or the legislature. Frequently these branches of government have established their own policies regarding access to records. Braverman and Heppler report that state laws follow either a liberal or conservative definition of a public record. *All records possessed by an agency* are deemed to be public records in those states with liberal definitions of a public record. But some state laws are more conservative and provide access only to those *records that are required to be kept by law.*

All state freedom of information laws provide exemptions to disclosure. Agencies *may* withhold material that falls under an exemption in some states; agencies *must* withhold this information in other states. Braverman and Heppler list the six most common substantive exemptions to the state open-records laws as follows:

1. Information classified as confidential by state or federal law
2. Law enforcement and investigatory information
3. Trade secrets and commercial information
4. Preliminary departmental memorandums (working papers)
5. Personal privacy information
6. Information relating to litigation against a public body

The attorneys report that although state laws vary widely, state courts have almost uniformly held that exemptions should be construed narrowly; that is, they should be read in such a way as to provide public access to the greatest amount of information. The federal Freedom of Information Act requires agencies to maintain an index of documents and records; not many state laws have the same requirement. But in every state except Indiana the right to inspect records includes the right to copy records. Procedures to gain access to state agency records follow the federal FOIA model. Two-thirds of the state statutes have provisions for judicial review of agency rulings where the state bears the burden to show that the record should remain undisclosed. But at least two states have tried to develop means that keep the question of access to records out of court.

Connecticut has established an independent commission to handle citizen appeals on denial-of-information requests. The three-member commission must meet within twenty days after receiving an appeal, hear the matter, and issue a ruling within fifteen days. The body can uphold the denial or make the agency provide access to the material. Either citizens or government agencies can appeal any decision by the commission to a court.

The New York State access law established a Committee on Public Access to Records. This committee has wide authority to issue regulations for the use of records and implementation of the new statute. There are seven members on the committee—three government officials and four persons appointed by the governor, two of whom must be from the media. The committee's function is different from the Connecticut commission, which acts as a review board. In New York the committee advises agencies and local government on access questions through guidelines, opinions, and regulations. It is supposed to recommend changes in the law when problems arise. In addition, to make the new law work more efficiently, the commission issues rules and guidelines: rules regarding the time and place records must be available, fees for copying, persons responsible for divulging records, and so forth. Finally, it is the job of the committee to ensure that the right of privacy of New York citizens is protected in connection with public access to the state's records. Some people criticize this last function, arguing that it makes little sense to make the same agency in charge of facilitating public access responsible for protecting the right of privacy.

This trend toward establishing public committees or commissions to handle access problems, to help interpret the law, and to issue guidelines is a very good one. It is far easier to complain to a commission when access is denied than to file a court suit. Committees like the New York Committee on Public Access to Records will make a state law far more meaningful and useful when a local government is dealt with. Access laws passed by states are often ignored at local levels because of ignorance or because citizens and press are unlikely to complain until a big issue arises. By providing guidelines and rules for local communities, a committee on public access immediately breathes life into an access law.

It is incumbent on all journalists and broadcasters to be as familiar as possible with the laws regarding access in their state. Knowledge of these kinds of laws is vital to efficient and complete reporting on government activities. Employees of public agencies are often as uninformed as average citizens about their responsibility to provide access to meetings, especially to records. Because of the normal adversary relationship between press and government, the natural tendency is to want to keep the reporter out of public documents and public meetings. Too often reporters are buffaloed by stubborn, uninformed, untruthful public employees who insist that they are not permitted by law to allow public inspection of certain records. If reporters know the law, they can recognize such bluffs on the spot and fulfill their responsibility to keep the public fully informed on the business and activities of government.

SUMMARY

All states have laws that govern access to public meetings and public records. Good state open-meetings laws have strong legislative declarations in support of public meetings, specifically define a public meeting by listing the number of members who must gather to constitute a meeting, and declare void all actions taken during a meeting that was improperly closed to the public. Most laws provide for closed sessions to discuss such matters as personnel actions, real estate transactions, and litigation.

State public-records laws tend to mirror the federal law. Both state and local agencies are governed by the laws and they apply to most governmental bodies except the legislature and the courts. Most state laws govern all records kept by these agencies, but a few are applicable only to records that are required to be kept by law. Exemptions to state open-records laws include material specifically excluded by other statutes, law-enforcement investigatory information, working papers, and highly personal information. Most laws provide for access to the judicial system in case a request for data is rejected, but both New York and Connecticut have established commissions to act as arbiters in these matters.

LAWS THAT RESTRICT ACCESS TO INFORMATION

Just as there are laws that provide for public access to government-held documents, there are laws that specifically preclude access to government-held information. There are provisions in scores of federal laws alone that limit the right of access. Tax statutes, espionage laws, legislation on atomic energy, and dozens of other kinds of laws are filled with limitations on the dissemination of information (e.g., personal information on taxes, national security questions, and matters relating to nuclear weapons). But in addition to these kinds of laws, the federal government has adopted in the past decade at least three rather broad sets of regulations regarding information held by the government. All three were adopted in the name of protecting the right to privacy, a value that seems to have replaced national security as the most commonly asserted reason the government uses to keep things secret. While these regulations cannot be considered here in a comprehensive sense, persons who gather information for a living need to be aware of their implications.

General Education Provisions Act

An amendment to the General Education Provisions Act (1974) is aimed at increasing both the parental access to and the confidentiality of educational records.* On the one hand, the law forces all federally funded schools and educational agencies to permit parents to inspect and review their children's educational records. On the other hand, the statute prohibits the distribution of personally identifiable information, excluding what is called directory data, to unauthorized persons without consent of the parents. The result is that student records or files must be kept confidential. This goal is hardly a hardship on the press in most instances. However, because of the stiff penalty in the law—possible loss to the school of federal funds—educators have occasionally overreacted and declared data that are actually unprotected by the statute to be confidential. In one absurd case a reporter-photographer indicated that school officials chased him off school property when he attempted to photograph children playing outside at recess. The officials cited the 1974 law as a reason that picture taking was no longer permitted on school property. Of course, instances like that are rare, and the significance of the law is its indication of the extreme interest in privacy today, rather than its threat to the legitimate news-gathering tasks of the press.

*Discussion of the General Education Provisions Act and the Federal Privacy Law, pages 296–298, is adapted from Don R. Pember, "The Burgeoning Scope of 'Access Privacy' and the Portent for a Free Press," 64 *Iowa Law Review* 1155, 1979.

The **Privacy Act** of 1974 has two basic thrusts. First, it attempts to check the misuse of personal data obtained by the federal government, the quantity of which has, of course, reached staggering proportions. Second, the law is intended to provide access for individuals to records about themselves that are held by federal agencies. The first objective of the law could be the more troublesome to the press.

The act requires that each federal agency limit the collection of information to that which is relevant and necessary, to collect information directly from the subject concerned when possible, and to allow individuals to review and amend their personal records and information. Also, under the act agencies are forbidden from disclosing what is called "a personally identifiable record" without the written consent of the individual to whom the record pertains. Since this section of the law is seemingly contradictory to the spirit of the federal FOIA, Congress was forced to clarify the responsibilities of federal agencies with regard to the law. A provision was added to the Privacy Act that declares that records required to be disclosed under the FOIA are not subject to the provisions of the Privacy Act and consequently cannot be withheld from inspection. To the government official with control of information, however, neither the Privacy Act nor the FOIA is unambiguous.

The difficulty in resolving aspects of the Privacy Act and the Freedom of Information Act is graphically illustrated by a recent case decided by the United States Court of Appeals for the District of Columbia. Frank Greentree was indicted and convicted in federal court on drug charges. He filed a civil suit to block state prosecution based on the same events. Greentree sought information from both the Drug Enforcement Administration (DEA) and the United States Bureau of Customs to assist him in his civil action. When the agencies refused to give him the material he sought, he filed both a Freedom of Information Act request and a Privacy Act request to get the information. The documents sought by Greentree were contained in something called the Investigations Record System, and this system of records has been declared to be exempt from the access provisions of the Privacy Act. Hence it was unavailable to Greentree through the federal privacy law. Because the information could not be released under the Privacy Act, the government argued that it was also unavailable under FOIA exemption three. Remember exemption three: it provides that the Freedom of Information Act does not apply to matters "specifically exempt from disclosure by statute." The material Greentree sought was exempt from disclosure under the federal privacy statute; therefore, the government argued, it was also exempt from disclosure under exemption three of the Freedom of Information Act. In two previous appellate court rulings this government argument was sustained. (See *Terkel* v. *Kelly,* 1979, and *Painter* v. *Federal Bureau of Investigation,* 1980.) But in Greentree the United States Court of Appeals for the District of Columbia denied the validity of this argument and ruled against the government. Judge Wald said that throughout its consideration of the Privacy Act, the Congress struggled to hold separate the Privacy Act and the FOIA. That effect was ultimately successful, he said. Judge Wald noted that section (b) (2) of the Privacy Act clearly states that "no agency shall disclose any record which is contained in a system of records . . . *unless disclosure of the record would be required under section 552 (The Freedom of Information Act) of this title* [author emphasis]." "We must conclude," Wald wrote, "that this section of the Privacy Act represents a congressional mandate that the Privacy Act *not* be used as a barrier to FOIA access." Congress could not have intended that a section of the Privacy Act could serve as a withholding statute under FOIA exemption three, the judge said. It is possible, he noted, that the information may not be available under exemption seven (the law enforcement exemption of the FOIA), but the government would have to prove that the material sought by Greentree was exempt from disclosure (*Greentree* v. *Customs Service,* 1982).

The Privacy Act imposes a cost on an agency if it releases a file that should remain private. To the bureaucrat, that presents a real dilemma, as was emphasized in the *Harvard Civil Rights/Civil Liberties Law Review* (1976):

> If government officials refuse to disclose the material, they risk being sued by the party who requested the file under the Freedom of Information Act. Under the FOIA the court may award to a successful plaintiff his costs and attorney's fees. If, on the other hand, agencies release material, they risk being sued under the Privacy Act by the person who is the subject of the file. In that case, the plaintiff might win by showing that the file was exempt from disclosure under FOIA. A successful Privacy Act plaintiff can collect not only his costs and attorney's fees, but also actual damage sustained because of disclosure.

Given this distinction between the statutes, it is easy to recognize that bureaucrats will choose to err on the side of caution—it is wiser to withhold the information and risk suit under the FOIA than possibly incur Privacy Act penalties.

Other conflicts exist in the administration of the two laws. Before passage of the Privacy Act, materials that were not required to be disclosed under the FOIA were nevertheless permitted to be disclosed at the discretion of a government agency. Now, information falling under an FOIA exemption, and thus not required to be disclosed, will routinely be withheld out of fear of violating the Privacy Act.

Criminal History Privacy Laws

In accordance with the broad scope of the Omnibus Crime Control and Safe Streets Act of 1968, the federal Law Enforcement Assistance Administration, an agency created by the Nixon administration to help local police forces fight crime, sought to develop a national computerized record-keeping system.* The system that was established permits any police department in the nation to have access to the records of virtually all other police departments.

*Discussion of Criminal History Privacy Laws, pages 298–300, is adapted from Pember, "Access Privacy and Free Press."

Congressional concern about the misuse of this record system led to limitations on access to the data. Police records have always contained a considerable amount of misinformation, information that is out of date, and information that is private. The centralized record-keeping system presents a problem referred to by some writers as the "dossier effect." The contrast between these computerized and centrally maintained records immediately accessible across the country and those police records of the past was sharp and immediately evident: fragmented, original-source records kept by a single police agency for a limited geographical area were not readily accessible because of their bulk and associated indexing problems. Hence, federal rules were adopted that require states, if they wish to participate in the national record-keeping system, to adopt rules that, among other things, limit the dissemination of some criminal history nonconviction data.

The *Code of Federal Regulations* ("Criminal Justice Information Systems") defines nonconviction data as follows:

> . . . arrest information without disposition if an interval of one year has elapsed from the date of arrest and no active prosecution of the charge is pending, or information disclosing that the police have elected not to refer a matter to a prosecutor, or that a prosecutor has elected not to commence criminal proceedings, or that proceedings have been indefinitely postponed, as well as all acquittals and all dismissals.

As a result of the state laws, press access to criminal history records kept by the police has been virtually eliminated unless data sought pertain to an incident for which a person is currently being processed by the criminal justice system, are conviction records, or are original records of entry, such as arrest records, that are maintained chronologically and are accessible only on that basis. Reporters can also obtain information about arrests not resulting in conviction, however, if they are aware of the specific dates of the arrests. It is hard to determine whether these laws have substantially affected the press's ability to report on the criminal justice system. A good police reporter usually can gain access to information he or she wants to see. Nevertheless, potential problems are apparent. In commenting on the social desirability of press access to criminal records, Steven Higgins ("Press and Criminal Record Privacy") recently noted:

> On the one hand, the uncontrolled dissemination and publication of certain criminal history records can adversely affect the individual himself. On the other hand, the public and the press must have access to basic records of official action if they are to effectively scrutinize and evaluate the operations of the police, the prosecuting agencies, and the courts.

The ability to achieve that scrutiny is important. For example, it is possible to envision a situation in which a prosecutor is accused of favoring friends or certain ethnic or racial groups when deciding whether to prosecute arrested persons. Without access to arrest records that can be compared with prosecution records, such a charge would be difficult to investigate. Persons within the criminal justice system could gain access to the needed records, but history indicates that these people must be prodded before they take action. And, of course, prodding is the function of the press.

There is another related, more serious problem that should be of great concern to persons earnestly worried about invasions of privacy. If the press cannot obtain official criminal history records, which admittedly are sometimes incorrect, journalists will rely on their own record-keeping systems, which are much more frequently inaccurate. Newspapers and broadcasting stations usually build record systems—called morgues—by saving clippings from newspapers and film from newscasts or storing data in their own computer systems. Errors in these original stories are seldom corrected. For example, suppose Jones was arrested in 1980 and charged with driving a stolen car. The local newspaper published incorrectly that he was arrested for car theft. Jones was never prosecuted. Fifteen years later he runs for the school board. The newspaper goes back into its own records—which it cannot verify with the police—and republishes its original error, that Jones was arrested for car theft. In such circumstances everyone—Jones, the press, the public—suffers.

To avoid such consequences, society would probably be served better if laws were passed that force law-enforcement agencies to continually monitor, update, and correct their criminal records but that nevertheless permitted public access to the records. Such laws could require, for instance, that when arrest data are released, disposition data must accompany the arrest data. There is, of course, no guarantee that the press or other agencies would publish the complete story—the arrest and the dismissal, for example, or the arrest and the subsequent acquittal—but no system that depends on a human element is risk free. In the end, public access to complete and accurate information is much to be preferred to a growing dependence on "private" media data banks.

State Statutes That Limit Access to Information

All states have statutes that limit access to information that would otherwise be available under a freedom of information law. The State of Washington, for example, has more than one hundred different laws that govern the access to particular information. Arizona has thirty-nine laws that block access to specific records. Some of these state statutes are aimed at blocking access to trade secrets; others limit access to information submitted to the state in compliance with environmental laws. The working papers of assessors, poll lists from prior elections, and reports from oil and gas companies are also frequently exempted from disclosure by a specific statute. State privacy laws are the most common kind of statutory limitation on the access to information.

Virtually every state has one or more statutes (sometimes this is the state's open-record law!) that limit access to government-held information on right-to-privacy grounds. While these laws are not traditionally thought of in the same terms as the tort of privacy (see chapter 4), they nevertheless have a similar impact. Tort law discourages the publication of private information by penalizing the press through the assessment of money damages. These statutes permit the state to institute civil or criminal action against the press for the publication of so-called private information or simply to bar access to this material so that it cannot be published.

SUMMARY

All of the states and the federal government have laws that specifically exclude certain kinds of information from the public scrutiny. Some of these exclusions were noted in the discussion of exemption three of the Freedom of Information Act. Today, the right to privacy has been erected as a substantial barrier to access to information held by government agencies. The federal government has adopted a law protecting the privacy of student records. The Congress passed a federal privacy law, which often conflicts with the provisions of the Freedom of Information Act. The federal government has also insisted that states pass statutes that control access to criminal history records. Much privacy legislation has been passed by the states themselves, and today the right to privacy is being used frequently to block access to public records.

ACCESS TO JUDICIAL RECORDS

Courts generally govern the access to information gathered through the judicial system. As a general rule, evidence introduced in a criminal or civil case is open to public inspection. Courts have found both a common law right of access and a First Amendment right of access to judicial records. The common law right is the weaker of the two, and may be rebutted with only a showing that countervailing interests (such as administrative concerns or privacy matters) heavily outweigh the public's interest in access. Under the First Amendment however, denial of access must be necessitated by a compelling government interest, and the denial must be narrowly tailored to meet that interest. Imagine that a court has entered a protective order sealing a file containing sixteen documents. When access is sought, the government can show that the release of two of these documents would be seriously harmful. The court must then fashion the order to protect the two documents, not all sixteen.

But simply getting access to evidence or documents is not always sufficient, especially if that evidence is contained on audio or videotape. The recent growth in popularity of government "sting" operations has resulted in many prosecutions based upon video or audiotaped evidence showing the defendant committing an illegal act. Frequently broadcasters seek to make copies of these tapes for airing on radio and television. Is this possible? In many instances it is; but the federal and state courts have not fully resolved the question. There seems to be a trend toward granting wider access to these tapes, but clearly this right of access to copy and broadcast is not absolute.

The lack of resolution of this issue is at least partially the result of a decision by the Supreme Court of the United States. Tapes made by President Richard Nixon at the White House were used as evidence in many of the Watergate trials of the seventies. Broadcasters sought to make copies of these tapes and broadcast them. The High Court agreed that there is a generally recognized right to access to inspect the evidentiary record in a case, but this is not an absolute right. "The decision as to access is one best left to the sound discretion of the trial court, a discretion to be exercised in light of the relevant facts and circumstances of the particular case," the Court said (*Nixon* v. *Warner Communications,* 1978; see also *Nixon* v. *Carmen,* 1982).

Judges have been exercising their own discretion in these cases, and not surprisingly different judges have reached different conclusions. The courts have considered a variety of factors in reaching a decision on whether to permit the broadcast or telecast of these kinds of electronic recordings. Whether transcripts of the recordings have already been published is an important factor. Courts have also considered whether the broadcast or telecast of the material would enhance public understanding of an important historical or public occurrence. The rights of the defendant are also considered: Would the broadcast of this material prejudice the right to a fair trial? In Atlanta recently, a federal court refused to permit broadcasters to copy and air tapes used as evidence in a trial involving charges of bribery until after the close of evidence in the case. The judge ruled that broadcast of the tape before the defendant had the opportunity to present his side of the story during the trial could possibly galvanize public hostility toward him to the point that some people might try to tamper with the jury by calling jury members and urging them to convict the defendant. The judge admitted this was a remote possibility, but nevertheless delayed release of the tapes to broadcasters (*U.S.* v. *Eaves,* 1988).

Most courts will insist upon clearer evidence that the broadcast or telecast of the material will harm the rights of the defendant or someone or something else. The United States Court of Appeals for the Third Circuit recently ruled that there is a strong presumption favoring access and that this presumption is not outweighed by mere speculations on the potential impact the telecast of the material may have on related proceedings (*U.S.* v. *Martin,* 1984). In Washington State the Supreme Court voided a contempt citation against a radio station that had broadcast, in violation of a court order, tape-recorded testimony that had been placed into evidence because the trial court had "accepted the most superficial showing of justification and then shifted to KHQ [the radio station] the burden of proving that the prior restraint was not necessary. . ." (*Washington* v. *Coe,* 1984).

It is often important whether the tapes that are sought have been introduced into evidence. When John Hinckley was tried for the attempted assassination of Ronald Reagan, the television networks sought to televise the videotaped deposition given by actress Jodie Foster in the case. The court refused the request, noting that the testimony was never admitted into evidence.

It was simply a statement from a witness; it just happened to be videotaped. No right existed to videotape and telecast the testimony of other witnesses. The videotaped deposition would not be an exception to that rule (in re *Application of ABC*, 1982). The New Mexico Supreme Court recently denied the press the right to copy and broadcast recordings of wiretaps that resulted in criminal indictments but were never played in open court or received into evidence (*New Mexico* v. *Brennan*, 1982). Who has been videotaped is also an important consideration when a court examines a request to broadcast the material. Videotapes of defendants and undercover police agents are more likely to be released than are recordings of innocent third parties. Jodie Foster was an "innocent witness" in the Hinckley case. She had been pulled into the case inadvertently. A United States district court in Minnesota rejected requests from broadcasters to air videotapes of a hostage recorded by her kidnapper. The court ruled that it would create serious hardship for the victim of the crime and would serve no proper purpose (in re *Application of KSTP*, 1980). A good way to outline the dimensions of this problem is to look at two different cases, one where access was granted and one where it was denied.

The government presented a considerable amount of evidence on both videotape and audiotape on Congressman John Jenrette and John Stowe in the Abscam trial. They were recordings of the defendants in the case making what the government alleged were illegal deals with undercover FBI agents. The networks sought to copy and broadcast these tapes. The United States District Court refused the request, fearing that if the tapes were televised it would be difficult to later impanel an impartial jury should a retrial be ordered by a higher court. The United States Court of Appeals for the District of Columbia disagreed and promulgated this test:

> Access may be denied only if the district court, after considering the relevant facts and circumstances of the particular case, and after weighing the interests advanced by the parties in light of the public interest and the duty of courts, concludes that justice so requires. . . . The court's discretion must clearly be informed by this country's strong tradition of access to judicial proceedings. In balancing the competing interests the court must also give appropriate weight and consideration *to the presumption—however gauged— in favor of public access to judicial records* [author emphasis].

Several factors favored release of the tapes, the court concluded. They were admitted into evidence and played to a jury at a public trial. The tapes contained only admissible evidence. This was a trial where the defendant was a high public official charged with betraying the public trust. The court admitted a retrial *might* be a problem, but there was no evidence that if there were a retrial, impartial jurors could not be found. What about protecting innocent third parties who were also pictured or heard in the tapes? There were only one or two instances of that, and the trial court can delete these sections, the court said. The tapes must be released (in re *Application of NBC*, 1981).

The United States Court of Appeals for the Fifth Circuit reached the opposite conclusion in another 1981 decision. The speaker of the Texas House of Representatives, two attorneys, and a labor leader were all indicted in an alleged bribery scheme. The speaker and the two attorneys were tried and acquitted. Broadcasters wanted to air audiotapes that had been made during the FBI sting operation that resulted in the indictments. These were discussions between the defendants and FBI undercover operatives that had been secretly recorded. The trial court refused on the grounds that the broadcast might make it difficult for the fourth defendant to have a trial by an impartial jury. The court of appeals supported this decision. The court noted that while there is a right in this country to inspect and copy judicial records and documents, it is not an absolute right. The trial court may exercise considerable discretion in granting or refusing to grant access to material. Clearly, the concern that the fourth defendant's trial might be prejudiced if the tapes were broadcast is a legitimate concern, the court said. It is not the job of the appellate courts to second-guess the trial courts on these matters. Finally, the court said it could not agree with decisions by the District of Columbia Court of Appeals and other courts that there exists a strong presumption in favor of access to this kind of evidence. The court said it could not find a basis for that presumption (*Belo Broadcasting* v. *Clark,* 1981). Other courts have recently followed the rationale of the *Belo* case, giving wide discretion to the trial judge in such instances (see *U.S.* v. *Webbe,* 1986, and *U.S.* v. *Beckham,* 1986).

The differences between these rulings represent to a certain extent the differences in the cases. The retrial was a distant possibility in the first case; the trial of the fourth defendant was about to take place in the second situation. But these rulings also represent differences in judicial philosophy. And as long as the Supreme Court is content to let the lower courts use their discretion in making these decisions, different rules will be applied in different parts of the nation.

Gaining public access to government-held information has been a problem for about as long as democracy has existed as a form of government. With the development of a corps of professional information and news gatherers in this century, the problem has become more visible. Couple this fact with the enormous growth of government in the past half-century, and a problem of rather large proportions develops. Until the last thirty years, most journalists depended upon friendship with sources and upon skill and wile to get the news from governments. Many reporters argue that this is still the best way to find out what is going on. The law plays an ever-increasing role today in gathering news and information. Much of the process of getting the news and keeping it has been institutionalized by statute and court decisions. At the same time the law has raised serious impediments to information gathering, which the press has thus far had difficulty in hurdling. Many of the most important press-government battles in the next decade will be fought over these issues, and at present the question of who will be the winner—the press, the government, or the public—is far from being answered.

BIBLIOGRAPHY

Here is a list of some of the sources that have been helpful in the preparation of chapter 5:

Books

Adams, John B. *State Open Meeting Laws: An Overview.* Columbia, Mo.: Freedom of Information Foundation, 1974.

Cross, Harold. *The People's Right to Know.* New York: Columbia University Press, 1953.

Gerth, H. H., and Mills, C. Wright, eds. *From Max Weber: Essays in Sociology.* New York: Oxford University Press, 1946.

How to Use the Federal FOI Act. 6th ed. Washington, D.C.: FOI Service Center, 1987.

Kirtley, Jane E., ed. *The First Amendment Handbook.* Washington, D.C.: The Reporters Committee on Freedom of the Press, 1986.

Marwick, Christine M., ed. *Litigation Under the Amended Freedom of Information Act.* 2d ed. Washington, D.C.: American Civil Liberties Union and Freedom of Information Clearing House, 1976.

Articles

Archibald, Sam. "The Revised F.O.I. Law and How to Use It." *Columbia Journalism Review,* July/August, 1977.

Beesley, Susan L., and Glover, Theresa. "Developments Under the Freedom of Information Act, 1986." 1987 *Duke Law Journal* 521, 1987.

Braverman, Burt A., and Heppler, Wesley. "A Practical Review of State Open Records Laws." 49 *George Washington Law Review* 721, 1981.

"The Definition of 'Agency Records' Under the Freedom of Information Act." 31 *Stanford Law Review* 1093, 1979.

Genovese, Margaret. "Reagan Administration Information Policies." *presstime,* April, 1985.

Hayes, Michael J. "Whatever Happen to 'The Right to Know'? Access to Government-Controlled Information Since Richmond Newspapers." 73 *Virginia Law Review* 111 (1987).

Malmgren, Lynn C. "First Amendment: Freedom of Press to Gather News." 20 *Villanova Law Review* 189, 1974.

Pember, Don R. "The Burgeoning Scope of 'Acess Privacy' and the Portent for a Free Press." 64 *Iowa Law Review* 1155, 1979.

Weinberg, Steve. "Trashing the FOIA." *Columbia Journalism Review,* January/February, 1985.

Wright, Anne H. "The Definition of 'Agency' Under the Freedom of Information Act as Applied to Federal Consultants and Grantees." 69 *Georgetown Law Journal* 1223, 1981.

Wright, William R. II. "Open Meeting Laws: An Analysis and a Proposal." 45 *Mississippi Law Review* 1151, 1974.

Cases

Anderson v. *WROC-TV,* 441 N.S.Y.2d 815 (1981).

in re *Application of ABC,* 537 F.Supp. 1168 (1982).

in re *Application of KSTP,* 504 F.Supp. 360 (1980).

in re *Application of NBC,* 653 F.2d 609 (1981).

Arieff v. *Navy,* 712 F.2d 1462 (1983).

Belo Broadcasting v. *Clark,* 654 F.2d 426 (1981).

BNA v. *Baxter, Environmental Defense Fund* v. *Office of Management and Budget,* 742 F.2d 1848 (1984).

Branzburg v. *Hayes,* 408 U.S. 655 (1972).

Browde v. *Navy,* 713 F.2d 864 (1983).

Chrysler Corp. v. *Brown*, 441 U.S. 281 (1979).

CNN v. *ABC et al*, 518 F.Supp. 1238 (1981).

Cohen v. *EPA*, 575 F.Supp. 425 (1983).

Common Cause v. *Nuclear Regulatory Commission*, 674 F.2d 921 (1982).

Crooker v. *Bureau*, 670 F.2d 1051 (1981).

Department of the Air Force v. *Rose*, 425 U.S. 352 (1976).

Dudman Communications Corp. v. *Air Force*, 815 F.2d 1565 (1987).

EPA v. *Mink*, 401 U.S. 73 (1973).

Epstein v. *Resor*, 296 F.Supp. 214 (1969), aff'd. 421 F.2d 930 (1970).

FBI v. *Abramson*, 456 U.S. 615 (1982).

Florida Publishing Co. v. *Fletcher*, 340 So.2d 914 (1976).

Forsham v. *Harris*, 445 U.S. 169 (1980).

Garrett v. *Estelle*, 556 F.2d 1274 (1977).

Goland v. *CIA*, 607 F.2d 339 (1978).

Greentree v. *Customs Service*, 674 F.2d 74 (1982).

Hardy v. *Bureau of Alcohol, Tobacco and Firearms*, 631 F.2d 653 (1980).

Heiser v. *Ripon Commonwealth*, see *News Media and the Law*, Summer 1987, p. 22.

Houchins v. *KQED*, 438 U.S. 1 (1978).

Justice Department v. *Julian*, 108 S.Ct. 606 (1988).

Justice Department v. *Reporters Committee*, 16 M.L.R. 1545 (1989).

Kissinger v. *Reporter's Committee*, 445 U.S. 136 (1980).

Knopf v. *Colby*, 502 F.2d 136 (1975).

Kurzon v. *Health and Human Services*, 649 F.2d 65 (1981).

Le Mistral, Inc. v. *CBS*, 402 N.Y.S.2d 815 (1978).

Long v. *IRS*, 596 F.2d 362 (1979).

MacEwan v. *Holm*, 359 F.2d 413 (1961).

Miami Herald v. *Small Business Administration*, 670 F.2d 65 (1982).

Miller v. *National Broadcasting Co.*, 232 Cal. Reptr. 668 (1986).

Natural Resources Defense Council, Inc. v. *Secretary of Energy*, 637 F.Supp. 116 (1986).

New Jersey v. *Lashinsky*, 5 M.L.R. 1418 (1979).

New Mexico v. *Brennan*, 645 P.2d 982 (1982).

New York Times v. *NASA*, 679 F.Supp. 33 (1987); aff'd. 852 F.2d 602 (1988).

Nixon v. *Carmen*, 670 F.2d 346 (1982).

Nixon v. *Warner Communications*, 435 U.S. 591 (1978).

Painter v. *FBI*, 615 F.2d 689 (1980).

Pell v. *Procunier*, 417 U.S. 817 (1974).

Philadelphia Newspapers v. *Nuclear Regulatory Commission*, 9 M.L.R. 1843 (1983).

Playboy v. *Justice Department*, 677 F.2d 931 (1982).

Providence Journal Co. et al v. *McCoy et al*, 49 F.Supp 186 (1950).

Public Citizen Health Research Group v. *Food and Drug Administration*, 704 F.2d 1280 (1983).

Publicker Industries v. *Cohen*, 733 F.2d 1059 (1984).

Reporters Committee for Freedom of the Press v. *Justice Department*, 816 F.2d 730 (1987).

Richmond Newspapers v. *Virginia*, 448 U.S. 555 (1980).

Rushforth v. *Council of Economic Advisers*, 762 F.2d 1038 (1985).

Russell v. *Air Force*, 682 F.2d 1045 (1982).

Saxbe v. *Washington Post*, 417 U.S. 843 (1974).

Sims v. *CIA*, 709 F.2d 95 (1983); rev'd 471 U.S. 159 (1985).

Society of Professional Journalists v. *Secretary of Labor,* 11 M.L.R. 2474 (1985), 832 F.2d 1180 (1987).

Stahl v. *Oklahoma,* 665 P.2d 839 (1983).

State Department v. *Washington Post,* 456 U.S. 595 (1982).

Stern v. *FBI,* 9 M.L.R. 1789 (1983).

Symons v. *Chrysler Corporation Loan Guarantee Board,* 670 F.2d 238 (1981).

Taylor v. *Army,* 684 F.2d 99 (1982).

Terkel v. *Kelly,* 599 F.2d 214 (1979).

Times-Picayune Publishing Co. v. *Lee,* 15 M.L.R. 1713 (1988).

U.S. Beckham, 789 F.2d 401 (1986).

U.S. v. *Martin,* 746 F.2d 964 (1984).

U.S. v. *Morison,* 604 F.Supp. 655 (1985), 844 F.2d 1057 (1988).

U.S. v. *Nixon,* 418 U.S. 683 (1974).

U.S. v. *Webbe,* 791 F.2d. 103 (1986).

Washington v. *Coe,* 101 Wis.2d 364 (1984).

WJW v. *Cleveland,* 686 F.Supp. 177 (1988).

Wolfe v. *Department of Health and Human Services,* 539 F.Supp. 276 (1982); aff'd 711 F.2d 1077 (1983).

Zemel v. *Rusk,* 381 U.S. 1 (1964).

6 PROTECTION OF NEWS SOURCES AND CONTEMPT OF COURT

In 1722 James Franklin, the less-publicized older brother of Benjamin Franklin, was jailed in a small cell for publishing a newspaper without the consent of the government of Massachusetts. He was the first of a host of American journalists who have been jailed for what they published about the government. Today in the United States journalists are still sometimes jailed. But not because of what they have published or revealed about the government; these men and women are jailed because they *refuse* to publish or reveal certain information.

Most journalists are highly efficient information gatherers. And a great deal of the information that journalists gather is not included in the newspaper stories or television reports they prepare. There is usually not space or time for everything. Sometimes sources ask that reporters not reveal their names. And sources often give reporters information "off-the-record" with the expectation that it will not be reported. In Minnesota recently, a jury awarded $700,000 to the public relations director of an advertising agency after he sued two local newspapers for failing to keep a promise that they would not identify him as the source of a news story. Both the *Minneapolis Star-Tribune* and the *St. Paul Pioneer Press* used Dan Cohen's name in their stories about a political candidate's twelve-year-old conviction for shoplifting. Cohen sued for breach of contract and misrepresentation (*Cohen* v. *Cowles Media,* 1988). The judgment was being appealed as this was written.

Reporters are not only efficient gatherers, they are excellent keepers too. They retain all sorts of unreported material in their notebooks or computer memories, on video or audio tape. Most of us don't care what reporters know but don't reveal in their stories. We have enough trouble getting through the stories that are published or broadcast. But for some persons, this undisclosed information is important, even vital. Law enforcement officials frequently want to know what a criminal suspect told a journalist during an interview—only parts of which have been published. Libel plaintiffs often need to know the identity of the sources used by reporters in preparation of a story in order to try to prove the story was untrue or fabricated or published with malice. Video recordings of a violent demonstration are often useful to police who seek to identify those who incited the violence or committed criminal acts. Hence, reporters are often asked to reveal information they have gathered but chosen not to publish or broadcast. In many instances journalists comply with such requests. At times, however, they refuse. When this happens, the persons interested in getting this information often get a court order, called a **subpoena,** to force the journalist to reveal the name of the news source or to disclose the confidential information. Or government agents may get a warrant to search a newsroom or a reporter's home to find the information they want.

In our society the press is supposed to represent a neutral entity as it gathers and publishes news and information. When the government or anyone else intrudes into the newsroom or the reporter's notebook, it compromises this neutrality. A news source who normally trusts journalists may choose not to cooperate if government agents can learn the source's name by threatening the journalist with a court order. Television news crews will hardly be welcome at protest rallies if the demonstrators know that the government will use the film to identify and prosecute the protestors. The effectiveness of the reporter as an information gatherer may be seriously compromised if government agents or civil and criminal litigants can force journalists to reveal information they choose not to disclose. Society also may ultimately suffer because the flow of information to the public may be reduced.

This chapter is about the problems a reporter can face when government agents or other persons use the power of the judicial system to gain access to the news-gathering processes. We will study the problems of source confidentiality and newsroom searches. We will also look at recent judicial and legislative attempts to resolve these issues. Finally, we will examine the powerful weapon the government may employ to get its way in these disputes: the contempt power. ♦

NEWS AND NEWS SOURCES

If news and information are the lifeblood of the press, then news sources are one of the wells from which that lifeblood springs. Many journalists, especially those who consider themselves investigative journalists, are often no better than the sources they can cultivate. News sources come in all shapes and sizes. Occasionally their willingness to cooperate with a reporter is dependent upon assurances from the journalist that their identity will not be revealed. Why would a news source wish to remain anonymous? There are undoubtedly many reasons. Often the source of a story about criminal activities has participated in criminal activities and has no desire to publicize this fact. Frequently the source of a story about government mismanagement or dishonesty is an employee of that government agency, and revelation of his or her identity could result in loss of the job for informing the press of the errors made by the employee's superiors. Some persons simply do not want to get involved in all the hassle that frequently results when an explosive story is published; by remaining anonymous they can remain out of the limelight.

Journalists have always used confidential sources and obtained information that government officials sought to uncover. The earliest reported case of a journalist's refusal to disclose his sources of information took place in 1848 when a reporter for the *New York Herald* refused to reveal to the United

States Senate the name of the person who had given him a secret copy of the treaty the United States was negotiating to end the Mexican-American War. He was held in contempt of the Senate and jailed. A United States Court of Appeals denied the journalist's petition for release (*Ex Parte Nugent,* 1848). But the issue of journalists protecting the identity of a confidential source surfaced infrequently in the next 120 years. In fact, from 1911 to 1968 only seventeen cases involving a reporter's confidential sources were reported, according to an article in the *California Law Review.*

In the past two decades requests to journalists to reveal confidential information or to share notes or video out-takes with government officials have become far more numerous. It is difficult to explain precisely why this has happened. In part it is probably due to changes that have occurred in the nature of reporting, which has become more oriented toward investigation. Reporters seem to have more valuable information than they had thirty years ago. The growth in the number of attempts to get information from journalists is also in part probably due to the changes in the nature of society. Illegal or quasi-legal activity seems more commonplace, corruption is more evident. There is a greater need to investigate today. There has also been a tremendous increase in litigation in the United States. The nation now has one-third of all the lawyers in the world, according to some reports, and these lawyers need something to do. Court actions are commonly at the root of requests to journalists to share unpublished information. Finally, the nature of reporters has changed as well. They are far more visible today and are therefore better targets of opportunity.

There are few viable options when a journalist is served with a subpoena and ordered to reveal confidential information or what is contained in his or her notebook. The reporter can cooperate with those who seek the information and reveal what it is they want to know. But this will likely damage the reporter/source relationship, and such cooperation usually carries with it an unfavorable stigma in the industry. The journalist can attack the subpoena and seek to have it quashed or annulled. This is expensive, and success can be elusive in many cases. Or, the journalist can refuse to cooperate, and very likely be held in contempt of court. This is when the prospect of a jail sentence arises. The choice for the journalist is not an easy one.

But the choice for society is difficult as well. The interests that are involved in this dilemma are basic to our system of government and political values. On the one hand, it is clearly the obligation of every citizen to cooperate with the government and testify before the proper authorities. This concept was so well-established by the early eighteenth century that it had become a maxim. John Henry Wigmore, in his classic treatise on evidence (*A Treatise on the Anglo-American System of Evidence*) cites the concept thus: "The public has a right to everyman's evidence." The Sixth Amendment to the United States Constitution guarantees us the right to have witnesses and to compel them to testify in our behalf. And surely this is a valuable right, both to society, and to the individual seeking to prove his or her innocence of charges of wrong-doing. The Supreme Court has said on many occasions that it is a citizen's duty to testify. In 1919 the Court wrote as follows on the duties and rights of witnesses (*Blair* v. *U.S.*):

> [I]t is clearly recognized that the giving of testimony and the attendance upon court or grand jury in order to testify are public duties which everyone within the jurisdiction of the government is bound to perform upon being properly summoned, . . . the personal sacrifice involved is a part of the necessary contribution to the public welfare.

On the other hand, society benefits from the free flow of information provided by the mass media. Many believe that when a reporter is forced to break a promise of confidentiality or is used as an arm of law enforcement investigators, it harms this free flow of information. People who know things, often important things, simply won't give this information to journalists for fear of being exposed if the reporter is squeezed for the information. The fragile reporter/source relationship may be damaged.

A recent survey of reporters who had been nominated for the Pulitzer Prize revealed that these journalists used confidential or off-the-record information in the preparation of about one-third of their news stories. Three-fourths of the respondents to this survey, prepared by attorney John Osborn and published in the *Columbia Human Rights Law Review,* said their ability to report the news would be substantially affected if they were routinely forced to disclose confidential or background data they had gathered. Others express doubts that the use of confidential sources is either so widespread or so important for most reporters. (See for example, Chamberlin, "Protection of Confidential News Sources: A Resolved Issue.") But even if the problem is a smaller one than some journalists like to believe, it nevertheless remains a problem for society, for any interruption in the flow of information is unhealthy.

The solution to this societal dilemma that has emerged in the past twenty years is to grant reporters a limited privilege in order to allow them to protect the confidentiality of names and information they have gathered. Individuals in other occupations—doctors, lawyers, members of the clergy, and in some instances, even accountants—enjoy a privilege that allows them to protect the confidentiality of discussions they have had with patients, clients, or parishioners. It should be no surprise, then, that reporters sought the same privilege.

But the privilege granted to reporters does not come in a nice neat package since its source varies in many instances. For example, there is a limited constitutional privilege that is applied by many courts, while in more than half the states it is a statutory privilege provided by the legislature. Finally, in at least one state (Washington) the common law is named as the source of the privilege.

The immediate task ahead is to outline the dimensions of the privilege, whether it is applied as a constitutional protection, a legislative protection or a common law protection. This section, especially the material on the constitutional privilege, is rife with generalizations that may not be applicable in every case or everywhere. We proceed with some caution.

CONSTITUTIONAL PROTECTION OF NEWS SOURCES

In 1972, the Supreme Court of the United States ruled, in a 5–4 decision, that there was no privilege under the First Amendment for journalists to refuse to reveal the names of confidential sources or other information when called to testify before a grand jury (*Branzburg* v. *Hayes*). This is the last word the nation's High Court has spoken on the subject. Yet today, there is a limited constitutional protection that has been applied by United States courts of appeal and United States district courts in many parts of the nation. The story of how judges in many of the lower and intermediate federal courts rewrote the *Branzburg* ruling is an example of the pragmatic genius of American law.

The Supreme Court consolidated three similar cases when it first faced the question of whether journalists could find a privilege in the First Amendment to permit them to refuse to testify when called before a grand jury. One case involved Paul Branzburg, a reporter for the *Louisville Courier-Journal*. Branzburg was called to testify in 1971 about drug use in Kentucky after he wrote two stories about drugs and drug dealers in the area. In the second case, Paul Pappas, a television reporter for a Massachusetts television station, was called before a grand jury to relate what he had seen and heard when he spent three hours at a Black Panther headquarters in July of 1970. Finally, *New York Times* reporter Earl Caldwell was subpoenaed to appear before a grand jury investigating the activities of the Black Panthers in Oakland, California. Caldwell, who was black, had gained the confidence of the leaders of the militant group and had consistently wrote illuminating stories about the Panthers that demonstrated an astute awareness of their activities. The decision in the three cases are referred to collectively as the *Branzburg* ruling.

In two instances—*Branzburg* and *Pappas*—lower courts had rejected arguments that the First Amendment provided a privilege for the reporters, a privilege which would permit them to refuse to testify. In *Caldwell,* however, the United States Court of Appeals for the Ninth Circuit ruled that forcing the journalist to even appear before a grand jury could damage the public's First Amendment right to be informed. The court therefore found that journalists enjoyed a qualified privilege that protected them when called to testify about confidential information. The government must show a compelling need for the witness' presence in order to overcome this privilege, the court ruled.

The Supreme Court fractured into three groups in deciding this case. Four justices, led by Byron White who wrote the Court's opinion, ruled that there was no First Amendment privilege for reporters called to testify before a grand jury. White said that while the Court was sensitive to First Amendment considerations, the case did not present any such considerations. There were no prior restraints, no limitations on what the press might publish, and no order for the press to publish information it did not wish to. No penalty for publishing certain content was imposed. White wrote (*Branzburg* v. *Hayes*, 1972):

> The use of confidential sources by the press is not forbidden or restricted. . . .
> The sole issue before us is the obligation of reporters to respond to grand jury subpoenas as other citizens do and answer questions relevant to an investigation into the commission of crime. Citizens generally are not constitutionally immune from grand jury subpoenas; and neither the First Amendment nor other constitutional provisions protect the average citizen from the disclosing to a grand jury information that he has received in confidence.

Reporters are no better than average citizens, White concluded.

The four dissenters differed sharply with the other justices. Justice William O. Douglas took the view that the First Amendment protection provides the press with an absolute and unqualified privilege. In any circumstance, under any condition, the reporter should be able to shield the identity of a confidential source. Justices Potter Stewart, William Brennan, and Thurgood Marshall were unwilling to go as far as Justice Douglas and instead proposed that reporters should be protected by a privilege that is qualified, not absolute. The three dissenters argued that the reporter should be able to protect the identity of the confidential source unless the government can show the following:

1. That there is a probable cause to believe that the reporter has information that is clearly relevant to a specific violation of the law
2. That the information sought cannot be obtained by alternative means less destructive of First Amendment rights
3. That the state has a compelling and overriding interest in the information

When the government cannot fulfill all three requirements, Justice Stewart wrote for the dissenters, the journalist should not be forced to testify.

Justice Lewis Powell provided the fifth vote needed for the Court to reject the notion of a constitutional privilege for reporters. But while Powell voted with those who could find no privilege in the First Amendment, his brief concurring opinion seemed to support the opposite proposition. "The Court does not hold that newsmen, subpoenaed to testify before a grand jury, are without constitutional rights with respect to the gathering of news or in safeguarding their sources," he wrote. No harrassment of reporters will be allowed, and a balance must be struck between freedom of the press and the obligation of all citizens to give relevant testimony. "In short, the courts will be available to newsmen under circumstances where legitimate First Amendment interests require protection," Powell wrote. Two years later, in a footnote in another case (*Saxbe* v. *Washington Post,* 1974) Powell emphasized that the High Court's ruling in *Branzburg* was an extremely narrow one and that reporters were not without First Amendment rights to protect the identity of their sources.

Lower Court Rulings

Most lower federal courts have treated *Branzburg* as an extremely narrow ruling. They have limited the holding to instances in which a grand jury has sought a reporter's testimony. Typical is the ruling by the United States Court of Appeals for the Third Circuit, where the court noted the *Branzburg* precedent.

> There, the Supreme Court decided that a journalist does not have an absolute privilege under the First Amendment to refuse to appear and testify before a grand jury to answer questions relevant to an investigation of the commission of a crime. No Supreme Court case since that decision has questions relevant to an investigation of the commission of extended the holding beyond that which was necessary to vindicate the public interest in law enforcement and ensuing effective grand jury proceedings (*Riley* v. *Chester,* 1979).

In cases that do not involve testimony before a grand jury, many jurists are taking Justice Powell's opinion to heart, rather than merely counting his vote. And they have recognized that Powell's concurrence fits more comfortably with Stewart's dissent outlining a qualified privilege than it does with White's blanket rejection of any privilege. At last count, nine of the twelve United States courts of appeal had accepted the notion that the First Amendment creates a qualified privilege that protects reporters who are subpoenaed to testify about confidential matters. This includes the first, second, third, fourth, fifth, eighth, ninth, tenth, and the D.C. courts of appeal. Other courts however, have rejected this notion. In 1987 the United States Court of Appeals for the Sixth Circuit refused to join this group. "Because we conclude that acceptance of the position . . . would be tantamount to our substituting, as the holding in *Branzburg,* the dissent written by Justice Stewart, we must reject that position." The judges therefore declined to join the other circuits. "That portion of Justice Powell's opinion certainly does not warrant rewriting the majority opinion to grant a First Amendment testimonial privilege to news reporters" the jurists added (*Storer Communications* v. *Giovan,* 1987).

Nevertheless, over the past eighteen years a qualified First Amendment privilege has emerged that protects reporters who are called upon to testify before grand juries, in court proceedings, and in other official government inquiries. The privilege has been fashioned by the trial and intermediate appellate courts in the federal system.

The successful application of this privilege depends upon several factors. What kind of a proceeding is involved is a key question. The privilege is more readily granted to a journalist involved in a civil suit than to one called before a grand jury, for example. And the privilege is qualified by various court tests, all of which mirror closely the test outlined by Justice Stewart in *Branzburg*. Is the information important? Is it clearly relevant to the proceedings? Is there somewhere else to get the information? In the next few pages we will attempt to sketch the rough outline of this reporter's privilege. It is important to remember, however, that without a binding Supreme Court ruling, the lower federal and state courts have been permitted to fashion their own rules; and there is distinct variance from state to state, federal circuit to federal circuit. Look to the court precedents in your region as the final authority in this matter.

Civil Cases

Most federal and state courts that have confronted the issue have granted to journalists involved in a civil action the qualified privilege to refuse to reveal the identity of a confidential source. The federal courts have found this privilege in the First Amendment. State courts have found the privilege in state statutes (see pages 326–329), the First Amendment, state constitutions, and even the common law.

The successful application of the privilege in these instances dates back to 1973, in the virtual shadow of the *Branzburg* ruling, when the Democratic party brought a civil action to win damages for the Watergate break-in. Ten reporters from the *New York Times, Washington Post, Washington Star-News, Time* magazine, and other publications were subpoenaed and told to bring their tapes, notes, letters, documents, and all other materials obtained during their reporting of the Watergate break-in. A United States district court quashed the subpoena, noting that the press is entitled to at least a qualified privilege to refuse to answer such questions under the First Amendment (*Democratic National Committee v. McCord*, 1973).

In 1977 the United States Court of Appeals for the Tenth Circuit refused to force filmmaker Arthur Hirsch to reveal confidential information he had obtained in connection with a civil action by the estate of Karen Silkwood against the Kerr-McGee Corporation. Hirsch was preparing a documentary film on the mysterious death of the young woman when he was subpoenaed by Kerr-McGee. The court ruled that a limited First Amendment privilege protected the filmmaker and that before he could be required to answer questions, the trial court was bound to consider whether the party seeking the information had independently attempted to obtain the information elsewhere and had been unsuccessful, whether the information sought from the reporter went to the heart of the matter before the court, and whether the information was of certain relevance in the case. In this case Hirsch did not have to testify (*Silkwood v. Kerr-McGee*, 1977). Courts in many jurisdictions have made similar rulings, granting a reporter an exemption from the normal requirement to testify.

Normally a court asks three questions before determining whether the privilege should be granted to the journalist:

1. Has the person seeking the information (normally the plaintiff) shown that the reporter's information is of *certain relevance* in the case?
2. Does the information go to the heart of the matter before the court?
3. Can the person who is seeking the reporter's information demonstrate that there is no other source for this information?

If *all* three questions can be answered yes, the chances are good the reporter will be required to testify. But this is a heavy burden for the plaintiff or the defendant to meet, and in most instances journalists are being excused from testimony (see in re *Consumers Union,* 1978; *Riley* v. *Chester,* 1979; and *McGraw-Hill* v. *Arizona,* 1982). In 1986 the United States Court of Appeals for the Fourth Circuit refused to force NBC reporters to disclose confidential sources they had used to prepare two television reports on Lyndon LaRouche. LaRouche said he needed this information for his libel action against the network and others, but the court ruled that he had not fully explored using alternative sources who might have the same information (*LaRouche* v. *NBC,* 1986).

In civil suits where the reporter is actually a party in the case, the courts have granted the privilege somewhat more grudgingly or not at all. A reporter can end up in a lawsuit either as a plaintiff or a defendant. If the reporter is a plaintiff in a lawsuit and has information that is critical to the case, it is unlikely that a court will permit the reporter to remain silent regarding these issues. Columnist Jack Anderson attempted to sue Richard Nixon and other former government officials for allegedly conspiring to deprive him of his civil rights. But he refused to cooperate with the defendants when they requested the names of confidential sources who gave the columnist information regarding the activities of Nixon and his White House associates. Citing the First Amendment, Anderson refused to reveal the names sought. But a federal district judge ordered him to give the information to the court if he hoped to continue his suit. The judge ruled that Anderson was attempting to use the First Amendment simultaneously "as a sword and a shield. . . . He cannot have it both ways. Plaintiff is not a bystander in the process, but a principal. He cannot ask for justice and deny it to those he accuses." Anderson was forced to withdraw his suit (*Anderson* v. *Nixon* et al., 1978).

A reporter usually ends up as a defendant in a lawsuit when a libel suit is filed because of something the reporter wrote or broadcast. Often the reporter based the allegedly libelous news report on confidential information or sources. It is important for the plaintiff in such a libel case to find out where the reporter obtained the information for the story to demonstrate that the journalist was negligent or that the material was published with actual malice (see pages 150–159 to refresh your memory about the meaning of these terms). It is much more difficult to predict how a court will respond to a plaintiff's demand that the reporter reveal confidential information in these kinds of instances. But some patterns have developed. For example, many courts insist that the plaintiff prove that the information sought is crucial to the matter of proving either negligence or actual malice. The 1972 ruling in *Cervantes* v. *Time* is a good example. The lawsuit was a twelve million dollar libel action against *Life* magazine for publishing a story suggesting that the mayor of St. Louis, Alfonso Cervantes, had underworld connections. The mayor wanted to know the names of the sources in the Federal Bureau of Investigation and Justice Department who supplied the information to reporter Denny Walsh. Cervantes said he could not prove malice without these names.

However, the information about the mayor was a small part of the story, which was extremely well documented. The charges against Cervantes comprised only four paragraphs of the eighty-seven-paragraph story. The court of appeals ruled, "To compel a newsman to breach a confidential relationship merely because a libel suit has been filed against him would seem inevitably to lead to an excessive restraint on the scope of legitimate news-gathering activity." The court said that if the plaintiff was able to provide persuasive evidence that this information was crucial to the question of malice, the privilege might then have to give way. However, in this case, "The mayor has wholly failed to demonstrate with convincing clarity that either the defendant acted with knowledge of falsity or reckless disregard of the truth." There was just no reasonable probability that the plaintiff would succeed in proving malice.

In *Senear* v. *Daily Journal American,* the Washington State Supreme Court ruled that a reporter for the Bellevue (Washington) *Journal-American* enjoyed a qualified common law privilege to refuse to reveal the identity of a source for a story he had written about a labor dispute. The state's high court ruled that the plaintiff could gain access to the information only if it could be shown that a libel claim against the newspaper had merit—it was not intended to merely harrass the newspaper; that the information sought went to the heart of the plaintiff's legal claim—it was critical to the cause of action; and that the plaintiff had exhausted other reasonable means to gain the information. Justice James Dolliver also noted that the trial court should determine that the reporter's interest in nondisclosure is supported by the need to preserve confidentiality, not simply a stance of noncooperation (*Senear* v. *Daily Journal American,* 1982).

In other libel suits, when reporters were asked to testify, the courts have ruled that the plaintiff need only show that there is a genuine issue of fact about the truth or falsity of the libelous material. It is not necessary to demonstrate that the reporter might have information that will resolve the issue. In a libel suit against the *Wall Street Journal,* the Massachusetts Supreme Judicial Court ruled that there was no privilege to protect the newspaper from revealing the name of the source of its story so long as questions material to the case remained to be resolved. "The obligation of newsmen, we think, is that of every citizen, *viz.,* to appear when summoned, with relevant written or other material when required, and to answer relevant and reasonable inquiries" (*Dow Jones* v. *Superior Court,* 1973). The New Hampshire Supreme Court ruled that a public-official libel plaintiff must satisfy the trial court that he or she has evidence to establish that there is a genuine issue of fact regarding the falsity of the publication. Once the plaintiff meets this burden, the privilege to withhold confidential information ceases to exist (*Downing* v. *Monitor Publishing Co.,* 1980). And the United States Supreme Court ruled in 1979 that plaintiffs may explore what the defendant was thinking about while preparing the story for publication or broadcast. The High Court ruled in *Herbert* v. *Lando* that as long as the public-figure libel plaintiff has a special burden of proof in a defamation case, denial of "discovery of editorial state of mind would make that burden unduly onerous." What this means is that the plaintiff can ask reporters or producers or editors if they had any doubts about the truth of the material when they published the story: Did they think they should check things a bit more before broadcasting the libelous charges? Were there other sources with whom they considered talking? And so forth.

On a few occasions, trial courts have reacted sharply when a reporter refused to reveal the name of a confidential source for a news story. The case of *Plotkin* v. *Van Nuys Publishing Co.* is a good example. Plotkin was one of the hostages held by Iranians for more than a year in the United States Embassy in Teheran. On the day he and the other hostages were released in 1981 the *Los Angeles Daily News* published a story alleging he was involved in drug trafficking and that he was under investigation by both the Drug Enforcement Administration (DEA) and the Los Angeles Police Department. Both agencies denied the story and Plotkin sued the newspaper for sixty million dollars. Before the trial began Plotkin sought the names of several confidential sources the reporters said they had relied upon. The reporters refused to reveal the names and the judge, without explanation, issued a default order and gave Plotkin the verdict and a sixty million dollar judgment. After considerable negotiation the judge reversed her order and ordered the trial to proceed. She told the journalists however, that if they continued to refuse to reveal the names of sources, she would rule as a matter of law that no such sources exist. The reporters later persuaded two DEA agents to testify and convinced the court that the other sources Plotkin sought had not provided them with the information that was used in the story.

The "no source" remedy has been used by courts in Idaho, Hawaii and New Hampshire as well. When applied it effectively strips away the libel defense for a newspaper or television station. The court is saying to the fact finder: you must presume there is no source for the story; the defendant surely fabricated it. While these kinds of ruling are rare, they are extremely frightening to the press. More typical in a civil suit is the aforementioned ruling that reporters enjoy a qualified privilege to refuse to testify, and this privilege can be overcome if the person seeking the material can show that the reporter's information is relevant, that it goes to the heart of the matter, and that alternative sources of this information have been exhausted.

Courts have granted the First Amendment privilege to reporters quite freely in civil actions in part, at least, because there is no competing constitutional right involved. In a criminal case, however, the privilege for the reporter must be balanced against the Sixth Amendment right of the defendant to compel testimony on his or her behalf. Consequently, it is somewhat less likely that a court will permit a reporter to refuse to answer questions about the identity of a confidential source or other confidential information. Courts most often apply slight variations of the Stewart test from the *Branzburg* case to determine whether or not the journalist will be compelled to testify.

In *United States* v. *Burke,* for example, the defendant was indicted for conspiracy in connection with a basketball point-shaving scheme at Boston College and attempted to impeach the testimony of the prosecution's chief witness, a reputed underworld figure. The defendant asked the court to subpoena the unpublished notes and drafts of *Sports Illustrated* reporter Douglas Looney, who had interviewed the witness. The United States Court of Appeals for the Second Circuit quashed the subpoena, noting that a court may order reporters to reveal confidential sources only when the information is (1) highly material and relevant, (2) necessary or critical to the defense, and (3) unobtainable from other sources (*U.S.* v. *Burke,* 1983).

In New York a reporter interviewed a key prosecution witness before a murder trial and the defendant subpoenaed the notes from that interview. The New York Supreme Court refused to require the reporter to produce these notes because, it said, the defendant failed to show that the information sought was "highly material and relevant," "necessary to his defense," and "unavailable from other sources" (*New York* v. *Bova,* 1983). In 1982 authorities called a reporter to testify in a criminal case against a physician who was charged with violating federal drug laws. Reporter Patrick Malone had written a story about the use and misuse of the drug Quaalude. The story included several statements that Malone attributed to the defendant in the drug case. The government wanted Malone to testify, to verify that Dr. Frederick Blanton had made the statements attributed to him in the article. The trial judge ruled that Malone did not have to appear as a witness because the government had failed to show it had exhausted all efforts to get the information elsewhere or that there was a compelling need to get this information at all (*U.S.* v. *Blanton,* 1982).

In 1984 the Washington State Supreme Court ruled that an *Everett* (Washington) *Herald* reporter did not have to reveal the names of several confidential sources he had used to prepare an article about alleged cult activities at an eighty-acre farm near rural Snohomish, Washington. The owner of the farm, Theodore Rinaldo, had been convicted of statutory rape, assault, coercion, and intimidating a witness. A year after his conviction, several persons who had testified on Rinaldo's behalf at his trial stepped forward and admitted they had committed perjury. It was during his second trial for tampering with witnesses and other offenses that Rinaldo tried to force reporter Gary Larson to reveal the names of persons who gave the reporter information for six articles that had brought the activities at the farm to the attention of local authorities. Justice James Dolliver, speaking for the court, ruled that Rinaldo would have to show that the information was necessary or critical to his defense and that he had made a reasonable effort to get the material by other means. He could not make such a showing, and the subpoena was quashed (*State* v. *Rinaldo,* 1984).

There are, of course, instances in which courts recognize a qualified privilege for the reporter but still force the reporter to testify. The case of *Kansas* v. *Sandstrom* in 1978 provides a good example. Milda Sandstrom was charged with murder in connection with the death of her husband. Reporter Joe Pennington testified at the trial that a confidential source had revealed to him that at a party shortly before Thad Sandstrom was killed, one of the state's witnesses had threatened to kill Sandstrom. Pennington said the informant had heard about the threat from another person who attended the party but refused to reveal the name of the informant. The Kansas Supreme Court ruled that in this instance Pennington did not enjoy a First Amendment privilege to refuse to identify the confidential informant.

The state's high court noted that lower courts that had applied the *Branzburg* ruling to criminal cases had generally concluded that the proper test for determining the existence of a reporter's privilege in a particular criminal case was to balance *the need of the defendant for a fair trial against the reporter's need for confidentiality* (author emphasis). "As a general rule, disclosure has been required only in those criminal cases where it is shown the information in possession of the news reporter is material to prove an element of the offense, to prove a defense asserted by the defendant, to reduce the classification or gradation of the offense charged, or to mitigate or lessen the sentence imposed," the court noted. In this case the trial court felt that the identity of the confidential informant could lead to information relevant to Mrs. Sandstrom's defense, and on appeal, the state high court concluded that this was a reasonable position to adopt.

In 1980 the United States Court of Appeals for the Third Circuit ruled that Jan Schaffer, a reporter for the *Philadelphia Inquirer,* had to testify about a conversation she had had with a prosecuting attorney before a criminal trial. The defendants in a government Abscam prosecution moved for a dismissal of the charges on the grounds that there had been massive pretrial publicity about the case that would prevent their getting a fair trial. The defendants charged that the publicity was the result of misconduct by the prosecutor, who they said had improperly given reporters details of the sting operation. The prosecutor admitted talking with reporters about the case, but the defendants sought the reporter's testimony to confirm the prosecutor's statements. The court, applying the three-part test, ruled that Schaffer would have to testify. The reporter obviously had the information—the prosecutor admitted talking with her about the case. There was a compelling need for the information—it was central to the defendant's charges of misconduct by the prosecutor. And the defense had attempted to get the information elsewhere—from the prosecutor himself. The reporter was the only source left (*U.S.* v. *Criden,* 1980).

Courts are even more reluctant to grant reporters the privilege to refuse to testify when what is sought is nonconfidential information; that is, information possessed by the journalist, but obtained without giving the source any promise of protection. For example, attorneys for Lyndon LaRouche recently sought videotape of an interview conducted by NBC with a man who was scheduled to be a key government witness at LaRouche's trial for mail fraud. NBC interviewed Forrest Lee Fick, a former paid consultant on the LaRouche staff, for an hour and forty minutes. Only one minute of the interview was broadcast and the LaRouche people wanted to see the rest. NBC refused, but the United States Court of Appeals for the First Circuit affirmed the trial court order that the videotape be given to the judge for an *in camera* (private) review. If he found that the material in the interview was relevant to the defense, the judge said he might later release it to LaRouche's attorneys. The court recognized that it was treading on interests close to the First Amendment, but noted that "When there is no confidential source of information at stake, the identification of First Amendment interests is more elusive." The court added that it recognized that forcing a reporter to reveal the name of a confidential source could jeopardize the ability of the media to get information, but no one has demonstrated how this chilling effect works when nonconfidential material is involved. The court emphasized its ruling was a narrow one—this was a criminal case and the material sought concerned a major witness, closely connected to the defendants, who was likely to be hostile. Material in the interview might permit the defendants to impeach this individual's testimony (*U.S.* v. *LaRouche Campaign,* 1988). The Maine Supreme Judicial Court issued a similar ruling in 1988 when it upheld the contempt conviction of a newspaper reporter who refused to testify at a murder trial about a news article he wrote that described his interview with the defendant. The court noted that this was a narrow question: Is there a qualified privilege for a reporter to refuse to testify concerning nonconfidential published information obtained from an identified source? The court said it was not convinced that requiring testimony in such a case would place an added burden on the press as it attempts to gather news and information. The reporter, Robert Hohler, was fined two thousand dollars and given a six month suspended jail sentence (*Maine* v. *Hohler,* 1988).

Regardless of the outcome of some of these cases, what is important is that most courts have recognized that there is a qualified privilege for reporters to refuse to reveal the names of confidential sources in criminal cases as well as in civil suits.

Grand Jury Proceedings

While the qualified privilege for reporters to refuse to reveal the identities of confidential sources in civil and criminal actions has been recognized by most lower federal courts and state supreme courts that have considered the question, these same courts have routinely refused to extend the First Amendment privilege to grand jury proceedings. This is true even though the grand jury's power to force disclosure is not constitutionally guaranteed, as is the criminal defendant's right to compel a witness to testify. The obvious explanation for this reluctance on the part of judges is that the single United States Supreme Court precedent on the question focused upon grand jury testimony and in that case, *Branzburg* v. *Hayes,* the High Court ruled that no privilege existed. Only a few reported decisions exist in which appellate courts have quashed or partially quashed a subpoena requiring a reporter to appear and testify before a grand jury.

Two reporters for the Black Panther newspaper, Brenda Presley and Sherrie Bursey, were called to testify before a grand jury in 1972, shortly after the *Branzburg* ruling. They wrote a story about a speech by Panther leader David Hilliard in which he either did or did not threaten former President Richard Nixon. They were called to testify before several grand juries. Although the reporters always answered some of the questions, they refused to answer all queries regarding confidential information and information regarding management of the Panther paper. The government presented sufficient evidence to convince the district court that there was a compelling and overriding national interest, and the women were called to testify. They refused to answer fifty-six different questions. On appeal, the United States Court of Appeals for the Ninth Circuit ruled that the two reporters had to answer seventeen of the fifty-six questions (*Bursey* v. *U.S.,* 1972). The court said the women did not have to answer queries about the people who worked at the newspaper or about how the paper was edited, but they did have to answer questions about whether they had seen firearms and explosives at Panther headquarters and about whether the Panther leaders conducted discussions concerning violent activities. The government interests were legitimate and compelling, the court said, and infringement upon the First Amendment was incidental.

In 1982 a United States district court in Colorado quashed a subpoena that called for the testimony of a wire-service reporter before a grand jury investigating the illegal removal of some photographs by a Secret Service agent from the home of the parents of John Hinckley, Jr., the man who shot President Reagan. The agent allegedly illegally removed the photos from the home while it was being searched and passed the pictures on to United Press International. The judge ruled that the grand jury hearing was not really involved with a criminal prosecution but had been instituted as an administrative proceeding aimed at gaining evidence to support the firing of the Secret Service agent. The court ruled that the reporter would not have to honor the subpoena unless the government could show that the reporter had information that would go to the heart of a pending *criminal investigation* (in re *Grand Jury Subpoenas,* 1982).

Finally, in a very unusual case in 1985, the United States Court of Appeals for the Third Circuit ruled that the author of a book did not have to appear before a grand jury, because the government had failed to articulate a compelling interest in gaining the disclosure of the author's notes, documents, and other records. Antoni Gronowicz wrote a purported biography of Pope John Paul II, entitled *God's Broker.* Gronowicz alleged that much of the material in the book came from two hundred hours of interviews he had had with the Pope. The Vatican denied this, and the publisher withdrew the book from circulation. The Justice Department launched an investigation in Philadelphia with the aim of prosecuting Gronowicz for mail fraud because of his promotion of the book. What the government was attempting to do was prove whether the book was true or false. This is an improper motive, the court ruled. The First Amendment protects citizens from government prosecution for false speech. "We will not enforce the grand jury subpoena in this case, where the government's purpose is admittedly to prove the truth of the book," the court ruled (in re *Gronowicz,* 1985).

These rulings are really atypical; more often than not reporters have found themselves forced to testify when subpoenaed to appear before a grand jury. If there is any good news in this state of affairs, it is that fewer and fewer such subpoenas are being issued today.

Telephone Records

The names of confidential news sources, reporters' notes, news film, and photographs are not the only records that have been sought by government agents through the use of a subpoena. The records of toll telephone calls made by reporters have also come under government scrutiny in recent years.

The telephone company maintains subscriber records for toll telephone calls for about six months. For long-distance calls billed to the subscriber's telephone number, these records indicate the telephone number called, as well as the date, time, and duration of the call. The records are no secret; a copy of the monthly toll-call record is provided to each subscriber with each month's bill.

In 1974 the American Telephone and Telegraph Company (AT&T) announced that in the future it would not release these records to the government without a subpoena and, as a general policy, would seek to notify subscribers immediately when their individual records had been subpoenaed by a government agency. However, when records were subpoenaed pursuant to a felony investigation, the telephone company said it would not notify the subscriber of the subpoena as long as the government certified that an official investigation was being conducted and that notification to the subscriber could impede the investigation.

The Reporter's Committee for Freedom of the Press challenged the telephone company's policy of releasing *any* records to the government, arguing that the government could use such records to determine reporters' sources. Journalists raised both the Fourth Amendment and the First Amendment as bars to this cooperation between AT&T and the government.

A United States court of appeals seemed unpersuaded that this cooperation created a real problem and ruled against the Reporter's Committee. The Fourth Amendment claim lacked merit, the court said, because the constitutional prohibition against illegal search and seizure "does not insulate all personal activity from official scrutiny." The First Amendment claim was similarly rejected. The court asserted that the First Amendment offers no additional protections against good faith criminal investigations beyond that afforded by the Fourth and Fifth amendments (*Reporter's Committee v. AT&T*, 1978):

> The principle is clear. To the extent individuals desire to exercise their First Amendment rights in private, free from possible good faith law enforcement investigation, they must operate within the zone of privacy secured by the Fourth Amendment. When individuals expose their activities to third parties, they similarly expose these activities to possible government scrutiny.

SUMMARY

In recent years more and more reporters have been called to testify in legal proceedings. Often they are asked to reveal confidential information to aid police in criminal investigations, to assist in the defense of a criminal defendant, or to help a libel plaintiff establish negligence or actual malice. Failure to comply with a court order can result in a citation for contempt of court. The Supreme Court of the United States ruled in 1972 that reporters were like all other citizens; they did not enjoy a First Amendment privilege that permitted them to refuse to testify before a grand jury. Despite this High Court ruling, the lower federal courts and state courts have fashioned a constitutional-common law privilege that often protects a journalist who has been subpoenaed to testify at a legal hearing. The privilege is qualified. In many instances a court will not require a journalist to testify unless the person seeking the information held by the journalist can demonstrate that the reporter has information that is relevant to the hearing, that there is a compelling need for the disclosure of this information, and that there are no alternative sources for this information.

Courts tend to apply this three-part test differently in different types of legal proceedings. Journalists are most likely to escape being forced to testify in a civil suit, especially if the reporter is not a party to the suit in some way.

Reporters are more likely to be forced to testify in a criminal case, but there are numerous examples of reporters being granted a qualified privilege to escape such testimony as well. Reporters called to testify before a grand jury, however, usually are required to honor the subpoena. A United States court of appeals has ruled that the records of toll telephone calls made by journalists may also be subpoenaed to further legitimate law enforcement proceedings.

LEGISLATIVE AND EXECUTIVE PROTECTION OF NEWS SOURCES	While the courts have erected limited barriers to protect journalists from subpoenas issued by government agencies, the state legislatures and the United States Department of Justice have attempted to protect reporters as well. Twenty-six states have passed statutes that shield reporters in one way or another from subpoenas that might force them to reveal confidential information. There is no federal shield law, but the Department of Justice has developed an extensive set of guidelines that sharply limit when and how federal agents may use subpoenas against journalists. First, let us look at the state statutes.
Shield Laws	In 1896 Maryland granted journalists a limited privilege to refuse to testify in court proceedings. By 1989, twenty-six additional states had adopted similar statutes called shield laws. The states that have such laws are Alabama, Alaska, Arizona, Arkansas, Delaware, Illinois, Indiana, Kentucky, Louisiana, Maryland, Michigan, Minnesota, Montana, Nebraska, Nevada, New Jersey, New Mexico, New York, North Dakota, Ohio, Oklahoma, Oregon, Pennsylvania, Rhode Island and Tennessee. In California, the state shield law was made a part of the state constitution.

These laws, in more or less limited terms, outline the reporter's privilege that has been established by the state. The statutes generally establish who can use the privilege (i.e. who is a reporter?), the kinds of information the privilege protects (i.e. confidential and nonconfidential; sources only or sources and information), and any qualifications that might accrue (i.e. the privilege is waived through voluntary disclosure of other parts of the material; instances when disclosure is mandated).

For example, the Alabama shield law provides:

> No person engaged in, connected with, or employed on any newspaper (or radio broadcasting station or television station) while engaged in a news gathering capacity shall be compelled to disclose, in any legal proceeding or trial, before any court or before a grand jury of any court, or before the presiding officers of any tribunal or his agent or agents, or before any committee of the legislature, or elsewhere, the sources of any information procured or obtained by him and published in the newspaper (or broadcast by any broadcasting station or televised by any television station) on which he is engaged, connected with, or employed.

Shield laws do provide important protection for reporters in many instances. In Illinois, for example, courts ruled that the state shield law prevented the editor of the *Journal of the American Medical Association* from being forced to reveal the name of a contributor who claimed he (she) had euthanized a terminally-ill patient. Under the statute, all other sources of information had to be exhausted and the disclosure of the information had to be essential to the public interest before the journalist could be required to reveal the information, the court ruled. The state's attorney failed to meet this burden (in re *Grand Jury Investigation,* 1988). The Oregon shield law recently helped Portland *Oregonian* editor Bill Hilliard avoid a stay in jail and a fine. At issue were photographs taken by a staff photographer at an antinuclear rally in Portland. Three demonstrators who were arrested for resisting arrest and harassing police sought all the photos taken that day (only a couple had been published) to aid them in their defense. They argued that the pictures were needed to test witnesses' recollection of events. The trial court ordered the photos disclosed, but Hilliard refused, arguing that the state shield law protected unpublished information obtained in the course of news gathering. The court of appeals agreed and said unless the defendants could specifically demonstrate that the photos were material and favorable to their defense, the trial court could not order disclosure (*Oregon ex rel Meyer* v. *Howell,* 1987).

Although these cases and others that could be cited show how shield laws have protected journalists, there are problems with these laws as well. Authorities who have studied the shield laws have found that they fail to give the news gatherer the same measure of protection as the First Amendment. Brian M. Cullen notes in the *Suffolk University Law Review:*

> Their disparate protection and their limited scope, as well as the narrow construction courts have accorded them, have permitted the frequent and arbitrary disclosure of confidential information. This lack of predictable protection has doubtlessly inhibited identity-conscious sources from revealing their stories to news gatherers. Moreover, the state shield statute must give way whenever it conflicts with the Constitution.

Cullen and Douglas Frazer, in an article in the *The Journal of Criminal Law and Criminology,* recently summarized some of the features of these state laws. Most of the shield laws apply to all formal state proceedings, administrative and legislative hearings as well as trials and grand jury investigations. But few of the laws give a protection that exceeds, or is even equal to, that given by the constitutional privilege. Four state shield laws claim to be absolute—those in Arizona, Nebraska, New Jersey, and Ohio—but only the New Jersey courts have ruled on this interpretation. The remaining twenty-two laws are qualified in many ways. In four states—Alaska, Louisiana, New Mexico, and North Dakota—the shield law can be overcome by a mere judicial determination that justice or public policy requires the privilege to yield to some other interest. Most state shield laws protect only the identity of confidential sources or information that would reveal the identity of the source. The First Amendment privilege, on the other hand, extends to unpublished information, outtakes, notes, tape recordings, and even photos.

Other qualifications abound in the laws. In some states a reporter waives the privilege upon the disclosure of any part of the confidential matter. In New Jersey, reporter Evan Schuman interviewed murder/kidnap suspect Gary Mayron, and the *New Jersey Herald* published several specific admissions made by Mayron about the crimes. While the New Jersey shield law has a broad privilege against compulsory disclosure of information gathered and the identities of the sources of that information, the Superior Court still required Schuman to testify about his interview with Mayron. By publishing specific information about the matter, along with the identity of the source, he had waived the privilege with respect to this information, the court ruled (in re *Schuman,* 1988).

And in New York there must be an understanding of confidentiality between the source and the reporter before the law will apply. Reporters at a Knight-Ridder television station in Albany conducted an interview with Donald Bent, whose wife had been missing for several days. Only one minute of the long interview was broadcast. When Mrs. Bent was found dead investigators served a subpoena on the television station, seeking the videotape containing the remainder of the interview. Since there was no evidence that Bent had originally asked that the interview be confidential, the New York Court of Appeals ruled that the state's shield law did not protect the television station (*Knight-Ridder Broadcasting* v. *Greenberg,* 1987).

State laws often exclude amateur news gatherers and free-lance writers. And these laws often don't cover what a reporter actually witnesses. In California for example, a reporter travelling with police witnessed the search and arrest of a criminal suspect. She was called on to testify at the trial, but refused, citing the state's shield law. The California Court of Appeals ruled that the shield law does not protect reporters from being compelled to give eyewitness testimony in criminal cases (*Delaney* v. *Superior Court,* 1988).

Finally, provisions in a state constitution will supersede the statutes, making them useless in some cases. In Pennsylvania recently the state supreme court ruled that the constitutional guarantee of the right of an individual to protect his or her reputation overrides the state shield law in a case where a libel plaintiff sought unpublished documentary evidence that had been gathered by the defendant, a Philadelphia television station. The court said it did not "believe that the legislature intended to preclude redress to an individual against the media for maliciously or negligently publishing false statements that damage the reputation" (*Hatchard* v. *Westinghouse Broadcasting Co.,* 1987).

Surely the existence of a shield law in a state is not a bad thing. The number of subpoenas that were never sent to journalists in the first place because of the existence of a shield law cannot be calculated. And in many instances the laws do provide real protection for journalists trying to do their jobs. But the privilege rooted in the First Amendment provides more protection because it is applied more broadly in most instances. And many reporters are uncomfortable knowing that they are expected to be watchdogs over the very branch of government—the legislature—that has granted them this protection. They fear that should push come to shove, the legislature can strip away this protection—something that cannot happen so easily with a privilege grounded in the First Amendment.

Federal Guidelines

As a kind of corollary to a shield law, the Department of Justice has adopted rules that define when and how a federal prosecuting attorney can obtain a subpoena against a working reporter. Here is a summary of the guidelines:

1. The Department of Justice must attempt to strike a balance between the public's interest in the free dissemination of ideas and information and the public interest in effective law enforcement when determining whether to seek a subpoena for a journalist's confidential information.
2. All reasonable attempts should be made to obtain the information from alternative sources before considering issuing a subpoena to a member of the news media.
3. Negotiations with the news media to gain the information sought shall be pursued in all cases in which a subpoena to a member of the news media is contemplated.
4. If the negotiations fail (if the reporter won't provide the material voluntarily), the attorney general must approve the subpoena based on the following guidelines:
   a. There must be sufficient evidence of a crime from a nonpress source. The department does not approve of using reporters as springboards for investigation.
   b. The information the reporter has must be essential to a successful investigation—not peripheral or speculative.
   c. The government must have unsuccessfully attempted to get the information from an alternative nonpress source.
   d. Great caution must be exercised with respect to subpoenas for unpublished information or where confidentiality is alleged.
   e. Even subpoenas for published information must be treated with care, because reporters have encountered harrassment on the grounds that information collected will be available to the government.
   f. The subpoena must be directed to specific information.

Telephone Records	Rules one through three in the guidelines just listed apply when federal agents seek to subpoena the toll telephone records of members of the media as well. If the negotiations to get the records fail, the agents must seek permission from the attorney general to issue the subpoena. In such a case the following guidelines apply:

1. There should be reasonable grounds to believe that a crime has been committed, and that the information sought is essential to the successful investigation of that crime.
2. The subpoena should be directed at only relevant information regarding a limited subject matter and should cover a limited period of time.
3. The government should have pursued all reasonable alternative means before seeking the subpoena.
4. Reporters must be given timely notice that the government intends to issue a subpoena.
5. Information obtained through the subpoena must be closely guarded so that unauthorized persons cannot gain access to it.

These federal guidelines have worked well. In some federal cases judges have insisted that the government must demonstrate that it has followed these guidelines before it will force a reporter to testify (*U.S.* v. *Blanton,* 1982, for example). Some state and local law enforcement agencies have adopted rules similar to these federal rules. The federal guidelines apply to criminal cases, civil matters, and subpoena of telephone records. It is true that these guidelines do not completely protect the working journalist, but the guidelines often work better than shield laws, and they go a considerable distance in reducing animosity that was mounting between the press, the police, and the courts.

Newsroom Searches	Does a newsroom or a journalist's home enjoy any constitutional protection from a search by the police or federal agents? The Supreme Court of the United States refused to extend the First Amendment in such a manner in 1978 (*Zurcher* v. *Stanford Daily*). Since then, however, the Congress and many state legislatures have provided qualified legislative protection for premises where news and scholarship are produced. The lawsuit that resulted in the Supreme Court ruling stemmed from the political turmoil of the early seventies, a period that generated many of the previously discussed cases regarding reporters' sources.

In April of 1971 police were asked to remove student demonstrators who were occupying the administrative offices of Stanford University Hospital. When police entered the west end of the building, demonstrators poured out of the east end, and during the ensuing melee outside the building, several police officers were hurt, two seriously. The battle between the police and the students was photographed by a student, and the following day pictures of the incident were published in the *Stanford Daily* student newspaper. In an effort to discover which students had attacked the injured police officers, law enforcement officials from Santa Clara County secured a warrant for a search of the *Daily*'s newsroom, hoping to find more pictures taken by the student photographer. It was hoped the pictures might provide visual evidence as to which students had battered the lawmen. There was no allegation that any member of the *Daily* staff was involved in the attack or other unlawful acts. No evidence was discovered during the thorough search.

This type of search is known as an innocent third-party search, or simply a third-party search. Police search the premises or a room for evidence relating to a crime, even though there is no reason to suspect that the owner of the premises or the occupant of the room is involved in the crime that is being investigated. Such searches are not uncommon, but in the lawsuit that followed, the student newspaper argued that this kind of search threatened the freedom of the press and should not be permitted unless police officials first obtain a subpoena—which is more difficult for lawmen to get than is a simple search warrant. The subpoena process would also provide the press with notice prior to the search and allow editors and reporters to challenge the issuance of the subpoena.

The newspaper argued that the unannounced third-party search of a newsroom seriously threatened the ability of the press to gather, analyze, and disseminate news. The searches could be physically disruptive for a craft in which meeting deadlines is essential. Confidential sources—fearful that some evidence that would reveal their identity might surface in such a search—would refuse to cooperate with reporters. Reporters would be deterred from keeping notes and tapes if such material could be seized in a search. All of this, and more, could have a chilling effect on the press, lawyers for the newspaper argued.

The Supreme Court, in a five-to-three ruling, disagreed with the newspaper. Justice Byron White ruled that the problem was essentially a Fourth Amendment question (i.e., was the search permissible under the Fourth Amendment?), not a First Amendment question, and that under existing law a warrant may be issued to search any property if there is reason to believe that evidence of a crime will be found. "The Fourth Amendment has itself struck the balance between privacy and public need and there is no occasion or justification for a court to revise the Amendment and strike a new balance . . . ," White wrote. The associate justice conceded that "where the materials sought to be seized may be protected by the First Amendment, the requirements of the Fourth Amendment must be applied with 'scrupulous exactitude.' " He added, "Where presumptively protected materials are sought to be seized, the warrant requirement should be administered to leave as little as possible to the discretion of the officer in the field." But Justice White rejected the notion that such unannounced searches are a threat to the freedom of the press, arguing that the framers of the Constitution were certainly aware of the struggle between the press and the Crown in the seventeenth and eighteenth centuries, when the general search warrant was a serious problem for the press. Yet the framers did not forbid the use of search warrants where the press was involved, White asserted. They obviously believed the protections of the Fourth Amendment would sufficiently protect the press (*Zurcher* v. *Stanford Daily,* 1978).

The decision by the Supreme Court reinforced existing law on the question and did not represent a dramatic change in policy. But prior to the search of the *Stanford Daily* in 1971, there had been only fifteen police searches of newsrooms in this country, ever, according to Anthony Lewis, columnist for the *New York Times.* The Supreme Court ruling seemed to suggest the value of such searches to law enforcement agencies across the United States, for in the next ten years nearly twenty newsroom searches were conducted. What happened at KBCI-TV in Boise, Idaho, is typical. There was a riot at the Idaho State Penitentiary in July 1980. Inmates invited Bob Loy, managing editor of KBCI-TV, to meet with them to hear their grievances. Loy toured the facility with a cameraman, who shot videotape of the fifteen million dollars in damage at the prison. After the riot was quelled, county prosecutor James Harris and police searched the KBCI newsroom for the videotapes taken at the penitentiary. The prosecutor obtained the search warrant on the grounds that he wanted to use the videotape in his prosecution of inmates for damaging the prison. After ninety minutes of what was described by *TV Guide* as "heavy-handed" searching, the tapes were found and confiscated. KBCI brought suit to have the search declared illegal and to get an injunction against future searches, but the case was dismissed by the Idaho district court, which cited the *Zurcher* ruling (*Reiss* v. *Harris,* 1980).

Incidents like these demonstrated the need for some kind of legislative relief, and Congress responded by passing the Privacy Protection Act of 1980. The law limits the way law officers and government agents can search for or seize materials that are in the hands of persons working for the mass media or persons who expect to publicly disseminate the material in some other manner (e.g., public speech). The statute designates two categories of material that are protected: work products and documentary materials. The law says a work product "encompasses the material whose very creation arises out of a purpose to convey information to the public." In layperson's language work products are reporters' notes, undeveloped film, out-takes, and so forth. Documentary materials are described as "materials upon which information is formally recorded," such as government reports, manuscripts, and the like. Congress based the statute on the commerce clause in the United States Constitution in order to extend the reach of the law to include state and local agencies, as well as federal law enforcement personnel. To obtain either work products or documentary materials, law enforcement agencies must obtain a subpoena; a search warrant will not do. There are, however, exceptions to the rule. A law enforcement agency may conduct a warranted search of a newsroom to find "work products" in either of the following two situations:

1. When there is a probable cause to believe that the person possessing such materials has committed or is committing a criminal offense to which the materials will relate.
2. Where there is reason to believe that the immediate seizure of such materials is necessary to prevent the death of or serious harm to a person.

A search warrant may be used instead of a subpoena to obtain documentary materials if either of the two conditions just listed are met or in either of these two situations:

1. There is reason to believe that the giving of notice pursuant to gaining a subpoena would result in the destruction, alteration, or concealment of such materials.
2. That such materials have not been provided in response to a court order directing compliance with a subpoena, all other legal remedies have been exhausted, and there is reason to believe that further delay in gaining the material would threaten the interests of justice.

In most instances, then, law enforcement personnel will be forced to seek a subpoena to gain access to information kept in a newsroom or a reporter's home. While the problem of newsroom searches has been alleviated, it has not been eliminated. In late 1988 The Reporters Committee for Freedom of the Press noted that numerous searches had been conducted in newsrooms in both Minnesota and California. In one of the Minnesota cases a United States district court ruled that the FBI's seizure of film from the *Minneapolis Star and Tribune* and WCCO-TV in the same city amounted to an unconstitutional prior restraint on publication in violation of the Privacy Protection Act (*Minneapolis Star and Tribune* v. *U.S.*, 1987).

HOW TO RESPOND TO A SUBPOENA

What should a reporter do if he or she is subpoenaed? You might first try to avoid the problem altogether. Don't give a promise of confidentiality to a source without first carefully considering whether such a promise is actually needed to get the story. Discuss the matter with an editor or the news director before agreeing to keep the name of a source confidential. Also, don't talk, even informally, with persons outside the newspaper about stories in which confidential information or sources are involved. Such discussions may later be ruled to constitute a waiver of the privilege you seek to assert at a later date.

But if a subpoena should arrive, the first thing to remember is that this does not mean the police are coming to your door to arrest you. It is simply an order that you have been called to appear at some type of proceeding or supply certain documents. So don't panic. Tell your editor or news director immediately. Ask to talk with your news organization's legal counsel. Don't attempt to avoid being served with the subpoena. While a reporter is under no obligation to make the job easier for the person serving the subpoena, resistance to this service may result in the subpoena being abandoned and a search warrant issued in its place. Don't ever accept a subpoena for someone else.

If the subpoena requests only published material, or video that has previously been broadcast, the newspaper or broadcasting station may simply provide this material without dispute. It is unlikely that the news organization will so readily provide other kinds of materials however. Journalists should be familiar with his or her news organization's policy on retaining notes, tapes, first drafts, etc. If there is no policy, it is worthwhile to ask management to consider adopting one. Once the subpoena has been served the material sought is considered official evidence, and if it is destroyed to avoid having to produce it, the reporter very likely will be held in contempt of court. So once you have been served, begin gathering the material together in case you have to surrender it at some later time.

If you believe that the material or names of sources should be withheld, and your news organization disagrees, it is in your interest to hire your own attorney to represent you. The company attorney is working for the company, not you. Finally, remember that the odds of being forced to give up the material or names are low. The law is, for the most part, on your side these days.

SUMMARY

State legislatures and the federal government have adopted statutes and rules that offer some protection to journalists who hold confidential information sought by government agents and other individuals. Twenty-six states have adopted so-called shield laws, which provide a qualified privilege for reporters to refuse to testify in legal proceedings. While sometimes these statutes can be helpful, they are not without problems. There is a lack of consistency among the state shield laws. These laws have definitional problems that permit courts to construe them very narrowly if they choose to. The laws usually protect only what someone tells a reporter, not what a reporter personally sees or hears. Often courts see the statutes as legislative interference with judicial prerogatives and go out of their way to interpret the laws in the least useful manner.

The Department of Justice has adopted rules that govern when and how federal agents may subpoena journalists, records possessed by journalists, and telephone toll records. The rules require federal agents to strike a balance between the public's interest in the free flow of information and effective law enforcement. Federal prosecuting attorneys are instructed to attempt to obtain information from alternative sources or to negotiate with the journalist to get the material before seeking a subpoena. The attorney general must approve all subpoenas under guidelines outlined in these rules.

Congress passed the Privacy Protection Act of 1980 in response to a ruling by the United States Supreme Court that the First Amendment does not ban searches of newsrooms or reporters' homes. This act requires federal, state, and local police agencies who seek a journalist's work products or other documentary materials to get a subpoena for these materials rather than seize them under the authority of a search warrant. The statute does provide exceptions to these rules. For example, premises may be searched and materials seized under a search warrant if police believe the reporter has committed a crime, if there is reason to believe someone will be harmed if the materials are not seized, or if police fear the materials might be destroyed if a subpoena is sought.

THE CONTEMPT POWER

We have seen that reporters have been subpoenaed to testify in a wide range of legal proceedings. Television news departments have been ordered to surrender films and videotapes. Broadcast journalists have been required under court order to supply audiotape recordings to police and prosecutors. And, of course, if journalists refuse to cooperate, they face severe penalty under the courts' power to punish for contempt. What is the contempt power? Without a thorough understanding of the contempt power, it is difficult to truly appreciate the predicament journalists can find themselves in when asked to produce the name of a news source or other confidential information.

History of Contempt

In 1631 in England a British subject was convicted of a felony, not a very uncommon event. This particular subject was angered at being found guilty, and after the sentence was read he threw a brickbat at the judge. The brickbat missed the judge, but the man was quickly seized, his right hand was cut off and nailed to the gallows, and he was immediately hanged in the presence of the court (this story is recounted by Ronald Goldfarb in *The Contempt Power*).

While such judicial retribution is an uncommon exercise of the contempt power, it nevertheless is a representative example of the power of judges to control what goes on in their courtrooms. Even as the end of the twentieth century approaches, disobedience of or disrespect for the court is normally put down swiftly by exercise of the power of contempt. Any act that interferes with the orderly processes of justice is usually promptly stopped and the offender is quickly punished. While other governmental bodies (legislative bodies, for example) can use the contempt power, its use by judges, which is the subject of this section, is far more common today.

In a nation like the United States with a long tradition of due process of law, the contempt power appears to be an anomaly, something out of character. One individual should not have the kind of unbridled power that a judge can wield via contempt. The contempt power can only be understood as an artifact of history. Hundreds of years ago in England the king dispensed justice to the people. The king was above the law, someone whose power was divinely inspired, and resistance to his orders was a sin, punishable by damnation. When judges eventually began to administer the courts on behalf of the monarch they retained much of this power since it was believed, though he was absent from the courtroom, the king nevertheless was spiritually guiding the hand of justice.

As representative democracy developed in England and royal influence of the government diminished, judges retained the contempt power, and it became institutionalized in common law courts in both Great Britain and the United States. Courts today rarely justify the exercise of the contempt power on the grounds that it protects the integrity of the judge. Instead, protection of the authority, order, and decorum of the court is the usual reason given for the use of the contempt power. Alternatively, the court will use contempt to protect the rights of the litigants using the court to settle a dispute.

Kinds of Contempt

Varieties of contempt are recognized through the common law and there have been efforts to label these varieties. But these efforts have been unsatisfactory; different courts call different kinds of contempt different things. No attempt will be made to resolve these discrepancies in this book. It is sufficient to note that judges use the contempt power for two purposes:

1. To protect the rights of a litigant in a legal dispute before the court. Imagine Jones wins a forty thousand dollar libel judgment against Smith, but Smith won't pay. The court can hold Smith in contempt for refusing to hand over the money. Or, a reporter refuses to name a source important to a plaintiff in a libel suit. To protect the plaintiff's rights, the judge can find the reporter in contempt.
2. To vindicate the law, the authority of the court, or the power of the judge. The defendant in a criminal trial refuses to be quiet and is constantly interrupting testimony. The judge can hold the defendant in contempt. Or, after a judge issues an order banning participants in a trial from speaking to members of the press, one lawyer holds a press conference. Again, a contempt citation might be issued against the attorney.

There are also two distinct forms of punishment for those persons found guilty of contempt. In some instances the judge can jail the guilty party in order to coerce a change of behavior. The jail sentence is indeterminate and can last, theoretically, forever. This form of punishment is generally used to protect the rights of litigants. Looking back at our earlier examples, a judge might jail Smith until he is willing to pay Jones the forty thousand dollars. Or the judge may jail the reporter until she agrees to cooperate and disclose the information sought.

Persons found to be in contempt of court can also be fined and given determinate jail sentences; that is, put in jail for thirty days or six months. This is strictly a punishment; there is no effort at coercion.

In some instances judges can use what is called summary contempt power, and this is perhaps the most onerous aspect of contempt. This power is usually limited to those occasions when the judge has first-hand knowledge of the contemptuous act: for example, the misbehavior occurs in the courtroom. When exercising this power, the judge will act as prosecutor ("I accuse you of. . . ."), jury ("I find you guilty of. . . ."), and judge ("I sentence you to. . . ."). When the summary power is applied the accused has few of the rights that normally are presumed under due process of law. There is no jury trial, no right to call witnesses in his or her behalf. The accuser and the judge are one and the same.

Any contempt conviction can be appealed. As in any other case, the appeal is taken to the next higher court in the state or in the federal system. Normally the punishment is suspended pending the outcome of the appeal.

Contempt and the Press The contempt power is broad and touches all manner of pesons who run afoul of a judge. Journalists are among persons at jeopardy. What kinds of situations are most likely to result in contempt problems for the press? To list a few:

1. Failure to pay a judgment in a libel or invasion of privacy case.
2. Failure to obey a court order. The judge rules that no photos may be taken in the courtroom, or orders reporters not to publish stories about certain aspects of a case. If these orders are disobeyed, a contempt citation may result.
3. Refusal to disclose sources or testify. This is the problem discussed in the bulk of this section.
4. Critical commentary about the court. This might be an editorial critical of the court or a cartoon mocking the judge. Contempt citations have been issued to punish the press in such cases.
5. Tampering with a jury. A reporter tries to talk with jurors during a trial, asking questions about their views on the defendant's innocence or guilt.

These are some of the more common ways that members of the press might become involved in a contempt problem, although the list is by no means exhaustive.

Limitations on Contempt Power	The early years of the twentieth century must be regarded as a high-water mark for the contempt power, because since that time the opponents of this power have succeeded in placing rather severe limitations upon its use. Make no mistake; it is not a sterile power. Judges can and still do use their contempt power. But in the last quarter of the twentieth century, judges throughout the United States have far less freedom in how they use this power than they had in the first quarter of this century.
Legislative Limits	One important limitation upon the power of the court to use contempt comes from legislatures. For example, for more than seventy years, the Congress has passed laws that limit use of the summary power by federal judges to dispose of contempt citations. The 1914 Clayton Antitrust Act, for example, requires that judges provide a jury trial in a contempt case when the contemptuous action is also a crime under federal or state law. In 1932, as a part of the Norris-LaGuardia Act, the Congress mandated jury trials for all contempts arising out of labor disputes. The 1957 civil rights law provided for a jury trial for contempt when the sentence imposed exceeded forty-five days in jail. The 1964 civil rights law contains the same provision.
Court-Imposed Limits	The bench itself imposes limitations upon the use of the summary power. The *Federal Rules of Criminal Procedure* requires that in many instances notice be given the contemnor and a hearing be allowed. In addition, there is the right to counsel, the right to cross-examine witnesses, the right to offer testimony, and in many instances the right to a jury trial. If the contempt citation is based upon criticism or disrespect of a judge, that judge is disqualified from the proceeding. Bail is also allowed. The courts and legislatures in many states also deem that a jury trial is a requirement in an indirect contempt.

In the instances just noted, the legislature or the bench itself grants the right to a jury trial. Is there a constitutional right to a jury trial in such cases? The United States Supreme Court has been grappling with this question since the 1960s.

In 1964 the High Court ruled that there is no constitutional right to a jury trial in a contempt case in upholding the contempt conviction of the governor of Mississippi, Ross Barnett, who willfully disobeyed an order of the Court of Appeals for the Fifth Circuit. As one might expect at that time and in that place, the substantive question involved was civil rights. However, a footnote to the Court's opinion states, "Some members of the Court are of the view that, without regard to the seriousness of the offense, punishment by summary trial without a jury would be constitutionally limited to that penalty provided for petty offenses" (*U.S.* v. *Barnett,* 1964).

Petty offenses generally carry a sentence of six months or less. What the Court seemed to be hinting at is that a jury trial is constitutionally required if the penalty exceeds more than six months in jail. A few years later in *Cheff* v. *Schnackenberg* (1966) the High Court specifically said what it had implied in the *Barnett* case—that sentences exceeding six months cannot be imposed in cases of criminal contempt without giving the accused a jury trial. Then in 1968, in *Bloom* v. *Illinois,* the High Court took the last step and ruled that criminal contempt is a crime in the ordinary sense and that since the United States Constitution guarantees the right to a jury trial in criminal cases, prosecutions by state courts for serious criminal contempts (those with more than a six-month penalty) must be heard by a jury.

In 1941 the United States Supreme Court placed a distinct limit on the power of federal judges to use their summary power in punishing contempts. An 1831 statute had limited the use of this power to contempts committed in the presence of the court or "so near thereto" as to obstruct the administration of justice. In 1918 the High Court ruled that the words "so near thereto" had a causal meaning. Any act that was in close relationship to the administration of justice could be punished summarily (*Toledo Newspaper Co.* v. *U.S.*). Twenty-three years later the Supreme Court reversed itself on this matter in the case of *Nye* v. *U.S.* Justice William O. Douglas cited research that had been done on the 1831 statute by legal scholars during the mid-twenties that showed Congress had intended the words to have a geographic, not a causal meaning. Before the summary power can be used, Douglas wrote, the misbehavior must be in the courtroom or in the physical proximity of the courtroom. Most people today believe this permits a federal judge to exercise the summary power to acts that take place in the courtroom, in the hallway outside the court and perhaps the lobby of the courthouse, but not much farther. Conceivably a noisy demonstration just outside the building might also be ruled to be "so near thereto" to affect the administration of justice.

Through various means, then, during this century the summary power of judges has been limited, and in turn the limitations have reduced the contempt power. Through statutes that explicitly limit the use of the summary power and through court rulings that limit the severity of punishment that may be applied in the absence of a jury, the absolute power of judges has been trimmed. Nevertheless, the summary power is still a threat. And even six months in jail is a long time!

First Amendment Limitations

The First Amendment was not raised as a barrier to contempt conviction until relatively modern times—in 1941 to be exact. In 1941, and again in 1946 and 1947, the United States Supreme Court ruled that freedom of the press to comment on the judiciary must be protected, except in those circumstances in which the commentary presents a serious threat to the proper functioning of the legal process. These three decisions—*Bridges* v. *California* and *Times Mirror Co.* v. *Superior Court, Pennekamp* v. *Florida,* and *Craig* v. *Harney*—stand as the bedrock support for the argument that the First Amendment protects the press in writing about the judiciary.

The first case, *Bridges* v. *California* and *Times Mirror Co.* v. *Superior Court* (1941), actually consisted of two appeals from decisions by California courts, and the cases were decided together as one case. In the first instance a newspaper, the *Los Angeles Times,* was ruled in contempt for publishing a series of anti-labor editorials. The trial court claimed that the editorials were aimed at influencing the disposition of cases before the court concerning labor unionists. In the second case, labor leader Harry Bridges was held in contempt of court when he publicly threatened to take the dockworkers out on strike if the courts attempted to enforce a judicial ruling going against Bridges and his union. While the spectre of a militant anti-labor union newspaper and a militant labor leader arguing on the same side of this question is remarkable, it is not as remarkable as the Court's decision, which voided both contempt citations.

In a five-to-four decision the High Court repudiated the idea that the contempt power is valid because it is deeply rooted in English common law. Justice Hugo Black wrote that even if this were the case, the idea ignores the generally accepted historical belief that "one of the objects of the Revolution was to get rid of the English law on liberty of speech and press." Black said that before a judge can use the contempt power to close off discussion of a case, there must be a "clear and present danger" that the discussion will produce interference with the proper administration of justice. In applying Holmes's famous World War I clear-and-present-danger sedition test to contempt, Black meant that only those threats to justice that are imminent or immediate can be punished. The substantive evil must be extremely serious and the degree of imminence extremely high before utterances can be punished, he wrote.

The government argued in these cases that commentary on a case is clearly proper, but only *after* the case is completed so that the course of justice cannot be influenced. Black rejected this notion, saying that it is while a trial is underway that the public interest about a case is highest. He wrote:

> We cannot start with the assumption that publications actually do threaten to change the nature of legal trials and that to preserve judicial impartiality it is necessary for judges to have a contempt power by which they can close all channels of public expression to matters touching on the pending cases.

It should be noted parenthetically that in using the clear-and-present-danger test to block contempt convictions, Justice Black made better use of those four words than did the High Court in its application of the test in sedition trials. For the clear-and-present-danger test indeed became an effective means of stopping contempt convictions against the press.

This concept was reinforced five years later when in the second case, *Pennekamp* v. *Florida* (1946), the court reviewed an appeal from the Florida Supreme Court involving a contempt citation against the *Miami Herald*. The *Herald* had been highly critical of the trial courts in Dade County, Florida, for many months. In at least two editorials, it was argued that the courts worked harder to protect the criminals than they worked to protect the people. But the newspaper's evaluation of the courts' performance was founded on serious misstatement of facts. The court found both the editor, John D. Pennekamp, and the newspaper in contempt and levied fines against them both.

The Supreme Court overturned the convictions, noting, "We are not willing to say under the circumstances of this case that these editorials are a clear and present danger to the fair administration of justice in Florida." Justice Stanley Reed wrote that while he could not precisely define clear and present danger, certainly the criticism of a judge's actions in a nonjury trial would not affect the legal process. What about the factual errors in the editorials? Justice Reed said the errors were quite immaterial. Free discussion, Reed said, is a cardinal principle of Americanism. Discussion after a trial ends might be inadequate and can endanger the public welfare. Freedom of discussion should be given the widest range compatible with the essential requirement of the fair and orderly administration of justice. "We conclude," Reed wrote, "that the danger under this record to fair judicial administration has not the clearness and immediacy necessary to close the door of permissible public comment. When that door is closed, it closes all doors behind it."

The following year, the Court once again reinforced the First Amendment barrier to the use of the contempt power in its decision in *Craig* v. *Harney* (1947), the third case. In this case a Texas newspaper had been highly critical of a judge who directed a jury to return a verdict against a well-liked citizen in a civil suit. The *Corpus Christi Caller-Times* was found in contempt of court, and again the High Court struck down the conviction. Justice William O. Douglas admitted that in the Court's opinion the critical articles were unfair because they contained significant errors about what had actually occurred at the trial. "But inaccuracies in reporting," he wrote, "are commonplace. Certainly a reporter could not be laid by the heels for contempt because he missed the essential point in a trial or failed to summarize the issues to accord with the views of the judge who sat on the case."

Douglas wrote that it took more imagination than the Court possessed to find "in this sketchy and one-sided report of a case any imminent or serious threat to a judge of reasonable fortitude. . . ." Douglas added, "Where public matters are involved, the doubts should be resolved in favor of freedom of expression rather than against it."

The three cases just discussed—*Bridges, Pennekamp,* and *Craig,*—represent three strong statements in favor of a broad discussion of judicial matters, of trials, and of the legal process. To some degree they also represent a limitation upon the contempt power of the courts. The clear-and-present-danger test is a formidable hurdle for any judge to clear before punishing a newspaper or television station with a contempt citation. However, lest we get swept away by the Court's rhetoric, it is important to look at what was involved in each of these cases, or rather what was not involved. In none of the cases did the judge first issue an order banning certain kinds of publicity about the case. In none of the cases could a jury have been influenced by the media publicity. In none of the cases did the press publish or broadcast evidence or statements prohibited at the trial. As a matter of fact, all three cases involved the same question—commentary or criticism directed toward a judge. From these cases it is clear that the Supreme Court expects the nation's judges to be strong, not to bend in the wind of public opinion, not to be influenced by journalistic commentary. But the Court has never indicated that it has the same expectations with regard to juries. It has never said that a judge must allow the press free rein in its comments on a pending case with regard to material evidence or the credibility of witnesses. The caution, then, is not to read more into these decisions than is actually there. *Bridges, Pennekamp,* and *Craig* stand for almost unlimited discussion of pending nonjury cases. That is about as far as we dare go, however.

Interference with the trial process, on the other hand, especially in a jury trial, will usually not be tolerated, First Amendment or not. During a 1982 criminal trial in Boulder, Colorado, the members of a venire—a panel of persons being examined to determine whether they will be seated as jurors—were instructed, in the presence of the press, not to talk with reporters or anyone else about the trial. But after many citizens complained that they thought that the venire members were being intimidated by attorneys during the examination process, two reporters for the *Boulder Daily Camera* contacted some prospective jurors to ask if they felt they were being intimidated. This was brought to the attention of the court and fourteen provisionally qualified jurors were dismissed. The examination procedure had to be started all over again. An angry judge, who said reporters were aware of his order to the venire, found the two reporters in contempt of court. An appellate court upheld the citation, and the reporters were forced to reimburse the state and the parties for the costs incurred because of the additional four days of trial during which the reexamination of the venire took place. The reporters also had to pay the costs for their own contempt trial (in re *Stone, 1985*).

| Present Status | When a journalist violates a court order, a contempt citation is probably forthcoming. But what if the court order appears to be illegal or unconstitutional on its face? Can a reporter still be held in contempt for violating such an order? This is perhaps the most perplexing problem the press faces today in relation to the contempt power. For there is no clear answer to these questions. The dilemma centers around what lawyers and judges call the collateral bar rule. This rule requires that court orders, even those that appear to be unconstitutional and are later deemed to be unconstitutional, must be obeyed. A person who violates a court order may not collaterally challenge the order's constitutionality as a defense to the contempt charge. Instead, that person must obey |

the order and then appeal the decision to a higher court. As legal scholar Richard Labunski of the University of Washington notes, "The rule in effect, requires journalists to either accept almost certain conviction for contempt, or obey the order, seek review, and forfeit the First Amendment rights they seek to exercise." A 1972 ruling, *U.S.* v. *Dickinson,* demonstrates how this collateral bar rule works.

In November 1971 a hearing was underway in federal court in Baton Rouge, Louisiana. A VISTA worker had been indicted by the state on charges of conspiring to murder the mayor of Baton Rouge. The defendant complained that the state had no evidence in the case and that prosecution was merely an attempt to harass him. The hearing in federal court was to determine the motives of the state in the prosecution. Since it was possible that the charges would be sustained and that the VISTA worker would be tried later in criminal court, the federal judge ruled that there could be no publicity about what took place during the hearing. The press could report that such a hearing was taking place, but that was all. Reporters Gibbs Adams and Larry Dickinson of the *Baton Rouge Morning Advocate and State Times* ignored the order, published a story about the hearing, and were found in criminal contempt and fined three hundred dollars each.

Upon appeal, the United States Court of Appeals for the Fifth Circuit struck down the trial court's no-publicity order but at the same time upheld the contempt convictions. The court cited a 1967 Supreme Court ruling—*Walker* v. *Birmingham*—as precedent. In that case Martin Luther King and seven other clergymen were arrested and held in contempt for violating a Birmingham, Alabama, court injunction banning all marches, parades, sit-ins, and so forth. The High Court ruled that while the ban on marches and parades was unconstitutional, Dr. King and the other defendants should have challenged the ban in court rather than just violate it. The contempt citations stood.

The same logic was applied in the *Dickinson* case. Judge John R. Brown wrote (*U.S.* v. *Dickinson,* 1972):

> The conclusion that the district court's order was constitutionally invalid does not necessarily end the matter of the validity of the contempt convictions. There remains the very formidable questions of whether a person may with impunity violate an order which turns out to be invalid. We hold that in the circumstances of this case he may not.

This decision perplexes many persons who cannot understand why the press, or anyone else for that matter, should be punished for not obeying an order that is not legal in the first place. It is probably best to have Judge Brown explain by quoting a lengthy passage from his opinion in the *Dickinson* case:

> We begin with the well-established principle in proceedings for criminal contempt that an injunction duly issuing out of a court having subject matter and personal jurisdiction *must be obeyed*, irrespective of the ultimate validity of the order. Invalidity is no defense to criminal contempt. "People simply

cannot have the luxury of knowing that they have a right to contest the correctness of the judge's order in deciding whether to wilfully disobey it. . . . Court orders have to be obeyed until they are reversed or set aside in an orderly fashion. . . ."

The criminal-contempt exception requiring compliance with court orders, while invalid nonjudicial directives may be disregarded, is not the product of self-protection or arrogance of judges. Rather it is born of an experience-proved recognition that this rule is essential for the system to work. Judges, after all, are charged with the final responsibility to adjudicate legal disputes. It is the judiciary which is vested with the duty and power to interpret and apply statutory and constitutional law. Determinations take the form of orders. The problem is unique to the judiciary because of its particular role. Disobedience to a legislative pronouncement in no way interferes with the legislature's ability to discharge its responsibilities [passing laws]. The dispute is simply pursued in the judiciary and the legislature is ordinarily free to continue its function unencumbered by any burdens resulting from the disregard of its directives. Similarly, law enforcement is not prevented by failure to convict those who disregard the unconstitutional commands of a policeman.

On the other hand, the deliberate refusal to obey an order of the court without testing its validity through established processes requires further action by the judiciary, and therefore directly affects the judiciary's ability to discharge its duties and responsibilities. Therefore, "while it is sparingly to be used, yet the power of courts to punish for contempts is a necessary and integral part of the independence of the judiciary, and is absolutely essential to the performance of the duties imposed upon them by law. Without it they are mere boards of arbitration whose judgments and decrees would be only advisory."

While most members of the press accept this logic to a point, they argue that the press presents a special case because time is a crucial factor in news gathering. Had the reporters in the *Dickinson* case, for example, not disobeyed the order but instead appealed the decision to a higher court, the trial they were covering would have been over before the restrictive order could have been declared invalid.

Judge Brown said that timeliness is an important aspect of news and that an appellate court should grant a speedy review of such orders. "But newsmen are citizens too," he wrote. "They too may sometimes have to wait. They are not yet wrapped in an immunity or given the absolute right to decide with impunity whether a judge's order is to be obeyed or whether an appellate court is acting promptly enough." Although Judge Brown seemed to see the need for speed, nine months elapsed between the original contempt citation and his ruling in the court of appeals.

The reporters appealed the ruling to the Supreme Court, but the High Court declined to hear the matter. Many authorities interpret the refusal as approval by the Court of the Fifth Circuit Court decision (*U.S. v. Dickinson*, 1972).

The implications of *Dickinson* are rather frightening. In a paper entitled "Judicial Restraints on the Press," Professor Donald Gillmor quotes Dickinson's attorney:

> If the heavy burden which must be borne by the government to support any prior restraint can be met merely by the assertion of the possibility of a conflict . . . between constitutional rights, then freedom of the press as we know it would be held hostage to the fertile imagination of judges.

Labunski reports in an article in the *American University Law Review* that courts in a handful of states have adopted rules relating to the validity of contempt citations based on unconstitutional orders. Courts in Washington and Illinois have rejected the reasoning of the *Dickinson* case and overturned contempt citations based on faulty orders. (See *State ex rel Superior Court* v. *Sperry*, 1971, and *Cooper* v. *Rockford Newspapers*, 1977.) Courts in Arizona (*Phoenix Newspapers* v. *Superior Court*, 1966, and *State* v. *Chavez*, 1979), California (in re *Berry*, 1968), Massachusetts (*Fitchburg* v. *707 Main Corp.*, 1976) and Alabama (*Ex Parte Purvis*, 1980) have also considered the question but have rendered more ambiguous decisions.

A recent case involving the press and the collateral bar rule unfolded in Providence, R.I. when a judge ruled the *Providence Journal* in contempt of court for publishing information about a reputed mob leader that had been obtained from an illegal government wiretap. The FBI had obtained the information illegally in 1962 and, in 1976, a United States court of appeals ruled that publication of the information would constitute an invasion of privacy. The matter arose again in 1985 and, on November 13, Judge Francis Boyle signed an order forbidding the publication of any of the information obtained from the wiretap. The *Providence Journal* published an article containing information from the wiretap on November 14. On November 19, Judge Boyle vacated his order forbidding the publication, acknowledging that it was likely to be found unconstitutional under the First Amendment. On March 17, 1986, however, he held the *Journal* and its editor, Charles Hauser, in contempt of court. He said the order should have been obeyed regardless of its legality. The newspaper was fined $100,000 and Hauser was sentenced to eighteen months probation and ordered to perform two hundred hours of public service work (in re *Providence Journal*, 1986).

The *Journal* appealed the contempt citation and in December of 1986 a three-judge panel of the United States Court of Appeals for the First Circuit ruled that a transparently invalid court order could not serve as the basis for a contempt citation. In other words, the court rejected the *Dickinson* precedent (in re *Providence Journal* 1986). Six months later, however, the entire panel of judges on the First Circuit issued a second ruling, modifying the December ruling. The court did not reverse its earlier decision voiding the contempt citation against the *Journal* and its editor, but added that from now on, publishers or broadcasters should first try to get an appellate review of the order before violating it. The judges said they appreciated the problems that could result by asking a newspaper to appeal an order rather than violate it. By appealing the order, "the right sought to be vindicated could be forfeited or the value of the embargoed information considerably cheapened," the judges noted. However, the court continued, "It is not asking much, beyond some additional expense and time, to require a publisher, even when it thinks it is the subject of a transparently unconstitutional order of prior restraint, to make a good faith effort to seek emergency relief from the appellate courts." If no timely access is available, or no decision is forthcoming, the publisher is free to go ahead and violate the order, knowing the right to later challenge the order will remain. All that is sought, the court said, is a good faith effort (in re *Providence Journal,* 1987). So while the court rejected the precedent from *Dickinson* in the Fifth Circuit, it was not ready to permit publishers and broadcasters to violate court orders, without at least first attempting to get an appellate review.

The ruling was appealed to the United States Supreme Court. Many hoped that with two circuits in obvious disagreement the High Court would settle the issue. But this was not to be. While the justices heard arguments on the case, they dismissed the appeal on a technicality. The special prosecutor who handled the appeal for the government had failed to obtain the proper authorization from the Solicitor General of the United States to petition for a writ of certiorari. "Absent a proper representative of the government as a petitioner in this criminal prosecution, jurisdiction is lacking and the writ of certiorari heretofore granted, is now dismissed," wrote Justice Blackmun for the court's majority (*U.S.* v. *Providence Journal,* 1988). The conflicting rulings by the First and Fifth Circuits therefore still stand.

SUMMARY

The power of a judge to punish for contempt of court is a remnant of the power of English kings. Today, courts have broad powers to punish persons who offend the court, interfere with legal proceedings, or disobey court orders. Contempt is used both to protect the rights of private persons who are litigating matters in the courts, and to punish a wrong committed against the court itself.

Some limits have been placed upon the contempt power. Legislatures often restrict the kinds of sentences judges may impose for contempt or require a jury trial before a contempt conviction. The Supreme Court has ruled that before criticism of a court may be punished by contempt, it must be shown that the criticism created a clear and present danger of the likelihood of interference with the administration of justice. In some jurisdictions appellate courts have ruled that persons must obey even unconstitutional contempt orders (the *Dickinson* rule).

BIBLIOGRAPHY

Here is a list of some of the sources that have been helpful in the preparation of chapter 6:

Books

Confidential Sources and Information. Washington, D.C.: Reporters Committee for Freedom of the Press, 1987.

Goldfarb, Ronald. *The Contempt Power.* New York: Columbia University Press, 1963.

Gordon, David. *Newsman's Privilege and the Law.* Columbia, Mo.: Freedom of Information Center, 1974.

Wigmore, John H. *A Treatise on the Anglo-American System of Evidence in Trials at Common Law.* 2d ed. Boston: Little, Brown & Co., 1934.

Articles

Berger, Robert G. "The 'No Source' Presumption: The Harshest Remedy." 36 *American University Law Review* 603, 1987.

Boyd, J. Kirk. "Legislative Response to *Zurcher v. Stanford Daily.*" 9 *Pepperdine Law Review* 131, 1981.

Chamberlin, Bill. "Protection of Confidential Sources: An Unresolved Issue." 44 *Popular Government* 18, 1978.

Cullen, Brian. "Circumventing *Branzburg:* Absolute Protection for Confidential News Sources." 18 *Suffolk University Law Review* 615, 1984.

Denniston, Lyle. "Court: Leave the Press Alone." *Washington Journalism Review,* June 1988.

Frazer, Douglas H. "The Newsperson's Privilege in Grand Jury Proceedings: An Argument for Uniform Recognition and Application." 75 *Journal of Criminal Law and Criminology* 413, 1984.

Goodale, James C. "*Branzburg v. Hayes* and the Development of a Qualified Privilege for Newsmen." 26 *Hastings Law Review* 709, 1975.

Labunski, Richard E. "The 'Collateral Bar' Rule and the First Amendment: The Constitutionality of Enforcing Unconstitutional Orders." 37 *The American Law Review* 323, 1988.

Lewis, Anthony. "The Big Chill." *The New York Times,* November 15, 1984.

Mullen, Lawrence J. "Developments in the News Media Privilege: The Qualified Constitutional Approach Becoming Common Law." 33 *Maine Law Review* 401, 1981.

Newman, Craig A. "A Qualified Privilege for Journalists *Branzburg v. Hayes:* A Decade Later." 61 *University of Detroit Journal of Urban Law* 463, 1984.

Osborn, John E. "The Reporter's Confidentiality Privilege: Updating the Empirical Evidence After a Decade of Subpoenas." 17 *Columbia Human Rights Law Review* 57, 1985.

Cases

Anderson v. Nixon et al, 444 F.Supp. 1195 (1978).
in re *Berry,* 463 P.2d 273 (1968).
Blair v. U.S., 250 U.S. 273 (1919).
Bloom v. Illinois, 391 U.S. 194 (1964).
Branzburg v. Hayes, 408 U.S. 655 (1972).
Bridges v. California and Times Mirror v. Superior Court, 314 U.S. 252 (1941).
Bursey v. U.S., 466 F.2d 1059 (1972).
Cervantes v. Time, 446 F.2d 986 (1972).
Cheff v. Schnackenberg, 384 U.S. 373 (1966).
Cohen v. Cowles Media, 15 M.L.R. 2288 (1988).
in re *Consumers Union,* 4 M.L.R. 2119 (1978).

Cooper v. *Rockford Newspapers*, 365 N.E.2d 746 (1977).
Craig v. *Harney*, 331 U.S. 367 (1947).
Delaney v. *Superior Court*, 249 Cal. Reptr. 60 (1988).
Democratic National Committee v. *McCord*, 356 F.Supp 1394 (1973).
Dow Jones v. *Superior Court*, 303 N.E.2d 487 (1973).
Fitchburg v. *707 Main Corp.*, 343 N.E.2d 149 (1976).
in re *Grand Jury Investigation*, 15 M.L.R. 1469 (1988).
in re *Grand Jury Subpoena*, 8 M.L.R. 1418 (1982).
in re *Gronowicz*, 750 F.2d 223 (1985).
Hatchard v. *Westinghouse Broadcasting Co.*, 532 A.2d 346 (1987).
Herbert v. *Lando*, 441 U.S. 153 (1979).
Kansas v. *Sandstrom*, 581 P.2d 812 (1978).
Knight-Ridder Broadcasting v. *Greenberg*, 518 N.Y.S.2d 595 (1987).
LaRouche v. *NBC*, 780 F.2d 1134 (1986).
McGraw-Hill v. *Arizona*, 680 F.2d 5 (1982).
Maine v. *Hohler*, 15 M.L.R. 1611 (1988).
New York v. *Bova*, 118 Misc.2d 14 (1983).
Ex Parte Nugent, 16 F.Cas. 471 (1848).
Ny504 U.S., 313 U.S. 33 (1941).
Oregon ex rel Meyer v. *Howell*, 86 Or.App. 570 (1987).
in re *Pappas*, 266 N.E.2d 297 (1971).
Pennekamp v. *Florida*, 328 U.S. 331 (1946).
Phoenix Newspapers v. *Superior Court*, 418 P.2d 594 (1966).
in re *Powers*, 4 M.L.R. 1600 (1978).
in re *Providence Journal*, 630 F.Supp. 993 (1986); 820 F.2d 1354 (1987).
Ex Parte Purvis, 382 So.2d 512 (1980).
Reiss v. *Harris*, No. 72454 (Idaho District Court, Ada County, 1980).
Reporter's Committee v. *AT&T*, 593 F.2d 1030 (1982).
Riley v. *Chester*, 612 F.2d 708 (1979).
in re *Schuman*, 537 A.2d 297 (1988).
Senear v. *Daily Journal-American*, 641 P.2d 1180 (1982).
Silkwood v. *Kerr-McKee*, 563 F.2d 433 (1977).
State v. *Chavez*, 601 P.2d 301 (1979).
State ex rel Superior Court v. *Sperry*, 483 P.2d 608 (1971).
State v. *Rinaldo*, 684 P.2d 608 (1984).
Storer Communications v. *Giovan*, 810 F.2d 580 (1987).
Toledo Newspaper Co. v. *U.S.*, 247 U.S. 402 (1918).
U.S. v. *Barnett*, 376 U.S. 681 (1964).
U.S. v. *Blanton*, 534 F.Supp. 295 (1982).
United States v. *Burke*, 700 F.2d 70 (1983).
U.S. v. *Criden*, 633 F.2d 346 (1980).
U.S. v. *Dickinson*, 465 F.2d 496 (1972).
U.S. v. *LaRouche Campaign*, 841 F.2d 1176 (1988).
U.S. v. *Providence Journal*, 108 S.Ct. 1502 (1988).
Walker v. *Birmingham*, 388 U.S. 307 (1967).
Zurcher v. *Stanford Daily*, 436 U.S. 547 (1978).

7 FREE PRESS AND FAIR TRIAL

In the past forty years the American judicial system has played an increasingly important role, both in our government and in our society. The number of laws, judges, courtrooms, and lawyers has risen dramatically at a pace far faster than the growth in American population over the same period. News about the criminal and civil justice systems has increasingly become grist for the information mills of the mass media. What is happening at the courthouse has become a staple of American journalism, a big story in many instances. But by focusing the spotlight of publicity upon the judicial system, the press has generated considerable tension in that community. Many believe that there is too much publicity, especially concerning crime. Others think the publicity is too intense, unrelenting at times. Many participants in the judicial process are brought there against their will. Jurors, witnesses, victims, and defendants often complain of invasions of privacy and intimidation as the news media attempt to relay to readers and viewers what is taking place.

An even more serious difficulty can result if massive press coverage of a criminal case results in deep and bitter prejudice against a defendant. At this point the dispute often takes on the dimensions of a constitutional dilemma. The Sixth Amendment promises criminal defendants a trial by an impartial jury. If jurors are selected from a community saturated with publicity about a case, can they be impartial? Can they decide the case solely on the facts presented during the trial? What should the court do? Stop the press from publishing this kind of information? Limit press access to information about the case? This sort of solution can run afoul of the First Amendment, the constitutional guarantee of freedom of expression.

Is a free press preferable to a fair trial? Or should we provide judges with the power and independence to control the press to insure that all those accused may enjoy a fair trial? United States Supreme Court Justice Felix Frankfurter argued in 1946 that we must have both:

> A free press is not to be preferred to an independent judiciary, nor an independent judiciary to a free press. Neither has primacy over the other; both are indispensable to a free society. The freedom of the press in itself presupposes an independent judiciary through which that freedom may, if necessary, be vindicated. And one of the potent means for assuring judges their independence is a free press (*Pennekamp* v. *Florida*).

As judicial activity in the United States has increased in the past four decades, and as press coverage of this activity has grown accordingly, the problem of balancing the rights of the press and the rights of criminal defendants and others enmeshed in the judicial system has become more difficult. In this chapter the dimensions of these problems and probable solutions to them are outlined.

351

First, the kinds of publicity many persons believe to be harmful to defendants are discussed, along with evaluation of the extent to which the mass media can in fact interfere with the trial process. In the remainder of the chapter the many schemes and ideas either proposed or enacted to solve the problem are outlined. It must again be remembered that in the free press–fair trial controversy, fifty-one different judicial systems are involved. That is, while the problem is clearly national, the solutions tend to be local or regional in scope. Consequently, generalizations about such a complex issue can sometimes be misleading. Reporters and broadcasters are urged to investigate the specific rules applicable to their state regarding publication of material about the judicial process. A simple way to do this is to talk to judges, members of bar associations, and veteran reporters. ◆

PREJUDICIAL CRIME REPORTING

It is quite easy to find examples of the kinds of news stories that many people believe might prejudice potential jurors. For example, the *Los Angeles Times* ran a story a few years ago beginning this way:

> A television sportscaster, Stan Duke, shot and killed a radio commentator, Averill Berman, early Sunday at the Wilshire District home of Duke's estranged wife, police reported. Duke was booked on suspicion of murder.

Readers probably wondered why Duke was arrested for suspicion of murder when it was patently obvious from reading the lead that Duke had committed the crime—or had according to the *Los Angeles Times*. Under the American system of justice a person is presumed innocent until proved guilty. In other words the state had to prove that Duke shot and killed Berman.

A newspaper in Washington State ran a far less sensational story, but in its own way it could have been even more damaging. The *Yakima Herald-Republic* headlined the story: "Innocent Not Tried, Claims Prosecutor." The first sentence stated, " 'Because of the screening process built into the criminal justice system in this county, innocent men never go to trial,' John Moore, Yakima County Deputy Prosecutor, said Wednesday." The people of that county probably spent a considerable amount of time wondering why they had courts at all if only the guilty went to trial. All that was really needed was an administrator of some kind to hand out sentences and fines.

The first story was written in the flush of journalistic excitement brought on by a sensational murder. The second story was written by a reporter who should have challenged the outrageous statement on the spot. Numerous other specific examples can be cited, but probably a better idea is to summarize the kinds of information many people agree can possibly interfere with the defendant's right to a fair trial. The following was taken from lists published by the American Bar Association and various state press-bench-bar committees.

1. Confessions or stories about the confession that a defendant is said to have made, including even alluding to the fact that there may be a confession. The Fifth Amendment says that a person does not have to testify against him or herself. Therefore a confession given to police may be subsequently retracted and often cannot be used against the defendant at the trial.

2. Stories about the defendant's performance on a test, such as a polygraph, or lie detector, or similar device, and about the defendant's refusal to take such a test. Most of this information is not permitted at the trial.

3. Stories about the defendant's past criminal record or that describe the defendant as a former convict. This information is not permitted at the trial. It may seem entirely logical to some people that when someone has committed ninety-nine robberies and is again arrested for robbery the accused probably did commit the crime. As a matter of fact, past behavior is immaterial in the current trial for robbery. The state must prove that the defendant committed *this* robbery.

4. Stories that question the credibility of witnesses and contain the personal feelings of witnesses about prosecutors, police, victims, or even judges. To illustrate: in the Sam Sheppard case, which will be discussed a little later, the judge was quoted as telling a reporter—before the trial started—that he thought Sam Sheppard was "guilty as hell," and the remark was published (*Sheppard* v. *Maxwell,* 1966).

5. Stories about the defendant's character (he or she hates children and dogs), associates (he or she hangs around with known syndicate gunmen), and personality (he or she attacks people on the slightest provocation).

6. Stories that tend to inflame the public mood against the defendant. Such stories include editorial campaigns that demand the arrest of a suspect before sufficient evidence has been collected; person-on-the-street interviews concerning the guilt of the defendant or the kind of punishment that should be meted out after the accused is convicted; televised debates about the evidence of the guilt or innocence of the defendant. All of these kinds of stories put the jury in the hot seat, as well as circulate vast quantities of misinformation.

Stories like these are less common today than they were half a century ago. Journalists tend to be much more careful about what they write and broadcast than they were in the heyday of police reporters, the first thirty years of this century. But such stories still occur too often. News of crime is a staple of local television news, where stations often use stories about the lurid in order to lure viewers to their channel. In daily newspapers, more serious stories about politics, government, world affairs and the environment usually push news of crime to the back page. But when a big case breaks, newspapers commonly descend upon it with a missionary zeal. Mass killings, sexual violence, serial murders are all prominently featured.

The first question that must be asked is whether intensive publicity about a criminal case does in fact jeopardize the right of the defendant in the case to enjoy a fair trial. Is the pool of jurors poisoned in such a way as to undermine the impartiality of the judicial process? This is a tough question, and one that has not yet been answered satisfactorily. Let's look at what we do know.

Impact on Jurors

For more than twenty-five years, social scientists have attempted to systematically examine the question of the impact of published prejudicial material on potential jurors. A major difficulty in this research has been the inability of the researchers to study the behavior of real jurors in actual trials. The law will not permit this. (Recently a judge in Milwaukee, Wisconsin, permitted a Public Broadcasting Service television crew to record jury deliberations and then broadcast a condensed version of the discussions on the *Frontline* series. This was a one-time event, however.) So researchers have instead conducted two kinds of studies: experiments in which they attempt to duplicate the trial process and surveys in which they interview nonjurors about actual crimes and criminal news.

The experiments have ranged from simple to elaborate and have often established some relationship between exposure to prejudicial material and the subject's increased willingness to find a hypothetical defendant guilty of a crime. But the findings are seriously flawed. The ersatz jurors know they are a part of an experiment; a real-life defendant's freedom or even life is not on the line. There is no robed judge to admonish these subjects to decide the case solely on the basis of the evidence presented at the trial and to insist that they ignore anything else they might have seen or read about the case. This is an important factor. In the single jury study done in recent times with real jurors and real trials, the researcher—Harry Kalven of the University of Chicago—reported, "We do . . . have evidence that jurors take with surprising seriousness the admonition [from the judge] not to read the paper or discuss the case with other people." The research cited by Kalven was part of a massive 1954 study in which actual jury deliberations were secretly recorded and studied. (Revelation of these practices prompted rules that permanently foreclosed the use of actual juries in such cases.) Finally, in real life a juror is not given newspaper articles about a defendant and then asked to judge that person guilty or innocent. This is what happened in the experiments and is patently phony. A trial, often a lengthy trial, will intervene in real life. So the experimental setting has been simply too unrealistic to determine whether or not the publication of prejudicial material may in fact cause problems for a defendant in real life.

Surveys conducted in some communities before the beginning of a major trial suggest that most persons are not affected by the publication of prejudicial pretrial material. Nearly two hundred persons were interviewed in one study before a sensational murder trial began in North Carolina, for example.

Only twenty-three percent of the persons contacted said they believed the defendant in the case was guilty. One-fifth of the persons surveyed told researchers they had never even heard about the case before. Similar results were obtained in similar studies.

This whole question is complicated today by research on other aspects of mass media that suggests we tend to remember far less of what we see and hear on television and what we read in the newspaper than many people might presume. Advertising research has demonstrated this for years; and recently, researchers at the University of Maryland found that a significant percentage of the one thousand persons they telephoned could not remember news stories that had been prominently reported only the week before the interview. In summary, the research we have does not support the argument that prejudicial publicity will damage the right of a defendant to a fair trial in every case. In a medium-to-large urban setting, it would indeed be rare if a jury of twelve citizens could not be found who knew little, even about a sensational crime, or who could not render a verdict based solely on the evidence presented in court. (See Pember, "Does Pretrial Publicity Really Hurt?") This is a fact that some courts are beginning to acknowledge. The United States Court of Appeals for the Ninth Circuit recently reversed an order by a trial court barring access by the press and public to certain pretrial documents in a highly publicized case. The court of appeals agreed that there had been massive publicity about the case, but noted that "Pretrial publicity does not, however, lead in every criminal case to an unfair trial." The judges added that "prejudicial publicity is less likely to endanger the defendant's right to a fair trial in a large metropolitan area such as Seattle" (*Seattle Times* v. *U.S. District Court,* 1988).

The Law and Prejudicial News

The definition of an impartial juror used by the courts in the United States is about 180 years old and stems from a ruling by Chief Justice John Marshall in the trial of Aaron Burr. Charges that the jurors were biased were made at the trial. In 1807 Marshall proclaimed that an impartial juror was one free from the dominant influence of knowledge acquired outside the courtroom, free from strong and deep impressions that close the mind. *"Light impressions,"* Marshall wrote, *"which may fairly be supposed to yield to the testimony that may be offered, which leave the mind open to a fair consideration of that testimony, constitute no sufficient objection to a juror . . ."* [author emphasis] (*U.S.* v. *Burr,* 1807).

While this definition is fairly precise, modern courts nevertheless have to cope with the problem of applying the definition to specific situations. It is appellate courts that most often must apply Marshall's definition to cases in which convicted defendants ask for a reversal on the grounds that the jury is not impartial, as guaranteed by the Sixth Amendment. Indeed, reversal is one important remedy the judicial system uses to cope with prejudicial publicity, that is, to simply reverse the guilty verdict and require that the defendant be retried.

Appellate courts appear to consider several factors in determining whether the defendant's trial was fair and impartial. Was there publicity about the case? Was the publicity prejudicial? Is there evidence that the jurors saw the prejudicial publicity? What kinds of information were contained in the publicity? It is not a simple task to uncover the answers to many of these questions, and not surprisingly, different courts often reach opposite conclusions in cases that appear to have similar facts. But even small differences in the facts can be important. For example, a United States court of appeals ruled in 1951 that a defendant's right to a fair trial was not damaged simply because a newspaper containing information about the case was found in a jury room. The judge had told the jury to disregard the contents of the news story and there was no evidence presented to the contrary (*Leviton* v. *U.S.*, 1951). Eight years later, however, the United States Supreme Court overturned a criminal conviction when evidence was presented that jurors had seen stories in newspapers, which were found in the courtroom, about a defendant's prior criminal record. The jurors told the judge they had read the stories but vowed they could decide the case solely on the evidence presented in court. The nation's High Court said it was not reasonable to believe that the jurors could be impartial in such a case (*Marshall* v. *U.S.*, 1959).

Appellate courts also pay attention to what the jurors tell judges in the pretrial questioning (voir dire) when they are asked about their knowledge of the case. Compare how the Supreme Court resolved these two appeals.

Leslie Irvin was arrested in connection with a series of sex murders. Statements that Irvin had confessed to all six killings received widespread publicity. At the trial, of 430 persons called as potential jurors, 375 told the judge that they believed Irvin was guilty. Of the twelve jurors finally selected, eight told the court they thought he was guilty before the trial started. The Supreme Court overturned the conviction, noting that in this case, in which so many persons so many times admitted prejudice, statements of impartiality could be given little weight (*Irvin* v. *Dowd*, 1961).

Fourteen years later Jack Murphy, the original "Murph the Surf," appealed his conviction for robbery and assault on the grounds that the jury had been prejudiced by extensive publicity about his previous criminal record and other extralegal exploits. The Supreme Court disagreed. Only twenty of the seventy-eight potential jurors who were questioned told the Florida trial judge they believed Murphy was guilty. The High Court said that this was not comparable to the evidence of hostility or overwhelming prejudice toward the defendant that was found in the Irvin case. The Constitution requires that the defendant have a "panel of impartial, indifferent jurors," ruled Justice Thurgood Marshall; "they need not, however, be totally ignorant of the facts and issues involved." It is sufficient that a juror can lay aside his or her impressions and personal opinions and render a considered opinion based on the evidence presented in court. Many people see this 1975 ruling in *Murphy* v. *Florida* as rejecting the often-asserted principle that publicity about a criminal case automatically results in bias toward the defendant.

In looking at the scores of decisions by appellate courts, one is persuaded that judges seem to have greater faith in jurors and the jury system than many social scientists who have studied these issues. Whether this is misplaced faith may never be known. Perhaps the answer is to be found in Professor Walter Wilcox's rhetorical question, "Could it be that the American jury confounds all the subtle nuances of the behavioral sciences and simply does its duty?" (in *Free Press and Fair Trial*, ed. Chilton R. Bush).

SUMMARY

The First Amendment to the United States Constitution guarantees freedom of the press; the Sixth Amendment guarantees every criminal defendant a fair trial. Many people believe these two amendments are in conflict because, often, publicity about a criminal case can prejudice a community against a defendant and make it impossible to find a fair and impartial jury in the case. The kinds of publicity that can be most damaging to a defendant include material about confessions or alleged confessions, stories about a past criminal record, statements about the defendant's character, and comments about the defendant's performance on scientific tests or refusal to take such tests.

Social science has not yet proved that such publicity does in fact create prejudice or that persons cannot set aside their beliefs about a case and render a verdict based on the facts presented at the trial. An impartial juror is not required to be free of all knowledge or impressions about a case; the juror must be free of deep impressions and beliefs that will not yield to the evidence that is presented in court during the trial.

COMPENSATING FOR PRETRIAL PUBLICITY

The law has many ways to minimize or even to eliminate the problem of prejudicial publicity in a criminal case. As a last resort a criminal conviction can be reversed by an appellate court if there is evidence that the trial was tainted by publicity.

Retrials cost the taxpayers money; considerable inconvenience results for witnesses, attorneys, and other participants. Defendants face continued hardship from uncertainty or even jail if they have not been released on bail. Most persons concerned with this problem consider reversal a remedy of last resort—something to do if all else fails.

Other remedies are considered far better in attempting to solve the problems that could result from pretrial publicity. These remedies fall into two broad categories:

1. Remedies that can be used by the trial court to compensate for the publication or broadcast of prejudicial publicity.
2. Remedies aimed at controlling the amount and kind of information that might be broadcast or published.

The remedies in the first category have existed for a long time and can be applied by trial judges with little difficulty in most instances. These include delaying the trial, moving the trial, carefully questioning the jurors to determine their biases, and other means. The impact upon both the judicial system and the press tends to be minimal when such remedies are applied.

The remedies in the second category can be more drastic and can cause serious problems, especially for the press. These remedies include issuing orders specifically limiting what can be published or broadcast, issuing orders that forbid participants in the trial process from talking about the case, and even barring public and press access to judicial records and proceedings. This latter category also includes nonbinding bench-bar-press guidelines, which have been adopted in many states. A close examination of all these remedies follows.

Traditional Judicial Remedies

Trial judges have at their disposal a battery of procedural tools that can be used to alleviate the impact of prejudicial publicity.

Voir Dire

Before prospective jurors finally make it to the jury box, they must pass a series of hurdles erected both by the attorneys in the case and the judge. These hurdles are designed to protect the judicial process from jurors who have already made up their minds about the case or who have strong biases toward one litigant or the other. In a process called **voir dire,** each prospective juror is questioned prior to being impaneled in an effort to discover bias. Pretrial publicity is only one source of juror prejudice. If the prospective juror is the mother of a police officer, she is likely to be biased if the defendant is on trial for shooting a police officer. Perhaps the juror is a business associate of the defendant. Possibly the juror has read extensively about the case in the newspapers and believes the police are trying to frame the defendant.

Both sides in the case question the jurors and both sides can ask the court to excuse a juror. This procedure is called challenging a juror. There are two kinds of challenges: **challenges for cause** and **peremptory challenges.** To challenge a juror for cause, an attorney must convince the court that there is a good reason for this person not to sit on the jury. Deep-seated prejudice is one good reason. Being an acquaintance of one of the parties in the case is also a good reason. Any reason can be used to challenge a potential juror. All the attorney must do is to convince the judge that the reason is proper. There is no limit on the number of challenges for cause that both prosecutor and defense attorney may exercise.

A peremptory challenge is somewhat different. This challenge can be exercised without cause, and the judge has no power to refuse such a challenge. There is a limit, however, on the number of such challenges that may be exercised. Sometimes there are as few as two or three and sometimes as many as ten or twenty, depending upon the case, the kind of crime involved, the state statute, and sometimes the judge. This kind of challenge is reserved for use against persons whom the defense or the prosecution does not want on the jury but whom the judge refuses to excuse for cause. An attorney may have an intuitive hunch about a potential juror and want that person eliminated from the final panel. Or the juror's social or ethnic background may suggest a problem to the attorney. In obscenity trials, for example, defense attorneys often look for persons with a college background, especially a liberal arts background; persons who are independent in their life-style, those who have had some exposure to pornography; and persons who have some artistic inclination. Studies have shown that Asian-Americans tend to be more tolerant of pornography than other ethnic groups. The prosecutor in an obscenity trial on the other hand, will look for other kinds of jurors. Less-educated jurors are more desirable, as are those with a religious background and persons who live close to the place where the pornographic material is distributed. Hispanic-Americans tend to be less tolerant of obscenity than most persons. An attorney will use the peremptory challenges to try to build the kind of jury he or she seeks. (See Seymour Wishman's *Anatomy of a Jury* for an interesting discussion of the elements involved in jury selection.)

Is voir dire a good way to screen prejudiced jurors? Seventy-nine percent of a large group of judges surveyed by Professor Emeritus Fred Siebert of Michigan State University said (in *Free Press and Fair Trial,* ed. Chilton R. Bush) that the questioning process was either highly effective or moderately effective in screening biased jurors. Most trial lawyers also agree, to a point. It is difficult, however, to argue with critics who say that voir dire uncovers only the prejudice that the prospective juror is aware of or is not too embarrassed to admit. Biased jurors can lie when questioned about their biases. They may not even know their minds are made up about the defendant's guilt. But these kinds of objections attack the root of the entire jury system. The only way to find jurors who are not biased in even a small way is to lock up babies when they are born and raise them as jurors, isolate them from the rest of the world until they are adults, and then release them to act only as jurors at trials. Nobody wants this kind of system. The faith that most persons have in the effectiveness of voir dire is comparable to their faith in the entire jury system.

Change of Venue

Many judges and legal authorities describe a **change of venue** as an effective means of dealing with massive pretrial publicity. Imagine for a moment that John Smith is arrested for a series of six brutal murders committed in River City over a period of six weeks and highly publicized by the local press. When Smith is arrested, the local news media saturate the community with stories about the killings, about the arrest, and about Smith. Day after day the newspapers and broadcasting stations focus on one new angle after another. Soon most of the people in River City know a tremendous amount about the suspect's past. One means to compensate for such publicity about a defendant in the community in which the crime takes place is to move the trial to another community. This procedure is called a change of venue. While the people in River City may be prejudiced against Smith by virtue of the reports in the news media, the people across the state in Ames may be ignorant of the matter.

Therefore, the trial, including the prosecutor and the defense attorney, the defendant, the judges, the witnesses, and assorted other trial participants, can be moved to Ames for the month or two of its duration. The jury will be selected from a panel of people who live in Ames. Seventy-seven percent of the judges surveyed think a change of venue is highly effective or moderately effective in controlling prejudicial publicity (*Free Press and Fair Trial*).

Change of venue is costly. Witnesses, attorneys, and other persons must be transported and housed and fed while the trial takes place in a distant city. The defendant must surrender the constitutional right to a trial in the district in which the crime was committed. Publicity about the case could appear in the media located in the community in which the trial is scheduled to be held, defeating the purpose of the change of venue. Often the effectiveness of the change of venue depends upon how far the trial is moved from the city in which the crime was committed. A trial judge in Washington State who was concerned about newspaper coverage of a local murder case granted a change of venue. But he moved the trial to an adjoining county, the only other county in the state in which the "offending" newspaper had significant circulation. The move accomplished very little, and the judge ultimately was forced to close portions of the proceedings to the press (*Federated Publications* v. *Kurtz,* 1980). Used wisely, a change of venue can be an effective device to protect the defendant's right to a fair trial, especially for crimes committed in rural counties where the number of potential jurors is small and where news often travels faster by word of mouth than through the mass media.

In some states it is possible for the defense to seek a change of veniremen rather than a change of venue. Instead of moving the trial to another city, the court will import a jury panel from a distant community. The judge and attorneys will visit the distant city, select a jury panel, and then transport the jurors to the community in which the trial will be held. This will cost the state less money, since all it must do is pay the expenses of twelve jurors for the duration of the trial.

Continuance

When a trial is continued, or a *continuance* is granted, the trial is delayed. By postponing a trial for weeks or even months, a judge expects that the people in the community will forget at least some of what has been written or broadcast about the case, and that is probably a legitimate expectation. However, before a trial may be postponed the defendant must sacrifice his or her right to a speedy trial, something guaranteed under the Constitution. Because the courtrooms in America are clogged, there are few truly speedy trials today, but a continuance delays a trial even longer. The defendant may spend this additional time in jail if bail has not been posted. It is also possible, even likely, then when the trial is finally set to begin, publicity about the case will reappear in the mass media.

But a continuance is a perfect solution in some cases. A judge told of how, just as he was scheduled to begin hearing a malpractice suit on a Monday morning, the Sunday paper, quite innocently, carried a long feature story on the skyrocketing costs of physicians' malpractice insurance because of the large judgments handed down in courts. The article pointed out that physicians passed the additional charges along to patients. The story was widely read. Jurors, who also pay doctors' bills, might hesitate to award a judgment to an injured patient knowing that it would raise insurance rates and ultimately cost patients more. The judge therefore continued the case for two months to let the story fade from the public mind.

Admonition to the Jury

Once a jury is impaneled, its members are instructed by the judge to render their verdict in the case solely on the basis of the evidence presented in the courtroom. Judges believe that most jurors take this **admonition** quite seriously. Jurors are also warned not to read newspaper stories or watch television broadcasts about the case while the trial is being held. Often jurors are excused from the courtroom while the trial judge hears arguments from the attorneys or even testimony from witnesses. In such instances the court usually wants to determine whether certain evidence is admissible in the case before the evidence is presented to the jury. The press may publish or broadcast reports about this evidence, whether or not it is admitted in the case. It would accomplish very little to keep such evidence from the jury during the trial if jurors could watch news stories about it during the evening television newscasts.

The following admonition, which is one used by King County, Washington, superior court judges, is typical:

> Do not discuss this case or any criminal case or any criminal matter among yourselves or with anyone else. Do not permit anyone to discuss such subjects with you or in your presence. . . . Do not read, view, or listen to any report in a newspaper, radio, or television on the subject of this trial or any other criminal trial. Do not permit anyone to read about or comment on this trial or any criminal trial to you or in your presence.

There is evidence that jurors follow these instructions closely. In the single major study in which real jury deliberations were examined to determine the impact of mass media publicity on the trial process, researchers found that jurors listen carefully to the cautionary instructions given to them by judges. The coordinator of that research project, Harry Kalven, noted in a letter to the director of the American Law Institute:

> We do . . . have evidence that the jurors take with surprising seriousness the admonition not to read the paper or discuss the case with other people. . . . Our overall impression . . . is that the jury is a pretty stubborn, healthy institution not likely to be overwhelmed either by a remark of counsel or a remark in the press.

For cases in which a high level of publicity is expected, publicity that might prove hard for a jury to avoid, the court has another device: **sequestration of the jury,** which means that once it is impaneled, the jury is put into seclusion. Jurors eat together, are housed at state expense at a hotel or motel, and are not permitted to visit with friends and relatives. Phone calls are screened, as is contact with the mass media. Jurors are allowed to read newspapers only after court officials delete stories that could be objectionable.

Sequestration is a costly process for both the state and the jurors. Sequestration for three or four days might be a lark, but the trials in which juries are normally sequestered are long trials, sometimes lasting as long as six months. Life can be seriously disrupted. The number of people who can afford the loss of income involved in such a situation is limited.

Although sequestered jurors are free from prejudicial publicity, attorneys fear the long quarantine produces a different kind of prejudice—prejudice against one or the other of the two sides in the case—wrought from keeping jurors away from friends and family for so long. Defense attorneys express this fear most often, feeling that jurors will tend to hold the defendant responsible for the inconvenience and therefore vote for conviction.

SUMMARY

Trial courts have many ways to compensate for the prejudicial pretrial publicity in a criminal case. Each citizen is questioned by the attorneys and the judge before being accepted as a juror. During this voir dire examination, questions can be asked of the potential jurors about the kinds of information they already know about the case. Persons who have already made up their minds about the defendant's guilt or innocence can be excluded from the jury.

Courts have the power to move a trial to a distant county to find a jury that has not been exposed to the publicity about the case that has been generated by local mass media. While such a change of venue can be costly, it can also be an effective means of compensating for sensational publicity about a case.

A trial can be delayed until the publicity about the case dies down. The defendant must waive the right to a speedy trial but, except in highly sensational cases, granting a continuance in a trial can thwart the impact of the massive publicity often generated in the wake of a serious crime.

Jurors are always admonished by the judge to base their decision on the facts presented in court and not to read or view any news stories about the case while they are on the jury. There is evidence that they take these warnings quite seriously.

In important cases it is always possible to seclude, or sequester, the jury after it is chosen to shield it from publicity about the trial.

The remedies just outlined have been used by trial judges for decades to reduce or eliminate the impact of prejudicial publicity. These remedies do not stop the publication of information about a criminal or civil case. Instead, they are used to compensate for the publication of prejudicial material. Such remedies are favored by the press because they have no direct impact upon the mass media.

However, many persons in the legal profession believe that compensating for publicity is a rather costly and sloppy way to solve the free press–fair trial dilemma. These compensatory remedies often create headaches for judges (extensive voir dire) or for trial participants (continuance, change of venue). They invariably cost all parties—especially the state—extra money, and they do not always completely compensate for massive publicity about a case, especially a sensational criminal case. Would it not be better if the press did not publish prejudicial information in the first place?

Agreements that attempt to limit certain kinds of publicity about criminal cases have been reached between the press and the courts in many states. These bench-bar-press guidelines are an effort to amicably resolve the free press–fair trial problem (these guidelines are discussed on pages 382–83).

But courts have also attempted other, more coercive means to limit publicity about criminal cases. Some trial judges have prohibited the press from publishing certain information about criminal cases. Violation of these orders, called restrictive orders by lawyers and judges and **gag orders** by journalists, can result in a citation for contempt of court. Other judges have barred journalists and other persons from attending pretrial hearings, and even trials, to keep information that might prejudice a jury out of the hands of reporters. No other aspect of mass media law has sparked more controversy in the past ten years than the restrictive-order–closed-courtroom issue. Since 1976 the Supreme Court of the United States has focused upon one or another aspect of this issue no less than ten times. This section of the text outlines these attempts to control the publication of information about criminal and civil matters. Restrictive orders are examined first; then the matter of closed courtrooms is discussed. Finally, we will outline the dimensions of bench-bar-press guidelines.

RESTRICTIVE ORDERS TO CONTROL PUBLICITY

Can a trial judge constitutionally forbid the press from publishing information about a criminal case that it has obtained legally? The answer is yes, a judge can issue an order restricting the news media from publishing prejudicial pretrial information. But such a **restrictive order** can be issued only when there is evidence that publication of the material will create a clear and present danger of interfering with the defendant's right to a trial by an impartial jury. The Supreme Court has ruled that such a restriction is permissible only if the judge has determined that "the gravity of the evil, discounted by its improbability, justifies such an invasion of free speech as is necessary to avoid the danger" (*Nebraska Press Association* v. *Stuart,* 1976). In order for such an order to be issued, there must be sufficient evidence to reasonably conclude that the following conditions prevail:

1. Intense and pervasive publicity concerning the case is certain.
2. No other alternative measure—such as a change of venue or continuance or extensive voir dire process—is likely to mitigate the effects of the pretrial publicity.
3. The restrictive order will in fact effectively prevent prejudicial material from reaching potential jurors.

Theoretically, then, a judge can bar the press from reporting on certain aspects of a trial. Practically, however, it is almost impossible for a judge to issue such an order today. It is simply too tough for a judge to meet the three-part Supreme Court test. In only a handful of instances in the past ten years has an appellate court permitted a gag order aimed at the press to stand. (See *KUTV* v. *Wilkinson,* 1984 for example.) Before examining the contemporary gag orders let's look at why such judicial tools developed in the past twenty years. Our story begins with a bizarre murder case that in turn provided the inspiration for one of the nation's most popular television series of the midsixties, "The Fugitive," starring David Janssen.

The *Sheppard* Case

Sam Sheppard, a prominent Ohio osteopath, was arrested for the bludgeoning death of his wife Marilyn. The doctor professed his innocence in the case, claiming that an intruder had entered their home at night, knocked him unconscious, and killed his wife. The Sheppard story broke during a slow-news Fourth of July weekend in 1954 and immediately caught the fancy of the nation's press. The publicity in the case was massive, far more extensive than the simple slaying merited. The coroner's inquest was held in a school gymnasium and broadcast live to the community. Debates were held about Sheppard's guilt or innocence. At the trial the press—much of it national rather than local press—dominated the courtroom. Participants in the case—police, prosecutors, defense attorneys, and witnesses—appeared to try to outdo themselves in offering extraneous, often outrageous, statements to reporters, who dutifully published these comments. One appellate court later described the trial as a Roman holiday for the press, an orgy of sensation. Sheppard was convicted.

The United States Supreme Court rejected Sam Sheppard's first appeal, in which he argued that his trial was prejudiced by the massive publicity. But years later, in 1966, the High Court agreed to hear the doctor's plea. In a stinging rebuke of trial Judge Blythin, the Court reversed Sam Sheppard's conviction for murder.*

*The state of Ohio chose to reprosecute Sheppard twelve years after the crime, but this time the middle-aged doctor was acquitted. Sheppard, who failed to reestablish his osteopathic career, died several years later.

Justice Tom Clark, who wrote the Supreme Court's opinion in the *Sheppard* case, came down hard on the press, noting that bedlam reigned during the trial and that "newsmen took over practically the entire courtroom, hounding most of the participants in the trial, especially Sheppard. . . ." Justice Clark saved his sharpest criticism for Judge Blythin, who conducted the trial, and the other officers of the court for allowing the publicity about the case and the coverage of the trial to get out of hand. Here are some excerpts from Clark's opinion (*Sheppard* v. *Maxwell*, 1966):

> Bearing in mind the massive pretrial publicity, the judge should have adopted stricter rules governing the use of the courtroom by newsmen . . . the court should have insulated witnesses [from the media]. . . . The court should have made some effort to control the release of leads, information and gossip to the press by police officers, witnesses and the counsel for both sides. . . . And it is obvious that the judge should have further sought to alleviate this problem by imposing control over the statements made to the news media by counsel, witnesses, and especially the coroner and police officers. . . . The court might well have proscribed extrajudicial statements by any lawyer, party, witness or court official which divulged prejudicial matters . . . the court could also have requested the appropriate city and county officials to promulgate a regulation with respect to dissemination of information about the case by their employees. In addition, reporters who wrote or broadcast prejudicial stories could have been warned as to the impropriety of publishing material not introduced in the proceedings.

The Supreme Court made it quite clear in the *Sheppard* decision that it holds the trial judge responsible for ensuring that the defendant's rights are not jeopardized by prejudicial press publicity. While the Court was critical of the press's behavior, no suggestion was made that the judicial system launch an attack on the press. Nevertheless, at a meeting following the decision, a professor of law, in explaining the High Court's opinion in *Sheppard*, suggested that the Court had proposed that judges use the contempt power to control the press. Justice Clark, who was at the same meeting, told the assembled trial lawyers that the professor misinterpreted the court's ruling (Friendly and Goldfarb, *Crime and Publicity*):

> The Court never held up contempt and it may well be that it will never hold up contempt because the restraint is too stringent. . . . The Court's opinion never mentioned any guidelines for the press. . . . I am not proposing that you jerk a newspaper reporter into the courtroom and hold him in contempt. We do not have to jeopardize freedom of the press.

As we will see shortly, the remarks by Justice Clark were soon forgotten.

Restrictive Orders and the First Amendment

Two years after the ruling in *Sheppard* v. *Maxwell*, the American Bar Association (ABA) proposed that trial judges use court orders to control the public statements and activities of the many participants in a trial—the prosecutor, witnesses, defense attorneys, jurors, and others. The bar association also recommended that judges use the contempt power against any persons who knowingly violated a valid judicial order not to disseminate information about the case. No state court system ever officially adopted the ABA recommendations, but the suggestions were taken to heart by many individual judges. Restrictive court orders became a common tool for a judge who sought to control the publicity about a pending criminal trial. One observer estimated that in the ten years between 1966 and 1976, trial courts issued almost 175 restrictive orders, 39 of which prohibited the press from reporting or commenting on some aspect of a pending criminal case. In addition, nearly all of the federal courts adopted standing orders regarding publicity in criminal cases.

Use of Restrictive
Orders

There is no such thing as a typical restrictive order; in fact, that is one of the virtues seen in them by judges. Each order can be fashioned to fit the case at hand. They often tend to be quite comprehensive. Orders aimed at the press usually limit the press coverage of certain specific details about a case; a defendant's confession or prior criminal record, for example. Orders aimed at the participants in a trial are usually much broader, forbidding comments by attorneys, witnesses, and others about any aspect of the case. In 1975 another sensational murder trial began, one that would ultimately bring the issue of pretrial publicity and gag orders before the Supreme Court.

Erwin Simants was arrested and charged in North Platte, Nebraska, with the murder of all six members of the Henry Kellie family. Like the *Sheppard* case, the arrest of Simants caught the eye of the national news media, and local Judge Hugh Stuart had his hands full with scores of reporters from around the state and the nation. Stuart responded by issuing a restrictive order barring the publication or broadcast of a wide range of information that he said would be prejudicial to Simants. The order was later modified by the Nebraska Supreme Court to prohibit only the reporting of the existence and nature of any confessions or admissions Simants might have made to police or any third party and any other information "strongly implicative" of the accused. The order was to stand in effect until a jury was chosen.

The press in the state appealed the publication ban to the United States Supreme Court, and in June 1976 the High Court ruled that Judge Stuart's order was an unconstitutional prior restraint upon the press (*Nebraska Press Association* v. *Stuart*, 1976). While all nine members of the Court agreed that the restrictive order in this case was a violation of the First Amendment, five members suggested that under the guidelines outlined at the beginning of this section (page 364), such an order might be proper. Chief Justice Burger wrote the opinion for the Court, in which he stressed that prior restraint was the exception, not the rule. There must be a clear and present danger to the defendant's rights before such a restrictive order might be constitutionally permitted, he said. But the Chief Justice did suggest that if the judge could demonstrate that the publicity about the case was intense and pervasive, that no other means could be used to compensate for such publicity, and that the restrictive order would be effective in keeping the prejudicial information out of the hands of prospective jurors, such an order might stand. In Simants's case, Burger said, while there was heavy publicity about the matter, there was no evidence that Judge Stuart had considered the efficacy of other remedies to compensate for this publicity. Also, the small community was filled with rumors about Simants and what he had told the police. Burger expressed serious doubts whether the restrictive order would have in fact kept prejudicial information out of public hands.

Of the remaining four members of the Court, Justices Stewart, Brennan, and Marshall stated that such prior restraints against the press would not be constitutional under any circumstance. Justice White implied that he agreed with that notion, but since he was not compelled to answer that question in the case before the Court, he would wait until another day to face the issue.

Please note, the Supreme Court did not declare restrictive orders aimed only at *trial participants* to be unconstitutional. This issue was not raised in the trial, but it is assumed that courts have much broader power to limit what attorneys, police, and other trial participants can say about a case out of court. *Guidelines on Fair Trial/Free Press,* issued by the United States Judicial Conference, for example, specifically recommends that federal courts adopt rules that limit public discussion of criminal cases by attorneys and court personnel and suggests that courts issue special rules in sensational criminal cases to bar extrajudicial comments by all trial participants. But, in light of the ruling in *Nebraska Press Association* v. *Stuart,* the conference *Guidelines* states:

> No rule of court or judicial order should be promulgated by a United States district court which would prohibit representatives of the news media from broadcasting or publishing any information in their possession relating to a criminal case.

In both 1978 and 1979 the Supreme Court issued opinions in cases that had the effect of reinforcing the rule from the *Nebraska Press Association* decision; that is, restrictions upon what the press may publish are to be tolerated only in very rare circumstances. In 1978 the High Court prohibited the state of Virginia from punishing the *Virginian Pilot* newspaper for publishing an accurate story regarding the confidential proceedings of a state judicial review commission (*Landmark Communications* v. *Virginia,* 1978). A Virginia State statute authorized the commission to hear complaints of a judge's disability or misconduct, and because of the sensitive nature of such hearings, the Virginia law closed the proceedings to the public and the press. The state argued that confidentiality was necessary to encourage the filing of complaints and the testimony of witnesses, to protect the judge from the injury that might result from the publication of unwarranted or unexamined charges, and to maintain confidence in the judiciary that might be undermined by the publication of groundless charges. While acknowledging the desirability of confidentiality, the Supreme Court nevertheless ruled against the state. Chief Justice Burger, writing for a unanimous Court, stated that the "publication Virginia seeks to punish under its statute lies near the core of the First

Amendment, and the Commonwealth's interests advanced by the imposition of criminal sanctions are insufficient to justify the actual and potential encroachments on freedom of speech and of the press. . . ." The court did acknowledge that the state commission could certainly meet in secret and that its reports and materials could be kept confidential. But while the press has no right to gain access to such information, once it possesses the information, it cannot be punished for its publication. In this sense the Court followed the *Nebraska Press Association* rule limiting restraints placed upon the press's right to publish.

In 1979 the High Court declared unconstitutional a West Virginia statute that made it a crime for a newspaper to publish, without the written approval of the juvenile court, the name of a youth charged as a juvenile offender (*Smith v. Daily Mail Publishing Company,* 1979). Again Chief Justice Burger wrote the opinion for the Court and stressed the fact that once the press has legally obtained truthful information, it cannot be stopped from its publication. In this case two Charleston, West Virginia, newspapers published the name of a fourteen-year-old boy who was arrested for the shooting death of a fifteen-year-old student. Reporters for the newspapers got the name from persons who had witnessed the shooting. "If the information is lawfully obtained," the Chief Justice wrote, "the state may not punish its publication except when necessary to further an interest more substantial than is present here."

Restrictive Orders Today

In the past decade the number of restrictive orders issued by trial courts has dropped substantially. Only a few have been aimed directly at the press, and most of those have been vacated by an appellate court. Restrictive orders aimed at participants are not uncommon today, but even many of these are failing to pass constitutional muster as appellate judges have started to apply the three-part *Nebraska Press Association* test against this type of gag order as well. Here are some examples of recent cases.

The Utah Supreme Court struck down a gag order aimed at the Salt Lake City media that prohibited the media from referring to a defendant in a 1981 rape trial as the "Sugarhouse rapist." Ronald D. Easthope, the man on trial, had been convicted in the early 1970s for a series of rapes in the Sugarhouse area of Salt Lake City. He was arrested again for rape after he was paroled. The state's high court first outlined the three standards raised in the *Nebraska Press Association* case:

1. Did the publicity threaten his right to a fair trial?
2. Would measures short of the judge's restrictive order insure the defendant a fair trial?
3. Will the restraint on the press achieve the desired results?

The state high court said the order was unconstitutional because the court had failed to consider any of these elements. The order was also invalid procedurally because the court had issued the order without notice or hearing. In addition, the state supreme court said it was hard to see how the term "Sugarhouse rapist" could harm Easthope, since he had admitted his previous crimes in open court (*KUTV* v. *Conder*, 1983).

The Arizona Supreme Court struck down a restrictive court order that blocked any courtroom sketching of the members of the jury unless the sketches were first approved by the court before they were telecast on the news. Applying the *Nebraska Press Association* test, the court said it could find little or no harm to the trial from the sketching. A few veniremen had expressed the fear of harm to their personal safety, but the vast majority of the 150 persons questioned had not. The trial court had not even considered other measures to cope with this limited threat. And finally, the order did not solve the problem since newspapers could print sketches of jurors. Also the trial was open; anyone could attend and see who was on the jury. "Jury fear was neither significant nor imminent enough to justify the censorship, less restrictive measures would have sufficed, and the sketch order promised very limited success in tempering the media involvement," the court said (*KPNX* v. *Maricopa County Superior Court*, 1984).

And the United States Court of Appeals for the Ninth Circuit struck down a court order that barred CBS from showing videotape it had legally obtained of John DeLorean meeting with FBI undercover agents in what the government said was a drug transaction. The court agreed that there had been widespread publicity about the case but added that "both precedent and experience indicate that widespread publicity, without more, does not automatically lead to an unfair trial." To restrain the publication or broadcast of material "the publicity must threaten to prejudice the entire community so that twelve unbiased jurors cannot be found," the court ruled. Looking at the impact on a single viewer or reader is not sufficient. The trial court had also failed to consider other alternatives, short of the restrictive order. It had rejected without any explanation using the voir dire process to screen out jurors who had seen the film on television. It had also failed to consider the "prophylactic effect of emphatic and clear instructions to the jury," the court of appeals said (*CBS* v. *U.S. District Court*, 1984). (DeLorean was later acquitted of these charges at his trial.)

One recent case in which a restrictive order was upheld occurred in Utah, where that state's high court permitted a trial court to bar the news media from reporting that a defendant was allegedly associated with organized crime. The press had reported such matters both before and after the trial began and the court had been forced to conduct a voir dire of the impaneled jurors. The court had asked the press to voluntarily restrain the publication of such material, but the news media had refused. The trial court said that waiver of a jury trial was too high a price for the defendant to pay and that sequestration of the jury during the long trial might prejudice the jury against the defendant. Strong admonitions to jurors might also result in such prejudice, the trial court concluded. The state supreme court ruled that the judge had met the burden of the *Nebraska Press Association* test and permitted the court order to stand (*KUTV* v. *Wilkinson,* 1984).

Court orders aimed at participants are more likely to be upheld. The United States Court of Appeals for the Fourth Circuit gave its approval to a restrictive order that prohibited several witnesses in a sensational criminal proceeding brought against several alleged members of the Ku Klux Klan and the Nazi Party from discussing their proposed testimony with reporters. The evidence supported the determination by the trial judge that there was a reasonable likelihood that the defendants would be denied a fair trial without this restriction on the witnesses, the court concluded (in re *Russell,* 1984). But even orders aimed at participants will be scrutinized carefully. A federal district court in California issued an order barring all attorneys in the espionage trial of FBI agent Richard Miller from making statements to the news media about any aspect of the case "that bears upon the merits to be resolved by the jury." The United States Court of Appeals for the Ninth Circuit ruled that the order was too broad. Many statements that bear upon the issues to be resolved by the jury present no danger to the administration of justice, the appeals court ruled. The district court must first determine what specific kinds of statements pose a real threat to the trial and then fashion a narrow restrictive order to proscribe them. The court of appeals then listed a half dozen kinds of comments that it might be permissible to block, regarding such matters as the identity or potential testimony of a witness or the contents of a statement made by the defendant (*Levine* v. *U.S. District Court,* 1985). And the appellate division of the New York Supreme Court ruled in 1986 that a court order to lawyers telling them to "refrain from any discussion of this case with the news media, to avoid any coverage of this case, or any attribution or any information in the media that would affect a fair trial of this case" was a violation of the First Amendment. The appellate judges ruled that the trial judge, who had told attorneys they could not even tell reporters what time court was supposed to convene, had not demonstrated that these extra-judicial statements by lawyers presented a "reasonable likelihood of a serious threat to the defendants right to a fair trial" (*NBC* v. *Cooperman,* 1986). In several recent cases courts have ruled that the press may legally challenge gag orders aimed only at trial participants because they interfere with a right to gather news (*Connecticut Magazine* v. *Moraghan,* 1987) or the right to receive information (in re *Dow Jones,* 1988). Once the potential of such interference is established the trial court must then justify its order under the standards enunciated by the Supreme Court in the *Nebraska Press Association* ruling.

A judge in Connecticut prohibited attorneys involved in a sensational murder trial from making any public statement to members of the press while the trial was in progress. The order was appealed to a United States district court on First Amendment grounds and the judge who applied the three-part test found the order wanting. Although there was substantial publicity about the case, the trial court had failed to even consider any less restrictive means that might have been used in place of the gag order. The order was therefore dissolved (*Connecticut Magazine* v. *Moraghan*, 1987). In Tennessee a trial judge issued an order prohibiting a congressman on trial for mail and bank fraud from commenting publicly on the case when he was not in Congress. The United States Court of Appeals for the Sixth Circuit ruled that the trial court had failed to establish that without the order, there was a clear and present danger to the trial process. "In the instant case, no facts were found which would suggest 'a serious and imminent threat,' and the order was neither narrowly tailored nor directed to any specific situation," the court said. Nor had the trial judge considered less restrictive alternatives to the order (*U.S.* v. *Ford*, 1987). The United States Court of Appeals for the Tenth Circuit rejected a trial judge's order forbidding jurors from discussing a case after it had ended. "While a court may broadly proscribe attorney and party contact with former jurors, it does not have the same freedom to restrict press interviews with former jurors," the court said (*Journal Publishing* v. *Mechem*, 1986). And in 1988 the appellate division of the New York Supreme Court ruled that a restrictive order aimed at the attorneys and their employees who were involved in a criminal trial was unconstitutional without the initial showing that the defendant's fair trial rights were in jeopardy (in re *New York Times*, 1988).

Restrictive orders that bar the press from publishing information about a criminal case have ceased to be a serious problem for journalists. Orders that limit what trial participants can say remain a nuisance, however, and probably do not serve the judicial system as well as many observers might imagine. Rumors tend to thrive in an atmosphere where the release of accurate information is stifled. It would be better perhaps to provide journalists bound to publish something about a case with accurate and truthful statements rather than push them to report what is ground out by a rumor mill.

SUMMARY

In some instances trial courts have attempted to limit the publication of prejudicial information about a case by issuing court orders restricting what the press may publish or what the trial participants may publicly say about a case. These restrictive orders grew out of a famous United States Supreme Court decision in the mid-1960s that ruled that a trial judge is responsible for controlling the publicity about a case.

In 1976 the Supreme Court ruled that the press may not be prohibited from publishing information it has legally obtained about a criminal case unless these conditions are met:

1. Intense and pervasive publicity about the case is certain.
2. No other reasonable alternative is likely to mitigate the effects of the pretrial publicity.
3. The restrictive order will prevent prejudicial material from reaching the jurors (*Nebraska Press Association* v. *Stuart*).

In two subsequent rulings the High Court reaffirmed its 1976 decision that confidential information legally obtained by the press may be published. These cases involved the name of a juvenile suspect in a murder case (*Smith* v. *Daily Mail*) and the names of judges whose conduct had been reviewed by a confidential state judicial commission (*Landmark Communications* v. *Virginia*).

While judges may still limit what trial participants say publicly about a case, even these restrictive orders have come under constitutional scrutiny in recent years.

CLOSED PROCEEDINGS

Trial judges were stripped of a potent weapon to control publicity about a criminal case when the United States Supreme Court barred the use of most restrictive orders aimed at the press. The state and federal judges quickly tried a new tack, the closing of trials and pretrial hearings to members of the press and the public. With the closing of these hearings, judges thus barred the press from gaining legal access to much of the prejudicial information that might be published or broadcast about a defendant. The damaging stories could not then be published, or so the judges argued. The closure of judicial hearings became the key First Amendment issue of the early 1980s. At least eight United States Supreme Court opinions have been handed down on this question, and these have been bolstered by scores of appellate court rulings from around the nation. The Supreme Court has focused upon two considerations relevant to whether a particular judicial proceeding or document should be open. First, the Court has considered whether the place and process has been historically open because "a tradition of accessibility implies the favorable judgment of experience" (*Globe Newspaper Co.* v. *Superior Court,* 1982). Second, the Court has examined whether public and press access to a particular hearing or document plays a significant positive role in the actual functioning of the proceeding or the judicial process generally.

On this basis we can summarize the rulings by the Court in this fashion:

A strong and virtually unqualified right for any citizen, including reporters, to attend a criminal or civil trial has been recognized.

A strong but qualified right for the press and public to attend pretrial hearings and gain access to most documents associated with the trial has also been recognized.

Trials

In 1980 the Supreme Court of the United States ruled in a 7–1 decision (Justice Powell took no part in this case) that the right of the public and the press to attend a criminal trial is guaranteed by both the common law and the First Amendment to the United States Constitution. The ruling, *Richmond Newspapers v. Virginia,* stemmed from a state court ruling in a Virginia criminal trial. In March 1976 John Stevenson was indicted for murder. He was tried and convicted of second degree murder, but his conviction was reversed. A second trial ended in a mistrial when a juror asked to be excused in the midst of the hearing. A third trial also resulted in a mistrial because a prospective juror told other prospective jurors about Stevenson's earlier conviction on the same charges. This was not revealed until after the trial had started. As proceedings were about to begin for the fourth time in late 1978, the defense asked that the trial be closed. The prosecution did not object and the court closed the trial. Richmond newspapers protested the closure to no avail. An appeal came before the United States Supreme Court in February 1980.

Chief Justice Burger wrote the Court's opinion, noting that "through its evolution the trial has been open to all who cared to observe." A presumption of open hearings is the very nature of a criminal trial under our system of justice, the Chief Justice added. While there is no specific provision in the Bill of Rights or the Constitution to support the open trial, the expressly guaranteed freedoms in the First Amendment "share a common core purpose of assuring freedom of communication on matters relating to the functioning of government," Burger wrote. "In guaranteeing freedoms such as those of speech and press the First Amendment can be read as protecting the right of everyone to attend trials so as to give meaning to those explicit guarantees," he added. The First Amendment, then, the chief justice noted, prohibits the government from summarily closing courtroom doors, which had been open to the public at the time that amendment was adopted.

But the chief justice refused to see the First Amendment as an absolute bar to closed trials. He noted that in some circumstances, which he explicitly declined to define at that time, a trial judge could bar the public and the press from a trial in the interest of the fair administration of justice. But, while the Court did not outline such circumstances, it was clear from both the tone and the language of the chief justice's opinion that in his mind such circumstances would indeed be unusual. Justices White, Stevens, Brennan, Marshall, Stewart, and Blackmun all concurred with the chief justice in five separate opinions. All but Stewart went further in guaranteeing access to trials than did Chief Justice Burger. Justice Rehnquist dissented.

In 1984 the United States Court of Appeals for the Third Circuit ruled that civil proceedings are also presumptively open to the public and the press. In *Publicker Industries* v. *Cohen* (1984), a lawsuit involving a corporate proxy fight, the court noted that a "survey of authorities identifies as features of the civil justice system many of those attributes of the criminal justice system on which the Supreme Court relied in holding that the First Amendment guarantees to the public and to the press the right of access to criminal trials. . . ." The right is not absolute, the court said, but absent a clear showing that closing the trial serves an important governmental interest and that closing the trial is the only way to serve this interest, the civil proceeding should be open. Numerous other federal and state courts have followed the rulings in *Richmond Newspapers* and *Publicker.* (See in re *Knight Publishing,* 1984, for example.)

In most instances a trial will be presumed to be open and the burden on the person seeking to close the trial is a heavy one. But there are occasions when a trial might be closed. Since 1980, courts have identified at least two such situations. The Vermont Supreme Court ruled in December 1981 that the ruling in the *Richmond Newspapers* case did not extend to juvenile proceedings. That is, the state may continue to hold such hearings—which are like trials—behind closed doors. The *Burlington Free Press* sought access to a juvenile proceeding in which a judge was to consider the status (adult or juvenile) of a fifteen-year-old boy who had murdered one young girl and assaulted another. Juvenile proceedings were supposed to be kept confidential under Vermont state law. The Vermont Supreme Court noted that there was no tradition of openness in these proceedings that mirrored the American tradition of public trials. In a juvenile proceeding there is no criminal conviction, often no punishment. "A juvenile proceeding is so unlike a criminal prosecution that the limited right of access described in *Richmond Newspapers* does not govern," the court ruled. In addition, there were many good reasons to keep such hearings closed, the court said. Publication of the name could impair the young person's opportunity for rehabilitation; confidentiality would protect the juvenile from carrying a stigma in the future. Publicity is often seen as a reward for a hard-core juvenile delinquent, the high court added (in re *J.S.,* 1981). But this does not mean that a juvenile proceeding cannot be open to the press and public. It is typical in most states for access to juvenile proceedings to be governed by statute. And frequently these statutes provide for open access to hearings involving juvenile offenders. The New York Court of Appeals recently ruled that sentencing proceedings in felony cases in which the defendant is a "youthful offender" (the defendant was between sixteen and nineteen when the crime was committed) are presumptively open. New York has a statute regarding youthful offenders, and under the statute "all felony offenders potentially treatable as youthful offenders, and this of course includes juvenile offenders, are subject to the full glare and publicity of adult offenders" (*Capital Newspapers* v. *Moynihan,* 1988).

Trials are often closed when juvenile sex offense victims testify. But sometimes the laws that mandate this closure are fashioned too broadly. In 1982 the Supreme Court ruled that a Massachusetts law that stated that the press and the public "shall" be excluded from the courtroom during such testimony was unconstitutional (*Globe Newspapers* v. *Superior Court,* 1982). The state argued that the law had two purposes: to encourage young victims to come forward to testify in such cases and to protect these young people from psychological harm once they come forward. The state law required the judge to close the trial when the victim testified; other portions of the trial could be closed at the judge's discretion. The flaw in the law, according to Justice William Brennan who wrote the Court's opinion, was that the trial judge was *required* to close the trial during the victim's testimony. Brennan agreed that protecting the physical and psychological well-being of a minor is a compelling interest:

> But as compelling as that interest is, it does not justify a mandatory-closure rule, for it is clear that the circumstances of the particular case may affect the significance of the interest. A trial court can determine on a case-by-case basis whether the closure is necessary to protect the welfare of a minor victim.

Under the statute the trial judge is not permitted to allow testimony in open court, even if the victim desires it, Brennan said.

Justice Brennan rejected the argument that a mandatory-closure law is more likely to prompt young victims of sexual assault to come forward to testify. He said there was no empirical support for this claim; in addition the argument was not logical. Reporters are permitted to attend the remainder of the trial, and can get the victim's name and details of the testimony from the transcript of the trial. The statute really does not do what the state thinks it should do, while it runs squarely against the presumption of open trials enunciated in the *Richmond Newspapers* case. Dissenters Burger and Rehnquist disagreed, arguing that the state has a long-standing right to protect juveniles, as well as a long tradition of excluding the public from trials involving victims of sexual assault. Justice Stevens also dissented because he said he believed the Supreme Court was improperly rendering an advisory opinion in the case, something the court is not supposed to do (*Globe Newspapers* v. *Superior Court,* 1982).

Other Hearings and Documents

The closure of a trial, even before the ruling in *Richmond Newspapers,* was an uncommon experience, but the closure of other parts of the judicial process was not uncommon. Time was when a trial was about the only proceeding that took place in the courtroom. Today, however, the judicial process is far more complicated. The kinds of proceedings and documents associated with a civil or criminal trial are myriad. There are presentence and postsentence hearings and reports. There is the voir dire process where the jury is selected. There are suppression hearings, plea hearings, sentence hearings. There are affadavits and mounds of other material developed during the discovery process. There are detention hearings, bail hearings, the list goes on. And what happens in a trial is often predetermined by what has happened in these other hearings, or by rulings made by the judge on motions and reports filed by the participants.

It was closure of the pretrial suppression hearings that first attracted press, and then appellate court, attention to the problem of access to these ancillary parts of the judicial process. The problems associated with publicity regarding these hearings are indicative of problems with other parts of the judicial process. And the dilemma of whether or not to open or close these hearings crystalizes the problems of access to other hearings and documents as well. So let's stop a moment and examine these hearings.

In most criminal cases the state and the defense will quarrel over the admittance of evidence at the trial. This evidence may be a weapon, a statement made by the defendant, the defendant's performance on a lie detector test, or something else of this nature. Usually the state will seek to have the evidence admitted at the trial, and the defense will attempt to block this effort. Fifty years ago this argument was normally carried out before the trial judge *after* the jury had been selected. The jurors were secreted in a safe place and did not hear the argument or the testimony that took place at such hearings. The judge would rule upon the admission of the disputed pieces of evidence and the trial would begin. The press attended such hearings, but of course the jurors were strongly admonished by the judge not to read or view or listen to anything about the case that might appear in the mass media. So if a judge ruled that the state could not introduce a weapon at the trial, and the press reported this ruling, the jurors would likely not see the story and never know such a weapon existed.

Evidentiary questions became somewhat more complicated following the numerous decisions regarding defendant's rights rendered by the Supreme Court in the 1960s. The pretrial hearing became more involved and often more lengthy. A practice soon developed of holding the hearing before the trial, often two or three weeks before the trial, even before a jury was chosen in the case. Press reports about the hearing would circulate in the community. If a judge barred the introduction of an important piece of evidence in a trial, citizens in the community—all potential jurors—could read these stories. Those selected as jurors, then, might very well know that such evidence existed even though it was not introduced at the trial. Before the ruling in *Nebraska Press Association* v. *Stuart,* a judge could use a restrictive order to bar the press from publishing or broadcasting information about the evidence. With that option gone, judges began to close the pretrial hearings. Reporters were barred from these traditionally open proceedings. The press protested but it was not until 1986, six years after the ruling in *Richmond Newspapers,* that the Supreme Court ruled that pretrial hearings are presumptively open. In a 7–2 ruling, the Court declared that there exists a qualified privilege for the press and the public to attend a pretrial hearing, even in the face of opposition from the defendant. A California trial court had closed the pretrial hearing for Robert Diaz, a nurse accused of killing as many as twelve patients in a hospital in which he worked. *The Riverside Press-Enterprise* protested the closure, but the California appellate courts ruled that while there was a First Amendment right for the public and press to attend a trial, no corollary right existed to attend a pretrial hearing. The United States Supreme Court disagreed. The preliminary hearing may be closed "only if specific findings are made demonstrating that first, there is a substantial probability that the defendant's right to a fair trial will be prejudiced by publicity, and, second, reasonable alternatives to closure cannot adequately protect the defendant's fair trial rights," wrote Chief Justice Burger. Mere risk of prejudice does not automatically justify refusing public access to hearings, Burger stressed. If the judge makes specific findings that the probability of such prejudice does exist, the closure order must be tailored very narrowly to serve that interest. In other words, if only two-hours worth of testimony during a three-day pretrial hearing might cause the probability of prejudice, the hearing should be closed only during those two hours. Trial judges should use other means, where possible, to protect the defendant. "Through voir dire, cumbersome as it is in some circumstances, a court can identify those jurors whose prior knowledge of the case would disable them from rendering an impartial verdict," Burger added (*Press-Enterprise* v. *Riverside Superior Court,* 1986).

It should be noted that the requirement that the defendant or the state show that there is a "substantial probability" of prejudice places a heavy burden upon the party seeking closure. Prior to this Supreme Court ruling some state courts and United States courts of appeal had applied a "reasonable likelihood of prejudice" test, which is far easier to overcome.

This decision is known among lawyers as *Press-Enterprise II,* to distinguish it from a 1984 ruling, also *Press-Enterprise* v. *Riverside Superior Court,* in which the Supreme Court ruled 9–0 that the public and the press have a right to attend the voir dire proceeding in which the jury is selected. The voir dire occurs just before the trial is to start, and after the pretrial hearings and motions. A California Superior Court in Riverside had closed all but three days of a six-week voir dire to protect the right of privacy of the jurors and the fair trial rights of the defendant. Chief Justice Burger wrote that the process of juror selection is a matter of importance, not simply to the adversaries but also to the criminal justice system. "No right ranks higher than the right of the accused to a fair trial. But the primacy of the accused's rights is difficult to separate from the right of everyone in the community to attend the voir dire which promotes fairness," he added. In some instances, Burger noted, the proceeding might be properly closed, but the presumption of openness may only be overcome by an overriding interest based on findings that closure is essential to preserve high values and is narrowly tailored to serve that interest. "The interest [is] to be articulated along with findings specific enough that a reviewing court can determine whether the closure order was properly entered,"

Burger said. In this case the judge's order was far too broad. Also, the judge had failed to articulate specific reasons for the closure and had failed to look to alternatives to closure as means of solving the problem (*Press-Enterprise v. Riverside Superior Court,* 1984).

Based on the court rulings regarding access to judicial proceedings, the following is the process a judge should go through in determining whether or not to close a particular proceeding or seal a particular file or document. Is the hearing or document presumptively open? This is the first question and will be answered by deciding (1) whether the proceeding or document has been historically or traditionally open and (2) whether openness plays a positive role in the functioning of the judicial process. If the hearing or document is presumed to be open, the presumption can only be overcome if the following takes place:

1. The party seeking closure, the defendant or the government or sometimes both, must advance an overriding interest that is likely to be harmed if the proceeding or document is open. The right to a fair trial or an invasion of privacy are such interests.

2. Whoever seeks closure must demonstrate that there is a "substantial probability" that this interest will be harmed if the proceeding or document remains open.

3. The trial court must consider reasonable alternatives to closure. A good voir dire might eliminate the possibility of prejudice that could result if a pretrial hearing remains open, for example.

4. If the trial judge deems closure is the only solution, the closure must be narrowly tailored to protect that interest. For example, imagine that during the voir dire prior to a rape trial, attorneys expect to ask prospective jurors whether they have ever been raped or sexually assaulted. Although this could prove embarrassing to some persons, closing the voir dire is not the solution. A narrowly-tailored order might permit those potential jurors who believe they would be embarrassed by answering such a question to request that their answers to that question be given in private. The remainder of the voir dire would be open.

5. The trial court must make adequate findings to support the closure decision. There must be a factual record for an appellate court to later examine if the closure order is challenged by the press or the public.

It is instructive to see how these rules have been applied by lower courts in the last few years. Let's take a brief look at a couple of cases.

In 1988 the United States Court of Appeals for the Ninth Circuit overturned a lower court ruling that closed the pretrial detention hearing for a woman accused of product tampering. Stella Nickell was charged with spiking Excedrin capsules with potassium cyanide to kill her husband, and then placing bottles with other doctored capsules on store shelves to try to make the murder look like a random killing. The court said that historically, pretrial detention hearings were not open, but such hearings have become much more important in recent years. It noted that public interest in the question of whether a defendant will be released to await trial is understandably very high because the community is directly affected and the hearing should therefore be open in this case. The court also ruled that there was no showing that an open hearing would create substantial probability of damaging Nickell's fair trial rights and that the trial court too easily dismissed potential alternatives. The hearing and the documents filed in connection with it must be open, the court said (*Seattle Times* v. *U.S. District Court,* 1988).

In Louisiana, however, the United States Court of Appeals for the Fifth Circuit ruled that it was permissible for a trial judge to question two jurors privately in his chambers about possible misconduct. This was during the second trial of former Louisiana governor Edwin Edwards. The first trial ended in a mistrial. During the second trial a juror reported to the marshal that another juror had remarked, "Did you know the last jury got paid for voting acquital?" The judge questioned both jurors in chambers about the matter. He said he did so to keep the matter away from other jurors. The same thing happened a few days later and the judge responded in the same fashion. After the trial ended the press sought a transcript and received an edited version with the jurors' names and other details stricken from the record.

The court of appeals supported the judge. It noted that historically such questioning of jurors has been conducted in private. Additionally, opening up such a hearing could be extremely harmful in this case, turning what the court called a "tempest in a teapot" into a mistrial. The court also supported the judge's decision to edit the transcript in order to protect the jurors from embarrassment (*U.S.* v. *Edwards,* 1987).

This is how the rules are supposed to work, then. What other kinds of proceedings and documents have been ruled to be open? Here is a brief summary of a few cases.

The United States Court of Appeals for the Fourth Circuit has ruled that plea and sentencing hearings in criminal cases are presumptively open (in re *Washington Post,* 1987). The United States Court of Appeals for the Third Circuit ruled in 1985 that indictments and informations are open to the public and the press (*U.S.* v. *Smith,* 1985). The West Virginia Supreme Court ruled that under that state's constitution, attorney disciplinary hearings must be open (*Daily Gazette* v. *West Virginia Bar,* 1984). The United States Court of Appeals for the Ninth Circuit ruled in 1985 that a United States district court erred when it sealed a postconviction motion to reduce a sentence together with the government's response. Such documents must be open, the court said, unless the proponents of closure demonstrate with specificity that compelling interests in support of closure override the presumption of access to such information (*CBS* v. *U.S. District Court,* 1985). And at least two United States courts of appeal have ruled that bail proceedings are presumptively open, the Fifth in *U.S.* v. *Chagra* (1983) and the First in in re *Globe Newspapers* (1984). The court in the *Globe* case, however, permitted the trial judge to close the hearing because the closure order was narrowly tailored and the judge had considered, but reasonably rejected, alternatives to closure to protect the rights of the defendant. Finally, the United States Court of Appeals for the Sixth Circuit recently ruled that the press and public do not enjoy a right of access to what is called a **summary jury trial,** a rather unusual judicial proceeding sometimes used in civil cases. The summary jury trial is a device used by courts to attempt to get the parties in the case to settle their dispute before going to a full-blown jury trial. In such a case the attorneys present much abbreviated arguments to jurors. There are no witnesses called, and objections to evidence or other matters are strongly discouraged. After hearing the arguments the jurors issue an informal verdict that can then be used to settle the case. For example, if plaintiff Jones loses the verdict in the summary jury trial, she may be more willing to settle the case without a normal trial. The court said there was no First Amendment right of access to such proceedings because such a right was not historically recognized, and that permitting access might actually work against the purpose of the summary trial, the settlement of the dispute (*Cincinnati Gas and Electric Co.* v. *General Electric Co.,* 1988).

A wide range of judicial documents have been ruled to be presumptively open as well. The United States Court of Appeals for the Ninth Circuit struck down a lower court order that sealed a large number of court records filed when the government prosecuted automaker John DeLorean. Pretrial proceedings are open, the court said and "There is no reason to distinguish between pretrial proceedings and the documents filed in regard to them." Such documents are often important to a full understanding of the way in which "the judicial process and the government as a whole are functioning," the court ruled (*AP* v. *U.S. District Court,* 1983). The court also ruled in 1988 that presentencing and postsentencing reports are presumed to be open records. The records were sought after a convicted felon was put on probation for a subsequent crime, and then murdered an attorney. The court said the trial judge had shown no compelling need to keep the records secret (*U.S.* v. *Schlette,* 1988). The United States Court of Appeals for the Second Circuit has ruled that a sealed plea agreement signed by a former union official who pled guilty to embezzlement of union funds should be made public, even though the court could keep the contents of one paragraph that contained extremely sensitive information secret (*U.S.* v. *Haller,* 1988). The United States Court of Appeals for the Third Circuit recently ruled that the terms of a settlement in a civil action that was sealed should be opened (*Bank of America* v. *Hotel Rittenhouse Assoc.,* 1986).

The one area in which the press has had little success in getting access to material is in obtaining records that are provided by litigants during discovery that are under a protective order. Remember, during the discovery process both sides in a legal dispute are permitted to explore the records and witnesses and other material held by the opposing party. The court assists in the process by compelling disclosure of this information when need be. Sometimes a party will refuse to disclose some material unless the court will guarantee that material will not be made public. The court then enters a protective order, shielding the material from public disclosure.

For example, a black couple filed a civil rights complaint against persons who had twice fire-bombed their home. In preliminary proceedings it was discovered that one of the defendants was an officer in the Ku Klux Klan. The plaintiffs sought from him a list of local Klan members and the court issued a subpoena ordering the production of the names. The Klansman resisted, but finally provided the list when it was put under a protective order, meaning that only the attorneys involved in the case could see the names. The court later sealed all access to the list in an effort to protect the privacy and associational rights of those named. The court of appeals upheld the ruling, noting that the list would never have been generated if it had not been for the protective order (*Courier-Journal* v. *Marshall,* 1987). The court in this case relied upon a United States Supreme Court ruling in 1984 regarding a somewhat similar issue. In that case, *Seattle Times Co.* v. *Rhinehart,* the High Court said that an order prohibiting the dissemination of information generated during the discovery process is not the classic kind of prior restraint that requires "exacting First Amendment scrutiny. . . . Where a protective order is entered on a showing of good cause . . . and does not restrict the dissemination of the information if gained from other sources, it does not offend the First Amendment." In all likelihood courts will continue to resist the disclosure of those documents that are generated during the discovery process and protected from public scrutiny by a court order.

The qualified right of access to judicial proceedings and documents has gone a long way to block attempts by courts to keep the public and the press out of the courtroom. Many trial judges, however, see closure as a simple solution to the problem of publicity about a criminal case. And often the motion for closure is made totally unexpectedly. What should a reporter do when faced with such a problem? Here are some tips for journalists from "*The Seattle Times* Newsroom Legal Guide" prepared by attorneys P. Cameron Devore, Marshall J. Nelson, and others at the Seattle law firm of Davis, Wright, and Jones.

Call the editor immediately so he or she can contact the company's lawyer. Try informally to remind the lawyer of the recent rulings and guidelines that provide for a presumptively open hearing. If that fails, the reporter should be prepared to make a formal objection to the closure, to try to hold the fort until legal help arrives. Reporters for *The Seattle Times* are prepared to read the following statement from a card they carry.

> Your honor, I am _____, a reporter for *The Seattle Times,* and I would like to object on behalf of my newspaper and the public to this proposed closing. Our attorney is prepared to make a number of arguments against closings such as this one, and we respectfully ask the court for a hearing on those issues. I believe our attorney can be here soon for the court's convenience and will be able to demonstrate that closure in this case will violate the First Amendment and article I, section 10, of the Washington State constitution. I cannot make the legal arguments myself, but our attorney can point out several issues for your consideration. If it pleases the court, we request the opportunity to be heard through counsel.

Such a statement would work in any court; simply cite the proper section of your own state constitution or any other relevant documents or guidelines. Reporters should be equipped to handle such an emergency.

SUMMARY

The public and the press have a right to attend trials and pretrial proceedings. This right is presumed when the proceeding has been historically or traditionally open, and when opening the hearing plays a significant positive role in the functioning of the judicial process. Although the right to attend a trial is not absolute, such a proceeding can be closed only in rare circumstances. Courts have permitted the closure of juvenile hearings, as well as a portion of the public testimony of rape victims. The right of access to pretrial proceedings and documents is qualified. The presumption that these hearings are open can only be overcome by a showing that there is an overriding interest that must be protected, that there is a "substantial probability" that an open hearing will damage this right, that the closure is narrowly tailored to deny access to no more of the hearing than is necessary to protect this interest, that the court has considered reasonable alternatives to closure, that closure of the hearing would in fact protect the interest that has been raised, and that the trial judge has articulated findings—which may be reviewed by an appellate court—that support the four points above.

BENCH-BAR-PRESS GUIDELINES

Both restrictive orders and the closure of court proceedings are admittedly effective ways of stopping publicity from reaching the hands of potential jurors, but they are equally dangerous in a representative democracy where information about how well government is operating is fundamental to the success of the political system. The bench, the bar, and the press in many states have found that cooperation, restraint, and mutual trust can be equally effective in protecting the rights of a defendant, while at the same time far less damaging to rights of the people.

In twenty-eight states the members of the bench, the bar, and the press have tried to reach a common understanding of the problems of pretrial news coverage and have offered suggestions as to how most of these problems might be resolved. These suggestions are usually offered in the form of guidelines or recommendations to the press and to participants in the criminal justice system. **Bench-bar-press guidelines** normally suggest to law enforcement officers that certain kinds of information about a criminal suspect and a crime can be released and published with little danger of harm to the trial process. The guidelines also suggest to journalists that the publication of certain kinds of information about a case (see the list of damaging kinds of statements on pages 352–53) can be harmful to the defendant's chances for a fair trial without providing the public with useful or important information. The guidelines are often presented in a very brief form; at other times they encompass several pages of text.

Bench-bar-press guidelines have existed in some states for more than twenty years. In some communities these guidelines work very well in managing the problems surrounding the free press–fair trial dilemma. A spirit of cooperation exists between press, courts, attorneys, and law enforcement personnel. In such communities it is rare to find a restrictive order or a closed courtroom. But most communities and states have found it takes considerable effort to make the guidelines work. Drafting the guidelines is only the first step. If after agreement is reached upon the recommendations, the bench, the bar, and the press go their separate ways, the guidelines usually fail as a means of resolving the free press–fair trial problems.

SUMMARY

In some states the press, attorneys, and judges have agreed to try to solve the problems surrounding the free press–fair trial controversy through voluntary bench-bar-press agreements. Such agreements usually contain suggestions to all parties as to what information should and should not be publicized about criminal cases. When the guidelines work, there is usually a cooperative, rather than a combative, spirit among the members of the press, the judiciary, and the bar. These guidelines often reduce or eliminate the need for restrictive orders or closed hearings.

CAMERAS IN THE COURTROOM

In 1976 journalists in all but two states were prohibited from bringing cameras or tape recorders into courtrooms. Today, such equipment is completely banned from only the federal courts, and courts in the District of Columbia, Indiana, Mississippi, Missouri, South Carolina, and South Dakota. In ten states—Delaware, Illinois, Kansas, Louisiana, Maine, Nebraska, North Dakota, Oregon, Texas, and Wyoming—recording equipment and cameras are permitted only in appellate courts. In the remaining thirty-five states such equipment is allowed in trial and appellate courtrooms, if only on an experimental basis for now. (See Dyer and Houserman, "Electronic Coverage of the Courts: Exceptions to Exposure.") The Supreme Court of the United States has ruled that the use of recorders and cameras by journalists during a trial does not by itself deprive the defendant of the constitutionally guaranteed right to a fair trial (*Chandler* v. *Florida,* 1981).

This swift reversal of the rules regarding the use of cameras in the courtroom climaxed a forty-year struggle by the press for relaxation of prohibitions that were instituted in the 1930s. At that time the press had conducted itself in an outrageous fashion in covering the trial of Bruno Hauptmann, who was charged with kidnapping the baby of Charles and Anne Lindberg. The trial judge, who had great difficulty in controlling the press, ordered that no pictures be taken during the court sessions. But photographers equipped with large, bulky, flash-equipped cameras moved freely about the courtroom, ignoring the judge's orders and taking pictures almost at will. As a result of this travesty, the American Bar Association (ABA) adopted rules prohibiting the use of cameras and other electronic equipment in courtrooms. The rules, known as Canon 35, were adopted in most states and were followed in practice in those states that did not officially adopt the rules. (See Frank M. White, "Cameras in the Courtroom: A U.S. Survey.")

After World War II when the photographic equipment became smaller and less obtrusive and faster film permitted photography indoors without flash equipment, the press began to agitate for changes in the rules. The television industry especially chafed under the proscriptions (the ABA rules had been amended in 1952 to include television), as they put broadcast reporters, who depended upon film to tell a story, at a distinct disadvantage in the competition with wordsmiths of the printed press. In the mid-1960s the United States Supreme Court had a chance to consider the constitutionality of the ban on cameras in the courtroom in a case that began in Texas, one of a handful of states that occasionally allowed photography and recording in the courtroom.

The defendant was Billie Sol Estes, who was accused of a swindle involving fertilizer tanks. The story was important in the Lone Star State; television was therefore permitted at the initial pretrial hearing, and still photographers were permitted throughout the trial. But there was disruption at the pretrial hearing. Twelve cameramen crowded into the tiny courtroom, cables and wires snaked across the floor, microphones were everywhere, and the distraction caused by this media invasion was significant. The situation improved during the trial when television and recording equipment was housed in a booth at the back of the courtroom. Estes appealed his conviction to the United States Supreme Court on the grounds that he had been denied a fair trial because of the presence of the cameras and recorders. The court agreed with the defendant. "While maximum freedom must be allowed the press in carrying out this important function [informing the public] in a democratic society, its exercise must necessarily be subject to the maintenance of absolute fairness in the judicial process," wrote Justice Tom Clark for the majority (*Estes* v. *Texas,* 1965). The photography and broadcasting equipment simply created too many impediments to a fair trial.

However, experimentation with cameras in the courtroom continued. Telecasting equipment improved. Journalists demonstrated to judges that they could act responsibly if they were permitted access to courtrooms with their cameras and recorders. More and more states began to permit telecasts and broadcasts of criminal and civil trials, as well as of the oral arguments at appellate hearings. In the early 1980s two former Miami police officers challenged the new rules in Florida that permitted cameras in the courtroom. They argued that television coverage of their trial in and of itself had deprived them of a fair trial. The Florida Supreme Court rejected their contention, and the United States Supreme Court agreed to hear the case. In a unanimous decision the High Court ruled that the mere presence of cameras in the courtroom or simply televising or broadcasting portions of a trial does not in and of itself cause prejudice to the defendant or interfere with the right to a fair trial. Chief Justice Burger wrote that at present "no one has been able to present empirical data sufficient to establish that the mere presence of the broadcast media inherently has an adverse effect on that [trial] process." It is true the presence of such equipment in the courtroom or the broadcast of a trial could endanger the defendant's right to a fair trial. But, Burger said, "an absolute constitutional ban on broadcast coverage of trials cannot be justified simply because there is a danger that, in some cases, prejudicial broadcast accounts of pretrial and trial events may impair the ability of jurors to decide the issue of guilt or innocence uninfluenced by extraneous matter." The chief justice said that in order to block the use of cameras and recorders at a trial, a defendant must demonstrate to the court how the trial will be adversely affected by the presence of this equipment. To overturn a conviction at a trial that has been televised, the defendant will need to show that the recording and photography equipment actually made a substantial difference in some material aspect of the trial. Proof that the jurors were aware of the cameras or that the presence of television cameras "told" jurors this was a big trial will not be sufficient to demonstrate prejudice, Burger wrote (*Chandler* v. *Florida,* 1981).

State courts have started to develop standards to assess complaints of prejudice from defendants who do not want their trials televised. In Florida, for example, the state supreme court has ruled that the trial court must hold an evidentiary hearing if a defendant or other participant in the trial protests the television coverage. Before cameras and recorders may be excluded, there must be a finding that electronic coverage of the trial would have an important "qualitatively different effect" on the trial than would other types of coverage (*Florida* v. *Palm Beach Newspapers,* 1981). Another Florida case demonstrates how such a difference might be shown. The defendant in the case had previously been found incompetent to stand trial. Treatment subsequently rendered her competent to proceed with the case. Her attorneys, armed with testimony from psychiatrists, asserted that television cameras in the courtroom would adversely affect the defendant's ability to communicate with her counsel and she might lapse into psychosis. The Florida Supreme Court ruled that this kind of evidence satisfied the standard for excluding television cameras (*Florida* v. *Green,* 1981). Some states provide exemptions from coverage to certain classes of trial participants such as juvenile offenders, victims of sex crimes, or police informants.

Cameras are not allowed in federal courtrooms, and federal judges have resisted all efforts to televise court hearings, even when the defendant sought to have cameras in the courtroom (see *U.S.* v. *Hastings,* 1983). The *Chandler* case stands for the principle that if the state decides to let cameras into the courtroom, their presence does not violate the constitutional guarantee of a fair trial. But nothing in the Court's opinion in *Chandler* suggests that states or the federal courts *must* permit cameras in the courtroom. (In 1988, the United States Court of Appeals for the Sixth Circuit ruled that prohibiting broadcasting or photographing of judicial proceedings does not impermissibly infringe on the First Amendment right of access to judicial proceedings *Conway* v. *U.S.* This was the fourth United States court of appeal to issue such a ruling.)

State rules on the admission of cameras to the courtroom vary. In some states cameras will not be permitted unless various key trial participants agree. In more states the cameras are allowed upon the discretion of the judge. If a participant objects to the admission of cameras to the courtroom, the press must honor this objection and refrain from photographing or recording this individual. Most states have adopted guidelines that establish the number of still and motion picture cameras permitted in the courtroom at any one time. Rules often specify where the cameras may be placed, require that all pictures be taken with available light, and even set standards of dress for photographers and technicians. The press must often be willing to share the fruits of the photography through pooling agreements, since most states have guidelines limiting movement and placement of cameras to when the court is in recess only.

SUMMARY

Until recently cameras and recorders were banned from courtrooms in nearly all states. But today such equipment may be used during a trial in about two-thirds of the states. The Supreme Court has ruled that the mere presence of cameras or recorders in the courtroom does not prejudice the defendant's right to a fair trial (*Chandler* v. *Florida*). To block the use of the cameras or to seek the reversal of a conviction at a trial that has been televised or recorded, a defendant will have to offer specific proof that the use of the electronic news-gathering equipment will or did interfere with the right to a fair trial.

A good deal of space has been devoted to the free press–fair trial problem because it is an important issue and because it continues to be a problem. Within both the press and the law, sharp divisions regarding solution of the problem remain. Many years ago during a battle over a free press–fair trial issue in one southern state, the national office of the American Civil Liberties Union filed an amicus curiae (friend of the court) brief supporting a free and unfettered press, while the state chapter of the same civil liberties group filed a brief in favor of the court's position supporting a fair trial.

Most journalists probably agree that we need more, not less, reporting on the justice system in the United States. In *Crime and Publicity* Alfred Friendly and Ronald Goldfarb write:

> To shackle the press is to curtail the public watch over the administration of criminal justice. . . . The press serves at the gatehouse of justice. Additionally, it serves in the manorhouse itself, and all along the complicated route to it from the police station and the streets, to the purlieus of the prosecutor's office, to the courtroom corridors where the pressures mount and the deals are made.

The two authors also point out that we do not want a press that is more or less free, just as we should not tolerate trials that are almost fair. "And to complicate the issue," they note, "it is evident that a free press is one of society's principal guarantors of fair trials, while fair trials provide a major assurance of the press's freedom."

Reporters dealing with the courts and the court system must be extremely sensitive to these issues. They should not be blinded to the sensitive mechanisms that operate in the courts to provide justice and fairness as they clamor for news. At the same time they should not let the authoritarian aspects of the judicial system block their efforts to provide the information essential to the functioning of democracy.

BIBLIOGRAPHY

Here is a list of some of the sources that have been helpful in the preparation of chapter 7:

Books

Buddenbaum, Judith M., et al. *Pretrial Publicity and Juries: A Review of Research.* Research Report No. 11, School of Journalism, Indiana University, 1981.

Bush, Chilton R., ed. *Free Press and Fair Trial: Some Dimensions of the Problem.* Athens: University of Georgia Press, 1971.

Friendly, Alfred, and Goldfarb, Ronald. *Crime and Publicity.* New York: Random House, Vintage Books, 1968.

White, Frank W. *Cameras in the Courtroom: A U.S. Survey.* 60 *Journalism Monographs,* 1979.

Articles

Dyer, Carolyn Stewart, and Hauserman, Nancy R. "Electronic Coverage of the Courts: Exceptions to Exposure." 75 *George Law Journal* 1633, 1987.

Landau, Jack C. "The Challenge of the Communications Media." 62 *American Bar Association Journal* 55, 1976.

Lindsey, Richard P. "An Assessment of the Use of Cameras in State and Federal Courts." 18 *Georgia Law Review* 389, 1984.

Pember, Don R. "Does Pretrial Publicity Really Hurt?" *Columbia Journalism Review,* September/October, 1984.

Trager, Robert, and Stonecipher, Harry W. "Gag Orders: An Unresolved Dilemma." 55 *Journalism Quarterly* 231, 1978.

Cases

in re *Application of NBC,* 653 F.2d 609 (1981).

Bank of America v. *Hotel Rittenhouse Assoc.,* 800 F.2d 339 (1986).

Branzburg v. *Hayes,* 408 U.S. 655 (1972).

Cable News Network, 824 F.2d 1046 (1987).

Capital Newspapers v. *Moynihan,* 525 N.Y.S.2d 24 (1988).

CBS v. *U.S. District Court,* 729 F.2d 1174 (1984).

CBS v. *U.S. District Court,* 765 F.2d 823 (1985).

Chandler v. *Florida,* 449 U.S. 560 (1981).

Cincinnati Gas and Electric Co. v. *General Electric Co.,* 854 F.2d 900 (1988).

Connecticut Magazine v. *Moraghan,* 676 F.Supp. 38 (1987).

Conway v. *U.S.,* 852 F.2d 187 (1988).

Courier Journal v. *Marshall,* 282 F.2d 361 (1987).

Daily Gazette v. *West Virginia Bar,* 326 S.E.2d 705 (1984).

Estes v. *Texas,* 381 U.S. 532 (1965).

Federal Publications v. *Kurtz,* 94 Wash.2d 51 (1980).

Florida v. *Green,* 395 So.2d 532 (1981).

Florida v. *Palm Beach Newspapers,* 395 So.2d 544 (1981).

Globe Newspapers v. *Superior Court,* 457 U.S. 596 (1982).

in re *Globe Newspapers,* 729 F.2d 572 (1984).

in re *Herald Co.,* 734 F.2d 572 (1984).

Irvin v. *Dowd,* 366 U.S. 717 (1961).

in re *J.S.,* 438 A.2d 1125 (1981).

Journal Publishing v. *Mechem,* 801 F.2d 1233 (1988).

Kansas City Star v. *Fossey,* 630 P.2d 1176 (1981).

Kearns-Tribune v. *Lewis,* 685 P.2d 515 (1984).

in re *Knight Publishing,* 743 F.2d 231 (1984).

KPNX v. *Maricopa County Superior Court,* 678 P.2d 431 (1984).

KUTV v. *Conder,* 668 P.2d 513 (1983).

KUTV v. *Wilkinson,* 686 P.2d 456 (1984).

Landmark Communications v. *Virginia,* 435 U.S. 829 (1978).

in re *Landmark Communications,* 12 M.L.R. 1340 (1985).

Levine v. *U.S. District Court,* 764 F.2d 590 (1985).

Leviton v. *U.S.,* 193 F.2d 848 (1951).

Marshall v. *U.S.,* 360 U.S. 310 (1959).

Miami Herald v. *Lewis,* 426 So.2d 1 (1982).

Murphy v. *Florida,* 421 U.S. 784 (1975).

NBC v. *Cooperman,* 116 A.2d 287 (1986).

Nebraska Press Association v. *Stuart,* 427 U.S. 539 (1976).

in re *New York Times,* 533 NYS2d 73 (1988).

Page Corp. v. *Lumpkin*, 292 S.E.2d 815 (1982).

Pennekamp v. *Florida*, 328 U.S. 331 (1946).

Press Enterprise v. *Riverside Superior Court*, 464 U.S. 501 (1984).

Press Enterprise v. *Riverside Superior Court*, 478 U.S. 1 (1986).

Richmond Newspapers v. *Virginia*, 448 U.S. 555 (1980).

in re *Russell*, 726 F.2d 1007 (1984).

Seattle Times v. *Ishikawa*, 640 P.2d 716 (1982).

Seattle Times v. *U.S. District Court*, 845 F.2d 1273 (1988).

Shepherd v. *Florida*, 341 U.S. 50 (1951).

Sheppard v. *Maxwell*, 384 U.S. 333 (1966).

Smith v. *Daily Mail Publishing Co.*, 443 U.S. 97 (1979).

Times-Picayune v. *Marullo*, 466 So.2d 1291 (1985).

U.S. v. *Brooklier*, 685 F.2d 1162 (1982).

U.S. v. *Burr*, 24 Fed. Cas. 49 No. 14692 (1807).

U.S. v. *Chagra*, 701 F.2d 354 (1983).

U.S. v. *Criden*, 675 F.2d 550 (1982).

U.S. v. *Edwards*, 823 F.2d 111 (1987).

U.S. v. *Ford*, 830 F.2d 596 (1987).

U.S. v. *Haller*, 837 F.2d 84 (1988).

U.S. v. *Hastings*, 695 F.2d 1278 (1983).

U.S. v. *Schlette*, 842 F.2d 1574 (1988).

U.S. v. *Smith*, 776 F.2d 1104 (1985).

in re *Washington Post*, 807 F.2d 383 (1986).

8 OBSCENITY

In an age when there is no shortage of real life and death issues, it is indeed strange that questions regarding the distribution, sale and even possession of obscene and erotic material command so much public attention. Year after year discussions about "what to do about obscenity?" flourish in this nation. Commissions study the problem; courts litigate the matter; protestors decry the material; civil libertarians defend it; and the mass media focus on the intensely emotional debates.

What is it about obscenity or other erotic material that provokes so much emotion in people? Why is it that the control of the distribution or sale or even possession of such material remains, year after year, such an important issue to so many people? United States District Judge H. Lee Sarokin noted recently that so-called adult book stores are estalished to sell merchandise intended to arouse sexual passion.

> They also seem to arouse passions of an entirely different sort. If a merchant announced his intention to open a store dedicated to murder mysteries, no matter how violent or bloody, nary a picket or protestor would appear. But should one announce that sex is to be the main theme, then organized opposition is inevitable (*E-Bru, Inc. v. Graves,* 1983).

Sarokin added that the public permits books, movies and television to inundate us with murder by gun or knife, strangling, rape, beatings and mayhem, all of which are illegal. But depictions of sexual acts, most of which are legal, are condemned with a furor. "We will tolerate without a murmur a movie showing the most brutal murder, but display a couple in the act of love and the outcry is deafening," Sarokin said.

The wisdom of Solomon, perhaps many Solomons, is needed to answer the questions raised above. For our purposes it is sufficient to note such passion and concern, and acknowledge that a great many Americans (and this is a peculiar American phenomenon) remain obsessed with what their neighbors read or watch.

The Supreme Court of the United States has defined what is legally obscene (see pp. 396–403). This particularly narrow range of material is considered beyond the ambit of First Amendment protection. Today, however, war is being waged against a far wider range of erotic material, much of it material that is not considered legally obscene. Song lyrics and music videos have been attacked. Public libraries have come under seige for owning admittedly frank but clinically sound sex education books. A coalition of conservative Christian groups, in league with a commission appointed by the Attorney General of the United States, successfully impaired the distribution of the so-called men's magazines like *Penthouse* and *Playboy.* In a few states efforts have been made to block the cablecasting of some R-rated movies. And a rock musician was recently prosecuted in California for including a reproduction of an erotic painting in an album jacket.

Why should there even be a chapter on the regulation of obscenity and pornography in a text on the law of mass communications that is concerned primarily with problems faced by journalists, advertising practitioners and public relations specialists? The persons involved in the business of producing, distributing and selling obscenity are surely among the dregs of civilized society. And the value of obscene material to society is probably insignificant. Yet we must remember that the rights of the best of us are no better than the rights of the worst of us. Obscenity mongers may not be the kinds of persons you would want to invite to your home for dinner. But John Peter Zenger was hardly a pillar of the community either. It is the people on the fringes of society who often push to extend civil liberties for all of us. And what if obscenity has little value to society? The same can be said about a considerable portion of advertising today, yet advertising enjoys the protection of the First Amendment.

There are compelling reasons for all of us to be concerned about the regulation of pornography and nonpornographic erotic material. The regulation of obscenity represents the proposition that the state can declare that one entire category of speech and press is without First Amendment protection—hardly a comforting proposition. It may only be obscenity that is banned today; it might be religious dogma or political speech tomorrow. The editor who applauds the clean-up of adult bookstores in her town should consider that the state might next attempt to clean up commentary critical of the government. And the Supreme Court has ruled that obscenity is without First Amendment protection largely on the basis of its conclusion that the Founding Fathers did not intend that obscenity should be protected by the First Amendment. This conclusion stands supported by only the barest of inconclusive evidence. Irrefutable evidence that such material is harmful to normal adults has not been brought forth.

The descriptions we use today to define obscenity, while surely better than descriptions of a half-century ago, remain amorphous. Because of this, self-censorship is exercised by many who deal in erotic material because they are unsure of just what it is that can be legally censored. The pressure noted earlier on record companies, music video producers, cable operators, magazine distributors and others has generally resulted in interruptions of the flow of perfectly legal material. The convenience store operator who drops the sale of *Playboy* to avoid a boycott limits the public accessibility to the monthly centerfold pictures and other salacious material. But also limited is public access to the not-infrequent news article or informative essay also contained in that magazine.

For these reasons and others, the regulation of obscenity and other erotic or sexually explicit material must remain a concern to all those who believe in freedom of expression; including persons employed in journalism, advertising and public relations. ◆

Early Obscenity Law

The Puritans, those sixteenth and seventeenth century religious reformers who came to North America from England to establish theocratic settlements, were not the first to pass laws against obscene books and pictures. Many persons argue that pre-Revolutionary laws against blasphemy also prohibited obscenity, but the best available evidence doesn't support this thesis. Substantial amounts of erotic material were in circulation in late eighteenth century America, some of it homegrown, some of it imported. As busy as he was with other matters, Benjamin Franklin still had time to write erotic literature. Some members of the Supreme Court have argued that when the First Amendment was drafted, it was not intended to protect the flow of obscenity. But there is no irrefutable evidence to support this argument, only the sense that it sounds logical to some persons.

The first recorded prosecution having to do with obscenity occurred in 1815, when a man named Jesse Sharpless was fined for exhibiting a painting of a man "in an imprudent posture with a woman." There are on record earlier convictions for offenses tied to obscenity; these were prosecutions under common law for crimes against God, not for merely displaying erotic pictures. In 1821 Peter Holmes was convicted for publishing a spiced up version of John Cleland's *Memoirs of a Woman of Pleasure.*

During the nineteenth century obscenity laws and prosecutions became more common, ebbing and flowing with major reform movements in the 1820s, 1830s and in the wake of the Civil War. The first federal obscenity statute, a customs law regulating the importation of obscene articles, was adopted in 1842. The most comprehensive federal statute adopted during the century became law in 1873. Known as the Comstock Act because of the intense pressure applied on the Congress by a young man named Anthony Comstock, the law declared that all obscene books, pamphlets, pictures and other materials were nonmailable. No definition of obscenity was provided by the Congress however. The Comstock law, as amended, remains the federal law today.

Federal agencies such as the Bureau of Customs and the Post Office Department were the nation's most vigilant obscenity fighters during the late nineteenth and first half of the twentieth centuries. Sometimes straying beyond what the law actually permitted, these agencies banned, burned and confiscated huge amounts of erotic materials including religious objects, pieces of art, books (including some of the best written during that era), magazines (including science and diving publications) and a wide array of material on birth control. When the motion picture industry began to grow in the early part of this century, local and state censors went after films that they believed to be obscene as well. The courts, especially the federal courts, became inundated with obscenity prosecutions and appeals. The Supreme Court of the United States seemed especially drawn to such litigation. Between 1957 and 1977, for example, the High Court heard arguments in almost ninety obscenity cases and wrote opinions in nearly forty of those cases. The remainder were decided by memoranda orders. (See p. 24 for a definition of this term.)

Defining Obscenity

Outlawing obscenity is one thing. Defining it is something else. Take a look at your dictionary. Among the meanings for the word obscene is indecent, lewd or licentious. Licentious is defined in the same book as meaning lewd or lascivious. What does lascivious mean? Something that is lascivious is inclined to be lewd or lustful. Lustful is defined as "having lewd desires." Finally, look at the definition of lewd. It means obscene or indecent. We are back where we started.

But it wasn't the people who prepared dictionaries (lexicographers) who had to provide the legal definition of obscenity—it was the courts. The first widely used definition of obscenity was the Hicklin rule, a description of obscenity borrowed from British law. Under the Hicklin rule a work is obscene if it has a tendency to deprave and corrupt those whose minds are open to such immoral influences (children for example) and into whose hands it might happen to fall. This is a very broad definition, and it facilitated the intense era of prosecutions by both federal and state authorities that followed.

It wasn't until 1957 that the United States Supreme Court officially abandoned the Hicklin rule, declaring that because of this rule American adults were permitted to read only what was fit for children to read. "Surely this is to burn the house, to roast the pig," Justice Felix Frankfurter noted (*Butler* v. *Michigan*). In abandoning the Hicklin rule the High Court was forced to fashion a new definition of obscenity, beginning with the case of *Roth* v. *U.S.* in 1957. Over the next nine years, in a variety of obscenity rulings, what we now remember as the *Roth-Memoirs* test was developed by the Supreme Court. The test has three parts.

First, the dominant theme of the material taken as a whole must appeal to prurient interest in sex. Implicit in this part of the test is the concept that the prurient (erotic) appeal of a book or film is determined by its impact upon the average man or woman, not upon a child or an extremely sensitive person. Also, the dominant theme of the work, not just selected passages or a few pages, must have this prurient appeal.

Second, a court must find that the material is patently offensive because it affronts contemporary community standards relating to the description or representation of sexual matters. Something that is patently offensive is something that is clearly indecent, and while we are hesitant to use this term, some people have argued that *patently offensive* means hard-core pornography. By contemporary standards the Court meant current standards, but the Court did not define what it meant by community: Were the standards local, state, or national?

Third, before something can be found to be obscene it must be utterly without redeeming social value. That means to have no social value at all.

Two aspects of this test should be noted: First, all three of these elements had to be present before something was obscene. Something that was patently offensive and had a prurient appeal was still not legally obscene if it had redeeming social value. All three elements must coalesce. Second, it was not a balancing test. Social value was not weighed against prurient appeal. If there was any social value at all, the material was then not obscene. And this fact, probably more than any other, made prosecution of obscenity cases very difficult. Utterly without redeeming social value is a difficult standard to prove. Some appellate court judges believed that if even only one or two persons found some value in a book or movie it was not *utterly* without redeeming social value. Consequently, the typical tack taken by defense attorneys was to bring in expert witnesses—psychiatrists, English professors, art critics, and the like—to testify that the work had some value as sexual therapy or as an example of a certain type of literature or art. Voila! Redeeming social value.

SUMMARY

Prosecutions for obscenity did not occur in this nation until the early nineteenth century. In the 1820s and 1830s many states adopted their first obscenity laws. The first federal law was passed in 1842. The government actively prosecuted obscenity in the wake of the Civil War, and in 1873 the Congress adopted a strict new obscenity law. Obscenity was defined as being anything that had a tendency to deprave and corrupt those whose minds might be open to such immoral influences and into whose hands it might happen to fall. This was called the *Hicklin rule.* The rule meant that if any part of a book or other work had the tendency to deprave or corrupt any person (such as a child or overly sensitive individual) who might happen to see the work, the material was obscene and no person could buy it or see it.

In the 1950s and early 1960s, the Supreme Court adopted a new definition or test, for obscenity, the *Roth-Memoirs* test. The test had three main parts:

1. The dominant theme of the material, taken as a whole, appeals to an average person's prurient interest in sex. This modified the *Hicklin* rule in two ways:
   a. Material that was offensive to children or overly sensitive persons was no longer declared obscene for all.
   b. The entire work, not just a part of a book or film, must be considered when determining whether it is obscene.

2. The material is patently offensive because it affronts contemporary community standards relating to sexual matters. It was assumed that there was a single, national standard that was applicable to all parts of the country.
3. The material is utterly without redeeming social value. It has no value at all.

Contemporary Obscenity Law

The *Roth-Memoirs* test for obscenity was used until 1973. By then significant changes in the composition of the Supreme Court had occurred, Richard Nixon was President, and a conservative mood of "let's get tough with obscenity" seemed to be surfacing. A commission appointed by President Lyndon Johnson in 1967 to study obscenity and pornography recommended that all laws restricting the consumption of erotic materials by consenting adults be repealed. But the recommendation was widely criticized, especially by those in government. Nixon vowed never to relax in the fight against obscenity. He rejected the commission's conclusion that regular viewing or reading of obscenity produced no harmful effects, "Centuries of civilization and ten minutes of common sense tell us otherwise," he said. Adding a phrase that would come back to haunt him in a different context within four years, President Nixon noted, "American morality is not to be trifled with."

The *Miller* Test

The court fashioned a new test of obscenity, beginning with the case of *Miller v. California,* in 1973.

Marvin Miller was convicted of violating the California Penal Code for sending five unsolicited brochures to a restaurant in Newport Beach. The brochures, which advertised four erotic books and one film, contained pictures and drawings of men and women engaging in a variety of sexual activities. The recipient of the mailing complained to police, and Miller was prosecuted by state authorities.

In *Miller*, for the first time since 1957, a majority of the Supreme Court reached agreement on a definition of obscenity. Chief Justice Warren Burger and four other members of the High Court agreed that material is obscene if the following standards are met:

1. An average person, applying contemporary local community standards, finds that the work, taken as a whole, appeals to prurient interest.
2. The work depicts in a patently offensive way sexual conduct specifically defined by applicable state law.
3. The work in question lacks serious literary, artistic, political, or scientific value.

As in the *Roth-Memoirs* test, the implications and ambiguities in these three elements create the need for fuller explanation. As a result of the *Miller* ruling and subsequent obscenity decisions handed down by the Court since 1973, some guidelines have emerged.

Community Standards

The first element of the test concerns community standards: To an average person, applying contemporary local community standards, the work, taken as a whole, appeals to prurient interest. While this standard resembles the *Roth-Memoirs* test, the Supreme Court emphasized that local rather than national standards are to be applied. The Supreme Court had previously been silent on this question. In 1964 in *Jacobellis* v. *Ohio,* Justice Brennan subscribed to the notion that the applicable community standard was a national one. Only one other justice joined Brennan in this opinion, but as the only word on the subject, it led many observers to believe that the community standards applicable under the *Roth-Memoirs* test were national standards. The chief justice rejected this in *Miller,* arguing that it was silly to suggest that persons in a small town in Utah shared the same standards as persons living in Los Angeles.

The application of local standards has placed significant emphasis upon the trier of fact in the case. This can be the trial judge, but more often it is the jury. The Supreme Court expects the trier of fact to rely upon his or her own knowledge of the standards in the community to determine the applicable standards in an obscenity case. In 1974 in *Hamling* v. *United States,* Justice Rehnquist wrote:

> This Court has emphasized on more than one occasion that a principal concern in requiring that a judgment be made on the basis of contemporary community standards is to assure that the material is judged neither on the basis of each juror's personal opinion nor by its effect on a particular sensitive or insensitive person or group.

The matter of instructing jurors in the question of determining community standards quickly surfaced as a problem. Jurors are not supposed to rely on their own subjective preference; the jury is not a distillation of the standards of the community. The jurors are supposed to apply standards that they believe to be the prevailing ones in the community, standards that can be more conservative or more liberal than their own. Justice Rehnquist noted in his *Hamling* opinion that the jury should not judge the material on the basis of how it might affect a particularly sensitive person. Yet there are sensitive persons in every community. Do not their tastes matter, too?

In California a trial judge, in giving jurors instructions in an obscenity trial told them to consider the effect of the material upon members of the community as a whole, including children and sensitive persons. In 1978 in *Pinkus* v. *U.S.,* the Supreme Court ruled that the instructions to the jury had been faulty. In considering community standards, "Children are not to be included for these purposes as part of the 'community' . . . ," wrote Chief Justice Burger. However, instructing the jury to consider the impact of the material upon sensitive or insensitive persons is permissible, so long as these persons are looked at as a part of the entire community. Burger wrote:

> In the narrow and limited context of this case, the community includes all adults who comprise it, and a jury can consider them all in determining relevant community standards. The vice is in focusing upon the most susceptible or sensitive members when judging the obscenity of the materials, not in including them along with all others in the community.

In summary, then, the jury is most often the fact finder of community standards. The jurors are supposed to rely upon their knowledge of the standards of the adult members of the entire community to determine whether the material appeals to prurient interest or is patently offensive. The jurors are not supposed to apply their own standards. One commentator notes that this approach, which places such heavy emphasis on the jury, assumes that jurors know the prevailing standards in the community as well as have the needed exposure to "all manner of descriptions or representations of sexual matters, whether spoken, written or performed." This assumption is largely untested.

Which community is meant? Chief Justice Burger ruled in *Miller* that local community standards must prevail. Does this mean state, county, city, or neighborhood? In many instances state standards are the ones that apply. In some instances state high courts have even ruled that cities and counties have no right to pass obscenity laws, since the states, through state statutes, have preempted the field of criminalizing obscenity (see *Spokane* v. *Portch,* 1979, for example). Yet for all practical purposes, since jurors are normally drawn from county or city voting lists and are expected to rely upon their knowledge of community standards, local standards are applied in determining the obscenity of the material.

In 1977 the Supreme Court was forced to consider an unusual case from Iowa that focused upon the role of the state in determining community standards. Between 1974 and 1978 Iowa state law prohibited only the distribution of obscene materials to minors. During this period Jerry Lee Smith used the United States postal service to distribute within Iowa several erotic magazines to adult recipients. His distribution did not violate state law, but he was charged with violating federal obscenity laws that prohibit the mailing of obscene material. At his trial Smith argued that since the state did not prohibit the distribution of such material to adults, his mailings had not offended the prevailing community standards. The federal trial judge nevertheless instructed jurors to draw upon their knowledge of the views of the people in the community to determine community standards. As part of their determination jurors could consider the state law, but the absence of statutes prohibiting the distribution of obscene material among adults was not a controlling factor in determining community standards. The Supreme Court, by a five-to-four vote, supported this position. The jury's discretion to determine community standards was not circumscribed by state law or the absence of state law (*Smith* v. *U.S.*, 1977). Justice Blackmun wrote that it would be inappropriate for a state legislature to attempt to freeze a jury to one definition of contemporary community standards. The state legislature can define within a statute the kinds of conduct that will be regulated by the state. It can adopt a geographic limit in the determination of community standards by defining the area from which the jury can be selected in an obscenity case. But it must leave to the jury the question of community standards. Blackmun also pointed out that this was a federal case. "The community standards aspects of the federal law present issues of federal law upon which a state statute such as Iowa's cannot have a conclusive effect," he added (*Smith* v. *U.S.*, 1977).

The question of applicable community standards is also an important factor in cases that involve the shipment of erotic material over long distances and its importation from abroad. Consider these hypothetical situations. A woman in New York mails obscene materials to a man in Nebraska. She is arrested and tried. At her trial, do the community standards of New York or the standards of Nebraska apply? Here is another case. A man in Florida orders erotic material from Sweden. The material enters this country in Boston and is seized, and the United States customs service calls for a determination of whether the material is obscene. What community standards should apply? Those of Boston or of Florida? The answers to these questions are tentative, but case law suggests the following guidelines.

In cases involving violation of postal laws, the government may choose to try the case in the community in which the material was sent or received or in any district through which the material passed (see section on postal censorship, pages 415–417). Consequently, the applicable standards are the standards existing in the community in which the trial is held. In the hypothetical cases just given, if the government chose to prosecute the defendant in New York, the standards of that community would apply. If the government chose to prosecute in Nebraska, those community standards would apply. Recently a postmaster in Oregon asked a postmaster in Wyoming to use a false name and solicit by mail erotic material distributed by an Oregon man. The defendant sent the material to Wyoming, was arrested and tried, and Wyoming community standards were applied. The record showed that the defendant had never resided in, traveled through, or had any previous business contact in Wyoming—prior to the time he sent the erotic matter through the mails to the Wyoming postmaster. Still, the Court of Appeals for the Tenth Circuit concluded (*U.S.* v. *Blucher*, 1978):

> So long as *Hamling* is the law, publishers and distributors everywhere who are willing to fill subscriptions nationwide are subject to the creative zeal of federal enforcement officers who are free to shop for venue from which juries with the most restrictive views are likely to be impanelled. . . .

A similar decision was reached in *U.S.* v. *McManus* (1976).

In cases involving import laws and customs regulations, the community standards of the district in which the material was seized—not of the district in which the addressee lives—are normally the applicable standards. In the hypothetical case just cited, Boston standards rather than Florida standards would be applied. When customs officials seized hundreds of printed articles in New York, they sent notices to all 573 intended recipients advising them that the material would be destroyed within twenty days because it was obscene, unless the recipients made a claim challenging the government determination that importation of the material was illegal. Fourteen persons made such claims and sought hearings. None of these persons lived in New York, yet the Court of Appeals for the Second Circuit ruled that since the material was seized in New York and since the obscenity hearing would be held in New York, New York community standards should be applied (*U.S.* v. *Various Articles of Obscene Merchandise,* 1977).

If the first element of the *Miller* obscenity test appears to give the trier of fact (judge or jury) almost total power in determining what is and is not obscene, the second element, as interpreted by the Supreme Court, limits that power.

Patent Offensiveness

The second element of the *Miller* test says that a work is obscene if it depicts in a patently offensive way sexual conduct specifically defined by applicable state law. There are two basic parts to the test: (1) patent offensiveness as determined by community standards and (2) sexual conduct specifically defined by applicable state law. Each of the two elements is important.

Patent offensiveness is to be determined by the trier of the fact, the judge or the jury, using contemporary community standards. But that phrase is deceptive, because the courts have ruled that the discretion of juror or judge in determining patent offensiveness is not unlimited. The kinds of conduct that may be labeled "patently offensive" in a prosecution for obscenity are hard-core types of conduct. A 1974 Supreme Court ruling illustrates this seeming contradiction. In 1974 in *Jenkins* v. *Georgia* the Supreme Court was faced with the decision by a Georgia jury that the movie *Carnal Knowledge* was obscene. The film was an R-rated movie, and while it had scenes that included partial nudity, it contained no explicit sexual scenes usually associated with X-rated films. Nevertheless, because in the *Miller* ruling the United States Supreme Court had given communities the power to determine community standards and because this jury found that *Carnal Knowledge* violated those standards, the Georgia Supreme Court upheld the conviction.

The United States Supreme Court reversed the ruling, saying that the Georgia courts obviously misunderstood the *Miller* decision. The jury did have the right to determine local standards, but only those descriptions or depictions of sexual conduct that are patently offensive can be censored, regardless of local standards. Justice Rehnquist noted that in the *Miller* case Chief Justice Burger gave two examples of the kind of patently offensive material he was talking about. These examples included "representations or descriptions of ultimate sexual acts, normal or perverted, actual or simulated," and "representations or descriptions of masturbation, excretory functions, and lewd exhibition of the genitals." Rehnquist said that while this catalog of descriptions was not exhaustive, it was "intended to fix substantive constitutional limitations . . . on the type of material . . . subject to a determination of obscenity" (*Jenkins* v. *Georgia,* 1974). Therefore, under the second part of the *Miller* test, a jury is limited in what it can find to be obscene to what commentators call hard-core pornography.

The second element in the Miller test seems to be confusing in another way. Chief Justice Burger wrote that the descriptions or depictions of sexual conduct that are banned have to be specifically defined by the applicable state law as written or authoritatively construed. This sounds as though before a state can prohibit a description of a certain kind of sexual conduct, the state must pass a specific law defining that kind of material.

How specific does the applicable state statute have to be? Not very. The High Court approved an Ohio statute that defined material as being obscene if it contained a display or description of nudity, sexual excitement, sexual conduct, bestiality, extreme or bizarre violence, cruelty, brutality, or human bodily functions or eliminations.

What if a state law does not define obscenity? What if it merely prohibits "obscene materials"? This is really not a problem, according to Chief Justice Burger, who ruled that it is sufficient in such states if the state supreme court rules that the term *obscene materials* in the law means specific descriptions of sexual conduct. For example, the Supreme Court in 1977 upheld the conviction of an individual who had been found guilty of selling two sado-masochistic publications. The defendant argued that the state law did not specifically prohibit the sale of such material. But Justice White and four members of the High Court ruled that such an argument had no merit, that such material had been held to violate Illinois state law long before the *Miller* ruling, and that such authoritative construction of the statute was sufficient to meet the test outlined under *Miller*. The examples cited by Chief Justice Burger in the *Miller* ruling, according to Justice White, were not exhaustive, but simply illustrative of the kinds of materials that could be considered patently offensive (*Ward* v. *Illinois,* 1977). Since 1973 most state obscenity statutes have been found to comply with the *Miller* standards, because of either specific descriptive language in the statute or authoritative construction by the state's high court.

Serious Value

To be obscene a work must lack serious literary, artistic, political, or scientific value. This is the third element of the *Miller* test. This element is designed to be a kind of check on the first two parts of the test, an effort to protect important works from obscenity prosecution. "The judicial role is more pronounced in the determination of the 'serious value' of the material, which is *not* [author emphasis] to be judged by the tastes of the average person or measured by community standards" (*Penthouse* v. *Mcauliffe,* 1981). While the first two prongs of the *Miller* test are to be applied using a community standards barometer, community standards are inapplicable when applying the third element of the test. "Just as the ideas a work represents need not obtain a majority approval to merit protection, neither insofar as the First Amendment is concerned does the value of the work vary from community to community based on the degree of local acceptance it has won," Justice Byron White wrote for the Supreme Court in 1987. "The proper inquiry is not whether an ordinary member of any given community would find serious literary, artistic, political or scientific value in allegedly obscene material, but whether a reasonable person would find such value in the material," White added for the five person majority (*Pope* v. *Illinois*). In applying the third standard then, jurors are to determine whether a reasonable person would see a serious value in the work. Does this reasonable person test permit more leeway for allegedly obscene material than a community standards test? The dissenters in the *Pope* case did not think so. Justice John Paul Stevens wrote that in many cases, reasonable persons could legitimately disagree about whether particular materials have social value. In addition, Stevens wrote, the use of the reasonable person test could foster "intolerable orthodoxy" in regulation of sexually explicit material. In fact, neither a community standards test nor a reasonable persons test gives a jury of lay citizens much help in determining whether a work has serious value or not.

It is probably unnecessary to point out that the third element in the *Miller* test—whether a work has serious literary, artistic, political, or scientific value— is considerably narrower than the "utterly without redeeming social value" standard from the *Roth-Memoirs* test. Material that may have some redeeming social value may totally lack any serious literary, artistic, political or scientific value. Both prosecutors and defendants often introduce "expert" testimony to persuade a judge that a film or book has some kind of serious value. Courts often have difficulty sorting out the conflicting statements from these witnesses because the Supreme Court has never defined "serious value" for the lower courts. In *Miller,* Chief Justice Burger warned lower courts to "always remain sensitive to any infringement on genuinely serious literary, artistic, political, or scientific value," but such an admonition does not help define the concept. Many courts have ruled that mere entertainment value in a film or book or the existence of a tenuous story line or the inclusion of an isolated idea are usually insufficient to redeem an otherwise obscene work (see *Penthouse* v. *Mcauliffe,* 1981, for example).

A United States district judge in Georgia defined serious value in this way when he was asked to determine whether the film *Caligula* was obscene (*Penthouse* v. *Mcauliffe,* 1981):

> We believe that by the phrase "serious value" the Supreme Court meant to extend constitutional protection to material which advocates ideas and in which the ideas are not used merely as a disguise or a sham for presenting

obscenity. The ideas must be a substantial part of the material and treated in a nonfrivolous manner. . . . We do not believe that the "serious value" test of *Miller* was meant to extend protection only to works which are artistic successes or which include textual political commentary. All political views and ideas, including historical narrative and social criticism, are protected, as are all serious artistic and intellectual efforts, whether they appeal to the average person or not.

The judge ruled that the film, which portrays violence and explicit sex in telling the story of the life of Roman Emperor Caligula during his reign from A.D. 37 to A.D. 41, had serious political and artistic value.

The Supreme Court has also instructed lower appellate courts not to hesitate to closely scrutinize trial court judgments regarding "serious value." Justice Blackmun in *Smith* v. *U.S.* noted that the determination of whether a book or magazine or film lacks value "is particularly amenable to appellate review." Hence, while an appellate court should be reluctant to second-guess a jury on a determination of contemporary community standards, it should not be hesitant in making an independent determination that a work either has or has not literary, artistic, political, or scientific value (*Smith* v. *U.S.,* 1977).

Some changes in obscenity law can be observed since the adoption of the *Miller* test. The Supreme Court is hearing far fewer obscenity cases than it did twenty years ago. Also, many communities have abandoned their attempts to regulate obscenity through criminal prosecution and today attempt to use civil suits or zoning regulations to control such erotic material (see pages 412–414 and 420–423 for a discussion of these means). Whether either of these changes is the result of *Miller* is unclear.

Selective Standards

Two other dimensions of the definition of obscenity that developed in the years prior to *Miller* seem to retain vitality today.

In 1966 in *Ginzburg* v. *U.S.,* the Supreme Court ruled that the manner in which material is marketed, advertised, and displayed can be a factor in determining whether a work is obscene or not. This case was the result of publisher Ralph Ginzburg's efforts to sell three different publications. In marketing these publications, Justice Brennan said, Ginzburg emphasized their erotic nature and thus was engaged in "**pandering**"—that is, in "the business of purveying textual or graphic matter openly advertised to appeal to the erotic interest of customers." This action can be a key factor in determining whether a publication or a film is obscene or not, Brennan said. Ginzburg's conviction was affirmed.

Richard Kuh, in *Foolish Figleaves,* cites as examples of pandering such schemes as using a provocative cover, using advertisements that list the previous bannings of the work, displaying the work along with other borderline items, and in various other ways promoting the erotic, deviant, or scatological appeal of the material. In 1977 in *Splawn* v. *California,* four members of the

Supreme Court agreed with Justice Rehnquist's majority opinion that "evidence of pandering to prurient interests in the creation, promotion, or dissemination of material is relevant in determining whether the material was obscene." One year later, in writing for a seven-man majority, Chief Justice Burger noted, "We have held, and reaffirmed, that to aid a jury in its determination of whether materials are obscene, the methods of their creation, promotion, or dissemination are relevant. . ." (*Pinkus* v. *U.S.,* 1978). Hence it seems assured that if proof of pandering is introduced by the prosecution, the jury may consider it evidence in determining the obscenity of the books or films or magazines.

The Supreme Court has also ruled that states may adopt **variable obscenity standards** for juveniles and for adults; that is, material acceptable for sale to adults may not be acceptable for sale to children. A bookseller or a theater owner can be prosecuted for providing obscene material to young people. This is a standard that emerged in 1968 in *Ginsberg* v. *New York* and was upheld as recently as 1975 in *Erznoznik* v. *City of Jacksonville.* In the latter case the city forbade drive-in theaters to show movies in which female buttocks and bare breasts were shown if the theater screen was visible from the street. The ordinance, which was justified in part as a means of protecting the city's youth from exposure to such material, was defective according to the Supreme Court. The High Court said that laws aimed at setting variable standards of obscenity for adults and for children were permissible but must be carefully constructed. "Only in relatively narrow and well-defined circumstances may government bar public dissemination of protected materials to children," Justice Powell wrote. Banning the showing of nudity is simply not narrow enough; only materials that have significant erotic appeal to juveniles may be suppressed under such a statute, he added. A simple ban on all nudity, regardless of context, justification, or other factors, violates the First Amendment.

Even if laws that erect a variable obscenity standard can pass constitutional muster, they nevertheless face a significant difficulty: in limiting what is accessible to children, the state cannot substantially reduce what is available to adults. Such laws are relatively simple to enforce when related to motion pictures; the theater owner can forbid all underage persons from entering the theater. But bookstores present a different problem. The state of Virginia recently adopted a law that prohibited the commercial display of sexually explicit material deemed harmful to juveniles. Books and magazines that included nudity, sexual conduct, or described "sexual excitement" were placed off-limits to persons under age eighteen. Such content is common to many books and magazines that are popular and perfectly legal for adults, however. So how does a bookseller deal with the problem? The store owners who challenged the Virginia law told the court they had only four options, none of which were acceptable. Persons under eighteen years of age could be prohibited from entering the store but this would result in a loss of sales of those books that are acceptable to young people. Also, the store would become an "adults only" establishment, an unattractive connotation to many adults. Booksellers could establish adult-only sections in their stores, but the ban on what is available to juveniles includes a wide variety of book categories. The book seller would need two different photography sections, one containing books with the occasional nude photograph, and one that young people could use. The same would apply to books on such subjects as science, medicine and mass media. Store owners could refrain from stocking any books covered by the ban, but this would turn their shops into what would amount to children's bookstores. Many best-selling novels and nonfiction works would be excluded. Finally, booksellers could stock the adults-only works behind the counter, but customers could not peruse these books, and it would require additional staff to serve the adult customers. A United States district court said the law was too broad, and placed a substantial restriction upon adult access to protected material (*American Booksellers v. Strobel,* 1985). The United States Court of Appeals for the Fourth Circuit reversed the ruling (*American Booksellers Association v. Virginia,* 1986), and the case wound up in the Supreme Court. In 1988 the High Court sent the case back to Virginia, asking the Virginia Supreme Court for an authoritative construction of the meaning of the statute. Justice William Brennan said that if the law were construed broadly, it might very well be a violation of the First Amendment. But if it was read very narrowly, it might pass constitutional muster. Brennan asked, for example: Would a bookseller be in compliance with the law if he or she did not segregate adult-only books, but prevented any juveniles he or she observed from looking at a restricted book or magazine? The High Court also said it wanted to know the breadth of the definition of restricted books. Did it cover, as booksellers alleged, a wide range of material? Or would it only make a small percentage of those books typically carried in a bookstore off-limits to young people?

In September of 1988 the Virginia Supreme Court answered both questions in such a manner as to construe the statute in a very narrow fashion so that it would pass First Amendment muster. What kinds of books and other materials are covered by the law? The court quoted the Virginia attorney general's statement that "A book will pass statutory muster [will not be covered by the statute] if it has serious value for a legitimate minority of juveniles, and in this context a legitimate minority may consist of older, normal adolescents." The court also said that the method chosen by the bookseller to display his or her wares is not the critical factor in determining the meaning of "knowingly display for commercial purposes." It is instead the opportunity the bookseller may afford to juveniles to take books off the shelves that they are unable to legally buy and read them in the store. To win a conviction under the statute, the court ruled, the state would have to show that the bookseller knowingly afforded juveniles an opportunity to peruse harmful materials or took no reasonable steps to prevent such perusal (*Virgina* v. *American Booksellers Association*, 1988). By forcing the Virginia high court to first construe its statute, the Supreme Court indirectly forced that court to interpret the statute in a very narrow fashion or face a ruling that it was unconstitutional. This should have an impact on the manner in which other state courts consider similar statutes aimed at keeping erotic material out of the hands of juveniles.

| Child Pornography | In 1982 the United States Supreme Court unanimously upheld a New York statute aimed at limiting the distribution of child pornography. The state law prohibits any person from knowingly promoting a sexual performance by a child under the age of sixteen years by distributing material that photographically depicts such a performance. The statute explicitly defines sexual performance as sexual conduct and lists the kinds of conduct that are not permitted to be shown. Justice Byron White wrote that child pornography defined in the statute is unprotected speech and can be subject to content-based regulation. The state has a strong state interest in protecting the well-being of children. To help prevent the abuse of children who are made to engage in sexual conduct for commercial purposes, the state can prohibit the distribution of material that shows children engaged in such conduct, even if this material might not be obscene under the three-part *Miller* test. White said that when a judge considers photographic depictions of live sexual performances by children the *Miller* formulation should be adjusted in the following respects: "A trier of fact need not find that the material appeals to the prurient interest of the average person; it is not required that sexual conduct portrayed be done so in a patently offensive manner; and the material at issue need not be considered as a whole." The value of permitting live performances and photographic reproductions of children engaged in lewd sexual conduct is exceedingly modest, the justice said. The law is aimed at stopping the sexual exploitation of children. One sure way to stop or at least reduce this exploitation is to ban the distribution of films in which children are depicted in sexual conduct. Distribution of written descriptions or other kinds of depictions (drawings) of children engaged in sexual conduct that are not otherwise obscene and that do not involve live performances are still protected by the First Amendment, White said (*New York* v. *Ferber*, 1982). |

A great many states have passed laws similar to the New York statute, and some of these laws are even more extensive. Susan J. Caughlan noted in a recent issue of the *Loyola Law Review* that some states have extended their statutes to prohibit the private possession of child pornography as well as the production and distribution of such material. The author suggests that such laws seem to be in conflict with a 1969 Supreme Court ruling, *Stanley* v. *Georgia*, in which the Supreme Court unanimously ruled that the Constitution protects the private possession of otherwise unprotected speech. "If the First Amendment means anything," Justice Thurgood Marshall wrote, "it means that the state has no business telling a man, sitting alone in his own house, what books he may read or what films he may watch." Caughlan therefore expects a constitutional challenge to the laws banning private possession.

In 1988 Congress passed its own child pornography law that requires anyone who produces material that includes images of sexual activity or lascivious exhibition of the genitals to keep records of the ages of the models or actors used. These performers must be at least 18 years old. Without these records to prove the ages of the participants, it would be presumed that the producer or photographer used minors in creating the work, and he or she could be prosecuted for selling obscene material. A coalition of groups challenged the law saying that it makes it very difficult in many instances for legitimate book and magazine publishers, and film and television producers to produce or distribute material with any sexual content, even if it is not obscene. The difficulty of getting such information about works produced in foreign countries was noted. Also, material that was produced before the law went into effect could not be re-issued without such age certification. A film made in 1985, for example, that lacked the age certification, could not be re-issued as a video cassette if it contained any sexual content. The presumption that minors were used in the production would apply. A decision in the lawsuit was pending in mid-1989.

Pornography and Women	One of the most concerted challenges to erotic material during the eighties came from an unlikely coalition of feminists and social conservatives such as the members of the Moral Majority. Ordinances drafted in Minneapolis, Indianapolis, Suffolk County, New York, and Los Angeles County, California, were aimed at blocking the sale and distribution of pornography on the grounds that it discriminates against women and fosters violence against women and children. The Minneapolis ordinance was drafted by two prominent feminists, Catherine MacKinnon, a professor of law at the University of Minnesota, and Andrea Dworkin, author of the 1981 book *Pornography: Men Possessing Women*.

Only the city of Indianapolis ultimately adopted such an ordinance, which created a civil cause of action for complainants aggrieved by any discriminatory practice prohibited by the ordinance, including the distribution of pornographic material. Complaints were to be investigated by the office of equal opportunity and if informal attempts to eliminate the discriminatory practice failed, a formal hearing could be held. Ultimately, the respondent in the case could face a court injunction blocking future discrimination, such as the distribution of certain magazines or books. Not all feminist organizations supported the ordinance, which was highly controversial because of its definition of pornography. The ordinance went far beyond the traditional definition of obscenity or pornography. It declared that pornography shall mean the graphic sexually explicit subordination of women, whether in pictures or in words, that also includes one of the following:

1. Women are presented as sexual objects who enjoy pain or humiliation.
2. Women are presented as sexual objects who experience sexual pleasure in being raped.
3. Women are presented as sexual objects—tied up, cut up, mutilated, bruised, or physically hurt—or as dismembered, truncated, fragmented, or severed into body parts.
4. Women are presented being penetrated by objects or animals.
5. Women are presented in scenarios of degradation, injury, abasement, or torture or are shown as filthy, inferior, bleeding, bruised, or hurt in a context that makes these conditions sexual.
6. Women are presented as sexual objects for domination, conquest, violation, exploitation, possession, or use or through postures or positions of servility, submission, or display.

Some observers noted that based on the final category alone, a large percentage of American advertising could be declared to be discriminatory (which it may well be) and hence be enjoined.

In June of 1984 an amalgam of booksellers, book distributors, publishers, and others sought to have the ordinance declared unconstitutional in federal court. Five months later United States District Judge Sarah Evans Barker granted the plaintiff's motion for summary judgment and ruled that the antipornography law was unconstitutional. The court ruled that the ordinance was unconstitutionally vague and that the kind of expression it sought to prohibit was protected by the First Amendment.

The proponents of the law had sought to avoid a confrontation with the First Amendment by arguing that the Indianapolis ordinance outlawed conduct, not expression. The law was aimed at stopping discrimination against women. And the Supreme Court, in *New York* v. *Ferber,* had recently approved of a New York statute that was aimed at blocking a kind of onerous conduct, the use of children in sexual performances. But Judge Barker ruled that even if the court accepts the findings of the city that the distribution of pornography conditions members of society to subordinate women, the means by which the city attempts to combat this discrimination is through the regulation of speech. Speech may only be restrained, the judge noted, if it falls into one of those widely recognized categories of expression that may be constitutionally regulated: obscenity, profanity, libel, fighting words, etc. While the kind of material outlawed by the ordinance is somewhat akin to the erotic material prohibited by obscenity laws, the definition of pornography in the ordinance goes far beyond the definition of obscenity in the three-part *Miller* test.

Proponents of the ordinance argued that in the *Ferber* ruling the Supreme Court permitted the state to regulate nonobscene expression because of a compelling state interest in protecting children. But the judge refused to accept the analogy between the protection of children and the protection of women, noting that adult women, unlike children, are capable of protecting themselves from being victimized by pornography (*American Booksellers Ass'n. v. Hudnut*, 1985).

The city appealed the ruling but lost when the United States Court of Appeals for the Seventh Circuit upheld the lower court ruling in August of 1985. Under the Indianapolis ordinance sexually explicit speech or expression is pornography or not, depending upon the perspective of the author, the court noted. Speech that subordinates women is pornographic, no matter how great the literary or political value of the work. Speech that portrays women in positions of equality is lawful, no matter how graphic the sexual conduct. "This is thought control," the court said. "It establishes an approved view of women, of how they may react to sexual encounters, of how the sexes may relate to each other. Those who espouse the approved view may use sexual images; those who do not, may not." The court added, "The power to limit speech on the ground that truth has not yet prevailed and is not likely to prevail implies the power to declare truth" (*American Booksellers Ass'n. v. Hudnut*, 1985).

The failure of this ordinance to pass constitutional muster will not end the debate over the question of pornography and women. But the law has also sparked sharp debate within the women's movement itself. Many found the coalition between ardent feminists and the conservative political right an unholy alliance that may in the end thwart other feminist goals. The Feminists Anti-Censorship Task Force, a group that opposed the ordinance, also questioned whether the images in books and magazines do actually cause violent acts against women and whether this type of law is the proper way to attempt to change the misogynist attitudes of many American males. (See "Is One Women's Sexuality Another Women's Pornography?" in *Ms.*, April, 1985, p. 37.)

SUMMARY

The *Miller* test is used today by American courts to determine whether something is obscene. It has three parts. Material is legally obscene under the following conditions:

1. An average person, applying contemporary local community standards, finds that the work, taken as a whole, appeals to prurient interest. This test requires the fact finder to apply local (usually state or county) standards rather than a national standard. The jury (or the judge if there is not a jury) determines the standard, based upon their knowledge of what is acceptable in the community.

2. The work depicts in a patently offensive way sexual conduct specifically defined by applicable state law. Again, the fact finder in the case determines patent offensiveness, based upon local community standards. But the Supreme Court has ruled that only so-called hardcore pornography can be found to be patently offensive. Also, either the legislature or the state supreme court must specifically define the kind of offensive material that may be declared to be obscene.

3. The material lacks serious literary, artistic, political, or scientific value. This is a question of law, not of fact, to be decided in large part by the judge.

The three-part *Miller-Hamling* test is the test that courts must use in defining obscenity in all cases except those involving juveniles. The Supreme Court has ruled that states may use a broader definition of obscenity when they attempt to block the sale or distribution of erotic material to children or when they attempt to stop the exploitation of children who are forced to engage in sexual conduct by pornographic filmmakers. But such laws must be careful so as not to unconstitutionally ban legal material as well. But the federal courts blocked an attempt by the city of Indianapolis to outlaw written and visual material that might result in discrimination against women or provoke violence against women and children.

CONTROLLING OBSCENITY THROUGH CRIMINAL PROSECUTION

For more than one hundred years, the typical manner in which the state has attempted to control obscenity has been through a criminal prosecution. Such lawsuits are complicated, and to be successful in these cases, prosecutors must follow carefully prescribed paths in deciding whether material is obscene, in collecting and seizing evidence, and in making arrests. Often persons charged with exhibiting or selling obscene materials seek to plea bargain with the state to reduce the charge. Booksellers, theater owners, and other merchants who deal in pornographic materials often do not want to fight the government in an obscenity prosecution. They are not in the business to crusade for the First Amendment. Their goal is to stay out of jail and to return to selling books or showing movies. If the state can be convinced to reduce the obscenity charge in exchange for a guilty plea, the defendant can often get by with paying a fine instead of going to jail and be back in business within a few days of the arrest. Prosecutors seem amenable to such plea bargaining because, as one noted, "Our business is to stop public distribution of certain obscene materials, not put people in jail."

If a case goes to trial, the judge and the jury are the ones who must determine whether the material sold or exhibited is obscene. The fact finder in the trial—the jury or the judge if there is not a jury—determines parts one and two of the *Miller* test, prurient appeal and patent offensiveness. A jury can also rule on the serious value of a work, but since this determination is normally regarded as a matter of law, a judge plays a far greater role in this determination. The instructions given to the jury by the judge are usually vitally important to the outcome of an obscenity case. The instructions, of course, tell the jury what the law is—in other words, how to determine whether the material is obscene. A trial judge generally bases the instructions both on a personal reading of the law and on personal experience. Judge David Soukup of the Washington State Superior Court, who has tried numerous obscenity cases, told researcher Kirk Anderson this about jury instructions:

> Basically the matter of deciding what to include in a set of instructions depends on what the judge himself feels is necessary such that the jury can make a knowledgeable and legally sound determination, a judgment that is predicated upon his own interpretation of the law and what it requires, in combination with what his practical experience tells him jurors need in order to best understand the criteria they must apply to the facts at hand. The result of this highly individualized process, which is also influenced by the judge's philosophy of his role under the law and his feeling about pornography in general, is that some judges will stick pretty close to the *Miller* test and the definitions of it provided by the Supreme Court, while others will attempt to embellish them by adding varying degrees of explanation arising from their own interpretations of the law. . . .

In addition to determining whether the material is obscene, jurors are also called upon to answer the question of whether the defendant was knowledgeable about the contents of what was being sold, distributed, or published. This is called **scienter,** or guilty knowledge. In a 1959 case, *Smith v. California,* the United States Supreme Court ruled that before a person can be convicted for selling obscene books the state has to prove that the seller was aware of the contents of the books, that he or she knew what they were about. The reason for this ruling is quite simple. As Justice William Brennan wrote more than thirty years ago, "If the bookseller is criminally liable without knowledge of the contents, . . . he will tend to restrict the books he sells to those he has inspected; and thus the state will have imposed a restriction upon the distribution of constitutionally protected as well as obscene literature . . ." (*Smith v. California,* 1959).

There has always been some confusion about exactly what a state or other jurisdiction must prove. For example, does the bookseller have to know the books are obscene? In the *Hamling* decision the Supreme Court tried to clarify this point by repeating that scienter merely means proving that the defendant has a general knowledge of the material in question—that a movie contains sadistic scenes for example. It is not necessary that the bookseller or the theater operator know that the material is legally obscene. Normally a prosecutor can demonstrate scienter without much trouble, but it is another question that the jury must decide.

What this process suggests is that, like other street crimes, the prosecution of obscenity in any community depends largely upon how the law is administered and interpreted *locally*. And within certain parameters, a community can read the books it wants to read, see the movies it wants to see, and buy the kinds of magazines it wants to buy. What the United States Supreme Court says about obscenity is relevant to most communities in only an indirect way. These practical realities regarding obscenity prosecutions suggest that the nation's appellate courts—especially the Supreme Court of the United States—probably spend far too much time contemplating this matter.

CONTROLLING OBSCENITY THROUGH CIVIL NUISANCE SUITS

Some communities have attempted to block the sale or exhibition of obscene material through the use of civil nuisance suits. Initially some states attempted to use their general nuisance statutes to block the distribution of obscene material. More recently, however, nearly a dozen states and a great many cities and towns have passed nuisance statutes specifically aimed at obscenity. These laws operate in this fashion. The statutes or ordinances define nuisance to include obscenity and then define obscenity using the three-part *Miller* test. Prosecutors are authorized by the statute to maintain a civil suit to abate the nuisance, much as they would bring an action against a factory that is polluting the community. A hearing is held to determine whether the defendant in the suit is in fact maintaining a nuisance; that is, whether obscene materials are being sold or exhibited. The court will determine whether or not the material is obscene, using the *Miller* test. If the materials are found to be legally obscene, an injunction is issued to abate the nuisance; the materials can no longer be sold.

Few find fault with the procedure thus far. But then the court can issue a second injunction, called a blanket or "standards injunction." This injunction forbids the defendant to sell or exhibit any other comparable obscene material; that is, material that the court has not yet seen but that would be obscene under the law. If the defendant violates this injunction, he or she will be held in contempt of court. Some persons have argued that this second injunction—banning the sale of material that has not yet been declared legally obscene—is an illegal prior restraint. But the courts have generally disagreed.

North Carolina, for example, passed a nuisance statute aimed at theaters regularly showing pornographic films and at adult bookstores that had coin-operated film projectors (peep shows) showing explicit sexual activity or sold pictorial magazines or photographs showing similar activity. The statute defined obscenity using the three-part *Miller* test. The state is obliged to prove that a bookstore owner or theater operator whom it takes to court deals predominantly and in the regular course of business with such obscene material. If the court agrees that the material is obscene and that it is a principal or substantial part of the defendant's stock in trade, an injunction will be issued barring the future sale or exhibition of comparable material. If this injunction is violated, the individual can be held in contempt of court and fined or jailed. The United States Court of Appeals for the Fourth Circuit upheld the North Carolina law despite protests by the defendant that it was a prior restraint (*Fehlhaber* v. *North Carolina,* 1982).

It appears that courts have upheld the constitutionality of such nuisance laws because they view the contempt hearing, at which the merchant may be punished for violating the second or the "standards injunction," as being almost identical with a criminal prosecution. "The courts validate the injunction because its prohibition is substantively identical to the prohibition of a criminal obscenity statute and because the contempt proceeding is similar in structure to a criminal obscenity trial," wrote Steven T. Catlett in an issue of the *Columbia Law Review.* The courts reason that since the two regulatory techniques are similar, if one is constitutional, the other must be also, Catlett notes. In the contempt hearing the state must prove that legally obscene material was sold or exhibited in violation of the injunction. The defendant enjoys the same procedural safeguards as a defendant in a criminal case. And the same kinds of punishment—fine or imprisonment—will be applied.

The United States Supreme Court has not ruled directly on the question of whether such laws are constitutional or not. In 1981 the High Court struck down a Texas statute that allowed a court to issue a temporary restraining order against a theater owner barring as a nuisance the exhibition of a film even before a court determined that the film was obscene (*Vance* v. *Universal Amusement,* 1980). The court never considered the question of the constitutionality of the second injunction, the "standards injunction," in this case. But in a dissent, Justice White did discuss the question and concluded that the enforcement of the standards injunction was "functionally indistinguishable from a criminal obscenity statute." Hence it is constitutional.

Some still aren't certain that such laws should be permitted. Circuit Judge Phillips dissented in the court of appeals ruling approving the North Carolina law. He noted (*Fehlhaber* v. *North Carolina,* 1982):

> The key feature of this civil nuisance statute remains . . . the power it gives the state courts to enjoin, under the peril of a contempt sanction, the sale and exhibition of materials that no judicial tribunal has yet determined to be obscene. This is a violation of the principles enunciated by the Supreme Court in *Near* v. *Minnesota.*

Four years after the *Fehlhaber* case the United States Court of Appeals for the Sixth Circuit invalidated a city of Paducah statute on the basis of the principle in the *Near* v. *Minnesota* ruling. Under the city ordinance, once a determination of obscenity was made by a board of commissioners and a bookstore was declared a public nuisance, abatement proceedings were initiated. If abated, the store owner lost all business licenses and permits— effectively putting him or her out of business, and stopping him or her from selling all books, not just obscene ones. The court of appeals ruled this was a prior restraint, the likes of which were seen in *Near* v. *Minnesota,* when Jay Near was not only stopped from publishing derogatory and offensive newspapers, but all newspapers (*City of Paducah* v. *Investment Entertainment Inc.,* 1986).

A NEW STRATEGY   The most recent attempts by the government to control the distribution of obscenity involve use of racketeering laws. The federal racketeering law, or RICO (Racketeer Influenced and Corrupt Organizations) law, was enacted in 1970 to fight organized crime. Its objective was to stop mobsters from channeling money from criminal enterprises such as drug trafficking into legitimate business used as fronts. The statute gives the government the power to confiscate the inventories of businesses the authorities suspect are laundering money for organized crime. This can occur before a trial takes place. The 1986 Meese Commission Report on Obscenity recommended that prosecutors use the racketeering statutes and the seizure approach to put pornographers out of business. Also, a conviction under a RICO statute carries with it a much harsher penalty than a conviction under a traditional obscenity statute. The Congress and 20 state legislatures quickly added obscenity to the list of racketeering offenses.

The statute in Indiana received the first court test and in 1989 the U.S. Supreme Court ruled that the First Amendment bars law-enforcement authorities from seizing the inventory of an adult book store prior to a trial at which the material has been ruled to be obscene. Three book stores in Ft. Wayne were emptied and then padlocked after their owners were charged, but not yet convicted, of engaging in a pattern of racketeering by repeatedly selling obscene books and films. Justice Byron White said the First Amendment's prohibition of prior restraint bars the state from confiscating material that has not yet been judged obscene. "The state cannot escape the constitutional safeguards of our prior cases by merely recategorizing a pattern of obscenity violations as racketeering," White said. The court was unanimous on this point.

But the high court did, with a 6 to 3 vote, sustain the use of the racketeering statutes to crack down on pornography, provided no confiscation takes place before a trial, even though the laws invoke a much harsher penalty. Left unanswered in the high court ruling was the question of whether the confiscation of the contents of an entire bookstore or video shop is appropriate even if the owner is found guilty of selling only a handful of obscene items. The three dissenters in the case, Justices Marshall, Brennan, and Stevens, rejected the argument that a racketeering statute could ever constitutionally apply to obscenity. (*Fort Wayne Books* v. *Indiana, Sappenfield* v. *Indiana,* 1989).

Postal Censorship

Use of the postal service to censor obscenity has a long tradition in the United States. In fact, it is largely through the postal system that the federal government becomes involved in the regulation of obscenity. The Post Office Department has long been an insensitive and moralistic censor of all sorts of material. Armed with congressional authority, as well as a nineteenth-century Supreme Court ruling that designated use of the mails a privilege and not a right (ex parte *Jackson,* 1878), the postal service has worked hard to keep the mails free of "smut," even smut in plain brown wrappers. While the government cannot tamper with first-class mail legally, publishers of magazines of all kinds—girly, nudist, art, anthropological, crime, true confessions—have long been plagued by postal inspectors. While the loss of much of this material would not be a severe blow to the nation's cultural heritage, it is still highly frustrating to publishers who must depend upon the postal service to deliver their wares. For most publications the Post Office Department runs the only game in town.

The Post Office Department has traditionally been plagued with administrative slovenliness that causes it to run afoul of the law. Federal courts have for years been telling the postal service that it cannot do this or that: institute a mail block, for example, deny due process of law in obscenity hearings, ban publications that do not contribute to "the public good," or force patrons to come to the post office to pick up mail from Communist countries. In 1968 the postal service took a new tack in regulating certain kinds of obscene material, a tack designed to take the service off the legal hot seat. What is known as the Anti-Pandering Law, or Section 3008 of Title 39 of the United States Code, was put into effect by Congress. It was designed to stop the delivery of unwanted obscene solicitations to mail patrons' homes. This had been a problem for years. Mailers were indiscriminate in sending out such material, and it was not uncommon for youngsters to receive lurid solicitations from publishers of magazines, books, and pictures.

Section 3008 allows postal patrons to remain free from such solicitations, but only after they have received such an advertisement. It works this way. Imagine that John Smith finds an advertisement for La Femme French postcards in his mailbox and is properly shocked. Under Section 3008 John can fill out a postal form, which is sent by the post office to the La Femme company, advising the mailer that Mr. Smith does not want to receive such solicitations in the future. If La Femme were to send John a subsequent mailing, the company could be subject to prosecution.

The interesting aspect of this law concerns the definition of obscenity—there is none. Postal patrons decide for themselves what is obscene. If they do not like the material, the dislike is all that is needed. Once the notice is sent to the mailer, *any* subsequent mailing is a violation of the law. John might decide that a *Time* magazine solicitation or an advertisement for seat covers or a record club is obscene. There must be solicitation, but that is the only requirement.

The distributors of erotic material challenged this law, since to remove a name from a mailing list is quite costly. Also they argued that the law violated their First Amendment rights and that because the law did not define obscenity, it was too vague and therefore a violation of Fifth Amendment rights. But the Supreme Court unanimously supported the law. The Court said that Congress intended to give the postal patron the right to decide on the obscenity of an advertisement, and this right eliminates the Post Office Department from a censorship role.

As far as the First Amendment right to communicate (if there is such a right) is concerned, the High Court ruled that the right of privacy is also guaranteed by the Constitution. This law does impede the flow of ideas, information, and so forth. However, Chief Justice Burger wrote (*Rowan* v. *Post Office,* 1970):

> . . . today everyman's mail is made up overwhelmingly of material he did not seek from persons he does not know. And all too often it is matter he finds offensive. It seems to us that a mailer's right to communicate must stop at the mailbox of an unreceptive addressee. . . . We categorically reject the argument that a vendor has a right under the Constitution or otherwise to send unwanted material into the home of another.

A more recent addition to the postal laws operates on somewhat the same principle and has caused the pornography distributors even more headaches. Section 3010 of Title 39, United States Code, called the Goldwater Amendment to the Postal Reorganization Bill, allows mail patrons the opportunity to get off a pornographer's mailing list even before they receive the first solicitation. Under this law John Smith can fill out a form at his local post office asserting that he does not want to receive any sexually oriented advertising. The postal service periodically publishes computerized lists of the names and addresses of persons who have signed this form. After a person's name has been on the list for thirty days, it is illegal to send that individual sexually oriented advertising matter. Mailers who ignore this are subject to both criminal and civil penalties.

Where do the mailers get the lists of names? They have to buy the lists from the government. When the law went into effect a few years ago, the cost of a master list was more than five thousand dollars. Of course supplements are published periodically, and they must be purchased as well.

Section 3010 is different from Section 3008 in that it defines sexually oriented material, whereas the Anti-Pandering Law lets postal patrons decide on their own. Here is how the statute defines sexually oriented material:

> . . . any advertisement that depicts in actual or simulated form, or explicitly describes, in a predominantly sexual context, human genitalia, any act of natural or unnatural sexual intercourse, or any act of sadism or masochism, or any other erotic subject directly related to the foregoing.

The law does not pertain to materials in which the sexually oriented advertisement comprises only a small and insignificant part of a larger catalog, book, or periodical. This statute was upheld by the federal courts (*Pent-R-Books* v. *U.S. Postal Service,* 1971). This law also provides that any envelope containing an advertisement that falls within the definition just given must carry a warning on the outside as to the nature of the contents.

Both of these statutes have been widely used and have solved one of the most serious problems relating to pornography—its shipment to people who do not want it. However, neither of these laws precludes the possibility of criminal obscenity prosecution against advertisers for sending out such material, even to people who want it. The 1974 *Hamling* case was based on just such an advertisement.

Regulating Films

The exhibition of films has often provoked an emotional reaction from community members and the government. Note the recent outcry at the showing of the R-rated film, "The Last Temptation of Christ," a movie that suggests that Jesus Christ was tempted by normal human sexual desires. Courts have always treated movies somewhat differently than they treat books, magazines, and artwork. Films have been censored for a great many reasons, including obscenity. Initially the Supreme Court refused to include films under the protection of the First Amendment. In 1915 in the case of *Mutual Film Corp.* v. *Industrial Commission of Ohio,* Justice Joseph McKenna wrote for the Court that while, indeed, movies may be mediums of thought, so are many other things, such as circuses and the theaters. "It cannot be put out of view," the justice wrote, "that the exhibition of moving pictures is a business, pure and simple, originated and conducted for profit, like other spectacles, not to be regarded . . . as part of the press of the country or as organs of public opinion."

This was the law until the 1950s, when the High Court ruled that film is a medium protected by the First Amendment and cannot be censored by a state, except in cases of obscenity (*Burstyn* v. *Wilson,* 1952). This seemed to put moviemakers on the same footing as magazine publishers, with one exception. The courts permitted prior censorship with regard to motion pictures; that is, a theater owner or film distributor could constitutionally be required to present the film to a board of censors for approval before showing it in the theater. In 1961 a film distributor challenged this practice and lost. In a five-to-four ruling the Court said that there is no complete and absolute freedom to exhibit, even once, any and every kind of motion picture (*Times Film Corp.* v. *Chicago*).

While approving prior censorship for motion pictures, the High Court also demands, within the censorship system, procedures that protect the rights of theater owners. Concerning such, the Court struck down several film censorship systems (for example, in Maryland and Dallas) that took too long to reach a decision, placed the burden of proof on the theater owner rather than on the government, and so forth (*Freedman* v. *Maryland,* 1965 and *Interstate Circuit* v. *Dallas,* 1968). In 1965 when the Court struck down the Maryland censorship law in *Freedman* v. *Maryland,* it outlined the constitutional requirements of a permissible film ordinance. But the Court was unable to find an ordinance that passed muster until 1974, when it summarily affirmed the judgment of a three-judge panel that approved the revamped Maryland law.

The Maryland law that was approved in *Star* v. *Preller* (1974) had these provisions:

1. Every film, including those in coin-operated loop machines, must have a license from the state board of censors before it can be shown. Showing a film without a license is a crime, regardless of whether it is obscene.

2. Once a film is submitted to the censorship board, the board must either issue a license or initiate an action in court against the film within eight days.

3. In a court action to determine whether the film is obscene, the censorship board must prove the film is obscene. The film distributor does not have to prove that it is not obscene.

4. A hearing must be held in court within five days after the action is filed.

5. The court must issue a ruling within two days after the hearing is over. There is also a provision for expedited appeals.

6. The film cannot be shown until the hearing is completed.

Given the fact that prior restraint is allowed, the benefit of this ordinance is that a film must be licensed or declared obscene in a maximum of fifteen days. Moreover, the state bears the burden of proof in any hearing that results. Perhaps this seems like crumbs for a starving man, but this system is nevertheless far superior to those of yesterday, in which motion pictures were often tied up for months with the censors and the theater owner or film distributor was forced to go into court and try to prove a negative: that a movie was not obscene.

Film prosecutions present problems. In the case of an obscene book, an undercover officer can buy a copy of the suspect edition, and it can be scrutinized and later used as evidence if a criminal action results. But the price of a movie ticket includes only the right to look, not to take. So the police and the courts experienced many years of pushing and shoving over what was and was not legal. For a while the police merely seized all copies of the film. But the courts did not approve of that, because whether or not the film was obscene was for the courts to decide. If the jury decided the film was not obscene, seizure then constituted a clear case of prior restraint. So the police were forced to use other means. In some cities the police videotaped portions of the movie for use as evidence in a trial. But the quality of the tape was poor, and often theater owners who were arguing about the high technical quality of a film complained that the police copy made the picture look worse than it actually was.

In 1973 in *Heller* v. *New York,* the Supreme Court handed down rules that clarified the matter, even though the new policies did not satisfy many people on either side. Under the *Heller* rules a film cannot be seized by police as evidence until a warrant is issued by a neutral judge or magistrate who has viewed the film and has ruled that it is obscene. The hearing in which the judge issues the warrant is not an adversary hearing, because the theater owner is not represented. This warrant is called an ex parte warrant. Only the state is represented, and all that the warrant says is that one judge has seen the film and thinks it is obscene.

The United States Court of Appeals for the Fifth Circuit modified these rules in 1979 when it decided that a judge or magistrate can also issue a warrant for seizure of the film on the basis of a government agent's *detailed* affidavit describing the film's content. The judge or magistrate does not actually have to see the film in order to issue the warrant (*United States* v. *Middleton,* 1979). Whether the United States Supreme Court will agree with this ruling has not been tested. The High Court will not permit so-called open-ended warrants. A police officer in New York bought two films at an adult bookstore and permitted a judge to view them. The judge declared the films to be obscene and gave the police officer a warrant to seize all copies of the two films and other obscene materials at the store. Police raided the store and seized eight hundred different items. The names and descriptions of these items were filled in on the warrant *after* they were seized. The Supreme Court unanimously ruled that such a procedure was a violation of the Fourth Amendment. "Our society is better able to tolerate the admittedly pornographic business of petitioner [the store owner] than a return to the general warrant era," Chief Justice Burger wrote (*Lo-Ji Sales* v. *New York,* 1979).

Following seizure of a film, an adversary hearing—a trial—is held to determine whether the film is in fact obscene. During the period between seizure and final judicial determination of obscenity, the theater owner can continue to show the motion picture if he or she has a second copy. If no second copy is available, the state must then permit the exhibitor to make a copy of the film that was seized so that exhibition of the movie can go on. Therefore, the police get their evidence and the theater owner can keep showing the movie until the trial is over. The only serious problem is that it is expensive for the theater owner to make a second copy of the movie.

SUMMARY

Postal censorship has historically been an important means used by the United States government to control the flow of obscene material in the United States. Today the postal service is less aggressive and permits postal patrons themselves to block the delivery of solicitations for adults materials and other obscene publications. Communities may also censor films before they are shown, so long as they follow strict procedures laid down by the United States Supreme Court.

REGULATION OF NONOBSCENE EROTIC MATTER

As the federal government moved to increase controls over legally obscene material during the 1980s, major efforts were also made to control nonobscene sexually-oriented material as well. Local communities attempted to use zoning laws to regulate the distribution of books and magazines and the screening of films; a presidential commission sought to slow the distribution of adult magazines; and pressure groups around the nation attacked the recording industry, music videos, cable television operators and others for the content of the material they were producing.

Zoning Laws

Many communities have attempted to use locational zoning ordinances to regulate businesses that sell or display sexually-explicit but not legally obscene material. Seattle passed a law in 1977 that requires all adult theaters to be located within a small area downtown. City officials said that the character and quality of Seattle neighborhoods could be preserved and protected by isolating this adult activity to a small area downtown. Detroit took just the opposite approach. A city law passed in 1972 prohibits adult theaters from being located within one thousand feet of other adult theaters; adult bookstores, cabarets, bars, taxi dance halls, hotels, pawnshops, pool halls, secondhand stores, and shoeshine parlors or within five hundred feet of areas zoned residential. The city did not want such businesses clustered together or near other types of "problem" businesses in the community. Both these statutes were upheld by the courts (*Northend Cinema* v. *Seattle*, 1978; *Young* v. *American-Mini Theaters, Inc.*, 1976).

The owners of these adult establishments have found that zoning, while perhaps inconvenient, provides them with a kind of safe haven from police harassment. They are normally permitted to operate their businesses without trouble unless they attempt to sell or exhibit material that is legally obscene (i.e., meets the definition of obscenity in the *Miller* test) or unless other criminal laws are violated as a result of the traffic into the adult establishments.

It must be remembered that these zoning schemes are aimed at regulating constitutionally protected material, not legally obscene material. Hence, there are clear limits that have been placed on such schemes. Foremost is the rule that a community cannot, under the guise of zoning, completely bar or even significantly reduce the number of bookstores, theaters, or newsstands that sell adult material. The ordinance in Detroit that was approved by the Supreme Court in the *Young* ruling did not substantially reduce the number of establishments selling adult material. And it left ample room for the introduction of new establishments. This point has been overlooked in some communities in which zoning regulations were used to try to close adult bookstores, theaters, and other businesses. In 1981 the Supreme Court struck down a Mount Ephraim, New Jersey, zoning regulation that effectively barred all live entertainment from the parts of the city zoned commercial. The High Court called the ordinance unreasonable and said that it excluded from the city a wide range of protected expression. The High Court also rejected Mount Ephraim's argument that its citizens had access to such entertainment, despite the zoning rules, because adult entertainment was readily available outside the city in nearby areas (*Schad* v. *Mount Ephraim*, 1981). The United States Court of Appeals for the Sixth Circuit threw out a Keego Harbor, Michigan, zoning law that prohibited adult theaters within five hundred feet of a tavern or bar, a church, or a school. There was no place in the small community that was not within five hundred feet of such an establishment (*Keego Harbor Company* v. *Keego Harbor*, 1981). The United States Court of Appeals for the Eighth Circuit voided a Minneapolis ordinance that effectively eliminated two-thirds of the adult bookstore locations in the city (*Alexander* v. *City of Minneapolis*, 1983). Finally, the United States Court of Appeals for the Sixth Circuit rejected an Ann Arbor, Michigan, ordinance that attempted to isolate adult bookstores to about a quarter of one percent of the city's land. The law required that any establishment having as a principal activity the sale of adult material (as defined by the law) be located in this small space. "Principal activity" was defined by the city as involving twenty percent or more of a merchant's business. The court said the law was too restrictive. "A limitation of adult materials up to twenty percent of a bookseller's wares conditions the constitutional right to speak in one way on the booksellers willingness to speak in a different way eighty percent of the time," the court said, adding that this was a violation of the First Amendment (*Christy* v. *Ann Arbor*, 1987).

These ordinances, which interfere with protected speech, must be strongly justified as furthering a substantial government interest. The city of Detroit provided a tremendous amount of data in defending its ordinance, data that demonstrated that concentrations of adult establishments caused neighborhood decay. The Detroit ordinance, then, was justified as preventing urban decay. Other communities have failed to do this, and their ordinances have been overturned. Keego Harbor, Michigan, provided little data at all to support its argument that the adult movie theaters created traffic problems and therefore had to be regulated by zoning. "When a city effectively zones protected activities out of a political entity, the justification required is more substantial than when the First Amendment burden is merely incidental as it was in *Young* v. *American-Mini Theaters*," the court noted (*Keego Harbor Company* v. *Keego Harbor*, 1981). Of course the First Amendment burden was incidental in *Young* because the law did not diminish the number of adult establishments. The United States Court of Appeals for the Fifth Circuit rejected a zoning ordinance adopted by the city of Galveston, Texas, modeled after the Detroit ordinance. The mayor and other city officials testified that they believed that the mere existence of adult theaters created crime and urban decay, but they offered no other evidence at the trial. "The paucity of evidence stands in sharp contrast to the facts of *American-Mini Theaters* v. *Young*," the court noted (*Basiardanes* v. *City of Galveston*, 1982). While a community must produce evidence to support its zoning regulation, it doesn't necessarily have to generate fresh evidence that relates directly to that community. It can rely upon the experience of other communities in the region. The city of Renton, Washington, a suburb of Seattle, relied upon the experience of other area cities (most notably Seattle) to justify its zoning statute. The United States Supreme Court ruled in 1986 that this was an acceptable practice. "The First Amendment does not require a city, before enacting such an ordinance to conduct new studies or produce evidence independent of that already generated by other cities," wrote Justice William Rehnquist, "so long as whatever evidence the city relies upon is reasonably believed to be relevant to the problem the city addresses" (*Renton* v. *Playtime Theatres*, 1986). Playtime Theatres owner Roger Forbes also objected to the Renton ordinance because, he argued, it forced all adult theaters to the outskirts of the community in an industrial area. In fact, only five percent of the entire city existed where the adult establishments were permitted; this made finding property very difficult, Forbes said. The seven-person Supreme Court majority was unsympathetic. "That respondents must fend for themselves in the real estate market, on an equal footing with other prospective purchasers and lessees does not give rise to a First Amendment violation," Justice Rehnquist wrote.

Finally, such a zoning ordinance must be narrowly drawn, so as not to restrict more speech than is necessary or to place a greater burden than necessary on the speech that is regulated. In the *Schad* case the city of Mount Ephraim had banned all forms of live entertainment, putting any sort of play or performance off-limits. This restricted more speech than needed to control adult entertainment. And the city of Galveston in the *Basiardanes* case defined an adult theater as any theater that regularly screened films that the state of Texas prohibited minors from seeing. Of course this includes all R-rated films. Again, the city went too far and banned too much expression. The city of Keego Harbor, on the other hand, might have used other methods— short of banning adult theaters—to handle its traffic problems, as Alfred X. Zen notes in the *Pepperdine Law Review*. "The court suggested that the increased ticketing of violators was a less intrusive means of serving the governmental interest involved," Zen wrote.

Zoning laws can be used to control the sale and exhibition of adult materials in a community. But only if they meet the three requirements outlined above: There can be no complete ban on such establishments or substantial reduction of the availability of such material in the community; a government must strongly justify—with evidence—such rules. And the laws must be narrowly drawn.

Meese Commission

In 1985 President Ronald Reagan appointed an Attorney General's Commission on Pornography to determine "the nature, extent, and impact on society of pornography in the United States" and to make recommendations about ways that pornography might be more effectively contained. Two things stand out immediately about this eleven-member group. First, its membership was tilted heavily toward persons who had already made up their minds that more censorship was the answer. Second, while the focus of the commission's inquiry was sexually explicit material, it was not necessarily legally obscene material. That is, the commission spent a great deal of time investigating erotic film, books, and magazines that are protected by the First Amendment. The Meese Commission, as it came to be known, held six public hearings to obtain testimony from approximately two hundred witnesses. It released its report in the summer of 1986. A majority of the commission members concluded that certain types of sexually explicit material are harmful, especially material oriented toward violent sex. This kind of material, the commissioners said, bears a causal relationship to sexual violence. Nonviolent pornography that depicts degradation, domination, subordination or humiliation also has an impact on fostering attitudes that women enjoy being raped, the commissioners said.

Two of the four women on the panel sharply disagreed with these conclusions, however. Columbia University psychology professor Judith Becker and Ellen Levine, editor of *Woman's Day,* said "The idea that eleven individuals studying in their spare time could complete a comprehensive report on so complex a matter in so constricted a time frame is simply unrealistic. . . . No self-respecting investigator would accept conclusions based on such a study." Others outside the commission also criticized the paucity (some said nonexistence) of evidence to support the commission's conclusions. But in the end, the Meese Commission recommended no new laws, only that existing federal and state laws be more vigorously enforced. Yet with state and federal prosecutors attempting to fight murder, rape, robbery, drug trafficking and other serious crimes with ever shrinking budgets, few believed the call for increased enforcement of obscenity laws would be widely heeded.

The most controversial aspect of the Meese Commission's work, however, was its efforts (inadvertent or otherwise) to stop the flow of several popular men's magazines and sexually oriented films and TV programs. During testimony in Los Angeles on October 17, 1985, the Rev. Donald Wildmon, the executive director of the National Federation of Decency, a conservative Christian-based pressure group, said that certain American corporations were engaged in the sale of pornography, including *Playboy* and *Penthouse.* Among those Wildmon criticized were CBS; *Time, Inc.;* RCA; and Coca-Cola for the films and television programming they distribute, and K-Mart; Southland Corp.

(7–Eleven stores); Dart Drug Co.; Stop N Go Stores; and other shops for carrying *Playboy, Penthouse,* and other "pornographic" magazines. The commission members seemed confused about whether Wildmon's testimony should be included in the final commission report, so they sent a letter to all twenty-six corporations. In part, the letter said ". . . the commission received testimony alleging that your company is involved in the sale or distribution of pornography. The commission has determined that it would be appropriate to allow your company an opportunity to respond to the allegations prior to drafting its final report section on identified distributors. . . . Failure to respond will necessarily be accepted as an indication of no objection (to the testimony)." The companies were not told that the allegations were based on the unsubstantiated testimony of one witness (out of a total of two hundred witnesses).

Some companies were outraged. *Time, Inc.* responded: "We cannot believe the United States Department of Justice would lend its name to this slipshod and misguided effort." Others responded in a different fashion. Southland pulled *Playbody, Penthouse,* and *Forum* out of its 7–Eleven stores. The company denied, however, it was bending to commission pressure. *Playboy* and *Penthouse,* stung by the loss of distributors and already suffering a sales slump, went to court. In July, a United States district court ruled that the letter sent by the commission threatened the First Amendment rights of the magazine publishers and distributors, and enjoined the publication in the commission report of the list of alleged pornography distributors. The court also ordered the commission to send a letter to all recipients of the first letter advising them that the original letter has been withdrawn and that no reply was required (*Playboy Enterprises* v. *Meese, 1986*).

Attacks on the Music Industry

The rock music industry came under attack in the mid-1980s for marketing what some persons called "porn rock"; that is, song lyrics, music videos, and album covers that some persons said were too sexually explicit, especially for the young persons who are the principal consumers of rock music. There is little question that rock music is protected by the First Amendment. Four different United States courts of appeal so ruled during the 1980s. (See *Cinevision Corp.* v. *City of Burbank,* 1984; *Reed* v. *Village of Shorewood,* 1983; *Tacynec* v. *City of Philadelphia,* 1983; and *Calash* v. *City of Bridgeport,* 1986.) The city of Burbank, for example, sought to prevent certain rock concerts that city officials said would attract drug users and other undesirable elements to the community. So city officials refused to issue concert permits for the Blue Oyster Cult, Jackson Browne, Roxy Music, Todd Rundgren, Patti Smith and Al Stewart. The "undesirables" they sought to keep out included homosexuals, blacks and anti-nuclear activists. The United States Court of Appeals for the Ninth Circuit ruled that music is a form of expression protected by the First Amendment, and the city's attempt to block certain concerts amounted to censorship.

In the mid-1980s activists nevertheless began to seek stronger limits on the recording industry. Some musicians noted that the growing pressure seemed to coincide with the reemergence of rock music as a political voice, as exhibited in the Farm Aid and Sun City concerts and the success of the overtly political rock group "U2." "Right now its sex and violence; before long it'll be, 'That's just too political,' " noted singer/songwriter John Cougar Mellencamp.

The PTA started the fight in 1984, attempting to both restrain what they called "porn rock," and force the industry to adopt some kind of standardized rating system for music similar to the one used by the motion picture industry. The rating system would identify songs that had profane or sexually explicit lyrics, contained references to the occult, glorified violence, or advocated drug or alcohol use. No one paid much attention to the crusade until a group of congressional wives formed the Parents Music Resource Committee (PMRC), and convinced some Members of Congress (including some of their husbands) to hold United States Senate hearings on the matter.

The industry rejected calls for a rating system. Spokespersons admitted that a few performers sometimes go off the deep end and exhibit questionable taste, but that these performers were obscure (until the hearings), their songs were not popular, and many of their recordings were not even released in the United States. Ratings would spur their sales, not slow them. The industry argued that a rating system would be unmanageable, since more than twenty-five thousand songs are released each year; far more than the five-hundred to six-hundred movies rated each year. Finally, industry spokespersons argued that labeling and ratings were a first step toward more overt censorship of music.

While the Senate committee took no action, the hearings did put the issue squarely in the public eye. And while the industry seemed to stand firmly in opposition to the proposed controls, there was a hidden factor that weakened its resolve. For several years the recording industry has sought from Congress a law that would place a royalty on the sale of all blank audio cassette tapes. This one dollar per tape royalty would be collected and distributed to the recording industry to compensate both artists and studios for the money supposedly lost when music fans tape music from records, other tapes, or radio broadcasts instead of buying records. An industry seeking help from Congress was hardly in a position to bite the hand that might feed it, and so it was not surprising that in November of 1985 the Parents Music Resource Committee and the Recording Industry Association of America, the industry trade group, announced a settlement. Record companies would either (their choice) place a PG label on records or print the potentially offensive lyrics on the album cover. In return, PMRC promised not to seek legislative support for a more formal ban. But the system really didn't work. In its first year of operation only two records carried the PG label and no albums carried printed lyrics as a warning.

Civil libertarians oppose the rating system for several reasons. They believe such a system will restrict public access to constitutionally protected material. This has happened with films that receive an X rating. Theater owners who show them are the target of community anger, many newspapers won't advertise them, and revenue from potential television sales is eliminated. Record store owners in malls reported that they were told by mall owners that their leases would be cancelled if they carried any records with warning labels, according to Seth Goodchild in an article in *Sports and Entertainment Law Journal.* Other stores said they would not stock such records due to pressure from various interest groups, especially religious groups. There is also a danger that the ratings will be too broad. The interpretation of song lyrics, like films, is very subjective, Goodchild points out. It is highly possible to have two different persons interpret the same song in different ways. This became obvious during the seventies when many radio stations mistakenly banned anti-drug songs in response to an FCC announcement that all broadcasters had to be careful about broadcasting music promoting drug use. (See page 535.) What about an album with one song with sexually explicit lyrics, but the remainder clean as a whistle? Should the entire album be labeled or banned? Many argued that those parents who were concerned about such things should monitor more closely the music played by their sons and daughters and not expect the government or the industry to do this for them.

By the end of the decade the issue was not resolved, but there was much less public attention given to the problem. Senator Albert Gore, whose wife Tipper was one of the leaders of the crusade, made an unsuccessful bid for the White House in 1988, and found that his participation in the hearings and his procensorship position hurt his chances among some potential supporters. But the pot is still simmering, ready to boil over again at the slightest provocation. Like the battle over R-rated movies on cable television (see pp. 542–543), the dispute over so-called "porn rock" in the recording industry will likely remain for many years.

SUMMARY

Significant efforts were made on many fronts during the eighties to control the flow of nonobscene, sexually explicit material. Many communities attempted to use locational zoning ordinances to regulate such material. These laws are permissible so long as they are strongly justified, don't exclude or substantially reduce the number of such businesses, and are drawn in a narrow fashion to limit only the narrowest possible range of speech. Less successful attempts to control sexually explicit material were made by the 1985 Attorney General's Commission on Pornography and by groups attempting to censor or regulate lyrics in rock music.

BIBLIOGRAPHY

Articles

Blakely, C. "Is One Woman's Sexuality Another Woman's Pornography?" *Ms.,* April, 1985.

Catlett, Steven T. "Enjoining Obscenity as Public Nuisance and the Prior Restraint Doctrine." 84 *Columbia Law Review* 1616, 1984.

Caughlin, Susan G. "Private Possession of Child Pornography: The Tensions Between *Stanley* v. *Georgia* and *New York* v. *Ferber.*" 29 *William and Mary Law Review* 187, 1987.

Courtler, Ann H. "Restricting Adult Access to Material Obscene as to Juveniles." 85 *Michigan Law Review* 1681, 1987.

Elkins, Susan. "Taking Serious Value Seriously: Obscenity, *Pope* v. *Illinois,* and an Objective Standard." 41 *University of Miami Law Review* 855, 1987.

Goodchild, Seth. "Twisted Sister, Washington Wives and the First Amendment: The Movement to Clamp Down on Rock Music." 3 *Entertainment and Sports Law Journal* 131, 1986.

Grunes, Rodney. "Obscenity Law and the Justices: Reversing Policy on the Supreme Court." 9 *Seton Hall Law Review* 403, 1978.

Maag, Marilyn J. "The Indianapolis Pornography Ordinance: Does the Right to Free Speech Outweigh Pornography's Harm to Women?" 54 *Cincinnati Law Review* 249, 1985.

Stein, Ronald M. "Regulation of Adult Businesses Through Zoning After *Renton.*" 18 *Pacific Law Journal* 351, 1987.

Van Dyke, Michael S. "Regulation of Pornography: Is Erotica Self-Expression Deserving of Protection?" 33 *Loyola Law Review* 445, 1987.

U.S. v. *Blucher,* 581 F.2d 244 (1978).

U.S. v. *McManus,* 535 F.2d 460 (1976).

U.S. v. *Middleton,* 599 F.2d 1349 (1979).

U.S. v. *Roth,* 237 F.2d 796 (1956).

Upper Midwest Booksellers v. *Minneapolis,* 602 F.Supp. 1361 (1985); aff'd. 780 F.2d 1389 (1985).

Vance v. *Universal Amusement,* 445 U.S. 308 (1980).

Virginia v. *American Booksellers Assoc.,* 484 U.S. 383 (1988); 372 S.E.2d 618 (1988).

Walker v. *Popenoe,* 149 F.2d 511 (1980).

Ward v. *Illinois,* 431 U.S. 767 (1977).

Young v. *American-Mini Theaters, Inc.,* 427 U.S. 50 (1976).

9 COPYRIGHT

What do Mick Jagger, George Harrison, Michael Jackson, the Bee Gees, and Ray Parker Jr. have in common? Sure, they're all contemporary pop musicians, but that's the easy answer. How about this for an alternate response; all have been sued recently for copyright infringement for songs they wrote. In 1988 a jury cleared Jagger of the charge that his song, "Just Another Night," was a copy of a song with the same name written by Patrick Alley. Harrison lost his case however when a court ruled he had unknowingly borrowed the structure of "My Sweet Lord" from the Chiffon's 1960s hit, "He's So Fine." Michael Jackson was sued unsuccessfully in 1983 over the song "The Girl in Mine." An Illinois jury found that the Bee Gees had copied the song "How Deep is Your Love" but an appellate court overturned the jury verdict. Finally, Ray Parker Jr. made an undisclosed out-of-court settlement because of the similarities between his song "Ghostbusters" and the song "I Want a New Drug" by Huey Lewis and the News.

Copyright is an area of the law that deals with intangible property—property that a person cannot touch or hold or lock away for safekeeping. This concept is sometimes confusing to people; how can the law protect something you can't hold or touch? One good way to explain this is to think for a moment about a personal letter you have written to your friend. After the letter has been received by your friend who owns it? Your friend owns the piece of paper that contains the words. That is his or her personal property now, and is protected by property law. But you retain ownership of the words and the words are protected by copyright law. Your friend could not publish the letter without your permission. But he could throw it away or set fire to it and destroy the paper. In such a case he is not using your words, your property, but merely destroying the letter.

Copyright is a close cousin to the law regulating patents and trademarks and to plagarism, which also affects intangible property. But all four of these areas protect something different. Copyright law protects "all works of authorship fixed in a tangible medium of expression." This includes writings, paintings, music, drama, and other similar works.

There are at least three different kinds of patent protections. There is one variety that protects inventions that have utility, such as a machine or a process. A typewriter can be patented; so can a specific way of reducing the hiss or noise on an audio tape. Patent law also protects designs—the appearance of an article of manufacture. The design of a piece of furniture or a tire tread or a belt buckle can be patented. A variety of patents also protect plants, but only those kinds that can be reproduced asexually through means other than seeds, like cuttings or grafting. Patent rights do not exist until the patent is issued by the United States government. Hence the famous abbreviation on many items, "pat. pending," which means the patent has been applied for and is pending.

Trademark protection extends to trademarks or brand names such as Ford or Coca-Cola, service marks such as Holiday Inn or McDonalds, certification marks such as Dolby on your cassette deck or Real (real dairy products) on your frozen pizza, and collective marks, such as Realtor, which is owned by the National Association of Realtors. These marks or words or symbols are used to distinguish that company's goods or services from those of another manufacturer. In order to maintain a trademark its owner must be constantly vigilant that the word or phrase does not become generic, or associated with a variety of sources. If this happens the word loses trademark status and can be used by any manufacturer or business. At one time trademark protection extended to the words cellophane and escalator. But no longer. However, only one company makes Popsicles, Q-Tips, or Jell-O, even though there are several brands of frozen confections, cotton swabs and gelatin desserts. Persons who work in the mass media will often get letters noting when they have failed to capitalize the first letter of a brand name such as Muzak or Lite beer or Lifesavers in a story or advertisement. It is through this and other means that a company can argue in court that it has worked to protect the meaning of its trademark to keep it from going into the public domain.

Plagiarism is the act of taking ideas, thoughts, or words from another and passing them off as your own. The notion of passing off someone else's work as your own is critical in a plagiarism case. Plagiarism protects the theft of ideas, whereas copyright protects only the specific expression of these ideas. We will focus exclusively on copyright law in this chapter. Persons who work in the mass media do not need to become copyright attorneys to avoid lawsuits in the 1990s. But newswriters, broadcasters, advertising copywriters and public relations practitioners should know both how to protect their own work from theft and how to avoid illegally taking the work of someone else. ♦

PROTECTING LITERARY PROPERTY

Protecting the rights of authors and other creators was not a problem prior to the development of mechanical printing. Each hand-copied manuscript was the result of the intensive labor of a copyist. Each book was an individual entity and could be protected by the law of personal property. The time and effort it took to reproduce even one book made the theft of a book through duplication an unattractive prospect. But the printing press changed all this, for it became possible to quickly and easily mass produce exact copies of a written work. Through the printing process two separate yet combined pieces of property emerged. The first was the book itself—a piece of physical property. The second was the arrangement and organization of the words or ideas in the book—a piece of intangible property.

The printing press was the first technological development that provided the inexpensive means of copying the work of others. As each new mass communications form has developed, the problem of protection of intangible property has arisen anew. Today it is the pirating of tapes, both video and audio, that is causing serious harm to the creators of motion pictures and musical performances. The film industry estimates that it loses as much as a billion dollars a year because of film and video tape piracy. The Motion Picture Association of America spent fifteen million dollars in 1988 alone trying to catch the pirates. And the recording industry has been seriously hurt for years as copies of LPs, CDs and cassettes are made legally by individuals for personal use and made illegally by well-organized gangs of pirates for resale.

Roots of the Law

Copyright law developed in Great Britain in the sixteenth century as the government sanctioned and supported the grant of printing privileges to certain master printers in exchange for their loyalty and assistance in ferreting out anti-government writers and publishers. But the rights of authors, as opposed to printers, were not protected until the early eighteenth century when the British Parliament passed the nation's first copyright law. The 1710 statute was called "An Act for the Encouragement of Learning, by Vesting the Copies of Printed Books in the Authors or Purchasers of Such Copies, during the Time Therein Mentioned." The law was passed in the eighth year of the reign of Queen Anne and hence became known as the "Statute of Eight Anne." The law gave the legal claim of ownership of a piece of literary property to the person who created the work or to a person who acquired the rights to the work from the author. The statute was a recognition by the Crown that in order to encourage the creation of books, plays and art, the creators of these works had to be assured that they would be rewarded for their labor. And that is the real logic behind copyright law, the fostering of the creative spirit. If a dramatist knew, for example, that as soon as her play was published she would lose control of the work because others could freely copy it, there would be little stimulation for the creation of plays.

British copyright law was applied in the colonies until American independence. American copyright law derives directly from the U.S. Constitution. In Article I, Section 8, of that document lies the basic authority for modern United States copyright law:

> The Congress shall have the power . . . To promote the Progress of Science and useful Arts, by securing for limited Times to Authors and Inventors the exclusive Right to their respective Writings and Discoveries.

This provision gives the Congress the power to legislate on both copyright and patent. The Congress did in 1790 by adopting a statute similar to that of Eight Anne. The law gave authors who were United States citizens the right to protect their books, maps, and charts for a total of twenty-eight years—a fourteen-year original grant plus a fourteen-year renewal. In 1802 the law was amended to include prints as well as books, maps, and charts. In 1831 the period of protection was expanded by fourteen years. The original grant became twenty-eight years with a fourteen-year renewal. Also, musical compositions were granted protection. Photography was given protection in 1865, and works of fine art were included five years later. Translation rights were added in 1870.

A major revision of the law was enacted in 1909, and our current law was adopted in 1976. The 1976 federal law preempted virtually all state laws regarding the protection of writing, music, and works of art. Hence, copyright law is essentially federal law and is governed by the federal statute and by court decisions interpreting this statute. Parenthetically it might be noted that in 1988 the Congress finally approved United States participation in the 102-year-old Berne Convention, the world's preeminent international copyright treaty. The United States had been hesitant in the past to join the treaty because of significant differences between United States and international law, but after the 1976 revision of United States copyright law, the differences were minimal. American media companies, anxious to expand their international business, sought to improve trade relations and strengthen United States influence on matters relating to international copyright law and therefore put pressure on the government to join the convention.

<table>
<tr><td>What May Be
Copyrighted</td><td>The law of copyright gives to the author, or the owner of the copyright, the sole and exclusive right to reproduce the copyrighted work in any form for any reason. Before a copyrighted work may be printed, broadcast, dramatized, or translated, the consent of the copyright owner must first be obtained. The law grants this individual exclusive monopoly over the use of that material.</td></tr>
</table>

What kinds of works are protected? The federal statute lists a wide variety of items that can be copyrighted, but this list is only illustrative. It includes:

1. Literary works
2. Musical works, including any accompanying words
3. Dramatic works, including any accompanying music
4. Pantomimes and choreographic works
5. Pictorial, graphic, and sculptural works
6. Motion pictures and other audiovisual works
7. Sound recordings

To quote the statute specifically, copyright extends to "original works of authorship fixed in any tangible medium of expression." The Congress has defined *fixed in a tangible medium* as that work which is "sufficiently permanent or stable to permit it to be perceived, reproduced, or otherwise communicated for a period of more than a transitory duration." Under these standards such things as newspaper stories or entire newspapers, magazine articles, advertisements, and almost anything else created for the mass media can be copyrighted. Performances, extemporaneous speeches, and improvised sketches are examples of materials that are not fixed in a tangible medium and are not protected by the federal copyright statute. But this does not mean that someone can film or record a performer's act, for example, without the performer's permission. This would be forbidden by other laws, such as the right to publicity (see chapter 4) and common law copyright.*

Copyright law is equally specific about what cannot be copyrighted:

1. Trivial materials cannot be copyrighted. Such things as titles, slogans, and minor variations on works in the public domain are not protected by the law of literary property. (But these items might be protected by other laws, such as unfair competition, for example.)

2. Ideas are not copyrightable. The law protects the literary or dramatic expression of an idea, such as a script, but does not protect the idea itself. "This long established principle is easier to state than to apply," notes law professor David E. Shipley. It is often difficult to separate expression from the ideas being expressed.

3. Utilitarian goods—things that exist to produce other things—are not protected by copyright law, according to William Strong in *The Copyright Book*. A lamp is a utilitarian object that exists to produce light. One cannot copyright the basic design of a lamp. But the design of any element that can be identified separately from the useful article can be copyrighted, according to Strong. The design of a Tiffany lamp can be copyrighted. The unique aspects of a Tiffany lamp have nothing to do with the utilitarian purpose of producing light; these aspects are purely decorative.

4. Methods, systems, and mathematical principles, formulas, and equations cannot be copyrighted. But a description, an explanation, or an illustration of an idea or system can be copyrighted. In such an instance the law is protecting the particular literary or pictorial form

---

*Under the 1909 law the United States had two kinds of copyright protection: common law copyright and statutory copyright. Much as it did in eighteenth-century England, the common law protected any work that had not been published. Common law protection was automatic; that is, the work was protected from the point of its creation. And it lasted forever—or until the work was published. In order to protect published works, the author, photographer, or composer had to register the book or picture or song with the United States government and place a copyright notice on the work. The 1976 statute does away with common law copyright for all practical purposes. The only kinds of works protected by the common law are works like extemporaneous speeches and sketches that have not been fixed in a tangible medium. They are still protected from the point of their creation by common law copyright. Once they are written down, recorded, filmed, or fixed in a tangible medium in any way, they come under the protection of the new law.

in which an author chooses to express her- or himself, not the idea or plan or method itself. For example, an individual writes and publishes a book in which she outlines a new mathematical formula. Although the book itself may be protected by copyright, the formula cannot be and others may use it freely. In other words, the copyright on an article or a book does not preclude the public from making use of what the book teaches.

| Original Works | Can all books and motion pictures be copyrighted? Not really. The law specifically says that only "original" works can be copyrighted. What is an original work? In interpreting this term in the 1909 law, courts ruled that the word *original* means that the work must owe its origin to the author. In 1973 a court reporter (an employee of the court who transcribes the proceedings) attempted to claim copyright over a transcript he had made of some of the proceedings during the investigation of the death of Mary Jo Kopechne. This young woman drowned when a car driven by Senator Edward Kennedy went off a bridge and into a creek near Chappaquiddick, Massachusetts. In *Lipman* v. *Commonwealth* (1973), a federal judge ruled that the transcript could not be copyrighted. "Since transcription is by very definition a verbatim recording of other persons' statements, there can be no originality in the reporter's product." |

In 1985 an organization called Production Contractors, Inc., or PCI, tried to block Chicago television station WGN from televising a Christmas parade on Thanksgiving Sunday. PCI, which put on the parade, sold the exclusive right to televise it to WLS. It claimed the parade was copyrighted, and WGN would be in violation of the law by televising it. A federal district court disagreed and ruled that a Christmas parade is not something that can be copyrighted; it is a common idea, not an event of original authorship (*Production Contractors* v. *WGN Continental Broadcasting,* 1985).

The work must be original. Must it be of high quality or be new or novel? The answer to both questions is no. Even common and mundane works are copyrightable. Courts have consistently ruled that it is not the function of the legal system to act as literary or art critic when applying copyright law. In 1903 Justice Oliver Wendell Holmes wrote in *Bleistein* v. *Donaldson Lithographing Co.,* "It would be a dangerous undertaking for persons trained only to the law to constitute themselves final judges of the worth of pictorial illustrations, outside of the narrowest and most obvious limits." Even the least pretentious picture can be an original, Holmes noted in reference to the posters involved in this case. Likewise, novelty is not important to copyright: the author does not have to be the first person to say something in order to copyright it. "All that is needed to satisfy both the Constitution and the statute is that the 'author' contributed something more than a merely trivial variation, something recognizably his own," one court ruled (*Amsterdam* v. *Triangle Publishing Co.,* 1951).

The key is how much of the author's own work is invested. In 1946 the *Philadelphia Inquirer* printed a copy of a map in connection with publication of a historical article. The map had been copyrighted by the Franklin Survey Company, which promptly sued for copyright infringement. The survey company had created the map by studying other maps; the company had done no surveying itself. It had obtained road numbers from the highway department and road names almost exclusively from other maps. There was no question that the Franklin Survey Company had spent a good deal of time assembling this material, but the fact was that the company did not create much of the material by its own labor. The court ruled that the survey company's copyright was invalid because the creative work by the plaintiff was not sufficient to make the map original (*Amsterdam* v. *Triangle Publishing Co.,* 1951). There must be at least a modicum of creative work in the map, the court said. Had Franklin not assembled this information in an original or unique fashion? This fact was immaterial, the court ruled. A map is protected only when the publisher gets some of the material "by the sweat of his brow." Originality is therefore the key; whether the work is novel or of artistic quality is not important.

News Events

Can an event or a fact be copyrighted? Suppose a reporter, Jane Adams, is standing next to a building that suddenly and violently collapses, killing scores of people trapped inside. Suppose the reporter is the only one who saw the building collapse. Can she write a news story about this disaster, copyright it, and then prohibit others from writing about the event as well? The answer is no.

This point was established in an interesting case. In 1917 the *New York Tribune* published a copyrighted story about the first large-scale use of submarine warfare by the Germans in World War I. The New York paper sold the republication rights for the story to the *Chicago Daily News.* Before the *Daily News* could print the story, the *Chicago Record-Herald* printed its own version of the story. The initial paragraph of the *Herald* version began, "The *Tribune* this morning in a copyrighted article of Louis Durant Edwards, a correspondent in Germany, says that Germany to make the final effort against Great Britain has plunged three hundred or more submersibles into the North Sea."

The remainder of the *Herald* story was comprised of five additional paragraphs, each of which was almost an exact duplication of a paragraph from the much longer *Tribune* story. The *Tribune* sued for infringement of copyright. The *Herald* answered by saying that a newspaper cannot copyright the news. Lawyers for the defendant argued that all the newspaper did was make use of facts that were in the public domain.

The circuit court of appeals agreed that as such news is not copyrightable. If the *Herald* story had been merely a summary or statement of the *Tribune* story, the *Tribune* would then have no case. However, the *Herald* did not stick to just a summary of the facts but used parts of the article, including the literary style and quality. The article itself, the way the words were organized, the style—the creative aspects of the report—can be (and in this case were) protected by copyright. The court said (*Chicago Record-Herald* v. *Tribune Association,* 1921):

> This is plainly more than a mere chronicle of facts or news. It reveals a peculiar power of portrayal and a felicity of wording and phrasing, well calculated to seize and hold the interest of the reader, which is quite beyond and apart from the mere setting forth of facts. But if the whole of it were considered as stating news or facts, yet, the arrangement and manner of statement plainly discloses a distinct literary flavor and individuality of expression peculiar to the authorship, bringing the article clearly within the purview and protection of the copyright law.

The court ruled that the fact that the *Herald* gave the *Tribune* credit did not alleviate the theft. On the contrary, the court said, it might have conveyed to the public the incorrect idea that the *Herald* had got permission from the *Tribune* to use the story.

Although news cannot be copyrighted, the expression of the news story—the style and manner in which the facts are presented—can be protected. Consider the imaginary building disaster story again. If reporter Jane Adams is the only one to witness the building collapse and publishes a copyrighted story about it, no one else can publish that exact story without her permission. But other news media can report that a building has collapsed and that scores of people have been hurt. They can summarize the facts presented in Adams' story. They should credit this information to Adams however, or face the possibility of being accused of misappropriating Adams' work. (See pp. 439–441).

A case in Florida recently raised an interesting question about the difference between facts and expression of facts. Gene Miller, a Pulitzer-Prize-winning reporter for the *Miami Herald,* wrote a book entitled *83 Hours Till Dawn,* an account of the kidnapping of Barbara Mackle. Miller said he had spent more than 2,500 hours on the book, and many aspects of the kidnapping case were uncovered by the journalist and reported only in his book.

Universal Studios wanted to film a dramatization of the 1971 incident but was unable to come to terms with Miller on payment for the rights. The studio produced the so-called docudrama anyway, and Miller sued for infringement of copyright. The similarities between Miller's book and the Universal script were striking—even some of the errors Miller had made in preparing the book were found in the film. But Universal argued that it was simply telling a story of a news event, and as such the research that Miller had done in digging out the facts regarding the story was not protected by copyright law. A United States district court agreed with Miller's contention.

"The court views the labor and expense of the research involved in the obtaining of those uncopyrightable facts to be intellectually distinct from those facts, and more similar to the expression of the facts than the facts themselves," the court said. The judge ruled that it was necessary to reward the effort and ingenuity involved in giving expression to a fact (*Miller* v. *Universal Studios,* 1978). But the United States Court of Appeals for the Fifth Circuit reversed the lower court ruling. "The valuable distinction in copyright law between facts and the expression of facts cannot be maintained if research is held to be copyrightable. There is no rational basis for distinguishing between facts and the research involved in obtaining the facts," the court said. To hold research copyrightable, the court said, is no more or less than to hold that the facts discovered as a result of research are entitled to copyright protection (*Miller* v. *Universal City Studios,* 1981). The court added: "A fact does not originate with the author of a book describing the fact. Neither does it originate with the one who 'discovers' the fact. The discoverer merely finds and records. He may not claim that the facts are 'original' with him, although there may be originality and hence authorship in the manner of reporting, i.e. the 'expression' of the facts."

The path followed by the United States Court of Appeals for the Fifth Circuit in the *Miller* case had been forged a year earlier by the United States Court of Appeals for the Second Circuit in a similar ruling. In March 1980 that court ruled that Universal Studios did not infringe upon the copyright of author A. A. Hoehling, who wrote *Who Destroyed the Hindenberg?* when it produced a film on the 1937 airship disaster. In writing his opinion Chief Judge Irving Kaufman noted that the Second Circuit Court had in the past refused "to subscribe to the view that an author is absolutely precluded from saving time and effort by referring to and relying upon prior published material. . . . It is just such wasted effort that the proscription against the copyright of ideas and facts . . . are designed to prevent" (*Hoehling* v. *Universal Studios,* 1980).

Misappropriation

While this chapter focuses upon copyright, an ancillary area of the law needs to be briefly mentioned, as it too guards against the theft of intangible property. **Misappropriation,** or unfair competition, is sometimes invoked as an additional legal remedy in suits for copyright infringement. Unlike copyright, which springs largely from federal statute today, misappropriation, or unfair competition, remains a creature of the common law. One of the most important media-oriented misappropriation cases was decided by the Supreme Court seventy years ago and stemmed from a dispute between the Associated Press (AP) and the International News Service (INS), a rival press association owned by William Randolph Hearst. (INS merged with the United Press in 1958 and today represents the *I* in *UPI*.)

The Associated Press charged that the International News Service pirated its news, saying that INS bribed AP employees to gain access to news before it was sent to AP member newspapers. The press agency also charged that the Hearst wire service copied news from bulletin boards and early editions of newspapers that carried AP dispatches. Sometimes INS editors rewrote the news, and other times they sent the news out on the wire just as it had been written by AP reporters. Copyright was not the question, because AP did not copyright its material. The agency said it could not copyright all its dispatches because there were too many and they had to be transmitted too fast. The International News Service argued that because the material was not copyrighted, it was in the public domain and could be used by anyone.

Justice Mahlon Pitney wrote the opinion in the seven-to-one decision. He said there can be no property right in the news itself, the events, the happenings, which are publici juris, the common property of all, the history of the day. However, the jurist went on to say (*Associated Press* v. *International News Service,* 1918):

> Although we may and do assume that neither party [AP or INS] has any remaining property interest as against the public in uncopyrighted matter after the moment of its first publication, it by no means follows that there is no remaining property interest in it as between themselves.

Pitney said there was a distinct difference between taking the news collected by AP and publishing it for use by readers and taking the news and transmitting that news for commercial use, in competition with the plaintiff. This action is unfair competition, he said—interference with the business of the AP precisely at the point where profit is to be reaped.

In 1963 a Pennsylvania broadcasting station was found guilty of pirating the news from a local newspaper and reading it over the air as if it were the fruits of its own news-gathering efforts (*Pottstown Daily News Publishing* v. *Pottstown Broadcasting,* 1963).

The decision in both these cases was based on the doctrine of unfair competition, or misappropriation. Courts have applied the doctrine in various instances of fraudulent or dishonest competitive business practices, but particularly in those instances where one seller attempts to substitute his or her own products for those of a well-known competitor by counterfeiting a trade name, package design, or trademark. For example, the owner of the Acme Motel remodels that building in the guise of a Holiday Inn, calls the remodeled creation Hollyday Inn, and attempts to lure weary travelers into this establishment on the basis of the reputation of the real Holiday Inn. This practice is considered unfair competition. In *Associated Press* v. *International News Service,* the Hearst wire service attempted to pass off Associated Press news as its own, and the court said the deception was unfair.

Another more recent case explores a different dimension of the problem. Orion Pictures bought the film rights to a French novel entitled $E = MC^2$ and prepared to make a film of the story entitled *A Little Romance*. Dell Publishing Company bought the translation rights to the same book and attempted to negotiate with Orion for a tie-in publicity campaign heralding the release of both the movie and the book. But Orion refused, claiming that the story had been changed so much in the film that it no longer resembled the book. Dell pushed on anyway and published the book using the movie title—*A Little Romance*—and the cover of the book stated "Now A Major Motion Picture." The promotional material for the book emphasized the tie-in with the film and was an attempt to boost sales of the book. Orion sued for unfair competition, arguing that the sale of the book could hurt the film. A federal judge agreed, noting that after he had read the book and seen the film he considered the motion picture to be substantially better than the novel. "It is the court's belief that if one were to read the book first, the entertaining achievement of the film would not be anticipated." The court said that the Dell book, through its title and cover promotion, gives the impression that it is the "official novel" version of the film and therefore has similar content. This misleads the public and constitutes unfair competition (*Orion Pictures* v. *Dell Publishing,* 1979). The book company was attempting to trade on the name of the picture in promoting the book. This practice is illegal, even though the title of a film cannot be copyrighted.

The critical legal issue in an unfair competition or misappropriation suit is whether there is a *likelihood* that an appreciable number of ordinarily prudent purchasers are likely to be misled, or simply confused, as to the source of the goods in question.

Duration of
Copyright
Protection

The length of time that a copyright will protect a given work depends upon when the work was created. The major revision of the copyright law in 1976 included a significant extension of the duration of copyright protection. Hence, there are two sets of guidelines for determining copyright duration. Any work created after January 1, 1978, will be protected for the life of the creator, plus fifty years. This allows creators to enjoy the fruits of their labor until death and then allows the heirs to profit from the work of their fathers, mothers, sisters, or brothers for an additional one-half century. After fifty years the work goes into what is called public domain. At that point it may be copied by any person for any reason without the payment of royalty to the original owner. The copyright on a work created by two or more authors extends through the life of the last author to die plus fifty years. A work for hire (i.e., where an author is paid to create a book for a corporation that then holds the copyright) is protected for seventy-five years after publication or for one hundred years after creation.

Under the previous copyright law, the 1909 statute, works could be copyrighted for only fifty-six years—two twenty-eight year terms. In 1976 Congress also extended the duration of protection for works created before 1978 (the date the new law went into effect), and these works are now protected for a total of seventy-five years. Under the statute, if a work is in its initial term of copyright, it is protected for the remainder of that twenty-eight year term plus forty-seven more years. Imagine a book was copyrighted in 1970. It will be protected until 1998 under its original twenty-eight year term, plus forty-seven more years, until 2045. But to gain the additional forty-seven years the copyright holder will have to renew the copyright as was required under the previous statute.

If the copyrighted work is already in its renewal term—the second twenty-eight years under the old law—it will be protected for a total of seventy-five years. Imagine, for example, that a song was originally copyrighted in 1940. The copyright was renewed in 1968, the end of the first twenty-eight year term. It will be protected for an additional forty-seven years from 1968, or until 2015. No renewal request is needed in this case.*

SUMMARY

American copyright law derives from rules and regulations established by the British government in the sixteenth and seventeenth centuries. The contemporary basis for the protection of intangible property is contained in the United States Constitution, and since 1789 the nation has had numerous federal copyright statutes. The current law, adopted in 1976, gives to the author or owner of a work the sole and exclusive right to reproduce the copyrighted work in any form for any reason. The statute protects all original works of authorship fixed in any tangible medium. Included are such things as literary works, newspaper stories, magazine articles, television programs, films, and even advertisements. Trivial items, utilitarian goods, ideas, and methods or systems cannot be copyrighted.

News events cannot be copyrighted, but stories or broadcasts that endeavor to describe or explain these events can be copyrighted. What is being protected is the author's style or manner of presentation of the news. Similarly, facts cannot be copyrighted, but works that relate these facts can be protected as expression. While news and facts cannot be copyrighted, anyone who attempts to present news or facts gathered by someone else as his or her own work may be guilty of breaking other laws, such as misappropriation, or unfair competition. In most cases copyrighted works are protected for the life of the author or creator plus fifty years. Different rules apply for works created before 1978 and for works made for hire.

*Additional information concerning duration of copyright is available in circulars *R15A* and *R15T,* which are published by the Copyright Office, Library of Congress, Washington, D.C., 20559.

FAIR USE

Owners of a copyright are granted almost exclusive monopoly over the use of their creations. The word *almost* must be used, for there are really four limitations upon this monopoly. Three of the limitations have been discussed already. First, the work must be something that can be copyrighted. There can be no legal monopoly on the use of something that cannot be protected by the law. Second, the monopoly only protects original authorship or creation. If the creation is not original, it cannot be protected. Third, copyright protection does not last forever. At some point the protection ceases and the work falls into the public domain.

The fourth limitation upon exclusive monopoly is broader than the other three, is certainly more controversial, and is concerned with limited copying of copyrighted material. This is the doctrine of fair use, which has been defined by one court as (*Triangle* v. *Knight-Ridder,* 1980):

> A rule of reason . . . to balance the author's right to compensation for his work, on the one hand, against the public's interest in the widest possible dissemination of ideas and information on the other.

This doctrine, then, permits limited copying of an original creation that has been properly copyrighted and has not yet fallen into the public domain.

Under previous copyright laws all copying of a copyrighted work was against the law. This absolute prohibition on copying constituted a hardship for scholars, critics, and teachers seeking to use small parts of copyrighted materials in their work. A judicial remedy for this problem was sought. It was argued that since the purpose of the original copyright statute was to promote art and science, the copyright law should not be administered in such a way as to frustrate artists and scientists who publish scholarly materials. In 1979 the United States Supreme Court ruled in *Baker* v. *Selden:*

> The very object of publishing a book on science or the useful arts is to communicate to the world the useful knowledge which it contains. But this object would be frustrated if the useful knowledge could not be used without incurring the guilt of piracy of the book.

The doctrine of **fair use** emerged from the courts, and under this judicial doctrine small amounts of copying were permitted so long as the publication of the material advanced science, the arts, criticism, and so forth.

The 1976 copyright law contains the common law doctrine of fair use. Section 107 of the new measure declares, "the fair use of a copyrighted work . . . for purposes such as criticism, comment, news reporting, teaching (including multiple copies for classroom use), scholarship or research is not an infringement of copyright."

In determining whether the use of a particular work is a fair use, the statute says that courts should consider the following factors:

1. The purpose and character of the use, including whether such use is of a commercial nature or is for nonprofit educational purposes
2. The nature of the copyrighted work

3. The amount and substantiality of the portion used in relation to the copyrighted work as a whole
4. The effect of the use upon the potential market for or value of the copyrighted work

Each factor on this list will be considered separately as the doctrine of fair use is explored. Interestingly, the fair-use criteria included in the statute and just listed here (1 through 4) are very close to the criteria that courts used under the old common law fair-use doctrine. This is no accident. In a report issued by committees in the House and the Senate on Section 107, the legislators said that the new law "endorses the purpose and general scope of the judicial doctrine of fair use" but did not intend that the law be frozen as it existed in 1976. "The courts must be free to adapt the doctrine to particular situations on a case-by-case basis. Section 107 is intended to restate the present judicial doctrine of fair use, not to change, narrow, or enlarge it in any way."

Purpose and Character of Use

The purpose and character of the use of a work is the initial factor to be considered. A use is more likely to be considered a fair use if it is a noncommercial or nonprofit use. But simply because material is used in a commercial venture doesn't disqualify it as a fair use. The United States Court of Appeals for the Second Circuit recently noted that according to committee reports compiled when the new copyright law was adopted, the Congress did not intend that only nonprofit educational uses of copyrighted works would qualify as fair use. The reports, said the court, are "an express recognition that . . . the commercial or nonprofit character of an activity, while not conclusive with respect to fair use, can and should be weighed along with other factors in fair use decisions" (*Maxtone-Graham* v. *Burtchaell,* 1986).

The law lists several categories of use that normally fall under fair use: criticism, comment, news reports, teaching, scholarship, and research. A book reviewer, for example, is clearly protected when quoting even long passages from a work being evaluated. A journalist could undoubtedly publish one or two stanzas from a poem by a poet who was named the winner of a Pulitzer Prize. Yet if a poster publisher took the same two stanzas of poetry, printed them in large type on eleven-by-fourteen stock, and tried to sell them for $2.50 each, the publisher would be guilty of an infringement of copyright. The purpose of the use in the case of the journalist was to give readers an example of the poet's work, but the poster publisher simply wanted to make a few bucks.

Another dimension of purpose or character focuses upon the use of the material to serve a public interest. In 1966 the Court of Appeals for the Second Circuit established a public-interest dimension of fair use in a complex copyright suit involving America's best-known recluse, the late Howard Hughes. Random House planned to publish a biography of Hughes in which a series of articles about Hughes in *Look* magazine were quoted rather extensively. When he learned of the Random House project, Hughes, who manifested almost a compulsion about his privacy, formed a corporation called Rosemont, which bought the rights to the *Look* magazine story. Rosemont then sued Random House for using material from the series. All these events took place even before the book was published.

Judge Lumbard ruled in favor of Random House, noting that the purpose of the copyright laws was not to stop dissemination of information about publicity-shy public figures. It would be contrary to the public interest, he said, to allow a man to buy up the rights to anything written about him to stop authors from using the material. Lumbard said that at least the spirit of the First Amendment applied to the copyright laws and that the courts should not tolerate the use of the copyright laws to interfere with the public's right to be informed regarding matters of general interest. Rosemont (Hughes) protested that such copying might be appropriate if the work in question were a scholarly biography of Hughes but that the Random House venture was commercial. Judge Lumbard said this fact was immaterial (*Rosemont* v. *Random House*, 1966):

> Whether an author or publisher reaps economic benefits from the sale of a biographical work, or whether its publication is motivated in part by desire for commercial gain, or whether it is designed for the popular market, i.e., the average citizen rather than the college professor, has no bearing on whether a public benefit may be derived from such a work. . . . Thus, we conclude that whether an author or publisher has a commercial motive or writes in a popular style is irrelevant to a determination of whether a particular use of copyrighted material in a work which offers some benefit to the public constitutes a fair use.

The decision in *Rosemont* represented a bold new step forward in copyright law, a step that many authorities felt was long overdue. On its face the case could not have been equitably decided any other way. Hughes's attempt to buy up his own life story was so patently obvious that the entire suit was really a farce—a mild diversion for the idle rich. Many persons asked: Will the public-interest ruling stand?

Two years later a federal district court in New York used the standard to allow the copying of several frames of very famous motion-picture film. An amateur photographer named Abraham Zapruder happened to be filming President John F. Kennedy when he was shot by an assassin in Dallas in 1963. The film is crude but is the only film available. *Life* magazine bought the rights to the film from Zapruder for $150,000 with the stipulation that the magazine would allow government agencies to use it in connection with investigation of the president's death. The Zapruder film became (and remains) a central piece of evidence in the death of John F. Kennedy, and many persons who believe that the Warren Commission was wrong, that there was a conspiracy, that there was more than one gunman, use the Zapruder film to attempt to prove their thesis. In this case the defendant wanted to publish several frames of the film in his book proposing a multi-assassin theory. When *Life* refused permission to use the film, the author used the frames anyway. Was this fair use?

Life said no, but the court disagreed. The judge said that there was little damage to the magazine as a result of publication of the pictures, that customers purchased the book because of its thesis, not because of its pictures, and that without the photographs the author's thesis was at best difficult to explain. "There is a public interest in having the fullest information available on the murder of President Kennedy. Thompson [the author] did serious work on the subject and had a theory entitled to public consideration." The public interest won out over the magazine's property rights (*Time, Inc.* v. *Bernard Geis Associates,* 1968).

But the public interest standard enunciated in *Rosemont* and *Zapruder* is not without boundaries. Copyright law cannot be ignored or abandoned simply because there is great public interest in the reporting of an event or a story about an important person. Both the American Broadcasting System (ABC) and the Columbia Broadcasting System (CBS) discovered that the fair-use doctrine has limits.

While James Doran was a student at Iowa State University, he produced a twenty-eight minute biography of wrestler Dan Gable. The film was financed by Iowa State and the Gable family, and the university held the copyright. Doran worked for ABC as a videotape operator during the 1972 Olympic Games, during which Gable won a gold medal in wrestling. Doran told ABC about his film while network reporters were scrambling for some biographical film about Gable. ABC broadcast long segments of the film during its telecast of the Olympic Games, without first obtaining permission from Iowa State University. The network claimed that these broadcasts were fair use in the copyright infringement suit that followed. The network said it was engaged in the laudable pursuit of disseminating the life story of an important public figure involved in an event of intense public interest. But the United States Court of Appeals for the Second Circuit rejected this argument. The network could have used other, noncopyrighted material for its film biography of the gold-medal-winning wrestler. The film was used at least in part for commercial exploitation by the network, the court ruled. No fair use (*Iowa State* v. *ABC,* 1980).

CBS found itself in a similar mess in 1982 after it had broadcast a copyrighted compilation of Charlie Chaplin films on the occasion of the great comedian's death. Roy Export Company owned the rights to the motion pictures excerpted in the thirteen-minute montage. This compilation of segments from six of Chaplin's greatest films had been put together by Roy Export for a one-time telecast on NBC during the 1972 Academy Award presentations, which featured a special segment on Charlie Chaplin. CBS had tried to buy the rights to the compilation from Roy Export, but the company refused the offer. When Chaplin died, CBS nevertheless obtained a copy of the film compilation from NBC, which had kept a videotape of the Academy Awards ceremony, and broadcast it as a memorial biography of the great comedian.

When the network was sued for copyright infringement, it claimed its telecast of the material was fair use. Chaplin's death was newsworthy, and a biography of the comedian's life would be incomplete without showing excerpts from some of his greatest films, the network argued. But the United States Court of Appeals for the Second Circuit disagreed. "The showing of copyrighted films was not essential to CBS's news report of Charlie Chaplin's death or to its assessment of his place in history," the court ruled. Other films that were in the public domain were available, the court said. Also, the public is generally familiar with Chaplin's work.

CBS also argued that the 1972 Academy Awards ceremony was a very important news event, since it marked the return of Charlie Chaplin to Hollywood after a twenty-year exile in Europe following the Communist witch-hunts in the film industry in the early 1950s. Again the court rejected the network's ideas. "The audiovisual news event, if there was one, was Chaplin's appearance, not the showing of his work," the judge ruled. The showing of the copyrighted compilation of Chaplin's film exceeded fair use (*Roy Export Co. v. CBS,* 1982).

It is important to note a difference between these latter two cases and the earlier decision on the Zapruder film, for this difference is a key to understanding what are perhaps one set of limits to the public-interest standard in fair use. Assume for a moment that comparable public interest exists in all three events—the Kennedy assassination, Dan Gable winning an Olympic gold medal, and the death of Charlie Chaplin. There was considerable noncopyrighted material available for the networks to use in reporting the latter two events. The broadcast of the copyrighted films was not essential to telling an important news story. In the case of the Zapruder film, however, much of the book's argument about the Kennedy assassination was based upon the Zapruder film. No suitable substitute existed.

Finally, the *Nation* magazine attempted to argue that its publication of an excerpt from the unpublished memoirs of Gerald Ford was fair use because the material contained information of great public interest. The article in *Nation* was approximately 2,250 words long and consisted almost entirely of paraphrases and quotations from portions of the 200,000 word draft memoirs, with little or no independent commentary. The article detailed Ford's recital of the events leading to the pardon of Richard Nixon, repeated stories about Henry Kissinger, John Connally, and others, and closed with some of Ford's observations about Nixon's character. *Time* magazine had purchased the right to print prepublication excerpts from the manuscript and had already paid Ford $12,500, half of the promised sum for the prepublication privilege. An unidentified source gave a copy of the draft memoirs to Victor Navasky, the *Nation* editor, and the weekly published its article on April 9, 1979, a full week before the excerpts in *Time* were scheduled to appear. *Time* cancelled its publication of the excerpts and refused to pay Ford the additional $12,500. Harper

& Row and the Reader's Digest Association, joint publishers of the Ford book (which was published in August of 1979) sued the *Nation* for copyright infringement.

A United States District court ruled that the *Nation* had indeed infringed upon the copyright on the work held by the book publishers (*Harper & Row Publishers* v. *Nation Enterprises*, 1983). But the United States Court of Appeals for the Second Circuit overturned this decision, declaring the publication of the material by the *Nation* was a fair use. The appeals court ruled that all but 300 words of the 2,250 word article was uncopyrightable news and history. The court found that the only possible infringement was the use of verbatim passages from the memoirs that had not appeared previously in other publications. Because of the great public import in the material, the court said it could excuse the verbatim appropriation of copyrighted material as "lending authenticity to this politically significant material." The court added, "Where information concerning important matters of state is accompanied by minimal borrowing of expression, . . . the copyright holder's monopoly must not be permitted to prevail over a journalist's communication." This was a broad assertion of a public-interest element of the fair-use defense in a copyright action (*Harper & Row Publishers, Inc.* v. *Nation Enterprises*, 1983).

But the victory for the *Nation* was short-lived, for the Supreme Court overturned the ruling by the court of appeals. Justice Sandra Day O'Connor, writing for the six-person majority, ruled that the promise of copyright would be an empty one if it could be avoided merely by dubbing the infringement a fair use because it contains news or information in the public interest. "In using generous verbatim excerpts of Mr. Ford's unpublished manuscript to lend authenticity to its account of the forthcoming memoirs, the *Nation* effectively arrogated to itself the right of first publication, an important marketable subsidiary right," O'Connor wrote. This was an important point in the ruling, for it surely narrowed the scope of the High Court's rejection of the public-interest component of fair use. The 1976 Copyright Act clearly recognizes the right of first publication for an author. The scope of fair use is narrowed where unpublished works are concerned. The Senate report that accompanied the 1976 law specifically states: "The applicability of the fair use doctrine to unpublished works is narrowly limited since, although the work is unavailable, this is the result of a deliberate choice on the part of the copyright owner. Under ordinary circumstances the copyright owner's 'right of first publication' would outweigh any needs of reproduction. . . ." Justice O'Connor concluded that the unpublished nature of a work is a key, though not necessarily determinative factor, tending to negate a defense of fair use (*Harper & Row Publishers* v. *Nation Enterprises*, 1985). While the Supreme Court decision appears to constitute a rejection of the public-interest dimension of the fair use defense, the decision was clearly a narrow ruling pegged to infringement of *unpublished* material. The broader public interest standard established in cases like *Rosemont* and *Zapruder* clearly remains intact for those cases involving the infringement of published works. Nevertheless be warned, for the public interest argument remains controversial and has taken root firmly only in the United States Court of Appeals for the Second Circuit, an admittedly liberal jurisdiction in many respects.

Nature of Copyrighted Work

Several considerations come to the fore when a court considers the nature of the copyrighted work. Is the work available? The use of material from a work that is out of print, for example, is more likely to be considered a fair use than the comparable use of material from a work that is in stock at local bookstores. As noted in the *Nation* case, courts take greater pains to protect unpublished works. The right of the author to first publication will generally outweigh a claim of fair use. Does the work contain consumable material, or is the book something that may be used over and over again? The copying of consumable material such as workbooks, books containing exercises, standardized tests, puzzles, and so forth is rarely considered fair use. Such works are intended to be purchased and consumed—not resold. Making photocopies, for example, of the pages of a biology workbook would clearly deprive the author of the sale of additional copies and would not be a fair use. On the other hand, courts appear to be more tolerant of copying from other kinds of works like newspapers, magazines and reference books. Use of this kind of material is rarely harmful to a publisher unless the copying is persistent and large scale.

Amount of a Work Used

The amount of a work used is often not as important as the relative proportion of a work used. Word counts, for example, really don't mean as much as percentages. The use of 500 words from a 450-page book is far less damaging than the use of 20 words from a 40-word poem. How much of the work, in relation to the whole, was used? Courts will consider exact copying when looking at this question; but they will also often consider paraphrasing. Pirates will find little refuge in a dictionary of synonyms. Ian Hamilton, a well-respected writer on literary topics, recently attempted to do a biography of J. D. Salinger, the man who wrote *Catcher in the Rye,* and an individual who surely rivals the late Howard Hughes as a recluse. Hamilton asked Salinger for cooperation, but the novelist refused because he did not want a biography written. Hamilton found collections of a series of unpublished letters written by Salinger to friends over a thirty-seven year period in public libraries. The interesting thing about a letter is that it has two owners. The recipient of the letter owns the paper and can surely donate it to a library, but the writer of the letter owns the words, and can control their later use. Salinger therefore attempted to block the publication of the book by copyrighting the letters and prohibiting Hamilton from using their content. The final revised manuscript contained only about two hundred words copied exactly from the Salinger letters. But in a great many other instances Hamilton had apparently closely paraphrased the original language in the letters. The United States Court of Appeals for the Second Circuit, noting again that these were unpublished letters, ruled that such use was not a fair use but an infringement and that closely paraphrasing Salinger's comments must be counted as a use. "What is protected is the manner of expression, the author's analysis or interpretation of events—the way he structures his material and marshalls facts, his choice of words and the emphasis he gives to particular developments," wrote Judge Jon O. Newman. The paraphrasing was too close to Salinger's own choice of words; to his creativity. There were forty-four letters involved and Hamilton had copied or paraphrased one-third or more of seventeen letters, and had copied or paraphrased more than ten percent of forty-two of the letters. Such material is on forty percent of the pages of Hamilton's manuscript, Judge Newman noted. The biographer had taken the "heart of the material" from the letters (*Salinger* v. *Random House,* 1987). Hamilton abandoned his initial effort and instead wrote *In Search of J. D. Salinger,* a book about Salinger's literary life (without the material from the letters) and his unsuccessful efforts to publish a biography of the reclusive author.

In some instances massive appropriation occurs, but defendants attempt to argue it is a fair use because it is for educational purposes. Courts seldom accept this argument. The Educational Services Board in Erie County, New York, rented educational and documentary films from various distributors and then made videotapes of them for future school use. The board copied films broadcast on television for future use as well. Five to eight full-time employees did the copying and made as many as ten thousand tapes in a single year. A court ruled that this was not a fair use regardless of the educational motives that the defendant alleged were the basis of the copying (*Encyclopaedia Britannica* v. *Crooks,* 1978).

More recently nine book publishers sued New York University, nine of its professors, and an off-campus copy center for copyright infringement. The suit charged that the faculty members repeatedly copied major amounts from many popular works such as Truman Capote's *In Cold Blood* and *The Final Days* by Bob Woodward and Carl Bernstein. The publishers argued that such copying was done semester after semester. The publishers dropped their suit in April 1983 in return for a pledge from the defendant school and faculty to adhere to copying guidelines.

One of the toughest tasks a judge must face is measuring fair use when someone presents a parody of a copyrighted work. To be successful a parody must conjure up in the viewers' or listeners' minds the original work; hence, it must use some aspects of the original work. But how much of the original can be used? "Saturday Night Live," a National Broadcasting Company television program, presented a parody of a New York City public relations campaign. The city had even commissioned the writing of a song—"I Love New York"—as a theme for the campaign. The NBC "Saturday Night Live" parody ended with the singing of "I Love Sodom" to the tune of "I Love New York."

The city claimed this was a copyright infringement, but the court disagreed. "A parody is entitled to conjure up the original. Even more extensive use would still be fair use, provided the parody builds upon the original, using the original as a known element of modern culture and contributing something new for humorous effect or commentary," the United States Court of Appeals for the Second Circuit ruled (*Elsmere Music* v. *NBC,* 1980). And the United States Court of Appeals for the Ninth Circuit recently ruled that it was a fair use for disc jockey Rick Dees to use the melody and some of the words from the first six bars of the song, "When Sunny Gets Blue," in his comic parody, "When Sonny Sniffs Glue." The lyrics in the original song are: "When Sunny gets blue, her eyes get gray and cloudy, then the rain begins to fall." In Dees' version: "When Sonny sniffs glue, her eyes get red and bulgy, then her hair begins to fall." The court noted that "like a speech, a song is difficult to parody effectively without exact or near-exact copying. If the would-be parodist varies the music or the meter of the original substantially, it simply will not be recognizable to the general audience." It is this special need for accuracy that gives the parodist some license in these cases, the court added (*Fisher* v. *Dees,* 1986). But see *MGM* v. *Showcase Atlanta,* 1981, for a parody that went too far.

It is important to remember that the amount of material that may be fairly copied is not an absolute but is always relative to the size of the total work from which the material is taken.

Effect of Use on Market The effect of the use upon the potential market for or value of the copyrighted work is the fourth criterion. While a cautionary note should be sounded against assigning relative weight to the four criteria, this final one—harm to the plaintiff—is probably given greater weight by most courts than any of the other three. In a Congressional Committee report on the 1976 law, the legislators noted that "with certain special exceptions . . . a use that supplants any part of the normal market for a copyrighted work would ordinarily be considered an infringement." And in the action by Harper & Row against the *Nation,* Justice Sandra Day O'Connor noted that "This last factor is undoubtedly the single most important element of fair use" (*Harper & Row* v. *Nation,* 1985). In the aforementioned *Salinger* case the market value of the unpublished letters was a significant factor in the determination that Hamilton's attempt to use them in a biography was not a fair use. The court estimated the current value of the letters at $500,000, and said: "For at least some appreciable number of persons, these phrases [in the biographical manuscript] will convey the impression they have read Salinger's words, perhaps not quoted verbatim, but paraphrased so closely as to diminish interest in purchasing the originals" (*Salinger* v. *Random House,* 1987). In 1977 a federal district court refused to grant a temporary order enjoining the publication of a cumulative 111-year name index of the 111 annually issued volumes of the

New York Times Index. The *Times* index is organized alphabetically within each annual volume. The *Roxbury Index* of the annual *New York Times Indexes* was to be organized alphabetically over the 111 years from 1863 to 1974. The index of the *Times* index would be of great benefit to researchers. For example, using only the *New York Times Index* for material on Charles Evans Hughes, a researcher would have to look in more than forty annual volumes spanning the late chief justice's life. But with the *Roxbury Index,* a researcher would need only to look in a single volume under Hughes's name for all the references during the forty-year period. While this would be a great boon to researchers, there was no question that by its very nature the *Roxbury Index* included much material copied from the copyrighted *New York Times Index.* The court ruled, however, that the effect of the personal-name index on the market for the *New York Times Index* appeared "slight or non-existent." As a matter of fact, persons could not use the *Roxbury Index* without also using the *New York Times Index,* so rather than being in competition with the annual index, the cumulative name index enhanced the value of the *New York Times* publication (*New York Times* v. *Roxbury Data Interface,* 1977).

The United States Court of Appeals for the Fifth Circuit ruled that it was fair use when the *Miami Herald* displayed copyrighted covers of *TV Guide* magazine in advertising for the newspaper's new television magazine. *TV Guide* had argued that such use was an infringement upon its copyright, since the advertisement for the *Herald* magazine was a blatantly commercial use of the *TV Guide* covers. The court conceded it was indeed a commercial use but noted that the use of the covers had absolutely no effect upon the potential market or value of the copyrighted *TV Guide* magazine covers. True, the advertisements for the *Herald* television magazine might hurt *TV Guide* sales, but the *advertising* did this, not the use of the covers of old editions of *TV Guide* (*Triangle Publications* v. *Knight-Ridder Newspapers, Inc.,* 1980). In this case the court said that the fourth factor, the effect of the use on the market for the copyrighted work, "is widely accepted to be the most important factor."

Finally, in the *Harper & Row* v. *Nation* case the Supreme Court looked at the direct economic impact of the publication of segments of the Ford memoirs in the *Nation*—the loss of $12,500 from *Time* magazine—as well as potential long-term losses. "More important," Justice O'Connor wrote, "to negate fair use one need only show that if the challenged use should become widespread, it would adversely affect the potential market for the copyright work."

The popularity of videocassette recorders (VCRs) presented one of the most interesting copyright problems in decades, and the fourth element, the economic impact wrought by the unauthorized use, was crucial in the ultimate resolution of the issue. Is it fair use when the owner of a home videocassette recorder copies television programs and motion pictures broadcast by television networks and local stations and then replays them for strictly personal use? Universal City Studios, Walt Disney Productions, and other program production companies brought suit in 1979 to stop such home recording. Named as defendants in the case were Sony Corporation of America and several distributors and sellers of the home video-recording equipment. Universal charged that the home copying of programs amounted to massive infringement of their copyrights on these programs. Sony and the other defendants argued that this was fair use of the material. The trial court ruled in favor of the defendants, noting that the copying was not undertaken for commercial purposes and that the harm to the plaintiffs in the case was purely speculative (*Universal City Studios* v. *Sony,* 1979). But the United States Court of Appeals for the Ninth Circuit reversed this decision and ruled against Sony. The court said such home recording was not fair use. The law states that *nonprofit educational* use may be fair use, but this is not the same as *noncommercial* use, the court said. The recording of entire programs was something certainly never contemplated when the fair-use standards were written, the court added. Finally, such copying could have a severe impact upon the plaintiffs. In the imminent future a large percentage of the nation's seventy-five million television households will have a videocassette recorder, and massive amounts of copying will take place, the court predicted. Viewers would watch the playback of programs they had copied, rather than new programs; commercials would be deleted in the playback; and the audience for rerun programming would be significantly reduced, the court concluded (*Universal City Studios* v. *Sony,* 1981).

Sony appealed the decision to the Supreme Court, which, in 1984, reversed the ruling by the court of appeals. Taping television programs at home for showing at a different time (called time shifting) is a noncommercial, nonprofit activity, wrote Justice John Paul Stevens for the five-person majority. But even a noncommercial, nonprofit use may impair the copyright holder's ability to obtain rewards that Congress intended the holder to have, Stevens noted. Then the economic impact of the use on the copyright holder must be considered. A majority of the High Court agreed completely with the trial court in its consideration of this factor. Universal City Studios and the other plaintiffs in the lawsuit had not shown that they had been harmed or might be harmed in the future because of such copying for home use. "Harm from time shifting is speculative and, at best, minimal," the justice wrote. "What is necessary is a showing by a preponderance of the evidence that some meaningful likelihood of future harm exists. If the intended use is for commercial gain, that likelihood may be presumed. But if it is for a noncommercial purpose, the likelihood must be demonstrated," he added. The motion picture and television program producers had failed to demonstrate this likelihood of harm. In fact, Stevens suggested, it was not implausible to suggest that time shifting, through the use of a videocassette recorder, increased the number of viewers who might see a program (*Sony Corp.* v. *Universal City Studios,* 1984).

SUMMARY

While the copyright statute gives the author or owner of a copyrighted work an exclusive monopoly over the use of that work, there has been recognition that it is important in some instances for other persons to be able to copy portions of a protected work. No liability will attach to such copying if the use is what the law calls a "fair use."

A court will consider four factors when determining whether a specific use is fair use:

1. What is the purpose of the use? Why was the material copied? Was it a commercial use or for nonprofit educational purpose? Was the use intended to further the public interest in some way?

2. What is the nature of the copyrighted work? Is it a consumable item such as a workbook, or is it a work that might more likely be borrowed from such as a newspaper or magazine article? Is the copyrighted work in print and available for sale? Has the work been previously published or is it unpublished?

3. How much of the copyrighted work was used in relation to the entire copyrighted work? Was it a small amount of a large work? or was it a large portion of a small work?

4. What impact does the use have on the potential market or value of the copyrighted work? Has the use of the material diminished the chances for sale of the original work? or is the use unrelated to the value or sale of the copyrighted material?

While a court considers each of these items closely, most courts tend to give extra weight to item four. In a close ruling the impact on the market or value of the copyrighted work often becomes the most crucial question.

COPYRIGHT NOTICE AND INFRINGEMENT

In order for a work to be protected under the copyright law, it must contain what is called a **copyright notice.** The law specifically prescribes the kind of notice required and states that it consists of three parts.

Proper Notice

A copyright notice must contain the word *Copyright,* the abbreviation *Copr.,* or the symbol © (the letter *C* within a circle; the symbol ℗ is used on phonorecords). The year of publication must also be included in the notice. For periodicals the date supplied is the date of publication. For books the date is the year in which the book is first offered for sale (e.g., a book printed in November or December 1991 to go on sale January 1992 should carry a 1992 copyright). The notice must also contain the name of the copyright holder or owner. Most authorities recommend that both the word *Copyright* and the symbol © be used, since the use of the symbol is required to meet the standards of the international copyright agreements. The symbol © protects the work from piracy in most foreign countries. A copyright notice should look something like this:

Copyright © 1992 by Jane Adams

The courts will be very strict with regard to the composition of the notice. Any old notice will not do. For example, a notice saying "This book was written by Jane Adams and is her property until 2005" will not qualify as proper notice. The new statute is virtually identical with previous statutes in prescribing the composition of the notice. In 1903 the Supreme Court ruled that since the statute states a specific way to give the reader proper notice, that is what the courts will demand. "In determining whether a notice of copyright is misleading, we are not bound to look beyond the face of the notice, and inquire whether under the facts of the particular case it is reasonable to suppose an intelligent person could actually have been misled" (*Mifflin* v. *H. H. White,* 1903).

The copyright notice can be placed anywhere that it "can be visually perceived" on all publicly distributed copies. (The rules are different for sound recordings, which by law cannot be visually perceived.) The Copyright Office of the Library of Congress has issued rules that implement the statutory description that the notice be visually perceptible. For example, the rules list eight different places where a copyright notice might be put in a book, including the title page, the page immediately following the title page, either side of the front cover, and so forth. For photographs, a copyright notice label can be affixed to the back or front of a picture or on any mounting or framing to which the photographs are *permanently* attached.*

The 1976 copyright law also provides that omission of the proper notice does not destroy copyright protection for the work if the notice is omitted from only a relatively small number of copies, if an effort is made within five years to correct the omission, or if the notice is omitted in violation of the copyright holder's express requirement that as a condition of publication the work carry a copyright notice.

At the same time the law protects persons who copy a work on which the copyright notice was inadvertently omitted. Such an innocent infringer incurs no liability—cannot be sued—unless this infringement continues beyond the time notice is received that the work has been copyrighted.

*Additional information is available in the bulletin *Methods of Affixation and Position of the Copyright,* published by the Copyright Office, and in the *Federal Register,* vol. 42, no. 247, for 23 December 1977, pp. 64374–78.

Registration

Proper notice is the only requirement that an author must fulfill to copyright a work. The work is then protected from the moment of creation for the life of the author plus fifty years. However, before a copyright holder can sue for infringement under the law, the copyrighted work must be registered with the federal government. To register a work the author or owner must do three things:

1. Fill out the proper registration form. The type of form varies, depending upon the kind of work being registered. The forms are available from the Information and Publications Section, Copyright Office, Library of Congress, Washington, D.C. 20559.
2. Pay a ten-dollar fee.
3. Deposit two complete copies of the work with the Copyright Office.

The statute gives an author or owner ninety days to get a work registered. What happens if the work is still not registered after ninety days and an infringement takes place? The owner can still register the work and bring suit. But a successful plaintiff in such a suit cannot win statutory damages (see pages 465–466) or win compensation for attorney's fees. It is best to get into the habit of registering a work as soon as it is published or broadcast.

The requirement of notice is a very important one. It allows all the works that no one wants to copyright to fall into the public domain immediately. It also tells the reader whether a work is copyrighted, was ever copyrighted, or is still copyrighted. It also identifies the owner of the work and the date of publication. The change in the law that protects authors who accidently forget to include a copyright notice on their works is healthy and worthwhile. But writers and broadcasters should get into the habit of putting the notice on all material that they believe to be valuable, whether it is published or not.

Infringement

It is important for authors to know how to protect their own work. It is equally important to know how to avoid being sued for stealing someone else's copyrighted material. Such theft does not always result in a successful suit, or even in a suit at all. Many times the owner of the copyrighted matter is unaware of the theft. Other times the harm to the copyright holder is insignificant. In copyright, as in other areas of mass media law, who you are is often more important than what you stole. For example, if the *East Ames Morning Dispatch and World Advertiser* publishes in its entertainment section, without permission, one complete act of a Neil Simon play, the newspaper might get a nasty letter from Simon's attorney, but probably not much more. But if the National Broadcasting Company presents the same act on one of its shows, it will surely get slapped with a copyright suit. Publication of the play in a small newspaper has not harmed the playwright significantly, and in addition the paper probably does not have much money. But presentation of even a single act of the play on NBC can diminish Simon's future royalties, since it would probably lessen the number of future stage productions of the play.

The United States copyright statute does not really define infringement. The law states that anyone who violates any of the "exclusive rights" of the copyright holder is an infringer of the copyright. That statement is of little help to courts attempting to determine whether an infringement has taken place. Consequently, courts continue to rely upon the definition of infringement forged during the past 150 years. Courts look to a variety of criteria to determine whether an infringement has taken place. We will focus upon three of these criteria that seem to be the most important: originality, access, and copying and substantial similarity. The burden of proof falls on the plaintiff in a copyright suit, but of course the defendant will do everything possible to prove that no copyright infringement has occurred. So both sides normally present evidence.

Originality

The copyright on the plaintiff's work must be valid before a successful infringement suit can be maintained. As has been previously noted, a work that is not original cannot be copyrighted. A central question, then, in many infringement suits is whether or not the plaintiff's work is original. Or is the plaintiff attempting to bring suit on the basis of the theft of material that cannot be legally copyrighted because it lacks originality or novelty?

History, for example, exists for all to use in a book or a story. Margaret Alexander brought an infringement suit against Alex Haley, claiming that he had copied portions of her novel *Jubilee* and her pamphlet *How I Wrote Jubilee* when he wrote and published his successful novel, *Roots*. But the court noted that most of what Alexander claimed Haley had stolen was history—the story of the slave culture in the United States, or material in the public domain such as folk tales about early American black culture. "Where common sources exist for the alleged similarities, or the material that is similar is not original with the plaintiff, there is no infringement," the court ruled (*Alexander* v. *Haley,* 1978).

An NBC employee recently tried to sue the network, arguing that he had originally proposed the concept for the highly successful "Bill Cosby Show" in 1980, some four years before the television program premiered. At that time NBC said it was not interested in the idea, the plaintiff said. But the court said that there was really nothing original in the concept proposed by plaintiff Hwesu Murray, or in the Cosby show itself for that matter. It merely combined two ideas that had been circulating for years: a family situation comedy, and the casting of blacks in nonstereotypical roles. The portrayal of a nonstereotypical black family in a half-hour show was a breakthrough in television broadcasting, the court noted, comparing the Cosby program with shows like "The Jeffersons," "Good Times," "Different Strokes," and "Sanford and

Son," all of which featured blacks in fairly stereotypical roles. But the fact that such a show had never before been broadcast does not necessarily mean that the idea for the program itself is novel. "Whereas here, an idea consists in essence of nothing more than a variation on a basic theme—in this case the family situation comedy—novelty cannot be found (*Murray* v. *NBC,* 1988).

Judith Rossner, the author of the successful book *Looking for Mr. Goodbar,* sued CBS for copyright infringement in 1985 when the network produced the film "Trackdown: Finding Mr. Goodbar." Both Rossner's book and the TV movie are based on the murder in 1973 of Roseann Quinn by John W. Wilson. Rossner's book leads readers up to the point of the murder; the CBS movie purportedly tells the story of the capture of the killer. Rossner claimed the use of the term "Mr. Goodbar" in the title of the movie violated her copyright. But a United States district court disagreed, noting that the term "Mr. Goodbar" had been used in newspaper stories about the killing before Rossner wrote her book. An author can't build a story around a historical incident and then claim exclusive right to the use of that incident, the court said. "To the extent that Rossner's characters were inspired by actual persons, she cannot prevent the future depiction of these characters through the individual creative efforts of others," the court ruled. Since the Mr. Goodbar concept was not original with Rossner, she could not claim it under copyright (*Rossner* v. *CBS,* 1985).

The author of a book entitled *Fort Apache* sued the producers of the film, "Fort Apache—The Bronx" for copyright infringement. Both the book and the movie focused upon the 41st Precinct of the New York City Police Department. Police officers had dubbed the South Bronx precinct Fort Apache because of the high incidence of violent crime in the area. Thomas Walker, a former police officer who was assigned to the 41st Precinct for fifteen months, wrote and published his book in 1976. The book was a series of stories about his work in the precinct, a narrative moving from one anecdote to the next with no real plot. The film, on the other hand, was intensely plotted, with several interrelated story lines, all taking place at once. Walker claimed the producers of the film had stolen his material, but a court of appeals disagreed. "To be sure, the book and the film share an identical setting, and police officers are central characters in both works," the court noted. "But the South Bronx and the 41st Precinct are real places known to the public through media coverage. Accordingly, the notion of telling a police story that takes place there cannot be copyrightable," the court ruled. The parts of the film that were similar to the book were not original with the book's author (*Walker* v. *Time-Life Films,* 1986).

Access

The second dimension of an infringement suit is access: the plaintiff must convince the court that the defendant had access to the copyrighted work. An opportunity to copy has to exist. If plaintiffs cannot prove that the so-called literary pirate had a chance to see and read the work, they are hard pressed to prove piracy. As Judge Learned Hand once wrote (*Sheldon v. Metro-Goldwyn-Mayer Pictures,* 1939):

> . . . if by some magic a man who had never known it were to compose anew Keats's, "Ode on a Grecian Urn," he would be an 'author' and if he copyrighted it, others might not copy that poem, though they might of course copy Keats's.

Here in contemporary terms is what Judge Hand said. If through some incredible coincidence a young composer were to write and publish a song called "Born in the U.S.A." that was an exact duplicate of the song by Bruce Springsteen, it would not be an infringement of copyright. Publishing a song exactly like a copyrighted song is not infringement; copying a copyrighted song is infringement. Moreover, if the young composer could prove that he had lived in a cave since birth, had never listened to the radio or records, and had never watched television or gone to the movies, and if Springsteen could not prove that the defendant had had access to "Born in the U.S.A.," he would lose his suit. It must be obvious that such a coincidence can never occur, but this illustration nevertheless makes the point. The *plaintiff* must prove access to the stolen work. The smaller the circulation of the copyrighted matter, the harder it is to prove access.

Failure to prove the defendant had access to a copyrighted book was fatal to a lawsuit brought by Sonya Jason against the writers and producers of the film *Coming Home.* Defendants Jane Fonda and others stated that their film was conceived in the late 1960s, that a first draft of the screenplay was completed by late 1973 and was revised in 1977. Jason's book, *Concomitant Soldier,* was first printed in April 1974. Only 1,100 copies were printed. About 500 copies were sold in New Jersey, 100 were sold through the plaintiff's church, 200 copies were returned to the printer because they were defective, and the remaining copies were sold in southern California. Jason claimed that a copy of the book might have been given to Nancy Dowd, a screenwriter for the film, but there was no evidence that Dowd or anyone else connected with the film had seen the book. Jason was only able to prove that several hundred copies of *Concomitant Soldier* were sold in southern California where Fonda, Dowd, and others associated with the film lived and worked. "That level of availability creates no more than a 'bare possibility' that defendants may have had access to plaintiff's book," the court said. "In and of itself, such a bare possibility is insufficient to create a genuine issue of whether defendants copied plaintiff's book" (*Jason v. Fonda,* et al., 1981).

Copying and Substantial Similarity

The final factor the court will consider is evidence that the defendant copied the plaintiff's work, or evidence that the two works are substantially similar. If the defendant has taken a chapter of the plaintiff's book, or long excerpts from the plaintiff's unpublished letters, or a character from a comic strip, this will surely support a finding of copying and probably infringement. A group aptly named Air Pirates copied Walt Disney characters for posters and T-shirts, but portrayed the loveable Disney creations in a hideous manner. This was copying and an infringement, the court said, despite the change in the nature of Mickey, Pluto, and the rest of the gang (*Walt Disney Productions* v. *Air Pirates,* 1972). Moving a character from one medium to another will not insulate the copying from a successful lawsuit either. A toymaker cannot make a plastic figure in the likeness of a movie character without first getting the permission of the copyright holder.

Such direct copying is often referred to as literal similarity—one work is literally like another. But more often than not direct or literal copying is not an issue. The story was not copied word for word, the character was not an exact duplicate of the defendant's character. In such a case the defendant is not accused of taking a particular line or segment of a work, but of appropriating "the fundamental essence or structure of the work." There must be more than minor similarities between the two works, they must be substantially similar. But this is another one of the instances where it is easier to state a rule than to apply it. How can you determine whether or not two works are substantially similar?

Courts have developed tests to be applied in making this determination and the one set of criteria that has recently been applied most often stems from a lawsuit by Sid and Marty Krofft Television Productions against the McDonald's corporation. The Kroffts, creators of "H. R. Pufnstuf," argued that the "McDonaldland" set featured in television commercials was a direct copy of the Living Island locale used in Pufnstuf. The United States Court of Appeals for the Ninth Circuit developed a two-part test to determine whether the two works were substantially similar. The first part of the test examines whether there is substantial similarity between the general ideas in the two works. Are the two works about the same thing? If the ideas are not similar, there is no infringement. But if the general ideas in the two works are similar, the court asks the second question: Is there substantial similarity in the manner in which the ideas are expressed in the two works? Are the major characters alike, are the dialogue and plot alike, are there similar scenes in the two works?

In the Krofft case the court found substantial similarity between the general ideas of both McDonaldland and the Living Island—mystical fantasy lands populated by strange and amusing beings. Is the idea of this fantasy land expressed in a similar fashion in both cases? The answer is yes. Both imaginary worlds are inhabited by anthropomorphic plants and animals. The topographical features of both places are the same—trees, caves, a pond, a road and a castle. Both works feature a forest with talking trees that have human faces. Both lands are governed by mayors who have large, round heads and long wide mouths. They are assisted by Keystone coplike characters. There are crazy scientists and multi-armed evil creatures in both lands. In a word it was a steal. In fact, McDonald's had hired some former Krofft employees to design and construct McDonaldland (*Sid and Marty Krofft Television Productions* v. *McDonald's Corporation,* 1977). While other tests exist to determine substantial similarity, the *Krofft* test is widely used. Here are some recent examples.

Warner Brothers, which owns the film rights to "Superman," sued ABC in the early 1980s for broadcast of the network series, "The Greatest American Hero." The general idea of both the "Superman" films and the ABC series is similar—a character, who wears a red and blue suit with a cape and is able to fly, battles the forces of evil. But the court ruled that Warner Brothers could not "claim a protected interest in the theme of a man dressed in a cape and tights who has the power to fly, resist bullets, crash through walls, break handcuffs, etc." The plaintiff must show that the concrete expression of the *Superman* idea has been appropriated. Warner Brothers could not do this. The characters in *Superman* and "The Greatest American Hero" are quite different. The hero of the ABC program is Ralph Hinckley, an ordinary man who reluctantly takes on abnormal abilities through a magic costume and is comically inept. Superman is naturally endowed with these powers, which he wields with grace and confidence. As a person Hinckley is the antithesis of the strong Superman character, the court said. In some ways the ABC show is a parody of Superman. "As a comedy that parodies American superheroes," Judge Motley wrote, " 'The Greatest American Hero' has a very different appeal from Superman, a real superhero, and plaintiffs have not sufficiently proven that it will reduce demand for movies and programs about Superman, and products bearing the Superman image" (*Warner Bros.* v. *ABC,* 1981).

The United States Court of Appeals for the Ninth Circuit was asked to determine whether writer/director Michael Crichton had stolen a screen treatment for his film called *Coma,* which was based on a book by Robin Cook. Plaintiff Ted Berkik in 1968 wrote a fifty-four-page screen treatment for a story he called "Reincarnation, Inc." Crichton apparently saw the screen treatment but did not use it ten years later when he wrote the screenplay for *Coma.* Berkik alleged that both the film and Robin Cook's book were taken from his screen treatment.

The stories have certain similarities, the court noted. Both deal with criminal organizations that murder healthy young people and then remove and sell their vital organs to wealthy people in need of organ transplants. And in both stories courageous young medical professionals investigate and finally expose the criminal organization. But these similarities are at a high level of generality. When one looks at the manner in which these similar ideas are expressed in the two works, the similarity ends. The plots of the two stories develop differently; the settings are different. *Coma* is replete with medical terminology and is an old-fashioned detective story; "Reincarnation, Inc." is more of a romance. Yes, there are some similarities, but general ideas are not protected. Nor are situations and incidents that flow naturally from a basic plot premise, so-called scènes à faire. "These familiar scenes [depictions of the small miseries of domestic life or romantic frolics at the beach] and themes are among the very staples of modern American literature and film. The common use of such stock material cannot raise a trial issue of fact on the plaintiff's copyright claim," the appellate court ruled. "It merely reminds us that in Hollywood, as in the life of real men generally, there is only rarely anything new under the sun" (*Berkik* v. *Crichton,* 1985).

Finally, the Trust Company Bank, which as a trustee holds the copyright to Margaret Mitchell's novel *Gone With the Wind,* sued the Putnam Publishing Group to block the United States distribution of the French novel, *The Blue Bicycle.* Mitchell's book is a Civil War era story set in the South. The plaintiffs argued that in *The Blue Bicycle* the characters and events from *Gone With the Wind* are simply moved from Georgia to France during the World War II era. The court agreed that the general idea of the two books is similar, but rejected the notion that there is similarity in expression of the idea. For one thing, the time and the setting of the stories is different. And while there are some similarities and parallels between the major characters in the two books, there are also significant differences. Some of the scenes are similar, and there is a similarity in the sequence of scenes, but the expression of the scenes is different. The total concept and feel of the two books is different, not substantially similar, the court ruled (*Trust Company Bank* v. *Putnam Publishing Group, Inc.,* 1988).

Is it impossible to win a suit based on substantial similarity? Of course not; the Kroffts won their suit. But the works have to be similar in many respects. There must be strong parallels. Universal City Studios successfully sued Film Ventures for copyright infringement when the company released a film called *Great White,* which was very similar to the movie *Jaws.* In this case the general idea of both films was obvious to an average filmgoer. But the similarities in the two pictures became even more apparent when the court objectively looked at the manner in which the ideas were expressed. Major characters were the same, the sequence of incidents was the same, the development and interplay of the major characters was the same, and even minor story points were the same. The court said the films were not identical but that "defendants have captured the total concept and feel of plaintiff's motion picture."

The court pointed to the following similarities in the films. In both films a local politician plays down the news of a great white shark in the interest of local tourism. Both films featured a salty English sea captain and a shark expert who go out to hunt the shark. The opening scenes of both films show innocent teenagers swimming on a beach who become the first victims of the shark. In both films a local fisherman's empty boat is found. In both films the shark approaches a small boat, bumps it hard, and causes a child to fall into the water. Finally, in both films the shark devours the English sea captain during the hunt but is finally killed when it swallows something that explodes in its stomach. "In light of the great similarity in expression, it would seem fair to conclude that the creators of *Great White* [which was titled *The Last Jaws* when it was released overseas] wished to be as closely connected with the plaintiff's motion picture *Jaws* as possible." The court issued an injunction to stop the exhibition of *Great White* and set a hearing to consider the award of damages (*Universal City Studios* v. *Film Ventures,* 1982).

It is not easy to prove infringement of copyright; yet surprisingly, a large number of suits are settled each year in favor of plaintiffs. In such instances the obvious theft of the material would generally appall an honest person. An individual who works to be creative in fashioning a story or a play or a piece of art usually has little to fear. The best and simplest way to avoid a suit for infringement is simply to do your own work, to be original.

SUMMARY

To protect the copyright of a work the author or owner must give proper notice and register the work with the government. A proper copyright notice looks like this:

Copyright © 1992 by Jane Adams (use the letter ℗ for phonorecords)

Notice must be placed where it can be visually perceived. Once notice is given, the work is protected. However, to gain the full benefits of the law, a work must be registered with the Copyright Office in the Library of Congress. The proper registration form along with ten dollars and two complete copies of the work must be sent to the Register of Copyrights.

When a plaintiff sues for infringement of copyright, the court will consider three important criteria. First, is the plaintiff's work original? If the plaintiff has attempted to copyright material that legitimately belongs in the public domain, the plaintiff cannot sue for infringement of copyright. Second, did the defendant have access to the plaintiff's work? There must be some evidence that the defendant viewed or heard the copyrighted work before the alleged infringement took place. Finally, is there evidence that the defendant actually copied the plaintiff's work? If no such evidence exists, are the two works substantially similar? In examining this latter issue, the court seeks to determine whether the ideas in the two works are similar. If the general idea of the two works is similar, is the expression of these ideas similar as well?

FREE-LANCING AND COPYRIGHT

What rights does a free-lance journalist, author, or photographer hold with regard to stories or pictures that are sold to publishers? The writer or photographer is the creator of the work; he or she owns the story or the photograph. Consequently, as many rights as such free-lancers choose to relinquish can be sold or given to a publisher. Beginning writers and photographers often do not have much choice but to follow the policy of the book or magazine publisher. Authors whose works are in demand, however, can retain most rights to the material for their future benefit. Most publishers have established policies on exactly what rights they purchase when they decide to buy a story or photograph or drawing. *The Writer's Market* is the best reference guide for the free-lancer. Here are some of the rights that publishers might buy:

1. All rights: The creator sells complete ownership of the story or photograph.
2. First serial rights: The buyer has the right to use the piece of writing or picture for the first time in a periodical published anywhere in the world. But the publisher can use it only once, and then the creator can sell it to someone else.
3. First North American serial rights: The rights are the same as provided in number 2, except the publisher buys the right to publish the material first in North America, not anywhere in the world.
4. Simultaneous rights: The publisher buys the right to print the material at the same time other periodicals print the material. All the publishers, however, must be aware that simultaneous publication will occur.
5. One-time rights: The publisher purchases the right to use a piece just one time, and there is no guarantee that it has not been published elsewhere first.

It is a common practice for publishers to buy all rights to a story or photograph but to agree to reassign the rights to the creator after publication. In such cases the burden of initiating the reassignment rests with the writer or photographer, who must request reassignment immediately following publication. The publisher signs a transfer of rights to the creator, and the creator should record this transfer of rights with the Copyright Office within two or three weeks. When this transaction has taken place, the creator can then resell the material. A ten-dollar fee must accompany either the original form or a certified copy of the transfer form when it is sent to the Register of Copyrights.

What if no agreement between the publisher and the writer or photographer is made? Well, this is a sloppy way to do business and shouldn't happen. And until recently authors suffered. Federal courts had ruled that in an absence of an agreement between the author and the publisher, the publisher retained extensive republication rights as well as the right to publish the piece in the magazine or book. But in 1989, in the case of *Community for Creative Non-Violence* v. *Reid,* the Supreme Court unanimously rejected that reading of the Copyright Act. Justice Thurgood Marshall wrote that the history of the copyright law did not support such a broad exception to the general principle that copyright vests in a work's creator. Under the ruling, businesses that pay a fee to a freelance artist or writer obtain the right to reproduce the material only once, unless they specifically agree to another arrangement. And even if an author assigns all rights to a publisher, he or she may reclaim them and the rights to any material derived from the original after 35 years.

Despite this fundamental change in the law, authors are urged to specify exactly what rights are being sold. This should be done in the query letter to the publisher, which, in the absence of a formal agreement, will be material in any future dispute. Free-lancers are also urged to beware of endorsements on payment checks from publishers.

It is not uncommon for a publisher to include a statement on a royalty check to the effect that "the endorsement of this check constitutes a grant of reprint rights to the publisher." In order to cash the check, the writer must agree to grant the reprint rights. In such cases writers should quickly notify the publisher that such an agreement is unacceptable and demand immediate payment for the single use of the story. Other pitfalls too numerous to mention await the inexperienced free-lancer. The best advice is to understand exactly what you are doing at all times during the negotiation of rights. Take nothing for granted; just because you are honest and ethical does not mean everyone else is. And if questions come up, consult a qualified attorney. Legal advice is costly, but it can save a writer or photographer money in the long run.

DAMAGES

Plaintiffs in a copyright suit can ask the court to assess the defendant for any damage they have suffered, plus the profits made by the infringer from pirating the protected work. Damages can be a little bit or a lot. In each case the plaintiff must prove to the court the amount of the loss or the amount of the defendant's profit. But, rather than prove actual damage, the plaintiff can ask the court to assess what are called statutory damages, or damage amounts prescribed by the statute. The smallest statutory award is $250, although in the case of an innocent infringement, the court may use its discretion and lower the damage amount to $100. The highest statutory award is $10,000. However, if the plaintiff can prove that the infringement was committed willfully, the maximum damage award can be as much as $50,000.

In addition the courts have other powers in a copyright suit. A judge can restrain a defendant from continued infringement, can impound the material that contains the infringement, and can order the destruction of these works. Impoundment and destruction are rare today.

A defendant might also be charged with a criminal offense in a copyright infringement case. If the defendant infringed upon a copyright "willfully and for purposes of commercial advantage or private financial gain," he or she could be fined up to $10,000 and jailed for not more than one year. The fines for pirating phonograph records and motion pictures are much higher: $25,000 and one year in jail for the first offense and $50,000 and up to two years in jail for subsequent offenses. Criminal actions for copyright infringement are rare today.

The law of copyright is not difficult to understand and should not be a threat to most creative persons in the mass media. The law simply says to do your own work and not to steal from the work of other persons. Some authorities argue that copyright is an infringement upon freedom of the press. In a small way it probably is. Nevertheless most writers, most authors, and most reporters—persons who most often take advantage of freedom of the press—support copyright laws that protect their rights to property that they create. Judge Jerome Frank once attempted to explain this apparent contradiction by arguing that we are adept at concealing from ourselves the fact that we maintain and support "side by side as it were, beliefs which are inherently incompatible." Frank suggested that we keep these separate antagonistic beliefs in separate "logic-tight compartments."

The courts have recognized the needs of society, as well as the needs of authors, and have hence allowed considerable latitude for copying material that serves some public function. Because of this attitude, copyright law has little, or should have little, impact upon the information-oriented mass media.

BIBLIOGRAPHY

Here is a list of some of the sources that have been helpful in the preparation of chapter 9:

Books

Cambridge Research Institute. *Omnibus Copyright Revision.* Washington, D.C.: American Society for Information Science, 1973.
Kaplan, Benjamin, and Brown, Ralph S., Jr. *Cases on Copyright.* 2d ed. Mineola, N.Y.: Foundation Press, 1974.
Nimmer, Melville B. *Nimmer on Copyright.* New York: Matthew Bender & Co., 1963.
Pipel, Harriet F., and Goldberg, Morton D. *A Copyright Guide,* 4th ed. New York: R. R. Bowker Co., 1969.
Strong, William. *The Copyright Book.* Cambridge, Mass.: The M.I.T. Press, 1981.

Articles

Bollier, David. "At War With Pirates." *Channels,* March 1987.
"Copyright: Hollywood Versus Substantial Similarity." 32 *Oklahoma Law Review* 177, 1979.
"Copyright Infringement and the First Amendment." 70 *Columbia Law Review* 320, 1979.
Kurtz, Leslie A. "The Independent Legal Lives of Fictional Characters." 1986 *Wisconsin Law Review* 429.
Morrill, Stephen S. "*Harper & Row Publishers* v. *Nation Enterprises:* Emasculating the Fair Use Accommodation of Competing, Copyright and First Amendment Interests." 79 *Northwestern University Law Review* 587, 1984.
Nimmer, Melville B. "Does Copyright Abridge the First Amendment Guarantees of Free Speech and Press?" 17 *UCLA Law Review* 1180, 1970.

Shaw, David. "Plagiarism: A Taint in Journalism." *The Los Angeles Times*, July 5, 1984.

Shipley, David E. "Conflicts Between Copyright and the First Amendment After *Harper & Row, Publishers v. Nation Enterprises*." 1986 *Brigham Young University Law Review* 983.

Cases

Alexander v. *Haley*, 460 F.Supp. 40 (1978).

Amsterdam v. *Triangle Publishing Co.*, 189 F.2d 104 (1951).

Associated Press v. *International News Service*, 248 U.S. 215 (1918).

Baker v. *Selden*, 101 U.S. 99 (1979).

Berkik v. *Crichton*, 761 F.2d 1289 (1985).

Chicago Record-Herald v. *Tribune Association*, 275 F.2d 797 (1921).

Community for Creative Non-Violence v. *Reid*, No. 88–293.

Elsmere Music v. *NBC*, 623 F.2d 252 (1980).

Encyclopaedia Britannica v. *Crooks*, 447 F.Supp. 243 (1978).

Harper & Row Publishers v. *Nation Enterprises*, 557 F.Supp. 1067 (1983), rev'd. 723 F.2d 195 (1983); rev'd. 471 U.S. 539 (1985).

Hoehling v. *Universal Studios*, 618 F.2d 972 (1980).

Iowa State v. *ABC*, 621 F.2d 57 (1980).

Jason v. *Fonda, et al.*, 526 F.Supp. 774 (1981).

Lipman v. *Commonwealth*, 475 F.2d 565 (1973).

Maxtone-Graham v. *Burtchaell*, 803 F.2d 1253 (1986).

MGM v. *Showcase Atlanta*, 7 M.L.R. 2190 (1981).

Miller v. *Universal City Studios*, 650 F.2d 1365 (1981).

Murray v. *NBC*, 844 F.2d 988 (1988).

New York Times v. *Roxbury Data Interface*, 434 F.Supp. 217 (1977).

Orion Pictures v. *Dell Publishing*, 471 F.Supp. 392 (1979).

Pottstown Daily News Publishing v. *Pottstown Broadcasting*, 192 A.2d 657 (1963).

Production Contractors v. *WGN Continental Broadcasting*, 622 F.Supp. 1500 (1986).

Rosemont v. *Random House*, 366 F.2d 303 (1966).

Rossner v. *CBS*, 612 F.Supp. 334 (1985).

Roy Export Co. v. *CBS*, 672 F.2d 1095 (1982).

Salinger v. *Random House*, 811 F.2d 90 (1987).

Sheldon v. *Metro-Goldwyn-Mayer Pictures*, 81 F.2d 49 (1939).

Sid and Marty Krofft Television Productions v. *McDonald's Corp.*, 562 F.2d 1157 (1977).

Sony Corp. v. *Universal City Studios*, 464 U.S. 417 (1984).

Time, Inc. v. *Bernard Geis Associates*, 293 F.Supp. 130 (1968).

Triangle Publications v. *Knight-Ridder Newspapers, Inc.*, 445 F.Supp. 875 (1978).

Trust Company Bank v. *Putnam Publishing Group, Inc.*, 14 M.L.R. 2340 (1988).

Universal City Studios v. *Film Ventures*, 543 F.Supp. 875 (1978).

Universal City Studios v. *Sony*, 480 F.Supp. 429 (1979); rev'd. 659 F.2d 963 (1982).

Walker v. *Time-Life Films*, 784 F.2d 44 (1986).

Walt Disney Productions v. *Air Pirates*, 345 F.Supp. 180 (1972).

Warner Bros. v. *ABC*, 523 F.Supp. 611 (1981).

10 REGULATION OF ADVERTISING

While a variety of icons might be used to exemplify American culture to a visitor from outer space in the last quarter of the twentieth century, the common advertisement might be the most appropriate. It seems that advertising is America in the 1990s, and America is advertising. Almost $110 billion was spent on advertising in 1988, and that does not include expenditures for direct marketing, sales promotion, and public relations. Someone has estimated that each of us is exposed to more than one hundred advertisements each day, a conservative estimate by most accounts. We have become, in a sense, walking advertisements ourselves, strolling through the malls with our Corona beer T-shirts or Ralph Lauren "Polo" sweaters, our branded Wrangler or Guess jeans, our Nike or Reebok labeled shoes. Try to buy a gym bag without a brand name on it. And automakers, not satisfied with small, decorous nameplates, now strip windows with large decals of car names. Many Americans love it and are willing to pay extra to prominently display a brand name.

But advertising is not without its critics. They argue that we end up paying a good deal more for products because of advertising. And that we buy more than we need because of advertising. And that advertising creates false images about who we are and what we value, and diverts our attention and our resources away from more serious concerns.

The regulation of advertising is a fairly recent phenomenon, if only because advertising as we know it today is a relatively modern phenomenon. Early American newspapers surely carried small commercial announcements along with other content. But modern American advertising—published attempts to convince a consumer that she needs a particular product as opposed to simple announcements that a merchant is selling a particular product—developed in the second half of the nineteenth century. Since that time we have moved from the point of having few, if any, regulations upon advertising, to having hundreds of laws that in one way or another regulate advertising. A recently published compilation, the "United States and Washington State Laws and Regulations Affecting Advertising," (compiled by Paul Conrad for the Allied Daily Newspapers) cites references to more than 450 statutes. They range from the regulation of advertising for abortions to the control of advertising for the sale of wine. These statutes not only focus upon matters of deceptive or untruthful advertising but on items such as whether the flag may be used in advertising, on which occupations and which professions can and cannot advertise, and on whether a sound truck may be used to sell liquor.

Persons in advertising, especially copywriters, need to have an understanding of many of these specific laws. There are useful compilations of them in most good law libraries, but there are simply too many of them to cover comprehensively in this short chapter. Instead, the focus in this section is upon larger questions regarding First Amendment protection for advertising, untruthful and deceptive advertising, and federal regulation of advertising through the Federal Trade Commission. ♦

ADVERTISING AND THE FIRST AMENDMENT

Commercial advertising currently enjoys qualified First Amendment protection. What is called the commercial speech doctrine first emerged from the Supreme Court of the United States in the mid-1970s. A majority of the High Court took the position that commercial advertising advances certain interests of the audience, including the promotion of informed consumer choices through the publication and broadcast of information on the availability of goods and services. This in turn promotes economic efficiency and helps society regulate the free enterprise system. The High Court has stated clearly that the First Amendment does not protect advertising for unlawful activities, or advertising that is false, deceptive or misleading. All other advertising is covered by the shield of the First Amendment however, and may be regulated only if the government can satisfy the following three requirements.

1. The government must assert a substantial state interest to justify the regulation.
2. The government must demonstrate that the regulation of the advertisement directly advances this state interest.
3. The regulation must be narrowly drawn, no more extensive than is necessary to serve the interest asserted by the state.

If the government can meet these three requirements, courts will normally permit the advertising in question to be restricted or banned altogether. But if the government interest advanced by the regulation is of little importance, or the government fails to assert a substantial state interest at all, or the ban on advertising is too broad (if it prohibits a wider range of commercial speech than is necessary to advance the state interest), then the regulation will likely be stricken as a violation of the First Amendment.

Before briefly reviewing the history and current status of this commercial speech doctrine two important points must be made. The first is that this doctrine is extremely new from a legal standpoint, and as such, is still being shaped. Second, the doctrine does not have the full support of the current membership of the United States Supreme Court. Recent decisions by the High Court indicate that Justices Brennan, Blackmun, Marshall and Kennedy seem tenacious in their support for the doctrine, Justices White and Stevens seem lukewarm, and Justices O'Connor, Scalia and Chief Justice Rehnquist seem somewhat hostile to the notion that commercial speech deserves First Amendment protection. Both of these points lead to the same conclusion: the commercial speech doctrine could be significantly modified at any time, or even abandoned altogether as a short-lived, bad experiment.

Growth of the Commercial Speech Doctrine

In 1942 the Supreme Court of the United States ruled that "the Constitution imposes no . . . restraint on government as respects purely commercial advertising." The decision came in an unusual case in which a man attempted to circulate handbills on a city street urging citizens to make a paid visit to a submarine he had moored at a nearby wharf (*Valentine* v. *Chrestensen,* 1942). Most authorities believed, despite the unusual nature of the case, that this decision settled the matter: advertising was not protected by the First Amendment. In 1964 the Supreme Court ruled that *political* or *editorial* advertising is protected by the First Amendment (*New York Times* v. *Sullivan*). But most authorities rationalized that the First Amendment is designed to protect political speech, and political advertising is certainly political speech. Hence, this was hardly a revolutionary decision.

It was not until the mid-seventies that the High Court ruled that *commercial* advertising enjoys the benefits of the First Amendment as well when it reversed the conviction of a Virginia newspaper editor who had been found guilty of publishing an advertisement that offered assistance to women seeking an abortion. Abortion was illegal in Virginia in 1971 when the advertisement was published. The Woman's Pavilion, a New York group, urged women who wanted an abortion to come to New York, where it was possible to have a legal abortion. Justice Blackmun wrote for the Court that speech does not lose the protection of the First Amendment merely because it appears in the form of a commercial advertisement. Blackmun distinguished this ruling from the High Court's ruling in *Chrestensen* by arguing that in that instance the Supreme Court merely upheld the New York ordinance as a reasonable regulation *of the manner in which commercial advertising can be distributed* [author emphasis]. Blackmun refused to open the door completely or to state explicitly how far this ruling opened the door. "We need not decide in this case," he wrote, "the precise extent to which the First Amendment permits regulation of advertising that is related to activities the state may legitimately regulate or even prohibit" (*Bigelow* v. *Virginia,* 1975).

In 1976 the Supreme Court clarified and expanded the extent to which advertising is protected by the First Amendment in the case of *Virginia State Board of Pharmacy* v. *Virginia Citizens' Consumer Council, Inc.* The Court ruled that a Virginia statute that had the effect of prohibiting pharmacies from advertising the price of prescription drugs violated the guarantee of freedom of expression in the First Amendment. Justice Harry Blackmun wrote:

> Advertising, however tasteless and excessive it sometimes may seem, is nonetheless dissemination of information as to who is producing and selling what product, for what reason, and at what price. So long as we preserve a

predominantly free enterprise economy, the allocation of our resources in large measure will be made through numerous private economic decisions. It is a matter of public interest that those decisions in the aggregate be intelligent and well informed. To this end, the free flow of commercial information is indispensable.

The High Court made it equally clear, however, that the government was completely free to continue to regulate commercial speech that is false, misleading, or deceptive or that proposes illegal transactions.

The next ruling on the commercial speech doctrine was handed down in 1977. The township of Willingboro, New Jersey, banned the display of "For Sale" and "Sold" signs on homes and lawns in the community. The motivation for the ban was the fear that such signs contributed to panic selling by white homeowners who feared that the township was becoming populated predominantly by black families and that property values would decline. The black population had increased in the community, while white homeowners moved elsewhere. Persons testified before the township council that "the reason eighty percent of the sellers gave for their decision to sell was that 'the whole town was for sale and they didn't want to be caught in any bind.' " Community leaders reasoned that banning "For Sale" signs might diminish the fear that "everyone is selling" and might also stabilize the population.

When the ban was challenged on First Amendment grounds, Willingboro attempted to justify the policy on two grounds: first, that homeowners had other means of communicating that their property was for sale, including newspaper advertising, and second, that the goal of the ban was to provide stable, racially integrated housing, two factors that the community and the region considered important. But Justice Thurgood Marshall and a majority of the Court rejected both arguments. Marshall wrote that advertising in the newspaper was not a satisfactory alternative because it was a costly and less-effective medium for communicating the specific message that a home was for sale. He added that while the goal of racial integration was important, so too were the goals asserted by the government in *Bigelow* and *Virginia Pharmacy*. Marshall asserted that the constitutional defect of the Willingboro ban was basic (*Linmark Associates* v. *Township of Willingboro,* 1977):

> The Township Council . . . acted to prevent its residents from obtaining certain information. That information . . . is of vital interest to Willingboro residents, since it may bear on one of the most important decisions they have a right to make: where to live and raise their families. . . . If the dissemination of this information can be restricted, then every locality in the country can suppress any facts that reflect poorly on the locality. . . . *Virginia Pharmacy* denies government such sweeping powers.

A decision two years later demonstrated that there are limits to the High Court's protection of commercial speech. The Court ruled that it was permissible for the State of Texas to constitutionally prohibit the practice of optometry under a trade name (i.e., Acme Optometrists). Customers could be misled or deceived through the use of such trade names, Justice Powell wrote for the majority of the High Court. "The trade name of an optometrical practice can remain unchanged despite changes in the staff of optometrists upon whose skill and care the public depends when it patronizes its practice," Powell noted. The jurist added that the use of an optometric trade name is strictly a business use; it does not provide consumers with information or knowledge useful in making an economic decision (*Friedman* v. *Rogers,* 1979).

In 1980 the Supreme Court handed down its most definitive ruling on commercial speech, establishing clearly for the first time the guidelines outlined at the beginning of this section (see page 470). Central Hudson Gas and Electric Corporation asked the Supreme Court to invalidate a New York Public Service Commission rule that forbade utilities to publish or broadcast any advertising that promoted the use of electricity. The commission justified the rule as a means of promoting energy conservation. The High Court struck down the ban in an eight-to-one ruling. Justice Powell noted that the utility's advertising did not promote an unlawful activity. Also, the state ban was aimed at all such advertising, not merely deceptive or misleading advertising. When advertising is truthful and does not promote an illegal activity, Powell said, the Court must examine the regulation itself more closely. What are the substantial state interests that are asserted in this case? New York argued that advertising that promoted electrical service interfered with the state's effort to convince citizens to conserve energy. The advertising also fostered inequities in the utility's rate structures, the state said. Powell agreed that the ban on advertising did further the state's interest in energy conservation and that this was a substantial interest. But he said the link between advertising and inequitable rate structures was tenuous at best. In other words, the ban on the ads did not directly advance this state interest.

Was the rule no more extensive than necessary to serve the state interest in energy conservation? Justice Powell said the rule was too broad. It prohibited Central Hudson Gas and Electric from advertising more efficient electrical energy devices such as heat pumps and electric power as a backup for solar energy. The energy conservation rationale, as important as it is, cannot justify suppressing all promotional advertisements, including those that would cause no net increase in total energy use, Powell wrote for the majority. The state failed to show that a more limited restriction on content would not adequately serve the same state interests (*Central Hudson* v. *Public Service Commission,* 1980; see also *Consolidated Edison* v. *Public Service Commission,* 1980, discussed on page 96).

The High Court ruled in June 1983 that a federal statute that barred the mailing of unsolicited advertisements for contraceptives was unconstitutional when applied to a contraceptive manufacturer's mailing of informational pamphlets that promoted its products but also discussed important public issues such as family planning and venereal disease. Justice Thurgood Marshall, writing for the Court, ruled that the government's interests asserted in support of the statute were insufficient to warrant the "sweeping prohibition" against mailing the advertisements. The government's interest in shielding persons from receiving mail that they are likely to find offensive "carries little weight," Marshall wrote. The government's second interest, aiding parents in directing the manner in which their children become informed about birth control, is substantial, Marshall conceded. But the statute goes too far, offering a "marginal degree of protection" only by "purging all mailboxes of unsolicited material that is entirely suitable for adults" (*Bolger* v. *Young Drug Products Corporation,* 1983).

The advertising of alcoholic beverages became an issue in the early 1980s as well. The United States Court of Appeals for the Tenth Circuit ruled that Oklahoma could require that cable television operators in that state delete all advertisements for alcoholic beverages contained in the out-of-state signals they retransmit to their subscribers. The state argued that the rule was designed to further its interest in discouraging the consumption of beer, wine, and liquor (*Oklahoma Telecasters Association* v. *Crisp,* 1983). The Supreme Court reversed this decision, however, but on the narrow grounds that the federal government had preempted the regulation of cable television and the state could not impose such a regulation on the electronic medium. The unanimous Supreme Court did not consider the First Amendment issue (*Capital Cities Cable* v. *Crisp,* 1984). Eight months earlier the United States Court of Appeals for the Fifth Circuit ruled that a Mississippi law that prohibited liquor and wine advertising on billboards, on newspapers printed and distributed in the state, and on radio and television stations operating within the state, and that required state broadcasters to delete such advertising from incoming network programming was not in violation of the First Amendment. The rule, the court said, had been shown to directly advance the substantial state interest in safeguarding the health of its citizens (*Dunagin* v. *Oxford,* 1984). Presumably, however, the subsequent ruling by the Supreme Court voids parts of the Mississippi ban, at least as it applies to broadcast media deleting commercials on incoming network programs, the exact issue in the *Crisp* case.

Finally, in an important ruling in mid-1986, the High Court ruled that Puerto Rico could restrict the advertising of casino gambling to persons who lived on the island, but continue to permit such advertising aimed at tourists (*Posadas de Puerto Rico Assoc.* v. *Tourism Co.,* 1986). Since 1948, Puerto Rico has permitted some forms of gambling, largely to enhance the tourist industry, but rules have prohibited the advertising of such games of chance to "the public of Puerto Rico." Puerto Ricans are not prohibited from gambling, local advertising for other types of gambling games is permitted (i.e., lottery and horse racing), and the casinos can maintain on-site advertising that can be seen by local residents. Still the state prohibited the casinos from promoting their games of chance among the people of the island territory.

A casino challenged the law as a violation of the First Amendment, but the Supreme Court, in a five-to-four ruling, upheld the regulation. The advertising was for a lawful activity and was not misleading, but Justice Rehnquist wrote that the government's interest in reducing the demand for gambling by Puerto Rican residents was a substantial interest. The regulations directly advanced this interest and the rule was no more intrusive than need be to accomplish this end. The casino argued that this was truthful advertising for a lawful activity. But Rehnquist responded that "the greater power to completely bar casino gambling necessarily includes the lesser power to ban advertising of casino gambling." In other words because the government could at will ban all gambling, it could certainly ban some advertising for gambling.

The High Court ruling in *Posadas* is a clear assertion that advertising for an entirely legal product or service can be banned under the First Amendment as applied through the *Central Hudson* test. This decision has given hope to many that Congress can—if it wants to—ban all tobacco advertising as well. Measures to accomplish just that have been introduced before the Congress and are currently being debated. Congress has already banned tobacco advertising on television, but this ban was instituted before the Supreme Court extended First Amendment protection to commercial advertising. In fact, the High Court in 1972 affirmed a lower court ruling upholding the Congressional ban (*Capital Broadcasting Co. v. Acting Attorney General,* 1972). Many observers believe that a Congressional ban on all tobacco advertising would stand a constitutional test. (See "First Amendment Values and the Constitutional Protection of Tobacco Advertising," 82 *Northwestern University Law Review* 145, 1987.) If the High Court was willing to accept that Puerto Rico needed to ban all advertising of legal gambling in order to further the state interest in reducing the demand for gambling, the High Court would likely accept the Congressional decision that a ban on all tobacco advertising is necessary to reduce demand for tobacco products, products which are hazardous to the health of individuals.

Advertising
Professional Services

The qualified constitutional protection for advertising just outlined is also applicable to advertising for professional services by doctors, dentists, lawyers, and other specialists. Yet the Supreme Court has demonstrated far greater concern for the potential deceptive nature of advertisements for such professional services. For example, while the High Court will clearly tolerate claims of quality service by plumbers, electricians, and piano teachers, lawyers and physicians may not make such claims in their advertisements. Such claims would be considered deceptive. Let us look briefly at the development of the rules regarding advertising by professionals.

In 1977 the Court struck down rules that prohibited lawyers from advertising and ruled that price advertising for routine legal services is protected by the First Amendment as long as it is not false or misleading. The High

Court would not tolerate however, advertisements regarding the quality of legal services, Justice Blackmun wrote for the Court's majority. Such advertisements (Jones and Jones Lawyers win more acquittals in drunk driving cases than any other lawyers in town) are not susceptible to verification and "might well be deceptive or misleading to the public, or even false" (*Bates and Van O'Steen* v. *Arizona,* 1977).

The *Bates* decision left confusion in the minds of many attorneys about just how far a lawyer could go in advertising services and just how far state bar associations could go in limiting such advertising. Personal solicitation by attorneys has always been banned, and in 1978 the High Court ruled that such rules did not run afoul of the First Amendment. Such advertising is distinctly different from price advertising, wrote Justice Blackmun for a majority of the Court (*Ohralik* v. *Ohio State Bar Association,* 1978).

But four years later the High Court ruled that the Missouri Bar Association had read the *Bates* ruling too narrowly and adopted rules that were far too restrictive. State bar rules in Missouri permitted lawyers to advertise only the following information:

1. Name, address, and telephone number.
2. Date and place of birth, schools attended, and foreign-language specialty.
3. Office hours, fee for initial consultation, availability of fee schedule, credit arrangements, and fixed fees for certain specific routine legal services.
4. Areas of practice.

Under areas of practice the bar association listed twenty-three specialties that could be listed.

The association reprimanded an attorney who included in his advertisement the statements that he was licensed to practice in both Missouri and Illinois, that he was admitted to practice law before the Supreme Court of the United States, and that he also carried two legal specialties not listed among the twenty-three approved for advertising by the bar association. Justice Powell, writing for a unanimous Supreme Court, ruled that the Missouri bar regulations prohibited far more than was necessary to prevent misleading advertisements. Regulation of such advertisements is permissible "only where particular advertising is inherently likely to deceive or where the record indicates that a particular form or method of advertising has in fact been deceptive," Powell wrote. The state can regulate truthful advertisements only if a substantial state interest is asserted and the interference with speech and press is in proportion to the state interest served by the regulation. In this case the advertisements were not misleading, and no substantial state interest was asserted, Powell wrote (in re *R. M. J.,* 1982).

In 1985 the Supreme Court broadened the right of attorneys to advertise to an even greater extent when it ruled that lawyers could solicit business for particular lawsuits, so long as the advertisements were not deceptive (*Zauderer* v. *Office of Disciplinary Council,* 1985). The Ohio Office of Disciplinary Council had disciplined attorney Philip Q. Zauderer for various misconduct, including an advertisement soliciting female clients who had suffered injuries from the use of the Dalkon Shield intrauterine device. The ad contained a line-drawing of the Dalkon Shield, a violation of the state rules. It stated that Zauderer was currently representing women suing the manufacturer of the contraceptive device and that he was willing to represent other women in similar suits. The attorney said he would handle the case on a contingent fee basis, and that if the suit was not successful, "no fees would be owed by the client." Ohio said the ad amounted to a solicitation of business and was misleading as well because it failed to inform potential clients that they would be liable for court costs if their suit failed. The state defended its prohibition on such advertising by arguing that it was inherently too difficult for regulators to distinguish accurate legal advertising from misleading legal advertising. "Were we to accept the state's argument in this case, we would have little basis for preventing the government from suppressing other forms of truthful and non-deceptive advertising simply to spare itself the trouble of distinguishing such advertising from false or deceptive advertising," said Justice Byron White, speaking for five members of the Court. "The First Amendment protections afforded commercial speech would mean little indeed if such arguments were allowed to prevail," he added. All eight justices ruled that the use of an accurate illustration was protected by the First Amendment, but in a six-to-two vote, the High Court affirmed the state's reprimand of Zauderer for failing to disclose to potential clients the likelihood that they would be assessed court costs if their suit failed.

The most recent ruling regarding professional advertising came in 1988, when the High Court struck down a Kentucky state ban on direct mail solicitation by lawyers (*Shapero* v. *Kentucky Bar Association*). The facts in the case fall somewhere in between the facts in *Ohralik,* in which the Supreme Court permitted a ban on personal, face-to-face solicitation by attorneys, and the facts in *Zauderer,* where the High Court struck down an Ohio ban on solicitation through newspaper advertising. Attorney Shapero asked the Kentucky Bar's advertising commission to approve a proposed letter to potential clients facing a mortgage foreclosure. In part the letter said:

> You may be about to lose your home. . . . You may call my office . . . for FREE information on how you can keep your home. Call NOW, don't wait. It may surprise you what I may be able to do for you.

The letter was not deemed to be false or misleading by the Kentucky Statute, but was prohibited under a rule forbidding the mailing of written advertising targeted to persons with known legal problems. Six of the nine members of the High Court ruled that the direct-mail ban violates the First Amendment.

The High Court refused to distinguish between newspaper and direct mail advertising. The Court also refused to accept the argument that the ban was justified because of the "serious potential for abuse." Direct mail advertising to targeted people did not present the same danger of overreaching and fraud as did face-to-face solicitation, wrote Justice Brennan:

> Unlike the potential client with a badgering advocate breathing down his neck, the recipient of a letter and the reader of an advertisement can effectively avoid further bombardment of his sensibilities simply by adverting his eyes.

The dissenters, led by Justice O'Connor, simply rejected Brennan's reasoning, arguing that unsolicited legal advice is simply not like other forms of commercial speech because "the quality of legal services is typically more difficult for most lay persons to evaluate . . . and an attorney has an obligation to provide clients with complete and disinterested advice." In commenting on the ruling, attorney P. Cameron Devore, an expert on the commercial speech doctrine, noted that "there is more than a suggestion in Justice O'Connor's dissent . . . that the whole commercial speech doctrine would be at risk in a decision in which these dissenters carried the day." Future rulings in the area of attorney advertising might in fact become the first major break in the wall erected by the commercial speech doctrine.

SUMMARY

American advertising is regulated by scores of laws adopted by all levels of government. Persons in advertising must be aware of such rules, as well as of all other regulations (libel, invasion of privacy, obscenity, etc.) that restrict the content and flow of printed and broadcast material. Since the mid-1970s commercial advertising has been given the qualified protection of the First Amendment because much advertising contains information that is valuable to consumers. The government may regulate or prohibit advertising (1) that promotes an unlawful activity or (2) that is misleading or untruthful. The state may also regulate truthful advertising for lawful activities and goods if it can prove (1) that there is a substantial state interest to justify the regulation, (2) that such regulation directly advances this state interest, and (3) that the regulation is no more extensive than needed to serve that important governmental interest. Advertising by professionals such as attorneys and physicians may be regulated in a somewhat more restrictive fashion.

THE REGULATION OF ADVERTISING

The regulation of deceptive or untruthful advertising is a large and difficult task policed by the advertising industry itself, the mass media, and various governmental agencies. Advertising in the eighties has become especially problematic because of the growth of comparative advertising, advertising in which the attributes of one product are placed squarely alongside those of another. There is also more advertising for more products than ever before. At about the same time advertising claims were increasing in intensity and in number, the federal government, a primary player in the regulation of advertising, pulled back from the aggressive stance it had taken during the 1970s. New means to control the content of commercial messages were explored. Let's briefly examine this process of regulation today.

Self-Regulation

Both the advertising industry and the mass media work to police American advertising. Television networks, for example, have guidelines regarding the content of commercials. The following are guidelines used by the National Broadcasting Company to judge the acceptability of comparative advertisements:

1. The products identified in the advertising must actually be in competition with one another.
2. Competitors shall be fairly and properly identified.
3. Advertisers shall refrain from discrediting, disparaging, or unfairly attacking competitors, competing products, or other industries.
4. The identification must be for comparison purposes and not simply to upgrade by association.
5. The advertising should compare related or similar properties or ingredients of the product, dimension-to-dimension, feature-to-feature, or wherever possible be a side-by-side demonstration.
6. The property being compared must be significant in terms of value or usefulness of the product to the consumer.
7. The difference of the properties must be measurable and significant.

Although the mass media screens advertising for taste as well, it is no guarantee that they present an unbreachable wall. Misleading, unfair, false and deceptive advertising is published and broadcast and because of this, the advertising industry has constructed a self-regulatory scheme to try to resolve as many problems as possible. The National Advertising Division (NAD) and the National Advertising Review Board (NARB) comprise a division of the Better Business Bureau designed exclusively to hear the complaints of one advertiser against another—they are not available for the resolution of consumer complaints. The NAD has heard more than three thousand cases since 1971, and resolved more than 100 cases in 1988. When a complaint is filed with the NAD, an investigation follows. The NAD decides whether or not there is substantiation for the advertising claim that has been challenged. If a finding of insufficient substantiation results, the NAD asks for modification in the advertisement, or that the entire advertisement be discontinued. Decisions are published in monthly reports. A NAD decision may be appealed to the NARB, a five-member review board, whose decision is final. It was reported in 1987 that during the previous sixteen years, from the creation of the NAD/NARB, no participant in the process had failed to abide by the NARB ruling. Although these decisions are not legally binding, they carry considerable force because the mass communications industry follows the NAD rulings. In other words, CBS will not broadcast an advertising claim that the NAD has found insufficiently supported by evidence.

In an era when almost twenty-five percent of all advertisements compare one product to another competing product, it is not surprising that the NAD/NARB have been kept busy. Here are some typical examples of how this self-regulatory process works. Coca-Cola, which manufactures Minute Maid products, complained to the NAD about advertisements by Country Time Lemonade Flavored Drink Mix stressing the idea that the peel of a lemon contains the richest flavor and that that is what makes Country Time taste like "good old-fashioned lemonade." Country Time contains lemon oil but no lemon juice. The NAD ruled the advertisements were not deceptive. Country Time then complained about an advertisement that said that Minute Maid Lemonade Crystals contain the juice of twenty lemons but that Country Time contains no lemon juice. After Country Time raised the issue, Minute Maid discontinued the advertisement. Next came an advertisement that proclaimed that Country Time tastes better than Minute Maid. Minute Maid complained; the NAD asked for proof. Country Time provided the results of a blind taste test that showed its drink was preferred by fifty-five percent of the drinkers. Issue ended.

Sometimes the NAD rules that an advertisement is in fact deceptive. During the great laxative wars of the early eighties, Nature's Remedy ran an advertisement that said that a competitor, Ex-Lax, contains an artificial chemical, whereas Nature's Remedy has "natural active ingredients." The advertisement was accurate enough, but the NAD said it was misleading in our health-conscious society where words like "artificial" and "chemical" have taken on health-threatening connotations. Both laxatives had been certified by the federal Food and Drug Administration (FDA) as safe and effective.

How effective is this kind of self-regulation? Critics point out correctly that because the decisions of the NAD are not binding, an advertiser can thumb his or her nose at a negative ruling. But that doesn't seem to happen. Two other weaknesses in the scheme are more significant. First of all, the NAD only hears complaints from advertisers against other advertisers, and only about national advertising, not local or regional advertising. Consumers can't complain to the NAD about advertising they find deceptive. The second problem with this self-regulation is the definition of the standard of deception. This is basically set by the advertisers, not the NAD. Advertisers are really only concerned that competing advertisers don't make false claims that give them an unfair advantage. If all advertisers are making the same deceptive claim, it is unlikely that anyone will complain to the NAD. For example, the advertising of analgesics has generated more claims and counterclaims of deception and deceit than the advertising for almost any other consumer product in the last ten years. The makers of Bayer Aspirin will fight advertising by the makers of Anacin, for example, that claims Anacin is a more effective pain reliever. This is an issue that can be resolved by the NAD. But neither analgesic maker is concerned about the validity of the claim made by virtually all analgesic makers that a brand-name product is superior to a generic aspirin, which is much cheaper for a consumer to purchase. Only a consumer would make this complaint—but the consumer has no access to NAD. Competing businesses fear the loss of sales because of a competitor's deceptive advertising. Consumers however, are concerned that all advertising, not just those that harm one of the competitors, be honest and truthful. Hence, self-regulation has a limited range of effectiveness and must be viewed more as a monitor of unfair business practices than as consumer protection.

Sometimes a competing advertiser does not believe a complaint to the NAD is sufficient to stop an advertisement or advertising campaign. Instead, a complaint is filed in court. That is another level of advertising self-regulation.

Lawsuits by Competitors and Consumers

Lawsuits for false advertising claims have been rare until recently. There is no deceptive advertising tort at common law, and few advertisers were willing to take the time and risk the expense of a lawsuit in the absence of case law to use as precedent. But since the early 1970s, and the rapid growth of comparative advertising, more and more advertisers have taken competitors to court over what they claim is deceptive and false advertising. American Home Products, the maker of Anacin and Advil, and Johnson & Johnson, the manufacturer of Tylenol, have been in court almost continually since 1976, regarding claims about the effectiveness or lack of effectiveness of their brand-name pain relievers. Half a dozen suits have already been tried and several more await trial. To distinguish among them, lawyers use roman numerals: Tylenol II or Anacin I. The federal judge involved in the latest series of battles, William C. Conner, has taken to wondering aloud if he is doomed to spend the rest of his days "as the czar of over-the-counter drug advertising," according to Charles Mann and Mark L. Plummer, in an article in a recent issue of *The Atlantic Monthly*. Conner became so frustrated at one point with these analgesic wars that he ruled in 1987 that both litigants were guilty of false advertising and told them to please settle their differences out of court. But the lawsuits go on.

It is the federal Lanham Act that makes such lawsuits possible. The law is aimed at stopping unfair competition in the marketplace, and section 43(a) makes an advertiser "civilly liable to another who is or is likely to be damaged by the false description or representation of goods and services." While the

Lanham Act was adopted in 1938, courts heard less than thirty false advertising cases brought under the statute between 1938 and 1968, according to Paul Pompeo in an article in the *Catholic University Law Review*. In 1974 a federal court established a five-part test to establish a case of false advertising under the statute (*Skil Corp. v. Rockwell Int'l Corp.*, 1974). A plaintiff must show:

1. The defendant, in its comparative advertisements, made false statements about the plaintiff's product.
2. That the advertisements actually deceived or have a tendency to deceive a substantial segment of the audience.
3. That such deception is material, in that it is likely to influence a purchasing decision.
4. That the defendant's falsely advertised goods are in interstate commerce.
5. That the plaintiff has been injured or is likely to be injured by the advertisements. This can be shown by demonstrating a diversion of sales from the plaintiff to the defendant, or through the lessening of goodwill that the plaintiff's product enjoys with buyers.

These five factors have been followed fairly closely (with some minor modifications) by other federal courts in establishing liability.

A plaintiff in a Lanham Act case will try to either obtain equitable relief—that is to stop or change the defendant's advertising—or to recover damages. Most commonly a plaintiff will try to win an injunction to eliminate the advertisements or to force the defendant to modify it. In 1976 American Brands won an injunction that forced R. J. Reynolds to remove the words "The lowest tar of all cigarettes" from advertising and promotional copy for "Now" cigarettes (*American Brands, Inc. v. R. J. Reynolds Tobacco Co.*, 1972). Ten years later Maybelline won a court order forcing the Noxell Corporation to halt distribution of its "Clear Lash" mascara, which it had falsely claimed was waterproof (*Maybelline v. Noxell Corp.*, 1986). Pompeo says equitable relief is usually sought because it is quicker and easier to win. To win an injunction the plaintiff need only show that the competitor's advertising is likely to deceive buyers; to win money damages, the plaintiff must show that the buying public was in fact deceived.

Damage awards in Lanham Act suits were uncommon until the 1980s. It is often difficult to prove that potential buyers have actually been deceived by a competitor's advertising, and that the false claim was relied upon by the consumer in making a purchasing decision. If money damages can be won, a plaintiff can pocket not only actual damages and court costs, but the profits made by the defendant through use of the false claim. A judge may double or triple this amount as well in cases of flagrant falsity. Oftentimes the court will rule that the monetary award be spent by the defendant in advertising to correct the misleading or false advertising. Avis sued Hertz in the mid-1980s when Hertz made the claim that "Hertz has more new cars than Avis has." At the time of the claim, Avis had 102,000 cars in its corporate and licensee fleet; Hertz had only 97,000. But Avis had only 95,000 cars available for rental. The trial court ruled that the claim was deceptive and enjoined Hertz from making any future comparisons between its own and Avis' fleet size. Hertz was also ordered to publish corrective advertising notices in the same magazines that had run the original advertisements (*Avis Rent-a-Car System* v. *Hertz Corp.,* 1985). An appellate court reversed the ruling, saying that the trial judge was too concerned with the word "cars" and not with the notion of "rental cars," something consumers cared about. According to Pompeo, Hertz produced a consumer survey for the court that demonstrated that eighty-seven percent of persons questioned understood the advertisement to mean rental cars, and Hertz did have more rental cars (*Avis Rent-a-Car System* v. *Hertz Corp.,* 1986).

Typical of other Lanham Act suits are the following cases. In early 1981 Budget Rent-A-Car filed a suit against Hertz, accusing the competing rental car company of falsely claiming Hertz had lowered its rates to meet Budget's rates. Cuisinarts Inc., a manufacturer of home food processors, sued rival Robot-Coupé, claiming false advertising and misappropriation of Cuisinart's reputation. The suit succeeded in blocking some Robot-Coupé advertisements. Twinoaks Products, the maker of a toilet bowl cleaner, also went to court in 1981 to stop Vanish commercials that claimed that long-lasting toilet bowl cleaners, like Twinoaks' 120 Automatic Bowl Cleaner, are harmful to plumbing while Vanish is not. The most publicized suit of the early eighties stemmed from the multibillion dollar "burger wars" between McDonalds restaurants and a host of competitors. Wendy's International and McDonalds both went to court to block Burger King television advertisements that claimed that people preferred the taste of Burger King burgers to those made by the other two fast-food franchisers. And in 1989 the Gillette Company took Swedish razor maker Wilkinson Sword to court over whose razor provides the most comfortable shave. At issue was which is slipperier, the little white plastic strip on Gillette's Atra Plus, or the little blue plastic strip on Wilkinson's Ultra Glide. It is around such monumental issues that these federal lawsuits often revolve.

Perhaps the most important Lanham Act case in recent years involved U-Haul and Jartran, firms that rent trucks and trailers to consumers. U-Haul had pretty much had its own way in this business, even in the face of new competition. But the Jartran advertising campaign (which won a prestigious marketing award) hurt U-Haul badly. The advertising featured price comparisons between the two companies that were computed in a manner unfair to U-Haul. The campaign also asserted that Jartran trucks were better. The size of the trucks pictured in the print advertising had been altered photographically to make the Jartran trucks appear larger. And nice, shiny new

Jartran trucks were compared with less desirable looking U-Haul models. U-Haul presented several consumer-perception surveys to the court that showed considerable consumer confusion regarding the advertising and charted a direct link between its lost sales and the Jartran campaign. During the year of the campaign Jartran experienced a ninety-two million dollar revenue increase, U-Haul, a forty-nine million dollar revenue decline. The court computed the damages by adding Jartran's advertising expense for the misleading campaign, about six million dollars, to the money spent by U-Haul to counteract the Jartran campaigning, close to fourteen million. The judge then doubled this total and awarded U-Haul forty million dollars in damages, the largest award by far ever given in a Section 43(a) case. Many people believe the size of this award will stimulate more advertisers to go to court to try to gain damages when they believe they have fallen victim to a false advertising campaign.

Consumers, as opposed to competitors, have a much more difficult time in maintaining an action for false advertising. As noted previously, there is no common law tort for deceptive advertising and the consumer has no standing to sue under the Lanham Act. (See *Colligan* v. *Activities Club of New York,* 1971.) Consumers can and do report false and deceptive advertising to the authorities, but as individuals they have few effective remedies at law for a deceptive advertisement. As George and Peter Rosden point out in their massive compendium *The Law of Advertising,* historically, common law courts have not been receptive to protecting consumers. "During the most formative period of common law," they write, "only a few goods in the marketplace were manufactured products so that the buyer was in an excellent position to judge for himself goods offered to him." Dairy products could be judged by their smell and texture; vegetables, meat, and fruit, by their looks. Judgments about wine, beer, and cloth were also easy to make. Protection was really necessary only in case of fraud such as watered beer. The basic slogan in those days was caveat emptor—buyer beware.

While today consumers are far better protected—they must be because of the thousands of consumer products about which they know little or nothing—there is little consumers can do themselves to attack the dishonest advertiser, short of reporting the advertisement to the proper authorities. Even if the law allowed a suit to redress an injury wrought by a false advertisement, where can a consumer find a lawyer to handle the case? Let us say you buy a certain toothpaste because the advertisements claim it will brighten your teeth and stop formation of cavities. If your teeth do not get brighter and you sue, your damages are for 94 cents. On a contingency fee the lawyer gets 40 percent, or about 38 cents. Even a suit over a $150 dental bill does not give an attorney-at-law much to work for, especially when a malpractice victim who wants to sue for $200,000 may be around the next corner.

The Rosdens point out that it is possible for a consumer to sue under product liability laws, but in such cases the advertisement must contain a commitment about the product that is not fulfilled after purchase by the consumer.

For example, an advertisement for a carpet cleaning product states that it will not damage carpets, but after a consumer uses the product, a large hole appears in the rug. The consumer would be able to sue (if he or she could retain a lawyer) for a new carpet.

A few states have also recently permitted consumers to sue advertisers under their unfair competition statutes. In late 1983 in California, for example, the state supreme court ruled that a group of parents of young children could sue General Foods, Safeway stores, and two major advertising agencies for damages allegedly caused by "a nationwide, long-term advertising campaign designed to persuade children to influence their parents to buy sugared cereals." Such rulings are not common, however, and this case never really came to fruition.

State and Local Laws

State regulation of advertising predates federal regulation by several years. This fact is not surprising when you consider that at the time the public became interested in advertising regulation—around the turn of the century—the federal government was a minuscule creature relative to its present size. Harry Nims, a New York lawyer, drafted a model law called the *Printers' Ink* statute (it was *Printers' Ink* magazine that urged passage of the law) in 1911. Many states adopted such legislation.

Enforcement of these local regulations, which is in the hands of attorney generals or local prosecutors, has been weak because these legal officers have many other statutes to enforce. When people are being murdered, robbed, maimed, or kidnapped, the fact that you or I have been deceived by an advertisement from a local furniture store seems relatively unimportant.

However, because of the consumer revolution of the last twenty years, many cities, counties, and states have strengthened their laws and their enforcement of false and deceptive advertising. In some areas prosecution is quite vigorous; in others, it is not. The laws vary from state to state, even from city to city. It is advised that persons involved in advertising obtain copies of all relevant laws regarding statutes in the area in which publication is made. The statutes make false or deceptive advertising a misdemeanor—a minor crime—and all but three states (Arkansas, Delaware, and New Mexico) have such laws on the books. But the general verdict is that these statutes have been fairly ineffective in dealing with false advertising.

The Federal Trade Commission

The Federal Trade Commission is the primary agent of the federal government for the regulation of advertising. The FTC was created by Congress in 1914 to police unfair methods of business competition. The agency was to make certain that "Company A" did not engage in practices that gave it an unfair advantage over its competitor, "Company B." And of course an unfair advantage may be gained through the use of false or misleading advertising. As originally conceived, the FTC was not worried about the impact of advertising upon consumers, only competitors. During the 1920's however, the FTC perceptively enlarged its mission in an effort to try to protect consumers as well. This effort was suddenly stopped in 1931 when the Supreme Court ruled the FTC had illegally enlarged its jurisdiction and that it could only attempt to regulate advertising that unfairly affected the advertiser's competitor (*FTC v. Raladam*).

In 1938 Congress adopted the Wheeler-Lea Amendment to the Trade Commission Act which gave the FTC the power to proceed against all unfair and deceptive acts or practices in commerce, regardless of whether they affect competition. Since that time the commission has developed into one of the nation's largest independent regulatory agencies. In addition to policing false advertising, the FTC is charged with enforcing the nation's anti-trust laws and several federal statutes such as the Truth in Lending Law and the Fair Credit Reporting Act. The five members of the commission are appointed by the president and confirmed by the Senate for a term of seven years. No more than three of the commissioners can be from the same political party. A chairperson, one of the five commissioners, is appointed by the president. While the agency is located in Washington, D.C., it has eleven regional offices throughout the nation.

The history of the agency reveals that it has often been swept by the political winds of the time. For years it was known as the "Little Gray Lady of Pennsylvania" because of its timid performance. During the late sixties and seventies in an era of consumer concern, the FTC showed new muscle and attacked some of the nation's largest advertisers, such as Coca-Cola and ITT Continental Baking. In the eighties the FTC reflected the spirit of deregulation that ran throughout Washington, D.C., as Ronald Reagan entered the White House. This, "get the government off our backs" philosophy accounts for the growth in civil lawsuits by one advertiser against another since the commission could no longer be counted upon to be an effective watchdog. As the new decade opens it is difficult to predict which way the FTC will move. As will be noted in the next section, it certainly has the power to be an aggressive agent in the battle against false and misleading advertising. But whether it also has the will to move in this direction is another question altogether.

SUMMARY

Self-regulation by the advertising industry has increased in recent years, especially with the growth of comparative advertising. The National Advertising Division and the National Advertising Review Board, divisions within the Better Business Bureau, are the primary agents for this self-regulation. Such regulation is geared toward satisfying the interests of advertisers rather than consumers, however. There has also been a rapid increase in lawsuits brought by advertisers against one another under Section 43(a) of the Lanham Act. An advertiser seeking redress under this fifty-year-old federal law can seek to either stop the misleading practice and/or win money damages. Again, this law provides little relief for consumers. Laws banning false advertising exist at both the state and local levels, but tend to be applied half-heartedly. The Federal Trade Commission remains the nation's most potent weapon against false or misleading advertising but this agency has recently reflected the national political mood of getting government "off the backs of business" and has taken a passive approach to problems in advertising.

FEDERAL TRADE COMMISSION POWERS

One of the Federal Trade Commissions most important responsibilities is to insure that consumers are not victimized by unfair, misleading, or deceptive advertising. Through custom and practice the agency has defined advertising as any action, method, or device intended to draw the attention of the public to merchandise, to services, to persons, and to organizations. Trading stamps, contests, freebies, premiums, and even product labels are included in this definition in addition to the more common categories of product and service advertising. Normally it is not difficult to distinguish an advertisement from some other kind of communication. Recently, however, this issue has been litigated because of an advertisement published by the R. J. Reynolds Company in 1985. The tobacco company published a full-page essay entitled "Of Cigarettes and Science" in several newspapers and magazines. Assertions were made in the body of this essay that the causal link between smoking and heart disease was mere opinion, not fact, because it was based on statistical correlations, not evidence of causation. Reynolds also asserted that even this correlation had been put under a shadow of doubt according to recent research called the "Mr. FIT" study. The FTC issued a complaint against Reynolds, claiming that the cigarette maker had misrepresented the findings in the study cited in the essay, and that it had omitted mentioning two material findings that tended to point to a connection between smoking and heart disease. An adminstrative law judge heard the complaint against Reynolds and threw out the FTC case. The administrative judge said that the essay was not an advertisement, but an editorial, expressing the company's opinion regarding the scientific method, the "Mr. FIT" study, and the smoking and health controversy. Therefore what R. J. Reynolds had to say on these matters could not be regulated. The five commissioners of the FTC reversed the ruling by the administrative law judge and enumerated several criteria that the judge should use in reconsidering whether or not the material in question is an advertisement; that is, whether it is commercial speech that can be regulated, or simply a paid editorial, noncommercial speech that cannot be regulated. The matter had not been resolved when this chapter was prepared. Normally, what the FTC declares to be an advertisement is considered an advertisement.

Does the FTC regulate all advertising? Legally, no, it cannot. But practically, it can regulate almost all advertising. Because the agency was created under the authority of Congress to regulate interstate commerce, products or services must be sold in interstate commerce or the advertising medium must be somehow affected by interstate commerce before the FTC can intervene. While many products and services are sold locally only, nearly every conceivable advertising medium is somehow affected by or affects interstate commerce. All broadcasting stations are considered to affect interstate commerce. Most newspapers ship at least a few copies across state lines. Even when a newspaper is not mailed across state lines, it is very likely that some of the news in the newspaper comes across state lines or that the paper on which the news is printed, the ink and type used to print the news, or parts of the printing machinery travel across state lines. The federal government became quite adept at demonstrating that businesses affect interstate commerce or are affected by interstate commerce as it learned to enforce civil rights laws like the Public Accommodations Act. The motel owner who declared that he did not have to abide by the federal law because his business was a local operation soon discovered that if the chickens or apples he served in his restaurant were shipped in from out of state, the courts were willing to say that his motel operation was a part of interstate commerce.

There are some other requirements that must be met before the FTC can act. It must be shown that the agency is acting in the public interest, which is really not too difficult since false advertising generally has an impact upon the public. If the FTC says it is acting in the public interest, courts usually take its word for it.

Once it has been shown that the action meets the agency definition of "advertisement" and that it affects interstate commerce in some way, one final element must be present before FTC powers are invoked—the advertisement must be deceptive or untruthful. The current FTC standard of deception has emerged during the past ten years as the agency moved from its aggressive stance of the seventies to its more passive position of the eighties. In fact, the current standard of deception is probably not fully refined, since in specific cases some commissioners attempt to offer slight alterations. (See, for example, in re *Southwest Sunsites, Inc.,* 1985.) But here is an outline of the three-part test that is currently in use.

1. *There must be a representation, omission, or practice that is likely to mislead the consumer.* The commission will consider the entire advertisement as well as all other elements of a transaction when making this determination. The issue is whether the act or practice is likely to mislead rather than whether it causes actual deception. The FTC recently ruled that two claims made by Figgie International about its Vanguard Heat Detectors were likely to deceive consumers. The company claimed that its heat detectors provided sufficient warning to allow occupants of a home to escape a fire, and that

heat detectors used with smoke detectors were significantly more effective than smoke detectors alone. The evidence did not support this, and potential purchases were likely to be led astray by these claims, the agency said (*Figgie International, Inc.,* 1986).

A deceptive statement may be made expressly, such as "Arcane Aspirin will cure the common cold," or the claim may simply be implied. Thomson Medical advertised its Aspercreme as an effective pain reliever for the symptoms of arthritis. The substance was to be applied directly to the body, and its effectiveness was compared with the effectiveness of aspirin in the advertising. There was a clear implication that the creme contained aspirin, which is known as an effective pain reliever, but it did not. The FTC ruled that it was deceptive to imply that it did since a consumer could be easily misled (*Thomson Medical Co.,* 1984).

The omission of important or material information in an advertisement can also be deceptive. For example, Beneficial Corporation, a finance company, advertised that it would provide a customer with an "instant tax refund" if the individual's tax return entitled him or her to a refund. But actually, what was unstated was that the customer had to first qualify for a loan, and there was nothing instant about the loan procedures. This omission was ruled to be deceptive by the FTC, and the agency ruling was upheld by a court of appeals (*Beneficial Corporation,* 1976). In early 1989 the FTC charged the Campbell Soup Company with deceptive advertising when it contended its soups could reduce the risk of heart disease because they were low in fat and cholesterol. The agency said that the soup company did not disclose that many of these same soups contained a high sodium content. Many health experts, including the United States Surgeon General, say that the consumption of substantial amounts of sodium can contribute to high blood pressure. Hence, the agency argued, the soups were not necessarily good for the heart merely because they had lower amounts of fat and cholesterol. Campbells soup said it stood by the claim and the case was set to go to a hearing. If an advertiser claimed that ninety-three percent of all its watches that have been sold since 1952 still keep perfect time would be deceptive if the advertiser did not reveal that the watches have only been on the market for the last five years. The FTC ruled that a claim by the makers of Wonder Bread that its bread is fortified with vitamins and minerals to help children grow up to be big and strong was deceptive because it did not reveal that nearly all commercially baked bread is fortified with vitamins and minerals. The FTC argued that by not disclosing that Wonder Bread is really no different from other bread, the baking company omitted an important element; it told only half the story (in re *ITT Continental Baking Co.,* 1971).

2. *The act or practice must be considered from the perspective of a consumer who is acting reasonably.* The test is whether the consumer's interpretation or reaction is reasonable. When advertisements or sales practices are targeted to a specific audience, such as those aimed at children, the elderly,

or the terminally ill, they will be viewed from the perspective of a reasonable member of that group. "For instance, if a company markets a cure to the terminally ill, the practice will be evaluated from the perspective of how it affects the ordinary member of that group," the commission noted in a 1983 policy statement. The terminally ill consumer is likely to be far more susceptible to exaggerated cure claims than is a healthy person. Also, advertising aimed at a special vocational group, such as physicians, will be evaluated from the perspective of a reasonable member of that group. A well-educated physician might be better able to understand a complicated pharmaceutical ad than the average individual.

The advertiser is not responsible for every interpretation or behavior by a consumer. The law is not designed to protect the foolish or the "feeble minded," the commission has noted. "Some people, because of ignorance or incomprehension, may be misled by even a scrupulously honest claim," one commissioner noted in 1963. "Perhaps a few misguided souls believe, for example, that all Danish pastry is made in Denmark. Is it therefore an actionable deception to advertise Danish pastry when it is made in this country? Of course not," the commissioner noted (in re *Kirchner,* 1963). When an advertisement conveys more than one meaning to a reasonable consumer, one of which is false, the seller is liable for the misleading interpretation. Here is a classic example: "Jones Garage will put a new motor in your car for only $350." What does this claim mean? One meaning is that the garage will sell you a new motor and install it for only $350. But an equally reasonable meaning is that the garage will install a motor that you already own for only $350. If the second meaning is intended, the seller may very well be held responsible for the first meaning—which is false—as well.

The commission will evaluate the entire advertisement when it examines it for misrepresentation. Accurate information in the text may not remedy a false headline, because a reasonable consumer may only glance at the headline. If a television announcer proclaims that a watch is one hundred percent waterproof, the advertiser cannot qualify this claim in a long printed message in small type that crawls across the bottom of the TV screen while the announcer tries to sell the product (*Giant Food, Inc. v. FTC,* 1963). Similarly, an advertiser cannot correct a misrepresentation in an advertisement with point-of-sale information. A seller cannot advertise a vacuum cleaner as having a one-hundred percent money-back guarantee and then expect to qualify that claim in a tag that is attached to the product as it is displayed for sale in a store. Qualifying disclosures must be legible and understandable, the FTC has ruled.

"The commission generally will not bring advertising cases based on subjective claims (taste, feel, appearance, smell)," according to the 1983 guidelines. The agency says it believes the typical reasonable consumer does not take such claims seriously and thus they are unlikely to be deceptive. Such claims are referred to as **puffery** and include representations that a store sells "the most fashionable shoes in town" or a cola drink is "the most refreshing drink around."

Finally, the commission has stated that when consumers can easily evaluate the product or service, when it is inexpensive, and when it is frequently purchased, the commission will scrutinize the advertisement or representation in a less critical manner. "There is little incentive for sellers to misrepresent . . . in these circumstances since they normally would seek to encourage repeat purchases," a 1983 statement proclaims. That means the advertiser of small, dry cell batteries, a relatively inexpensive product purchased often by most consumers, will be given a bit more leeway in advertising than the advertiser of a six-hundred dollar home generator.

3. *The representation, omission, or practice must be material.* A material misrepresentation or practice is one that is likely to affect a consumer's choice of a product. In other words, according to the commission policy statement, "it is information that is important to the consumer." The FTC considers certain categories of information to be more important than others when deciding whether a claim is material or not. Express claims as to the attributes of a product are always considered material. Advertising claims that significantly involve health and safety are usually presumed to be material. Information pertaining to the "central characteristics of the product or service" are usually considered to be material. Information has also been found to be material where it concerns the purpose, efficacy, or cost of the product or service. Claims about durability, performance, warranties, or quality have also been considered material. An example of a claim that was not considered material is a statement made by Chevron in the advertising of a gasoline additive, F-310. In both television and print advertising, a company spokesperson claimed to be standing in front of the Chevron research laboratories while he made the pitch for the product. In fact, he was standing in front of a county courthouse. The statement was false, but was it material? An administrative law judge said it was not. The location of the spokesperson is immaterial to a consumer judging the product.

Demonstrations or mock-ups often become the subject of FTC inquiries, and the question of materiality is often raised. For many years a shaving cream manufacturer claimed that its product was so good that it could be used to shave sandpaper. In a TV demonstration Rapid Shave was spread on sandpaper and then, a few moments later, the sand was shaved off. The demonstration was phony. What the announcer shaved was not sandpaper, but sand sprinkled on glass. The FTC argued that this was deceptive and that the claim that Rapid Shave could be used to shave sandpaper was a material representation. The Supreme Court agreed, despite the plea from Colgate-Palmolive that the product really could shave sandpaper if it was left on the paper long enough, but because the sand and the paper were the same color, a TV demonstration did not work. Hence the company had to use sand on glass (*FTC v. Colgate-Palmolive Co.,* 1965). But the High Court did not say that all mockups were deceptive. Only those that are used to support a material product claim must be restricted. For example, plastic ice cubes may be substituted for the real thing in an advertisement for a soft drink because no claim about the quality of the ice cubes is involved. But plastic ice cubes can not be used in a television commercial aimed at selling ice cubes if the advertisement extolls the attributes of these marvelous, uniform-sized, crystal clear ice cubes. The phony ice cubes are then being used to demonstrate a material claim for the product.

Some lawyers who represent advertisers take the cynical view that an advertisement is deceptive when the FTC says it is, regardless of the content of policy statements or other official pronouncements. There is undoubtedly some truth to this argument. If an ad is ruled to be deceptive, what happens next? Let's now look at the means the FTC has at its disposal to control or correct false and deceptive advertising.

Means to Reduce Deceptive Advertising	In dealing with false advertising the FTC's greatest enemy is the time needed to bring an action against an advertiser. Since advertising campaigns are ephemeral, the FTC often has difficulty in catching up with the advertiser before the short-lived campaign has been replaced with something else. But if time is the greatest enemy, publicity is the FTC's strongest ally. Advertisers don't like the publicity that accompanies a charge of false advertising. A recent study by the commission of 122 false advertising cases acted upon between 1962 and 1985 revealed that the stock of companies charged usually dropped sharply after the charges were published. This can cost a company millions of dollars. In addition, consumer reaction to the charges often results in lost sales as well.

In addition to the informal sanction of publicity, the FTC has a wide range of remedies to deal with advertising. Let's briefly look at this arsenal.

Guides	The FTC issues industry guides on a variety of products and services. These are basically policy statements that alert the advertisers before the fact to what the agency believes are permissible claims and what may be problematic claims. For example, the FTC has issued a guide on the use of the word "free" and when it can and cannot be legitimately used. Guides have also been issued, for example, for advertising private vocational schools, home study courses, and decorative wall paneling. The guides are designed to help the advertiser keep within the law. But they do not carry the force of law and if and when an advertiser makes a claim that exceeds what is listed as permissible in a guide, the FTC must proceed against the advertiser with other remedies and prove that the claim is in fact deceptive.

Industry guides apply only to prospective advertising campaigns, events that have not yet occurred. The next remedy on the ladder is voluntary compliance and is used for advertising campaigns that are over or nearly over. Imagine that a company is nearing the end of an advertising campaign in which it has advertised that its mouthwash can prevent a consumer from getting a common cold. The FTC believes that the claim is deceptive. If the advertiser has had a good record in the past and if the offense is not too great, the company can voluntarily agree to terminate the advertisement and never use the claim again. In doing this, the advertiser makes no admission and the agency no determination that the claim is deceptive. There is just an agreement not to repeat that particular claim in future advertising campaigns. Such an agreement saves the advertiser considerable legal hassle, publicity, and money, all especially desirable since the advertising campaign is over or almost over.

The next remedy seems to be similar to voluntary compliance but is more complicated and more binding. The remedy is called a **consent order** and is a written agreement between the commission and the advertiser in which the advertiser again makes promises concerning future advertising. The advertiser is asked to agree not to do certain things and may also be asked to do certain other things. If the advertiser signs the agreement, the FTC takes no further action.

Recently Ogilvy and Mather agreed to cease advertising that Aspercreme contains aspirin. Tomy Corporation agreed to discontinue representation that any collection of products (dollhouses, accessories, etc.) is a set unless depicted products can be bought as a set. Great North American Industries, Inc., agreed to halt claims that its engine oil additive will result in substantial fuel economy unless the claims were based on competent, scientific tests. These are typical of the kinds of consent orders drafted by the FTC.

As will be noted in the discussion of FTC procedures, there is considerable pressure on the advertiser to agree to a consent order. The chance of winning a case before the FTC is usually slim, the litigation is costly, and the publicity that results from such litigation often does the product more harm than any FTC sanction.

If after accepting the consent order the advertiser then violates the agreement, the company is subject to a severe fine, up to $10,000 a day while the violation continues (i.e., while the advertising campaign continues). RJR Foods paid a $70,000 civil penalty for violating a 1973 order involving the disclosure of the fruit juice content in Hawaiian Punch. And R. J. Reynolds Tobacco Company was fined $100,000 for allegedly violating a 1972 order requiring a clear and conspicuous lettering in disclosing the health warning.

What happens if the advertiser really believes its claim is truthful and does not want to sign a consent order? The commission may issue a **cease and desist order.** Under terms of such an order, the advertisements must stop or the advertiser faces a severe civil penalty: again, a fine of up to $10,000 a day. In the long-running (eleven years) Geritol case, for example, the commission issued an order in 1965 prohibiting the J. B. Williams Company from implying in its advertising for Geritol that its product could be helpful to persons who were tired and run-down (in re *J. B. Williams Co.,* 1965; in re *J. B. Williams Co.* v. *FTC,* 1967). The commission contended that medical evidence demonstrated that Geritol, a vitamin-and-iron tonic, helps only a small percentage of persons who are tired and that in most persons tiredness is a symptom of ailments for which Geritol has no therapeutic value. The J. B. Williams Company violated the cease and desist order (at least, that is what the commission alleged) and in 1973 was fined more than $800,000. A court of appeals threw out the fine in 1974 and sent the case back to district court for a jury trial, which the advertisers had been denied the first time around (*U.S.* v. *J. B. Williams Co.,* 1974). The jury was to decide whether the Geritol advertisements did in fact violate the cease and desist order. At a second hearing in 1976, the FTC won a $280,000 judgment against the patent medicine manufacturer.

In 1976 the manufacturer of STP was ordered to stop making false claims regarding the effectiveness of its oil treatment. In 1978 a court found that the advertisement violated the order, and a $500,000 fine was levied.

Standard Oil of California was ordered to stop claiming that its Chevron gasolines with F-310 produce pollution-free exhaust. The commission banned television and print advertisements in which the company claimed that just six tankfuls of Chevron will clean up a car's exhaust to the point that it is almost free of exhaust-emission pollutants.

In 1983 the FTC ordered the manufacturers of Bufferin, Excedrin, Bayer Aspirin, Cope, Vanquish, and Midol to stop claiming that these products were superior to or safer than similar products. The agency said that Sterling Drugs and Bristol-Myers Co., the patent medicine manufacturers, could only make such claims if they had well-controlled clinical tests to prove the claims. Such studies do not exist, the FTC said. The commission said that Bristol-Myers had wrongly claimed that doctors recommend Bufferin more than other nonprescription pain relievers. This claim was false, FTC Commissioner David A. Clanton said. The commission said that claims made by Sterling Drugs that Bayer Aspirin had greater purity, stability, freshness, and disintegration speed were also unproven. The order issued by the agency states that advertising claims must be proven by two well-controlled clinical studies, although other forms of proof may be acceptable on a case-by-case basis. This kind of substantiation is noted in the next section.

Few advertisers are willing to carry a case as far as the cease and desist order. Those who do are usually prepared to go a lot farther—to a court of appeals to challenge the FTC's ruling. The appeal process is explored in the discussion of FTC procedures (page 501).

The pressure is heavy upon advertisers to voluntarily comply or to sign a consent order, especially since in neither case is there admission of wrongdoing and in both instances the legal processes will take so long that the offensive advertising campaign will probably be finished before the case is heard. Many people feel that the FTC does its job if it gains compliance voluntarily, for the mission of the agency is, after all, to stop deceptive advertising, not to punish advertisers. Other observers disagree, however, and argue that without stronger sanctions the advertiser is not motivated to refrain from future illegal acts. This kind of argument prompted the FTC to undertake new regulatory schemes, which we will now examine.

Substantiation

Advertising substantiation has been an important part of the FTC regulatory scheme since 1972. The basis of the program is simple: the commission asks advertisers to substantiate claims made in their advertisements. The FTC does not presume that the claims are false or misleading. The advertiser is simply asked to prove the claims are truthful. The substantiation process has been modified at least three times since it was initiated. Initially the commission demanded that all advertisers in a particular industry—such as soap and detergent makers—provide documentation for all their claims. This resulted in tremendous grumbling from advertisers, as well as mountains of studies and reports for the FTC. The agency was drowned in documentation. The process is therefore streamlined today. Panels of experts scrutinize advertisements and target for documentation those claims that seem most suspect. The most recent commission policy statement on substantiation was issued in July 1984. Under this new policy express substantiation claims, such as "doctors recommend" and "specific tests prove," require the level of proof advertised. Otherwise, advertisers will be expected to have at least a "reasonable basis" for claims in their advertising, wrote attorney Thomas J. McGrew in a 1985 article in the *Los Angeles Daily Journal*. The degree of substantiation that will be deemed reasonable varies with "the type of claim, the product, the consequences of a false claim, the benefits of a truthful claim, the cost of developing substantiation . . . , and the amount of substantiation experts in the field believe is reasonable," the policy statement said.

On its face substantiation seems like a fairly benign regulatory tool. But from the standpoint of legal process, it has had a major impact upon regulation of advertising. It has shifted the burden of proof in a great many advertising cases from the FTC, which in the past had to prove that a claim was false, to the advertiser, who must now prove that the claim is truthful. If the case goes to litigation and a hearing, the burden reverts back to the FTC, which must then prove that the advertising claim is false or misleading. But most cases are settled far short of litigation through a consent agreement or a cease and desist order.

Corrective Advertising **Corrective advertising** is a highly controversial scheme based on the premise that to merely stop an advertisement is in some instances insufficient. If the advertising campaign is successful and long running, a residue of misleading information remains in the mind of the public after the offensive advertisements have been removed. Under the corrective advertising scheme, the FTC forces the advertiser to inform the public that in the past it has not been honest or has been misleading. One commentator called the scheme "commercial hara-kiri."

Under what circumstances will the FTC ask for corrective advertising sanctions? The commission has resisted issuing a specific policy regarding this question. For example, in 1979 it responded to a request for such a policy from the Institute for Public Representation in Washington, D.C., by saying it would continue to deal with corrective advertising problems on a case-by-case basis. In the past, however, the agency has adopted this rather vague standard for the imposition of corrective advertising:

> If a deceptive advertisement has played a substantial role in creating or reinforcing in the public's mind a false and material belief which lives on after the false advertising ceases, there is clear and continuing injury to competition and to the consuming public as consumers continue to make purchasing decisions based on the false belief.

In such a case, corrective advertising is appropriate, according to the FTC.

The FTC first attempted to force what it calls affirmative or corrective disclosures in 1950, but a court of appeals ruled that it lacked the power to do so under the Federal Trade Commission Act. The court ruled in *Alberty* v. *FTC* (1950) that the agency lacked the authority to encourage or require informative advertising. Ten years later, however, in *Feil* v. *FTC* (1960), the courts reversed the *Alberty* decision. The FTC threatened to use the remedy against the Campbell Soup Company to correct the misperception created when the company put clear marbles in the bottom of a bowl of vegetable soup to force the vegetables to the top (*Campbell Soup Co.*, 1970). The first corrective advertisement did not appear until 1971. It was the result of a consent order signed by the ITT Continental Baking Company with regard to its advertising for Profile Bread. The television version of the corrective advertisement was this:

> I'm Julia Meade for Profile Bread. And like all mothers I'm concerned about nutrition and balanced meals. So I'd like to clear up any misunderstanding you may have about Profile Bread from its advertising or even its name. Does Profile have fewer calories than other breads? No, Profile has about the same per ounce as other breads. To be exact Profile has seven fewer

calories per slice. But that's because it's sliced thinner. But eating Profile Bread will not cause you to lose weight. A reduction of seven calories is insignificant. It's total calories and balanced nutrition that counts. And Profile can help you achieve a balanced meal, because it provides protein and B vitamins as well as other nutrients.

This corrective advertisement was in response to a Profile campaign that led some people to believe that one could lose weight by eating Profile Bread.

The commission required that corrective advertisements like this one constitute twenty-five percent of the advertising for Profile Bread during the year following the agreement. This is the typical percentage in a corrective-advertising agreement, although at times the FTC has agreed to allow advertisers to allot only fifteen percent of their advertising budget for corrective advertisements.

Only a few other manufacturers of well-known nationally advertised products have been forced to make corrective disclosures. One was the company making Ocean Spray Cranberry Juice, which for years advertised that its cranberry juice had more food energy than other juices. Since food energy is really only another way of saying caloric value, the FTC ordered the juice maker to tell people that fact in a corrective advertisement (*Ocean Spray Cranberries, Inc.,* 1972).

Corrective advertising, once feared by advertisers as a serious threat to the sales of their products, has been used sparingly in recent years. Paul Heard, in a recent article in the *University of Chicago Law Review,* suggests an explanation for this: "The FTC hesitates to order corrective advertising injunctions because the effectiveness of such orders is subject to much debate. Several studies indicate that corrective advertising injunctions do not fully undeceive consumers."

Injunctions

When Congress passed the Trans-Alaska Pipeline Authorization Act in 1973, attached to that piece of legislation was a bill that authorized the FTC to seek an injunction to stop advertisements that it believed violated the law. Attorneys for the FTC can seek these restraining orders in federal court. An injunction is clearly a drastic remedy and one that the agency has said it will not use often. Spokesmen for the FTC have said that the agency will use the power only in those instances in which the advertising can cause harm, in those cases where there is a clear law violation, and in those cases where there is no prospect that the advertising practice will end soon.

The first time the FTC used its new power was in 1973, when it sought and got a restraining order against several west coast travel agents who promoted trips to the Philippines for "psychic surgery." The FTC said that many Americans were being fleeced by so-called psychic surgeons who supposedly performed bloodless operations on patients by using their minds rather than scalpels. The agency won its case. More recently the FTC won a preliminary injunction against the National Commission on Egg Nutrition to block advertising claims that no scientific evidence exists linking egg consumption to a higher risk of heart disease. A lower court ruled that an injunction was too severe, limiting public debate on the cholesterol issue and damaging the advertisers financially. But a court of appeals reversed the lower court ruling and granted the injunction (*FTC* v. *National Commission on Egg Nutrition*, 1977). The ruling by the court suggests that the FTC will be permitted to enjoin an advertising practice when the danger to the public is immediate.

Trade Regulation Rules

In January 1975 President Ford signed the Magnuson-Moss Warranty—Federal Trade Commission Improvement Act, the most significant piece of trade regulation legislation since the Wheeler-Lea Amendment in 1938. The new law did many things, but basically it greatly enlarged both the power and the jurisdiction of the FTC. Until the bill was signed, the FTC was limited to dealing with unfair and deceptive practices that were "in commerce." The new law expanded the jurisdiction to practices "affecting commerce." The change of a single word gave the FTC broad new areas to regulate. The law also gave the agency important new power.

Three sections of the act expanded the remedies the FTC can use against deceptive advertising. First, the agency was given the power to issue trade regulation rules defining and outlawing unfair and deceptive acts or practices. The importance of this power alone cannot be overestimated. In the past the agency had to pursue deceptive advertisements one at a time. Imagine, for example, that four or five different breakfast cereals all advertise that they are good for children because they contain nine times the recommended daily allowance of vitamins and minerals. Medical experts argue that any vitamins in excess of one hundred percent of the recommended daily allowance are useless; therefore, these advertisements are probably deceptive or misleading. In the past the FTC would have had to issue a complaint against each advertiser and in each case prove that the statement was a violation of the law. Under the new rules the agency can issue a trade regulation rule—as it had done for nutritional claims—which declares that claims of product superiority based on excessive dosage of vitamins and minerals are false and misleading. If advertisers make such claims, they are in violation of the law. All the commission must prove is that the advertiser had actual knowledge of the trade regulation rule, or "knowledge fairly implied from the objective circumstances."

The advantages of the **trade regulation rules,** or TRRs as they are called, are numerous. They speed up and simplify the process of enforcement. Advertisers can still litigate the question, challenge the trade regulation rule, seek an appeal in court, and so forth. In most cases they probably will not go to that expense. Trade regulation rules should have a great deterrent effect, as they comprehensively delimit what constitutes an illegal practice. In the past after the commission issued a cease and desist order, businesses frequently attempted to undertake practices that fell just outside the narrow boundaries of the order. The TRRs are much broader and make it much harder for advertisers to skirt the limitations. Finally, via TRRs the FTC is able to deal with problems more evenhandedly. An entire industry can be treated similarly, and just one or two businesses are not picked out for complaint.

While the FTC had issued TRRs since 1962, it had done so sparingly, since it was unsure of its power to take this action. In 1974 a court of appeals upheld the right of the agency to promulgate such rules (*National Petroleum Refiners Association* v. *FTC,* 1974). This court decision was made law by Congress in the FTC Improvement Act. Since that time, according to one FTC representative, the commission has been busy promulgating rules, so that this aspect of regulation is more visible now.

The two other aspects of the new law that improved FTC remedies are these. The FTC may seek civil penalties against anyone who knowingly violates the provisions of a cease and desist order, even if that person was not originally the subject of the order. To wit: Chemical company A sells a spray paint that is toxic if used in a closed area, but the product is advertised as being completely harmless. The FTC moves against the company and issues a cease and desist order that states that in the future the firm must not advertise the product as being completely harmless. Chemical company B also sells a spray paint that has the same toxicity and is advertised the same way. If it can be shown that company B was aware of the provisions of the order against company A and continued to advertise its product as being completely safe, B can be fined up to $10,000 per day for violating the order, even though the order is not directed against B.

The new law gave the FTC the right to sue in federal court on behalf of consumers who have been victimized by practices that are in violation of a cease and desist order or by practices that are in violation of a TRR, a right which the agency has been reluctant to use.

SUMMARY

The Federal Trade Commission has the power to regulate virtually all advertising that is deceptive or misleading. To be deceptive an advertisement must contain a representation, omission, or practice that is likely to mislead the consumer; the advertisement or practice must be considered from the perspective of a reasonable consumer; and the representation, omission, or practice must be material. The FTC has many remedies that may be applied to attempt to regulate deceptive or untruthful advertising:

1. Guides or advisory opinions that attempt to outline in advance what advertisers may say about a product.
2. Voluntary agreements by advertisers to terminate a deceptive advertisement.
3. Consent orders or written agreements signed by advertisers promising to terminate a deceptive advertisement.

4. Cease and desist orders to advertisers to terminate a particular advertising claim, failure to comply with which can result in severe penalty.

5. Substantiation of advertisements in which the advertiser must prove all claims made in an advertisement.

6. Corrective advertising in which an advertiser must admit in future advertisements that past advertisements have been incorrect.

7. Injunctive power to immediately halt advertising campaigns that could cause harm to consumers.

8. Trade regulation rules that can be issued to regulate advertising throughout an entire industry.

THE REGULATORY PROCESS

To understand the importance of the regulatory process, students should be familiar with procedures followed in a deceptive advertising case, be aware of the kinds of advertising that can be considered deceptive, and be familiar with the defenses to a charge of deceptive advertising.

Procedures

Most cases come to the attention of the FTC from letters written either by consumers or by competitors of the offending advertiser. The legal staff of the agency then does a preliminary investigation. If the complaint counsel, an FTC staff attorney, feels there is no substance to the charge, the case ends. But if the attorney believes there is a provable violation, he or she writes a memorandum to the commission. A proposed complaint and a proposed consent order accompany the memorandum. The agency has recently established an evaluation committee at the FTC to review prospective cases and weed out the weak cases that consume staff resources and time.

After the proposed complaint has been prepared by the staff and reviewed, the commissioners vote on it. If they agree with staff lawyers—and they normally do—the advertiser is notified that a complaint is about to be issued. The advertiser is given the opportunity to sign the consent order or to negotiate a more favorable consent order. At this point there can be three results. First, the advertiser can agree to the consent order, and the commission can vote to accept the consent order. Second, the commission can vote not to accept the order. Third, the advertiser can reject the consent order. If the first happens, the order is published and is made final sixty days later.

If either the commission or the advertiser rejects the consent order, a complaint is issued, and a hearing is scheduled before an administrative law judge, who works within the FTC and officiates at commission hearings. At the hearing that follows—which is a lot like an informal trial—the burden of proof rests upon the FTC staff lawyers—complaint counsels—to show a violation of the law. In a criminal trial for robbery or murder, the evidence must show "beyond a reasonable doubt" that the defendant is guilty. In a civil case, liability must be established by "preponderance of evidence." In a hearing before an administrative law judge, all the complaint counsel must show is that there is "substantial evidence" of a violation of the law. While what substantial evidence is, is hard to define, it is less evidence than is required in either a criminal suit or a civil suit. After the hearing the judge either orders the case dismissed or issues a cease and desist order. The decision is final unless either the complaint counsel or the advertiser appeals. If that happens, the entire commission decides the matter. Overruling an administrative law judge is not uncommon. For example, after the hearing on Chevron F-310 the commission overruled the judge's decision to dismiss the charges. More recently the commission overruled a judge's cease and desist order against several television advertisements for Dry Ban spray deodorant. The judge agreed with complaint counsel that the advertisements implied that the spray "went on dry" but in fact was wet when it hit the skin. The FTC disagreed and said that all the advertisement implied was that Ban went on the skin drier than other antiperspirant sprays. A court of appeals must finalize either a consent order or a cease and desist order, but this is a routine matter.

If the FTC dismisses the cease and desist order, the matter ends there. If it supports the order, the advertiser can still appeal to the courts for relief. This is not a common practice, however. It is difficult for courts to reverse an FTC ruling. There are only a handful of reasons that a judge can use to overturn the commission decision. The case goes to the court of appeals and there is no new finding of fact: what the FTC says is fact, is fact. The following are all instances in which a court can overturn a FTC ruling (1) "convincing evidence" that the agency made an error in the proceedings, (2) no evidence to support the commission's findings, (3) violation of the Constitution—for example, the agency did not provide due process of law, (4) the action goes beyond the agency's powers, (5) facts relied upon in making the ruling are not supported by sufficient evidence, and (6) arbitrary or capricious acts by the commission. Such an event is an extreme rarity. An appeal of an adverse ruling by a circuit court can be taken to the Supreme Court, but only if certiorari is granted.

The enforcement powers of the FTC are limited but can nevertheless be effective. Violation of either a cease and desist order or a consent order can result in a penalty of 10,000 dollars per violation per day. A fine such as this can add up fast! As a result of the *Geritol* case, the agency can be forced into district court to prove to a jury that in fact the orders were violated. This action impedes the enforcement procedure, for a jury trial is time-consuming and costly. As an alternative the agency can go back to the court of appeals that finalized the consent order or the cease and desist order and seek a civil contempt citation against the advertiser. The penalty is then up to the judge and will probably be much smaller, since civil contempt damages are considered remedial and are not intended as a deterrent.

A question that is often raised about the regulation of advertising is whether or not an advertising agency has any responsibility in an FTC false-advertising case. In the 1940s the FTC announced that an advertising agency could be held jointly responsible with the advertiser for false advertising. The agency reasoned that if the agency was active in preparation of the advertisement and if it had relatively extensive product knowledge, it could be held accountable. So the extent of agency participation in the ad campaign will generally determine whether or not the agency will be held responsible, according to Marcella Tyler, who prepared a special report on the FTC for the Institute for Communication Law Studies at the Catholic University School of Law.

Examples of Deceptive Advertising

There are a few special problems regarding deceptive advertising that deserve special mention before we leave this topic.

Testimonials

Even casual television viewers must be aware of the growth in recent years of testimonial advertising, commercial pitches hurled at viewers by some of America's leading celebrities and sports stars. Providing endorsements for American business and industry can be very lucrative for these cultural icons. Michael Jackson and Lionel Ritchie signed on with Pepsi Cola for fees estimated at 5 million dollars each. James Garner's work for Polaroid earned him an estimated 3 million dollars. For a few week's work for Coca-Cola and General Foods in 1985, Bill Cosby earned an estimated 1.5 million dollars. And the "experts" in the business estimate that a Super Bowl win automatically means between 500,000 and 1 million dollars in endorsements for the quarterback on the winning team. To a great many people, especially television viewers, a recommendation to purchase a product by one of their close friends (television friends, that is) can be highly persuasive.

Endorsements have been regulated by the FTC for many years. Prior to 1932, when a company paid for a testimonial—any testimonial—that fact had to be revealed in the advertisement. Many people believe that that is what the law should still be. Obviously an advertiser cannot fake a testimonial and claim that Cher chews Tuity Fruity gum, for example. Not only is that a deceptive claim, but the advertiser would face liability for invasion of privacy as well. (Remember the appropriation tort pp. 204–218.) And an unsolicited testimonial must in fact be unsolicited. Finally, a statement cannot be altered to make it sound like an endorsement, if it was not originally intended as such. Imagine this movie review: "If you like movies with a stupid plot, wooden acting, unimaginative direction, and poor photography, you'll love this film.

This is the worst movie of the year." Enter a clever advertising copywriter with a box full of ellipses who turns a negative review into an endorsement. "The critics say, . . . you'll love this film. This is the . . . movie of the year!" This is deceptive advertising.

The FTC adopted a new set of rules for testimonial advertising in 1975. Experts who endorse products must now have the expertise to evaluate the products. The law is quite rigid concerning products that relate to health and safety. The FTC ruled that an "expert" endorsement by former astronaut Gordon Cooper of a product that supposedly increased automobile performance, reduced smog emission, and cleaned an engine was improper. Cooper's skill related to space missions; he did not have the education or training to qualify as an "expert" in the field of automobile engineering (in re *Leroy Gordon Cooper,* 1979).

A celebrity or expert endorser must be a bona fide user of a product at the time of the endorsement. This means the individual must use the product more than "now and then," or "once in a while." And endorsers must use a product because they like it and approve of it. The advertiser can continue to use the endorsement only so long as there is good reason to believe that the endorser still uses the product.

When an organization—like the National Football League—endorses a product, there must be evidence that the endorsement represents the collective judgment of the members of the organization, not just the judgment of the executive director or the management council of the group.

Payment made to an expert or celebrity endorser does not have to be revealed as long as there is no representation made in the advertisement that the endorsement was given without compensation. Payment made to a non-famous endorser (the typical man on the street) need be revealed only if the endorser knows that a favorable review of a product might result in the use of the endorsement as an advertisement. Here is an example. An advertiser announces that it is looking for man-on-the-street endorsements for Snappy Soda and invites persons to taste it and give their reactions to the drink. The fact that the tasters know in advance that a favorable review might get them a lucrative television commercial could color their reactions to the drink. But if the advertiser secretly records an individual's reactions to Snappy Soda and has not told this person such reactions might be used as a television endorsement, no disclosure of subsequent payment need be made.

Celebrity endorsements must also reveal a material connection between endorsers and products if one exists. Pat Boone was fined by the FTC for failing to meet this rule in his endorsements of Acne-Statin, a skin-blemish medication. Cooga Mooga Corporation, owned and operated by Boone for the purpose of promoting the performer's business interests, was one of several companies marketing and promoting the skin medication. Boone received twenty-five cents for each nine-dollar bottle sold. In this case Boone also implied that his four daughters had used the preparation successfully, which was not completely true, and that Acne-Statin was superior to other similar products, an expert evaluation he was not qualified to make (in re *Cooga Mooga, Inc. and Charles E. Boone,* 1978). This was the first time a celebrity had been held directly responsible for deceptive endorsement. The singer paid a large fine and was ordered to pay partial restitution to persons who had bought the product. The link between a product and a celebrity endorser does not have to be as direct as the connection between Boone and Acne-Statin to require disclosure. Former astronaut Gordon Cooper was paid for his endorsement of the previously noted automotive product on the basis of the number of devices sold. The more products sold, the more money he received. The FTC ruled that this was a material connection between the product and the endorser and should have been revealed in the endorsements (in re *Leroy Gordon Cooper,* 1979).

An endorser cannot make any statement that an advertiser cannot make; that is, the endorser also must have support for his or her conclusions. The makers of a cough syrup cannot honestly say that their product cures a cough. A housewife who endorses the cough syrup cannot make that statement either. If an endorser changes his or her view and decides the product is no good, the advertiser must stop using that testimonial.

Endorsements that claim to be from typical consumers must be made by consumers, not by actors playing the part of consumers. Note that most "man/woman on the street" testimonials never make the claim that the endorsers—who are normally actors—are typical consumers. That is a conclusion advertisers hope we reach as viewers, but since no such claim is made, the ads are permissible. Laypersons cannot endorse the effectiveness of drug products. If an endorser says she removes facial hair safely with a depilatory, her experience must be typical of most consumers. She cannot be the exception to the fact that the product damages the skin of most women who use it.

Bait-and-Switch Advertising

One of the classic false advertising games is what is called **bait-and-switch advertising.** Here is the general idea. An appliance store advertises in the newspaper that it is selling a brand-new washing machine for 57 dollars. The advertisement is the bait to get customers into the store. When customers come to the store to grab up this bargain, the salespeople are very honest about the advertised washer and say that it is a pile of junk (and it probably is!): it has no dials, it tears fine fabrics, it tends to leak, its motor is loud, and so forth. However, over in a corner is a really good buy, a snappy model that is on sale for 595 dollars. This high-pressure selling is the switch. If customers insist on buying the bait, chances are they will be told the machines have all been sold. The merchant had never intended to sell that model. The whole idea is to use the bait to lure people into the store who are in the market for washing machines, and then skillful, if not honest, salespersons switch customers to a more costly model via high-pressure selling—convenient monthly payments and so forth.

Bait-and-switch advertising is illegal. Technically the law says that it is deceptive to advertise goods or services with the intent not to sell them as advertised or to advertise goods and services with the intent not to supply reasonably expected public demand, unless limitation on the quantity is noted in the advertisement (see Title 16 *Code of Federal Regulations,* 238).

Bait-and-switch advertising is not the same as loss-leader advertising, legal in many places, in which a merchant offers to sell one item at below cost (the leader) in order to get customers into the store in the hope that they will then buy additional merchandise at regular cost. Supermarkets use this scheme and so do other retail outlets. Those states that outlawed this practice did so because of pressure from small merchants who cannot afford to sell anything at a loss and do not want to be put at a marketing disadvantage with high-volume sellers.

Free Offers

It is deceptive to be untruthful about matters of cost and price; to say that the price of an item is reduced when it is not; to advertise a factory discount price when it is not; to advertise a special introductory price when it is not. The use of the word *free* causes many problems. If a merchant gives a free toothbrush to all persons who come into the store, the merchant can advertise that free toothbrushes are being given away. The word *free* may be used in connection with mail-order giveaways, even if the customer is charged a small fee for postage and handling, fifteen or twenty-five cents. However, to advertise a free set of drinking glasses and then require people to pay three dollars postage and handling is illegal.

The word *free* can be used even when the customers are required to buy another item before getting the free item so long as this fact is made clear in the advertisement: a free toothbrush with every purchase of a tube of toothpaste. However, this rule applies only so long as the price of the toothpaste is not inflated to cover even partial cost of the toothbrush. The toothpaste must be sold at the regular price. The same limitation applies to two-for-one sales: the first item must be sold at regular price, not at an inflated price.

Defenses

The basic defense against any false advertising complaint is truth; that is, proving that a product does what the advertiser claims it does, that it is made where the advertiser says it is made, or that it is as beneficial as it is advertised to be. While the burden is upon the government to disprove the advertiser's claim, it is always helpful for an advertiser to offer proof to substantiate advertising copy.

Another angle that advertisers can pursue is to attack a different aspect of the government's case rather than try to prove the statement true. For example, an advertiser can argue that the deceptive statement is not material to the advertisement as a whole, that is, it will not influence the purchasing decision, or that the advertisement does not imply what the government thinks it implies. For example, to say, as Dry Ban did, that a deodorant "goes on dry" does not mean that it is dry when it is applied, merely that its application is drier than that of other antiperspirants.

The success rate in defending false-advertising cases is not high. As with most legal problems, it is best to consult legal counsel before a problem arises and not after a complaint has been issued.

Publisher Liability

Can a publisher or broadcasting station be held liable for publishing or broadcasting advertising for a product or service that turns out to be harmful? Almost fifty years of case law says no, according to attorney P. Cameron Devore, a leading authority on the law relating to commercial speech. Devore asserts that this principle is rooted deeply in common law and in the perceived unfairness of imposing otherwise unlimited liability on publishers for not investigating copy submitted to them or collected by them in the normal course of business. "The principle is now also firmly based on First Amendment analysis, with actual malice required to establish liability," Devore said recently in a speech at the Practicing Law Institute in New York.

But a United States district court in Texas recently ruled exactly the opposite in holding the magazine *Soldier of Fortune* liable in a wrongful death action. In 1984 a man named John W. Hearn placed this advertisement in the personal services section of the magazine's classified advertising: "Ex-Marine—67–69 Nam Vets—ex D.I.—weapons specialist—jungle warfare, pilot, M.E high risk assignments U.S. or overseas." A phone number accompanied the advertisement. Robert Black Jr. contacted Hearn and paid him ten thousand dollars to kill his wife, Sandra Black. Hearn was caught and convicted of the crime and is now serving three life sentences in Florida for that murder and two other contract killings. Robert Black was convicted as well and in 1988 he was on death row in a Texas prison for his part in the slaying.

Sandra Black's mother and son sued the magazine and in March of 1988 a jury awarded the pair 9.4 million dollars. The federal court ruled in this case that the First Amendment protection of commercial speech did not foreclose a simple negligence action by the survivors against the magazine. The court said it did not intend to impose on every publisher the burden of investigating every advertisement submitted to it, but rather intended to limit this holding to the facts in this case. "The reasonableness of its [the advertisement] publication in defendant's magazine without investigation, however, is not clear given the nature of the magazine and its readership and given the fact that many advertisements submitted for publication in the personal services column expression offer criminal services," the judge wrote. The plaintiffs in the case used expert testimony during the trial to establish that many advertisements in the magazine that were harmless on their face were understood in the context of the magazine to offer criminal services. The court also said it did not intend its holding to affect otherwise protected noncommercial speech; only commercial advertising (*Eimann* v. *Soldier of Fortune,* 1988). *Soldier of Fortune* has appealed the ruling with the expectation—shared by most experts— that the ruling will be overturned.

Advertising law is complicated, involved, and constantly changing. Even advertisers who set out to honestly follow the straight and narrow run into difficulty once in a while. The best way to cope with these problems is by thorough understanding of both the law and the way the law operates.

SUMMARY

Complaints against advertisers are prepared by the FTC staff and approved by a vote of the commission. Administrative law judges can hold hearings, which are somewhat like trials, to determine whether the FTC charges are valid. A United States court of appeals can review all commission orders. Advertisers need to take special care when dealing with testimonials and endorsements. The law outlaws bait-and-switch advertising in which customers are lured to a store with promises of low prices but then are pushed by salespersons to buy more expensive products.

BIBLIOGRAPHY

Here is a list of some of the sources that have been helpful in the preparation of chapter 10:

Books

Howard, John A., and Hulbert, James. *A Staff Report to the Federal Trade Commission.* Washington, D.C.: Federal Trade Commission, 1974.
Rohrer, Daniel M., ed. *Mass Media, Freedom of Speech, and Advertising.* Dubuque, Ia.: Kendall/Hunt, 1979.
Rosden, George E., and Rosden, Peter. *The Law of Advertising.* New York: Matthew Bender & Co., 1986.

Articles

Berman, Jeffrey A. "Constitutional Realism: Legislative Bans on Tobacco Advertisements and the First Amendment." 1986 *University of Illinois Law Review* 1193, 1986.
Cornell, Arthur B. Jr. "Federal Trade Commission Permanent Injunction Actions Against Unfair and Deceptive Practices: The Proper Case and the Proper Proof." 61 *St. John's Law Review* 503, 1987.
DeVore, P. Cameron. "Commercial Speech: 1988." Remarks to Communications Law 1988 Practicing Law Institute, New York City, November 10, 1988.
Edwards, Krista L. "First Amendment Values and the Constitutional Protection of Tobacco Advertising." 82 *Northwestern University Law Review* 145, 1987.

Heald, Paul. "Money Damages and Corrective Advertising: An Economic Analysis 5." 55 *University of Chicago Law Review* 629, 1988.

Jones, Michael E. "Celebrity Endorsements: A Cause for Alarm and Concern for the Future." 15 *New England Law Review* 521, 1980.

Karns, Jack E. "The Federal Trade Commissions Evolving Deception Policy." 22 *University of Richmond Law Review* 399, 1988.

Kogan, Jay S. "Celebrity Endorsement: Recognition of a Duty." 21 *The John Marshall Law Review* 47, 1987.

Langworthy, Elisabeth A. "Time, Place, or Manner Restrictions on Commercial Speech." 52 *George Washington Law Review* 127, 1983.

McGrew, Thomas J. "Advertising Law: Inactive FTC, Activism in Courts." *The Los Angeles Daily Journal,* January 17, 1985.

Mann, Charles C., and Plummer, Mark L. "The Big Headache." *The Atlantic Monthly,* October, 1988.

Morris, Brian. "Consumer Standing to Sue for False and Misleading Advertising Under Section 43(a) of the Lanham Trademark Act." 17 *Memphis State University Law Review* 417, 1987.

Pompeo, Paul E. "To Tell the Truth: Comparative Advertising and Lanham Act Section 43(a)." 36 *Catholic University Law Review* 565, 1987.

Townley, Rod. "No Hitting Below the (Money) Belt." *TV Guide,* August 7, 1982.

Tyler, Marcella A. "Federal Trade Commission Regulation of Advertising Today." Institute for Communication Law Studies, Catholic University School of Law, 1984.

Waltzer, Garrett J. "Monetary Relief for False Advertising Claims Arising Under Section 43(a) of the Lanham Act." 34 *UCLA Law Review* 953, 1987.

Whelan, Margaret. "Common Sense and Commercial Speech." 48 *University of Pittsburgh Law Review* 1121, 1987.

Cases

Alberty v. *FTC,* 182 F.2d 36 (1950).

American Brands, Inc. v. *R. J. Reynolds Tobacco Co.,* 413 F.Supp. 1352 (1972).

Aronberg v. *FTC,* 132 F.2d 165 (1942).

Avis Rent-a-Car Systems v. *Hertz Corp.,* 726 U.S.P.Q. 95 (1985), rev'd 782 F.2d 381 (1986).

Bates and Van O'Steen v. *Arizona,* 433 U.S. 350 (1977).

Beneficial Corp. v. *FTC,* 542 F.2d 611 (1976).

Bigelow v. *Virginia,* 421 U.S. 809 (1975).

Bolger v. *Young Drug Products Corp.,* 463 U.S. 60 (1983).

Campbell Soup Co., 77 F.T.C. 664 (1970).

Capital Broadcasting Co. v. *Acting Attorney General,* 405 U.S. 1000 (1972).

Capital Cities Cable v. *Crisp,* 467 U.S. 691 (1984).

Central Hudson v. *Public Service Commission,* 447 U.S. 557 (1980).

Colligan v. *Activities Club of New York,* 442 F.2d 686 (1971).

in re *Cooga Mooga, Inc. and Charles E. Boone,* 92 F.T.C. 310 (1978).

Dunagin v. *Oxford,* 718 F.2d 738 (1984).

Eimann v. *Soldier of Fortune,* 15 M.L.R. 1026 (1988).

Feil v. *FTC,* 285 F.2d 879 (1960).

in re *Figge International, Inc.,* 107 F.T.C. 313 (1986).

Friedman v. *Rogers,* 440 U.S. 1 (1979).

FTC v. *Colgate-Palmolive Co.,* 380 U.S. 374 (1965).

FTC v. *Inecto, Inc.,* 70 F.2d 370 (1934).

FTC v. *National Commission on Egg Nutrition,* 570 F.2d 158 (1977).

FTC v. *Raladam,* 283 U.S. 643 (1931).

Giant Food, Inc. v. *FTC,* 322 F.2d 977 (1963).

in re *ITT Continental Baking Co.,* 79 F.T.C. 248 (1971).

in re *J. B. Williams Co.,* v. *FTC,* 381 F.2d 884 (1967).

in re *Kirchner,* 63 F.T.C. 1282 (1963), aff'd. 337 F.2d 751 (1964).

in re *Leroy Gordon Cooper,* 94 F.T.C. 674 (1979).

Linmark Associates v. *Township of Willingboro,* 431 U.S. 85 (1977).

Maybelline v. *Noxell Corp.,* 643 F.Supp. 294 (1986).

National Petroleum Refiners Association v. *FTC,* 340 F.Supp. 1343 (1972); rev'd. 482 F.2d 672 (1974).

Ocean Spray Cranberries, Inc., 70 F.T.C. 975 (1972).

Ohralik v. *Ohio State Bar Association,* 436 U.S. 447 (1978).

Oklahoma Telecasters Association v. *Crisp,* 699 F.2d 490 (1983).

Posadas de Puerto Rico Assoc. v. *Tourism Co.,* 478 U.S. 328 (1986).

in re *R. J. Reynolds Tobacco Co.,* 51 Antitrust & Trade Reg. Rep. 219 (1988).

in re *R. M. J.,* 455 U.S. 191 (1982).

Shapero v. *Kentucky Bar Association,* 108 S.Ct. 1916 (1988).

Skil Corp. v. *Rockwell Int'l Corp.,* 375 F.Supp. 77 (1974).

in re *Southwest Sunsites, Inc.,* 105 F.T.C. 7 (1985).

in re *Thompson Medical Co.,* 104 F.T.C. 313 (1984).

U.S. v. *J. B. Williams Co.,* 498 F.2d 414 (1974).

Valentine v. *Chrestensen,* 316 U.S. 52 (1942).

Virginia State Board of Pharmacy v. *Virginia Citizens' Consumer Council, Inc.,* 425 U.S. 748 (1976).

Warner-Lambert v. *FTC,* 562 F.2d 749 (1977).

Zauderer v. *Office of Disciplinary Council,* 471 U.S. 626 (1985).

11

BROADCAST REGULATION

From 1927 until the end of the 1970s, almost forty-five years, the United States broadcasting industry operated under the blanket of a comprehensive and fairly stringent collection of federal regulations. These rules had a single, if diffuse, purpose: to insure that broadcasters operated first their radio, and later their television stations, in the public interest. In 1980 this regulatory scheme began to be dismantled by the very agency assigned to make it operate—the Federal Communications Commission (FCC). During this past decade scores of technical, business and content regulations were repealed or watered down. The public interest service standard has been all but abandoned, according to critics of deregulation. The Commission began to treat the broadcasting industry just like any other American business. Indeed, Mark Fowler, the chairman of the FCC during most of the past decade, once publicly described television as "just a toaster with pictures."

The 1980s ended with considerable uncertainty about what will happen next in broadcast regulation. Ronald Reagan left the White House, and with him went many of the conservative ideologues who carried out the massive deregulation of the broadcast as well as other industries, deregulation that was tentatively started in some industries during the Carter administration. President George Bush's posture on these matters is not at all clear at this point. Indeed the industry itself does not speak with a singular voice. Some within broadcasting say they don't favor less regulation. Nearly all within the broadcasting industry favor heavier regulation of the cable industry. And those in the cable industry seek less regulation for themselves, but want other telecommunications industries (like the telephone companies) regulated to diminish their strength as competitors.

The Congress, which has been more liberal than the President for the past twenty years, seems frustrated, some say fed up. In the late 1980s the House of Representatives thwarted many efforts by the FCC to deregulate the broadcasting industry to an even larger extent, blocking attempts by the commission to end rules on personal attacks and political editorials (see pages 563–565), and network ownership of programming, for example. Often nothing official happened. The FCC would announce the consideration of a rule change, a bill would be introduced in Congress that would void the possible FCC action, and the commission would back off. Other times however, Congressional efforts were not sufficient. A Presidential veto killed efforts by the Congress to reenact the fairness doctrine (see pages 554–557) and rules governing advertising on television programs aimed at children (see pages 536–538). The federal judiciary began to play a more critical role as well, striking down important rules governing cable television, and raising questions regarding the age-old rationale that supported government regulation of broadcasting in the face of the First Amendment.

Changes in the pattern of regulation of broadcasting are occurring rapidly, even as we stand on the edge of what may be a new regulatory era in Washington. And trying to describe this changing regulatory scheme is like trying to describe a swiftly moving train. The cars have passed by before the words leave the mouth. Dealing with just the fairness doctrine plays havoc with an author's attempt to be current and comprehensive. The FCC announced in 1987 that it would no longer enforce the fairness doctrine; the Commissioners said they believed it was unconstitutional. Congress voted overwhelmingly to reenact the fairness doctrine as a statute. President Reagan vetoed the law. What now, then, is the status of the fairness doctrine? In the spring of 1989 new fairness doctrine legislation was introduced in Congress. During the Presidential campaign George Bush suggested he would veto such legislation if elected President. Will he? Will Congress be able to override the veto? Will the courts rule on the matter even before Congress has a chance to act? On radio the announcer can simply invite listeners to "tune in tomorrow." Authors of books don't have that luxury.

In this chapter we will describe contemporary broadcast regulation, such as it is, with both an eye to the past and an eye to the future. We will first briefly recount the history of broadcast regulation. Next we will examine the political/social philosophy that supported the regulatory scheme for almost fifty years, and the political/economic theory that has been raised to support the deregulation of the broadcasting industry. The bulk of the remainder of the chapter focuses on contemporary regulations and the regulators themselves. Finally, we will outline the regulation of cable television, something that is changing as rapidly as anything else in this area.

The regulation of telecommunications in America today is a massive and complicated affair. It involves the regulation of broadcasting and video programming by cable and ancillary services such as multichannel multipoint distribution services (MMDS), regulation of telephone and telegraph services, and regulation of other interactive communications systems. It also involves easements for the stringing of phone lines and television cable, and myriad other problems that are beyond the scope of this chapter. Much of this is very technical and is rightly the province of the specialist. Let's begin this chapter with a short explanation of why our broadcasting system was not given the same First Amendment rights granted to the printed press. ♦

REGULATION HISTORY AND RATIONALE

The individuals who created our system of regulation of broadcasting adopted what some call a trusteeship model for a pattern. The model suggests that the broadcaster should act as a public trustee, using the valuable broadcast airwaves for the benefit of the public. It was no accident that this model was adopted. It was dictated in no small part by the early history of radio. Let us examine that history briefly. Then we can attempt to outline the basic rationale that supports this trusteeship model.

Development of Radio

Radio is not the invention of a single individual. Rather, it represents an accumulation of many ideas that emerged during the last years of the nineteenth century. At first only simple radio signals were transmitted. But gradually transmission of more complicated voice signals became possible. The basic hardware of radio had been developed by 1910, but the medium grew far differently than did the print medium. Remember, printing came at a time when people were groping for a means of spreading propaganda, and the printing press became a major weapon in the battle for democracy and religious freedom in England. The press was used as a means of spreading information and ideas. Radio has never really been dedicated to those ends. Initially it was a gadget that tinkerers built as a plaything for talking with friends and neighbors and for listening to strangers in distant places. The military was first to see the practical value of radio. The navy used radio as a means of keeping track of its ships out of port and for transmitting messages to captains on the high seas. The army too saw radio as an effective device for improving military communications. After World War I the armed forces made one concerted push to have the government take control of all radio communication, but the effort failed.

Aside from the military, few persons could see the practical side of radio, especially of radio broadcasting. The giant radio manufacturers were the first to reason that if they used radio to broadcast entertainment, people would want to buy radio sets. Commercialism took a big step forward in the early twenties when the concept of broadcasters selling broadcast time to sponsors developed.

Radio Act of 1912

The regulation of broadcasting in the United States dates from 1910, when Congress ruled that all United States passenger ships must carry a radio. Two years later the lawmakers passed the **Radio Act of 1912** in response to considerable pressure from the army and navy, which asserted that increasing numbers of amateur broadcasters interfered with military transmissions. The 1912 law required that all radio transmitters be licensed by the federal government and that operators of the transmitters be required to have a license. The secretary of labor and commerce, who was delegated the job of administering the law, was given authority to assign specific broadcast wavelengths to specific kinds of broadcasting (military wavelength, ship-to-shore wavelength, etc.). The secretary also had the power to determine the time periods when broadcasts could be carried, but he had no discretionary power to license. Anyone walking in the door and filling out an application could get a license.

The popularity of radio in the early 1920s caused a serious problem for the government. Too many persons wanted a license and too many radio broadcasters wanted to transmit at the same time. In 1923 a frustrated Secretary of Commerce Herbert Hoover refused to grant a license to an otherwise qualified applicant, claiming he enjoyed this discretion under the 1912 law. A federal court ruled that Hoover had gone beyond the law. "The duty of issuing licenses to persons or corporations coming within the classification designated in the act reposes no discretion whatever in the secretary of commerce. The duty is mandatory," Judge Van Orsdel wrote (*Hoover* v. *Intercity Radio Co., Inc.,* 1923).

While Hoover was defeated in the courts, conscientious broadcasters and other persons concerned with the future of radio continued to urge the secretary to set up regulations to control broadcasting. At the Fourth National Radio Conference in 1925 (Hoover called yearly meetings to draft broadcasting regulations which Congress annually rejected), the secretary of commerce outlined his philosophy with regard to broadcast regulation. This philosophy remains an important pillar of support for the trusteeship model of regulation:

> We hear a great deal about freedom of the air, but there are two parties to freedom of the air, and to freedom of speech for that matter. Certainly in radio I believe in freedom for the listener. . . . Freedom cannot mean a license to every person or corporation who wishes to broadcast his name or his wares, and thus monopolize the listener's set. We do not get much freedom of speech if one hundred fifty people speak at the same time at the same place. The airwaves are a public medium, and their use must be for the public benefit. The main consideration in the radio field is, and always will be, the great body of the listening public, millions in number, countrywide in distribution. There is no proper line of conflict between the broadcaster and the listener. Their interests are mutual, for without the one the other could not exist.

Under pressure from leading broadcasters and emboldered by the consensus that the annual radio conferences seemed to indicate, Hoover continued to act beyond his legal authority in regulating broadcasting. In 1926 his actions were again challenged, this time by Eugene F. McDonald who operated station WJAZ in Chicago on an unauthorized wavelength and at times not authorized by his license. His challenge to Hoover was joined in federal district court and again Hoover lost. Judge Wilkerson ruled, "There is no express grant of power in the [1912] act to the secretary of commerce to establish regulations" (*U.S.* v. *Zenith Radio Corp.,* 1926).

Hoover insisted that the United States attorney general appeal the ruling, but in a lengthy opinion Acting Attorney General William J. Donovan stated that he agreed with Wilkerson's interpretation of the law. Donovan wrote that while stations were required to have licenses to operate, the secretary of commerce had no authority to assign specific stations to specific wavelengths, to limit hours of operation, or to place limitations on the amount of broadcast power used by a station. Donovan added:

> It is apparent from the answers contained in this opinion that the present legislation is inadequate to cover the art of broadcasting, which has been almost entirely developed since the passage of the 1912 act. If the present situation requires control, I can only suggest that it be sought in new legislation, carefully adopted to meet the needs of both the present and the future.

Hoover capitulated, and the chaos, which the secretary's illegal regulations had somewhat abated, returned to the airwaves. Finally, Congress could no longer ignore the mounting pressure and adopted federal legislation by passing the comprehensive **Radio Act of 1927.**

Radio Act of 1927

The nation had operated without substantial regulation of broadcasting for about twenty years, but nonregulation did not seem to work. A traffic cop was obviously necessary to make certain that broadcasters transmitted on assigned wavelengths, that they operated during assigned hours, and that they operated at assigned levels of power. Only with this kind of regulation could listeners use the medium. The Radio Act of 1927 created much more than a traffic cop however. As former FCC Commissioner Glen Robinson notes in *The Administrative Process,* "Even a cursory examination of the act, however, indicates that the regulatory powers granted to the Federal Radio Commission (and later to the FCC) exceeded those minimally required to avoid electronic interference." The new law governed programming, licensing and renewal, and many other aspects of radio not associated with broadcast signals and electronic interference.

The years immediately following the passage of the new law brought order to broadcasting. The courts upheld the power of the federal government to regulate the broadcast media, and a system of regulations began to take shape. The 1927 act also provided the basic philosophical foundation for broadcasting regulation. The law asserted that the radio spectrum, the airwaves, belongs to the public and that broadcasters merely use this public resource while they operate a licensed station. The law established that the broadcaster must operate in "the public interest, convenience or necessity" at all times. This was the standard of conduct that would be used to evaluate licensees at renewal time. An independent agency, the Federal Radio Commission, was also established to supervise the regulation of broadcasting.

While the 1927 legislation was satisfactory in dealing with the problems of broadcasting, it became evident, following a study initiated by President Franklin D. Roosevelt in 1933, that the radio industry and the telephone and telegraph industries were interdependent. In 1934 Roosevelt urged Congress to adopt a new law that would be broad enough in scope to govern all these media. After extensive hearings and debates, the Federal Communications Act of 1934 was approved. This law has been amended frequently since 1934, but it stands as the basic regulation of the broadcast industry today (47 *United States Code*, Section 151, 1970).

Justifications and Challenges to Regulation

The decision to regulate American broadcasting, made by Congress in the face of what can only be described as chaos in the industry, nevertheless represents more than an expedient solution to a difficult problem. The regulatory scheme rests upon a philosophical foundation, and this foundation rests upon at least three major supports. These supports are the justification for what we call the trusteeship model of broadcast regulation.

Scarcity in the Spectrum

There is a real and absolute limit on the number of persons who can broadcast over the airwaves at any given time. What engineers call the broadcast spectrum is finite, and we have yet to discover a way to enlarge this spectrum. Therefore, not everyone who wants to operate a radio or television station can do so. Persons who want to use the spectrum to operate radio and television stations also face competition for space on the spectrum from persons who want to use mobile telephones or shortwave radios or who want to transmit electronic data. Someone must decide who shall be permitted to use this valuable broadcast spectrum.

Service to the Public

The radio or television broadcaster who uses the spectrum to transmit radio or television signals is using a valuable public resource, a resource that belongs to all of us. Since only a selected few are chosen to use the airwaves, some person or some agency must insure that those who do use this public resource serve the needs of the people—fulfill the public interest. The government has chosen to do this in the name of the people, and by doing so it reaches toward a goal traditionally fostered by the First Amendment. As Justice Byron White said in 1969, "There is nothing in the First Amendment which prevents the government from requiring a licensee to share his frequency with others and to conduct himself as a proxy or fiduciary with obligations to present those views and voices which are representatives of his community. . . ." It is the right of the public to receive suitable access to social, political, esthetic, moral and other ideas and experiences, which is crucial here, he added (*Red Lion Broadcasting* v. *FCC,* 1969).

Fear and Harm

The corollary to the notion that the broadcaster should serve the public interest, is that the broadcaster should not harm the public interest. Broadcast media are powerful and potentially dangerous in the wrong hands. They can invade the home by the mere flick of a switch. Radio and television can spread lies or rumors far and wide in an instant. Radio and television can exacerbate social problems by teaching anti-social behavior. The broadcast media can also teach unacceptable values such as materialism or hedonism.

Under the trusteeship model, the government is assigned the responsibility of controlling broadcasting. Because of the scarcity of broadcast frequencies, the government must assign those frequencies to those persons who can best serve the nation. Because these frequencies are a public resource, the government must act to ensure that those broadcasters who use the scarce frequencies serve the public interest—the greatest good for the greatest number. And because broadcasting is powerful and could cause harm, the government must ensure that the electronic media are not used in an improper manner. Under the trusteeship model the government will maintain ownership of the public airwaves in behalf of the people and temporarily assign broadcast frequencies to private individuals who are expected to act as trustees for the public in the use of this valuable resource. The public interest will be served through government regulation of these trustees.

Challenge to the
Trusteeship Model

The trusteeship model of regulation was challenged in the late 1970s by those who proposed regulation by the marketplace; that is, regulation by listeners and viewers and advertisers and others who actually use the media. In proposing this new concept, proponents of marketplace regulation rejected many of the assumptions underlying the trusteeship model. Here is a brief summary of their assertions.

Scarcity as a justification for regulation simply will not hold. Today there are many more radio and television stations than there are newspapers in a community, and the printed press is not regulated. Theoretically at least, cable television is a medium of unlimited channels. We have broken the bounds of the finite spectrum through new technology.

The marketplace is a better regulator of the industry than government. The best evidence of the public interest is what people will listen to and watch. If members of the audience or advertisers are unhappy with what a station is doing, they will turn their back on the station. And this will force the station owner to change the programming.

While broadcasting may have the potential to cause harm, so may the printed press. Why are newspapers and magazines not more heavily regulated? Because of the First Amendment. If broadcasting is the most pervasive medium, if it is the one that can touch its audience most deeply, then broadcasting, among all mass media, deserves First Amendment protection. The guarantees of freedom of speech and press are hollow if they are only applied to largely ineffectual mass communications. Since television is (according to some surveys) the most widely used source for news and information today, it should be free from government interference.

Who is right and who is wrong in this argument? And is that important? In deciding to regulate broadcasting the nation was making a policy decision, not declaring the revelation of universal truths. While the advocates of marketplace regulation are correct when they say there seems to be no scarcity of communications media today, this argument in a sense misses the point. There are still more people who want to own a radio or television station than the spectrum will permit. And someone must select who owns and who doesn't. It is argued that the marketplace can make this decision. Afterall the market decides who owns parcels of land and buildings through pricing practices. In fact this happens now in broadcasting when stations are offered for sale. But who has the most money is not always the best indicator of who will best serve the communication needs of the society.

The marketplace can act as an effective regulator only if there is a wide variety of goods. There is a sameness, especially in television, that limits public choices in the broadcasting marketplace. Even public television must strive to please a wide audience today to sustain itself in the face of sharp budget reductions from the federal and state governments that were supposed to support it. Many point out that under the recent regime of "marketplace regulation" there has been a substantial increase in the quantity of "sleazy" programming on radio and television, that many children's programs have become thirty minute commercials, and that trafficking in radio and television licenses has left listeners and viewers bewildered as each new owner changes formats or programming schemes. The amount of news on radio decreased dramatically at most stations, according to recent studies, when the requirement to broadcast news was dropped. Even supporters of the marketplace approach have a difficult time pointing out a positive public value that has accrued under this scheme of regulation or, more appropriately, nonregulation. At best they can say that broadcasting is considerably freer today than it was ten years ago. And this is true: it is freer to broadcast important but controversial programming, freer to take a stand on critical issues, freer to serve the needs it defines for the community. It is also freer to relegate public service to the back burner, freer to increase profits at the expense of quality programming, freer to ignore those portions of programming that don't meet the advertiser's demographic profiles. In the end, of course, that is what freedom is all about.

Freedom from government control is a value that can't be dismissed too readily. There is no question that traditional First Amendment interests have been compromised through both regulation and the threat of regulation. President John F. Kennedy and the National Democratic Committee used the fairness doctrine and the FCC to try to silence right-wing radio critics (see Friendly, *The Good Guys, the Bad Guys and the First Amendment*). And many local television stations were intimidated when FCC Chairman Dean Burch requested copies of all analyses of televised speeches made by President Richard

Nixon. Burch was the former chairman of the Republican party, hardly a disinterested observer of criticism of the embattled president. The GOP also organized license renewal challenges against television stations owned by the *Washington Post,* a major thorn in Nixon's side. And in 1984 the Central Intelligence Agency asked the FCC to consider refusing to renew the broadcast licenses of stations owned by ABC because the network had broadcast a news report highly critical of the agency, a report that CIA boss William Casey said violated the fairness doctrine. It has also been argued that many timid broadcasters simply refuse to exercise their full constitutional rights of free expression because they mistakenly fear government intervention. And this reduces, rather than enhances, the flow of news and information to the public.

The argument that broadcast regulation is wrong because of the First Amendment is perhaps the most difficult to challenge in some ways. It should be remembered, however, that there are really three distinct kinds of regulation of broadcasting. First, the government places limits on the accumulation of broadcasting properties; one person can own only twelve television, twelve AM radio, and twelve FM radio stations. Second, the government exercises control over who may use the airwaves for broadcasting; these are the licensing requirements. Finally, the communications act and FCC policies restrict the content of broadcast programming through rules such as the candidate access and equal opportunity, as well as regulations regarding the broadcast of indecent material.

Each of these kinds of rules relates somewhat differently to the First Amendment. Limiting the number of broadcast properties any individual may own has few First Amendment implications. It is hard to argue that someone who owns thirty-six broadcasting stations is being denied freedom of expression because the government forbids that person from owning one more radio or television station. But there are those who will make that argument. Licensing regulations certainly have greater First Amendment implications. How these rules are written determines how serious these implications will be. The government can surely regulate the speakers in a public park so that four or five people don't try to speak at the same time in the same place—so long as all have a chance to speak sometime. Broadcast licensing rules could be written in the same fashion. But current rules are far more complex and because one applicant for a license is often selected over another on the basis of what kind of programs he or she proposes to broadcast, there is no question but that the government is acting as a kind of censor. Rules regulating content most clearly run counter to our traditional views of freedom of expression. Only those persons who are willing to accept the newer access theory of the First Amendment (see pages 48–49) or who view broadcasting as entirely different from the printed press can view the fairness doctrine and other similar rules as being a constitutional exercise of government power.

These then are the arguments for and against the deregulation of broadcasting. Before considering the implications of the changes, let's now briefly look at exactly how broadcasting has been deregulated.

The Deregulation of Broadcasting	While this book is generally about what is rather than what was, it is still important to understand just what has happened to the regulation of broadcasting in the past decade. There are two reasons for this. First, it is possible that some of these deregulatory actions will be rescinded in the near future. Congress is unhappy with many of these changes and it may have the muscle to get many of these rules back on the books. Second, in order to evaluate the regulation of broadcasting today, it is important to be able to see it from the perspective of the past as well. Many of these changes are so recent that we have not really begun to feel the full impact of this deregulation.

The FCC has been the prime mover in deregulation, but the agency can only relax those administrative rules it has adopted in the past. The FCC cannot rescind a rule contained in the communications act, only Congress can change those rules. Courts can also void rules, but only if they somehow clash with the Constitution or are adopted through an illegitimate use of either administrative or congressional authority.

Ownership Rules

Under previous rules no individual or company could own more than twenty-one broadcast properties, seven television stations, seven AM radio stations, and seven FM radio stations. Additionally, only five of the seven television stations could be VHF channels 2 through 13. The VHF stations are more powerful than UHF stations (channels 14 through 83), can reach a much wider audience, and are generally more profitable. Under new rules an individual can own as many as twelve AM radio and twelve FM radio stations. If two of each kind of the stations have fifty percent minority ownership, an individual or company can own fourteen of each. A single individual or company can own as many as twelve television stations; the distinction between owning VHF and UHF stations has been modified. If two of the stations are on the UHF band or if two have 50 percent minority ownership, the total number one individual may own is raised to fourteen. However, no owner may reach more than 25 percent of the total U.S. audience with his or her stations. Consequently, a company like Capital Cities/ABC, which owns eight television stations that reach 24.4 percent of United States television households, cannot own the maximum of twelve or fourteen stations. At one point the FCC had proposed abolishing all ownership restrictions, but Congress forced the agency to back down on this proposal. Finally, the FCC in 1982 abandoned a rule that required a broadcaster who purchased a station to operate it for at least three years before selling it. The rule imposed a kind of stability on the broadcasting industry and inspired, many thought, a sense of connection between the broadcaster and the community. In the wake of this rule change radio and television stations have sometimes been treated more like pork belly shares than communications enterprises. "What has developed is a new breed of broadcasters; fast-buck artists who buy and sell stations on speculation and dump them when they can turn a quick profit," said United States Representative Edward J. Markey, the chairperson of the House Telecommunications Subcommittee.

The FCC has not been able to make drastic revisions in the rules on licensing and relicensing. Congress has been petitioned by broadcasters, with the support of the commission, to modify the current regulations on relicensing broadcast stations and drop what is called the comparative hearing requirement. Currently, the FCC is supposed to hold a full hearing when a challenger seeks to gain a license currently held by a broadcaster (see pages 531–534). The commission is supposed to evaluate both the current license holder and the challenger on several criteria and award the license to the individual or company that will best serve the community interest. Under various congressional proposals this requirement would be abandoned. The broadcast license would automatically be renewed unless the commission finds that the actions of the current license holder demonstrated such serious disregard for the provisions of the communications act or FCC rules that the application for renewal should be denied. Only after the renewal is denied could the applications of challengers be considered. Congress has yet to take action on the proposal which is considered a high priority item by the broadcasting industry.

But while licensing rules per se have not been changed by the commission, many other rules that have an impact on relicensing have been relaxed. These are rules that govern performance standards for the broadcasters. By eliminating such standards the FCC has made it much easier for broadcasters to live up to the statutory mandate that they serve "the public interest, convenience and necessity." Commercial radio and television stations are no longer required to provide a minimum amount of local programming, informational programming, and nonentertainment programming. There are no longer limits on the number of commercial minutes per hour that may be broadcast. Requirements that broadcasters undertake a formal process of ascertainment to determine the needs and interests of their local community and then propose programming to meet these needs have also been dropped. Broadcasters are no longer required to keep program logs that list all programs, as well as the type and source of each program. The agency has eliminated eighty-four percent of all bookkeeping formerly required. Myriad other rules have been eliminated as well, including FCC policies concerning licensee distortion of audience ratings, conflict of interest, sports announcer selection, and use of a station for personal advantage in other business activities. The changes listed above represent a small portion of the regulations that have been dropped.

The agency has, where it is possible, relaxed rules regarding program content. In two separate actions the agency modified long-held rules regarding children's programming. In the past the broadcaster was required to demonstrate how the station had met the needs of various groups of child viewers, such as preschoolers, elementary-school-age children, and others. In 1984 the commission modified this rule and refused to adopt mandatory children's programming rules. The FCC said that the rules were not needed unless the video market *as a whole* does not exhibit a clear failure to serve the needs and interests of the child. What this means in practical terms is this: If the needs of children are being met by a public television station in the community and through cable channels or other over-the-air stations, a broadcaster would not necessarily have to provide programming for young people. The decision was challenged, but a United States court of appeals upheld the ruling (*Action for Children's Television* v. *FCC,* 1985). At the same time the agency also dropped rules that limited the number of commercial minutes that could be broadcast in children's programs. A proliferation of children's programs with toy tie-ins ("GI Joe" and "Care Bears"), resembling thirty-minute commercials, has been the result. (See pages 536–538 for more on this.)

In 1987 the FCC repealed the fairness doctrine (see pages 554–557), a policy which required broadcasters to air programming about controversial community issues, and to present these issues in a fair and balanced manner. Congress tried to overturn this action, but its legislation was vetoed by President Reagan. In February of 1989 the District of Columbia United States Court of Appeals ruled that the FCC did not abuse its discretion by repealing the fairness doctrine, but declined to rule that the doctrine was unconstitutional (*Syracuse Peace Council* v. *FCC,* 1989). Congress did succeed in blocking FCC efforts to abandon rules regarding political editorialization and personal attacks however. (See pages 563–565.) The FCC cannot repeal the equal opportunity doctrine, which provides that broadcasters shall make available equal time for candidates for public office, and the candidate access rule, which gives candidates for federal office an opportunity to purchase broadcast time on radio and television stations. These rules are both contained in federal statutes. But the FCC is the agency that applies these rules and through half-hearted application, the agency has reduced their effectiveness.

Many persons argue that the commission has consistently undercut the intent of the equal opportunity rule. Under this regulation if a broadcaster allows one candidate for a particular office to use his or her broadcast facility, all other candidates for the same office must be given the same opportunity. But in recent years the FCC has declared that a candidate's news conference is not covered by the law and that debates between candidates may be staged by the news media without triggering the equal opportunity rules (see pages 549–550). By interpreting the rule in such a narrow fashion and the exceptions to the rule in such a broad fashion, the FCC has significantly reduced the effectiveness of this regulation as well.

What has been discussed in this section is barely the tip of the iceberg, an outline of some of the more visible rules that the Federal Communications Commission has abandoned in the past decade. Scores of other business and technical rules have also been set aside. The agency has even proposed—but not yet permitted—some users to decide how to use the space they occupy on the electromagnetic spectrum. Near the end of the 1980s the commission suggested that users of the UHF television spectrum, channels fifty through fifty-nine, should be permitted to also use these broadcast channels for land mobile telephone communications, including cellular telephones. Land mobile phone users have long been attempting to gain an additional share of the spectrum. UHF channels fourteen through twenty and seventy through eighty-three have already been dedicated to that use. Under this FCC proposal, however, a purchaser of a UHF television station could, without FCC approval, abandon the television operation and lease the channel to mobile phone users. The market would decide the use based on who would pay more for the channel. Giving a user the power to change the kind of communication service designated for a particular channel without government approval was previously simply unheard of in this country.

Whether the deregulation will continue into the 1990s remains unknown. Retrenchment is just as possible. Regardless, there are still a vast array of rules and regulations still on the books, and those are what the remainder of this chapter is all about.

SUMMARY

American broadcasting has been regulated almost from its inception. Regulation has been based on the trusteeship theory, which rests upon three philosophical pillars: the scarcity of broadcast frequencies, the need for those selected to use these frequencies to serve a broader public interest, and the fear that broadcasting can be harmful if not regulated. Proponents of the deregulation of broadcasting have raised an alternative theory: the notion that the marketplace is the best regulatory of the industry. These persons deny that there is scarcity in the age of cable television, and argue that the public users of radio and television, not the government, are best able to define the public interest. They also argue that the First Amendment should protect the electronic media to the same extent that it protects the printed press.

The FCC has already abandoned scores of rules regarding such things as the owernship and sale of television and radio stations, performance standards for broadcasters, and certain content rules. Congress has attempted to block some of these efforts, but has been frustrated by presidential vetoes. Whether deregulation continues, or some of the abandoned rules are reinstated depends in large part on the posture of the Bush administration toward broadcasting and regulation.

REGULATION THROUGH LICENSING

As already mentioned, the broadcasting industry is regulated by the Federal Communications Commission. It has the power to grant licenses to broadcast and to renew those licenses.

Federal Communications Commission

The 1934 Federal Communications Act provided that a seven-member **Federal Communications Commission** regulate the broadcast industry. In 1982 Congress reduced the size of the commission to five members as an economy measure. Members of the FCC are appointed by the president, with the approval of the Senate, to serve a seven-year term. (The Congress was considering a bill to reduce the term of FCC appointees to five years to give the Congress greater oversight of the commission. Final action on the proposal was pending as this chapter was written.) One member is selected by the president to be chairman. No more than a simple majority of the commission (three members) can be from the same political party.

Like all administrative agencies, the FCC is guided by broad congressional mandate—in this case the Federal Communications Act. The agency has the power to make rules and regulations within the broad framework of the act, and these regulations carry the force of the law. With regard to some matters the 1934 law is very specific. For example, Section 315—the equal opportunity provision (or equal time rule)—details regulations concerning the use of the broadcast media by political candidates. But in other areas Congress was eloquently vague. The mandate that broadcasters operate their stations in "the public interest, convenience or necessity" can mean almost anything a person wants it to mean. Consequently, the FCC developed a great many rules and policies in its effort to implement the public interest requirement.

Procedures

The commission employs a large staff and is divided into various divisions. The Mass Media Bureau, for example, deals exclusively with broadcasting and cable television problems. Other divisions work with telephone and telegraph problems and with safety and special services. Administrative law judges, who are assigned to the FCC by the Civil Service Commission, are independent of control and direction by the agency. The administrative law judges are responsible for conducting inquiries for the agency and have powers that are normally incident to conducting trials and hearings. Their decisions on matters such as controversies involving alleged violations of the equal opportunity rules and license revocation are final unless an exception is filed by any of the parties in a case. If there is an exception, the FCC commissioners themselves normally hear the dispute and render a decision. Here is an example of this procedure.

Imagine that a candidate for Congress, Ruth Right, accuses television station WKTL of violating the candidate access rule, section 312(a) of the communication act. (See pages 544–547 for a complete description of this rule.) This statute obligates broadcasters to make commercial time available to candidates for federal office during an election campaign. Ruth Right files a complaint with the FCC, which the Mass Media Bureau then investigates. Assume that after its investigation the Mass Media Bureau concludes that the station did violate the law. A complaint is then filed against WKTL-TV. The station can accept the complaint and punishment, or contest the matter. If that happens, an administrative law judge conducts a quasi-judicial hearing in the case, with the attorneys from the Mass Media Bureau arguing that the candidate access rule was violated, and representatives of the station arguing it was not. Let's imagine that the judge rules against the station in this case. This decision is final unless WKTL-TV files an exception to the ruling within thirty days. The matter then goes before the five members of the commission for a hearing. The Mass Media Bureau may also file an exception to a ruling against it by the administrative law judge and have a hearing before the FCC. If the FCC finally rules against the station, WKTL-TV can ask a United States court of appeals to review the decision.

An appellate court cannot substitute its own judgment for that of the Federal Communications Commission. The judges do not review the factual record to see whether they reach the same conclusion. FCC decisions, like the decisions of all administrative agencies, cannot be overruled except for quite specific reasons. The court can check to see whether the petitioner (the party who brings the appeal) has been afforded due process of law. It can investigate various other issues. Were there procedural irregularities? Did the FCC make an adequate finding of the facts? Did the commission state the reasons for its decision? Are the findings of the agency supported by the evidence in the record? Did the action by the FCC conform to its congressional mandate or did it go beyond the authority granted in the communications act?

While theoretically these are the only kinds of issues a court can examine, courts on occasion have gone beyond these limits to examine the factual questions. Some judges have been reluctant to refrain from examining the substantive issues involved and sometimes have even reached conclusions different from those reached by the FCC. The United States Supreme Court is available for the final appeal.

We have briefly reviewed how the FCC operates. Other aspects of FCC procedures are considered when licensing and programming controls are discussed in detail. Let us next take a quick look at FCC powers as invested by the Federal Communications Act of 1934.

Powers

An important aspect of the 1934 law is the affirmation of the philosophy in the 1927 measure, which established a privately owned broadcasting system operating over the public airwaves. This was a kind of compromise between establishing complete government control of broadcasting, as in most nations, and allowing the broadcasting industry to operate like most other industries, that is, with no government regulation.

The Congress approved the 1934 law under the authority of the commerce clause of the United States Constitution, which gives the federal legislature the exclusive power to regulate interstate commerce. This means that states, counties, and cities have no regulatory power over broadcasting stations. The federal government has *preempted* the law in this area. Under the

1927 act the question had arisen of whether this clause meant that the federal government lacked power to regulate broadcasters whose signals did not cross state lines, stations that were not engaged in interstate commerce. In 1933 in *FRC* v. *Nelson Brothers,* the United States Supreme Court ruled that state lines did not divide radio waves and that national regulation of broadcasting was not only appropriate but also essential to the efficient use of radio facilities.

While the Federal Communications Act branded telephone and telegraph companies common carriers (because they are monopolies, they have to be common carriers; that is, they must accept business from anyone who wishes to use their services), broadcasting stations were not so designated. Because broadcasters are not common carriers, they may refuse to do business with anyone or any company. Broadcasters do not have to make their facilities available to all members of the public. In addition the commission lacks the power to set rates for the sale of broadcasting time. Broadcasting is founded on the basis of free competition among holders of broadcast licenses.

The act makes it clear that while broadcasters may freely compete, they in no way assume ownership of a frequency or wavelength by virtue of using it for three years or for three hundred years. When a license is granted, the broadcaster must sign a form in which any claim to the perpetual use of a particular frequency is waived.

Technically the FCC lacks the power to censor broadcasters. Section 326 of the act states:

> Nothing in this act shall be understood or construed to give the commission the power of censorship over radio communications or signals transmitted by any radio station, or condition shall be promulgated or fixed by the commission which shall interfere with the right of free speech by means of radio communication.

No censorship, then. At least that is what Section 326 states. But that is not the way this section has been interpreted. The FCC has chosen to interpret Section 326 (with the approval of the courts) to mean that it may not censor specific programs, that is, forbid a broadcaster to carry programs on radical politicians or programs that picture members of a minority group in a derogatory fashion. However, at license renewal time the agency can consider the kind of programming the licensee broadcasts, and if the agency finds the programming objectionable, this fact can be held against the licensee. The United States Supreme Court adopted this understanding of Section 326 in its 1978 ruling in *FCC* v. *Pacifica Foundation* when the Court sustained the agency's censure of WBAI-FM for broadcasting George Carlin's monologue "Seven Dirty Words" (see pages 540–541). Most people would call this censorship. Section 326, then, has limited meaning and is of limited value to broadcasters.

The commission has broad-ranging powers in dealing with American broadcasters. Section 303 of the act outlines some of the basic responsibilities of the agency, which include classification of stations, determination of the power and technical facilities licensees must use, and specification of hours during the day and night stations can broadcast. The FCC also regulates the location of stations, the area each station can serve, the assignment of frequency or wavelength, and even the designation of call letters. There are not many things that broadcasters can do without first seeking the approval or consent of the Federal Communications Commission.

The key powers held by the FCC, however, focus on licensing and renewal of licenses and the authority to regulate programming and program content. It is toward these powers that primary consideration is directed in the remainder of this chapter.

Licensing

Issuing and renewing broadcast licenses are perhaps the most important functions of the FCC. These functions are very important to broadcasters as well, for without a license there can be no broadcasting. Virtually everything the broadcaster does is tied in some way to having the license renewed. In addition to getting a license for a new station, the broadcaster must also seek FCC approval for most operational changes, such as increasing power, changing the antenna height or location, selling the station, transferring ownership, and so forth. Broadcasting licenses are granted to radio stations for seven years; a license to operate a television station lasts only five years.

The **licensing process** is very complex and loaded with small but important details. An applicant for a new broadcast license must complete an incredible amount of paperwork in order to be considered by the FCC. A person who is seeking a new broadcast license must first obtain a construction permit, permission to start building the station. Obtaining this permit is actually the biggest hurdle. If the permit is granted, if construction of the station conforms to technical requirements, and if the work is completed within the time specified in the permit, the license is routinely issued.

What kinds of qualifications must the prospective licensee meet? The applicant must be a United States citizen, must be capable of building and operating the station for one year without taking in any revenue, and must possess (or be able to hire people who possess) the technical competence to construct and operate a broadcasting station. The applicant must also be honest and open in dealing with the commission and must have generally good character. The applicant must meet the qualifications under the multiple-ownership rules. No individual may own more than twelve television stations (fourteen if two are fifty percent minority owned or UHF stations), provided the total number of stations can reach no more than twenty-five percent of United States households. Similarly, no one may own more than twelve AM and twelve FM radio stations. Again, fourteen of each kind of station may be owned if two of the stations have fifty percent minority ownership. This is an effort by the FCC to increase minority ownership of broadcasting properties.

There are additional rules that limit ownership of multiple broadcasting properties and newspapers and broadcasting stations within a city or market area (these regulations are discussed in more detail in chapter 12). The applicant has to endeavor to ascertain the needs and interests of the people in the community to be served by the station and then prepare a programming scheme that will serve those needs and interests. If the applicant shows the commission that he or she is in compliance with these requirements and if there is no competing applicant or community protest against granting the permit, the permit to construct the station will be granted. The license then follows when construction is completed.

Competing Applicants

What happens when more than one person wants the same broadcast license? The government must decide who shall get it. The qualifications of both candidates are studied (a list of the kinds of criteria used by the FCC is given on page 532) and the most deserving gets the license. In the spring of 1989 the FCC proposed that a random lottery be used to select license holders when multiple applicants sought the same new broadcast license. This would replace the existing competitive process, which FCC members described as costly and time consuming. Under the proposal all applicants for the license would be screened to ensure they are qualified. Any or all applicants could be challenged by community groups or other interested parties. The process would give extra weight to minority applicants, and to those applicants whose selection would enhance the diversity of ownership of broadcast properties. But in the end, all things being equal, the selection of the licensee would be made on the basis of chance. The FCC had not yet decided to adopt this plan when this chapter was prepared.

An applicant for a new license might also be challenged by someone who already holds a broadcast license in the same area and believes that the local market cannot absorb another broadcasting station. The existing license holder can argue in one of two ways to try to convince the FCC not to grant the new license:

1. The addition of another broadcast signal will damage the quality of the owner's existing broadcast signal.
2. The addition of a new station will cause economic harm to the owner of the existing station. There is not enough advertising revenue in the community to support an additional station without harming the existing station.

The FCC can accept the second argument only if the station operator can show that the reduced revenues will *adversely affect program service.* Demonstrating only a potential loss in profits is not sufficient. The United States Court of Appeals for the District of Columbia noted in 1958 that "to license two stations where there is revenue for only one may result in no good service at all" (*Carroll Broadcasting Co.* v. *FCC,* 1958).

Renewal of Licenses   Broadcast licenses are granted for limited periods of time. Television stations are licensed for five years; radio stations are licensed for seven years. These broadcast licenses must be renewed by the FCC before the broadcaster can continue to operate. The FCC recently established and the federal courts have affirmed a simplified renewal procedure that drastically reduced the documentation required by the commission in routine renewal cases.

To gain renewal of a license, the broadcaster must provide the FCC with data about the broadcast operation. This points out an important fact about renewal: the FCC does not conduct an independent investigation of the licensee. Rather, the broadcaster (and sometimes other interested parties) provides the commission with nearly all material relevant to the renewal. The data provided to the FCC focus upon technical matters, business matters, and programming matters. If the FCC is not satisfied with what it sees, it can schedule a formal hearing on the renewal application. A formal hearing is prerequisite to both nonrenewal and revocation of a license before expiration.

If a problem does arise during renewal, it often takes years for the FCC to resolve the matter. In 1975, for example, the FCC voted to strip the licenses from all the public television stations in Alabama because they had discriminated against blacks in the 1960s. By 1975, when the FCC took its action, these public broadcasting stations had solved the problems of the 1960s, served the minority community with high-quality programming, and were considered model broadcasting operations with regard to the employment of minority persons. In 1976 the FCC voted to deny renewal to station WHBI in Newark, New Jersey, for failing to adequately supervise its programming. The action had started seven years earlier in 1969 when the station sought renewal of its license (*Cosmopolitan Broadcasting Corp.*, 1976).

The commission may refuse to renew a broadcast license if the licensee has violated any important provision of the Federal Communications Act or FCC rules. Stations that broadcast fraudulent advertising have been denied the renewal of their licenses (*May Seed and Nursery Co.*, 1936). The renewal of a license for a station that was used solely to promote the causes of its owner was denied (*Young People's Association for the Propagation of the Gospel*, 1938). If a station does not adequately supervise the programming it carries, its license may not be renewed (*Cosmopolitan Broadcasting Corp.*, 1976). Federal courts have ruled that denial of a license renewal does not violate the First Amendment. Acknowledging that a First Amendment issue might arise when a licensee is stripped of the power to broadcast, the United States Court of Appeals for the District of Columbia nevertheless ruled more than a half-century ago (*Trinity Methodist Church, South v. FRC*, 1932):

> This does not mean that the government, through agencies established by Congress, may not refuse a renewal of license to one who has abused it to broadcast defamatory or untrue matter. In that case there is not a denial of freedom of speech, but merely the application of the regulatory power of Congress in a field within the scope of its legislative authority.

The previous year another United States court of appeals judge had ruled that the commission had a perfect right to look to past programming practices of a renewal applicant to determine whether the license should be renewed. Invoking the biblical injunction "by their fruits ye shall know them," the court affirmed that past programming is a central issue in consideration of service in the public interest (*KFKB Broadcasting Association* v. *FRC*, 1931).

When a license renewal is denied, the broadcaster can appeal the FCC ruling to a United States court of appeals, and sometimes the court will reverse the decision by the agency. In one of the most widely publicized license renewal disputes of recent times, the United States Court of Appeals for the District of Columbia partially overturned a commission ruling that stripped RKO General, one of the nation's largest broadcasting chains, of television licenses in New York, Boston, and Los Angeles. The FCC had ruled in 1980 that the broadcaster and its parent company, General Tire and Rubber Company, had engaged in "extensive and serious" misconduct and could no longer be trusted as broadcasters. The agency upheld several charges that had been first levied against RKO General in 1974. The commission ruled that the renewal of licenses for stations WOR-TV in New York and KHJ-TV in Los Angeles were conditioned on the outcome of a hearing that was held to determine whether the license for WNAC-TV in Boston should be renewed. At the conclusion of the hearings on WNAC-TV, the FCC found misconduct in four areas and refused to renew any of the valuable licenses. RKO General appealed this decision. The court of appeals ruled that three of the four reasons given by the FCC for denial of the license renewal applications were invalid. The fourth reason—that RKO General had failed to be candid with the FCC during the Boston hearing about problems its parent company (General Tire) was having with the Securities and Exchange Commission—was sufficient to deny the renewal of the license for WNAC-TV, but not the television licenses for WOR and KHJ (*RKO* v. *FCC,* 1981). RKO General remained unsatisfied and sought to win back its Boston license through an appeal to the United States Supreme Court. But the High Court declined to hear the case. The FCC action against RKO General both angered and frightened radio and television station owners and spurred the broadcast industry in its efforts to win deregulation. Litigation in this case was still pending in early 1989, another example of the snail-like pace of the regulatory process.

Persons who seek to gain a new television license or renew an old one must in some manner consider the needs of the listeners and viewers in the community and show the FCC how they are being responsive to these needs. In the past the agency required that a broadcaster use formal ascertainment methods, which were quite specific and required the broadcaster to do a full study of the community and interview scores of community leaders and others. The FCC has dropped the formal ascertainment requirement for both radio and television stations.

The renewal of most broadcast licenses is a routine matter. There are instances, however, where members of the community ask the commission to deny the renewal of a broadcast license or another individual seeks to gain control of the license and operate a broadcasting station.

Public challenges to the renewal of a license are a relatively modern phenomena and today are quite rare. It wasn't until 1966 that citizens were even permitted to take part in the renewal process and, then, only after a United States court of appeals ordered the FCC to change its policies. A group of persons from Mississippi were blocked by the FCC in their attempt to stop the renewal of a television license for a station in Jackson, Mississippi, that citizens accused of racist policies. The FCC said the group lacked "standing" to take part in the hearing. "Standing" is a legal word that means a direct and substantial interest in the outcome of the hearing. Judge Warren Burger (who became the nation's chief justice) wrote in *Office of Communication, United Church of Christ* v. *FCC* (1966) that the action of the FCC:

> . . . denies standing to spokesmen for the listeners, who are often most directly concerned with and intimately affected by the performance of the licensee. . . . The theory that the commission can always effectively represent the listener interests in a renewal proceeding without the aid and participation of legitimate listener representatives . . . is one of the assumptions we collectively try to work with so long as they are reasonable and adequate. When it becomes clear, as it does to us now, that it is no longer a valid assumption which stands up under the realities of actual experience, neither we nor the commission can continue to rely upon it.

Recent FCC rulings have made it far more difficult for a citizen to challenge the renewal of a license. Because a station no longer is forced to keep many records that were at one time routine, it is often hard for a citizens' group to document its charges against the broadcaster. More importantly, however, the FCC has substantially lowered performance standards for radio and television stations. Stations no longer must program for children on a regular basis or broadcast nonentertainment programming, for example. This has sharply reduced the number of issues that a citizens' group might raise in challenging the renewal of the license.

More commonly the challenge to the licensee comes from another broadcaster who seeks the license for himself or herself. Since only one person can broadcast on the same frequency in the same community at the same time, the FCC must choose which of these two individuals should have the right to use the broadcast license.

Under the current law the FCC must hold what is called a **comparative license hearing** whenever there are two or more applicants for the same license. Broadcasters consider this an onerous rule and are seeking to have it changed. Several bills have been introduced in Congress in recent years that could forbid the FCC to consider the application of another person for a license unless the agency first denies renewal for the current license holder. And the FCC could only deny renewal of the license if it found that the actions of the broadcaster had demonstrated a serious disregard for the provisions of the Federal Communications Act and other FCC rules. This would effectively kill comparative license renewals—a result the industry wants. But Congress has indicated it is reluctant to even consider such a measure unless the broadcasting industry is willing to accept the reenactment of many FCC regulations that imposed important public service responsibilities upon the broadcaster, regulations that have been abandoned over the past decade (see H.R. 1140, 100th Congress). The industry seems unwilling to accept such regulations and a kind of stalemate has developed. Lobbying by the broadcast industry continues, however.

At the present time broadcasters must face the comparative renewal hearing. In the hearing the FCC attempts to determine which of the two license applicants will best serve the public interest. In 1965 the FCC outlined a list of seven items it said it would consider in looking at the applications from competing applicants:

1. Diversification of control of the media: Persons holding existing media (like a newspaper or a second broadcasting station) in the area or having significant media holdings elsewhere will not be considered as favorably as those without or with fewer media holdings.

2. Full-time participation in station operation by the owners: The FCC will favor working owners over absentee owners.

3. Proposed program service: What does the applicant propose to do with the frequency? Supposedly, applicants who plan to devote more time to programs on public affairs and education and information will be favored over those who plan to program heavily with entertainment.

4. The past broadcast record of the current license holder, as well as the record of other broadcasters who seek the license: If the past record is average, it is disregarded. If it is exceptional, with unusual attention to public needs and interests, or if it is especially poor with regard to serving the public interest, the past record then becomes a factor.

5. Efficient use of the frequency: This is a technical question and has to do with judicious use of the spectrum.

6. Character of applicant: Does the applicant have a record free of criminal prosecution? Is the applicant considered honest and trustworthy? and so forth.

7. Other factors: The report did not outline these additional factors.

Theoretically, based on these criteria, the best applicant in a comparative broadcast license hearing will be given the license. But theory does not always rule in such hearings, and the actions of the FCC with regard to competing applicants have often been erratic during the past two decades. It sounds quite simple to say that the FCC should score each applicant on seven criteria and announce a winner. But is it fair to compare the real programming records of an existing broadcaster with the promises of a challenger? Is it not possible that an individual who holds several broadcast properties might be better qualified—by virtue of this experience—to operate another station than someone without other broadcast holdings? Why should applicants' activities outside the broadcast industry be used against them in a comparative hearing? All of these questions, and many more we could list, raise difficult issues. And taking away a broadcast license is not a simple matter. The license holder has millions of dollars tied up in property and equipment that would be unusable without the license. Rulings by the FCC in comparative hearings reflect the problems inherent in these proceedings. And time and again the federal courts have overturned FCC decisions, adding to the confusion in this area. A ruling regarding a Florida broadcasting station is a good case in point.

Cowles Communication, Inc., held the license for a Daytona Beach television station, WESH-TV. In 1969 Cowles was challenged when it sought renewal of that license by a group entitled Central Florida Enterprises, Inc. Despite findings that the Cowles company had violated an FCC rule by moving a production studio without first getting permission, that some principals in the Cowles organization had pleaded no contest to charges of mail fraud for a *Look* magazine subscription scheme, and that Central Florida was rated more highly on the diversification and integration of ownership and management criteria, the FCC returned the license to Cowles after the comparative hearings. The commission concluded that Cowles had provided substantial service in the past, which should provide the owners with a "renewal expectancy." In 1978, nine years after the renewal application was filed, the United States Court of Appeals for the District of Columbia called the decision unreasonable and overturned it. The court said it was simply unfair to place so much weight upon past performance when the challenger was superior on other criteria (*Central Florida Enterprises, Inc.* v. *FCC*, 1978). "The fly in the analysis is that the commission judges incumbents largely on the basis of their broadcast records," wrote Judge Wilkey, "to which there will be nothing comparable on the side of the challenger in any case." Four months later in an unusual statement, Judge Wilkey tried to clarify his earlier ruling in denying the FCC's petition to rehear the case:

> Our principal reason [for setting aside the renewal] . . . was that the commission's manner of balancing its findings was wholly unintelligible, based as it was said, on "administrative feel." Admittedly, licensing in the public interest entails a good many discretionary choices, but even if some of them rest inescapably on agency intuition . . . , we may at least insist that they do not contradict whatever rules for choosing do exist.

Wilkey added, however, that an incumbent broadcaster could be given an advantage in a comparative renewal hearing for meritorious service. The matter was remanded to the FCC for further action and again, the agency voted in favor of Cowles on the basis of the station's past service, indicating that in the interests of industry stability, a renewal expectancy is necesssary where meritorious service has been provided. The ruling was again appealed, but this time the court upheld the commission's action and said it approved of the FCC policy that renewal expectancy is a factor to be weighed with all other factors and that the better the past record, the greater the renewal expectancy weight (*Cowles Florida Enterprises, Inc. v. FCC,* 1982).

The prospect of a renewal challenge certainly causes apprehension among broadcasters, probably far beyond what it should. On only two occasions has the FCC ever taken away a broadcaster's license during a comparative renewal hearing.

SUMMARY

The five-member Federal Communications Commission has been established by law to regulate the broadcasting industry. The agency has the responsibility to supervise all over-the-air broadcasting as well as any other electronic communication that has an impact upon over-the-air communications. While the FCC is forbidden by law from censoring the content of broadcast programming, the agency nevertheless has considerable control over what is broadcast by radio and television. By licensing and relicensing broadcasting stations, the FCC can ensure that broadcasters meet certain standards, including programming standards.

Television stations are licensed for five years; radio stations are licensed for seven years. To gain a license to broadcast, an applicant must meet several important criteria that have been established by the Congress and by the FCC. When two or more persons seek the same license, the FCC must decide which applicant would best serve the public interest.

When a licensee seeks to renew a broadcast license, other interested persons may challenge the license holder. A citizen watchdog group may ask the FCC to deny the renewal of a license in order to force the broadcaster to change what group members believe to be onerous policies. Other persons who seek to use the broadcast license may also challenge the license holder at renewal time. Under current law the FCC must hold what is called a comparative hearing when such a challenge is made. Congress, however, is considering changing the law to protect license holders. Under a proposed new law a hearing would be needed only if the record of the current license holder contains serious deficiencies.

REGULATION OF PROGRAM CONTENT

The regulation of program content is not directly tied to license renewal, but the failure of a broadcaster to observe FCC rules regarding programming can certainly be considered at renewal time. Despite the rule against censorship in the Federal Communications Act (see page 526), the commission has extensive control over a wide range of programming matters. Content controls range from specific federal statutes (the laws that prohibit the broadcast of obscenity) to rather vague commission guidelines (such as the policy statement regarding broadcasters' responsibility for phonograph records played over the air). Many programming rules are contained in the Federal Communications Act; others have been generated by the FCC under the agency mandate to regulate broadcasting in the public interest, convenience, and necessity.

The FCC has a wide range of sanctions with which to enforce these rules. These include, in order of magnitude, the following:

1. A letter of reprimand that is put in a licensee's file and may be material at renewal time
2. Cease and desist order, which is rarely issued but can be used to stop a broadcaster from doing something the commission does not believe should be done
3. Forfeiture or fine, which can range up to twenty thousand dollars for a serious violation (the FCC has asked the Congress to give it the authority to raise the limits on forfeitures to one million dollars for serious violations)
4. Short-term renewal, from six months to two years, while the FCC studies the broadcaster's record to determine whether the license should be renewed at all
5. Nonrenewal or revocation of the license, the nuclear bomb of broadcast regulation (rarely used as a sanction)

Sometimes the commission will simply write a letter to a broadcaster inquiring about a programming practice. This letter alerts station management that the FCC is aware of the practice or even concerned about the practice. Often the letter of inquiry results in the station changing the programming practice. Some people call this "regulation by raised eyebrow."

Broadcasters have many programming responsibilities that are supervised by the FCC. In the broadest sense the radio or television station owner must carry programming that serves the needs of the community as they have been determined by the station. There was a time when the FCC required each and every broadcaster to carry a wide variety of programming: religious, educational, agricultural, news, sports, weather, and many other kinds. At renewal time a checklist was prepared to be certain the broadcaster fulfilled the station's responsibilities in all these areas. This is not done any longer, but a broadcaster is still expected to meet these kinds of needs if they exist in the community.

In a narrower sense, there are many simple little program rules that have been promulgated by both the Congress and the commission. Stations, for example, are required to identify themselves periodically. Broadcasters must announce when the station or program receives a gratuity in return for an advertising plug on the air. A station may not knowingly broadcast fraudulent advertisements. It is illegal for a station to broadcast a lottery (a lottery is a contest in which a person trades something of value for the chance to win a prize). The license for station WWBZ in Vineland, New Jersey, was not renewed in 1955 at least partially because it had broadcast information on lotteries—in this case horse races. Giving the race results from the local track as a part of the evening news is one thing, but broadcasting up-to-the-minute race results from racetracks around the country is something else altogether. At least the FCC thought so and ruled that such information is useful primarily to persons involved in illegal gambling (in re *Community Broadcasting Service, Inc.,* WWBZ, 1955). The broadcast or telecast of information about state lotteries, however, including live coverage of prize drawings, is considered news coverage.

Contrary to popular belief, the government has never had general rules regarding the number or length of commercials that may be broadcast on radio or television. For many years the industry trade association, the National Association of Broadcasters (NAB), had a "Code of Good Practices" and members who followed the code voluntarily limited the number of commercial minutes each hour. The code, which had many facets, was abandoned by the NAB in the early eighties after the United States Justice Department brought an anti-trust action against the association (see page 600). The one exception to the commission's no-limit on commercials policy was for programming aimed at children. Until 1984 the agency limited the number of commercial minutes during an hour of children's programming to 9.5 minutes on weekends and 12 minutes on weekdays. In addition, television stations had to broadcast a minimum amount of educational and informational programming as a requirement for license renewal. But in 1984 these rules were abandoned. In a terse two-sentence statement, the FCC attempted to justify its decision:

> Elimination of the policy [on children's programming] is consistent with the commission's general deemphasis regarding quantitative guidelines. . . . Moreover, the commission has consistently noted the importance of advertising as a support mechanism for the presentation of children's programming.

The result of this and other FCC action on children's television was immediate. Many stations increased the number of commercial minutes in their children's programming. More importantly, the FCC action paved the way for what are really program-length commercials, cartoon shows built around popular toys like "G.I. Joe" and "Smurfs." In many instances toy companies actually subsidized the production of these programs from their promotion budgets and offered them to television station at rates far below what the station would have to pay for a nontoy-oriented program. Some broadcasters even partook in revenue sharing with the toy companies, earning a percentage of the profits from the toys. In 1987 Peggy Charren, the head of Action for Children's Television, (ACT) estimated that there were seventy-five such programs on the air.

ACT went to court and won a technical victory. The United States Court of Appeals for the District of Columbia ruled that the FCC had failed to jusify changing its policies regarding children's television. "Far be it from us to demand long-winded, tiresome explanations. But the commission's barebones incantations of two abbreviated rationales cannot do service as the requisite 'reasoned basis' for altering its long-established policy," the court ruled. The court noted that for the past fifteen years the FCC had justified its policy regarding television for children on the assumption that the marketplace doesn't work when children are in the audience. Now, the agency embraces a conclusion that the marketplace did work. This conclusion has to be more fully explained, the court ruled (*Action for Children's Television* v. *FCC,* 1987).

While the FCC was rethinking its assumptions regarding children's television, Congress decided to act. In 1988 a bill was passed that limited commercial minutes during an hour of children's programming to 10.5 on weekends and 12 on weekdays. In addition, the measure reimposed minimum requirements upon the broadcaster to carry educational and informational programming for children. The measure passed in the House on a vote of 328 to 78, and was approved on a voice vote in the Senate. (On a voice vote, a single member of the Senate can block approval.) President Reagan, however, used a pocket veto to kill the measure. Reagan failed to sign the bill within the ten days required by law, after Congress had adjourned its final session. Similar legislation was reintroduced in the Congress in 1989. No action had been taken on the matter when this chapter was prepared. This discussion demonstrates graphically, however, how seemingly simple changes—like lifting the cap on commercial minutes—can result in fundamental programming changes.

Can the FCC control a broadcast station's format as part of its regulation of programming content? For many years the FCC resisted efforts by citizens' groups to force the agency to get involved when a radio station dropped one kind of music format, classical, for example, and adopted another format, let us say rock. But listeners went to federal court, and the FCC was ordered in 1970 to *review* a format change by a station when the abandonment of a unique format produced community protests (*Citizens Committee to Preserve the Voice of the Arts in Atlanta* v. *FCC,* 1970). The United States Court of Appeals for the District of Columbia went one step further in 1974 and ordered the FCC to *hold a hearing* whenever a unique format was being abandoned by a radio station and persons in the community objected (*Citizens' Committee to Save WEFM* v. *FCC,* 1974). A unique format would be one that no other station in the market used. The loss of this format would deny the citizens in the community access to a particular kind of music or programming. Normally it has been supporters of classical music who have protested when a local station drops the classical format. But in Seattle in 1981 New Wave rock fans mounted a protest when the community's only (at that time) New Wave music station abandoned that format. Despite the earlier court rulings, the FCC continued to argue through the late seventies that the marketplace should determine the broadcaster's format; the government should not get involved. And in 1981 the Supreme Court of the United States supported the agency and overturned a lower federal court decision calling for a hearing on a format change. Justice Byron White, writing for the seven-person majority, stated, "We decline to overturn the commission's policy statement which prefers reliance on market forces to its own attempt to oversee format changes at the behest of disaffected listeners." Justice White warned the agency, however, to be alert to the consequences of its policies and stand ready to change its rules if necessary to serve the public interest more fully (*FCC* v. *WNCN Listeners Guild,* 1981).

Obscene or Indecent
Material

The Federal Communications Commission has spent much of its time during the past eight years cloaked in the mantle of the First Amendment, abandoning rules that restricted broadcasters' programming practices. But there is one exception: the agency has materially attempted to tighten the screws that limit the broadcast of obscene or indecent material. Section 1464 of the United States Code gives the FCC the power to revoke any broadcast license if the licensee transmits obscene or indecent material over the airwaves. As noted previously in this book, having the power to ban obscenity and indecency is one thing; defining obscenity and indecency is another.

The Supreme Court has assisted the FCC in regulating obscenity by defining what is and is not legally obscene. And actually the broadcast of obscenity has never really been a serious problem for FCC regulators since radio and television stations just don't go that far. The matter of indecency is far different, however, since the courts have not been as helpful as we will see shortly.

Television, and to a large extent radio, have always been conservative media, trying to lure large audiences to their windows so advertisers can display their wares. The television industry itself has tended to set standards somewhere to the right of prudishness, fearful of offending even a small segment of the potential audience. In 1975 the three commercial networks—under the watchful eye of the FCC and with the cooperation of the NAB—instituted what was called "the family hour." Stations that subscribed to the NAB Code of Good Practices were told that the hours from seven to nine each evening were to be set aside for family viewing and that programs with sexual overtones and excessive violence were taboo in this period. The censorship undertaken by the networks was heavy-handed. The word *virgin* was cut from one program (*innocent* was substituted). Censors began to look anew at Cher's navel and a braless guest on the "Phyllis" show was redressed before filming began. Programs that had been broadcast in the eight P.M. time slot for several years were either moved or toned down to meet the new family-hour standards. But the rule was challenged by the creators of television programs.

Writers and directors in Hollywood, where most television programs are produced, went to court, and in 1976 federal Judge Warren J. Ferguson of the District Court for Southern California ruled that the "adoption of the family viewing policy by each of the three networks constituted a violation of the First Amendment." The judge ruled that the policy had been motivated by informal statements from the Federal Communications Commission, which threatened government action against the industry should not the family hour or something like it be adopted (*Writers Guild* v. *FCC*, 1976). The judge's conclusion is more than substantiated in Geoffrey Cowan's fascinating book *See No Evil*, the story of the genesis of the family hour.

A United States court of appeals later overturned the lower court ruling on the grounds that the federal district court had no jurisdiction in the case, that the Federal Communications Commission should have heard the issue (*Writers Guild* v. *ABC*, 1979). The networks, however, made no effort to reestablish the policy.

Law professor Harry Kalven noted years ago in the *Michigan Law Review* that while a regulation may not directly interfere with free speech, "in operation it may trigger a set of behavioral consequences which amount in effect to people censoring themselves in order to avoid trouble with the law." Or what people believe will be trouble with the law. Such is the case with the regulation of indecency in broadcasting. The family hour is a good example of this tendency.

Because of the general conservatism of the broadcasting industry, the FCC has had few problems with regard to indecent broadcasting. There are but a few recorded instances of FCC action during the past thirty years. In 1962 the commission refused to renew the license of radio station WDKD at least partially because a disc jockey at the station habitually told "off-color" or "indecent" jokes on the air (in re *Palmetto Broadcasting Co.*, 1962). A college radio station was fined one hundred dollars for broadcasting "indecent" four-letter words over the air in 1970 (in re *WUHY-FM, Eastern Educational Radio*, 1970). A two thousand dollar fine was levied against an Illinois radio station in 1973 for broadcasting a discussion between an announcer and a listener about oral sexual practices (*Sonderling Broadcasting Corp.*, 1973). The discussion stemmed from the station's call-in "topless radio" format. A federal court of appeals upheld the judgment two years later (*Illinois Citizens Committee for Broadcasting* v. *FCC*, 1975).

Until recently it has generally been the small radio station, often on the FM band, and a listener-supported operation, that has most often run afoul of the FCC regarding indecency. It was a broadcast on such a station that gave rise to the most important court ruling on the subject. In 1978, the Supreme Court of the United States upheld an FCC ruling that radio station WBAI in New York City had violated the federal law when it broadcast a recorded monologue by comedian George Carlin on the English language. The recording, which was played in midafternoon after the announcer warned listeners that it might be offensive to some, contained seven four-letter words that were used many times. The record was played as part of a program on society's attitude toward language. The FCC got one complaint and as a result took action against the station on the grounds that it had broadcast indecent language. The agency defined indecent language as "language that describes in terms patently offensive as measured by contemporary community standards for the broadcast medium, sexual or excretory activities and organs, at times of the day when there is a reasonable risk children may be in the audience." The FCC said the WBAI broadcast met this definition. The latter phrase, "when there is a reasonable risk children may be in the audience," meant that the agency believed it was permissible to broadcast adult programming during what it called a "safe harbor," from 10 P.M. to 6 A.M.

Pacifica Foundation, which owns and operates the station, challenged the ruling, and in March 1977 the United States Court of Appeals for the District of Columbia overturned the FCC action, ruling that the commission's order was overbroad and vague. Two years later, however, the Supreme Court reversed the court of appeals and sustained the FCC ruling. Justice John Paul Stevens wrote the opinion for the Court, noting that because of its unique characteristics, broadcasting has traditionally received the least First Amendment protection of all media. Stevens said broadcast was uniquely pervasive, that it can have an impact upon persons not only in public, but also in the privacy of their own home. Prior warning cannot completely protect the listener or viewer, he added. Also, "The ease with which children may obtain access to broadcast material . . . amply justifies special treatment of indecent broadcasting," Stevens wrote. The majority denied that the order was vague or overbroad. Stevens said that the ruling would deter only the broadcast of offensive references to excretory and sexual organs and activities. "While some of these references may be protected, they surely lie at the periphery of First Amendment concern," he said. The associate justice added that the Court's ruling did not involve Elizabethan comedy or even citizens band transmission. "We have not decided that an occasional expletive in either setting would justify any sanction . . . ," Stevens noted, adding that the FCC decision rested on a nuisance rationale—"putting the right thing in a wrong place." Stevens added, "Like a pig in a parlor" (*FCC* v. *Pacifica Foundation,* 1978).

While upholding the FCC, the Supreme Court ruling substantially narrowed the agencies definition of indecency. Broadcasters were forbidden to broadcast anything that contains the repeated use, for shock value, of words similar or identical to those used by Carlin at a time when children may be in the audience—presumably before ten P.M.

In 1978 few broadcasters saw this as a problem but things have changed dramatically in the broadcasting industry in the subsequent ten years. The tremendous popularity of cable television and videocassette recorders has seriously drained off the audience for over-the-air television. Not only are viewers finding new programming and movies to watch on their television sets, they are finding a range of explicit content not available on over-the-air television. Cable television is not governed by the same rules as those that govern over-the-air broadcasting, and viewers can rent movies that suit many different tastes. The competition in radio has become more intense as well, as FM stations with their stereo sound and crisper signal threaten to push listeners off the AM dial. So competition in both radio and television have heated up, so to speak. Shock radio and trash television have become symbols of our culture.

The FCC (and others in the conservative Reagan administration like the Meese Commission, see chapter 8) tried to close the door on some of this new sexually-explicit broadcasting. In 1987 the FCC came down on three broadcasting stations for carrying indecent programming. WYSP-FM in Philadelphia was cited for comments made by a morning drive-time disc "shock jockey" named Howard Stern. A student-run station at the University of Santa Barbara, KCSB-FM, was cited for playing a song entitled "Makin' Bacon" between ten and eleven P.M. one night. And KPFK-FM in Los Angeles, a Pacifica station and perennial FCC target, was hit for broadcasting a serious drama, "The Jerker," concerning AIDS in the gay community. It was aired after ten P.M. following a warning from the station to listeners.

In its decision against the three stations the FCC seemingly ignored the Supreme Court's language in *Pacifica* and reapplied the rather broad definition of indecency it first used in the Carlin case. Indecency was defined by the agency as "exposure of children to language that describes in terms patently offensive as measured by contemporary standards for the broadcast media, sexual or excretory activities and organs." Several months later the FCC announced it was narrowing the so-called safe harbor for adult material, previously from ten P.M. to six A.M., to midnight to six A.M. As if to add an exclamation point to its new standards, the commission for the first time ever in early 1988 fined a television station for airing "indecent material," an R-rated film called "Private Lessons" that was broadcast at eight P.M. The film is described in Leonard Maltin's *TV Movies and Video Guide* in this way: "Male adolescent from wealthy family finds sexual delight with the maid, unaware that she has other plans for him. Surprise box-office hit is pretty mild piece of sleaze. Written by humorist Dan Greenberg." (*Leonard Maltin's TV Movies and Video Guide,* 1989 edition. New York: New American Library, p. 840.) The station, KZKC in Kansas City, Missouri, was fined two thousand dollars, the maximum under the law.

After its policy changes, the commission was faced with significant criticism from both the political left and right. Conservatives like United States Senator Jesse Helms said they thought the safe harbor (midnight to six A.M.) concept was nonsense. "What kind of sense is it," Helms asked, to rule that something is indecent and then, "come the stroke of midnight, bong, bong, bong—it is OK?" More savage criticism came from moderates and liberals who saw the impact of the decision as reducing prime-time television programs to only what was fit for children.

Action for Children's Television and others filed a lawsuit against the FCC, challenging the new standards, and in 1988 the protestors won a partial victory. The court upheld the agency's definition for indecency. The FCC can surely prohibit indecent programming in the morning and afternoon, the court said. But the judges ruled that the FCC had no evidence upon which to base its postmidnight-only safe harbor. The FCC said it had rating data showing a substantial number of people aged twelve through seventeen in the audience in the late evening hours. The court called the findings "unsubstantial and more ritual than real." The fact that there are young people in the audience does not support a finding that there are young people watching indecent programming. The court also questioned the FCC's new definition of children, those twelve to seventeen. In the past the agency had indicated it had been concerned primarily with those under the age of twelve. The agency must reconsider its new policy regarding the safe harbor the court said. "The fact is," the court ruled, "the commission has no scientific body of information that conclusively establishes one time as more appropriate than another as the critical hour after which to permit broadcast of indecent speech—which unlike obscenity is still protected by the First Amendment." The court even suggested that the FCC should consider permitting the broadcast of adult programming in the evening hours, when children and their parents would likely be in the viewing audience. The parents can then assume the task of deciding whether or not to expose their children to such programs. It is not the FCC's function to supervise what children see and hear, the court said. The agency may only intervene to assist parents in exercising control when they, the parents, see fit (*Action for Children's Television* v. *FCC,* 1988). While the courts were pondering this questions, Congress was acting. Senator Helms proposed that there should be no safe haven for broadcasting indecency; not before midnight, not after midnight, not ever. Helms attached his proposal as an amendment to an approporations bill that won congressional support in mid-1988. In December 1988 the FCC, bowing to the will of the legislature, totally banned the broadcast of indecent programming. Most observers, including at least one FCC commissioner, Patricia Diaz Dennis, said they believed the total ban was unconstitutional. A court challenge to the total ban was pending in the spring of 1989.

Meanwhile, the discussion continues. Many people strongly believe that television and radio should not contain sexually-explicit programming. Others disagree, noting that while some parents might believe this is true, others do not, and parents should not be denied the opportunity of making a choice for themselves. As the level of adult-oriented material creeps up each year and as commercial television fights to keep its adult audience, this battle is likely to be joined again and again.

The courts have made it clear that they will not tolerate local or state interference with the broadcast of indecency on cable television. Utah, for example, adopted a criminal statute in 1981 to punish any person who distributed by wire or cable any pornographic or indecent material to subscribers.

A United States district court ruled that such a statute could only prohibit the distribution of hard-core pornography as defined in *Miller* v. *California* (see pages 396–397). The Utah statute was too broad because it defined indecent material to include nudity, which has not been ruled to be legally obscene by the Supreme Court. The state argued it sought to protect children from such adult fare. The court urged the legislators to read the rulings in *Butler* v. *Michigan* (see page 394) and *Erznoznik* v. *City of Jacksonville* (page 404) where the Supreme Court said that a state could not regulate materials for adults on the basis of what is fit for children. The judge added (*Home Box Office* v. *Wilkinson,* 1982):

> That's one of the nice things about TV—not just cable TV, but also regular broadcast channels that are allocated, licensed and regulated by the government. There is no law that says you have to watch. There is no law that says you have to purchase a television set. There is no law that says you have to subscribe to a cable TV service any more than you have to subscribe to the *Salt Lake Tribune.*

Subsequent rulings have reinforced the decision by the court (see *Cruz* v. *Fere,* 1983, *Community Television* v. *Wilkinson,* 1985 and *Jones* v. *Wilkinson,* 1986). The Cable Communications Policy Act of 1984 clearly states that all levels of government—federal, state and local—can prohibit, limit, and penalize the exhibition of obscene programming on a cable system. (However, a cable operator cannot be held liable for the obscene programming appearing on the public access channels.) But the law really did not resolve the matter of whether government may ban the broadcast of indecent programming on cable. Michael Myerson, writing in a recent edition of the *Georgia Law Review,* suggests that the act is open-ended on the question of indecency. Congress did not want to go beyond the Supreme Court in permitting indecent cable programming, yet it recognized that the federal courts have ruled that cable is different from over-the-air television and permitted indecent material to be cablecast. But if the Supreme Court were to rule that cable television could be treated like broadcast television for the regulation of indecency, the act will not preempt local laws, Myerson wrote.

SUMMARY

The FCC has broad control over the content of broadcast programming. To enforce this control the agency has a wide variety of sanctions, which include letters of reprimand, fine or forfeiture, and nonrenewal or revocation of broadcast licenses. Content regulations involve a wide range of broadcast programming. In the broadest sense the broadcaster must program to meet the needs of the community. But programming rules also involve simple regulations, such as the requirement to present station identification at various times of the broadcast day.

The FCC has chosen not to attempt to control the selection of format by a broadcaster. Citizens' groups have urged the FCC to hold hearings when a radio station drops one program format and adopts a new one. In the early seventies federal courts supported these citizen protests, but in 1981 the United States Supreme Court ruled that the government need not get involved when a broadcaster decides to switch from one format to another.

Federal law prohibits the broadcast of any obscene or indecent material. In 1979 the Supreme Court ruled that a radio or television station can be punished for broadcasting material that is not legally obscene, but is merely indecent. The court based its ruling on the fact that children might be present during the broadcast. In the late 1980s the FCC broadened its definition of indecent material but ruled that it was permissible to broadcast such content between midnight and six A.M. A federal court accepted the new definition but asked the FCC to justify its decision to allow such material only after midnight.

Several states have attempted to adopt laws that limit the transmission of indecent material, including adult R-rated films, over pay cable television. Federal courts have struck down these laws on the basis that only legally obscene material can be barred from such nonbroadcast television transmission.

REGULATION OF POLITICAL PROGRAMMING

The guarantees of freedom of speech and freedom of the press were added to the Constitution in large measure to protect the political debate in this nation from interference by the government. Yet the government is permitted to regulate some aspects of this kind of broadcasting. Opponents of such regulation argue that these regulations fly directly in the face of the First Amendment and are dangerous to the political process. Those who support such regulation argue that it is because political and public affairs broadcasting is so important that it must be regulated. The broadcaster doesn't take his/her public service responsibility seriously enough and must be prodded by the government; without regulation, broadcasters—who tend to be of a like mind—will favor one political adversary over another. Let's examine briefly the kind of regulation that exists.

Candidate Access Rule

Broadcasters cannot completely block candidates for federal office from buying airtime on the station to promote their candidacies because of the existence of the **candidate access rule.** Section 312 (a) (7) of the Federal Communications Act, adopted in 1971 by the Congress, states that a broadcast license can be revoked for willful and repeated failure "to allow reasonable access to or to permit the purchase of reasonable amounts of time for the use of a broadcasting station by a legally qualified candidate for federal elective office on behalf of his candidacy." This statute applies only to candidates for federal office: presidents and vice-presidents and United States senators and representatives. The FCC has asked the Congress to repeal this law in its effort to deregulate broadcasting.

Federal courts have provided two important interpretations of this statute. Both cases stemmed from the 1980 presidential election campaign. The Carter-Mondale presidential committee sought to buy thirty minutes of time on all three networks in early December 1979 for President Jimmy Carter to announce that he would be a candidate for reelection and to present a film outlining Carter's record as president. The request was made in October 1979. NBC refused. ABC said it could not reach a decision on the question. CBS offered two five-minute segments, one at 10:55 P.M. and one during the day. Privately, all three networks were fearful of breaking into their prime time entertainment schedules for a political broadcast. But publicly the broadcasters argued that the political campaign had not yet started; it was too early (the election was scheduled for November 1980) to begin to carry political programming.

The FCC ruled against the networks, the United States Court of Appeals for the District of Columbia ruled against the networks, and the Supreme Court of the United States ruled against the networks. The High Court ruled in its six-to-three decision that a broadcaster could not institute an across-the-board policy rejecting all requests from federal candidates for air time. Chief Justice Burger wrote that once a political campaign begins, a broadcaster must give reasonable and good faith attention to access requests from legally qualified candidates (*CBS* v. *FCC,* 1981):

> Such requests must be considered on an individualized basis, and broadcasters are required to tailor their responses to accommodate, as much as reasonably possible, a candidate's stated purpose in seeking air time. In responding to access requests, however, broadcasters may also give weight to such factors as the amount of time previously sold to the candidate, the disruptive impact on regular programming, and the likelihood of requests for time by rival candidates under the equal opportunities provision of Section 315 (a). These considerations may not be invoked as pretexts for denying access; to justify a negative response, broadcasters must cite a realistic danger of substantial program disruption—perhaps caused by insufficient notice to allow adjustments in the schedule—or of an excessive number of equal time requests.

Burger added that broadcasters must explain their reasons for refusing air time or making limited counteroffers so the FCC can review these decisions if needed. Each of the networks had argued, however, that the 1980 presidential campaign had not really started. After all, the time period sought by Carter was eleven months prior to the election. In this case the networks should not be bound by Section 312, they asserted. The majority of the Supreme Court rejected this argument, noting the following evidence that the campaign had started:

1. Ten Republican candidates and two Democratic candidates had announced they were running for president.
2. The selection of delegates to the national political conventions had started in many states.
3. Many candidates were making speeches in an effort to raise money.
4. The Iowa caucuses to select convention delegates were scheduled for January, one month after the broadcast time sought by Carter.
5. Newspapers had been covering the national political campaign for at least two months.

Burger rejected the notion that Section 312 created a right of access to the media. None is created by this decision, he added. But a licensed broadcaster is "granted the free and exclusive use of a limited and valuable part of the public domain; when he accepts that franchise it is burdened by enforceable public obligations" (*CBS* v. *FCC,* 1981).

The Supreme Court's ruling means that a broadcaster cannot adopt an across-the-board policy of rejecting all requests for air time. Each request must be considered individually, and can be rejected only if the broadcaster can demonstrate good cause.

Section 312 implies that the candidate can seek to buy time on a station or ask for free time. Does this mean a broadcast station must *give* a candidate for federal office free time if fulfilling such a request would not interfere substantially with the broadcast schedule or would not prompt requests for equal time from other candidates? The United States Court of Appeals for the District of Columbia answered no when that question was asked. On March 14, 1980, President Carter delivered a thirty-minute speech on the economic condition of the nation. The speech was carried on all three networks. This was four days before the presidential primary in Illinois. Senator Ted Kennedy, who was also seeking the Democratic nomination for president, requested that the networks *give* him thirty minutes of air time to respond to the president's speech. The networks said they would sell Kennedy the time, but would not give it to him. Kennedy argued that they were obliged to provide him thirty minutes at no cost because of Section 312. The court of appeals supported the FCC's denial of Kennedy's request. The law does not confer upon a candidate the privilege of using a broadcaster's facilities without charge. Broadcasters may meet the demands of Section 312 by either giving the candidate free time or making time available for purchase, the court said. The networks had already given Kennedy's campaign considerable free time through its news coverage of the candidate (*Kennedy for President Committee* v. *FCC,* 1980).

Supporters of Section 312 see it as a means to permit candidates for federal office to use the important broadcast communication channels in this nation to talk to prospective voters. Opponents say it is government interference in broadcasters' operation of their business, and it can cause severe financial hardship if programming schedules are disrupted to facilitate political broadcasts.

When Congress adopted Section 312 in 1971, it also specified the highest rates that a broadcaster can charge a candidate for federal office for using station facilities. The general rule is: Forty-five days before a primary election and sixty days before a general election, the charge to a candidate cannot exceed the lowest rate the station charges its local advertisers for that particular time slot. At other times the rate must be "comparable" to what the station charges other advertisers. There are considerable details in these rules that are important but are too involved to outline here. Students who intend to enter broadcast sales should closely study Section 312 of 47 *United States Code*.

One final note. Section 312 applies only to candidates for federal office. However, a broadcast station has an obligation to serve the public interest. The FCC could surely find that a broadcaster who consistently refuses to provide access to candidates for state or local office was not properly serving the public interest.

Equal Opportunity Rule

Section 315 contains the equal opportunities or **equal time rule.** It has been a part of the Federal Communications Act since the law was passed in 1934. It was significantly changed by the Congress in 1959. Section 315 is not really difficult to understand. If a broadcasting station permits one legally qualified candidate for public office to use its facilities, it must afford equal opportunity to all other such legally qualified candidates for the same office. Section 315 also specifically prohibits the station from censoring material in broadcasts by political candidates. The FCC fined a Stamford, Connecticut, radio station ten thousand dollars for censoring the paid political broadcasts of two mayoral candidates (see *Kuczo* v. *Western Connecticut Broadcasting,* 1977).

What does equal opportunity mean? It means equal time, equal facilities, and comparable costs. If John Smith buys one-half hour of television time on station WKTL to campaign for the office of mayor, other legally qualified candidates for that office must be allowed to purchase one-half hour of time as well. If Smith is able to use the station's equipment to prerecord his talk, other candidates must have the same opportunity. If the station charges Smith one hundred dollars for the one-half hour of time, the station must charge his opponents one hundred dollars.

The station does not have to solicit appearances by the other candidates; it merely must give them the opportunity to use the facilities if they request such use within one week of Smith's appearance. Finally, Section 315 clearly states that broadcasters do not have to allow any political candidates the use of their facilities if they so choose. However, if they allow one candidate to use the facilities, they must allow the same use to all seeking the same office. Of course the provisions of Section 312 of the Federal Communications Act are also relevant to use of a station's facilities by a candidate.

Use of the Airwaves
Section 315 states that "use" by one candidate of a broadcast facility entitles all opponents to "use" the facility as well. A key question then is, What does the word *use* mean? What constitutes an appearance by a candidate in the eyes of the law? It is easiest to begin by listing those things that do not constitute a use:

1. The appearance by a candidate in a bona fide or legitimate newscast does not constitute use of the facility in the eyes of the law. Section 315 will not be triggered. The FCC has ruled that appearances by political candidates on ABC's "Good Morning America," NBC's "Today" and the CBS's "This Morning" are exempt from provisions of Section 315. The agency considers all three programs bona fide newscasts. However, if the newscaster or reporter who reads the news is a candidate for public office, this exemption does not apply to that candidacy. In an unusual case TV reporter William Branch, a general assignment reporter for KVOR-TV in Sacramento, announced he was a candidate for town council in a nearby community. The station told him he would have to take an unpaid leave of absence if he chose to run for office because it could not afford to give his opponent free time equal to the time Branch appeared in the newscasts. Branch sought help from the FCC, arguing that his appearances in a bona fide newscast would not trigger Section 315. The FCC disagreed and a United States court of appeals supported the regulatory agency. "When a broadcaster's employees are sent out to cover a news story involving other persons . . . the bona fide news event is the activity engaged in by those other persons, not the work done by the employees covering the event," the three-judge panel ruled. Branch argued that this ruling extinguished his right to hold public office. The court disagreed; the ruling simply says the station will have to provide equal time for opposing candidates if the reporter is a candidate (*Branch* v. *FCC,* 1987).

2. The appearance of a candidate in a bona fide news interview program does not constitute a use. The key words are *bona fide.* An appearance on "Meet the Press," which is a bona fide news interview show, is not use of a broadcasting facility. But an appearance on "Meet the Candidates," a public-affairs show created by a television station for the express purpose of interviewing candidates prior to an election is use because it is not a bona fide news interview show. The show was created especially for the election campaign by the station and is not broadcast when electioneering is not in progress.

3. The appearance of a candidate in the spot news coverage of a bona fide news event is not use. When candidate Smith is interviewed at the scene of a bad fire about the problems of arson in the city, this is not use in terms

of Section 315. Political conventions are considered bona fide news events; therefore an appearance by a candidate at the convention can be broadcast without invoking Section 315.

4. The appearance of a candidate in a news documentary is not a use if the appearance is incidental to the presentation of the subject of the program. Example: During the spring months of the 1968 political campaign, CBS broadcast a documentary on reform of the federal income tax laws. An interview with Senator Robert Kennedy, who was leading a fight in the United States Senate for tax reform, was included in the program. At that time Kennedy was a candidate for the presidency, but his appearance in the documentary did not activate the equal opportunity rule because the program was about tax laws. Kennedy's appearance was incidental to that subject. A news documentary about Kennedy would have been a different story and would have triggered the Section 315 sanction. In the documentary the network was merely talking to Kennedy about a national problem on which he was an expert.

Debates between political candidates are considered bona fide news events, and the broadcast of these events will not initiate use of Section 315. This is true even if the broadcaster sponsors the debate, according to a 1984 ruling by the FCC. Prior to this ruling an outside third party had to sponsor the debate before it was considered a news event. In both 1976 and 1980, for example, the League of Women Voters sponsored presidential debates that included only the candidates from the Democratic and Republican parties. Feminist Sonia Johnson, who ran for president with the Citizens Party in 1984, challenged this FCC policy after she was not permitted to take part in the nationally televised debates. She argued that exclusion from the debates effectively excluded her from winning the election, and denied voters who were sympathetic to her cause, but who were unacquainted with her, the opportunity to vote for her. A United States court of appeals disagreed, ruling that Johnson did not enjoy a right under any federal law to be included in the televised debates (*Johnson* v. *FCC,* 1987). In 1988 there was little pretense of outside sponsorship of the debates.

Press conferences held by political candidates are also normally considered bona fide news events and are exempt from the provisions of Section 315. A press conference held by President Jimmy Carter in February 1980, several months after he announced he was a candidate for reelection, was broadcast live by all the television networks. Carter's opponent for the Democratic nomination, Ted Kennedy, sought time from the television networks under the equal opportunity rule. The networks said no. The FCC agreed with the broadcasters; the press conference was a bona fide news event. The agency had ruled in 1975 that all press conferences featuring political candidates were exempt from Section 315 as news events. Kennedy appealed the ruling to the United

States Court of Appeals for the District of Columbia and lost. The court said that to determine whether the coverage of a news conference can be considered spot coverage of a bona fide news event three criteria must be examined:

1. Was the press conference broadcast live? Coverage of spot news should be live coverage.
2. Was there any evidence of favoritism on the part of the broadcaster? Did the station just carry Carter's press conferences and ignore his opponent's conferences?
3. Finally, did the broadcaster make a good-faith judgment that the news conference was a bona fide news event?

In this case the press conference was carried live, the networks had covered Kennedy press conferences, and it was obvious that a determination had been made by the broadcasters that this was an important news event (*Kennedy for President Committee* v. *FCC*, 1980).

With these exceptions, all other appearances by a candidate are considered use in the meaning of Section 315. A paid political broadcast, a spot announcement, and even a five-minute interview on the "Tonight Show" are all appearances that will invoke Section 315. Opposing candidates would have the right to ask for equal opportunity. During Ronald Reagan's campaigns for the presidency, stations had to refrain from showing his old movies and segments of "Death Valley Days" in which he appeared as the host (see *Adrian Weiss,* 1976). Pat Paulsen's quadrennial run for the White House forced television stations and networks to pull movies in which he appeared out of their libraries until the election was over. Once, Johnny Carson interviewed the mayor of Burbank, California, on his program in recognition of the fame that town had gained by being the butt of a joke on Rowan and Martin's "Laugh-In." But Carson's staff had not done their homework, for the mayor was in the midst of a campaign for reelection. The NBC affiliate in Los Angeles was forced to give each of the mayor's dozen or so opponents equal time.

Legally Qualified Candidates

One of the most confusing aspects of Section 315 regards the FCC's definition of a legally qualified candidate. It is a long definition filled with lots of *ands* and *ors* and needs clarification.

A legally qualified candidate is any person (1) who publicly announces that he or she is a candidate for nomination or election to any local, county, state, or national office, *and* (2) who meets the qualifications prescribed by law for that office, *and* (3) who qualifies for a place on the ballot or is eligible to be voted for by sticker or write-in methods, *and* (4) who was duly nominated by a political party that is commonly known and regarded as such or makes a substantial showing that he or she is a bona fide candidate.

There should be no question about number one in the definition: the candidate must be an announced candidate. Number two merely states that the person must be eligible to hold the office to which he or she aspires. Henry

Kissinger, for example, is not eligible to be president, since he is not a natural-born citizen. Despite the fact that he may be an announced candidate for that office, he is not a legally qualified candidate. Number three is self-explanatory: the person's name must appear on the ballot or he or she must be an eligible write-in or sticker candidate. Number four is the confusing qualification. Who knows what a substantial showing really is? What is a political party "commonly known and regarded as such"? Answers to these questions are judgment calls, and broadcasters with questions can solicit answers from the FCC. In fact, it is through the solicitation of such questions that the agency makes most of its Section 315 rulings.

Many critics charge that a smart politician can refrain from announcing his candidacy for reelection, for example, and just make many television appearances and not be in violation of Section 315. That is true. But stations should be able to see what the candidate is doing and can refuse to allow appearances by an unannounced candidate, especially appearances that are clearly political in nature. A station that is not careful in this regard can be subject to problems at renewal time.

Equal opportunity cases are rare. Normally the broadcaster asks the agency for guidance and then follows the recommendations of the commission, or files an appeal if the answer is not what the station wants to hear. In early 1987 the KING Broadcasting Co. in Seattle asked the FCC to declare exempt, under Section 315, two proposed program formats for the coverage of major party presidential candidates. The first format consisted of two thirty-minute pre-taped statements by the Republican and Democratic candidates outlining their essential campaign message. The two half-hour statements would be shown back to back. In the second format the two candidates would be interviewed individually for 45 minutes by a journalist. Again, both interviews would be shown back to back. Finally, the station proposed giving both candidates a few minutes at the end of the statements and interviews for rebuttal. The FCC refused to declare the formats exempt, saying they were neither bona-fide news interviews or on-the-spot news coverage. KING appealed the ruling. The United States court of appeals ruled that formats were not exempt because they were interviews, but that the FCC needed to reconsider whether they could qualify for an exemption as on-the-spot news coverage. The agency had to determine why the debates were exempt as news coverage, but the formats proposed by KING were not (*KING Broadcasting Co. v. FCC,* 1988). The final FCC ruling was pending in the spring of 1989.

The FCC has granted two qualifications for the application of the equal opportunity doctrine, one of which appears much more important than it really is. The first qualification is broad: In primary elections, Section 315 applies to intraparty contests rather than to interparty contests. In a primary election, the contest is not Republicans versus Democrats, it is Republican versus Republican and Democrat versus Democrat. Only opponents can get equal opportunity. Imagine Jane Adams is a Republican candidate for governor. She is one of four Republicans seeking to win the primary. Six Democrats are also seeking to win the primary election and gain the nomination for the governorship in their party. Ms. Adams appears on KLOP for fifteen minutes. What are the station's obligations? The station is obliged to give equal opportunity to the other three Republican candidates, since they are the ones against whom Jane is running. The Democrats are not running against Ms. Adams at this time. While this qualification is broad, it makes a good deal of sense.

The second qualification turns out to be not much of a qualification at all, although it appears to be on its face. The only appearance that can trigger use of Section 315 is an appearance by the candidate. Under Section 315 appearances by friends, relatives, supporters, and so forth, do not require the station to give equal opportunity to opponents. However (this is an important however), the FCC has decided that such noncandidate appearances do require the station to provide an opportunity for appearances by supporters of the other legally qualified candidates.

This is known as the **Zapple rule** and was formulated a few years ago in response to a letter from Nicholas Zapple, formerly a staff member of the Senate Subcommittee on Communications. It was restated in the FCC's 1972 *Report Regarding the Handling of Political Broadcasts*. This is what the FCC said:

> The commission held in "Zapple" that when a licensee sells time to supporters or spokesmen of a candidate during an election campaign who urge the candidate's election, discuss the campaign issues, or criticize an opponent then the licensee must afford comparable time to the spokesmen for an opponent. Known as the quasi-equal opportunity or political party corollary to the fairness doctrine, the "Zapple" doctrine is based on the equal opportunity requirement of Section 315 of the Communications Act; accordingly, free reply time need not be afforded to respond to a paid program.

The Zapple rule is a fairly specific formulation of one part of what had been vague FCC policy for some time, that is, that during political campaigns, programs that do not invoke Section 315 would fall under the ambit of the Fairness Doctrine (see pages 554–560). This means that licensees are required to play fair with all candidates. Broadcasters are therefore obliged to scrutinize even those programs that are exempt from Section 315, such as newscasts, to ensure that a balance of some sort is maintained.

Three last points need to be made about Section 315. First, since broadcasters are not permitted to censor the remarks of a political candidate, they are immune from libel suits based on those remarks. In 1959 the Supreme Court ruled that since stations cannot control what candidates say over the air, they should not be held responsible for the remarks. The candidate, however, can still be sued (*Farmers Educational and Cooperative Union of America v. WDAY*, 1959). Second, ballot issues like school bond levies, initiatives, and referendums do not fall under Section 315 but have been treated as controversial issues under the Fairness Doctrine. Finally, in 1986, a United States court of appeals ruled that the provisions of the equal opportunity rule do apply to electronic data transmission processes, such as teletext. Teletext is a system whereby the sender encodes data on the unused portion of a standard television signal and sends it through the airwaves. With proper decoding equipment the receiver sees that data as text on the television screen. The FCC had ruled previously that none of the political affairs content regulations—Section 315, Section 312 or the Fairness Doctrine—applied to such data transmission services. The court of appeals agreed that neither Section 312 nor the Fairness Doctrine were applicable to teletext. But it said that the FCC could not exclude the application of Section 315, at least not without a rational reason. The court noted that teletext was capable of generating high resolution graphics. It would seem, the court ruled, that if a pictorial representation of the candidate were transmitted via teletext with a message, this would satisfy the statutory definition of use under the federal statute (*Telecommunications Research and Actions Center* v. *FCC,* 1986).

SUMMARY

Several rules govern political broadcasts carried by radio and television broadcasters. Section 312 of the Federal Communications Act states that broadcasters cannot have an across-the-board policy rejecting all paid and nonpaid appearances by candidates for federal office. A candidate's request must be evaluated and can be rejected only if it could cause serious disruption of program schedules or might prompt an excessive number of equal time requests. While this rule applies only to requests from candidates for federal office, the government's mandate that broadcasters operate their stations in the public interest may very well include similar standards for the treatment by broadcasters of requests for access to air time from state and local candidates.

Section 315 states that if a broadcaster provides one candidate for office with the opportunity to use a station's broadcast facilities, all other legally qualified candidates for the same office must be given the same opportunity. The use of the station's facilities includes all appearances on the station with the exception of the following:

1. Bona fide newscasts
2. Bona fide news interview programs
3. Spot news coverage
4. Incidental appearance in a news documentary

Candidate press conferences and debates between candidates are considered spot news events. During primary elections Section 315 applies only to candidates from the same political party running against each other to win the party's nomination to run in the general election.

The FCC treads a bit softer when it comes to dealing with news programming. There have been instances in which charges were made that stations and networks falsified the news. Congress also gets into such debates, as it did in the controversy over the CBS broadcast "The Selling of the Pentagon," but usually takes no action. The FCC is also reluctant to act in such cases. Distortion or falsification of news involves a good deal more than simply a news source disagreeing with the manner in which a news story was reported. The deliberate distortion rule states that the distortion or staging must be deliberately intended to slant or mislead—and this allegation must be supported by extrinsic evidence. For example, independent witnesses must testify that they saw the staging. Also, the distortion or staging must involve a significant part of the news event, not a minor or incidental part of the news report. The FCC has refused to investigate "inaccurate embellishments concerning peripheral aspects of news reports or attempts at window dressing which concerned the manner of presenting the news, as long as the essential facts of the news stories to which these presentational devices were related were broadcast in an accurate manner" (*Galloway* v. *FCC*, 1985).

Complaints were made to the commission about such programs as "The Selling of the Pentagon" and "Hunger in America." The Columbia Broadcasting System was accused of careless editing in the program on the Pentagon, editing that took quotations from various parts of a speech and made it appear that these separate statements were actually one statement. There were other questionable editing practices as well. In "Hunger in America" the same network showed viewers a baby that it claimed had died of malnutrition. While many babies do die each week of malnutrition, the one photographed by the network had, in fact, died of other causes. The response of the FCC in "The Selling of the Pentagon" case is typical of how that agency handles such complaints. "Lacking evidence or documents that on their face reflect deliberate distortion, we believe that this government licensing agency cannot properly intervene," the commission ruled. "As we stated in the 'Hunger in America' ruling, the commission is not the national arbiter of truth." While taking a hands-off action itself, the agency reminded broadcasters, "The licensee must have a policy of requiring honesty of its news staff and must take reasonable precautions to see that news is fairly handled. The licensee's investigation of substantial complaints . . . must be a thorough, conscientious one, resulting in remedial action where appropriate." From this statement one can presume that obvious and blatant staging of news will be considered a disservice to the public interest but that the FCC is not capable of evaluating or monitoring the editing techniques of thousands of news departments. Errors will have to be fairly serious and well documented before the commission will intervene.

The Fairness Doctrine

For almost forty years the Fairness Doctrine was the most controversial of all broadcast regulations. Then in 1987 the Federal Communications Commission abolished the rule. More than a year later a federal court ruled that the agency's action was not arbitrary and repealing the Fairness Doctrine was permissible (*Syracuse Peace Council v. FCC,* 1989). The action by the FCC remained controversial. Congress attempted to enact the fairness doctrine through statute, but President Reagan vetoed the measure. Efforts began in Congress again in early 1989 to try to establish the controversial regulation, but it was expected President Bush was likely to veto such a law as well. At least that is what the Department of Justice recommended that he do. Quite possibly, then, by the time you reach this portion of the text, the Fairness Doctrine will be dead and buried, once and for all. It is also possible that it will be alive and well. Consequently, I have retained material about the Fairness Doctrine in this chapter, reasoning it is easier to skip over a section (if the doctrine is finally abandoned) than it is to scramble to find information about the Fairness Doctrine (if Congress readopts it and it becomes law).

The Fairness Doctrine is a deceptively simple rule. It requires broadcasters to provide adequate time for the discussion of controversial public issues. Also, the broadcaster must insure that the coverage of these issues is fair; that is, that important contrasting views on these issues are presented. Many persons, especially those in broadcasting, consider the Fairness Doctrine to be a flagrant affront to the First Amendment. Other persons argue, with the same passion, that the Fairness Doctrine is the only thing that makes freedom of expression a reality in broadcasting because it permits all persons, not just the broadcaster, the opportunity to speak.

The Fairness Doctrine is a creature of the FCC; it was not a part of the Federal Communications Act of 1934. In fact, attempts to include such a rule in the 1934 law at the time of its passage failed. The doctrine emerged in the late 1940s after the FCC had studied the problem of editorialization by broadcasters. The agency had ruled in 1941 that broadcasters could not editorialize on their stations (in re *Mayflower Broadcasting Corp., WAAB,* 1941). Many persons protested this decision, and in 1949 the FCC reversed itself. The commission said it was permissible for broadcasters to editorialize as a part of fulfilling their responsibility to provide time for the presentation of programming devoted to the discussion of important public issues. The commission added that while the broadcaster could present a point of view on these issues, it was the licensee's responsibility to make certain that other responsible points of view were presented as well (*In the Matter of Editorialization by Broadcast Licensees,* 1949). This was the genesis of the Fairness Doctrine.

In 1959 Congress amended Section 315, the equal opportunity rule, to exclude news programming from the ambit of this regulation. Many persons believe that at this time the Congress, through certain language in the amendment, codified the Fairness Doctrine as a part of the Federal Communications Act. Indeed the FCC said it believed this until 1980, when it sought to deregulate broadcasting. Swept in on Ronald Reagan's very long coattails, the deregulators invaded Washington at the end of the 1970s and set about to do what the president had promised—"Get government off of the back of business." As one of the most regulated industries, broadcasting became an immediate target for change, and abolishing the Fairness Doctrine became the centerpiece of the deregulatory effort.

Mark Fowler, Reagan's choice to head the FCC, publicly announced that he would ask Congress to kill the Fairness Doctrine as well as other regulations. But Congress was unsympathetic, and little happened. By 1985 Reagan appointments filled the FCC however, and in that year the commission issued a thirty-seven page report following an inquiry into the Fairness Doctrine. The report concluded that the Fairness Doctrine no longer served the public interest. "We have found," the commissioners wrote, "that far from filling its intended purpose, the doctrine has a chilling effect on broadcaster's speech." The agency, however, did not eliminate the doctrine, unsure as it was of its own power to do so. If in fact, as many believed, the Fairness Doctrine had been codified in 1959 by the Congress, the FCC could not repeal it. Only Congress can change a federal statute.

At least one judge did not think that Congress had codified the Fairness Doctrine in 1959. In a ruling on whether or not certain FCC content regulations pertained to teletext (see pages 552–553) Judge Robert Bork noted that "We do not believe that language adopted in 1959 made the Fairness Doctrine a binding statutory obligation; rather it ratified the commission's long standing position that the public interest standard authorized the Fairness Doctrine (*Telecommunications Research and Action Center* v. *FCC*, 1986)." On the heels of this decision legal challenges to the doctrine mounted. If the FCC did not believe in the Fairness Doctrine and Congress did not mandate it, how could the commission continue to enforce it (*Meredith Corp.* v. *FCC*, 1987). Fearing that the agency would abandon the Fairness Doctrine, Congress tried to preempt the commission. In the spring of 1987 the House of Representatives voted 302 to 102 to make the Fairness Doctrine the law; the Senate followed with a 59–31 vote. In June Ronald Reagan vetoed this legislation and the Democratic leadership in the Senate acknowledged that votes did not exist to override the veto. Within two months, on August 4, the FCC announced it was abandoning the Fairness Doctrine. The FCC commissioners made several arguments. They argued that because of the growth in broadcast technology, scarcity of channels was no longer a problem. Consequently, one station no longer had to present all points of view to insure the public was well informed. Also, the chilling effect on broadcasters who became timid rather than risk Fairness Doctrine violations hurt rather than helped the public discussion of controversial issues. In addition, the agency said it could find no evidence that the Congress had ever made the doctrine a part of the law. Finally, the commissioners said the Fairness Doctrine was a violation of the First Amendment. In making this assertion the FCC flatly contradicted the Supreme Court which in 1967 had ruled that the Fairness Doctrine was indeed constitutional (*Red Lion Broadcasting Co.* v. *FCC*, 1967).

In March of 1988 the FCC voted not to reconsider its decision to abolish the Fairness Doctrine nor consider any less stringent alternatives. "The FCC has done the right thing in terms of service to the public interest and the First Amendment," said commission chairperson Dennis Patrick. As noted previously, this action was sustained by a United States court of appeals (*Syracuse Peace Council v. FCC,* 1989). What follows is a brief outline of the Fairness Doctrine as it stood, just before it was repealed.

What the Doctrine Means

The first mandate of the Fairness Doctrine is that the broadcaster must provide adequate time for the discussion of controversial public issues. This is not an order that a broadcaster carry news and information programming, something the FCC has ruled is no longer a requirement. But if the issues arise, the broadcaster should devote time to an exploration of these issues. How much time? The agency has never specified an amount of time. "It is the individual broadcaster who, after evaluating the needs of his particular community, must determine what percentage of the limited broadcast day should be devoted to news and discussion or consideration of public issues," the FCC said.

An FCC ruling in 1976 helped clarify what is adequate time for the discussion of public issues. Representative Patsy Mink, the sponsor of an anti-strip-mining bill in Congress, asked a West Virginia radio station to broadcast an eleven-minute audiotaped discussion of her bill. The station refused, noting that it had not carried any pro-strip-mining broadcasts and consequently was not required to carry an anti-strip-mining program. Representative Mink complained to the FCC that the station had not fulfilled its obligations under the Fairness Doctrine to provide an adequate amount of time for a discussion of public issues. The station argued that it had covered the issue by presenting Associated Press news reports on the issue during its regular newscasts.

The FCC ruled against the station, reaffirming that "the Fairness Doctrine imposes two affirmative responsibilities on the broadcaster: coverage of issues of public importance must be adequate and must fairly reflect differing viewpoints." The commission noted that the requirement to present contrasting viewpoints would not make much sense without a corresponding obligation to cover issues of public importance. While acknowledging that the licensee was not obligated to address each and every issue that may be important to the public, the commission ruled (*Patsy Mink,* 1976):

> Where, as in the present case, an issue has significant and possibly unique impact on the licensee's service area, it will not be sufficient for the licensee as an indication of compliance with the Fairness Doctrine to show that it may have broadcast an unknown amount of news touching on a general topic related to the issue cited in a complaint. Rather it must be shown that there has been some attempt to inform the public of the nature of the controversy, not only that such a controversy exists.

What is a reasonable opportunity for opposing viewpoints? The Fairness Doctrine does not require—as does Section 315—one-to-one precision in granting time for opposing viewpoints. So long as all sides of the issue are reasonably aired, the strictures of the Fairness Doctrine will have been met. A United States court of appeals spoke to the question of balance in a 1983 ruling on a Fairness Doctrine complaint brought by the Democratic National Committee (DNC) against both NBC and CBS television networks. Both networks had broadcast a series of thirty-second paid spots, prepared by the Republican National Committee, that supported President Reagan's economic policies. The DNC argued that the networks did not balance these spots with material about the negative aspects of the administration's economic program. In hearing the complaint the FCC accepted the validity of the assertions by the Democrats that the spots, coupled with other reports on the administration, created a frequency of presentation ratio in which pro-administration views enjoyed a three-to-one advantage on CBS and a four-to-one advantage on NBC. But the FCC said this was not a glaring disparity; coverage was not out of balance. The court of appeals ruled that this was a reasonable conclusion on the part of the FCC and refused to overrule the agency. The balance required in the context of the Fairness Doctrine is measured not in terms of equal time or identical treatment, but rather in terms of fairness and reasonableness—with ample deference given to the broadcaster's conception of what reasonableness entails, the court said (*Democratic National Committee* v. *FCC,* 1983).

Do all viewpoints have to be aired? What about that fellow in the valley whose ideas are different from those of everyone else? No, it would be unreasonable to require the broadcaster to include all opinions. The commission requires an airing only of those viewpoints that have a significant measure of support or viewpoints that reflect the ideas of a significant segment of the community. But it is the duty of the broadcaster to make certain that these views are aired, and in this way the Fairness Doctrine is sharply different from Section 315. The Equal Opportunity Rule is a passive rule. The candidate must come forward and seek equal time. The Fairness Doctrine requires the active participation of the broadcaster, who has an affirmative duty to find someone to speak to all sides of the issue or present all sides of the issue himself.

What is a controversial issue of public importance? In actual practice the broadcaster decides what is controversial and what is not. Some of the factors which the FCC suggests that the licensee take into consideration when determining whether an issue is controversial include the following:

1. The degree of media coverage of the issue.
2. The degree of attention the issue receives from government officials and other community leaders.
3. The impact the issue is likely to have on the community at large.

A ruling by the FCC, supported by the Court of Appeals for the District of Columbia, indicates that a controversial issue is expected to be rather specific and narrow. A conservative political-action group calling itself American Security Council Foundation (ASCF) undertook a content analysis of CBS television news broadcasts in 1975 and 1976 and concluded that the network's coverage of the national security issue was not balanced. The group called the coverage "too dovish." The FCC rejected the complaint, noting among other things that ASCF had not defined a controversial issue with sufficient specificity in its complaint. A United States court of appeals upheld this ruling in 1979, arguing that the items included under the umbrella of "national security" were simply too diverse to be bunched together under a single national security heading. The ASCF looked at such items as NATO, détente with China and the Soviet Union, SALT treaties, amnesty for persons prosecuted during the Vietnam War for a wide range of offenses, the Vietnam War itself, Middle East issues, and others. "The issues analyzed by ASCF arose independently in time and were largely discussed and acted upon on an independent basis," the court ruled. "Consideration of the issues together, rather than individually, would not provide a basis for determining whether the broadcaster presented a reasonable balance of conflicting views, because views on any one issue do not support or contradict views on the others," the six-person majority noted. What does NATO have to do with détente in China? or what does amnesty have to do with SALT? the court asked. An issue is not a "particular, well-defined" issue for Fairness Doctrine purposes if the separate issues comprising it are so indirectly related that a view on one does not, in a way that would be apparent to an average viewer, support or contradict a view on any other (*American Security Council Foundation* v. *FCC,* 1979).

In 1980 the FCC dismissed a complaint made against all three networks by the National Committee for Responsive Philanthropy. The committee alleged that the networks had failed to balance the issue raised by broadcast of spot announcements urging persons to support the United Way fund drives ("Thanks to you, it's working."). The United States Court of Appeals for the District of Columbia upheld the dismissal by the agency, noting that the committee's complaint failed to show that such announcements meaningfully addressed a controversial issue of public importance. The Fairness Doctrine only applies, the court said, when a broadcast statement amounts to advocacy of a position on one side of an ongoing public debate and obviously and substantially addresses that issue in a meaningful way (*National Committee for Responsive Philanthropy* v. *FCC,* 1981).

By and large it comes down to whether the broadcaster believes that an issue is important, is controversial, and does stimulate debate within the community.

The FCC does not monitor for violations of the Fairness Doctrine but relies instead on complaints from viewers and listeners. In a typical year the FCC receives between seven thousand and ten thousand complaints. Most are telephone calls and the vast majority of these complaints never amount to anything. The amount of actionable complaints, that is, complaints where the agency staff actually investigates the matter, are remarkably small. The reason for this is that it is very difficult to make a proper Fairness Doctrine complaint. It was made even more difficult by the Reagan FCC of the 1980s when it placed a much heavier evidentiary burden on the person making a Fairness Doctrine complaint.

To file a proper complaint, a listener or viewer must inform the commission of the name of the station and the date and time of the offending broadcast. That is only the beginning. Next the complainant must demonstrate "by objectively quantifiable information" that the issues discussed were controversial and of public importance. Then the listener or viewer must demonstrate that the program or programs complained of "meaningfully discussed" the identified issues of public importance. Finally, the complainant must demonstrate that in its overall programming the licensee failed to present contrasting viewpoints to sufficiently meet its obligations.

It is not always easy even to convince the FCC that the broadcast focused upon a controversial issue. For if the broadcaster says that the issue is not controversial or is not important, the FCC must accept the answer unless there is evidence that the broadcaster has acted in an arbitrary or capricious manner in making this determination. So long as the broadcaster makes a good-faith judgment that the issue is not controversial, there is nothing the FCC can do. The broadcaster has the discretion to decide what is and what is not controversial. Furthermore the FCC cannot substitute its judgment for that of the broadcaster. Clearly if the broadcaster ignores overwhelming evidence that the people are interested or ignores the fact that a vigorous public debate is underway, the FCC can then rule that the determination is not made in good faith. But this is a very rare kind of ruling. Generally the agency takes the licensee's word.

In 1972 NBC broadcast a program entitled "The Broken Promise," a documentary about private pension plans. It was very critical of certain private pension plans and graphically showed how millions of Americans had been ripped off and cheated. Narrator Edwin Newman told viewers *that most private pension plans are good,* that they provide a real benefit to the workers. Most of the NBC program, however, dealt *with bad pension plans.*

A Fairness Doctrine complaint was lodged against the network by a conservative watchdog organization called Accuracy In Media. The FCC asked NBC whether the program dealt with a controversial issue. The network said no, and this was its reasoning. The program talked about bad private pension plans. There were no allegations that all pension plans were bad. In fact, quite the opposite: it was stated that most plans are good. NBC focused on the bad plans. Everybody agrees that some plans are bad. There is no controversy about that. Since the program focused only on the bad plans, it did not deal with a controversial issue.

The FCC did not accept this logic. But when the decision was appealed to a court of appeals, the agency had its hand slapped. The court said that so long as the network had made a good-faith judgment, NBC was to exercise discretion as to whether the issue was controversial (*NBC* v. *FCC,* 1974). The FCC could not come to a different conclusion on the basis of the same evidence. That was not permitted. What the agency must ask is this: Was there any evidence that could lead the network to decide that the issue was not controversial? And if there was, then NBC's determination was made in good faith.

Other questions can also pose problems for someone who seeks to make a Fairness Doctrine complaint. In the mid-1980s citizens of Dodge City, Kansas, complained that radio station KTTL was presenting a series of programs hosted by right-wing, fundamentalist clergy who consistently attacked Jews, Roman Catholics, blacks and other minorities. The programming was a violation of the Fairness Doctrine, they argued. Despite the documented fact of unbalanced programming by the station, the complaint was dismissed. The FCC said the petitioners had failed to show that the issues discussed on the programs were controversial or important, and they also failed to show that these discussions constituted a meaningful discussion of any issues. The FCC instead characterized the attacks as "incoherent monolgues and tirades" (*Cattle Country Broadcasting,* 1985).

The final requirement is often the most difficult to meet for persons seeking to file a complaint. The broadcaster's overall programming must be unbalanced and unfair. The Fairness Doctrine does not mandate fairness within the context of a single program or even a single day's programming. What is required is that over the long haul—weeks, maybe even months—the station makes a balanced presentation of the issue. What this means is that unless a complainant has the capacity to monitor a broadcaster's programming day and night, week after week, it is difficult to assert that overall programming has been unbalanced. Therefore, most complaints that make any headway through the commission are filed by professional media monitoring organizations like Accuracy in Media. These special-interest groups have staffers watching television around the clock, hoping to catch a violation of one kind or another.

If the FCC is satisfied with the complaint it will forward a letter to the broadcaster asking for a response to the matter. Does the broadcaster agree that the subject was a controversial issue? If so, how has the broadcaster fulfilled the fairness doctrine obligations? At this point what the FCC is looking for is not necessarily evidence of balanced programming by the broadcaster. Instead, what is sought is assurances and evidence that the broadcaster has made a good faith effort to provide the balance required by the law. Unless the licensee has really fouled up, the FCC is usually satisfied with the answer.

This is at least partially why between 1982 and 1986, for example, the FCC decided only a single Fairness Doctrine complaint against a broadcaster, out of the likely thirty thousand complaints initially filed with the agency.

<table>
<tr><td>Advertising</td><td>

The Fairness Doctrine has been applied to advertising for a commercial product only one time, and the FCC has said since that application that it was a mistake to do it even once. In 1967 in response to a petition from a young attorney named John Banzhaf, the commission ruled that stations that carry advertisements for cigarettes must carry free public service messages showing the dangers of smoking as well (*WCBS-TV: Applicability of the Fairness Doctrine to Cigarette Advertising,* 1967). The United States Court of Appeals for the District of Columbia sustained the ruling in *Banzhaf v. FCC* (1969). Cigarette smoking was a controversial subject. Later, of course, Congress passed a law that banned cigarette advertisements from the airwaves completely.
</td></tr>
</table>

Following the *Banzhaf* ruling, other public interest groups sought to have broadcasters balance advertisements for gasoline and automobiles with messages about environmental protection. But the FCC did not agree to these proposals. The commission argued that the smoking decision was unusual, that smoking is a habit that can disappear, that the government urged the discontinuance of cigarette smoking, that government studies showed the danger of smoking, and so forth. In other words the problem of smoking is different from the problem of pollution. So the Friends of the Earth went to court, and in 1971 the Court of Appeals for the District of Columbia reversed the FCC ruling. The court said it could not see the distinction between the cigarette case and that case (in re *Wilderness Society and Friends of the Earth,* 1971):

> Commercials which continue to insinuate that the human personality finds greater fulfillment in the larger car with the quick getaway do, it seems to us, ventilate a point of view which not only has become controversial but involves an issue of public importance. Where there is undisputed evidence, as there is here, that the hazards to health implicit in air pollution are enlarged and aggravated by such products, then the parallel with cigarette advertising is exact and the relevance of *Banzhaf* inescapable.

The court said, however, that stations do not have to broadcast anti–big-car advertising, as in the cigarette advertisements case. The key is overall programming. If the licensees carry programming that discusses the environmental dangers of pollution and the diminution of resources, the Fairness Doctrine will be satisfied.

In a 1974 report on the Fairness Doctrine the FCC discussed the application of the doctrine to advertising. The commission said that it would apply the doctrine to editorial advertising—commercials that consist of direct and substantial commentary on important public issues—but not to product advertising, not even to controversial products. It said that the cigarette decision was a mistake; if it had to decide the case today, it would not make the same decision. "We believe that standard product commercials," the commissioners wrote, "make no meaningful contribution toward informing the public on any side of any issue." (This, of course, is a little different position than the Supreme Court has taken on the question of the value of advertising in the evolution of the commercial speech doctrine. See chapter 10.) The courts have upheld this decision by the FCC, most recently in 1977 (*National Citizens Committee for Broadcasting* v. *FCC,* 1977). The commission also rejected a proposal by the Federal Trade Commission that the FCC require stations to offer rebuttal time to public interest groups to answer commercials that raise controversial issues, commercials that make claims that are based on disputed scientific premises, and commercials that are silent about the negative aspects of the advertised products (like too many aspirin can be harmful). The FCC said that almost all commercials raise controversial issues for some people, that such a "counteradvertising proposal" could have an adverse economic effect on broadcasting, and that it did not believe that the Fairness Doctrine was an appropriate vehicle with which to correct false and misleading advertising.

The case of *Public Media Center* v. *FCC* (1978) is an example of the kind of advertising to which the FCC will apply the Fairness Doctrine. In this case, in which eight California television stations were charged with violating the Fairness Doctrine for broadcasting commercials for the Pacific Gas and Electric Company advocating development of nuclear power without presenting the views of opponents of such development, a United States court of appeals upheld the commission ruling. The court also remanded the case to the FCC to clarify why it had not made the same ruling regarding four other stations that had also broadcast the same television commercials.

One additional note: the FCC has not applied the Fairness Doctrine to entertainment programs, even to controversial shows such as the two-part "Maude" episode concerning abortion (*Diocesan Union of Holy Name Societies of Rockville Centre and Long Island Coalition for Life,* 1973).

Personal Attacks and Political Editorials

The Fairness Doctrine is a fairly nebulous policy that has been outlined primarily on a case-by-case basis. But the commission has drafted specific rules, related to the doctrine, that deal with personal attacks and political editorials. The FCC considered dropping these rules, but was stymied by Congress. Here are the specific rules:

Personal attacks
   (a) When, during the presentation of views on a controversial issue of public importance, an attack is made upon the honesty, character, integrity or like personal qualities of an identified person or group, the licensee shall, within a reasonable time and in no event later than one week after the attack, transmit to the person or group attacked (1) notification of the date, time and identification of the broadcast; (2) a script or tape (or an accurate summary if a script or tape is not available) of the attack; and (3) an offer of a reasonable opportunity to respond over the licensee's facilities.

(b) The provisions of paragraph (a) of this section shall not be applicable (1) to attacks on foreign groups or foreign public figures; (2) to personal attacks which are made by legally qualified candidates, their authorized spokesmen, or those associated with them in the campaign, or other such candidates, their authorized spokesmen, or persons associated with the candidates in the campaign; and (3) to bona fide newscasts, bona fide news interviews, and on-the-spot coverage of a bona fide news event (including commentary or analysis contained in the foregoing programs, but the provisions of paragraph (a) of this section shall be applicable to editorials of the licensee).

Political editorials

(c) Where a licensee, in an editorial, (i) endorses or (ii) opposes a legally qualified candidate or candidates, the licensee shall, within twenty-four hours after the editorial, transmit to respectively (i) the other qualified candidate or candidates for the same office or (i) the candidate opposed in the editorial (1) notification of the date and time of the editorial; (2) a script or tape of the editorial; and (3) an offer of a reasonable opportunity for a candidate or a spokesman of the candidate to respond over the licensee's facilities: *Provided, however,* that where such editorials are broadcast within seventy-two hours prior to the day of the election, the licensee shall comply with the provisions of this paragraph sufficiently far in advance of the broadcast to enable the candidate or candidates to have a reasonable opportunity to prepare a response and to present it in a timely fashion.

The personal attack rules stem from FCC rulings in 1962 stating that when licensees broadcast what amounts to a personal attack upon an individual or group within the community, they have an affirmative obligation to notify the target of the attack of the broadcast and offer the target an opportunity to respond. In 1967 these earlier decisions were clarified and made more specific with the publication of the personal attack rules.

As you can see from the rules, the licensee's obligations are quite specific. It is important to remember that just naming someone in an editorial or commentary does not necessarily constitute a personal attack. On the other hand the rules apply to attacks made by everyone, not just by the station itself.

Paragraph (b) of the rules exempts attacks made by candidates and their followers upon other candidates and their followers. Newscasts, news interviews, and on-the-spot news coverage are also exempted from the personal attack rules but not from the more general provisions of the Fairness Doctrine. Paragraph (c) outlines licensee obligations with regard to editorial endorsements of candidates.

Soon after the personal attack rules were published, they were challenged in court. A small radio station in Pennsylvania challenged an FCC ruling requiring it to provide free time to Fred Cook, an author, who had been attacked by right-wing evangelist Billy James Hargis. The United States Court of Appeals for the District of Columbia upheld the constitutionality of both the personal attack rules and the Fairness Doctrine (*Red Lion Broadcasting*

Co. v. *FCC,* 1967). While this case was being litigated, the Radio and Television News Directors' Association and other broadcasting organizations petitioned the United States Court of Appeals for the Seventh Circuit in Chicago to review the constitutionality of the Fairness Doctrine. In this case the court of appeals struck down both the personal attack rules and the Fairness Doctrine as being in violation of the First Amendment (*Radio and Television News Directors' Association* v. *U.S.,* 1968). With two circuit courts at odds on the question, the Supreme Court had to decide the issue.

In a unanimous decision in 1969, the High Court upheld the constitutionality of both the personal attack rules and the Fairness Doctrine with the argument that the First Amendment operates as a command to the government to protect the public from one-sided presentations of public issues. Going back to the original congressional mandate that the broadcaster operate in the public interest, the Court said the public interest is served only when the community receives exposure to all sides of controversial matters. As far as the First Amendment is concerned, wrote Justice Byron White, the licensed broadcaster stands no better off than those to whom the licenses are refused (*Red Lion Broadcasting Co.* v. *FCC,* 1969):

> A license permits broadcasting, but the licensee has no constitutional right to be the one who holds the license or to monopolize a radio frequency to the exclusion of his fellow citizens. There is nothing in the First Amendment which prevents the government from requiring a licensee to share his frequency with others and to conduct himself as a proxy or fiduciary with obligations to present those views and voices which are representative of his community and which would otherwise, by necessity, be barred from the airwaves.

Later in the opinion Justice White asserted, "It is the right of the public to receive suitable access to social, political, esthetic, moral and other ideas and experiences, which is crucial here. That right may not constitutionally be abridged either by the Congress or by the FCC."

The First Amendment

Broadcasting stations are not common carriers; that is, they have the right to refuse to do business with anyone they choose. During 1969 and 1970 two groups, the Democratic National Committee and a Washington, D.C., organization known as Business Executives Movement for Peace, sought to buy time from television stations and networks to solicit funds for their protest of the Vietnam War and to voice their objections to the way the war was being waged by the government. Broadcasters rebuffed these groups on the grounds that airing such controversial advertisements and programming would evoke the Fairness Doctrine, and they would then be obligated to ensure that all sides of the controversy were aired. Such action was a nuisance and could be costly. The broadcasters told the Democratic committee and the businessmen that one of their basic policies was not to sell time to any individual or group seeking to set forth views on controversial issues.

When this policy was challenged before the FCC, the commission sided with the broadcasters, noting that it was up to each individual licensee to determine how best to fulfill Fairness Doctrine obligations. But the United States Court of Appeals for the District of Columbia reversed the FCC ruling, citing the *Red Lion* decision that the right of the public to receive information is deeply rooted in the First Amendment. A ban on editorial advertising, the court ruled, "leaves a paternalistic structure in which licensees and bureaucrats decide what issues are important, whether to fully cover them, and the format, time and style of coverage. . . ." This kind of system, the court ruled, is inimical to the First Amendment (in re *Business Executives Movement for Peace* v. *FCC,* 1971):

> It may unsettle some of us to see an antiwar message or a political party message in the accustomed place of a soap or beer commercial. . . . We must not equate what is habitual with what is right or what is constitutional. A society already so saturated with commercialism can well afford another outlet for speech on public issues. All that we may lose is some of our apathy.

The victory of the businessmen and Democrats was short-lived, for by a seven-to-two vote, the United States Supreme Court overturned the appellate court ruling (*CBS* v. *Democratic National Committee,* 1973). Stations have an absolute right to refuse to sell time for advertising dealing with political campaigns and controversial issues. To give the FCC the power over such advertising runs the risk of enlarging government control over the content of broadcast discussion of public issues.

In response to the argument that by permitting broadcasters to refuse such advertising, we place in their hands the power to decide what the people shall see or hear on important public issues, Justice Burger wrote:

> For better or worse, editing is what editors are for; and editing is the selection and choice of material. That editors—newspaper or broadcast—can and do abuse this power is beyond doubt, but that is no reason to deny the discretion Congress provided. Calculated risks of abuse are taken in order to preserve high values.

The Court was badly fractured on this case and Justices Brennan and Marshall dissented. Only two other justices—Stewart and Rehnquist—joined the chief justice in his opinion. The remainder joined in overturning the court of appeals ruling, but for their own reasons. Broadcasters are required to present programming on public issues and to do so in such a manner as to ensure that all sides get a fair hearing. How this is to be accomplished is the business of the broadcaster. The Fairness Doctrine does not provide right of access to television or radio.

Finally the High Court used the First Amendment to strike down a Congressional statute that forbad all noncommercial educational broadcasting stations that receive money from the Corporation for Public Broadcasting (CPB) from editorializing on any subject at all. The government attempted to justify the law on two grounds. It argued that a ban on editorials was needed to prevent noncommercial broadcasting stations from being coerced, as a result of getting money from the federal government, into becoming vehicles for government propaganda. Also, it said the law was needed to keep stations from becoming convenient targets for capture by private-interest groups wishing to express their own partisan viewpoints. These justifications were insufficient, wrote Justice William Brennan for the five-member majority. The ban on all editorials by every station that receives CPB funds is too broad and far exceeds what is necessary to protect against the risk of governmental interference or to prevent the public from assuming that editorials by public broadcasting stations represent the official views of government. "The regulation impermissibly sweeps within its prohibition a wide range of speech by wholly private stations on topics that do not take a directly partisan stand or that have nothing whatever to do with federal, state or local government," Brennan wrote. And the ban really isn't effective, since the very same opinions that cannot be expressed by the station's management may be aired by someone appearing on a program as a guest. Chief Justice Burger and Justices Rehnquist, White, and Stevens dissented (*FCC* v. *League of Women Voters,* 1984). Public broadcasting stations are still prohibited from endorsing political candidates, however.

SUMMARY

The government may exercise control over the content of public affairs programs. While the FCC has thus far rejected complaints that television news coverage was slanted or staged, the agency may attempt to enforce the Fairness Doctrine. This rule states that a broadcaster must devote time for the discussion of controversial community issues and that the coverage of these issues must reflect contrasting community viewpoints on the issues. The Fairness Doctrine, which was abandoned by the FCC in 1987 after several years of controversy, put an affirmative responsibility upon the broadcaster to ensure that coverage was fair; it was insufficient for a radio or television station operator to present one side of an issue and then invite persons with opposing viewpoints to appear as a means of fulfilling Fairness Doctrine responsibilities.

The FCC has refused to define "adequate time" for the discussion of public issues. Affording a reasonable opportunity for opposing viewpoints means making certain that those views that reflect the ideas of significant segments of the community are aired. The broadcaster can decide what is a controversial issue of public importance. An examination of the media coverage of the issue, the impact the issue may have on the community, and the degree of attention the issue has received from community leaders may be used to guide the broadcaster in making this judgment.

It is difficult for a citizen to make an effective complaint against a broadcaster for violating the Fairness Doctrine. So long as the licensee has made a good-faith effort to present balanced coverage of important community issues, the FCC is reluctant to take action against the broadcaster. The Fairness Doctrine applies to editorial advertising (trying to sell an idea), but not to product advertising. A specific section of the Fairness Doctrine called the personal attack rules requires a broadcaster to notify a person or group that it plans to attack on the air and provide free time for the individual or group to respond to the attack.

The Supreme Court ruled in the Red Lion case that the Fairness Doctrine does not violate the First Amendment. The Supreme Court has ruled that broadcasters do not have to sell time to persons who wish to broadcast messages about controversial public issues. The Court has also ruled that a congressional ban on editorializations by public television stations is unconstitutional.

REGULATION AND NEW TECHNOLOGY

One of the most perplexing aspects of contemporary mass media law is the attempt by the government to regulate or control the bewildering array of new electronic information-transmitting technology that has burst upon the scene in recent years. In the pages that follow we will focus upon the regulation of the newer broadcast services, especially cable television. We will also briefly consider some aspects of the regulation of low-power TV (LPTV), multipoint distribution services (MDS), satellite master antenna television (SMATV), and private earth stations or dish antennas. No attempt is made to discuss the regulation of the many kinds of electronic data-transmission services or two-way nonbroadcast systems, just as regulation of telephone and telegraph is not a part of this book. Attempts to regulate the new mass media are coming at every level and occur at a pace equal to the introduction of the new technology. Comprehensive rules regarding such technology will take a long time to develop. Cable television has been around since the late 1940s, yet it was not until late 1984 that the Congress got around to adopting what might be called comprehensive cable television regulations.

Cable Television

Cable television is the oldest of the new technologies. Community antenna television (CATV), the forerunner of what we now call cable television, began in the late 1940s. The FCC first asserted jurisdiction over cable television in 1962; until then the industry was regulated by a hodgepodge of local and state rules. But from the very beginning the commission was forced to move tentatively toward the regulation of cable, because its jurisdiction was simply not clear. Cable is not broadcast; signals travel through wires, not the airwaves. There is no scarcity of spectrum, an important foundation for broadcast regulation. Cable is not a common carrier, as are telephone or telegraph; FCC authority to regulate these two-way communication devices does not clearly imply that the FCC has authority to regulate cable. At first rules were issued only for cable systems that used microwave relays as well as wire to transmit television signals. These microwave transmissions were similar to over-the-air broadcast and seemed to provide a jurisdictional foothold for the commission. These actions were sustained by the courts (in re *Carter Mountain Transmission Corp.*, 1962, 1963). In 1966 the agency issued rules that affected all cable systems, those that used the microwave relays and those that did not. Cable operators argued that the agency had no power to regulate cable transmission that did not use the broadcast spectrum, which was transmitted exclusively by wire. But the Supreme Court supported the FCC in a 1968 ruling. Justice Harlan wrote for the Court (*U.S. v. Southwestern Cable Co.*, 1968):

> The commission has been charged with broad responsibilities for the orderly development of an appropriate system of local television broadcasting. . . . The commission has reasonably found that the successful performance of these duties demands prompt and efficacious regulation of community antenna television systems [cable systems]. We have elsewhere held that we may not, "in the absence of compelling evidence that such was Congress' intention . . . prohibit administration action imperative for the achievement of an agency's ultimate purpose. . . ." There is no such evidence here, and we therefore hold that the commission's authority over "all interstate . . . communication by wire or radio" permits the regulation of CATV systems.

Justice Harlan added that the FCC can regulate cable television, at least to the extent "reasonably ancillary to the effective performance of the commission's various responsibilities for the regulation of television broadcasting."

Given a green light by the Supreme Court, the FCC began in the late 1960s and early 1970s to issue more and more wide-ranging regulations. The agency imposed equal time rules, sponsor identification rules, and the Fairness Doctrine upon all programming originated by cable casters. In addition, the FCC ruled that all cable systems having more than 3,500 subscribers would have to operate "to a significant extent as a local outlet by originating cable casting." In other words, the cable operators could no longer merely scoop the signals of other broadcasting stations out of the air and send them into a home via wire. They had to create programs themselves, which required programming facilities far beyond the needs of the simple automated services thus far originated by cable operators.

The Midwest Video Corporation challenged this rule. Again the Supreme Court upheld the authority of the FCC. In a five-to-four decision the Court ruled (*U.S. v. Midwest Video Corp.*, 1972):

> The effect of the regulation, after all, is to assure that in the retransmission of broadcast signals viewers are provided suitably diversified programming. . . .
> In sum, the regulation preserves and enhances the integrity of broadcast signals and therefore is "reasonably ancillary" to the effective performance of the commission's various responsibilities for the regulation of television broadcasting.

Cable television operators argued, as did Justice Douglas in a strong dissent, that the FCC was forcing them into the broadcasting business when they did not want to be licensed for that business. A majority of the Court disagreed, however, noting that the cable operators voluntarily engaged themselves in providing that service and that "the commission seeks only to ensure that it satisfactorily meets community needs within the context of their undertaking." Given this broad, sweeping power, the FCC issued a comprehensive set of cable regulations in 1972, the *Fourth Report and Order on Cable Television Service.*

In 1976 the FCC refined these rules to the extent that all cable systems with more than 3,500 subscribers carrying over-the-air broadcast signals had to develop a minimum twenty-channel capacity by 1986, had to make certain channels available for access by third parties, and had to furnish equipment and facilities for the creation and broadcast of this "access" programming. Again Midwest Video challenged the commission's ruling. This time the cable company won when the Supreme Court in April 1979 struck down the FCC order, saying that the commission was going beyond its authority. Justice Byron White, writing for the six-person majority, said that these rules were not reasonably ancillary to the effective performance of the commission's responsibility to regulate over-the-air television. White said the access rules transferred control of cable television from the cable operator to the public seeking to use the medium. "Effectively," White wrote, "the commission has regulated cable systems . . . to common carrier status," something which Congress has always rejected for broadcasting in the past (*FCC v. Midwest Video Corp.,* 1979). Earlier, the Court of Appeals for the Eighth Circuit had been even more critical of the commission when it struck down the cable access rules in 1978. The court said the FCC had no jurisdiction to promulgate such rules (*Midwest Video Corp. v. FCC,* 1978):

> Jurisdiction is not acquired through visions of Valhalla. An agency can neither create nor lawfully expand its jurisdiction by merely deciding what it thinks the future should be like, finding a private industry that can be restructured to make that future at least possible, and then forcing that restructuring in the mere hope that if it's there it will be used.

By 1980 the theme of deregulation, which was beginning to dictate changes in the regulation of broadcasting, also began to influence the regulation of cable television. In 1980 the FCC abandoned its rules that limited the number of distant signals a cable company could import for its subscribers. Distant signals are broadcast signals coming from more than thirty-five miles away from a cable system in a large market or more than fifty-five miles away from a cable system in a smaller market. The FCC also abandoned rules that stopped cable systems from transmitting programs carried by stations outside the area if the same programs were carried by local stations. These were called program exclusivity rules. (In the spring of 1989, the FCC announced it would reimpose these program exclusivity rules on January 1, 1990. But the ruling generated controversy and whether or not it would be implemented was unclear.) While relaxing its own rules, the FCC worked to strengthen the local regulation of cable systems.

Until 1984 the FCC jurisdiction to regulate cable had been justified because of the commission's statutory responsibility to regulate television generally. But in *Capital Cities* v. *Crisp* (see page 474 for a fuller discussion of this case) a unanimous Supreme Court struck down an Oklahoma State ban on liquor advertising on cable TV on the grounds that the federal government had preempted this area of regulation. In its ruling the High Court suggested that the FCC had virtually unbounded authority over cable television. The High Court asserted that "the commission's authority extends to all regulatory actions necessary to ensure the achievement of the commission's statutory responsibilities." Those responsibilities were defined to include "ensuring that the substantial benefits provided by cable of increased and diversified programming are secured by the maximum number of viewers" (*Capital Cities* v. *Crisp,* 1984). This decision seemed to open the door that had been partially closed in *Midwest II* and seemed to signal the Court's willingness to approve comprehensive cable regulation by the FCC.

Shortly after the Supreme Court ruling, Congress adopted the Cable Communications Policy Act of 1984, a comprehensive statute that firmly defined the jurisdiction and responsibilities of the FCC with regard to cable television. (The substance of this law will be outlined shortly.) In less than six months the commission's jurisdiction to regulate cable television had been clarified, first by the courts and then by the Congress.

But there are apparent limits to FCC jurisdiction. The power to regulate the cable industry does not in itself imply the complete authority to regulate what is cablecast via the medium. At least that is what is suggested by a pair of recent rulings regarding an important cable regulation, the must-carry rules. These are regulations that force a cable company to carry the signals of all commercial television stations within thirty-five miles of the community served by the cable system. The rules were originally adopted to protect local broadcasting. Many feared that if the cable operator could import signals into the community, local television stations would lose their audience and ultimately die. But the court of appeals ruled that the regulations violated the cable operator's rights of freedom of expression. "It is now clearly established that cable operators engage in conduct protected by the First Amendment," the court said. Government regulation of broadcasting has always been justified on the grounds of scarcity of broadcast signals in the spectrum, wrote Judge Skelly Wright. But such a rationale has no place in evaluating government regulation of cable television. Wright and the two other members of the court could find no other compelling reasons why the government should regulate the cable industry either. Cable television is much closer to film or the printed press than it is to broadcasting, Wright noted. The must-carry rules were designed to protect local broadcasters and in doing so are favoring certain classes of speakers over other speakers. Government cannot do this. Cable operators complained that on small cable systems, those with twelve or so channels, there were few channels left for cable network programming (MTV, CNN, and others) if the cable operator had to transmit all the local stations. They argued that this impinged upon their editorial discretion to program the channels that they wanted to program. The court agreed and noted that the rules also interfered with the wishes of the subscribers—who may want to watch something other than the local stations. Judge Wright pondered whether the rules were designed to protect localism in broadcasting, a worthy goal, or local broadcasters. Government assumes a heavy burden of justification for any rule that impinges upon the First Amendment. In this case the government failed to carry the burden, the court said (*Quincy Cable* v. *FCC,* 1985).

In the autumn of 1986, with the support of both the cable and the broadcasting industries, the FCC announced it had adopted a modified version of the must-carry rules which were to last for only five years. The FCC said during the five-year period viewers could become adjusted to using what is called an input selector device. When hooked to a television, this device permits the viewer to select to watch either cable television or over-the-air television. The switch, which costs about $7.50, is tied into an antenna, which costs a good deal more. By switching to the over-the-air mode the viewer is able to watch a local channel that is not being carried by the cable system. Under the new rules, cable systems must devote only a portion of their capacity to carrying local television signals. Systems with less than a twenty-channel capacity must carry only a public broadcasting station; cable systems with between twenty-one and twenty-seven channels must devote seven channels to local broadcast signals; and systems with more than twenty-seven channels must devote twenty-five percent of their capacity to local television station signals. (Local stations are defined as those located within fifty miles of the cable community.)

In late 1987, in *Century Communications* v. *FCC,* a United States court of appeals ruled that these rules also violated the cable operator's First Amendment rights. The court ruled that the FCC had not demonstrated that the new rules furthered a substantial government interest—a requirement for a rule to outweigh the First Amendment interest involved. The court said the FCC had failed to bring forth evidence to prove that it would take viewers five years to learn how to use these input selection switches. It also failed to demonstrate that during the sixteen months that elapsed after the *Quincy Cable* decision, cable operators were in fact dropping local stations.

A study funded by the cable industry suggests that local stations are not being dropped. The Price Waterhouse research report concluded in late 1988 that ninety-eight percent of all stations that would have qualified to be carried under the old rules were still being carried. But at what price? In South Carolina one cable company is charging a local television station twenty four thousand dollars per year to stay on the system, according to an article in *Channels* magazine. And in Florida, a cable company's conditions for carrying local stations include forbidding the station to use the term "free TV" in its advertising. Elsewhere, according to Frank Lovece, author of the article, cable operators have refused to carry local stations that offer local advertisements in order to deter competitors. In late 1988 the FCC announced it would probably abandon the must-carry rules.

A United States court of appeals ruled that cable is protected by the First Amendment; the Supreme Court has certainly implied that it is as well. In 1986, a year before the *Century Communications* decision, the High Court ruled that the operator of a cable television system engages in activities that "plainly implicates First Amendment interests." The case involved a California cable operator who could not get a franchise to wire a section of Los Angeles and challenged the right of the city to limit which cable operators could and could not wire the city. Writing for a unanimous Supreme Court, Justice Rehnquist said, "Cable television partakes of some of the aspects of speech and the communication of ideas as do the traditional enterprises of newspaper and book publishers, public speakers and pamphleteers." Obviously, none of the "traditional enterprises" listed by Rehnquist are regulated as heavily as cable television or broadcasting generally. The High Court made no ruling on the constitutionality of the city's franchising authority, but sent the case back for construction of a better factual record at a trial. But the message was clear. Not only were judges of the court of appeals beginning to look at cable television operators more as a newspaper than a broadcasting station, but members of the Supreme Court had some of the same ideas (*Los Angeles* v. *Preferred Communications,* 1986).

Cable Communications Policy Act of 1984	The Cable Communications Policy Act of 1984 (hereafter Cable Act) was adopted after decades of crazy-quilt regulation at the federal, state, and local levels. The act was needed because some state and local governments were attempting to assert increased control over an industry that had become increasingly national in scope. In the summer of 1988, in a decision regarding the right of the FCC to establish certain technical standards for cable television, the Supreme Court read the new Cable Act in an expansive fashion, giving the FCC assurances that its regulation of the medium would be supported under the law (*New York City* v. *FCC,* 1988). Attorney Michael Meyerson points out in the *Georgia Law Review* that to understand the law it is important to recognize that it is a compromise. Representatives of the cable industry and the cities—the government units that award cable franchises—negotiated for three years before a bill was drafted that both could find acceptable.

The purposes of this legislation are enumerated in Section 601 of the Cable Act itself. They are as follows:

1. To establish a national policy concerning cable communciations

2. To establish franchise procedures and standards that encourage the growth and development of cable systems and that assure that cable systems are responsive to the needs and interests of the local community

3. To establish guidelines for the exercise of federal, state, and local authority with respect to the regulation of cable systems

4. To assure and encourage that cable communications provide the widest possible diversity of information sources and services to the public

5. To establish a process that protects cable operators against unfair denials of renewal by franchising authorities and that provides for an orderly process for consideration of renewal proposals

Jurisdiction and Franchises

The law clearly asserts federal jurisdiction over the control of cable but limits the FCC's broad discretion over cable policy. This is an indication that many members of the legislative body feared the commission would preempt local authority over cable television and then deregulate the industry. Consequently, under the new act most of the obligations imposed on the cable operator will come from local government rather than the FCC, but the local government must operate within the policy framework erected by the Congress in the Cable Act. The local government will be the "franchising authority" and grant the franchise to the cable operator.

While the statute outlines some policies regarding the content of the franchise, other matters—such as duration and timetable for construction of a system—are in the hands of the local government. The statute speaks of "services" and "facilities and equipment." *Services* generally means programming. *Facilities and equipment* refers to hardware of the system and the physical capabilities of the system, such as channel capacity, two-way or one-way, etc. Local governments are generally barred from establishing requirements for service or programming but are given a wide latitude to establish standards for equipment and facilities. The local government can insist that a cable operator provide broad categories of programming to meet the needs of children, different ethnic groups, or others and can insist that the cable operator provide public access channels for citizens to use. But critics of the law, such as Michael Botein of the New York Law School, point out that cable operators are permitted under the law to renege on these promises if they turn out to be "commercially impractical."

The act permits local govenment to charge a cable operator a franchise fee of up to five percent of the operator's gross revenues. But a recent ruling by the United States Supreme Court (see *Minneapolis Star and Tribune Co.*

v. *Minnesota Commissioner of Revenue,* 1983) strongly suggests that there is a constitutional limit on such a fee that may be lower than the one set by statute. Observers, such as Michael Meyerson, suggest that any fee collected can only be used to finance the operation of the franchise system. It cannot be collected simply to raise revenue. So a local government may be forced to charge a lower fee if the five percent assessment generates too much revenue.

The act permitted local governments to regulate the rates a cable operator could charge for basic cable service for two years, until December 29, 1986. After that time the franchising authority could regulate the rates for basic service only if the cable system were without "effective competition" in the community. The act did not define effective competition but required the FCC to define the term within six months, and in mid-1985 the commission ruled that there was effective competition to a cable system in a community if there were three over-the-air broadcast channels available to viewers. Most communities meet this profile, so local government is largely without any power to regulate what the cable operator can charge for basic service—the local over-the-air channels, the public access channels, and whatever else the cable operator includes in the package. Some members of the Congress, however, have expressed concern that cable operators may be attempting to take advantage of this provision. In mid-1988 United States Senator Howard Metzenbaum noted that there had been a fifty percent rate boost in ninety-three markets since Congress deregulated rates in 1986. He said the industry had to demonstrate that such rates were needed and were not adjusted simply to earn higher profits, or face the prospect of legislation to prevent such abuses. The prices charged to subscribers for the premium or pay channels are presently not regulated under the law.

The law makes it somewhat easier for a cable operator to renew a franchise, another provision of the act that some critics don't like. A franchising authority can deny the renewal of a franchise if the cable operator has not "substantially complied with the material terms of the existing franchise"— that is, has failed to live up to past promises—or if the cable operator's renewal proposal is not "reasonable to meeting the future cable-related community needs and interests." But the act also requires the local government to go through a set of formal procedures before it can deny a renewal, and critics charge that the burden of these procedures will tend to discourage cities from denying renewals.

Freedom of Speech

The Cable Act has established that third parties—that is, persons other than the cable operator or the local government—must have access to the cable system. Several means are provided for such access. The local franchising authorities are permitted to require that the cable operator provide public access and government and educational access channels. A public access channel is set aside for free public use on a nondiscriminatory, first-come, first-served basis. Neither the cable operator nor the government can censor what appears on such a channel. The franchising authority can prescribe limited (content-neutral) time, place, and manner rules for the public access channel, such as deciding that the access channel will give each user thirty minutes of time or that persons must sign up three days before the date they wish to use the channel. But that is about all. The government and educational channels are used either by schools or to broadcast public hearings or city council meetings. These channels are to be programmed as the government sees fit.

Commercial access channels must also be provided by the cable operator. The law provides that a certain number of channels must be set aside for use by "unaffiliated programmers" at reasonable rates. The cable operator cannot control the content of these programs. The number of channels that must be set aside for commercial access depends upon the number of activated channels in the cable system. An activated channel is one that is being used or is available for use. Systems with fewer than thirty-six channels need not have any commercial access channels; those with thirty-six to fifty-four channels must set aside ten percent of the channels for commercial access. Systems with more than fifty-four channels must reserve fifteen percent of these channels for commercial access. The cable operator can set the price and conditions of use for these channels, so long as they are "reasonable." Costs cannot have anything to do with content; that is, a cable operator cannot charge someone who puts on a conservative talk show one hundred dollars per hour and someone who puts on a liberal talk show five hundred dollars. However, the cable operator can set different rates for different categories of program; i.e., news programs cost fifty dollars per hour, movies one hundred dollars per hour.

As noted earlier the act permits all levels of government to prohibit and penalize the broadcast of obscene material over cable television. The law is somewhat less clear regarding the authority of local government to regulate the broadcast of indecent material. But federal courts have interpreted the statute in such a way as to give the FCC and only the FCC jurisdiction in this area (see pages 542–543). However, the act requires that every cable operator provide upon the request of a subscriber a lockbox device that permits the subscriber to block out the reception of specific channels. This permits parents to control what children can watch when the parents are not at home. Local governments can control the cablecasting of obscenity over the commercial access channels, but it is much harder for the franchising authority to control the transmission of obscenity over the public access channels. Whoever runs the public access channels can ask a user to sign an agreement that he or she will not broadcast obscenity while on the air, and of course any programmer who does broadcast obscenity can be punished after the telecast. But the public access channels are supposed to be free from close government scrutiny. That is why the law relieves the cable operator of any liability for the broadcast of any obscenity, libel, false advertising, or invasion of privacy that appears on the access channels.

One purpose of the law is to make available to as many persons as possible the fruits of the burgeoning communications technology. The act deals with this issue in several ways. It does not permit a cable operator to redline; that is, refuse to wire one portion of a franchise area because the citizens are poor or most persons would not subscribe to the cable. The act makes legal the use of the private earth stations, the so-called dish antennas, to receive unscrambled satellite transmissions. Under the Federal Communications Act such reception was often a violation of the law. However, cable channels and others who use satellite transmissions are permitted to scramble their signals under the new law—and many have begun to do so, much to the distaste of the 2.1 million dish owners. Both the FCC and local governments have the authority to regulate the use of the private earth stations in other ways. Local governments have attempted to use zoning rules or other regulations to keep the often unsightly and large antennas out of the community. But the FCC has ruled that local governments can only ban backyard or rooftop antennas when the TV receiving equipment violates "reasonable and clearly defined health, safety or aesthetic" considerations.

Protection of subscribers' right to privacy is a special concern in the Cable Act. The prospect of widespread use of two-way cable television—something that hasn't happened yet—gives the cable company the opportunity to gather an immense amount of data on subscribers. Products that are ordered via television, films that are watched, votes on public referenda are all recorded by the system's computer for legitimate reasons. But the use of this kind of data by the cable company for other purposes would surely violate the privacy of the subscriber. Yet there were no laws prohibiting such use. Users of one-way cable even provide the cable company with some kinds of information subscribers might not like to have widely known. The names of persons who subscribe to adult movie channels is one example. The Cable Act states that a cable company can only collect "personally identifiable information" for two purposes: (1) to obtain the information that is necessary to serve the subscriber and (2) to search for unauthorized reception of the cable signal. All personally identifiable information must be destroyed once it has been used for the purpose it was gathered, and the cable operator cannot disclose such information, even to government, unless the government can establish that it has a compelling reason to have this data that outweighs the subscriber's right to privacy. The subscriber must be told at least once a year what kind of data is being collected and is permitted to see this information and correct it if it is in error.

The Cable Act is a comprehensive attempt to provide both a cable policy and a regulatory framework. But it focuses almost exclusively on broadcast services. It says little about the regulation of data transmission over common carrier-type services; it skirts the issue of whether states, rather than the federal government, have a right to regulate such services. Can the FCC preempt the states in such regulation? What does the *Crisp* decision (see page 574) mean in this regard? These are issues that are still very much alive.

Other Broadcast Services	The FCC maintains the right to regulate other new broadcast services. Multipoint distribution services (MDS) have the configuration of traditional over-the-air broadcasting stations and are controlled by the FCC rather than local government. An MDS is wireless cable; the operator transmits television signals via microwave signals to subscribers who are equipped with a special antenna and a device that converts the microwave signals to one that can be received through a television set. Operation of such systems is regulated by federal law. In 1983 the FCC decided to allocate eight microwave channels per market for commerical use, setting off a stampede for the MDS licenses. The FCC scheduled lotteries to determine which of the sixteen thousand applicants would get the thousand licenses, but it took two years for the lotteries to occur. Even then they were held under a legal cloud as minority and female applicants challenged the FCC licensing process.

The Cable Act has given the local governments some control over the regulation of satellite master antenna television. The SMATVs are really private cable companies that service large apartment and condominum complexes. The complex owner sets up antennas and provides residents with television services. Congress was concerned that these television viewers recieve as many of the benefits of cable television as regular cable subscribers and gave local government limited power to franchise such operations and establish levels of performance, as they can with cable operators.

In 1982 the FCC authorized the development of what is called low-power television, or LPTV. LPTV stations broadcast no more than ten miles in one direction. They are really neighborhood stations. The process of licensing these stations through lotteries has gone very slowly. There is room for about four thousand such stations in the lower forty-eight states but only a small percentage of that number are now broadcasting. The federal government is solely responsible for the regulation of such stations.

The regulation of these exotic new technologies is just beginning and in some ways government—and that means we the people as well as the bureaucracy—seems ill-prepared to handle the challenge we have been given. While the nation now has a cable policy, it still lacks a broader communications policy. And until that is developed, it will be difficult to use regulation in a "creative" rather than a "control" manner to insure the greatest benefits from these amazing new technologies for all the people.

SUMMARY

The power of the FCC to regulate cable television was a clouded issue for many years. Slowly, but surely, the commission, with the permission of the courts, moved to regulate this new technology. In 1984 both the Supreme Court and the Congress gave the FCC what seemed to be clear jurisdiction to set broad rules for government cablecasting. But a subsequent court of appeals ruling has cast some doubt on all government regulation of cable.

The Cable Communications Policy Act of 1984 is a comprehensive measure setting policies and standards for the regulation of cable television. Local governments are given the primary responsibility under this measure to regulate the cable systems in their communities. They may issue franchises, collect franchise fees, and renew franchises. Regulation of the cost of basic service, however, will no longer be common. The act also provides for the inclusion of public, government, and commercial access channels. It also makes provisions to protect subscribers' right to privacy. The FCC does retain the power to regulate other forms of communications technology, however, including MDSs, earth stations, and low-power television.

BIBLIOGRAPHY

Here is a list of some of the sources that have been helpful in the preparation of chapter 11:

Books

American Enterprise Institute. *Broadcast Deregulation.* Washington, D.C.: American Enterprise Institute for Public Policy Research, 1985.

Cowan, Geoffrey. *See No Evil.* New York: Simon & Schuster, 1979.

Friendly, Fred. *The Good Guys, The Bad Guys and the First Amendment: Free Speech and Fairness in Broadcasting.* New York: Random House, 1976.

Ginsberg, Douglas. *Regulation of Broadcasting: Law and Public Policy Towards Radio, Television and Cable Communications.* St. Paul, Minn.: West Publishing Co., 1979.

Pember, Don R. *Mass Media in America.* 5th ed. Chicago: Science Research Associates, 1987.

Powe, Lucas A. Jr. *American Broadcasting and the First Amendment.* Berkeley: University of California Press, 1982.

Robinson, Glen O., and Gelhorn, Ernest. *The Administrative Process.* St. Paul, Minn.: West Publishing Co., 1974.

Articles

Bernstein, Andrew A. "Access to Cable, Natural Monopoly and the First Amendment." 86 *Columbia Law Review* 1663, 1986.

Bloch, Susan L. "Orphaned Rules in the Administrative State: The Fairness Doctrine and Other Progeny of Interactive Deregulation." 76 *Georgetown Law Journal* 59, 1987.

Bollier, David. "The Strange Politics of Fairness." *Channels,* January/February, 1986.

Bolton, Michael J. "In Stark Contravention of Its Purpose: Federal Communications Commission Enforcement of the Fairness Doctrine." 20 *Journal of Law Reform* 799, 1987.

Botein, Michael. "Who Came Out Ahead in the Cable Act." *Channels,* March/April, 1985.

Brown, Les. "Why Deregulation Won't Last." *Channels,* September/October, 1984.

Brown, Rhonda. "Ad Hoc Access: The Regulation of Editorial Advertising on Television and Radio." 6 *Yale Law and Policy Review* 449, 1988.

Cummings, Gary. "The Dark Side of Fairness." *Washington Journalism Review.* September, 1987.

Ecabert, Gayle S. "The Demise of the Fairness Doctrine: A Constitutional Reevaluation of Content-Based Broadcasting Regulations." 56 *Cincinnati Law Review* 999, 1988.

"FCC Launches Attack on Indecency." *Broadcasting*, April 20, 1987.

Fields, Howard. "Congress All Fed Up with Runaway FCC; Full-time Parent Now." *Television/Radio Age*, July 6, 1987.

Fogarty, Joseph R., and Spielholz, Marcia. "FCC Cable Jurisdiction: From Zero to Plenary in Twenty-five Years." 37 *Federal Communications Law Journal* 361, 1979.

Gregory, Robert S. "Regulating Cable Television: *Quincy Cable's* Unnatural Approach to Cable's Natural Monopoly." 31 *New York School Law Review* 591, 1986.

Johnson, Nicholas. "FCC Gets Down on Dirty." *Washington Journalism Review*, July/August, 1987.

Lovece, Frank. "Muddling Through the Must-Carry Mess." *Channels*, September, 1988.

Meyerson, Michael. "The Cable Communications Policy Act of 1984: A Balancing Act on the Coaxial Wires." 19 *Georgia Law Review* 543, 1985.

Robbins, Vicky H. "Indecency on Cable Television—A Barren Battleground for Regulation of Programming Content." 15 *St. Mary's Law Journal* 417, 1985.

"Should the Government Decide What's Best for Viewers?" *TV Guide*, December 12, 1987.

Simon, Jules F. "The Collapse of Consensus: Effects of the Deregulation of Cable Television." 81 *Columbia Law Review* 612, 1981.

Spong, Lawrence. "Cable Television Right of Way: Technology Expands the Concept of Public Forum." 20 *Journal of Law Reform* 1293, 1987.

Cases

Action for Children's Television v. FCC, 756 F.2d 899 (1985).
Action for Children's Television v. FCC, 821 F.2d 741 (1987).
Action for Children's Television v. FCC, 852 F.2d 1332 (1988).
Adrian Weiss, 58 FCC 2d 342 (1976).
American Security Council Foundation v. FCC, 607 F.2d 438 (1979).
Banzhaf v. FCC, 405 F.2d 1164 (1969).
Branch v. FCC, 824 F.2d 37 (1987).
in re *Business Executives Movement for Peace v. FCC*, 450 F.2d 642 (1971).
Capital Cities v. Crisp, 467 U.S. 691 (1984).
Carroll Broadcasting Co. v. FCC, 258 F.2d 440 (1958).
in re *Carter Mountain Transmission Corp.* 32 FCC 459 (1962); aff'd 321 F.2d 359 (1963); 375 U.S. 951 (1963).
Cattle Country Broadcasting, 50 Fed. Reg. 37, 272 (1985).
CBS v. Democratic National Committee, 412 U.S. 94 (1973).
CBS v. FCC, 453 U.S. 567 (1981).
Central Florida Enterprises, Inc. v. FCC, 598 F.2d 37 (1978).
Century Communications v. FCC, 835 F.2d 292 (1987).
Citizens Committee to Preserve the Voice of Arts in Atlanta v. FCC, 436 F.2d 263 (1970).
Citizens' Committee to Save WEFM v. FCC, 506 F.2d 246 (1974).
in re *Community Broadcasting Service, Inc., WWBZ*, 20 FCC 168 (1955).
Community Television v. Wilkinson, 611 F.2d 1099 (1985).
Cosmopolitan Broadcasting Corp. 59 FCC 2d 558 (1976).
Cowles Florida Enterprises, Inc. v. FCC, 683 F.2d 503 (1982).
Cruz v. Fere, 571 F.Supp 125 (1983).
Democratic National Committee v. FCC, 717 F.2d 1471 (1983).
Diocesan Union of Holy Name Society of Rockville Centre and Long Island Coalition for Life, 41 FCC 2d 497 (1973).
In the Matter of Editorializing by Broadcast Licensees, 13 FCC 1246 (1949).

Farmers Educational and Cooperative Union of America v. *WDAY*, 360 U.S. 525
(1959).
FCC v. *League of Women Voters*, 468 U.S. 912 (1984).
FCC v. *Midwest Video Corp.* 440 U.S. 689 (1979).
FCC. Pacifica Foundation, 438 U.S. 726 (1978).
FCC v. *WNCN Listeners Guild*, 450 U.S. 582 (1981).
Fourth Report and Order on Cable Television Service, 37 Fed. Regs. 3251 (1972).
FRC v. *Nelson Brothers*, 289 U.S. 266 (1933).
Galloway v. *FCC*, 778 F.2d 16 (1985).
Home Box Office v. *Wilkinson*, 531 F.Supp. 987 (1982).
Hoover v. *Intercity Radio Co., Inc.* 286 F. 1003 (1923).
Illinois Citizens Committee for Broadcasting v. *FCC*, 515 F.2d 197 (1975).
Johnson v. *FCC*, 829 F.2d 157 (1987).
Kennedy for President Committee v. *FCC*, 636 F.2d 417 (1980); 636 F.2d 432
(1980).
KFKB Broadcasting Association v. *FRC*, 47 F.2d 670 (1931).
King Broadcasting Co. v. *FCC*, 860 F.2d 465 (1988).
Kuzco v. *Western Connecticut Broadcasting*, 424 F.Supp. 1324 (1977).
Los Angeles v. *Preferred Communications, Inc.*, 476 U.S. 488 (1986).
in re *Mayflower Broadcasting Corp., WAAB*, 8 FCC 333 (1941).
May Seed and Nursery Co., 2 FCC 559 (1936).
Meredith Corp. v. *FCC*, 809 F.2d 863 (1987).
Midwest Video Corp. v. *FCC*, 571 F.2d 1025 (1978).
Minneapolis Star and Tribune Co. v. *Minnesota Commissioner of Revenue*, 460
U.S. 575 (1983).
National Citizens Committee for Broadcasting v. *FCC*, 567 F.2d 1095 (1977).
National Committee for Responsive Philanthropy v. *FCC*, 652 F.2d 589 (1981).
NBC v. *FCC*, 516 F.2d 1101 (1974).
New York City v. *FCC*, 108 S.Ct. 1637 (1988).
Office of Communications, United Church of Christ v. *FCC*, 359 F.2d 994 (1966).
in re *Palmetto Broadcasting Co.*, 33 FCC 250 (1962).
Patsy Mink, 59 FCC 2d 984 (1976).
Public Media Center v. *FCC*, 587 F.2d 1322 (1978).
Quincy Cable v. *FCC*, 768 F.2d 1434 (1985).
Radio and Television News Director's Association v. *U.S.*, 400 F.2d 1002 (1968).
Red Lion Broadcasting Co. v. *FCC*, 381 F.2d 908 (1967); aff'd 395 U.S. 367
(1969).
RKO v. *FCC*, 670 F.2d 215 (1981).
Sonderling Broadcasting Corp., 27 P & F Rad. Regs. 287 (1973).
Syracuse Peace Council v. *FCC*, 867 F.2d 654 (1989).
Telecommunications Research and Actions Center v. *FCC*, 801 F.2d 501; 806 F.2d
1115 (1986).
Trinty Methodist Church South v. *FRC*, 62 F.2d 650 (1932).
U.S. v. *Midwest Video Corp.*, 406 U.S. 649 (1972).
U.S. v. *Southwestern Cable Co.*, 392 U.S. 157 (1968).
U.S. v. *Zenith Radio Corp.*, 12 F.2d 616 (1926); 35 Op. Att'y. Gen. 126 (1926).
WCBS-TV, 8 FCC 2d 381 (1967); aff'd Applicability of the Fairness Doctrine to
Cigarette Advertising, 9 FCC 2d 921 (1967).
in re *Wilderness Society and Friends of the Earth*, 30 FCC 2d 643 (1971); rev'd
Friends of the Earth v. *FCC*, 449 F.2d 1164 (1971).
Writers Guild v. *ABC*, 609 F.2d 355 (1979).
Writers Guild v. *FCC*, 423 F.Supp. 1064 (1976).
in re *WUHY-FM, Eastern Educational Radio*, 24 FCC 2d 408 (1970).
Young People's Association for the Propagation of the Gospel, 6 FCC 178 (1938).

12 REGULATION OF THE MEDIA AS A BUSINESS

The primary purpose of this book is to focus upon the censorship and regulation of what is printed in the press or broadcast over radio and television—the content of mass media communication. Yet mass media face other regulation as well, regulation based not on content, but on other criteria. In the United States newspapers, broadcasting stations, film companies, and magazines are usually private businesses, and as such these media businesses face the myriad rules and regulations confronting other businesses in this nation. Rules regarding minimum wages, maximum working hours, safety, health, taxation, and many other areas apply to the mass media as well as to automobile manufacturers, furniture companies, and beauty salons.

Two factors stand out regarding these rules. First, they are applied to the media regardless of content. Magazines that aim to contribute to the essential political debate in this country have to meet the same minimum wage rules as do romance magazines, which appeal to the emotions. The makers of serious films must meet the same safety standards at their studios as do the makers of sleazy sex-oriented films. The point is this: Whereas in some areas the law is applied differently to businesses thought to serve the public interest than to those that do not, no such variable application occurs when the media are looked at as businesses.

Second, while the First Amendment has been at the center of our discussion of press regulation to this point in the book, the guarantees of freedom of expression mean very little when the media are regulated as businesses. The First Amendment might protect a newspaper that erroneously labels a politician a crook or a magazine that publishes the intimate secrets of the life of a public official, but it will not protect the publisher who fails to meet fire code regulations or the broadcaster who refuses to pay legitimate taxes. More than fifty years ago the Supreme Court made this abundantly clear when it upheld the constitutionality of the National Labor Relations Act, which at the time was under a First Amendment challenge launched by the Associated Press (AP). "The business of the Associated Press is not immune from regulation because it is an agency of the press," wrote Justice Owen Roberts for the five-man majority. "The publisher of a newspaper has no special immunity from the application of general laws" (*AP* v. *NLRB,* 1937). Broadcasting station operators and publishers often have to be reminded of this. In 1981 a United States district court in Massachusetts ruled that a newspaper has no First Amendment right to decline to participate in the quarterly financial report program of the Federal Trade Commission (FTC). The court said the FTC only sought financial data and did not intrude upon the exercise of editorial judgment (*U.S. v. Nanlo*, 1981). The press must meet all its legal responsibilities as a business, regardless of the First Amendment. ♦

GOVERNMENT AND THE MASS COMMUNICATION BUSINESS

No attempt will be made in this chapter to outline all the broad areas of regulation affecting the media as a business. The mass media, like all businesses, face myriad federal, state, and even local regulations. In labor relations alone the printed press must cope with rules on worker health and safety, pay, the employment of juvenile workers (newspaper carriers) and a wide range of other matters. Recently, for example, the *Washington Post* was taken to court by ninety-nine editors, reporters and photographers who claimed the newspaper had violated provisions of the United States Fair Labor Standards Act. They complained that they were not paid time-and-a-half for overtime work as they should be. But under the law, professionals are considered exempt from the overtime pay provisions, and The *Post* argued that these workers were professionals. A United States district court agreed, noting that the Department of Labor defines "professionals" as persons who do original and creative work in a recognized field of endeavor, work that depends primarily upon the invention, imagination or talent of the employee. The *Post* staffers "produce original and creative writing of high quality within the meaning of the regulations," the court ruled (*Sherwood* v. *Washington Post Group*, 1988). Scores of other such labor relations cases abound. But consideration of these rules and other business regulations more properly reside in a class in business law. Only two areas of commercial regulation will be outlined in this chapter, since both have implications beyond simple business regulation. The regulation of the ownership and operation of the media through antitrust laws and FCC policies is significant because it can have an important impact on who can own the press and, in some instances, the content of media communication. Taxation of the press will be noted briefly also, since on at least some occasions taxation has been used as a means to indirectly censor the press.

Antitrust Laws and Newspapers

The government's primary weapons against economic concentration and restraint of trade in industry are the antitrust laws. The Sherman Act of 1890 and the Clayton Act of 1914 provide the legal bases for the Department of Justice to bring both criminal and civil suits against businesses that use monopolistic tactics to endanger free competition. The press is not immune from such legal pressure, yet surprisingly it has been an infrequent target of government antitrust action. One author notes that between 1945, when the Supreme Court ruled that the First Amendment did not shield the press from action by the government to stop monopolistic practices, and 1969, only twelve antitrust suits were initiated against the press. In 1976, when seventy-two different newspapers changed hands (most were bought up by newspaper chains), there were no antitrust actions against newspaper interests. Why? Catherine B. Roach offered one opinion in an article in the *Memphis State University Law Review:*

> Because of the structure of the communications industry—basically a collection of local circulation and advertising markets—anti-trust enforcers have encountered difficult problems of proof as to anticompetitive effects in relevant markets.

In an effort to explain some of the anticompetitive problems the federal government has sought to control in the press, here is a summary of some of the litigation in the past forty years.

Restrictive Membership Rules

As noted previously, it was in 1945 that the Supreme Court first gave approval to the prosecution of antitrust action against members of the press. The occasion was a suit by the government against the Associated Press, the giant news cooperative and wire service. Marshall Field had founded the morning *Chicago Sun* and sought an AP membership for his newspaper. But under AP bylaws the owners of the rival *Chicago Tribune* were given the opportunity to approve or disapprove Field's application for membership. Without this approval, the applicant needed the consent of a majority of all AP members for the membership application to be accepted. These rules effectively kept newspapers that competed with AP members from getting the highly desirable membership and access to the AP wire service.

The federal government brought an antitrust action against the AP, charging that its membership laws resulted in an illegal monopoly in restraint of trade—a violation of the Sherman Act. Among the AP responses to the suit was the vigorous assertion that the Department of Justice lawsuit against the news cooperative represented a serious infringement upon the constitutionally guaranteed freedom of the press. But the High Court ruled that the Associated Press membership provisions were in fact a violation of the Sherman Act. And Justice Hugo Black, writing for the majority, dismissed the argument that the AP was shielded from such legal action by the First Amendment. "Member publishers of the AP are engaged in business for profit exactly as are other businessmen who sell food, steel, aluminum or anything else people need or want," Black wrote. He said that the inability to buy news from the news agency could have serious effects upon a publication and actually endanger its ability to continue to operate successfully. And then Black penned one of his most memorable passages regarding freedom of the press (*AP* v. *U.S.,* 1945):

> The [First] Amendment rests on the assumption that the widest possible dissemination of information from diverse and antagonistic sources is essential to the welfare of the public, that a free press is a condition of a free society. Surely a command that the government itself shall not impede the free flow of ideas does not afford nongovernmental combinations a refuge if they impose

restraints upon that constitutionally guaranteed freedom. Freedom to publish means freedom for all and not for some. Freedom to publish is guaranteed by the Constitution, but freedom to keep others from publishing is not.

The First Amendment, then, provides no safe house for the business person who violates laws or rules designed to foster free competition. And as we have noted earlier, this generalization rings as true with regard to other commercial regulations as it does with antitrust laws.

Local Monopolies

Six years after the *AP* case, the Supreme Court heard arguments in another antitrust action involving the press. This case focused upon what was essentially a monopoly newspaper business in a medium-sized town. The newspaper refused to accept advertising from businesses that also used other community advertising media.

The *Lorain* (Ohio) *Journal* and the *Times Herald* were owned by the same publisher. The combined daily circulation of the two papers reached nearly one hundred percent of the families in the community. The only print competition came from the weekly *Sunday News*. In 1948 a radio station began operation in the community. Shortly thereafter the publisher of the two daily papers announced that the newspapers would no longer accept advertising from businesses and industries in the community that also broadcast advertisements over the radio station. The Department of Justice brought an antitrust action against the Lorain Journal Company, charging that the publishing firm was attempting to monopolize interstate commerce and to force advertisers to boycott the radio station. Justice Harold Burton, writing for a unanimous Supreme Court, ruled that the newspaper's policy violated the Sherman Act, "A single newspaper, already enjoying a substantial monopoly in its area, violates the 'attempt to monopolize' clause [of the Sherman Act] . . . when it uses its monopoly to destroy threatened competition." A publisher has the right to refuse to publish any advertisement, but he cannot use this right as "a purposeful means of monopolizing interstate commerce." The First Amendment afforded the paper no special protection: "The injunction applies to a publisher what the law applies to others," Burton wrote (*Lorain Journal Co. v. U.S.*, 1951).

Two years later the Supreme Court was forced to scrutinize a tie-in, or combination advertising rate scheme, used by a New Orleans publisher. The Times-Picayune Company published both the morning *Times-Picayune* and the evening *States*. There was also a competing afternoon paper published in the city, the *Item*. Advertisers who wanted to purchase an advertisement in either the *Times-Picayune* or the *States* had to purchase an advertisement in both. The government brought a civil action against the Times-Picayune Company, charging that its forced combination advertising policy was an unreasonable restraint of trade.

The Supreme Court ruled in a five-to-four decision that the combination advertising rate was not a violation of the law. Justice Tom Clark admitted in his opinion for the majority that such an advertising scheme could hurt competition. Clark cited statistics that showed that of the 598 daily papers that had begun publication between 1929 and 1950, more than 225 of them survived at the end of that period. Of these 598, 46 dailies had encountered combination advertising-rate schemes like the one in New Orleans. Of those 46 papers, only 5 survived in 1950.

According to the Supreme Court, however, such an advertising-rate combination or "tying" arrangement was illegal only if a business with a dominant position in the market coerced its customers into buying an unwanted inferior product along with the desired product. The government argued that the *Times-Picayune* was the dominant, desired product and the afternoon *States* was the unwanted, inferior product that advertisers were forced to buy. The crucial questions in the case, according to Clark, were whether the *Times-Picayune* held a dominant market position and whether the *States* was really an inferior product. The five-man majority answered both questions negatively. The *Times-Picayune* had the greatest circulation, published the most pages, and had the highest amount of advertising, but it was not dominant in the relevant market—the advertising market. The morning paper carried about 40 percent of the classified and display advertising published by the three papers. If all papers had an equal share, the *Times-Picayune* would have still had about 33 percent. The circulation for the *Times-Picayune* was 190,000; for the *States*, 105,000; and for the *Item*, 115,000. The third paper, the *Item*, was flourishing, Clark wrote. He added, "The record in this case thus does not disclose evidence from which demonstrably deleterious effects on competition may be inferred." A majority of the High Court rejected the argument that the *Times-Picayune* was the desired product and the *States* was the inferior product. The products were identical, Clark added (*Times-Picayune* v. *U.S.*, 1953):

> Here . . . two newspapers under single ownership at the same place, time and terms sell indistinguishable products to advertisers; no dominant "tying" product exists . . . no leverage in one market excludes sellers in the second, because for present purposes the products are identical and the market the same.

Five years after the ruling, the Times-Picayune Company purchased the *Item* and created the *States-Item*, making it the only afternoon paper in the city.

Despite the loss in the *Times-Picayune* case, the Department of Justice pushed on with a similar antitrust action in Kansas City against a rate-combination, or tie-in, advertising policy. This time the government was successful in proving the market dominance of the Kansas City Star Company, something it could not prove with regard to the Times-Picayune Company.

The defendant owned the morning *Kansas City Times* and the afternoon *Kansas City Star.* The two papers were circulated to ninety-six percent of the homes in the area. In addition, the Kansas City Star Company published the *Sunday Star* and owned WDAF radio and WDAF-TV stations. Through all its holdings, the company received ninety-four percent of all advertising revenue spent in the area. The only competition in the print media field were weekly and suburban papers.

In order to subscribe to any one of the three Star Company–owned newspapers, a resident had to subscribe to all three: both dailies and the Sunday edition. Advertisers were also required to run advertising in all three newspapers. The Star Company used this monopoly power ruthlessly. Examples documented by the government included threats by the newspaper to stop the news coverage of a professional baseball player who bought space in a competing paper to advertise his florist shop. Also, it was reported that advertisers who failed to buy space in the defendant's newspapers received less favorable treatment in getting advertising on WDAF-AM and WDAF-TV. The United States Court of Appeals for the Eighth Circuit ruled that such circulation and advertising tie-ins violated the Sherman Act in light of the market dominance by the Star Company. With regard to the First Amendment the court said, "To use the freedom of the press guaranteed by the First Amendment to destroy competition would defeat its own ends, for freedom to print news and express opinions as one chooses is not tantamount to having freedom to monopolize" (*U.S.* v. *Kansas City Star,* 1957).

The conviction in this criminal antitrust action was just the beginning for the Star Company. A subsequent civil suit was settled by the firm through a consent order (this legal device is described on page 493), under which the Star Company agreed to sell its broadcasting properties and to stop the tie-in policies with regard to advertising and circulation. Additional civil suits were generated by media competitors in the Kansas City area, and it is estimated that in the end the Star Company paid out several hundred thousand dollars in damages.

Chain Ownership

Ten years elapsed before a federal court again ruled in an important media antitrust action. And for the first time the government action against the press was initiated because of something other than newspaper policy regarding advertisers or subscribers. In this case the target of the federal suit had merely purchased a nearby newspaper.

Serious concern was generated by many thoughtful students of the media during the sixties with regard to the shrinking number of independently owned newspapers in the United States. Similarly, competition between papers in major cities shrunk rapidly to the point where communities with competing daily newspapers were considered unusual. The statistics tell the story graphically. In 1923 daily newspapers were published in nearly 1,300 American cities. Of that total, 502 cities had two or more competing daily papers. Forty years later in 1963, daily newspapers were published in 1,476 cities, but only 51 communities had competing papers. Today there are truly competing newspapers in only about 20 American cities. Many feared the demise of the independent newspaper in the United States. The dearth of competition between papers in communities augured a less-vital press and fewer outlets for the publication of ideas and protests. The first real government response to these fears came in southern California when the Department of Justice brought a civil antitrust action against the Times-Mirror Corporation for purchasing a large newspaper company in an adjoining county.

Since 1948 the morning *Los Angeles Times* had had the largest circulation in California. It was an important force in southern California. In the mid-1960s the firm bought the Sun Company, which published the morning *Sun,* the afternoon *Telegram,* and the *Sunday Sun-Telegram* in San Bernardino County, which adjoins Los Angeles County on the east. Until its purchase by the Times-Mirror Corporation, the Sun Company had been the largest independent publisher in southern California. The government argued that the purchase of these newspapers by the Times-Mirror Corporation resulted in a restraint of interstate commerce, in violation of the Sherman Act, and had the impact of lessening competition in the area, which is a violation of the Clayton Act.

In ruling in favor of the government, Judge Warren Ferguson noted that the purchase of the Sun Company newspapers by Times-Mirror was only the latest of a series of actions that had reduced the number of independently owned California newspapers from fifty-nine percent in 1952 to twenty-four percent in 1966. "The acquisition of the *Sun* by the *Times* was particularly anticompetitive," Judge Ferguson wrote, "because it eliminated one of the few independent papers that had been able to operate successfully in the morning and Sunday fields." Since the purchase of the Sun Company newspapers by the Times-Mirror Corporation, Ferguson noted, two daily newspapers had been closed and two more newspaper mergers in San Bernardino County had occurred. The federal district judge ruled that the acquisition of the Sun Company newspapers by the Times-Mirror Corporation "has raised a barrier to entry of newspapers in the San Bernardino County market that is almost impossible to overcome." Ferguson said that the market for new papers was effectively closed, and "no publisher will risk the expense of unilaterally starting a new daily newspaper there." The judge pointed to the fact that even the prestigious *New York Times* failed to break into the market with a West Coast edition of its successful newspaper. Divestiture was ordered by the court, and the Supreme Court affirmed this ruling one year later (*U.S.* v. *Times-Mirror Corporation,* 1968).

Following divestiture the Sun Company newspapers were purchased by the Gannett newspaper chain, the largest chain in the nation. Many persons questioned whether the people in San Bernardino County gained or lost as a result of the government lawsuit and the subsequent purchase of the paper by

Gannett. Gannett ownership of the *Sun* and the *Telegram* did create a "second owner" in the community, but was the owner a better owner or as good an owner? Both the Times-Mirror Corporation and Gannett are absentee owners not living in the community in which the newspapers are published. But the Times-Mirror Corporation resided just over the county line and certainly was familiar with the problems and people in the area. Gannett has corporate offices in New York State, completely across the nation. The *Los Angeles Times* is one of the most prestigious newspapers in the United States. It remains speculative whether Gannett has fused this quality into the Sun Company newspapers. The opportunity did exist. However, few Gannett newspapers have risen above a mediocre or adequate level. Chances of producing a superior paper for the people of San Bernardino County seem significantly lower with the Gannett ownership. Finally, while the Times-Mirror Corporation is a large media corporation in its own right, its newspaper holdings remain miniscule compared with the growing Gannett chain, which in 1989 owned more than 90 daily newspapers in the nation. What was accomplished, many persons asked, by taking the Sun Company newspapers away from a small newspaper chain and giving it to a large one? The answers to these questions reflect directly on government antitrust policy, which appears to focus on the competition among economic units—advertisers and competing newspapers—rather than on the impact upon the reading public.

Joint-Operating Agreements

A year later the Justice Department's next major newspaper antitrust suit reached the Supreme Court. In this action the Department of Justice sought to break up the **joint-operating agreement** between the Citizen Publishing Company and the Star Publishing Company in Tucson, Arizona. The joint-operating arrangement (JOA) had been in effect for nearly thirty years in Tucson, and similar agreements existed between newspapers in more than twenty other American cities. The arrangement was simple. Two independent newspapers merged their advertising, printing, and circulation operations to form a third company. The news departments of the two papers remained separate and independent. The third company, Tucson Newspapers Incorporated, handled all advertising and circulation and printing for the evening *Citizen* and the morning and Sunday *Star*. Profits were pooled and shared.

The joint-operating agreement had two clear effects in the community. First, it provided lower costs for both papers and made it possible for two newspapers to be published in situations where only one might survive in pure head-to-head competition. At the same point, however, the lowered costs for the two newspapers made it difficult, if not impossible, for a third newspaper to compete. The government attacked several provisions of the arrangement as being violations of the Sherman Act. Specifically the lawyers for the Department of Justice argued that the setting of advertising and subscription prices by Tucson Newspapers was price-fixing. They also objected to profit pooling and to the fact that both the Star Publishing Company and the Citizen Publishing Company agreed not to engage in other media business in the area.

After considerable time in the lower courts, the Supreme Court in 1969 declared the arrangement to be a violation of the law (*U.S.* v. *Citizen Publishing Company,* 1969). Justice Douglas wrote that through a joint-operating agreement the two publishers had gained market control over the newspapers in Tucson. The Court did allow the *Star* and the *Citizen* to share some of the same facilities but struck down policies on profit pooling, establishment of joint-advertising and subscription rates, and other similar agreements.

In the months immediately following the ruling in *Citizen Publishing Company,* scores of bills were introduced in Congress to salvage the joint-operating agreement. If such policies were against the law, as the Supreme Court had ruled, then the law would have to be changed, the publishers argued. And it was. In 1970, after an intensive lobbying effort by the publishing industry, the Congress adopted the Newspaper Preservation Act. Taking a clue from Justice Douglas's opinion in the *Citizen Publishing Company* case, Congress enacted legislation that permitted newspapers to continue to function under joint-operating agreement so long as at the time at which the agreement is made, one of the two papers is in "probable danger of failing." Papers seeking to enter into joint-operating agreements in the future have to first gain permission from the attorney general if they expect to be exempted from the antitrust rules provided for by the law. The measure had the impact of legalizing the twenty-two agreements in effect in 1970, including the one that the Supreme Court had declared illegal in Tucson. The merits of the law have been hotly debated along lines similar to the debate over the joint-operating agreements themselves. While legalizing these agreements has ensured that in twenty-two cities, at least, newspaper news and editorial competition will survive, the law at the same time makes it practically impossible for other publishers to compete with the two monopoly papers that boast lower operating costs.

After several years of trying to compete with the *San Francisco Examiner* and the *Chronicle,* which have operated under a joint agreement since 1965, Bay Area publisher Bruce Brugman went to court in July 1971 and charged that the Newspaper Preservation Act violated his freedom of the press by encouraging journalistic monopoly. Brugman, who published the monthly *Bay Guardian,* told the court that his small paper had difficulty getting advertisers because of the lower joint-advertising rates set by the two newspapers. Many advertisers could not afford to or chose not to advertise beyond the two large San Francisco dailies. Federal district judge Oliver Carter showed little sympathy for Brugman's arguments, however, and in 1972 ruled that the congressional measure did not authorize a monopoly (*Bay Guardian Publishing Company* v. *Chronicle Publishing Company,* 1972). Carter wrote:

> Here the act was designed to preserve independent editorial voices. Regardless of the economic or social wisdom of such a course, it does not violate the freedom of the press. Rather, it is merely a selective repeal of the antitrust laws. It merely looses the same shady market forces which existed

before the passage of the Sherman, Clayton and other antitrust laws. Such a repeal, even when applicable only to the newspaper industry, does not violate the First Amendment.

The law regarding joint-operating agreements has changed little in the past twenty years, although some litigation has ensued. In 1979 the E. W. Scripps Company sought Department of Justice approval of a joint-operating agreement between its *Cincinnati Post* and Gannett's *Cincinnati Enquirer.* For the first time a public hearing was held on the question. While the government ultimately agreed that the Scripps publication met the requirements of a failing newspaper, attorneys for the Department of Justice raised the interesting question of whether a newspaper could truly be termed "failing" when the parent company (Scripps) might be benefitting financially from the tax write-offs accorded by the *Post*'s losses. The matter was not pressed at that time by the government, and the application for the joint-operating agreement was approved.

A hearing was also held before the Department of Justice gave its approval to a joint-operating agreement between the *Seattle Times* and the *Seattle Post-Intelligencer.* Persons protesting the agreement argued that the Hearst Corporation, owner of the *Post-Intelligencer,* was not in danger of failing. They argued that Hearst had taken money out of the newspaper in order to put it in the position of a failing newspaper. They also argued that the corporation had made no effort to try to sell the newspaper so that another owner might keep it independent; in fact Hearst had rejected all offers to purchase the paper. The hearing judge rejected all contentions and approved the joint-operating plan. Attorney William French Smith also approved of the pact, despite arguments from the antitrust division of the Department of Justice that the *Post-Intelligencer* was not legally a "failing newspaper." A court challenge to Attorney General Smith's approval of the agreement was mounted, and in late August 1982 a United States district court ruled that Smith had acted improperly when he approved the joint-operating proposal. Judge Barbara Rothstein rejected plaintiff's contentions that the Newspaper Preservation Act was a violation of the First Amendment. But she did agree that before the *Post-Intelligencer* could qualify as a failing newspaper, there must be a showing by those persons seeking the approval of the agreement that no other viable alternatives existed for maintaining the newspaper's independent editorial voice. Hearst did not have an obligation under the law to try to seek out buyers for the paper. But in this case there was evidence that buyers were interested in the newspaper. Hearst would have to demonstrate that because of existing economic conditions and other factors, a new owner of the newspaper could not make the *Post-Intelligencer* succeed (*Committee v. Smith,* 1982). But less than one year later, the United States court of appeals for the Ninth Circuit reversed the district court ruling and held that the Hearst Corporation had met its burden of showing that the alleged alternative owners did not offer a solution to the financial difficulties experienced by the *Post-Intelligencer.* Six people did inquire into the possibility of buying the newspaper, but these were not offers. And these inquiries did not show that the *Post-Intelligencer* could in all probability be sold to a buyer who would continue its operation as an independent newspaper. The critical question in the case, the court of appeals opinion noted, was whether the newspaper was suffering losses that more than likely could not be reversed. There was no evidence that any new owner might be successful in reversing the *Post-Intelligencer's* financial difficulties. In fact, the court said, there was sufficient evidence in the record supporting a negative answer (*Committee for an Independent P–I v. Hearst,* 1983).

In 1986 the *Detroit Free Press,* owned by the Knight–Ridder newspaper chain, and the *Detroit News,* owned by the Gannett Company, announced they would enter into a joint-operating agreement. Many questioned how anyone could seriously contend that either paper was in danger of failing when their corporate owners were so prosperous. Nevertheless, owners of the *Free Press* and the *News* identified the former as the failing paper and sought permission to merge their production, circulation, and advertising operations. In August of 1986, an assistant United States attorney general recommended that a hearing be held to determine the need for the joint agreement. After studying the situation, he said he had concluded that a joint-operating agreement did not appear necessary to maintain both editorial voices in Detroit. He noted that recently the *Free Press* had shown both advertising and circulation gains, and that the paper had yet to realize the promise of added revenue from an expanded and modernized printing plant. The newspaper did not appear to match the picture of a newspaper in a downward spiral, the traditional plight of a failing newspaper. True, the *Free Press* had lost forty million dollars in the past five years, but Assistant United States Attorney General Douglas Ginsberg noted that the losses came in an effort to achieve market dominance by offering cut-rate subscriptions and lower advertising rates. "When a newspaper owner consciously and deliberately decides to sacrifice short-term profits in a quest for greater long-term profits, indeed potential monopoly profits, should a JOA be available as a 'second best' alternative?" Ginsberg asked.

A hearing was held on the issue during which the anti-trust division of the Department of Justice opposed the approval of the joint-operating agreement. In December of 1987 the administrative law judge who heard the case urged the rejection of the proposed agreement. He ruled that the *Free Press* was not dominated by the *News,* that the *Free Press* was not in a downward spiral toward ultimate failure, and that the applicants had failed to prove that there exists in Detroit an irreversible market condition that would cause the *Free Press* to fall into this downward spiral. In short, the *Free Press* is not a failing newspaper, the judge ruled. "The losses incurred by the *Free Press* and the *News* are attributable to their strategies of seeking market dominance and future profitability at any cost along with the expectation that failure to achieve these goals would result in a favorable consideration of a JOA application," wrote administrative law judge Morton Needelman.

The final decision rested with Attorney General Edwin Meese, who in August of 1988, said he accepted the administrative law judge's findings, but rejected his conclusions. He approved the joint-operating agreement, arguing that the continuing losses by the *Free Press* clearly put the newspaper in danger of failure. A citizens law suit was filed to attempt to block the agreement, but in late 1988 a United States district court ruled that the attorney general had not acted in an arbitrary and capricious manner in approving the JOA. The court said that "it would make little sense to hold that a newspaper should be denied a JOA and forced to close because of financial reasons simply because the publication has not entered a stereotypical 'downward spiral.' The test must be one of probabilities, not certainties." Thus the court changed a basic criteria for qualification for a JOA. Instead of requiring that one of the newspapers meet the profile of a probable failing newspaper, the court said it was sufficient to show that one of the newspapers may become a failing newspaper if conditions did not change. The court noted that speculation by the administrative law judge that if both papers would stop trying to destroy each other with cut-rate pricing they could "again bask in the sun of profitability" was only speculation. The judge said he was somewhat disconcerted by Attorney General Meese's response to the proposition put forth by the anti-trust division and the administrative law judge that both papers adopted the price-cutting strategies knowing that if they failed to gain market domination they could fall back on the joint-operating agreement rather than suffer financial ruin. The court noted that the attorney general had "failed to address the subtlety of the dual issue motive" (*Michigan Citizens for an Independent Press* v. *Attorney General*, 1988).

An appeal was taken to the United States Court of Appeals for the District of Columbia, but those opposed to the Detroit JOA lost again. Judge Silberman ruled that Attorney General Meese's conclusion that the *Free Press* was in danger of failing with no prospect of reversal was certainly "debatable," but "hardly unreasonable." Silberman noted that the real difficulty in the case is the potential impact of the approval of the JOA on other newspapers. "It is feared that the statute authorizing a JOA creates a self-fulfilling prophecy. Newspapers in two newspaper towns will compete recklessly because of a recognition that the loser will be assured of a soft landing," he wrote. This problem emerges from the rather ambiguous phrase that remains the test in each case, is one of the newspapers in "probable danger of financial failure?" But the Congress delegated to the Attorney General, not to the courts, the responsibility of "putting content" into that ambiguous phrase," Silberman concluded in the 2–1 ruling (*Michigan Citizens* v. *Thornburgh*, 1989). The appellants sought an en banc review of the ruling by the Court of Appeals, but this was denied (*Michigan Citizens* v. *Thornburgh,* 1989). In a move that took most observers by surprise, the Supreme Court agreed on May 1, 1989, to hear an appeal in the case.

At least two more JOAs have been proposed. Two small dailies in York, Pa., have applied to the Justice Department to merge all non-editorial functions. And in California a proposed JOA would join the *Manteca Bulletin,* a morning paper with a paid circulation of 6,500, plus a free circulation of 13,000 for the Friday paper, and the *Manteca News,* which is delivered to 5,600 paid subscribers on Friday and to 18,600 nonpaying readers on Wednesday. This would be the first JOA between a daily and nondaily, if it is approved.

In Washington, D.C., a bill was introduced in Congress that would permit JOA newspapers to engage in activities currently not authorized by the Newspaper Preservation Act, including the operation of electronic news and advertising delivery systems, and the publication of total market coverage papers— free circulation publications. No action was taken on the measure in the 100th Congress that adjourned in 1988. It is expected that the measure will be reintroduced in the 101st Congress.

What most people regard to be the most serious anticompetitive newspaper phenomenon of the 1980s is the rapid growth of newspaper chains and the concurrent demise of the independent newspapers. But the Department of Justice seems unwilling to move against such acquisitions. The antitrust division of the department did investigate the merger of the Gannett newspaper chain with Combined Communications, a large broadcasting chain that also owned two newspapers. But following the investigation *Editor and Publisher* quoted the assistant attorney general for antitrust, John H. Shenefield, as saying:

> The antitrust laws do not flatly prohibit media conglomerates anymore than they prohibit other kinds of conglomerates. Under present law, some measurable impact on competition in some market must be proven before a merger or acquisition will be held to violate the antitrust laws. Indeed, the courts have been generally reluctant to condemn conglomerate mergers where such an impact has not been shown, regardless of the social or other objections that have been asserted.

In an effort to enhance the government's ability to attack the growth of the giant conglomerates, Senator Edward Kennedy introduced a bill in 1979 that, if enacted, would have prohibited companies with more than 2.5 billion dollars in annual sales or more than 2 billion dollars in assets from merging. In addition, under the Kennedy proposal companies with 350 million dollars in annual sales or 200 million dollars in assets could merge only if they could convince the government that such a merger would enhance competition or produce efficiencies of benefit to consumers. The Kennedy proposal would have had little impact upon media conglomerates, as most are not as large as the companies the Kennedy proposal sought to regulate. The Kennedy plan has not yet been adopted by the Congress.

Today the most common kind of antitrust action brought against a newspaper is brought by a competing publication. Serious wars are being waged in many communities between newspapers and competing free-circulation shoppers or direct-mail advertisers. For many years the newspaper was the only important carrier of print advertising in a community. Free-circulation shoppers developed in the 1950s and became a thorn in the side of many newspapers. The shoppers gave an advertiser total market coverage; newspapers, of course, were delivered only to subscribers. Recent changes in the postal laws caused the newspaper industry even more headaches. Formerly the United States Postal Service required postage on each piece of mail delivered. But the law has been revised. Today it is possible for a direct-mail company to insert several different advertisements in a single circular or wrapper and pay a single postage fee for the entire package. This is called marriage mail. The shoppers and marriage-mail packagers began to pull advertisers away from the newspapers. In retaliation many newspapers began offering advertisers their own total market service: a shopper or even a direct-mail package. This competition has resulted in a great many lawsuits in which the owner of a shopper or direct-mail operation has brought a civil action against the newspaper for antitrust law violations. Most of these suits never go to trial, but are settled. The newspapers have generally won the few that have gone to trial, but not in every case. A federal court in Virginia ruled against a daily newspaper that used illegal practices to try to kill a competing free-circulation weekly newspaper and shopper. The newspaper began issuing its own shopper and offered advertising rates below those in the weekly shopper, rates that were actually below the daily newspaper's costs. The federal judge ruled that the Sherman Act outlaws the use of monopoly power to destroy threatened competition. Below-cost pricing in and of itself is not illegal, the court ruled. But evidence of below-cost pricing along with evidence that advertisers who went into the daily newspaper's shopper got rebates and special tie-in rates for advertising in the daily paper does suggest monopolistic practices. There was also testimony in the case that the publisher of the newspaper had said that the weekly shopper would not be in business much longer. The court enjoined the publication of the daily newspaper's shopper unless its advertising rates were raised and all tie-in and rebate advertising arrangements were ended. That the daily newspaper already controlled eighty-five percent of all print advertising in the community was an important factor in the victory for the weekly publisher (*Advantage Publications* v. *Daily Press*, 1983).

Broadcasting
Monopolies

The Department of Justice has carried the largest burden in attempting to control the competitive practices of the newspaper industry. But in broadcasting the Federal Communications Commission (FCC) has taken the lead in regulating the ownership of radio and television stations, and only recently has the Department of Justice moved against members of the industry.

The Federal Communications Commission has closely regulated the business practices of broadcasters by means of the license renewal procedures and other commission policies. Congress has passed statutes with regard to some matters such as the rates a broadcaster may charge a candidate for public office. The FCC itself has issued scores of rules regarding business and advertising practices. It has also been the FCC that has attempted to control both the growth of broadcast chains and other ownership practices of the members of the industry.

The commission's first rules on ownership were issued in 1940, when it declared that no single individual or company could own more than three television stations and six frequency modulation (FM) radio stations. Amplitude modulation (AM) radio ownership was not limited. These numbers were revised continually until the 1980's when rules were adopted that stand today. A single individual or company cannot own more than twelve AM stations, twelve FM stations, and twelve television stations. If some stations are at least fifty percent minority owned or if two of the television stations are on the UHF rather than the VHF band, it is permissible for a single individual to own up to fourteen of each kind of station (see page 520 for detailed information on this rule).

In 1968 the FCC adopted what is called its "one to a customer rule," which was modified in 1971 and is the rule that exists today. The commission will not permit any broadcasting company to own more than a single VHF television station in a given market or one AM-FM radio combination. The 1971 rule was applied prospectively; that is, the agency did not force the owners of existing very high frequency TV–AM-FM combinations to sell one of their properties. It simply announced it would no longer approve the formation of such combinations in the future. The agency took a more flexible position on the ultrahigh frequency TV–AM-FM combinations, announcing that it would rule upon requests for such combinations on a case-by-case basis in the future.

In 1975 the agency attempted to thwart what it saw as another problem: the ownership of broadcast properties by newspaper companies in the same city. The rules promulgated by the commission were rather simple but provoked a serious court battle. The commission said that in the future it would bar the ownership of a broadcast license by a newspaper operating in the same city. All but a handful of the existing newspaper-broadcast combinations were allowed to remain intact. However the FCC did seek divestiture in communities in which there was common ownership of the only daily newspaper and the only broadcasting station. Similarly, in communities where there was more than one broadcasting station, the agency sought to break up the common ownership of the only daily newspaper and the only television station. Sixteen such forbidden combinations existed, and the license holders were given five years to divest themselves of either the broadcasting property or the newspaper.

The National Citizens Committee for Broadcasting challenged the FCC rules, arguing that while it supported the prospective cross-ownership ban, the FCC should have forced *all* existing combinations to sell either their newspapers or broadcasting properties. In other words, the public interest groups opposed the grandfather clause in the FCC rules. The United States Court of Appeals for the District of Columbia agreed and ruled that the FCC must order divestiture of all the jointly owned newspaper-broadcast combinations except in "those cases where the evidence clearly discloses that cross-ownership is in the public interest" (*National Citizens Committee for Broadcasting v. FCC,* 1977). Judge McGowan wrote that "although we do not disturb the commission's prospective rules, we conclude that the divestiture order is inconsistent with its long-standing policy that 'nothing can be more important than insuring that there is a free flow of information from as many divergent sources as possible.' "

The FCC appealed the ruling by the court, and in 1978 the Supreme Court reversed the lower court decision. Justice Thurgood Marshall, writing for the unanimous Court, said the court of appeals was mistaken in ruling that the FCC could have no rational reason for not ordering divestiture of the existing combinations. The agency's arguments that it would disrupt the industry, that it would deny to many meritorious broadcast station owners the opportunity to continue service to the public, and that it would likely result in an increase in the growth of broadcast chains as locally owned broadcast properties were sold under the divestiture orders were substantial, Marshall argued. "We believe that the limited divestiture requirement reflects a rational weighing of competing policies," the justice concluded for the Court (*FCC v. National Citizens Committee for Broadcasting,* 1978).

As in other areas of broadcast regulation, the FCC during the late 1980s attempted to loosen some of these ownership rules. It first granted temporary waivers to media magnate Rupert Murdoch that permitted his News America Publishing Company to own both newspapers and television stations in New York and Boston. Congress did not approve of this action and attached an amendment to a budget resolution that effectively voided these waivers. Murdoch went to court and in 1988 the United States Court of Appeals for the District of Columbia ruled the congressional action unconstitutional. The court said that a review of the history of the amendment made it clear that the action voiding the FCC waivers was aimed solely at Murdoch. This was discriminatory and violated the First Amendment (*News America Publishing v. FCC,* 1988).

In August of 1988 the FCC proposed ending its long-standing ban on the ownership of cable television systems by national television networks. Action was pending on this proposal in early 1989. Earlier in 1988 the FCC proposed repealing parts of the "one-to-a-customer rule" noted previously. The commissioners said the proposal was motivated by problems faced by many struggling AM radio stations. Permitting them to own an FM station and a UHF television station in the same community as well as the AM station may permit them to continue to operate the AM station. Congress moved quickly and signalled to the agency that it would attempt to block this proposal. The Senate in July 1988 adopted legislation that forbade the FCC to loosen these rules. Nothing was adopted during the 100th Congress, and the matter was unresolved in early 1989.

Antitrust Action

Another important action aimed at broadcasters in the 1970s was a Department of Justice antitrust suit against the three major television networks: ABC, CBS, and NBC. The Department of Justice filed the actions in 1972, but the complaints were dismissed without prejudice. In 1974 the Justice Department refiled the actions, which asserted that the networks had violated the Sherman Act by trying to monopolize the programs shown in prime-time evening hours. The government originally sought a court order that would have accomplished the following:

1. Prohibited the networks from obtaining any interest (other than showing the program for the first time) in any entertainment television program, including feature films, made by others.
2. Prohibited the networks from the syndication of such programs.
3. Prohibited the networks from offering to another network any such programming produced by the network itself or any other network.
4. Prohibited the network from offering any other commercial network programs it produced.

The thrust of what the government sought was to take the television networks out of the program production business. Three years after the litigation began, NBC surprisingly agreed to sign a consent decree that was considerably more limited than the original order sought by the government. In the decree the network agreed to specific restrictions in bargaining with independent program producers, agreed not to acquire syndication rights or other distribution or profit shares in programs produced by others, agreed not to enter into reciprocal arrangements with either CBS or ABC in the purchase or sale of programming rights, and agreed to limit the broadcast of programs it had produced. Under the terms of the settlement, the network agreed that for the next ten years it would limit the broadcast of programs it produced itself to two-and-one-half hours per week during prime time, eight hours per week during daytime hours, and eleven hours per week during fringe hours. However, this programming limitation would only apply if both CBS and ABC either agreed to similar limitations or similar limitations were forced upon them through court order. CBS and ABC came to similar terms with the Justice Department. These agreements will expire in the early 1990s.

The Justice Department also attacked television trade association rules that it believed too monopolistic. A majority of television stations belong to the National Association of Broadcasters. The association promulgated an advertising code, that member stations were expected to follow. Rules included a limit on the number of commercials that could be broadcast each hour, the number of commercial interruptions in a particular program, and the number of different products that could be advertised in a commercial lasting less than one full minute. The latter rule, known as the multiple-product rule, prohibited a sponsor from advertising more than one product in a thirty-second commercial, the unit of time that has become the industry standard. The Justice Department said the rule had the effect of compelling some advertisers to purchase more commercial time than they need or want and this prohibition artificially increased the demand for commercial time. Since all three networks and most television stations subscribed to the association code, the Justice Department said these rules violated the Sherman Act, that they were a restraint of trade.

A United States district court agreed in 1982 (*U.S.* v. *NAB*). The court noted that:

> . . . a relatively small business which is able to promote one successful product in a series of thirty-second commercials is precluded by that standard from using any portion of that thirty seconds to launch a second product, the sale of which will not, or not yet, support a commercial of its own.

The court noted that association member stations were monitored and code violations could result in discipline. The association argued that it was promoting the public interest in preventing overcommercialization of television. The court disagreed: "Congress has determined where the public interest lies when antitrust liability is at issue: it lies in fair and free competition" (*U.S.* v. *NAB*, 1982).

When the multiple-product standard was struck down, the association was forced to reexamine all its advertising rules. It apparently determined it was vulnerable to antitrust prosecution on other grounds as well, for it abandoned all enforcement of its advertising code. The association had dropped enforcement of its programming standards after the 1976 ruling that voided the family viewing hour. Consequently the National Association of Broadcasters completely closed its doors on such code enforcements in late 1982.

While these events were taking place in the broadcasting industry, the film industry was also under scrutiny by the government for anticompetitive practices that were first banned more than twenty-five years ago.

Antitrust Laws and the Movies

The movie industry has faced government scrutiny for possible antitrust violations since the late 1930s. A succession of officials within the Department of Justice, including Thurman Arnold, Francis Biddle, and Tom Clark, attacked the Hollywood studios for a variety of commercial practices deemed to be anticompetitive. Particularly onerous was the fact that in the 1930s and 1940s most of the major studios owned vast chains of theaters. By controlling the film industry from the initial creative stages through the sale of popcorn during the exhibition of a film, the studios exercised powerful dominance in the media. Independent theaters found it extremely difficult to obtain good motion pictures to exhibit—the studios kept those for their own theaters. And independent filmmakers, of which there were few, found it difficult to compete with the large studios. A film made by a major studio was bound to be shown in a good theater—one owned by the film company—and generally costs at least were made. Independent producers had no guarantee that their films would be exhibited at all, let alone at a "good house."

Independent distributors and theater owners also faced a second problem: the block-booking policies of the major studios. Under **block-booking** a distributor or theater owner was forced to "buy" a package of movies to exhibit. Generally this package included the popular and quality films the studio produced, but the package was also laced with a great many poorer films, often the lower grade B pictures that the Hollywood studios produced to keep their vast number of salaried technical employees busy and to develop new creative talent within the studio. Theater owners would often lose a considerable amount of money by exhibiting these second-rate films but had to take them as part of the package containing the good films that would be profitable to exhibit.

By the end of the 1940s, through a series of protracted antitrust litigation, the Department of Justice had succeeded in forcing the major studios to revise many of their policies. In 1948 the courts declared the block-booking practices to be a violation of the Sherman Act (*U.S.* v. *Paramount Pictures,* 1948). The studio policy of forcing independent theaters to charge minimum admission prices (so the independent owners could not undercut the admission prices at the studios' own theaters) was also declared illegal. Henceforth independent theaters were allowed to competitively bid for the right to show any of the films made by the major studios, and there could be no requirement that a theater had to take a bad picture to get a good one. The following year the studios agreed to sell their chains of theaters, a move that broke the backs of some of the weaker studios. By 1950 most of the serious anticompetitive practices the industry had developed in its fifty-year history had ended. But while this was a positive step for those in competition with the major studios, some students of film found that the government action hurt the creative end of the motion picture industry. Charles Higham in his book *Hollywood at Sunset* notes:

> . . . in practical terms the victory of the Department of Justice and the independents over wicked Hollywood had incalculably disastrous effects on the film industry and the very character of film entertainment itself. For confidence in a product, the feeling that it could flow out along guaranteed lines of distribution, was what gave many Hollywood films before 1948 their

superb attack and vigor. Also, the block-booking custom, evil though it may have been, ensured that many obscure, personal, and fascinating movies could be made and released, feather-bedded by the system and underwritten by more conventional ventures.

Higham concluded that the successful antitrust action was a victory for justice, but a defeat for entertainment.

But the illegal practices by the major studios did not altogether cease after 1950. In 1962 the Department of Justice brought an action against Loew's, Inc., Screen Gems, and other film distributors for using the block-booking techniques in selling movies to television. In Washington WTOP-TV had complained that in order to get quality films such as *Casablanca, Sergeant York,* and *Treasure of Sierra Madre,* the station had to accept a large number of weak, less popular films. The Supreme Court followed its earlier precedents and declared the practice to be illegal under the Sherman Act (*U.S. v. Loew's, Inc.,* 1962). In 1988 20th Century Fox was fined $500,000 after being found guilty of contempt of court by block booking films in 1984 and 1985. The Studio said it would appeal. Instances of block booking still arise from time to time. The selling of films in blocks is quite common (and not illegal) in the sale of pictures by their owners to pay television services and to videocassette distributors.

The configuration of the film industry in the 1980s makes such illegal practices almost unnecessary, as the business is dominated by seven major studios that control the distribution of more than eighty percent of the films exhibited in the United States. The 1978 Task Force on the Motion Picture Industry reported that "major producers/distributors are effectively limiting competition by maintaining tight control over the distribution of films, both by their failure to produce more films and by their failure to distribute more films produced by others." As of today, this practice has not been investigated and probably is legal under our current interpretation of antitrust laws. The task force noted that there was no evidence of criminal intent on the part of the film companies, but they have nevertheless agreed to "tacitly limit production among themselves and . . . create sufficient barriers to entry to effectively squash new competition." Independent Hollywood producers are attempting themselves to beat this system by forming their own distribution systems, but it is a difficult and expensive task. Time will tell whether such schemes loosen the rein the major studios have over competition.

In addition to attempting to maintain control of distribution, the major studios are also getting back into the theater business. The Department of Justice has announced, informally at least, that it is no longer interested in enforcing the provisions of the consent agreement signed by the studios forty years ago, prohibiting them from owning theaters. Most of the major studios have made substantial investments in the purchase of theater chains.

If the First Amendment has failed as a defense against antitrust action by the government, it has fared somewhat better as a means for blocking government taxes aimed at harrassing or hurting the press. And that is the next subject of this chapter.

Taxation and the Press

The First Amendment guarantees that the press shall be free from unfair and discriminatory taxes that have an impact upon circulation or distribution. In this area the classic case concerns a United States senator from a southern state and the daily press of that state (*Grosjean* v. *American Press Co., 1936*).

During the late 1920s and early 1930s, the political leader of Louisiana was Huey P. Long. Long was a demagogue by most accounts and in 1934 held his state in virtual dictatorship. He controlled the legislature and the state house and had a deep impact upon the judicial branch as well. Long started his career by attacking big business—Standard Oil of California, to be exact. He became a folk hero among the rural people of Louisiana and was elected governor in 1928. In 1931 he was elected to the United States Senate, and many people believe that he would have attempted to win the presidency had he not been assassinated in 1935.

In 1934 the Long political machine, which the majority of the big-city residents had never favored, became annoyed at the frequent attacks by the state's daily newspapers against the senator and his political machine. The legislature enacted a special 2 percent tax on the gross advertising income of newspapers with a circulation of more than 20,000. Of the 163 newspapers in the state, only 13 had more than 20,000 subscribers, and of the 13, 12 were outspoken in their opposition to Long. The newspapers went to court and argued that the tax violated the First Amendment as well as other constitutional guarantees. The press won at the circuit court level on other grounds, but the state appealed. Then in 1936 the Supreme Court ruled in favor of the newspapers squarely on First Amendment grounds.

The state of Louisiana argued that the English common law, which it claimed the American courts had adopted after the Revolution, conferred upon the government the right to tax newspapers and license them if need be. Justice George Sutherland, who wrote the opinion in this unanimous Supreme Court decision, said however that such taxes upon newspapers were the direct cause of much civil unrest in England and were one of the chief objections Americans had had to British policy—objections that ultimately forced independence.

The justice wrote:

> It is impossible to concede that by the words "freedom of the press" the framers of the amendment intended to adopt merely the narrow view then reflected by the law of England that such freedom consisted in immunity from previous censorship. . . . It is equally impossible to believe that it was not intended to bring within the reach of these words such modes of restraint as were embodied in . . . taxation."

Sutherland asserted that the tax not only restricted the amount of revenue the paper earned but also restrained circulation. Newspapers with less than twenty thousand readers would be reluctant to seek new subscribers for fear of increasing circulation to the point where they would have to pay the tax as well. The justice added that any action by the government that prevents free and general discussion of public matters is a kind of censorship. Sutherland said that in this case even the form in which the tax was imposed—levied against a distinct group of newspapers—was suspicious. He then wrote:

> The tax here involved is bad not because it takes money from the pockets of the appellees [the newspapers]. If that were all, a wholly different question would be presented. It is bad because, in the light of its history and of its present setting, it is seen to be a deliberate and calculated device in the guise of a tax to limit the circulation of information to which the public is entitled in virtue of the constitutional guaranties. A free press stands as one of the great interpreters between the government and the people. To allow it to be fettered is to fetter ourselves.

Therefore in *Grosjean* v. *American Press Co.,* the Supreme Court struck down a discriminatory tax against the press. An interesting footnote to the case concerns the opinion. Justice Sutherland's opinion is one of the most eloquent ever penned in defense of free expression. The justice was not normally such an articulate spokesman. What happened in this case? Speculation is that Sutherland's opinion incorporates a concurring opinion by Justice Benjamin Cardozo, perhaps the greatest writer ever to serve on the Court, and the eloquence of the *Grosjean* opinion is really Cardozo's, not Sutherland's.

Despite the fact that Justice Sutherland specifically noted in his opinion that the ruling in *Grosjean* did not mean that newspapers are immune from ordinary taxes, some newspaper publishers apparently did not read the opinion that way, but saw it instead as a means of escaping other kinds of taxes. After *Grosjean,* for example, unsuccessful attempts were made to have a sales tax in Arizona declared inapplicable to newspapers because it was a restriction on freedom of the press (*Arizona Publishing Co.* v. *O'Neil,* 1938). Since 1953 when the United States Supreme Court refused to hear an appeal from a California decision affirming the constitutionality of a general business tax on newspapers, the matter has been fairly well settled. The California case involved the *Corona Daily Independent,* which challenged a business tax imposed by the city of Corona. A license tax of thirty-two dollars had been levied for many years against all businesses. In 1953 the newspaper refused to pay the levy on the grounds that the tax violated its First Amendment rights to freedom of expression. The *Grosjean* case prohibited such taxation, lawyers for the publication argued. The trial court ruled in favor of the newspaper, but the California Appellate Court disagreed and reversed the ruling (*City of Corona* v. *Corona Daily Independent,* 1953). Justice Griffin wrote that there is ample authority to the effect that newspapers are not made exempt from ordinary forms of taxation. Justice Griffin said that the newspaper had not shown that the amount of the tax was harsh or arbitrary, that the tax was oppressive or confiscatory, or that the tax in any way curtailed or abridged the newspaper's right to disseminate news and comment:

> We conclude that a nondiscriminatory tax, levied upon the doing of business, for the sole purpose of maintaining the municipal government, without whose municipal services and protection the press could neither exist nor function, must be sustained as being within the purview and necessary implications of the Constitution and its amendments.

The United States Supreme Court refused to review the ruling in *City of Corona* v. *Corona Daily Independent,* and most people believed the refusal signaled concurrence with the opinion of the California court.

But in 1983 the United States Supreme Court did review an unusual tax placed on a handful of Minnesota newspapers. Since 1971 Minnesota had imposed a use tax on the cost of the paper and ink products consumed in the production of a publication. The law was amended in 1974 to exempt from the tax the first $100,000 worth of paper and ink used. After the exemption was adopted, only about fifteen newspapers in the state were forced to pay the tax. And the Minneapolis Star and Tribune Company ended up paying about two-thirds of all the revenues collected under the tax. The Star and Tribune Company challenged the tax, and in March 1983 the High Court ruled that the levy against the newspapers was invalid.

Justice Sandra Day O'Connor described the tax as a "special tax that applies only to certain publications protected by the First Amendment." She added: "A power to tax differentially, as opposed to a power to tax generally, gives a government a powerful weapon against the taxpayer selected." Such a tax could be used to censor the press, a clear violation of the First Amendment. The tax law is also deficient because it ends up hitting only a few of the newspapers in the state. "Whatever the motive of the legislature in this case," Justice O'Connor wrote for the Court's majority, "we think that recognizing a power in the State not only to single out the press but also to tailor the tax so it singles out a few members of the press presents such a potential for abuse that no interest suggested by Minnesota can justify the scheme" (*Minneapolis Star* v. *Minnesota Commissioner of Revenue,* 1983).

The Supreme Court voided another tax scheme in 1987 because, Justice Thurgood Marshall said, "the taxing scheme was based solely on the content of the publication." Arkansas had a sales tax on tangible personal property. Several items were exempt from the tax including newspapers and "religious, professional, trade and sports journals and/or publications printed and published in the state." The publisher of a general interest magazine sued to be exempt from the tax. The publisher argued that his magazine was published in the state and therefore should be exempt. The Arkansas Supreme Court ruled that the publisher had read the statute incorrectly. The law only exempted religious, professional, trade and sports publications that were printed in the state, not all magazines printed in the state. This tax was unconstitutional because it was discriminatory, because its applicability depended solely on the content of the publication, the High Court said. This is a violation of the First Amendment (*Arkansas Writers' Project* v. *Ragland,* 1987). The High Court heard arguments in the autumn of 1988 in a similar case, *Texas Monthly* v. *Bullock,* in which a Texas statute exempted religious periodicals from the general state sales tax. The publisher of the *Texas Monthly* argued that the law not only discriminated against certain publications based on their content, but also violated the separation of church and state clause in the First Amendment. In February of 1989, by an 6–3 vote, the Supreme Court declared the Texas tax invalid. Justice William Brennan, writing the court's opinion, said the tax violated the establishment clause of the First Amendment (*Texas Monthly Inc.* v. *Bullock,* 1989).

The basic rule of First Amendment law regarding taxes on the press is this: Newspapers, broadcasting stations, and other mass media must pay the same taxes as any other business. Taxes that are levied only against the press and tend to inhibit circulation or impose other kinds of prior restraints (such as very high taxes that keep all but very wealthy people from publishing newspapers) are unconstitutional. Also, decisions by the state to tax or not tax cannot be based solely on the content of the publication.

Regulation of the commercial aspects of the mass media is not new. Yet as the media continue to grow as giant businesses and more and more take on the configuration of modern American industry, commercial regulation will increase. The former Chief Justice of the United States suggested as much in 1978 in a concurring opinion in the case of *First National Bank of Boston* v. *Bellotti.* The case involved a Massachusetts state law that forbade banks and corporations from making contributions or expenditures for the purpose of "influencing or affecting the vote on any question submitted to the voters." The Court struck down the statute as running afoul of the First Amendment. Chief Justice Warren Burger noted in his concurrence:

> A disquieting aspect of Massachusetts's position is that it may carry the risk of impinging on the First Amendment rights of those who employ the corporate form—as most do—to carry on the business of mass communications, particularly large media conglomerates. This is so because of the difficulty, and perhaps impossibility, of distinguishing, either as a matter of fact or constitutional law, media corporations from corporations such as the appellants [a bank] in this case.

John Oakes, editorial page editor of the *New York Times,* noted that Burger's opinion "may lead to a questioning of the need for special protection of the press as such, under a First Amendment that was in fact designed to insure the free flow of information and opinion, and not the accretion of corporate power." Oakes added, during a speech at the 1978 Conference on Media and the Public at the Washington Journalism Center, that the growth of concentration of the ownership of the media into fewer hands could lead to a grave dislocation between the press and the public:

> The quality of the product turned out by the conglomerates' publishing and broadcasting arms may be less important in the long run than the loss of public confidence in the press engendered by fears of "the sinister effect of riches" upon the institution of the press.

Oakes added that he feared that public disillusionment with the press could even adversely influence the judiciary's normal strong adherence to the guarantees of a free press.

SUMMARY

Mass media businesses are regulated by the government just like any other businesses, and the First Amendment offers no special protection from such regulation.

The government has brought many antitrust actions against mass media companies. Action by the Justice Department against newspapers has focused upon industry rules that limit the profitable entry into the newspaper business (the *AP* case) and upon discriminatory newspaper advertising and circulation rules. Antitrust law has been found to be largely ineffective to block the growth of vast chains of newspapers but has been used to stop concentration of ownership of newspapers in specific local areas. Congress adopted the Newspaper Preservation Act in 1970, which permits monopolistic joint-operating agreements between newspapers in situations where one of the two papers is in danger of failing without such a cost-saving agreement. The law has been ruled to be constitutional by the federal courts.

The government has not used antitrust laws against the concentration of ownership in broadcast because the Federal Communications Commission has adopted ownership rules that limit such concentration, but many of these rules are currently under examination at the FCC and may be abandoned. The government has, however, forced the television networks to stop monopolizing the programs shown in prime time. It has also forced abandonment of industry codes that artificially increased the demand for advertising time on television.

Antitrust actions against the film industry in the late forties forced the major film production studios to sell off their chains of motion-picture theaters and prohibited them from such discriminatory practices as block-booking the films they distributed.

While the courts have ruled that newspapers cannot be subject to discriminatory taxes that have the tendency to restrain circulation, publishers and broadcasters are expected to pay normal business taxes. The First Amendment cannot be raised as a bar to such levies.

BIBLIOGRAPHY

Here is a list of some of the sources that have been helpful in the preparation of chapter 12:

Books

Gerald, J. Edward. *The Press and the Constitution.* Minneapolis: University of Minnesota Press, 1948.
Higham, Charles. *Hollywood at Sunset.* New York: Saturday Review Press, 1972.
Oppenheim, S. Chesterfield, and Shields, Carrington. *Newspapers and Antitrust Laws.* Charlottesville, Va.: Michie Company, 1981.

Articles

Clift, Eleanor. "Waiving Goodbye: Congress Ambushes Murdoch." *Washington Journalism Review,* March 1988.
Picard, Robert G. "JOA Amendment Looms." 28 *Grassroots Editor* 3, 1987.
"Proposed JOA Between Daily, Non-Daily Would be Smallest." *Presstime,* May, 1988.
Roach, Catherine B. "Media Conglomerates, Anti-Trust Law, and the Marketplace of Ideas." 9 *Memphis State University Law Review* 257, 1979.

Cases

Advantage Publications v. *Daily Press,* 9 M.L.R. 1761 (1983).
AP v. *NLRB,* 301 U.S. 130 (1937).
AP v. *U.S.,* 326 U.S. 1 (1945).
Arizona Publishing Co. v. *O'Neil,* 22 F.Supp. 117; aff'd 304 U.S. 543 (1938).
Arkansas Writers' Project v. *Ragland,* 481 U.S. 221 (1987).
Bay Guardian Publishing Company v. *Chronicle Publishing Company,* 344 F.Supp. 1155 (1972).
City of Corona v. *Corona Daily Independent,* 252 P.2d 56 (1953).
Committee for an Independent P–I v. *Hearst,* 704 F.2d 467 (1983).
Committee v. *Smith,* 549 F.Supp. 985 (1982).
FCC v. *National Citizens Committee for Broadcasting,* 436 U.S. 775 (1978).
First National Bank v. *Bellotti,* 435 U.S. 765 (1978).
Grosjean v. *American Press Co.,* 297 U.S. 233 (1936).
Lorain Journal Co. v. *U.S.,* 342 U.S. 143 (1951).
Michigan Citizens for an Independent Press v. *Attorney General,* 15 M.L.R. 1943 (1988).
Michigan Citizens v. *Thornburgh,* 868 F.2d 1285 (1989); rhr'g den., 868 F.2d 1315 (1989).
Minneapolis Star v. *Minnesota Commissioner of Revenue,* 460 U.S. 575 (1983).
National Citizens Committee for Broadcasting v. *FCC,* 555 F.2d 938 (1977).
News America Publishing v. *FCC,* 844 F.2d 800 (1988).
Sherwood v. *Washington Post Group,* 15 M.L.R. 20 (1988).
Texas Monthly v. *Bullock,* 109 S.Ct. 890 (1989).
Times-Picayune v. *U.S.,* 345 U.S. 594 (1953).
U.S. v. *Citizen Publishing Co.,* 394 U.S. 131 (1969).
U.S. v. *Kansas City Star,* 240 F.2d 643 (1957).
U.S. v. *Loew's, Inc.,* 371 U.S. 38 (1962).
U.S. v. *NAB,* 536 F.Supp. 149 (1982).
U.S. v. *Nanlo,* 519 F.Supp. 723 (1981).
U.S. v. *Paramount Pictures,* 334 U.S. 131 (1948).
U.S. v. *Times-Mirror Corp.,* 274 F.Supp. 607 (1967); aff'd 390 U.S. 712 (1968).

GLOSSARY

absolute privilege An immunity from libel suits granted to government officials and others based on remarks uttered or written as part of their official duties.

absolutist theory The proposition that the First Amendment is an absolute, and that government may adopt no laws whatsoever that abridge freedom of expression.

actual damages Damages awarded to a plaintiff in a lawsuit based upon proof of actual harm to the plaintiff.

actual malice A fault standard in libel law: knowledge before publication that the libelous material was false or reckless disregard of the truth or falsity of the libelous matter.

administrative agency An agency, created and funded by the Congress, whose members are appointed by the president and whose function it is to administer specific legislation, such as law regulating broadcasting and advertising.

admonition to a jury Instructions from a judge to a trial jury to avoid talking to other persons about the trial they are hearing and to avoid news broadcasts and newspaper or magazine stories that discuss the case or issues in the case.

Alien and Sedition Laws of 1798 Laws adopted by the Federalist Congress aimed at stopping criticism of the national government by Republican or Jeffersonian editors and politicians.

amici curiae "Friends of the court"; persons who have no legal right to take part in a lawsuit but are allowed to appear on behalf of one of the parties in a case.

appellant The party who initiates or takes the appeal of a case from one court to another.

appellate court(s) A court that has both original and appellate jurisdiction; a court to which cases are removed for an appeal.

appellee The person in a case against whom the appeal is taken; that is, the party in the suit who is not making the appeal.

appropriation In the law of privacy, use of a person's name or likeness without consent for advertising or trade purposes.

arraignment The first official court appearance made by a criminal defendant at which he or she is formally charged with an offense and called upon to plead guilty or not guilty to the charges contained in the state's indictment or information.

ascertainment A procedure established by the Federal Communications Commission that instructs broadcast licensees in the manner in which they are to determine important problems and issues in a community.

bait-and-switch advertising An illegal advertising strategy in which the seller baits an advertisement with a low-priced model of a product but then switches customers who seek to buy the product to a much higher-priced model by telling them that the cheaper model does not work well or is no longer in stock.

bench-bar-press guidelines Informal agreements among lawyers, judges, police officials, and journalists about what should and should not be published or broadcast about a criminal suspect or criminal case before a trial is held.

block-booking An illegal scheme in which a motion-picture distributor requires a theater owner to book a poor film in order to book a popular film.

bond; bonding A large sum of money given by a publisher to a government to be held to ensure good behavior. Should the publisher violate a government rule, the bond is forfeited to the government, and the newspaper or magazine cannot be published again until a new bond is posted.

candidate access rule Section 312 of the Federal Communications Act, which forbids a broadcaster from instituting an across-the-board policy that denies all candidates for federal office the opportunity to use the station to further a political campaign.

case reporter(s) A book (or books) containing a chronological collection of the opinions rendered by a particular court for cases that were decided by the court.

cease and desist order An order issued by a court requiring the cessation of a particular behavior or practice.

challenge for cause The request by a litigant in a criminal or civil case that a juror be dismissed for a specific reason.

change of venue Moving a trial to a distant community in order to find jurors who have not read or viewed prejudicial publicity about the defendant.

citation The reference to a legal opinion contained in a case reporter that gives the name, volume number, and page number where the opinion can be found. The year the opinion was rendered is also included in the citation.

civil complaint A written statement of the plaintiff's legal grievance, which normally initiates a civil suit.

civil contempt That variety of contempt of court in which the act of disrespect or disobedience is aimed at one of the parties in the lawsuit, rather than at the court itself.

commercial speech doctrine The legal doctrine that states that truthful advertising for products and services that are not illegal is normally protected by the First Amendment to the United States Constitution.

common law Principles and rules of law that derive their authority not from legislation but from community usage and custom.

comparative license hearing A hearing to evaluate potential licensees when two or more persons seek the same broadcast license, as required by a Federal Communications Commission rule.

concurring opinion A written opinion by an appellate judge or justice in which the author agrees with the decision of the court but normally states reasons different from those in the court opinion as the basis for his or her decision.

consent A defense in both libel and invasion of privacy cases that provides that individuals who agree to the publication of a libelous story or the appropriation of their name cannot then maintain a lawsuit based upon the libel or the appropriation.

consent order or decree A document in which an individual agrees to terminate a specific behavior, such as an advertising campaign, or to refrain from a specific action, such as making a certain advertising claim.

constitution A written outline of the organization of a government that provides for both the rights and responsibilities of various branches of the government and the limits of the power of the government.

contempt of court An act of disobedience or disrespect to a judge, which may be punished by a fine or jail sentence.

continuance The delay of a trial or hearing; that is, the trial is postponed.

copyright That body of law which protects the works created by writers, painters, photographers, performing artists, inventors, and other persons who create intangible property.

copyright notice The words "Copyright © 1989 by Don R. Pember," for example, which indicate to a user that a work is copyrighted by the author or creator.

corrective advertising scheme Rules established by the Federal Trade Commission that require an advertiser to correct the false impressions left by deceptive advertising in a certain percentage of future advertisements.

court's opinion The official opinion of an appellate court that states the reasons or rationale for a decision.

criminal contempt That variety of contempt of court in which the act of disrespect or disobedience is aimed directly at the court.

criminal history privacy laws State laws that limit the access of non-law enforcement-personnel to criminal records maintained by states.

criminal libel A libel against the state, against the dead, or against a large, ill-defined group (such as a race) in which the state prosecutes the libel on behalf of the injured parties.

criminal suit A legal action brought by the state against an individual or group of individuals for violating state criminal laws.

criminal syndicalism laws Laws that outlaw advocacy, planning, or processes aimed at establishing the control over industry by workers or trade unions.

damages Money awarded to the winning party in a civil lawsuit.

defamation Any communication that holds a person up to contempt, hatred, ridicule, or scorn and lowers the reputation of the individual defamed.

defendant The person against whom relief or recovery is sought in a civil lawsuit; the individual against whom a state criminal action is brought.

demurrer An allegation made by the defendant in a lawsuit that even if the facts as stated by the plaintiff are true they do not state a sufficient cause for action.

de novo A new or fresh. In some instances a court of general jurisdiction will hear an appeal from a case from a lower court and simply retry the case. This is a de novo hearing.

devisable right A right that may be passed on to an heir.

Dickinson Rule A rule emanating from a decision by the United States Court of Appeals for the Fifth Circuit stating that even a patently unconstitutional court order must be obeyed until it is overturned by an appellate court.

dicta Remarks in a court opinion that do not speak directly to the legal point in question.

direct appeal The statutorily granted right of an aggrieved party to carry the appeal of a case to the Supreme Court of the United States. The High Court can deny this right if the appeal lacks a substantial federal question.

direct criminal contempt A criminal contempt that is committed in the presence of the court, that is, in the courtroom or near the courtroom.

dissenting opinion A written opinion by a judge or justice who disagrees with the appellate court's decision in a case.

en banc; sitting en banc A French term to describe all the justices or judges of an appellate court sitting together to hear a case. This situation is the opposite of the more typical situation in which a small group (called a panel) of judges or justices in a particular court hears a case.

Equal Time Rule Section 315 of the Federal Communications Act, which states that when broadcasters permit a legally qualified candidate for elective office to use their broadcasting facilities, all other legally qualified candidates for the same elective office must be given the similar opportunity.

equity A system of jurisprudence, distinct from the common law, in which courts are empowered to decide cases upon the basis of equity or fairness and are not bound by the rigid precedents that often exist in the common law.

Espionage Act A law adopted by the Congress in 1917 that outlawed criticism of the United States government and its participation in World War I in Europe.

executive privilege An asserted common law privilege of the president and other executives to keep presidential papers, records, and other documents secret, even from the Congress.

executive session A popular euphemism for a closed meeting held by a government body such as a city council or school board.

fair comment A libel defense that protects the publication of libelous opinion that focuses upon the public activities of a person acting in a public sphere.

Fairness Doctrine A Federal Communications Commission rule that requires that broadcasters devote a reasonable portion of broadcast time to the discussion of important public issues and that the coverage of these issues be fair in the sense that all important contrasting views on the issues are presented.

fair use A provision of the copyright law that permits a limited amount of copying of material that has been properly copyrighted.

false light That portion of privacy law which prohibits all publication or broadcast that falsely portrays an individual in an offensive manner.

FCC See Federal Communications Commission.

Federal Communications Act The law, adopted in 1934, that is the foundation for the regulation of broadcasting in the United States.

Federal Communications Commission A five-member body appointed by the president whose function is to administer the federal broadcasting and communications laws.

Federal Open Meetings Law (Government in Sunshine Act) A federal law that requires approximately fifty federal agencies and bureaus to hold all their meetings in public, unless a subject under discussion is included within one of the ten exemptions contained in the statute.

Federal Trade Commission A five-member body appointed by the president whose function it is to administer the federal laws relating to advertising, antitrust and many other business matters.

Fighting Words Doctrine A legal doctrine that permits prior censorship of words that create a clear and present danger of inciting an audience to disorder or violence.

FOIA See Freedom of Information Act.

Freedom of Information Act A federal law that mandates that all the records created and kept by federal agencies in the executive branch of government must be open for public inspection and copying, except those records that fall into one of nine exempted categories listed in the statute.

FTC See Federal Trade Commission.

gag order(s) A restrictive court order that prohibits all or some participants in a trial from speaking about a case or that stops publications and broadcasting stations from reporting on certain aspects of a case.

Government in Sunshine Act See Federal Open Meetings Law.

grand jury A jury whose function it is to determine whether sufficient evidence exists to issue an indictment or true bill charging an individual or individuals with a crime and to take such persons to trial. It is called a grand jury because it has more members than a petit, or trial, jury.

identification As used in a libel suit, the requirement that the plaintiff prove that at least one person believes that the subject of the libelous remarks is the plaintiff and not some other person.

impeachment A criminal proceeding against a public officer that is started by written "articles of impeachment" and followed by a trial. The House of Representatives, for example, can issue articles of impeachment against the president, who is then tried by the Senate.

indictment A written accusation issued by a grand jury charging that an individual or individuals have committed a specific crime and should be taken to trial.

indirect criminal contempt A criminal contempt committed outside the presence of the court, that is, not in the courtroom or near the courtroom.

information A written accusation issued by a public officer rather than by a grand jury charging that an individual or individuals have committed a specific crime and should be taken to trial.

intrusion An invasion of privacy committed when one individual intrudes upon or invades the solitude of another individual.

invasion of privacy A civil tort that emerged in the early twentieth century and contains four distinct categories of legal wrongs: appropriation, intrusion, publication of private facts, and false light.

joint-operating agreement An exemption to the federal antitrust law that permits two newspapers in a community to merge advertising, circulation, and printing functions but maintain separate editorial departments.

judgment of the court The final ruling of a court, which determines the outcome of a lawsuit. It is different from the verdict, which is the decision of the jury in a trial.

judicial decree A judgment of a court of equity; a declaration of the court announcing the legal consequences of the facts found to be true by the court.

judicial instructions A statement (often written) made by a judge to the members of a jury informing them about the law (as distinguished from the facts) in a case.

judicial review The power of a court to declare void and unenforceable any statute, rule, or executive order that conflicts with an appropriate state constitution or the federal constitution.

jury A group of men and women called together in a trial court to determine the facts in a civil or criminal lawsuit. It is sometimes called a petit jury to distinguish it from a grand jury.

legal brief(s) (brief) Written legal argument presented to the court by one or both parties in a lawsuit.

libel Published or broadcast communication that lowers the reputation of an individual by holding him or her up to contempt, ridicule, or scorn.

licensing process The process by which a government gives a publisher or a broadcaster prior permission to print a newspaper or operate a broadcasting station. Revocation of a license can be used as punishment for failing to comply with the law or the wishes of the government. Licensing of the printed press in the United States ended in the 1720s.

litigant A party in a lawsuit; a participant in litigation.

memorandum order The announcement by an appellate court of a decision in a case that does not include a written opinion containing the rationale or reasons for the ruling.

misappropriation Taking what belongs to someone else and using it unfairly for one's own gain; for example, attempting to pass off a novel as part of a popular series of novels written and published by someone else. It is often called unfair competition.

Missouri Plan A system used in some states by which judges are appointed to the bench initially and then must stand for reelection on a ballot that permits citizens to vote to retain or not retain the judge.

NAD See next entry.

National Advertising Division (NAD) of the Council of Better Business Bureaus An industry organization that evaluates and rules upon the truthfulness of advertising claims. Complaints are normally brought to the NAD by competing advertisers.

negligence A fault standard in libel and other tort law. Negligent behavior is normally described as an act or action that a reasonably prudent person or a reasonable individual would not have committed. In libel law, courts often measure negligence by asking whether the allegedly libelous material was the work of a person who exercised reasonable care in preparation of the story.

neutral reportage An emerging libel defense or privilege that states that it is permissible to publish or broadcast an accurate account of information about a public figure from a reliable source even when the reporter doubts the truth of the libelous assertion. The defense is not widely accepted.

nonjusticiable matter An issue that is inappropriate for a court to decide because the jurists lack the knowledge to make the ruling, because another branch of government has the responsibility to answer such questions, or because a court order in the matter would not likely be enforceable or enforced.

open meetings laws State and federal statutes that require that certain meetings of public agencies—normally in the executive branch of government— be open to the public and the press.

open records laws State and federal statutes that require that certain records of public agencies—normally in the executive branch of government—be open for inspection and copying by the public and the press.

opinion The written statement issued by a court that explains the reasons for a judgment and states the rule of law in the case.

oral argument An oral presentation made to a judge or justices in which the litigants argue the merits of their case.

original jurisdiction Jurisdiction in the first instance, as distinguished from appellate jurisdiction. A court exercising original jurisdiction determines both the facts and the law in the case; courts exercising appellate jurisdiction may only rule upon the law and the sufficiency of the facts as determined by a trial court.

pandering The business of purveying textual or graphic material openly advertised to appeal to the erotic interest of customers. This criterion is sometimes used in obscenity prosecution to determine whether the material in question is obscene.

per curiam opinion An unsigned court opinion. The author of the opinion is not known outside the court.

peremptory challenge A challenge without stated cause to remove a juror from a panel. Litigants are given a small number of such challenges in a lawsuit.

personal attack rules Specific rules issued by the Federal Communications Commission that outline the responsibilities of a broadcast licensee if and when an attack upon an individual or identifiable group is made during a radio or television broadcast. The licensee must inform the individual or group of the attack and provide an opportunity for a reply, among other requirements.

petitioner One who petitions a court to take an action; someone who starts a lawsuit, or carries an appeal to a higher court (appellant). This person is the opposite of a respondent, one who responds to a petition.

plaintiff An individual who initiates a civil lawsuit.

pleadings The written statements of the parties in a lawsuit that contain their allegations, denials, and defenses.

precedent An established rule of law set by a previous case. Courts should follow precedent when it is advisable and possible.

preferred position theory A theory on how the First Amendment should be interpreted that states that when the guarantees of freedom of speech and freedom of the press are balanced against other important rights, the rights of freedom of expression are to be given extra weight, to be preferred. Legally this proposition requires that persons who would restrict freedom of expression bear the burden of proving that such restrictions are justified and not a violation of the First Amendment.

pretrial hearing A meeting prior to a criminal trial at which attorneys for the state and for the defense make arguments before a judge on evidentiary questions; that is, whether a confession made by the defendant should be admitted as evidence at the trial. This type of hearing is sometimes called a suppression hearing.

Printers' ink statute A model law drafted in 1911 to control false or misleading advertising. Most states adopted some version of this model in the early twentieth century. Such laws are largely ineffective because they are not normally enforced.

prior restraint Prepublication censorship that forbids publication or broadcast of certain objectionable material, as opposed to punishment of a perpetrator after the material was published or broadcast.

Privacy Act A federal statute that forbids the disclosure of specific material held by federal agencies on the grounds that its release could invade the privacy of the subject of the report or document.

publication In libel law, exposing an allegedly libelous statement to one person in addition to the subject of the libel.

publication of private information In privacy law, publicizing embarrassing private information about an individual that is not of legitimate public concern.

puffery Often expansive hyperbole about a product that does not contain factual claims of merit. Normally puffery is permitted by the law (e.g., "this is the best-looking automobile on the market today").

punitive damages Money damages awarded to a plaintiff in a lawsuit aimed not to compensate for harm to the injured party, but to punish the defendant for his or her illegal conduct.

qualified privilege In libel law, the privilege of the reporter (or any person) to publish a fair and accurate report of the proceedings of a public meeting or public document and be immune from lawsuit for the publication of libel uttered at the meeting or contained in the document.

Radio Act of 1912 The first federal broadcast law, which imposed only minimal regulation on the fledgling broadcast industry. Radio operators were required to have a license under this statute.

Radio Act of 1927 The first comprehensive national broadcast law, which provided the basic framework for the regulation of broadcast that was later adopted in the Federal Communications Act of 1934.

reasonable access rule See candidate access rule.

reporter-source privilege The privilege asserted by a reporter to shield the identity of the source of confidential information used in a news story.

respondent The person who responds to a petition placed before a court by another person; the opposite of the petitioner. At the appellate level, the respondent is often called the appellee.

restrictive order A court order limiting the discussion of the facts in a criminal case both by participants in the case and by the press. See also gag order.

retraction In libel law, a statement published or broadcast that attempts to retract or correct previously published or broadcast libelous matter. A timely retraction will usually mitigate damages, and in some states that have retraction laws, plaintiffs must seek a retraction before beginning a lawsuit or they lose the ability to collect anything but special damages.

right of publicity An offshoot of privacy law that protects the right of persons to capitalize upon their fame or notoriety for commercial or advertising purposes.

right of reply A little-used libel defense that declares as immune from a lawsuit a libelous remark made against an individual in reply to a previously published libelous remark made by that individual.

scienter Guilty knowledge. In many criminal prosecutions the state must prove that the accused was aware of the nature of his or her behavior. In an obscenity case, for example, the state must normally show that the defendant was aware of the contents of the book he or she sold.

Section 312 See candidate access rule.

Section 315 See equal time rule.

Sedition Act of 1918 An amendment to the Espionage Act adopted in the midst of World War I that severely limited criticism of the government and criticism of United States participation in the European war.

seditious libel Libeling the government; criticizing the government or government officers. It is sometimes called sedition.

sequestration of the jury Separating the jury from the community during a trial. Usually a jury is lodged at a hotel and members are required to eat together. In general, sequestration means to keep jurors away from other persons. The exposure of the jury to news reports is also screened to shield jurors from news reports about the trial.

shield laws State statutes that permit reporters in some circumstances to shield the name of a confidential news source when questioned by a grand jury or in another legal forum.

single mistake rule In libel law, a rule that states that it is not libelous to accuse a professional person or business person of making a single mistake (e.g., "Dr. Alan Jones incorrectly diagnosed the patient's illness").

slander Oral defamation.

Smith Act A federal law adopted in 1940 that makes it illegal to advocate the violent overthrow of the government.

special damages Damages that can be awarded to a plaintiff in a lawsuit upon proof of specific monetary loss.

stare decisis "Let the decision stand." This concept is the operating principal in the common law system and requires that judges follow precedent case law when making judgments.

statute of limitations A law that requires that a legal action must begin within a specified period of time (usually one to three years for a civil case) after the legal wrong was committed.

statutes Laws adopted by legislative bodies.

statutory construction The process undertaken by courts to interpret or construe the meaning of statutes.

strict liability A doctrine in tort law that declares that a defendant is liable for even an unintentional and nonnegligent act that causes harm to a plaintiff. Libel law was formerly governed by the doctrine of strict liability.

subpoena A court document that requires a witness to appear and testify or to produce documents or papers pertinent to a pending controversy.

substantiation A Federal Trade Commission rule that requires an advertiser to prove the truth of advertising claims made about a product or service.

summary contempt power The power of a judge to find an individual guilty of a contempt of court and impose a sentence without giving the individual the benefit of a jury trial.

summary judgment A judgment granted to a party in a lawsuit when the pleadings and other materials in the case disclose no material issue of fact between the parties, making it possible for the case to be decided on the basis of the law by the court. A summary judgment avoids a costly jury trial.

summary jury trial An abbreviated jury trial where jurors hear arguments but no witnesses are called and little evidence is presented. The jurors can issue an informal verdict which can be used as the basis for a settlement of the case, thus avoiding a full-blown and costly trial.

survival statute A statute that permits an heir to continue to maintain a lawsuit though the plaintiff died after the suit was filed, but before it was resolved.

time, place, and manner restrictions or rules Rules, when justified by a substantial government interest, that can regulate the time, place, and manner of speaking or publishing and the distribution of printed material.

trade libel Product disparagement, and not considered true libel; disparaging a product as opposed to the manufacturer or maker of the product.

trade regulation rules Rules adopted by the Federal Trade Commission that prohibit specific advertising claims about an entire class of products. For example, makers of fruit drinks that contain less than ten percent fruit juice cannot advertise these products as fruit juice.

trespass Unlawful entry upon another person's land or property.

trial court(s) Normally the first court to hear a lawsuit. This court is the forum in which the facts are determined and the law is initially applied, as opposed to an appellate court, to which decisions are appealed.

unfair competition See misappropriation.

variable obscenity standards A Supreme Court doctrine that permits states to prohibit the sale, distribution, or exhibition of certain kinds of nonobscene matter to children, so long as these laws do not interfere with the accessibility of this material to adults.

verdict The decision of a trial jury based upon the instructions given to it by the judge.

voir dire A preliminary examination the court makes of persons chosen to serve as jurors in a trial. Persons can be challenged for cause or on the basis of a peremptory challenge by either side in the legal dispute.

writ of certiorari A writ by which an appellant seeks the review of a case by the Supreme Court of the United States. When the writ is granted, the Court will order the lower court to send up the record of the case for review.

Zapple Rule A corollary to the equal time rule that states that when the supporters of a legally qualified candidate are given time on a radio or television broadcast, the supporters of all other legally qualified candidates for the same office must also be given equal opportunity.

Table of Cases

Index